Everything

DO NOT REMOVE
CARDS FROM POCKET

Everything Baseball

JAMES MOTE

PRENTICE HALL PRESS

New York   London   Toronto   Sydney   Tokyo

Prentice Hall Press
Gulf + Western Building
One Gulf + Western Plaza
New York, New York   10023

Library of Congress Cataloging-
in-Publication Data

Mote, James.
   Everything baseball / James
Mote.—1st ed. p.   cm.
   Includes index.
   ISBN 0-13-292889-2
   1. Baseball—United States—
Miscellanea.   I. Title.
GV863.A1M67   1989   88-28816
796.357′0973—dc19   CIP

Manufactured in the United
States of America

10 9 8 7 6 5 4 3 2 1

First Edition

Acknowledgments

Many people and institutions supplied information and materials that I am pleased to acknowledge. My requests to scholars and professionals in fields unrelated to baseball invariably met with helpful and enthusiastic replies. To these people —and, of course, to the baseball community as a whole—I wish to extend my deepest gratitude.

I wish to thank Thomas R. Heitz, Librarian of the National Baseball Library, Cooperstown, New York, for permitting me full use of that facility, and Peter P. Clark, Registrar of the National Baseball Hall of Fame and Museum in Cooperstown, New York, for allowing me access to the museum's collection of fine art and other holdings. The generous assistance accorded me by the National Baseball Library staff of Patricia Kelly, Jon Blomquist, Bill Deane, Helen Kubis, Betty McCarthy, and Dylis Burdt is sincerely appreciated.

A number of museums and libraries were utilized during the preparation of this book, notably the New York and Los Angeles public libraries; the Performing Arts Research Center at Lincoln Center, New York; Margaret Herrick Library, Academy of Motion Picture Arts and Sciences, Beverly Hills, California; Film Study Center, Museum of Modern Art, New York; Film Stills Archive, Museum of Modern Art, New York; Museum of Broadcasting, New York; Television Information Office, New York; Frick Art Reference Library, New York; and the National Art Museum of Sport, West Haven, Connecticut. To the curators and staffs of these institutions I extend a special note of gratitude.

I would also like to thank the following people for their expert assistance: Dr. Roderick Bladel, Billy Rose Theater Collection, Performing Arts Research Center at Lincoln Center; Edwin M. Matthias and Cooper C. Graham, Motion Picture, Broadcasting and Recorded Sound Division, Library of Congress; Bruce McIntosh, Librarian, First Interstate Bank Athletic Foundation, Los Angeles; Christine Hennessey, Inventory of American Paintings, National Museum of American Art, Washington, D.C.; Carol Sue Whitehouse, Special Collections, Newberry Library, Chicago; Sherry A. O'Brien, Harris Collection, Brown University Library; Victoria Jennings, Research Division, The Phillips Collection, Washington, D.C.; Ann M. Loyd, Pennsylvania Division, Carnegie Library of Pittsburgh; Maurice A. Crane, Director, G. Robert Vincent Voice Library, Michigan State University; Elizabeth Fernandez-Gimenez, Research Division, Milwaukee Art Museum; Heidi D. Shafranek, Permanent Collection Division, Whitney Museum of American Art, New York; and Shelly Mehlman Dinhofer, Director, Museum of the Borough of Brooklyn.

Grateful acknowledgment is also made to Al Feilich, vice-president, Information and Research, Broadcast Music, Inc. (BMI), New York; Bruce MacCombie, director of publications, G. Schirmer, Inc., New York; Mindy Keskinen, Goodspeed Opera House, East Haddam, Connecticut; Brian Robinette, NBC Television, Burbank, California; the publicity departments of ABC, CBS, NBC, WNET-TV, New York, Home Box Office, and the Disney Channel; and to the following officers and members of the Society to Preserve and Encourage Radio Drama, Variety and Comedy (SPERDVAC), Hollywood, California, for generously providing materials on baseball-related radio programs: John Gassman, Larry

Gassman, Barbara J. Watkins, Tom Price, and Andrew S. Love. The radio index is considerably improved for their many kindnesses extended me.

I am profoundly indebted to Jim Walsh of *Hobbies* magazine for his definitive discography of early baseball-related recordings; to Andy Strasberg, director of marketing, San Diego Padres, and Michael Brown, New York, for providing catalogs and photographs of their outstanding collections of baseball-related recordings and sheet music; to John Hillyard, Los Angeles, John Bertelsen, San Pedro, California, Tom Leonard, Phoenix, Arizona, Bob Claster, Los Angeles, Mike Keiffer, Hawthorne, California, Steve Propes, Long Beach, California, Ted T. Nichols, Westmont, Illinois, Cliff Hoyt, Buckeystown, Maryland, Dennis Tucker, Maineville, Ohio, Frank Merrill, Macomb, Illinois, Allen E. Paul, Richmond, Indiana, and Bob Bindig, Orchard Park, New York, for contributing needed information and materials. I am also indebted to Peter Glass, East Hartford, Connecticut, for his outstanding photographic services.

I would like to thank the 26 major league baseball clubs and the Society for American Baseball Research (SABR), Cooperstown, New York, for providing materials useful to my research.

Many film and television production companies, art galleries, book and music publishers, and theater and recording companies generously provided photographs and other materials. I am equally indebted to a number of creative artists whose works are herein described, who graciously provided original source materials or copies of their works. Their assistance is deeply appreciated.

During the preparation of this book I resided in southern California and central Connecticut, where I made extensive use of three local libraries, I wish to thank the staffs of the Hawthorne (California) Public Library, the Raymond Library, East Hartford, Connecticut, and the Welles-Turner Memorial Library, Glastonbury, Connecticut, for providing much needed services and filling my many requests.

I am particularly grateful to my editor at Prentice Hall Press, Paul Aron, for his encouragement and expert assistance.

On a personal note, I wish to thank my nephew Jason for his enduring faithfulness. My friends Doug Nelson, Bill Studebaker, Harry and Carla Burgess, Gregory Nelson, and Tom Ito offered support when it was needed most, which was often. To each of them I extend a grateful handshake in thought.

While this book bears no formal dedication, it is to my brothers John, Phil, and Bill that the greatest debt is owed. This book, then, is a testimony not only of a love for baseball but a deeper love among brothers.

—James Mote
East Hartford, Connecticut

Contents

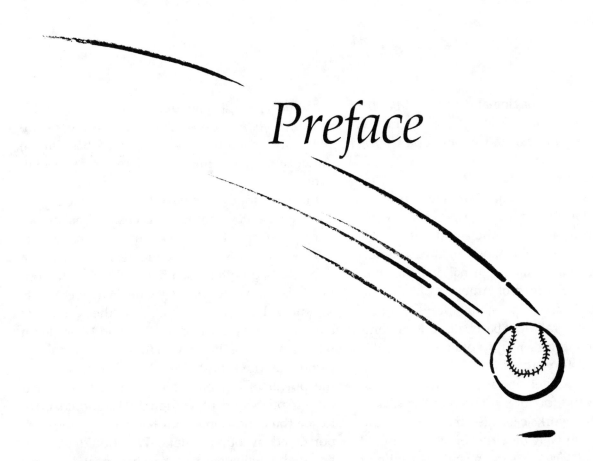

Preface

Anyone whose life has been enriched by the rhythms, the rituals, and the lyric romance of baseball, whose childhood was consumed by an inexhaustible passion for swinging a bat or throwing a ball, knows that there are two kinds of baseball that are played in our lives. One is the real game of baseball: played with a real ball and bat and, always to be preferred, on real grass and in real sunlight. This is the game that is played in vacant lots and playgrounds, in country pastures and in city streets, and which now is as intrinsic to the American landscape as the California redwood or the New England maple. It is the game of our forebears, played when behind every outfield lay an uncharted wilderness of unbounded wealth and splendor. It is the game that has been a companion to more than a hundred of our summers and will likely be a never-disappointing harbinger to a thousand more of our springs.

And then there is the other, interior game of baseball. This is the game that is played in the dreams of children and in the memories of old men and in the imagination of anyone who has ever wished, if only for a moment, that he or she could have been a big league baseball player. It is the mythical, magical game that transcends innings and outs and seasons—and lifetimes. It is the baseball we relive, reshape, and invent anew, and it is played—in winter as in spring—in fields as fertile as the human imagination. It is the game that makes dreamers and storytellers of us all, and it has become as ingrained in the American consciousness as Mark Twain's glorious river or the Lone Ranger's heroic west.

In the other game of baseball, the Dodgers still play in Ebbets Field in Brooklyn, and Joe DiMaggio still patrols the Yankee Stadium center field. In this game, personal favorites of ours—players who are perhaps short on talent but great of heart—become perennial all-stars and, eventually, the occupants of our private halls of fame.

In the baseball we imagine and create, it is possible for us to follow Mickey Mantle in the lineup, to have embraced a weeping Lou Gehrig on his day, or to have witnessed Willie Mays's amazing over-the-shoulder catch in the 1954 World Series—even though we were born in 1955. In the baseball of our dreams, our memories, and our myths, everyone—and not just the ballplayers on the field—joins in the summer-long Maypole dance that is our national pastime.

This book is a record of America's lively, enduring warm-hearted, passionate, and joyously uninhibited celebration of baseball. It documents —for the first time in one volume—baseball's fascinating history in virtually every area of American daily life: in art, cinema, drama, poetry, fable and folklore, story and song. Taken as a whole, the works cataloged in these pages— everything from *Bang the Drum Slowly* to *Casey at the Bat* to *Eight Men Out*—represent the canon of an original American mythology, not unlike that which has been created about the cowboy. In more ways than we may realize, baseball is our Arabian Nights, our King Arthur's Roundtable, and its heroes are our Galahads, our Greek gods. In these pages are found all the legends and lore of our national pastime, which, it can be said, are as compelling as the epic tales of the ancients.

Baseball—the real and the mythologized—is indelibly woven into the fabric of American culture. It has been fused into our language, our humor, our ideals, into the order and pattern of our lives. As one thumbs through the pages of this book, one cannot help but be constantly surprised—astounded—at baseball's extraordinary presence in American daily life. Hardly a day passes, it seems, when the game is not the subject of a newly released movie or song, or a novel that's just been published or a television program that's just been aired. Indeed, baseball's significance in American culture is so far-reaching that

it can only be apprehended in its totality. To this end, *Everything Baseball* presents the most complete and comprehensive view of baseball in American art and life ever offered in any publication.

But why should we wish to explore the mythical, magical, *other* game of baseball? If, as scholar and philosopher Jacques Barzun once wrote, "Whoever wants to know the heart and mind of America had better learn baseball," then the opposite is almost doubtlessly true. Whoever wants to know baseball—the soul of the game, its charm and wonder and allure—had better learn what Americans have written and felt about the game they love best. We should want to learn the power of our baseball dreams as expressed by our poets and playwrights. We should want to see the evocation of our baseball memories as portrayed by our painters. We should want to enjoy the fellowship of baseball nostalgia and folklore as created by our moviemakers and novelists. We should want to examine the ideas and sentiments, the memories and myths, of our artists, writers, thinkers, and self-professed fans. Only in this way can we understand the magical hold baseball has upon us, how it not only diverts us but makes us laugh, makes us dream, and makes us somehow more human if only because the game itself is so irrepressibly alive.

Collected in these pages are the best and worst of American art and life, the significant and the trivial, the timeless and the ephemeral, the obscure and the celebrated. Listed are works that interpret the nature and spirit of the game, that capture the joy and freedom of its participants, re-create the challenges and moral dilemmas as found on the fields of human possibilities. And there are works that simply re-create the dramatics—or, more accurately, the melodramatics of the sport, that merely draw upon the widely accepted presumptions about the game. But mostly, the works cataloged in these pages are the spontaneous expressions of a unique community of people: those who were moved by a genuine fascination—in many cases, a profound passion—for the game of baseball. Theirs are the works that will explain to future millenniums what it was about this child's game that enthralled a nation for more than a hundred and fifty years. Here, then, is baseball's time capsule. Here are the creative efforts of a restless, driving, energetic people concerning their love for a gentle, pastoral, slow-moving game. Here is baseball's legacy. Here is the heart and mind of America.

Directions for Use

Everything Baseball has been designed so that catalog entries as diverse as published music and motion pictures could have a similar appearance and a readily comprehensible text. Because nonprint as well as printed materials are listed, it has been necessary to devise a bibliographical format that accommodates each of the various art forms. For this reason, extensive use of symbols, codes, and abbreviations has been avoided, and differences in terminology (e.g., author, playwright, screenwriter, composer, etc.) have been standardized. The result is a work that serves many levels of interest—in sport, the arts, and mass culture—and as many levels of expertise.

Included in *Everything Baseball* are detailed listings, containing sources and descriptions, of artistic or creative works relating to baseball in America. Succeeding variants of baseball such as softball, stickball, etc., are also listed. Antecedents to baseball, such as stool-ball, rounders, and cricket, are not included in the catalog. All forms of baseball in America—professional, amateur, youth, and sandlot—are represented in *Everything Baseball*.

Only first editions and original issues are listed. Subsequent printings or productions are noted only if the work has been expanded or significantly revised. In each case, the difference between the original and subsequent edition is clearly stated.

Works produced or published after January 1, 1988 are not included in this edition of *Everything Baseball*. Those works will be included in a future edition.

TITLES

Titles of baseball-related works are listed exactly as copyrighted or otherwise presented, including misspellings and lapses of grammar. When a title misspelling of a proper noun exists, the error is corrected in the annotation. No attempt has been made to correct or standardize the title spelling of such baseball terminology as *homerun* or *home run*, as these may indicate the era or the spirit in which the work was created.

It is important to note that the antiquated spelling of *base ball* is retained as originally stated in the titles of early baseball-related works. For purposes of easy identification, however, the words *base ball* are to be considered as one word. All titles beginning with the words *base ball* or *base-ball* are filed under the spelling of *baseball*.

Works bearing no formal title—notably a few paintings or other works of art—can be found under *Untitled*. A few works whose titles are unknown or unverifiable can be located under *Title Not Known*. Only works judged to be historically or artistically significant are listed without actual titles. It is hoped that by their inclusion in *Everything Baseball*, titles to these works will be uncovered and included in a later edition.

Title variants, when known, are listed in the annotation. In each case, the actual or earliest documented title is used in the entry heading.

Works bearing the same title are listed chronologically. When works have the same title and year of origin, the alphabetical arrangement is by the writer or artist's last name.

Titles beginning with an *A, An,* or *The* are arranged alphabetically under the word succeeding the article. Accordingly, a work titled *Base Hit* (1960) will be located after a similar work titled *A Base Hit* (1959), when articles are ignored and the year of origin is considered.

ARTISTS' NAMES

Names of writers and creative artists are standardized throughout *Everything Baseball*. Misprintings or other variant spellings of artists' names are corrected without annotation.

JOSEPH DANIEL TOOMEY JR.
2 CHICAGO W

COLLECTIONS

Library, museum, and other significant holdings of nonprint materials are listed whenever possible. Sources and collections of published materials, with few exceptions, are not listed in *Everything Baseball.*

For selected nonprint works, the Library of Congress card catalog number is given. For other nonprint materials, notably film and television photoplays and documentaries, the United States copyright registration dates and numbers are listed. It is important to note that the absence of a copyright or copyright renewal number is not an indication that a copyright or copyright renewal has not been secured.

CROSS REFERENCES

When a work has been adapted in another form, *see also* is listed for the original and all corresponding titles. Unless noted, the adaptation bears the same title as the original work.

ANNOTATIONS

The purpose of the descriptive annotations is to place a work in a cultural or historical perspective and to relate the work to significant patterns of creative expression; for example, baseball as a folk celebration, as an American symbol, as a metaphor for the human condition, etc. Particular attention has therefore been given to a description of the theme, and not the plot, of narrative works. Metaphorical or allegorical allusions to baseball or baseball players are annotated whenever possible.

For works that have been adapted to other forms, the annotation will be found in the entry listing for the original work. It is important, therefore, to note the *see also* for works bearing no descriptive annotations.

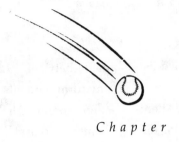

Chapter

1

Baseball in Film

The following catalog contains a comprehensive listing of feature-length and short theatrical photoplays relating to baseball. Included in this section are silent-era comedies and melodramas, baseball serials, film adaptations of baseball-related novels, plays and short stories, original dramas and musicals relating to baseball, and photoplays dramatizing the lives and lore from baseball's past. Also included are baseball-related photoplays available in home video format.

Not included in this section are documentary and historical films relating to baseball. For a lising of these films, *see:* Baseball in Documentary and Miscellaneous Films. For a listing of full-length movies produced for television, *see:* Baseball in Television.

In 1898, just four years after Thomas Edison startled the world with history's first motion picture, *Fred Ott's Sneeze,* Edison released *The Ball Game,* a straightforward look at baseball as played by two local amateur clubs. Ninety years and a few hundred baseball films later, baseball remains a popular—if mostly unsuccessful—theme for the movies. While the early history of baseball films is tainted by low comedy and high melodrama, more recent movies such as *The Natural* and *Eight Men Out* indicate that a new era of serious baseball films may be at hand.

A few of the earliest baseball movies—those produced between 1890 and 1912—can be viewed at the Motion Picture Division of the Library of Congress. In the early days, paper prints of films were deposited in the Library of Congress for purposes of securing copyrights. These paper prints—unlike nitrate-stock film, which decomposes rapidly—are remarkably well preserved. Having recently been converted to film, these historic movies are available for viewing at the Library today.

Unfortunately, the vast majority of baseball movies

made between 1912 and 1939 are no longer extant in any form, and all that is known of these films is what contemporary film reviews tell us. However, a small number of baseball films produced during this era—and many from the later years—are contained in the collections of the American Film Institute at the Library of Congress, the Film Study Center at the Museum of Modern Art in New York, the Yale Film Study Center, and the UCLA Film Center in Los Angeles. In addition, scripts, reviews, books, and other historical materials relating to baseball films are located at the Billy Rose Theatre Collection in the Performing Arts Research Center at Lincoln Center in New York, and the Margaret Herrick Library at the Academy of Motion Picture Arts and Sciences in Beverly Hills, California.

Titles to films contained in this catalog are listed as copyrighted, as shown in the body of the film, as stated on the script, or as given in published reviews. Listings for members of the cast include featured as well as principle players and are not all-inclusive in most cases. Major league baseball players portrayed in each film are listed whenever possible.

Photographs in this section have been provided by the Museum of Modern Art/Film Stills Archive, the National Baseball Library in Cooperstown, New York, and through the courtesy of Allied Artists Productions, Inc., Paramount Pictures, Metro-Goldwyn-Mayer, Universal, Warner Bros., Twentieth Century-Fox, Columbia Pictures, Tri-Star Pictures, and RKO Radio Pictures.

Home video cassettes are available for many baseball films listed in this catalog. For further information regarding home video and other historical and collectible film materials, consult the Selected Guide to Sources and Dealers located at the back of the book.

E X P L A N A T O R Y   N O T E S

1. Title of the photoplay, year of release.

2. Name of the film series in parentheses, if applicable.

3. Name of releasing company.

4. Name of production company.

5. Length of the photoplay in minutes or reels, silent or sound, black and white or color.

6. Writer(s) of photoplay.

7. Director of photoplay.

8. Producer of photoplay.

9. Cast of photoplay.

10. Copyright date and registration number.

11. Name of film library holding a print of the photoplay.

12. Annotation. Description of the photoplay. *Home video* (given when the film is available in home video format).

ALIBI IKE, 1935
Warner Bros.
73 minutes, sound, black and white
Based on the story by Ring W. Lardner, published in the *Saturday Evening Post,* July 31, 1915
Written by William Wister Haines
Directed by Ray Enright
Cast: Joe E. Brown as Frank X. Farrell, Olivia de Havilland as Dolly Stevens, Ruth Donnelly as Bess, Roscoe Karns as Carey, and William Frawley as Cap
See also: Baseball in Radio; Baseball in the Spoken Arts—Recorded

Oafish pitching star becomes involved with gamblers.

ANGELS AND THE PIRATES, 1951
See: Angels in the Outfield

ANGELS IN THE OUTFIELD, 1951
MGM
102 minutes, sound, black and white
Based on the story by Richard Conlin
Written by Dorothy Kingsley and George Wells
Directed and produced by Clarence Brown
Cast: Paul Douglas as Guffy McGovern, Janet Leigh as Jennifer Paige, Donna Corcoran as Bridget White, Keenan Wynn as Fred Bayles, Spring Byington as Sister Edwitha, and Ellen Corby as Sister Veronica
Copyright date and number: August 24, 1951, LP 1159
See also: Baseball in Radio

Crusty manager believes in guardian angels, and a perennial last-place club suddenly contends for the pennant. Released in Europe under the title, Angels and the Pirates.

AROUND THE BASES, 1926
(The Collegians)
Universal Pictures Corp.
Junior Jewel
Two reels, silent, black and white
Written by Carl Laemmle, Jr.
Cast: George Lewis, Eddie Phillips, and Dorothy Gulliver
Copyright date and number: December 21, 1926, LP 23457; May 24, 1954, R 130954

AS THE WORLD ROLLS ON, 1921
Elk Photo Plays
Andlauer Productions
Seven reels, silent, black and white
Cast: Jack Johnson and Blanche Thompson
American Film Institute, Washington, D.C.

The one and only Babe Ruth and Anna Q. Nilsson in a scene from the 1927 silent comedy, Babe Comes Home. *The newlyweds are spatting because the Babe, who had promised to give up his tobacco-chewing habit, had seemed too genuinely pleased by the dozens of tobacco plugs and spittoons he'd received as wedding gifts. (First National Pictures, 1927.)*

A youth, harassed by neighborhood toughs, is taught how to box and play baseball. Features an "all black all-star cast."

AUNT MARY, 1979
See: Baseball in Television

BABE COMES HOME, 1927
First National Pictures
Six reels, silent, black and white
Based on the story, "Said With Soap" by Gerald Beaumont, published in *Redbook*, April 1925, pp. 52–55
Written by Louis Stevens
Directed by Ted Wilde
Cast: Babe Ruth as Babe Dugan, Anna Q. Nilsson as Vernie, Lou Archer as Peewee, and Tom McGuire as the manager
Copyright date and number: April 28, 1927, LP 23893; March 10, 1955, R 145570
American Film Institute, Washington, D.C.

Tobacco-chewing slugger falls into a slump after quitting the habit for his sweetheart.

BABE RUTH BASEBALL SERIES, 1932
(Christy Walsh All-America Sport Series)
Universal Pictures Corp.
Series of films
One reel each, sound, black and white
Written by Lou Breslow
Directed by Ben Stoloff and Lou Breslow
Cast: Babe Ruth

Series of photoplays incorporating baseball instruction from Babe Ruth. Includes: Slide, Babe, Slide; Just Pals; Perfect Control; Fancy Curves; Over the Fence.

THE BABE RUTH STORY, 1948
Allied Artists Productions, Inc.
106 minutes, sound, black and white

William Bendix in the title role of The Babe Ruth Story. *(Allied Artists Productions, Inc., 1948.)*

Written by Bob Considine and George Callahan
Directed and produced by Roy Del Ruth
Cast: William Bendix as Babe Ruth, Claire Trevor as Claire Ruth, Charles Bickford as Brother Matthias, Fred Lightner as Miller Huggins, William Frawley as Jack Dunn, and Mark Koenig as himself
Copyright date and number: August 14, 1948, LP 1877
See also: Baseball in Radio

Fictionalized biography of Babe Ruth. Home video.

THE BAD NEWS BEARS, 1976
Paramount Pictures
102 minutes, sound, color
Written by Bill Lancaster
Directed by Michael Ritchie
Cast: Walter Matthau as Morris Buttermaker, Tatum O'Neal as Amanda Whurlitzer, Vic Morrow as Roy Turner, Joyce Van Patten as Cleveland, and Jackie Earle Haley as Kelly Leak
See also: Baseball in Television; Baseball in Juvenile and Miscellaneous Fiction. *See: The Bad*

In a horrendous slump because he misses his favorite chaw, Babe Dugan, star of the Angels, steps to the plate in a crucial game. A moment later his wife will toss a plug from the stands and the Babe, naturally, will whack a four-bagger to clinch the flag. (First National Pictures, 1927.)

Having already hit three home runs that game, Babe Ruth (William Bendix) prepares to take his final at bat as a player for the Boston Braves. (Allied Artists Productions, Inc., 1948.)

The transformation of Morris Buttermaker (Walter Matthau)—an oafish, beer-guzzling coach of an impudent, inept Little League team—from unwilling volunteer to win-at-all-costs taskmaster is the substance of the irreverent comedy, The Bad News Bears. (Paramount Pictures, 1976.)

News Bears Go to Japan; The Bad News Bears in Breaking Training

Middle-aged alcoholic coaches an inept, irreverent team of Little Leaguers. Home video.

THE BAD NEWS BEARS GO TO JAPAN, 1978
Paramount Pictures
91 minutes, sound, color
Written by Bill Lancaster
Directed by John Berry
Cast: Tony Curtis as Marvin Lazar, Jackie Earle Haley as Kelly Leak, David Pollock as Rudi Stein, Matthew Douglas Anton as E. R. W. Tillyard III, Erin Blunt as Ahmad Rahim, and George Gonzales as Migel Agilar
See also: Baseball in Juvenile and Miscellaneous Fiction. *See:* The Bad News Bears; The Bad News Bears in Breaking Training

Streetwise Little League team outwits their huckster coach who attempts to exploit them for financial gain.

Nothing to Wink At

It can be said of Babe Ruth, as it was once said of another great man, that "the world will not soon look upon the likes of him again." It has been over fifty years since Babe Ruth last played a game of big league baseball, and we've not seen anyone remotely like him stride up to the plate, swing the bat with the sweeping force of a hammer thrower, launch a stupendous drive that seemed propelled by its own engine, trot around the bases in his inimitable pigeon-toed style, thumb his oversized nose at the opposing dugout, doff his cap appreciatively to his adoring fans, and look over his prominent belly to touch home plate and clinch the tour. Not in fifty years

has there been anyone quite like the Babe. It's unlikely there'll be anyone in a thousand and fifty.

Of Babe Ruth's many appealing qualities, one of the most special was the engaging way in which he melded man to myth. On those occasions when an impossibly mythic achievement was attributed to him—which aroused the skepticism of even the most worshipful street urchin —the Babe often would simply wink. It was his way of saying that the feat could have been accomplished if only it had occurred to him to have done it.

In his lifetime Babe Ruth winked at an amazing

number of inventions about him, some of which were forgotten none too quickly, but most of which were entered into the Ruthian canon as indisputable fact. One bit of Ruthiana that can never be forgotten—or winked at—is the motion picture travesty *The Babe Ruth Story*.

Who can forget—or forgive—such scenes as the Babe being implored by a tearful, freckle-faced boy not to let his dog Pee Wee die? Or the look upon the paraplegic child's face when he miraculously rises to his feet at the Babe's off-handed greeting, "Hiya, kid"? Or the Babe's seemingly unending soliloquy at Miller Huggins's deathbed? Or the puttied nose affixed Cyrano-like upon actor William Bendix's face? No one can. No more than Fred Merkle or Mickey Owen could ever forget their misfortunes, either.

For all its rank silliness and grating ineptitude, the film's real fault is in its utter lack of irony, or to put it another way, the Babe's self-knowing wink. In one of the first scenes in the film, we see a ball crashing through a window at St. Mary's Industrial School in Baltimore, causing a perfect baseball-sized hole to be made at the center of the curiously shatterproof glass. Who hit that prodigious blast, Father Matthias is asked by a visitor. The schoolboy Babe is told to come over to where Baltimore Orioles manager Jack Dunn and Father Matthias are standing. Sure, the Babe can hit. But can he also throw? Why, the Babe will show you. William Bendix winds and uncorks a Baltimore-to-Washington perfect strike right into the very baseball-sized hole in the window, not enlarging the hole one iota. Not a gasp but a Ruthian wink is called for here. The scene, like the entire movie, is played as though William Bendix were Charlton Heston and Babe Ruth were Moses, not as an embellishment of sports-page mythology but as gospel.

It is unfortunate that much of what the world knows about Babe Ruth is based upon this movie

and other exaggerated tales, because the real Babe Ruth is eminently worth knowing. This extraordinary ballplayer—possibly the greatest baseball player ever to have played the game—was not a buffoonish braggart but a man who possessed a boundless affinity for people and zest for life. While he was indeed gluttonous in the extreme, and notoriously licentious within the special province of the locker room, the bar-room and the hotel suite (he was, after all, a jock), Babe Ruth was far from being an uncivilized lout. If anything, the Babe's affable warmth and humanity, his magnetic presence, encouraged the boisterousness in others, especially the men who wanted to shake his hand, the kids who wanted his autograph, and the adoring women who wanted the pleasure of his company.

A journalist once told a story of a time during his childhood when Babe Ruth and the touring New York Yankees played his small-town minor league heroes at the local ballpark. After his heroes had been thoroughly drubbed by the major leaguers, the boy's father—attempting to cheer up the child—arranged an introduction with the Babe. The journalist recalled how as a child he would not shake the hand that had been kindly offered him. The Babe, sensing the boy's disappointment at the outcome of the game, said to the father as he drove away: "Tell the boy we were lucky today."

This sensitive and ennobling remark is hardly the demurral of the swaggering buffoon portrayed in the film.

Babe Ruth—the real Babe Ruth—was a consummate professional on the ball field. He took baseball, children, food, his fans, and lovemaking seriously and enjoyed each voraciously. But everything else he winked at: money, U.S. presidents, speed limits, people's names, the Great Depression, pint-sized managers, and the shamelessly overblown folklore of deifying sportswriters. The Babe would be a great pitcher or a great home run hitter, whatever was asked of him. He would eat hot dogs or the finest steaks, whichever was available. He could be as happy with a group of frenzied kids or a bevy of beautiful women, it didn't matter which. But Babe Ruth could not be anything but completely himself. Give the Babe his appetites and his passions and the world could have the rest of him—and make of him whatever it wished.

Because the Babe never bothered to dispel the myths, and as he took great pains never to disappoint or deflate his fans, who were the keepers of the myths, Babe Ruth remained not only bigger than life but bigger than the myths that were created about him. It took a special human being to be Everyman and Superman at one and the same time, particularly as he plied his trade in a game as capricious as baseball. But somehow the Babe was able to live his whale-sized life in the proverbial fish bowl—and achieve his incredible hitting heroics—without seeming to elevate himself at the expense of the common man. Indeed, there was not a move the Babe made, whether attending a wedding of a business associate or playing nine holes on the local links, that his adoring public did not experience with him—

either in person or through detailed newspaper accounts the following day. Throughout Babe Ruth's public and baseball life, the whole world was a worried and doting Aunt Polly to his mischievous Tom Sawyer.

In story and song, drama, and verse, Babe Ruth was mythologized with flagrant—but not necessarily unscrupulous—disregard to the truth. In this respect, *The Babe Ruth Story* differs from previous treatments of the Babe's life. Unlike the other mythological tales in which the Babe was present—and winking—at their telling, the film was produced while the Babe lay dying of cancer in a New York hospital. Had Babe Ruth enjoyed good health he would have thrown all the world a wink to let everyone know that the movie was harmless hokum and nothing more. But his death two days after the film's New York premiere forever recast the picture from a shallow recapitulation of popular mythology to hopeless parody. One simply cannot watch this awful film without thinking that the Babe had been unforgivably betrayed.

Even now, decades after his death, Babe Ruth remains bigger than life, far bigger, of course, than baseball. But in this priggish movie, the Babe is never any bigger than the tabloid sports pages. ◆

THE BAD NEWS BEARS IN BREAKING TRAINING, 1977
Paramount Pictures
100 minutes, sound, color
Written by Paul Brickman
Directed by Michael Pressman
Cast: William Devane as Mike Leak, Jackie Earle Haley as Kelly Leak, Jimmy Baio as Carmen Ronzonni, David Pollock as Rudi Stein, and Chris Barnes as Tanner Boyle
See also: Baseball in Juvenile and Miscellaneous Fiction. *See: The Bad*

News Bears; The Bad News Bears Go to Japan

Motley Little League team plays for the championship. Home video.

BANG THE DRUM SLOWLY, 1973
Paramount Pictures
Rosenfield Productions
97 minutes, sound, color
Written by Mark Harris from his novel of the same name
Directed by John Hancock

Cast: Michael Moriarty as Henry Wiggen, Robert DeNiro as Bruce Pearson, Vincent Gardenia as Dutch Schnell, Phil Foster as Joe Jaros, Ann Wedgeworth as Katie, Patrick McVey as Mr. Pearson, and Tom Ligon as Piney Woods
See also: Baseball in Television; Baseball in Fiction; Baseball in Miscellaneous Recordings

Star pitcher Henry Wiggen befriends a second-string catcher who is secretly dying of an incurable disease. Home video.

BASEBALL, A GRAND OLD GAME, 1914
Biograph Co.
One reel, silent, black and white
Copyright date and number: August 26, 1914, LU 3261

BASEBALL AND BLOOMERS, 1911
Thanhouser Co.
One reel, silent, black and white
Cast: William Garwood

BASEBALL AND BLOOMERS, 1919
(Facts and Follies Series)
Physical Culture Photoplays, Inc.
One reel, silent, black and white
Directed and produced by Bernarr MacFadden
Copyright date and number: December 3, 1919, LP 14509

BASEBALL AND TROUBLE, 1914
Lubin Manufacturing Co.
One reel, silent, black and white
Written by O. A. Nelson
Copyright date and number: December 31, 1914, LP 4110

BASEBALL AT MUDVILLE, 1917
Selig
One reel, silent, black and white
Written by J. J. Roberts
Directed by Norval MacGregor
Cast: Lee Morris, John Lancaster, and William Hutchinson

Men's baseball club, disguised as the Milligan Bloomer Girls, plays a roughneck game against a gentlemanly local team.

BASEBALL BILL, 1916
Universal Film Manufacturing Co., Inc.
Series of six films
One reel each, silent, black and white

Series of comic melodramas featuring Baseball Bill. Includes: Baseball Bill (premiere

Pitcher Henry Wiggen (Michael Moriarty) and third-string catcher Bruce Pearson (Robert DeNiro) attempt to keep an agonizing secret from their teammates in the 1973 film adaptation of Mark Harris's classic novel, Bang the Drum Slowly. *Pearson's impending death serves as a backdrop to explore the value and meaning of male relationships and friendships. (Paramount Pictures, 1973.)*

episode); Flirting with Marriage; The Black Nine; Baseball Madness; A Box of Tricks; Strike One.

BASEBALL BILL, 1916
(Baseball Bill)
Universal Film Manufacturing Co., Inc.
Laemmle
One reel, silent, black and white
Written and directed by Billy Mason
Credits: Al Russell
Copyright date and number: June 22, 1916, LP 8558
See: Baseball Bill

Premiere chapter in a series of six films.

THE BASEBALL BUG, 1911
Thanhouser Co.
One reel, silent, black and white

Cast: John W. Noble and Florence LaBadie

The wife of a conceited small-town player exposes his limited baseball abilities with the aid of Hall of Fame pitcher Chief Bender and two of his Philadelphia A's teammates, Rube Oldring and Jack Coombs.

THE BASEBALL FAN, 1908
Essanay
One reel, silent, black and white
Written and directed by G. M. (Broncho Billy) Anderson

Slapstick adventures of a fan's visit to a Chicago White Sox game.

THE BASEBALL FAN, 1914
Powers Co.
Released April 10, 1914

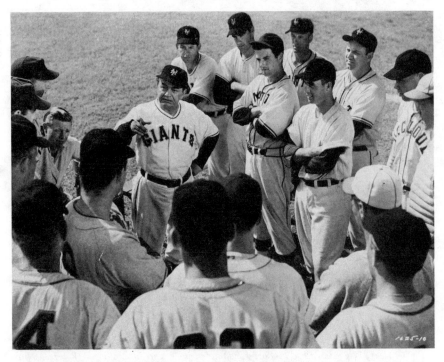

Coach Hans Lobert (Edward G. Robinson) is a director of a Florida tryout camp in the 1953 film, The Big Leaguer. Among the two hundred big league hopefuls are Adam Polachuk, whose coal-mining father thinks he is studying to be a lawyer, Bobby Bronson, a brash show-off from the midwest, Julie Davis, a New York street tough, and a famous ballplayer's son who'd rather pursue a career as an architect than a life as a baseball player. Hall of Famer Carl Hubbell shows up to give a few pointers and to lend authenticity to the melodrama. (Metro-Goldwyn-Mayer, 1953.)

THE BASEBALL FANS OF FANVILLE, 1914
Joker Co.
Cast: William Franey

BASEBALL MADNESS, 1917
(Baseball Bill)
Universal Film Manufacturing Co., Inc.
Victor
One reel, silent, black and white
Directed by Billy Mason
Credits: Al Russell
Cast: Billy Mason, Orin Jackson, Countess Du Cello, Gloria Swanson, and Marc Fenton
Copyright date and number: April 21, 1917, LP 10614
See: Baseball Bill

BASEBALL'S PEERLESS LEADER, 1913
Patheplay
Two reels, silent, black and white
Cast: Frank Chance, Gwendolyn Pates, and Ned Burton

Romantic drama starring the Chicago Cubs' famed first baseman.

BASEBALL STAR FROM BINGVILLE, 1911
Essanay
One reel, silent, black and white
Released June 27, 1911

Comedic adventures of an overweight small-town player.

BASEBALL, THAT'S ALL!, 1910

George Melies
One reel, silent, black and white
Released September 8, 1910

Office clerk's obsessive interest in baseball costs him his job and nearly wrecks his marriage.

THE BASEBALL UMPIRE, 1913
Majestic
Released September 23, 1913

BATTER UP, 1927
(Mermaid Comedies)
Educational Film Exchanges, Inc.
Two reels, silent, black and white
Directed by Stephen Roberts
Produced by Jack White
Copyright date and number: August 17, 1927, LP 24372

THE BATTLING ORIOLES, 1924
Associated Exhibitors
Pathe Exchange
Hal E. Roach Studios
Six reels, silent, black and white
Directed by Ted Wilde and Fred Guiol
Cast: Glenn Tryon as Tommy Roosevelt Tucker, Blanche Mehaffey as Hope Stanton, John T. Prince as Cappy Wolfe, and Noah Young as Sid Stanton
Copyright date and number: September 25, 1924, LP 20608
American Film Institute, Washington, D.C.

Aged members of the champion 1874 Orioles attempt to develop the son of a deceased teammate into a big leaguer.

BETRAYED, 1925
(Play Ball)
Two reels, silent, black and white
Copyright date and number: June 23, 1925, LP 21580; October 10, 1952, R 100757
See: Play Ball (1925)

THE BIG LEAGUER, 1953
MGM

73 minutes, sound, black and white
Written by Herbert Baker
Directed by Robert Aldrich
Cast: Edward G. Robinson as John B.
"Hans" Lobert, Vera-Ellen as Christy,
Jeff Richards as Adam Polachuk,
Richard Jaeckel as Bobby Bronson,
William Campbell as Julie Davis, and
Carl Hubbell and Al Campanis as
themselves
Copyright date and number: July 13,
1953, LP 2765

*Son is determined to play professional baseball
against his father's wishes.*

THE BINGO LONG TRAVELING ALL-STARS AND MOTOR KINGS, 1976

---

*Star slugger for the Baltimore Elite Giants,
Leon Carter (James Earl Jones), strides to the
plate to face trick-pitcher Bingo Long. Carter's
home run prompts Long to invite the slugging
catcher to join his touring all-star club. (Universal, 1976.)*

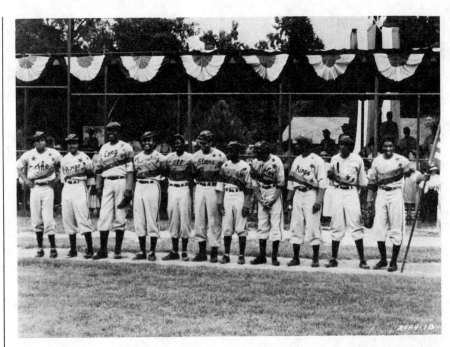

The lineup of the 1930s-era all-black touring all-stars, The Bingo Long Traveling All-Stars and
Motor Kings. *Billy Dee Williams stars as pitcher Bingo Long, James Earl Jones as Leon Carter, and
Richard Pryor as Charlie Snow. (Universal, 1976.)*

Universal
110 minutes, sound, color
Based on the novel by William
Brashler
Written by Hal Barwood and
Matthew Robbins
Directed by John Badham
Cast: Billy Dee Williams as Bingo
Long, James Earl Jones as Leon
Carter, Richard Pryor as Charlie
Snow, Stan Shaw as Esquire Joe, and
Ted Ross as Sallison Potter
*See also: Baseball in Fiction; Baseball in
Miscellaneous Recordings. See: Bingo!*
(Baseball in Theater)

*Misadventures of a barnstorming team of black
all-stars during the 1930s.* Home video.

THE BLACK NINE, 1917
(Baseball Bill)

Universal Film Manufacturing Co.,
Inc.
Special Victor
One reel, silent, black and white
Written and produced by Billy Mason
Copyright date and number: January
10, 1917, LP 9968
See: Baseball Bill

BLUE SKIES AGAIN, 1983
Warner Bros.
Lantana
96 minutes, sound, color
Written by Kevin Sellers
Directed by Richard Michaels
Cast: Robyn Barto as Paula Fradkin,
Harry Hamlin, Mimi Rogers, Kenneth
McMillan, Dana Elcar, and Marcos
Gonzales

*Woman aspires to become the first female major
league baseball player.* Home video.

Second basewoman Paula Fradkin (Robyn Barto) prepares to take her first at bat in a big league spring training game in the film, Blue Skies Again. *The former fast-pitch softball star is attempting to become the first woman to play in the major leagues. (Warner Bros., 1983.)*

A BOX OF TRICKS, 1917
(Baseball Bill)
Universal Film Manufacturing Co., Inc.
Special Victor
One reel, silent, black and white
Directed by John Stepping
Credits: Harry Wulze
Copyright date and number: May 22, 1917, LP 10814
See: Baseball Bill

BREAKING INTO THE BIG LEAGUE, 1913
Kalem
Series of two films
One reel each, silent, black and white
Cast: Harry Millarde, Marguerite Courtot, Henry Hallam, John McGraw, and Christy Mathewson

BREWSTER'S MILLIONS, 1985
Universal Pictures
97 minutes, sound, color
Based on a novel by George Barr McCutcheon
Written by Herschel Weingrod and Timothy Harris
Directed by Walter Hill
Cast: Richard Pryor as Montgomery Brewster, John Candy as Spike Nolan, Lonette McKee as Angela Drake, Stephen Collins as Warren Cox, Jerry Orbach as Charley Pegler, and Pat Hingle as Edward Roundfield

Minor league pitcher inherits $300 million on the condition that he spends $30 million in 30 days. Home video.

BROTHER RAT, 1938
Warner Bros.
90 minutes, sound, black and white

Based on the play by John Monks, Jr. and Fred R. Finklehoffe
Written by Richard Macaulay and Jerry Wald
Directed by William Keighley
Cast: Priscilla Lane as Joyce Winfree, Eddie Albert as Bing Edwards, Wayne Morris as Billy Randolph, Ronald Reagan as Dan Crawford, and Jane Wyman as Claire Adams
See also: Baseball in Theater. See: About Face; Brother Rat and a Baby (Baseball in Film: Appendix)

BULL DURHAM, 1988
Orion Pictures Corp.
North State Films, Inc.
115 minutes, sound, color
Written and directed by Ron Shelton
Produced by Thom Mount and Mark Burg
Cast: Kevin Costner as Crash Davis, Tim Robbins as Ebby Calvin (Nuke) LaLoosh, Susan Sarandon as Annie Savoy, Trey Wilson as Skip, Robert Wuhl as Larry, and Max Patkin as himself

Two small-town minor league teammates fall in love with a flamboyantly eccentric woman baseball fan.

BUMPTIOUS PLAYS BASEBALL, 1910
Edison Manufacturing Co.
One reel, silent, black and white
Copyright date and number: October 7, 1910, J 146436–39

Mr. Bumptious, an overweight, self-important man, plays baseball.

THE BUSHER, 1919
Thos. H. Ince Corp.
Five reels, silent, black and white
Based on the story by Earle Snell
Written by R. Cecil Smith
Directed by Jerome Storm
Cast: Charles Ray as Ben Harding,

Colleen Moore as the girl, and Otto Hoffman as the deacon
Copyright date and number: May 7, 1919, LP 13709

Big league pitcher, released for intemperance and insubordination, returns home in disgrace.

THE BUSH LEAGUER, 1917
Selig
One reel, silent, black and white
Cast: Lee Morris, John Lancaster, and William Hutchinson

Pitcher exerts hypnotic powers over opposing batters.

THE BUSH LEAGUER, 1927
Warner Bros.
Seven reels, silent, black and white
Based on the story by Charles Gordon Saxton
Written by Harvey Gates
Directed by Howard Bretherton
Cast: Monte Blue as Specs White, Clyde Cook as Skeeter McKinnon, Leila Hyams as Alice Hobbs, and William Demerest as John Gilroy
Copyright date and number: August 8, 1927, LP 24278
American Film Institute, Washington, D.C.

Rookie pitcher proves his allegiance to his team —and his love for its female owner—by hitting a home run in the clutch.

BUTTER FINGERS, 1925
Pathe Exchange, Inc.
Mack Sennett, Inc.
Two reels, silent, black and white
Directed by Del Lord
Cast: Billy Bevan
Copyright date and number: June 23, 1925, LU 21583

A batted baseball lands in a barrel of tar and wreaks havoc on a game fixed by gamblers.

CASEY AT THE BAT, 1899
Thomas A. Edison

Fabled pitcher Christy Mathewson and manager John McGraw of the New York Giants were the stars of this 1913 series of two one-reelers. The poster for this silent film is an extremely rare collector's item today. (Kalem, 1913.)

One reel, silent, black and white
Copyright date and number: April 22, 1899, 27968

Documentary-style dramatization bearing no relation to the famous ballad.

Wallace Beery stars as a gullible braggart who refuses a bribe in the 1927 silent comedy, Casey at the Bat. *After making it to the major leagues as a slugger for the New York Giants, the small-town hero finds the lure and excitement of the big city too much to resist, and, naturally, he fans in a pinch. But the mighty Casey is exonerated when it's discovered that he had not taken a bribe after all but had struck out on an illegally thrown pitch. (Paramount Pictures, 1927.)*

Wallace Beery and small-town sweetheart ZaSu Pitts are pictured in this lobby card for Casey at the Bat. *(Paramount Pictures, 1927.)*

CASEY AT THE BAT, 1913
Vitagraph
One reel, silent, black and white
Written and directed by James Young
Cast: Harry T. Morey, Norma Talmadge, Harry Northrup, and Kate Price

CASEY AT THE BAT, 1916
Fine Arts-Triangle
Five reels, silent, black and white
Written by William Everett Wing
Directed by Lloyd Ingraham
Cast: DeWolf Hopper as Casey, Kate Toncray as Casey's sister, May Garcia as Casey's daughter, Carl Stockdale as Hicks, and William H. Brown as Judge Blodgett

Hopper is better known for his popular recordings of the famous ballad. (See: Baseball in Comedy and Light Verse—Recorded).

CASEY AT THE BAT, 1920
John Franklin Meyer
Copyright date and number: December 18, 1920, MP 1811

CASEY AT THE BAT, 1927
Paramount Pictures
Famous Players-Lasky
Six reels, silent, black and white
Written by Hector Turnbull and Jules Furthman
Directed by Monte Brice
Cast: Wallace Beery as Casey, Ford Sterling as O'Dowd, ZaSu Pitts as Camille, and Sterling Holloway as Putnam
Copyright date and number: March 5, 1927, LP 23753; March 22, 1954, R 12763
American Film Institute, Washington, D.C.

After being framed by gamblers, a gullible Casey is struck out by an illegally thrown pitch.

Quigley, Rita Hayworth, Patricia Farr, and John Gallaudet
Copyright date and number: June 8, 1937, LP 7193; April 15, 1965, R 359447

The star of a women's softball team investigates the murder of a teammate.

GOODBYE, FRANKLIN HIGH, 1978
Cal-Am Artists
94 minutes, sound, color
Written by Stu Krieger
Directed by Mike MacFarland
Cast: Lane Caudell as Will Armer, Ann Dusenberry, Darby Hinton, Julie Adams, and William Windom

A high-school senior must decide between college and a baseball career.

GRACIE AT THE BAT, 1937
Columbia Pictures Corp. of California, Ltd.
Two reels, sound, black and white
Written by Elwood Ullman and Al Giebler
Directed by Del Lord
Cast: Andy Clyde, Louise Stanley, Leora Thatcher, Ann Doran, and Bud Jamison
Copyright date and number: October 4, 1937, LP 7471; August 18, 1965, R 367088

A male coaches a women's softball team.

THE GREAT AMERICAN PASTIME, 1956
MGM
89 minutes, sound, black and white

Directed by Herman Hoffman
Cast: Tom Ewell, Anne Francis, Ann Miller, Dean Jones, and Ruby Dee
Copyright date and number: November 15, 1956, LP 7377

An attorney coaches a suburban Little League team.

HAL CHASE'S HOME RUN, 1911
Kalem
One reel, silent, black and white
Cast: Hal Chase

A ninth-inning home run by New York Yankees' star Hal Chase helps a teammate to win the affection of a lady friend.

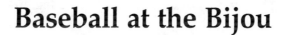

Baseball at the Bijou

While Hollywood has portrayed baseball with considerably less élan than it has children and dogs, cowboys and horses, or even mad scientists and oversized lizards, the depiction of baseball on the silver screen has not been as woeful as tradition would have us believe. True, Orson Welles never offered the world *Citizen O'Malley*, and D. W. Griffith never contemplated *The Birth of Baseball*. And the fact is that films such as *The Babe Ruth Story* and *The Kid from Cleveland* not only poisoned the genre but nearly made cricket fans of us all. But the truth remains that Hollywood, despite its penchant for showing the game as low-level melodrama, has made a number of worthy contributions to baseball lore and even a cinematic gem or two.

The first motion picture ever made on a baseball subject was Thomas Edison's *The Ball Game* in 1898. It consists of a few short scenes showing two amateur baseball clubs playing a makeshift game. The next year Edison released *Casey at the Bat*, a crude burlesque in which a baseball player pummels an umpire after striking out. The film bears no relation to the famous ballad of the same name.

Several short comedies were produced in the years immediately following, including Edison's *How the Office Boy Saw the Ball Game* in 1906, but the first feature film relating to baseball appears to have been *His Last Game*, released by the Independent Motion Picture Company in December 1909. In this bewildering melodrama, the Choctaw Indian baseball team, led by star pitcher Bill Going, is slated to play the local Jimtown club, made up of local cowboys. Interest in the game is at a fever pitch and wagering among the

Hal Chase, the free-spirited player-manager of the New York Highlanders and star of the 1911 silent film, Hal Chase's Home Run. *(National Baseball Library.)*

menfolk in the small Arizona town is intense. Two cowboys, intending to make good on their bets, approach the Native American with an offer of a bribe, which the proud Going declines. Later, after he nearly imbibes a drink that had been drugged, the pitcher confronts the two gamblers and kills one of them in self-defense. Going is quickly arrested and sentenced to death —but he is granted a temporary reprieve out of respect for his unswerving scrupulousness. He is allowed to participate in the all-important baseball game, which, of course, he wins singlehandedly with his pitching and hitting heroics. The movie concludes with the Choctaw pitcher sitting cross-legged at the edge of an open grave, calmly smoking a pipe. The abrupt ending prompted *Variety* to suggest that some form of censorship might have been applied, as the exe-

cution appeared to have been mysteriously edited out. The film, at any rate, was a success, as movies about Native Americans—virtually all of them portraying degrading stereotypes—were the rage in the early 1900s. *His Last Game* was just one of fifty motion pictures incorporating an Indian theme released in 1909 alone.

The first major leaguer to star in a feature film was a free-thinking, high-spirited, audacious Californian, named Hal Chase, who appeared in *Hal Chase's Home Run* in 1911. The player-manager of the New York Highlanders (now Yankees) was a natural for the movies: handsome, athletic, graceful, ebullient, and self-assured. He was the greatest fielding first baseman of his time (his specialty was charging bunts, a critical skill during deadball-era baseball), and was an excellent hitter. In 1911, the year the movie was released, Chase hit .315 with 32 doubles and 36 stolen bases. He was known by his fans—and they were legion—as Prince Hal.

Chase's role in the film was relatively minor. A baseball-crazy friend of his is courting a woman who resents her man's fanatical interest in the game. In a fit of petulance, the woman demands that the New York club win the pennant or else the engagement is off. The friend desperately enlists the aid of Hal Chase, who obligingly hits a home run in the bottom of the ninth to bag the pennant and his friend's marriage as well.

It was not to be a life of movie-star fame and baseball glamour for Chase, however. Rumors circulated in baseball that Prince Hal was involved in game fixing, and while nothing was ever proved, his teammates and managers—especially the venerated Christy Mathewson— were convinced of Chase's culpability. After being effectively blackballed from the major leagues, Chase continued playing outlaw and semipro baseball wherever he could hang his glove. But rumors continued to dog the exiled first baseman. Added to others were those concerning his alleged involvement in the 1919 "Black Sox" scandal. He died, an alcoholic and a pauper, at age 64.

Frank Chance, the Chicago Cubs player-manager, starred in *Baseball's Peerless Leader* (also titled *The Peerless Leader*) in 1911, and Frank "Home Run" Baker, a third baseman in the Philadelphia Athletics' celebrated "$100,000 Infield," was the star of *A Short-Stop's Double* in 1913 and *"Home Run" Baker's Double* in 1914. The great Ty Cobb starred in *Somewhere in Georgia* in 1916, a melodramatic romance written by Grantland Rice, which critic Ward Morehouse later recalled as "absolutely the worst movie I ever saw." Christy Mathewson and manager John McGraw were the stars of a two-part feature titled *Breaking into the Big League* in 1913. Thereafter it was common for baseball stars to appear in motion pictures, although none ever came close to achieving the success in celluloid that he enjoyed on the diamond.

One famous ballplayer of the day, outfielder Mike Donlin of the New York Giants, aspired to be something more than a curiosity on the screen. In 1915 he produced and starred in his own feature, titled *Right Off the Bat*, a self-mythologizing autobiography detailing the slugger's rise from small-town hero to big league star. The picture was generally well received by the critics. *Variety* said of Donlin's effort: "Mike was a distinct surprise and, contrary to custom, could pass as a film lead on ability alone." Indeed, Donlin went on to appear—mostly in minor roles and usually as a gangster—in dozens of films, talkies as well as silents. His *Right Off the Bat*, however, was his only starring film role.

Most early baseball films, even those made before the 1919 "Black Sox" scandal came to light, focused on the game-fixing angle. Inevitably, a baseball player is approached by gamblers with a

Frank "Home Run" Baker, who led the American League with eight home runs in 1914, was the popular star of two early silent baseball movies. (National Baseball Library.)

bribe too good to refuse. The ballplayer, a member in good standing in the baseball priesthood, refuses the bribe and heroically attempts to defend baseball's honor through the use of physical force—a struggle he invariably loses. The game fixers then kidnap the ballplayer in order to secure their bets and do away with a witness to their crime. But without fail, the hero shows incredible resourcefulness in a crisis and escapes, usually as the ninth inning is about to begin, to hit a home run in the clutch and win the game.

Typical of this genre was the 1924 silent movie

Life's Greatest Game, in which a small-town player refuses to throw a game for a gambler, who gets even by stealing the ballplayer's family away. Jack Donovan, the ballplayer, believing his family has perished in an ocean liner accident, goes on to become a major league star, and, twenty years later, manager of the New York Giants. One day his son joins the Giants as a star pitcher and, to spite his father who he believes had abandoned him, resolves to throw a World Series game. The manager, unaware that the pitcher is his son, attempts to mold the young star into an exemplary major leaguer, and in the end it works. The lad pitches his team to a World Series victory over the Yankees. The film is noteworthy because the director, despite making a serious effort to portray baseball realistically, still allowed the picture to lapse into maudlin melodrama. The trend was simply too strong to buck.

Latter-day Hollywood, contending with a tradition of baseball as surefire box office poison, played it safe from the 1940s to the early 1960s, producing a number of light baseball comedies such as *It Happens Every Spring, Angels in the Outfield,* and *Take Me Out to the Ball Game,* or biographical dramas such as *The Winning Team, The Stratton Story,* and *The Pride of the Yankees.* Although the hoary melodrama was largely avoided, baseball films from this era were mediocre at best. Even the much-celebrated *Pride of the Yankees* was mawkish and as predictable as a Wade Boggs .300 season.

Fear Strikes Out, the story of Boston Red Sox outfielder Jimmy Piersall's emotional breakdown, was a decided cut above the usual baseball movie. Though criticized for actor Anthony

Perkins's distinct unathleticism (he even wore shoulder pads under his uniform to give himself a broader appearance), Piersall's mental anguish and his family's inability to comprehend the depth of his suffering were effectively portrayed. The scene in which the father implores the child Piersall to catch balls that were thrown increasingly hard and fast is unforgettable, as is the haunting scene in which the major leaguer Piersall climbs the backstop screen to seek his father's approval.

Other notable films include *Damn Yankees,* an appealing adaptation of the long-running theatrical hit; *The Jackie Robinson Story,* clearly the best of the baseball bioflicks, probably because a winning Jackie Robinson portrayed himself in the film; and *Bang the Drum Slowly,* a somewhat ponderous but still riveting adaptation of Mark Harris's novel. In 1976 Hollywood scored its first box office smash hit with a baseball movie with the release of *The Bad News Bears,* a hilarious and irreverent treatment of Little League baseball and the win-at-all-costs mentality that pervades our culture. But it was not until *The Natural* was released in 1984 that a baseball movie was taken seriously as adult entertainment. While the film was a popular and visual success, its too-earnest attempts at importance and meaningfulness give virtually every scene an overbearingly studied tone. But the film convinced Hollywood that a baseball movie, unencumbered by melodramatics or gimmickry, will appeal to a popular audience. *Bull Durham* and *Eight Men Out,* two recent motion pictures intended for adult viewership, may be harbingers of more to come. ◆

HEADIN' HOME, 1920
Cine-Vintage Films
Yankee Co.
Five reels, silent, black and white

Subtitles written by Arthur "Bugs" Baer
Directed by Lawrence Windom
Cast: Babe Ruth, Ruth Taylor, Tom

Cameron, James A. Marcus, Ricca Allen, Ann Brody, and Margaret Seddon

THE BABE AS THESPIAN

Babe Ruth starred in two films, *Headin' Home* and *Babe Comes Home*, and made cameo appearances in several other movies, notably *Speedy* and *The Pride of the Yankees*. Although there was little question that his presence on the screen matched his charisma on the baseball field, opinions regarding Ruth's acting abilities were somewhat less than unanimous.

A Yankee teammate of the Babe's, shortstop Mark Koenig, recalled flatly: "He couldn't act worth crap." And yet a *New York Times* reviewer said of Ruth's brief but amusing appearance in *Speedy* that, "The big Babe does some excellent acting. . . ." And *Variety* offered the Babe an unqualified, if backhanded compliment on his role in *Headin' Home* by declaring, "He, and he alone, makes it worth five minutes of anybody's time."

Perhaps it was the Babe himself who provided the most telling assessment of his cinematic career. He once wrote, with unsparing irony: "There never was a movie quite like *Headin' Home*. Thank God."

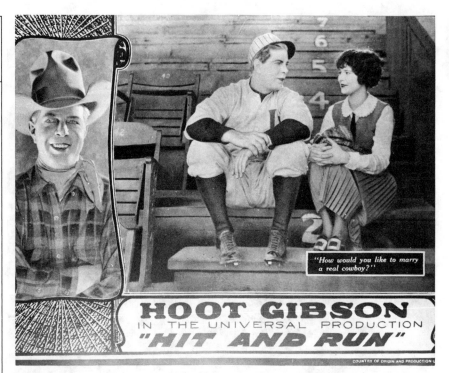

Cowboy actor Hoot Gibson was the star of the 1924 silent baseball film, Hit and Run, *in which he and his sweetheart (Marion Harlan) are kidnapped by gamblers intent on fixing the World Series. The slugger uses a little cattle-punching know-how to lasso his way to freedom and win the game with a home run in the pinch. (Paramount Pictures, 1924.)*

A small-town slugger wins fame, fortune, and love.

THE HECKLER, 1940
Columbia Pictures
Two reels, sound, black and white
Directed by Del Lord
Cast: Charley Chase, Bruce Bennett, Richard Fiske, Stanley Brown, Don Beddoe, and Robert Sterling
Copyright date and number: February 4, 1940, LP 9399

An avid baseball fan behaves obnoxiously at the ballpark. Remade as Mr. Noisy.

HERE COME THE TIGERS, 1978
Filmways Pictures
American International Pictures
90 minutes, sound, color
Written by Arch McCoy
Directed by Sean S. Cunningham
Cast: Richard Lincoln as Coach Eddie Burke, James Zvanut, Samantha Grey, William Caldwell, and Manny Lieberman

Inept Little League team wins a championship, a la Bad News Bears.

HER FIRST GAME, 1917
Metro Pictures Corp.
One reel, silent, black and white
Cast: Mr. and Mrs. Sidney Drew, and Wally Pipp
Copyright date and number: August 13, 1917, LP 11247; April 11, 1945, R 139160

Misadventures of a woman attending her first baseball game.

HIS LAST GAME, 1909
Independent Motion Picture Co.
Laemmle
One reel, silent, black and white
Released December 6, 1909

In this earliest-known dramatic photoplay relating to baseball, the star player for an all-Indian baseball team hits a home run in the clutch after refusing a bribe from cowboy gamblers.

Clubhouse melodrama in the 1942 film, It Happened in Flatbush. *The batboy for the Brooklyn Dodgers intercedes on behalf of Frank Maguire (Lloyd Nolan), whose hard-nosed win-at-all-costs managing (not to mention his romance with the woman owner of the team) has incited the players to circulate a petition demanding his removal from the helm. (Twentieth Century–Fox, 1942.)*

HIT AND RUN, 1924
Universal Pictures
Six reels, silent, black and white
Written by Edward Sedgwick and
Raymond L. Schrock
Directed by Edward Sedgwick
Cast: Hoot Gibson as Swat Anderson,
Marion Harlan as Joan McCarthy,
Cyril Ring as George Collins, and
Mike Donlin as Red McCarthy
Copyright date and number: July 14,
1924, LP 20389
American Film Institute, Washington,
D.C.

Slugger is kidnapped by gamblers but escapes to win the game.

A HOME PLATE WEDDING, 1925
(Play Ball)
Two reels, silent, black and white
Copyright date and number:
September 25, 1925, LP 21848;
October 10, 1952, R 100764
See Play Ball (1925)

HOME RUN AMBROSE, 1918
L-Ko Motion Picture Kompany
Two reels, silent, black and white
Directed by W. S. Fredricks
Cast: Mack Swain
Copyright date and number: January
8, 1918, LP 11917

"HOME RUN" BAKER'S DOUBLE, 1914
Kalem
Two reels, silent, black and white
Written and directed by Kenean Buel
Cast: Frank "Home Run" Baker,
Marguerite Courtot, Henry Hallam,
Ben Ross, and Helen Lindroth

HOME RUN BILL, 1919
Universal Film Manufacturing Co.,
Inc.
Nestor
One reel, silent, black and white
Cast: Billy Mason
Copyright date and number: March 4,
1919, LP 13479

HOT CURVES, 1930
Tiffany Productions
Nine reels, sound, black and white
Based on the story by A. P. Younger
and Frank Mortimer
Written by Earle Snell
Directed by Norman Taurog
Cast: Benny Rubin as Benny
Goldberg, Rex Lease as Jim Dolan,
Alice Day as Elaine McGrew, and
Mike Donlin as the scout
Copyright date and number: June 18,
1930, LP 1380
American Film Institute, Washington,
D.C.

Two fun-loving ballplayers vindicate themselves in the clutch.

HOW JONES SAW THE BASEBALL GAME, 1907
S. Lubin
One reel, silent, black and white
Copyright date and number: October
26, 1907, H 101654

Jones uses subterfuge in order to attend a baseball game.

HOW THE OFFICE BOY SAW THE BALL GAME, 1906
Thomas A. Edison

One reel, silent, black and white
Copyright date and number: July 10,
1906, H 80456–64

Office boy escapes from work to see a baseball game.

I'LL BUY YOU, 1956
Shochiku
113 minutes, sound, black and white
Based on a novel by Minoru Ono
Written by Zenzo Matsuyama
Directed by Masaki Kobayashi
Cast: Keiji Sata, Keiko Kishi, Minoru Oki, and Yunosuko Ito

Japanese-language film—titled, Anata Kaimasu—*in which an unscrupulous scout uses every means at his disposal to pressure a young baseball player into signing a contract.*

INSIGNIFICANCE, 1985
Island Alive, Inc.
Recorded Picture Company and
Zenith Productions
105 minutes, sound, color
Written by Terry Johnson from his play of the same name
Directed by Nicolas Roeg
Cast: Michael Emil as The Professor, Theresa Russell as The Actress, Tony Curtis as The Senator, Gary Busey as The Ballplayer, and Will Sampson as The Elevator Attendant
See also: Baseball in Theater

Four unnamed characters—inspired by Albert Einstein, Marilyn Monroe, Joseph McCarthy, and Joe DiMaggio—meet in a Manhattan hotel room during the early 1950s. Home video.

INTO SEGUNDO'S HANDS, 1925
(Play Ball)
Two reels, silent, black and white
Copyright date and number:
September 11, 1925, LP 21810;
October 10, 1952, R 100763
See: Play Ball (1925)

The stars of The Jackie Robinson Story *(left to right): Richard Lane, Ruby Dee, Jackie Robinson, and Minor Watson as Brooklyn Dodgers' owner Branch Rickey. (Eagle-Lion, 1950.)*

IT HAPPENED IN FLATBUSH, 1942
Twentieth Century-Fox
80 minutes, sound, black and white
Written by Harold Bushman and Lee Loeb
Directed by Ray McCarey
Cast: Lloyd Nolan as Frank Maguire, Carole Landis as Kathryn Baker, Sara Allgood as Mrs. McAvoy, William Frawley as Sam Sloan, and Robert Armstrong as Danny Mitchell

Maverick woman baseball club owner incurs the wrath of columnists, fans, umpires, and fellow club owners.

IT HAPPENS EVERY SPRING, 1949
Twentieth Century-Fox
80 minutes, sound, black and white
Written by Valentine Davies from his novel of the same name
Directed by Lloyd Bacon
Cast: Ray Milland as Vernon Simpson, Paul Douglas as Monk Lanigan, Jean Peters as Deborah Greenleaf, Ed Begley as Stone, and Ted de Corsia as Dolan
See also: Baseball in Radio; Baseball in Fiction

IT'S GOOD TO BE ALIVE, 1974
See: Baseball in Television

IT'S MY TURN, 1980
Columbia Pictures
Rastar
91 minutes, sound, color
Directed by Claudia Weill
Cast: Michael Douglas as Ben, Jill

Ruby Dee stars as Rachel Robinson and Jackie Robinson as himself in The Jackie Robinson Story. *(Eagle-Lion, 1950.)*

Clayburgh as Kate, Charles Grodin, Beverly Garland, Steven Hill, Teresa Baxter; and Elston Howard, Roger Maris, Mickey Mantle, and Bob Feller as themselves

Ex-ballplayer and career woman are involved in a modern-day romance. Home video.

THE JACKIE ROBINSON STORY, 1950
Eagle-Lion
76 minutes, sound, black and white
Written by Lawrence Taylor and Arthur Mann
Directed by Alfred E. Green
Cast: Jackie Robinson as himself, Ruby Dee as Rae Robinson, Louise Beavers as Mrs. Robinson, Joel Fluelien as Mack Robinson, Billy

Wayne as Clyde Sukeforth, and Minor Watson as Branch Rickey

Film biography of the Hall of Famer. Home video.

JIM THORPE—ALL AMERICAN, 1951
Warner Bros.
107 minutes, sound, black and white
Written by Russell J. Birdwell
Cast: Burt Lancaster as Jim Thorpe, Charles Bickford, Steve Cochran, Phyllis Thaxter, and Dick Weston

Film biography of the famed athlete and major league baseball player. Home video.

JUST PALS, 1932
(Babe Ruth Baseball Series)
One reel, sound, black and white

Copyright date and number: February 2, 1932, LP 2817; December 17, 1959, R 248576
See: Babe Ruth Baseball Series

JUST THE BEGINNING, 1977
Yung Bang Films
105 minutes, sound, color
Written by Suh Yoon Sung
Directed by Jong In Yup
Cast: Jin Yoo Young, Ha Myoung Jung, Kang Juttee, and Doh Kum Bong

Korean-language film in which a misfit youth-league baseball team wins the championship, a la Bad News Bears.

THE KID COLOSSUS, 1954
See: Roogie's Bump

THE KID FROM CLEVELAND, 1949
Republic Pictures Corp.
89 minutes, sound, black and white
Written by John Bright
Directed by Herbert Kline
Cast: George Brent as Mike Jackson, Lynn Bari as Katherine, Rusty Tamblyn as Johnny Barrows, Tommy Cook as Dan Hudson, Johnny Berardino as Mac, Bill Veeck as himself, and the Cleveland Indians as themselves

A youth is rescued from delinquency when he is made a batboy for the Cleveland Indians.

THE KID FROM LEFT FIELD, 1953
Twentieth Century-Fox
80 minutes, sound, black and white
Written by Jack Sher
Directed by Harmon Jones
Cast: Dan Dailey as Larry (Pop) Cooper, Anne Bancroft as Marian, Billy Chapin as Christy, Lloyd Bridges as Pete Haines, Ray Collins as Whacker, and Johnny Berardino as Hank Dreiser

MUSH BALL

The Kid from Cleveland, released in 1949, is the quintessential kids' baseball movie. It's moralistic, overly nice, features real live baseball heroes, and it's a deadly bore. Here are some unanimous—and pungent—opinions on this masterwork of baseball mush:

"I would like to buy every print of the film and burn it. Boy, that picture was a dog."
—Lou Boudreau, one of the 1949 Cleveland Indians players cast in the film.

"I have one unwritten law at home that I adhere to: I never allow my kids to mention or see that abortion."
—Bill Veeck, owner of the 1949 Cleveland Indians and one of the stars of the film.

"The only mild salvation of this sentimental fable . . . is a reasonably decent conclusion and a general intention to do some good. Whether this purpose will be realized by the picture is questionable."
—Bosley Crowther, *New York Times* film critic.

Copyright date and number: July 22, 1953, LP 2924
See also: Baseball in Television

Pirates' batboy is made the manager of the team after his advice—received surreptitiously from his peanut-vending father—proves to be successful.

THE KID FROM LEFT FIELD, 1979
See: Baseball in Television

Batboy Johnny Barrows (Rusty Tamblyn) thinks that the Cleveland Indians are just about the nicest bunch of guys a kid could ever want to meet in The Kid From Cleveland. (Republic Pictures, Corp., 1949.)

KILL THE UMPIRE, 1916
Universal Film Manufacturing Co., Inc.
Nestor
One reel, silent, black and white
Written by Ben Cohn
Directed by Eddie Lyons and Lee Moran
Cast: Eddie Lyons, Eileen Sedgwick, Lee Moran, and Mina Cunard
Copyright date and number: July 8, 1916, LP 8658

KILL THE UMPIRE, 1950
Columbia Pictures
78 minutes, sound, black and white
Written by Frank Tashlin
Directed by Lloyd Bacon
Cast: William Bendix as Bill Johnson, Una Merkel as Betty Johnson, Ray Collins as Jonah Evans, and William Frawley as Jimmy O'Brien
Copyright date and number: May 1, 1950, LP 307
See also: Terrible Tempered Tolliver (Baseball in Television)

Unable to hold a job, a baseball fanatic becomes an umpire.

LADIES' DAY, 1943
RKO Radio Pictures
62 minutes, sound, black and white
Based on the play by Robert Considine, Clark Lilley, and Bertrand Robinson
Written by Charles E. Roberts and Dane Lussier
Directed by Leslie Goodwins
Cast: Lupe Velez as Pepita Zorita, Eddie Albert as Wacky Walters, Patsy Kelly as Hazel, Max Baer as Hippo, and Jerome Cowan as Updike

Misadventures of a baseball player's stormy marriage.

LIFE'S GREATEST GAME, 1924
Film Booking Offices of America
Seven reels, silent, black and white
Written by Emilie Johnson
Directed and produced by Emory Johnson
Cast: Tom Santschi as Jack Donovan, Johnnie Walker as Jack Donovan, Jr.,

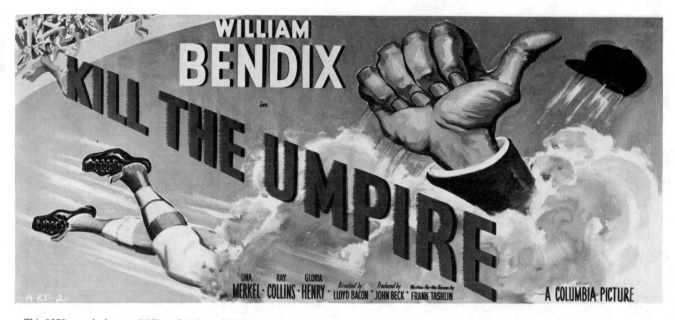

This 1950 comedy features William Bendix as Bill "Two Call" Johnson, whose double vision causes him to call every play twice. (Columbia Pictures, 1950.)

Jane Thomas as Mary Donovan, David Kirby as Mike Moran, and Gertrude Olmstead as Nora Malone
Copyright date and number: October 5, 1924, LP 20660
American Film Institute, Washington, D.C.

Manager's son, believed to be deceased, is a pitcher for his father's club.

LITTLE LEAGUE MOOCHIE, 1959
See: Moochie of the Little League (Baseball in Television)

LONG GONE, 1987
See: Baseball in Television

THE LOUD MOUTH, 1932
Paramount Pictures
19 minutes, sound, black and white
Directed by Del Lord
Cast: Mat McHugh, Ray Cooke, and Franklin Pangborn

Obnoxious fan attempts to rattle the team he has bet against.

LOVABLE TROUBLE, 1941
Columbia Pictures
Two reels, sound, black and white
Written by Harry Edwards and Al Giebler
Directed by Del Lord
Cast: Andy Clyde, Esther Howard, Ann Doran, Luana Walters, and Vernon Dent
Copyright date and number: October 21, 1941, LP 10825

A male coaches a baseball team comprised of beautiful show girls.

A LOVE AFFAIR: THE ELEANOR AND LOU GEHRIG STORY, 1978
See Baseball in Television

LOVE AND BASE BALL, 1914
Bison
Two reels, silent, black and white
Cast: Christy Mathewson

Melodramatic romance in which the Hall of

Famer wins fame, fortune, and love with his pitching and hitting heroics.

LOVE, DYNAMITE AND BASEBALLS, 1916
Mutual
Directed by Jack Dillon
Cast: Jack Dillon, Priscilla Dean, Arthur Moon, and Russell Powell

Star pitcher is involved in a crime ring.

LUCAS TANNER, 1974
See: Baseball in Television

THE MCGUERINS FROM BROOKLYN, 1942
See: Two Mugs From Brooklyn

MILLION DOLLAR INFIELD, 1982
See: Baseball in Television

A MISSION OF HATE, 1925
(Play Ball)
Two reels, silent, black and white

Rolin Film Co.
One reel, silent, black and white
Cast: Harold Lloyd, Snub Pollard,
and Bebe Daniels
Copyright date and number: August
25, 1917, LU 11293

Inept athlete hits a home run in the clutch.

OVER THE FENCE, 1932
(Babe Ruth Baseball Series)
One reel, sound, black and white
Copyright date and number: February
29, 1932, LP 2891; December 17, 1959,
R 248580
See: Babe Ruth Baseball Series

THE PENNANT PUZZLE, 1912
Selig Polyscope Co.
One reel, silent, black and white
Cast: John Lancaster

*A baseball fan's obsession with a baseball board
puzzle involves the police, other fans, and the
players and managers on the field.*

PERFECT CONTROL, 1932
(Babe Ruth Baseball Series)
One reel, sound, black and white
Copyright date and number: February
9, 1932, LP 2836; December 17, 1959,
R 248581
See: Babe Ruth Baseball Series

*A schoolboy daydreams about playing baseball
with Babe Ruth.*

THE PINCH HITTER, 1917
Triangle-Ince-Kay-Bee
Five reels, silent, black and white
Written by C. Gardner Sullivan
Directed by Victor L. Schertzinger
Cast: Charles Ray as Joel Parker,
Sylvia Breamer as Abby Nettleton,
Joseph J. Dowling as Obadiah Parker,
Jerome Storm as Jimmie Slater, and
Louis Durham as Coach Nolan

*College team mascot pitches his club to victory
and wins the hand of his sweetheart. Reedited
and reissued in 1923. Remade in 1925.*

*The star player for the Williamson College team is injured and no one is available to take his place
except the team's mascot Joel Parker (Charles Ray), a shy, unathletic rube and the perennial butt of
college jokes. He promptly whacks a pinch-hit home run, wins the game and the hand of his sweetheart,
and becomes the campus hero in this 1917 silent comedy, The Pinch Hitter. (Triangle-Ince-Kay-
Bee, 1917.)*

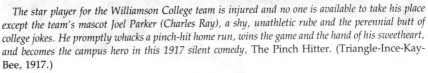

THE PINCH HITTER, 1923
Tri-Stone Pictures
Kay-Bee Pictures
Five reels, silent, black and white
American Film Institute, Washington,
D.C.

Reedited from the 1917 film.

THE PINCH HITTER, 1925
Associated Exhibitors
Seven reels, silent, black and white
Written by C. Gardner Sullivan
Directed by Joseph Henabery
Cast: Glenn Hunter as Joel Martin,
Constance Bennett as Abby
Nettleton, Jack Drumier as Obadiah
Parker, and Reginald Sheffield as
Alexis Thompson
Copyright date and number:

December 30, 1925, LU 22201
American Film Institute, Washington,
D.C.

*Mascot of the college team hits a home run in
the clutch. Remake of the 1917 film.*

PLAY BALL, 1917
(Pokes and Jabbs)
Jaxon Film Co.
One reel, silent, black and white

*Office clerk daydreams about his exploits as a
baseball star.*

PLAY BALL, 1925
Pathe Exchange, Inc.
Series of ten films
Two reels each, silent, black and
white

Based on stories suggested by John J. McGraw
Written by Frank Leon Smith
Directed by Spencer G. Bennet
Cast: Allene Ray, Walter Miller, J. Barney Sherry, Harry Semels, Mary Milnor, and Wally Oettel

Baseball player falls in love with the daughter of a wealthy businessman, who is suspected of funding a disposed monarch's coup d'état.

Includes: To the Rescue; The Flaming Float; Betrayed; The Decoy Wire; Face to Face; The Showdown; A Mission of Hate; Double Peril; Into Segundo's Hands; A Home Plate Wedding.

PLAY BALL ON THE BEACH, 1906
American Mutoscope and Biograph Co.
One reel, silent, black and white

Copyright date and number: June 1, 1906, H 78529

Slapstick vaudeville sketch in which a male umpires a women's baseball game.

THE PRIDE OF ST. LOUIS, 1952
Twentieth Century-Fox
93 minutes, sound, black and white
Based on the story by Guy Trosper
Written by Herman H. Mankiewicz
Directed by Harmon Jones
Cast: Dan Dailey as Dizzy Dean, Joanne Dru as Patricia Nash Dean, Richard Hylton as Johnny Kendall, Richard Crenna as Paul Dean, and Stuart Randall as Frankie Frisch
Copyright date and number: April 11, 1952, LP 1731
See also: "Movietime USA" (Baseball in Radio)

Film biography of Hall of Fame pitcher Dizzy Dean.

THE PRIDE OF THE YANKEES, 1942
RKO Radio Pictures
127 minutes, sound, black and white
Based on the story by Paul Gallico
Written by Jo Swerling and Herman Mankiewicz
Directed by Sam Wood
Cast: Gary Cooper as Lou Gehrig, Teresa Wright as Eleanor Gehrig, Walter Brennan as Sam Blake, Babe Ruth as himself, Ernie Adams as Miller Huggins, Harry Harvey as Joe McCarthy; and Bill Dickey, Bob Meusel, and Mark Koenig as themselves
See also: Baseball in Radio; Baseball in Comic Art—Collected: Appendix; Baseball in Miscellaneous Recordings

Dramatization of the life of Hall of Famer Lou Gehrig. Home video.

RHUBARB, 1951
Paramount Pictures
95 minutes, sound, black and white

Two stars of the 1942 film The Pride of the Yankees: *Babe Ruth, who appeared as himself, and Gary Cooper, whose portrayal of Lou Gehrig won him an Academy Award nomination. (RKO Radio Pictures, 1942.)*

Based on the novel by H. Allen Smith
Written by Dorothy Reid and Francis Cockrell
Directed by Arthur Lubin
Cast: Ray Milland as Eric Yeager, Jan Sterling as Polly, Gene Lockhart as T. J., Elsie Holmes as Myna Banner, and William Frawley as Len Sickles
Copyright date and number: September 1, 1951, LP 1183
See Also: Baseball in Comic Art—Collected: Appendix; Baseball in Fiction

RIGHT OFF THE BAT, 1915
Mike Donlin Productions
Five reels, silent, black and white
Cast: Mike Donlin as himself, Roy Hauck as young Mike Donlin, Henry Grady as Mike Donlin's father, Fan Bourke as Mike Donlin's mother, Rita Ross Donlin as Viola's friend, and John McGraw as himself

Melodramatized autobiography of the New York Giant outfielder's rise from a small-town ambidextrous pitcher to a big league slugger.

ROOGIE'S BUMP, 1954
Republic Pictures Corp.
John Bash Productions
Eight reels, sound, black and white
Based on the story by Joyce Selznick and Frank Warren
Written by Jack Hanley and Dan Totheroth
Directed by Harold Young
Cast: Robert Marriot as Roogie Rigsby, Ruth Warrick as Mrs. Rigsby, William Harrigan as Red O'Malley; and Roy Campanella, Billy Loes, Carl Erskine, and Russ Meyer as themselves
Copyright date and number: August 4, 1954, LP 4144

The spirit of a deceased star pitcher endows an awkward youth with extraordinary pitching skills. Retitled The Kid Colossus *for release in Europe.*

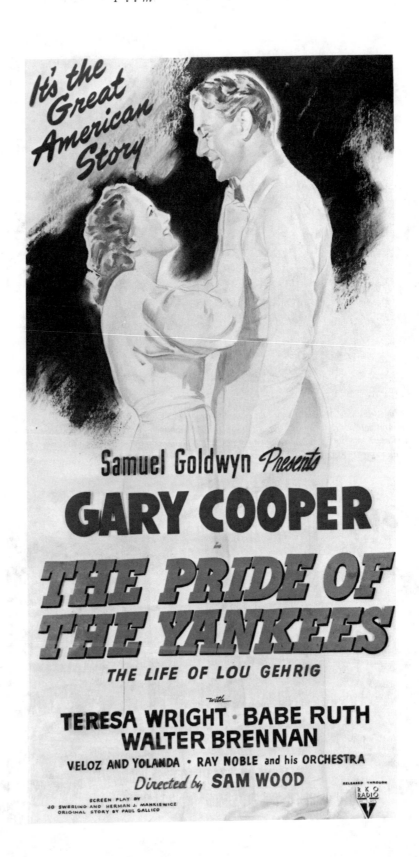

It's the Great American Story

Samuel Goldwyn *Presents*

GARY COOPER

in

THE PRIDE OF THE YANKEES

THE LIFE OF LOU GEHRIG

with

TERESA WRIGHT · BABE RUTH WALTER BRENNAN

VELOZ AND YOLANDA · RAY NOBLE and his ORCHESTRA

Directed by **SAM WOOD**

RELEASED THROUGH
RKO RADIO

SCREEN PLAY BY
JO SWERLING AND HERMAN J. MANKIEWICZ
ORIGINAL STORY BY PAUL GALLICO

A seldom-seen kids' baseball movie stars real-life Brooklyn Dodger heroes Russ Meyer, left, Carl Erskine, and catcher Roy Campanella, right, in the 1954 fantasy, Roogie's Bump. *Little Roogie Rigsby (Robert Marriot) is endowed with a magical bump on his arm that allows him to throw the ball at lightning speed. (Republic Pictures Corp., 1954.)*

SAFE AT HOME!, 1962
Columbia Pictures Corp.
Naud-Hamilburg Productions
83 minutes, sound, black and white
Based on the story by Tom Naud and Steve Ritch
Written by Robert Dillon
Directed by Walter Doniger
Cast: William Frawley as Bill Turner, Bryan (Kurt) Russell as Hutch Lawton, Patricia Barry as Johanna Price; and Mickey Mantle, Roger Maris, Ralph Houk, and Whitey Ford as themselves
Copyright date and number: April 1, 1962, LP 22252

Ten-year-old boy falsely claims a friendship with Mickey Mantle and Roger Maris and promises to produce them for his team's Little League banquet.

A SHORT-STOP'S DOUBLE, 1913
Selig Polyscope Co.
One reel, silent, black and white
Written by Arthur P. Hankins
Cast: Frank "Home Run" Baker
Copyright date and number: July 24, 1913, LU 989

THE SHOWDOWN, 1925
(Play Ball)
Two reels, silent, black and white
Copyright date and number: August 17, 1925, LP 21724; October 10, 1952, R 100760
See: Play Ball (1925)

SHUT OUT IN THE NINTH, 1917
Thomas A. Edison, Inc.
Two reels, silent, black and white
Written by Edward H. Griffith and Sumner Williams
Cast: Howard Brooks, Andy Clark, William Wadworth, Ogden Childs, Peggy Adams, Charles Frohman, and Jessie Stevens
George Kleine Collection, Library of Congress

THEY'RE ALL CHEERING ROOGIE, THE MIRACLE KID WITH THE SUPER ZOOM BALL!

REPUBLIC PICTURES presents A JOHN BASH PRODUCTION

ROOGIE'S BUMP

THEY'RE ALL HERE... Featuring THE BROOKLYN DODGERS

ROY CAMPANELLA
BILLY LOES
RUSS MEYER
CARL ERSKINE

THE GREAT O'MALLEY, HE STARTED IT ALL

INTRODUCING **ROBERT MARRIOT**
WITH RUTH WARRICK · ROBERT SIMON · OLIVE BLAKENEY
Screen Play by JACK HANLEY and DAN TOTHEROH · Original Story by FRANK WARREN and JOYCE SELZNICK · Directed by HAROLD YOUNG · A REPUBLIC RELEASE

ESQUIRE BOOT POLISH

The M & M boys ... the toast of baseball and the stars of the po... kids' film, Safe at Home! *after their recor... king 1961 season. Roger Maris, left, hit 61 h... runs and Mickey Mantle, right, hit 54 to pac... New York Yankees to yet another World S... championship. Coach Bill Turner (William ... ley) looks on as the Yankee sluggers give ...tch Lawton (Bryan Russell) a few batting ...ters. (Columbia Pictures Corp., 1962.)*

Two teenage baseball players compete for the affection of an attractive girl.

SLIDE, BABE, SLIDE, 1932
(Babe Ruth Baseball Series)
One reel, sound, black and white
Copyright date and number: January 7, 1932, LP 2741, December 17, 1959, R 248589
See: Babe Ruth Baseball Series

SLIDE, KELLY, SLIDE, 1910
Essanay

SLIDE, KELLY, SLIDE, 1927
MGM
Eight reels, silent, black and white
Written by A. P. Younger
Directed by Edward Sedgwick
Cast: William Haines as Jim Kelly, Sally O'Neil as Mary Munson, Harry Carey as Tom Munson, Karl Dane as Swede Hansen; and Mike Donlin,

Irish Meusel, Bob Meusel, and Tony Lazzeri as themselves
Copyright date and number: April 1, 1927, LP 23805; January 5, 1955, R 142831
American Film Institute, Washington, D.C.

Conceited New York Yankees pitcher loses the support of teammates and loved ones.

SLIDE, NELLIE, SLIDE, 1936
The Vitaphone Corp.
Two reels, sound, black and white
Written by Bert Granet
Directed by Murray Roth
Cast: Joe Cunningham, Herman Bing, and Bert Granet
Copyright date and number: February 17, 1936, LP 6136; July 11, 1963, R 318851

Two women's softball teams vie in a comedic game.

SLIDE, SPEEDY, SLIDE, 19...
Mack Sennett, Inc.
18 minutes, sound, black and whi...
Written by John A. Waldron, Earle Rodney, Del Lord, Walter Weems, and Harry McCoy
Directed by Babe Stafford
Cast: Daphne Pollard, Wade Boteler, and Tom Dugan
Copyright date and number: July 19, 1931, LP 2453

THE SLUGGER'S WIFE, 1985
Columbia Pictures Corp.
Rastar
114 minutes, sound, color
Written by Neil Simon
Directed by Hal Ashby
Cast: Michael O'Keefe as Darryl Palmer, Rebecca DeMornay as Debby Palmer, Martin Ritt as Burly De Vito, Randy Quaid as Moose Granger,

Busher Jim Kelly (William Haines) shows up at the New York Yankees' training camp to demonstrate his batting style in the 1927 silent melodrama Slide, Kelly, Slide. *(Metro-Goldwyn-Mayer, 1927.)*

A tense World Series moment for the Yankees in Slide, Kelly, Slide. *Jim Kelly (William Haines), second from left, is a conceited and boorish pitcher who must hurl the game of his life to regain the support of his teammates and the hand of his sweetheart. (Metro-Goldwyn-Mayer, 1927.)*

Cleavant Derricks as Manny Alvarado, and Lisa Langlois as Aline Cooper

See also: Baseball in Miscellaneous Recordings

Atlanta Braves' slugger is consumed with love for a beautiful entertainer. Home video.

SOMEWHERE IN GEORGIA, 1916

Sunbeam Motion Picture Corp.
Six reels, silent, black and white
Based on the story by Grantland Rice
Written by L. Case Russell
Directed by George Ridgwell
Cast: Ty Cobb, Elsie MacLeod, Harry Fisher, Will Corbett, Ned Burton, and Eddie Boulden

Melodrama in which a baseball star wins fame, fortune, and love.

SPIT-BALL SADIE, 1915

Pathe Exchange, Inc.
Rolin Film Co.

A curtain call for Atlanta Braves outfielder Darryl Palmer (Michael O'Keefe) in the Neil Simon comedy, The Slugger's Wife. *(Columbia Pictures Corp., 1985.)*

One reel, silent, black and white
Cast: Harold Lloyd, Gene Marsh, and Eleanor Whitney

Man disguises himself as "Spit-Ball Sadie" in order to enjoy the company of an all-women baseball team.

SQUEEZE PLAY, 1980
Troma, Inc.
92 minutes, sound, color
Directed by Samuel Weil
Cast: Jim Harris, Jenni Hetrick, Al Corley, Rick Gitlin, and Helen Campitelli

Battle of the sexes is fought on the softball field. Home video.

STEALING HOME, 1988
Warner Bros.
98 minutes, sound, color
Written and directed by Steven

Kampmann and Will Aldis
Produced by Thom Mount and Hank Moonjean
Cast: Mark Harmon as Billy Wyatt, William McNamera as Billy Wyatt at age 14, Jodie Foster as Katie Chandler, Blair Brown as Ginny Wyatt, Harold Ramis as Alan Appleby at age 38, and Jonathan Silverman as Alan Appleby at age 16

Light-hearted look back at a minor league ball-player's coming of age in 1960s suburbia.

STEALIN' HOME, 1932
(Rufftown Comedies)
RKO Pathe Pictures
Two reels, sound, black and white

Based on a story by Arthur "Bugs" Baer
Written by Ralph Cedar
Cast: James Gleason, Eddie Gribbon, and Mae Busch
Copyright date and number: May 6, 1932, LP 3016

Comedic misadventures of a small-town pitcher.

THE STRATTON STORY, 1949
MGM
106 minutes, sound, black and white
Written by Douglas Morrow and Guy Trosper
Directed by Sam Wood
Cast: James Stewart as Monty

James Stewart, second from left, stars as Monty Stratton in The Stratton Story, *the dramatization of the Chicago White Sox pitcher's return to professional baseball after a hunting accident resulted in the amputation of one leg. Equipped with an artificial limb, Stratton served as the White Sox batting practice pitcher for two years before startling the baseball world in 1946 by winning 18 games in the Class-C East Texas League. (Metro-Goldwyn-Mayer, 1949.)*

Stratton, June Allyson as Ethel, Frank Morgan as Barney Wile, Agnes Moorehead as Ma Stratton, Bruce Cowling as Ted Lyons, Dean White as Luke Appling; and Gene Beardon, Jimmy Dykes, Mervyn Shea, and Bill Dickey as themselves
See also: Baseball in Radio

True story of pitcher Monty Stratton's return to professional baseball after the amputation of one leg.

STRIKE ONE, 1917
(Baseball Bill)
Universal Film Manufacturing Co., Inc.
Nestor
One reel, silent, black and white
Story and direction by Craig Hutchinson
Written by C. B. Hoadley
Cast: Dave Morris, Gladys Tennyson, Charles Cook, Charles Dorian, and Rube Miller
Copyright date and number: November 9, 1917, LP 11701
See: Baseball Bill

SWELL-HEAD, 1935
Columbia Pictures Corp.
Seven reels, sound, black and white
Based on the story by Gerald Beaumont
Written by William Jacobs
Directed by Ben Stoloff
Cast: Wallace Ford
Copyright date and number: April 2, 1935, LP 5446; December 5, 1962, R 306053

Boorish slugger is humbled after being struck and blinded by a pitched ball.

TAKE ME OUT TO THE BALL GAME, 1910
Essanay
Directed by G. M. (Broncho Billy) Anderson
Released August 24, 1910

A CINEMATIC LINEUP

Since there is no way to bring back the Hollywood Stars of the old Pacific Coast League, here is the next best thing. The following is an all-star lineup of fictional characters from Hollywood's most famous (and infamous) baseball movies:

Center field: Joe Hardy (Tab Hunter), *Damn Yankees*
Second base: Paula Fradkin (Robyn Barto), *Blue Skies Again*
Right field: Babe Dugan (Babe Ruth), *Babe Comes Home*
Third base: Frank Baker (Frank "Home Run" Baker), *"Home Run" Baker's Double*
Designated hitter: Leon Carter (James Earl Jones), *The Bingo Long Traveling All-Stars and Motor Kings*
Left field: Roy Hobbs (Robert Redford), *The Natural*
First base: Nat Goldberg (Jules Munshin), *Take Me Out to the Ball Game*
Catcher: Crash Davis (Kevin Costner), *Bull Durham*
Shortstop: Dennis Ryan (Frank Sinatra), *Take Me Out to the Ball Game*
Pitcher: Elmer Kane (Joe E. Brown), *Elmer the Great*
Manager: Morris Buttermaker (Walter Matthau), *The Bad News Bears*

Baseball fanatic becomes so involved with the home team's victory that he leaves the ballpark without his wife.

TAKE ME OUT TO THE BALL GAME, 1949
MGM

---

93 minutes, sound, color
Based on the story by Gene Kelly and Stanley Donen
Written by Harry Tugend and George Wells
Directed by Busby Berkeley
Cast: Frank Sinatra as Dennis Ryan, Gene Kelly as Eddie O'Brien, Jules Munshin as Nat Goldberg, Esther Williams as K. C. Higgins, and Tom Dugan as Slappy Burke
Copyright date and number: March 1, 1949, LP 2174
See also: Baseball in Music and Song—Recorded

Two baseball stars are vaudevillians during the off-season. Released in Europe as Everybody's Cheering. *Includes the song, "O'Brien to Ryan to Goldberg." (See:* Baseball in Music and Song—Recorded.) *Home video.*

THEY LEARNED ABOUT WOMEN, 1930
MGM
Eleven reels, sound, black and white
Based on the story by A. P. Younger
Written by Arthur "Bugs" Baer and Sarah Y. Mason
Directed by Jack Conway and Sam Wood
Cast: Joseph T. Schenck as Jack, Gus Van as Jerry, Bessie Love as Mary, and Mary Doran as Daisy
Copyright date and number: March 3, 1930, LP 1117
American Film Institute, Washington, D.C.

Two baseball stars become vaudevillians after their success in the World Series.

TIGER TOWN, 1983
See: Baseball in Television

TITLE NOT KNOWN, 1915
(Serial of baseball humor)
Written by Ring W. Lardner
Produced by Hans Moss

The title of the serial is unknown and no print
of the film has been located.

TOO MANY WOMEN, 1932
(The Boy Friends)
MGM
Hal Roach
Two reels, sound, black and white
Directed by Anthony Mack and Lloyd
French
Cast: Mickey Daniels, Grady Sutton,
Gordon Douglas, Mary Korman,
Harry Bernard, and Tiny Sandford
Copyright date and number: October
3, 1932, LP 3295

*Star pitcher's baseball abilities decline when his
sweetheart marries another man.*

TO THE RESCUE, 1925
(Play Ball)
Two reels, silent, black and white
Copyright date and number: June 23,
1925, LP 21578; October 10, 1952, R
100755
See: Play Ball (1925)

TRIFLING WITH HONOR, 1923
Universal Pictures Corp.
Eight reels, silent, black and white
Based on the story, "His Good
Name" by William Slavens McNutt,
published in *Collier's*, July 22, 1922,
pp. 3–4
Written by Frank Beresford and
Raymond L. Schrock
Directed by Harry A. Pollard
Cast: Rockliffe Fellowes as the Gas-
Pipe Kid, Fritzi Ridgeway as Ida
Hunt, Buddy Messinger as Jimmy
Hunt, and Hayden Stevenson as
Kelsey Lewis
Copyright date and number: April 24,
1923, LP 18898
American Film Institute, Washington,
D.C.

*Ex-convict, idolized as a clean-living baseball
star, refuses to throw a game for blackmailers
who threaten to reveal his past.*

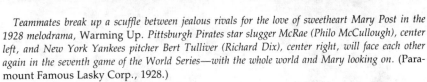

*Teammates break up a scuffle between jealous rivals for the love of sweetheart Mary Post in the
1928 melodrama,* Warming Up. *Pittsburgh Pirates star slugger McRae (Philo McCullough), center
left, and New York Yankees pitcher Bert Tulliver (Richard Dix), center right, will face each other
again in the seventh game of the World Series—with the whole world and Mary looking on. (Paramount Famous Lasky Corp., 1928.)*

TWO MUGS FROM BROOKLYN, 1942
Favorite Films
Directed by Kurt Neumann
Produced by Hal Roach
Cast: William Bendix, Max Baer,
Marjorie Woodworth, and Joe Sawyer

*Misadventures of two semipro baseball players
who are framed by mobsters. Subsequently
released by United Artists under the title,* The
McGuerins from Brooklyn.

WARMING UP, 1928
Paramount Famous Lasky Corp.
Eight reels, sound, black and white
Based on the story by Sam Mintz
Written by Ray Harris
Cast: Richard Dix as Bert Tulliver,
Jean Arthur as Mary Post, Claude

King as Mr. Post, Philo McCullough
as McRae, and Mike Donlin as the
veteran
Copyright date and number: August
4, 1928, LP 25507
American Film Institute, Washington,
D.C.

*Rival baseball stars compete for the love of a
woman.*

WHAT LOLA WANTS, 1958
See: Damn Yankees

WHISTLING IN BROOKLYN, 1944
MGM
87 minutes, sound, black and white
Written by Nat Perrin and Wilkie
Mahoney

Ronald Reagan stars as Hall of Famer Grover Cleveland Alexander in the 1952 film biography, The Winning Team. *The veteran pitcher is about to strike out Tony Lazzeri with two out and the bases loaded in the famous 1928 World Series between the St. Louis Cardinals and the New York Yankees.* (Warner Bros., 1952.)

Directed by S. Sylvan Simon
Cast: Red Skelton as Wally Benton, Ann Rutherford as Carol Lambert, Jean Rogers as Jean Pringle, William Frawley as Detective Ramsey, and the Brooklyn Dodgers as themselves
Copyright date and number: September 24, 1943, LP 12334

Inept detective, pursued by gangsters, disguises himself as a pitcher for the Battling Beavers baseball team.

A WINNER NEVER QUITS, 1986
See: Baseball in Television

THE WINNING TEAM, 1952
Warner Bros.
98 minutes, sound, black and white
Written by Ted Sherdeman, Seeley Lester, and Merwin Gerard
Directed by Lewis Seiler
Cast: Ronald Reagan as Grover Cleveland Alexander, Doris Day as Aimee, Frank Lovejoy as Rogers Hornsby, Eve Miller as Margaret, and James Millican as Bill Killefer
Copyright date and number: June 23, 1952, LP 1795

Film biography of the Hall of Fame pitcher Grover Cleveland Alexander.

Appendix to Chapter 1

This appendix contains a listing of nonbaseball-related photoplays featuring a significant baseball-related character or scene. Also included in the catalog are nonbaseball-related films in which a major league baseball player is cast in a starring or featured role. In most cases the relation to baseball—and not the film's plot or theme—is annotated.

For *Explanatory Notes* to this section, *see:* Baseball in Film.

ABOUT FACE, 1952
Warner Bros.
94 minutes, sound, color
Based on the film *Brother Rat*
Cast: Gordon MacRae and Eddie Bracken
See also: Brother Rat and a Baby. See: Brother Rat (Baseball in Film)

AMAZING GRACE AND CHUCK, 1987
Tri-Star Pictures
115 minutes, sound, color
Written and produced by David Field
Cast: Joshua Zuehike as Chuck Murdock, and Alex English as Amazing Grace Smith

A 12-year-old youngster gains national attention when he refuses to pitch in a Little League game as a protest against nuclear armaments.

AMERICATHON, 1979
86 minutes, sound, color
Cast: Harvey Korman, Fred Willard, and Zane Buzby

Features Los Angeles Dodgers manager Tom Lasorda in a minor role. Home video.

BLACK GUNN, 1972
98 minutes, color, sound
Cast: Jim Brown and Martin Landau

Includes Oakland A's star pitcher Vida Blue in a minor role.

BOYS' RANCH, 1946
MGM
Written by William Ludwig
Cast: James Craig as Dan Walker

Former ballplayer operates a Texas ranch for homeless boys.

BROTHER RAT AND A BABY, 1940
Warner Bros.
87 minutes, sound, black and white
Cast: Wayne Morris, Eddie Albert, and Ronald Reagan
See also: About Face. See: Brother Rat (Baseball in Film)

THE CAMERAMAN, 1928
MGM
Directed by Edward Sedgwick
Cast: Buster Keaton as Luke, and Marceline Day as Sally

Contains a comical pantomime of a one-man baseball game.

CANNERY ROW, 1982
MGM
120 minutes, sound, color
Cast: Nick Nolte as Doc

Doc is a baseball player turned marine biologist. Home video.

THE CEREMONY, 1971
Shibati Organization
122 minutes, sound, color
Directed by Nagisa Oshima
Cast: Kenzo Kawarazaki, Atsuko Kaku, and Atsuo Nakamura

Japanese-language film in which a son humiliates his perfectionist parents by committing an error in a crucial game.

CHU CHU AND THE PHILLY FLASH, 1981
Twentieth Century-Fox
100 minutes, sound, color
Cast: Alan Arkin and Carol Burnett

The Philly Flash is an alcoholic former all-star pitcher.

C'MON, LET'S LIVE A LITTLE, 1967
Paramount Pictures
85 minutes, sound, color
Cast: Bobby Vee and Jackie De Shannon

Includes Houston Astros pitcher Bo Belinsky in a minor role.

EXPERIMENT IN TERROR, 1962
Columbia Pictures Corp.
123 minutes, sound, black and white
Cast: Glenn Ford, Lee Remick, and Stefanie Powers

Final scene occurs in Candlestick Park during a night baseball game. Home video.

THE GEISHA BOY, 1958
York Pictures Corp. in association with Paramount Pictures
98 minutes, sound, color
Copyright date and number: December 1, 1958, LP 12534

Includes a scene at a Japanese baseball game.

HAWAIIAN BUCKAROO, 1938
Principal Productions, Inc.
Seven reels, sound, black and white
Written by Dan Jarrett
Directed by Ray Taylor
Cast: Lou Gehrig and Smith Ballew
Copyright date and number: January 24, 1938, LP 7849

I'LL FIX IT, 1934
Columbia Pictures
68 minutes, sound, black and white
Written by Ethel Hill and Dorothy Howell
Directed by Roy William Neill
Cast: Jack Holt, Mona Barrie, Edward Brophy, and Jimmy Butler
Copyright date and number: September 28, 1934, LP 4994; July 2, 1962, R 297683

A father attempts to manipulate his son's scholastic status so that the youngster can play on the school baseball team.

IRONWEED, 1988
Tri-Star Pictures
145 minutes, sound, color
Written by William Kennedy
Cast: Jack Nicholson as Francis Phelan, and Meryl Streep as Helen
See also: Baseball in Fiction

I WONDER WHO'S KISSING HER NOW, 1947
Twentieth Century-Fox
Directed by Lloyd Bacon
Cast: June Haver and Mark Stevens

Includes the song, "The Umpire Is a Most Unhappy Man." (See: Baseball in Music and Song—Recorded.)

LARCENY, INC., 1942
Warner Bros.
95 minutes, sound, black and white
Cast: Edward G. Robinson and Broderick Crawford
Copyright date and number: May 2, 1942, LP 11250

A prison baseball game is included.

MAIN STREET TO BROADWAY, 1953
MGM
102 minutes, sound, black and white
Cast: Tom Morton, Mary Murphy, and Agnes Moorehead

Includes a cameo appearance by Leo Durocher. Home video.

MANHATTAN MERRY-GO-ROUND, 1938
Republic Pictures Corp.
80 minutes, sound, black and white
Copyright date and number: November 13, 1937, LP 7597

Segment: Joe DiMaggio delivers a humorous lecture on baseball with the aid of newsreel clips. Home video.

MAX DUGAN RETURNS, 1983
Twentieth Century-Fox
98 minutes, sound, color
Written by Neil Simon

Features Kansas City Royals' batting coach Charlie Lau as himself. Home video.

MEET JOHN DOE, 1941
Warner Bros.
132 minutes, sound, black and white
Directed by Frank Capra
Cast: Gary Cooper as "John Doe," and Barbara Stanwyck as Ann Mitchell
Copyright date and number: May 5, 1941, LP 10453

An ex-ballplayer becomes a populist hero. Home video.

MOONLIGHT IN HAVANA, 1942
Universal Pictures Corp.
63 minutes, sound, black and white
Cast: Allan Jones, Jane Frazee, Don Terry, and William Frawley

Big leaguer is torn between a career as a baseball player and nightclub singer.

MR. DYNAMITE, 1941
Universal Pictures Corp.
Directed by John Rawlins
Cast: Lloyd Nolan as Tommy Thornton, and Irene Hervey as Vicki Martin

Baseball player is caught in a web of international intrigue.

THE NAUGHTY NINETIES, 1945
Universal Pictures Corp.
76 minutes, sound, black and white
Cast: Bud Abbott and Lou Costello

Segment: Abbott and Costello perform their famous "Who's on First?" routine. (See also: The World of Abbott and Costello.) See: "Who's on First?" (Baseball in Miscellaneous Plays and Sketches; Baseball in Comedy and Light Verse—Recorded); "Broadcast of June 13, 1944" (Baseball in Radio).

THE PREMONITION, 1976
94 minutes, color, sound
Cast: Sharon Farrell, Richard Lynch, and Jeff Corey

Features New York Yankees' outfielder Roy White in a minor role. Home video.

RADIO DAYS, 1987
Orion Pictures Corp.
90 minutes, sound, color
Written and directed by Woody Allen

Includes a comedic scene in which a blind man plays baseball. Home video.

RAWHIDE, 1938
Principal Productions, Inc.
Six reels, sound, black and white
Written by Dan Jarrett and Jack Natteford
Directed by Ray Taylor
Cast: Lou Gehrig as himself, and Smith Ballew as Larry Kimball
Copyright date and number: April 8, 1938, LP 8051

Musical western in which cowboy Lou Gehrig refuses to join a corrupt cattlemen's association. Home video.

A SOLDIER'S STORY, 1984
Columbia Pictures Corp.
99 minutes, sound, color
Cast: Howard E. Rollins, Jr. and Adolph Caesar

Includes a scene of an Army baseball game.
Home video.

SPEEDY, 1928
Paramount Famous Lasky Corp.
Eight reels, silent, black and white
Directed by Ted Wilde
Cast: Harold Lloyd as Speedy Swift,
Ann Christy as Jane Dillon, and Babe
Ruth as himself

Speedy takes Babe Ruth for a madcap taxi ride.

STEPPING FAST, 1923
Fox Film Corp.
Five reels, silent, black and white
Directed by Joseph J. Franz
Cast: Tom Mix as Grant Malvern, and
Claire Adams as Helen Durant
Copyright date and number: May 13,
1923, LP 19146; August 17, 1950, R
65955
American Film Institute, Washington,
D.C.

STRATEGIC AIR COMMAND, 1955
Paramount Pictures
114 minutes, sound, color
Cast: James Stewart as Col. Robert
"Dutch" Holland
Copyright date and number: April 21,
1955, LP 4673

*Baseball player is recalled to Air Force duty at
the peak of his career. Home video.*

THAT TOUCH OF MINK, 1962
Universal-International
99 minutes, sound, color
Cast: Cary Grant, Doris Day, and Gig
Young
Copyright date and number: May 24,
1962, LP 24721

*To impress a lady friend, a suitor introduces
her to members of the New York Yankees—
including Mickey Mantle, Roger Maris, and
Yogi Berra. Home video.*

UP THE RIVER, 1930
Fox Film Corp.
Directed by John Ford
Cast: Spencer Tracy, Claire Luce, and
Humphrey Bogart
Copyright date and number:
September 16, 1930, LP 1598; October
31, 1957, R 201140
American Film Institute, Washington,
D.C.

Includes a prison baseball game.

WHEN NATURE CALLS, 1985
Troma, Inc.
85 minutes, sound, color
Cast: David Orange as Greg, and
Barbara Marineau as Barb

*Includes Willie Mays in a cameo role. Home
video.*

WOMAN OF THE YEAR, 1942
MGM
112 minutes, sound, black and white
Cast: Spencer Tracy as Sam Craig,
and Katharine Hepburn as Tess
Harding

*Female political reporter and male sportswriter
fall in love. Includes a humorous scene at a
baseball game. Home video.*

A WOMAN UNDER THE INFLUENCE, 1974
155 minutes, sound, color
Cast: Peter Falk and Gena Rowlands

*Features former Cleveland Indians' slugger
Leon Wagner in a minor role.*

THE WONDERFUL COUNTRY, 1959
United Artists
96 minutes, sound, color
Cast: Robert Mitchum as Martin
Brady

*Features Satchel Paige in the role of Sergeant
Sutton.*

THE WORLD OF ABBOTT AND COSTELLO, 1965
75 minutes, sound, black and white
Narrated by Jack E. Leonard
Cast: Bud Abbott and Lou Costello

*Documentary includes the famous "Who's on
First?" comedy routine. (See also: The
Naughty Nineties.) See: "Who's on First?"
(Baseball in Miscellaneous Plays and Sketches;
Baseball in Comedy and Light Verse—
Recorded); "Broadcast of June 13, 1944"
(Baseball in Radio).*

YOUNG MAN OF MANHATTAN, 1930
Paramount-Publix Corp.
Eight reels, sound, black and white
Cast: Norman Foster as Toby
McLean, and Claudette Colbert as
Ann Vaughn
American Film Institute, Washington,
D.C.

*A New York sportswriter is sent to St. Louis to
cover the World Series.*

ZAPPED!, 1982
Embassy Pictures
96 minutes, sound, color
Directed by Robert J Rosenthal
Cast: Scott Baio, Heather Thomas,
and Scatman Crothers

*Misadventures of a high school baseball player
who can telekinetically alter the flight of a
baseball. Home video.*

Baseball in Documentary and Miscellaneous Films

The following catalog contains a listing of baseball-related theatrical newsreels, documentaries, and miscellaneous films of historical or cultural interest. Included in this section are silent-era films relating to early 1900s baseball, player biographies, team histories, instructionals, educational films produced for young people, and film documentaries profiling the events and personalities from baseball's past. Also included are documentary and miscellaneous films produced for home video viewing.

Not included in the catalog are regular-season or All-Star Game highlights, American or National League highlights, or World Series highlights since 1916.

For *Explanatory Notes* to this section, *see:* Baseball in Film.

AMERICAN LEAGUE STARS AND BASEBALL FUNDAMENTALS, 1970
Ex Cell O Corp.
30 minutes, sound, color
Narrated by Tony Kubek

Kubek describes the essentials in becoming a good baseball player.

AND THIS IS PEE WEE REESE, 1954
(This Is Baseball)
One reel, sound
Copyright date and number: August 10, 1954, LP 3948

Number eleven in the series. See: This Is Baseball.

THE ART OF HITTING, 1986
Morris
60 minutes, sound, color

Batting fundamentals as shown by former Cincinnati Reds outfielder Vada Pinson. Home video.

BABE RUTH, HOW HE MAKES HIS HOME RUNS, 1920
(Babe Ruth Instructional Films)
One reel, silent, black and white
See: Babe Ruth Instructional Films

BABE RUTH INSTRUCTIONAL FILMS, 1920
Educational Pictures
Series of films
One reel each, silent, black and white

Contains scenes from actual baseball games. Includes: Babe Ruth, How He Makes His Home Runs; Play Ball with Babe Ruth.

BALL AND BAT, 1926
(Grantland Rice Sportlight)
Pathe Exchange, Inc.
Written and produced by John L. Hawkinson
Copyright date and number: July 22, 1926, MU 3491

THE BALL GAME, 1898
Thomas A. Edison
One reel, silent, black and white
Copyright date and number: May 20, 1898, #31442

First baseball game ever filmed depicts a Newark, New Jersey amateur team playing an unknown opponent.

BASEBALL—A HAPPY SUMMER EVENING, c. 1965
Modern Talking Picture Service, Inc.
Chrysler Corp.
30 minutes, sound

Baseball tips from Ted Williams and the Boston Red Sox.

BASEBALL, AN ANALYSIS OF MOTION, 1919
One reel, silent, black and white

Players are shown in slow motion—an innovation at the time—in order to depict grace and skill.

BASEBALL BATS AND SAMURAI SWORDS, 1977
VidAmerica, Inc.
60 minutes, sound, color

American and Japanese all-star teams play in Nishinomiya Stadium. Home video.

BASEBALL BATTER, 1931
(Models in Motion)
Eastman Teaching Films, Inc.
One reel
Written by George W. Hoke
Copyright date and number: April 29, 1931, MP 2634

BASEBALL: FUN AND GAMES, 1977
VidAmerica, Inc.
60 minutes, sound, color

Odd plays, trivia, and quirks of baseball history are featured. Home Video.

BASEBALL FUNDAMENTALS, 1942
Coronet Productions
David A. Smart
One reel, sound, black and white
Written by Emmet Branch McCracken
Copyright date and number: May 12, 1942, MP 2034

BASEBALL FUNDAMENTALS AND TECHNIQUES, 1950
Ideal Pictures, Inc.
National Exhibition Co.
40 minutes, sound, black and white

Narrated by Russ Hodges

Features Leo Durocher and the New York Giants.

BASEBALL IN THE NEWS, 1985
The Great American Pastimes Company
Series of three films
55 minutes each, sound

Edited theatrical newsreels in three volumes: 1951–1955; 1956–1960; 1961–1967. Home video.

BASEBALL PITCHER, 1931
(Models in Motion)
Eastman Teaching Films, Inc.
One reel
Written by George W. Hoke
Copyright date and number: May 13, 1931, MP 2635

BASEBALL'S ACROBATIC ACE, 1955
(Grantland Rice Sportlight)
Paramount Pictures Corp.
9 minutes, sound, black and white
Narrated by Ward Wilson
Copyright date and number: April 8, 1955, MP 5832

Features baseball trickster Jackie Price.

BASEBALL'S MAIN STREET, 1955
30 minutes, sound, color

Documentary profile of the 1955 Milwaukee Braves.

BASEBALL THE PETE ROSE WAY, 1986
Embassy
60 minutes, sound, color

Baseball instructionals for youngsters. Home video.

BASEBALL TODAY, 1949
Official Sports Films Service
30 minutes, sound

Rules and fundamentals of baseball are explained.

BASEBALL/TV, 1979
Written and produced by Stuart Sherman
2 minutes

Abstract study of two popular American pastimes.

BAT BOY, 1953
(Sportscope)
RKO Pathe, Inc.
8 minutes, sound, black and white
Copyright date and number: September 3, 1953, MP 4176

BATTER UP, 1936
AudiVision, Inc.
One reel
Copyright date and number: March 11, 1936, MP 6340

BATTER UP, 1949
(Sports News Review)
Warner Bros.
The Vitaphone Corp.
10 minutes, sound, black and white
Written and directed by Robert Youngson
Narrated by Don Donaldson
Copyright date and number: May 17, 1949, MP 4072

Highlights and history of baseball.

BATTING FUNDAMENTALS, 1946
Coronet Instructional Films
One reel, sound, black and white
Copyright date and number: March 5, 1946, MP 2149

BIG LEAGUE, 1937
(Bill Corum)
The Van Beuren Corp.
One reel, sound, black and white
Copyright date and number: May 7, 1937, MP 7566

BIG LEAGUE BASEBALL FOR LITTLE LEAGUERS, c. 1965
Modern Talking Picture Service, Inc.
Chrysler Corp.
30 minutes, sound
Narrated by George Kell

Baseball tips from the Detroit Tigers.

BIG LEAGUE GLORY, 1948
(Grantland Rice Sportlight)
Paramount Pictures, Inc.
10 minutes, sound, black and white
Directed by Russell T. Ervin and Rod Warren
Narrated by Ted Husing
Copyright date and number: June 11, 1948, MP 3145

The various levels of the New York Giants' minor league system are detailed.

BIG LEAGUERS, 1939
(RKO Pathe Sportscope)
Pathe News, Inc.
9 minutes, sound, black and white
Produced by Frederic Ullman, Jr.
Copyright date and number: April 21, 1939, MP 9414

BIG LITTLE LEAGUERS, 1951
(Grantland Rice Sportlight)
Paramount Pictures Corp.
One reel, sound
Copyright date and number: March 16, 1951, MP 1199

History of Little League baseball.

BOBBY SHANTZ, 1952
(Sportscope)
RKO Pathe, Inc.
One reel, sound
Copyright date and number: December 13, 1952, MP 3620

Newsreel profile of the Philadelphia A's pitcher and American League Most Valuable Player for 1952.

THE BOSTON RED SOX, 1957
Borden Productions
21 minutes, sound

Highlights of the 1956 Red Sox season.

THE BOYS OF SUMMER, 1983
VidAmerica, Inc.
VCA Programs, Inc.
90 minutes, sound, color
Based on the book by Roger Kahn
Narrated by Sid Caesar
See also: Baseball in the Spoken Arts—Recorded

Interviews with members of the Brooklyn Dodgers of the 1940s and 1950s. Home video.

THE BRAVES FAMILY, 1947
40 minutes, sound, color

Features Boston Braves' players, coaches, and front office personnel. Home video.

BULLPEN, 1974
W & W Films, Inc.
22 minutes, sound, color

Relief specialists Joe Page, Jim Konstanty, Roy Face, Hoyt Wilhelm, Ron Perranoski, and Tug McGraw are featured.

BUSH LEAGUE TO BRIGHT LIGHTS
Video Tape Network
60 minutes, sound, color

Profile of two players struggling to succeed in baseball.

THE CARDINAL TRADITION, 1958
Modern Talking Picture Service, Inc.
Premiere Film and Recording Corp.
30 minutes, sound, black and white
Copyright date and number: January 13, 1958, MP 8728

Highlights and history of the St. Louis Cardinals baseball club.

CASEY AT THE BAT, 1972
(Reading Poetry Series)

12 minutes, sound, color
Produced by Art Evans
Narrated by George Maharis

Narration of the famous ballad over a scene showing children playing baseball, and a rereading over a slow motion scene of an actual big league game.

CATCHING IN BASEBALL, 1947
Encyclopaedia Britannica Films, Inc.
One reel, sound
Copyright date and number: February 11, 1947, MP 1713

Features instructions from Jimmy Dykes and Hollis Thurston.

CHRISTY MATHEWSON, NEW YORK NATIONAL LEAGUE BASEBALL TEAM, 1907
The Winthrop Moving Picture Co.
Copyright date and number: May 24, 1907, H 94486

Early newsreel footage of the Hall of Fame pitcher in action.

CHUCK TANNER
Oxford Films
Tele-Sports
22 minutes, sound, color

Profile of the Chicago White Sox manager.

CIRCLING THE BASES, 1947
A. G. Spalding and Bros.
20 minutes, sound, black and white
See also: Baseball in Comic Art—Collected: Appendix

Baseball fundamentals and instruction with an emphasis on base-running.

CONNIE MACK, 1950
(Sportscope)
RKO Pathe, Inc.
8 minutes, sound, black and white
Copyright date and number: December 15, 1950, MP 1026

Newsreel profile of the Hall of Fame manager of the Philadelphia A's.

DIAMOND DEMON, 1947
(Pete Smith Specialty)
MGM
One reel, sound, black and white
Produced and narrated by Pete Smith
Copyright date and number: January 2, 1947, MP 1601

Features Jackie Price, baseball trickster.

DIAMOND DUST, 1939
(Grantland Rice Sportlight)
Paramount Pictures, Inc.
One reel, sound, black and white
Narrated by Ted Husing
Copyright date and number: May 12, 1939, MP 9389

DIAMOND SHOWCASE, 1949
(Sportscope)
RKO Pathe, Inc.
9 minutes, sound
Copyright date and number: November 18, 1949, MP 4966

DIAMONDS IN THE ROUGH, 1974
National Film Board of Canada
Zolov Productions
26 minutes, sound, color

Documentary profile of the Montreal Expos.

DONKEY BASEBALL, 1935
(MGM Oddities)
MGM
One reel, sound, black and white
Narrated by Pete Smith
Copyright date and number: February 26, 1935, MP 5439; February 26, 1962, R 291719

Fad of playing this unusual variation of baseball is featured.

THE FENCE BUSTER, 1954
(Movietone News)
Fox
15 minutes, sound, black and white

Newsreel biography of Babe Ruth.

50 YEARS OF BASEBALL MEMORIES, 1980
Major League Baseball Productions
30 minutes, sound
Narrated by Lew Fonseca

Highlights and history of baseball.

FUTURE BASEBALL CHAMPS, 1957
Twentieth Century-Fox Film Corp.
One reel, sound
Copyright date and number: April 3, 1957, MP 8152

FUTURE MAJOR LEAGUERS, 1951
(World of Sports)
Columbia Pictures Corp.
11 minutes, sound, black and white
Copyright date and number: May 31, 1951, MP 1718

Baseball fundamentals from the New York Giants.

GENE MAUCH
Oxford Films
Tele-Sports
22 minutes, sound, color

Profile of the Montreal Expos manager.

THE GIANTS–WHITE SOX WORLD TOUR, 1914
John J. Gleason
Written by Frances McGlynn
Copyright date and number: May 7, 1914, MU 166

THE GIANTS–WHITE SOX WORLD TOUR, 1914
Eclectic Film Co.
Written by Jack Gleason
Copyright date and number: August 20, 1914, MU 229

GREATEST LEGENDS OF BASEBALL, c. 1975
Viacom International

60 minutes, sound, color

GREAT MOMENTS IN BASEBALL, 1977
Major League Baseball Productions
60 minutes, sound, color

Highlights and history of baseball. Home video.

THE HISTORY OF BASEBALL
Major League Baseball Productions
120 minutes, sound, color

Highlights and history of baseball. Home video.

HOLLYWOOD ON THE BALL, 1952
(Screen Snapshots)
Columbia Pictures Corp.
9 minutes, sound, black and white
Library of Congress number: Fi 52-994

HOME RUN ON THE KEYS, 1937
The Vitaphone Corp.
One reel, sound, black and white
Directed by Roy Mack
Credits: Cyrus D. Wood
Cast: Babe Ruth and Zez Confrey
Copyright date and number: July 12, 1937, LP 7263; September 13, 1964, R 345343
See also: Baseball in Music and Song

Babe Ruth performs a musical number—a baseball parody of "Kitten on the Keys."

HORSE-HIDE HEROES, 1951
Warner Bros.
Vitaphone Corp.
10 minutes, sound, black and white
Copyright date and number: April 25, 1951, MP 1062

Newsreel tribute to the all-time greats of baseball.

INSIDE BASEBALL, 1931
(Bill Cunningham Sports Review)
Brown Nagel Productions, Inc.

10 minutes, sound
Copyright date and number: October 11, 1931, LP 2664

KING OF DIAMONDS, 1954
(Movietone News)
Fox
15 minutes, sound, black and white

Newsreel biography of Lou Gehrig.

KING OF THE HILL, 1974
National Film Board of Canada
60 minutes, sound, color
Directed by Donald Brittain and William Canning

Profile of Ferguson Jenkins, the first Canadian to achieve stardom in the major leagues. Home video.

LEGION AT BAT, 1953
Columbia Pictures Corp.
Produced in association with the National Americanism Commission and the American Legion
One reel, sound, black and white
Copyright date and number: March 26, 1953, MP 4122

History of American Legion Junior Baseball, including the "Little World Series."

LET'S GO METS, 1963
New York Metropolitan Baseball Club
30 minutes, sound
Copyright date and number: December 11, 1963, MP 14078

LET'S GO METS!, 1986
Vestron
30 minutes, sound, color
See also: Baseball in Music and Song—Recorded

Includes highlights, interviews, and the music video to the song, "Let's Go Mets!" Home video.

LITTLE LEAGUE BASEBALL, 1949

Little League Baseball Association
20 minutes, sound, black and white
Directed by Emerson Yorke
Narrated by Joe Hasel

Highlights and history of Little League baseball.

LITTLE LEAGUE'S OFFICIAL HOW-TO-PLAY BASEBALL BY VIDEO, 1986
MasterVision
90 minutes, sound, color

Offensive and defensive fundamentals of baseball are explained. Home video.

THE LONG WINTER OF HENRY AARON, 1973
Video Tape Network
60 minutes, sound, color

Profile of Atlanta Braves' slugger Hank Aaron, who finished the 1973 season with 713 career home runs—one short of Babe Ruth's all-time record.

MEET BABE RUTH, 1985
CEL Communnications, Inc. in association with ESPN
30 minutes, sound, black and white
Narrated by Bernie Barrow

Documentary profile of Babe Ruth. Home video.

MICKEY MANTLE'S BASEBALL TIPS FOR KIDS OF ALL AGES, 1986
CBS-Fox
90 minutes, sound, color

Features instructionals from New York Yankee greats Mickey Mantle, Whitey Ford, and Phil Rizzuto. Home video.

MR. BASEBALL, 1954
(Movietone News)
Fox
15 minutes, sound, black and white

Newsreel biography of Hall of Fame manager Connie Mack.

MY NAME IS TED WILLIAMS
30 minutes, sound
Narrated by Tom Harmon

THE NAME OF THE GAME IS BASEBALL, c. 1975
Prudential Insurance
30 minutes, sound, color
Narrated by Curt Gowdy

Youngsters learn baseball fundamentals from big league stars.

THE NAME OF THE GAME IS FUN, 1966
American League of Professional Baseball Clubs
Chrysler Corp.
30 minutes, sound
Copyright date and number: November 23, 1966, LP 34278

Chronicle of major league baseball from spring training through the regular season.

1915 WORLD'S CHAMPIONSHIP BASEBALL SERIES, 1915
World Series Film Co.
Copyright date and number: October 21, 1915; November 11, 1915, MU 446

THE OLD BALL GAME, 1963
60 minutes, sound, black and white
Narrated by Branch Rickey

Rickey outlines the highlights and history of baseball.

OPEN TRAILS, 1922
(A Sport Pictorial)
Arrow
Produced by Jack Eaton
National Film Archive, The British Film Institute, London

Includes newsreel footage of Babe Ruth batting.

PLAY BALL, 1938
(News World of Sports)
Columbia Pictures Corp. of California, Ltd.

One reel, sound, black and white
Narrated by Jack Kofoed and Ford Bond
Copyright date and number: April 18, 1938, MP 8412; February 10, 1966, R 379750

Spring training with the New York Yankees.

PLAY BALL, 1950
(This is America)
RKO Pathe, Inc.
13 minutes, sound, black and white
Copyright date and number: May 26, 1950, MP 405

PLAY BALL, PLAY SAFE, 1965
Aetna Life Insurance Co. in association with Babe Ruth League Baseball and the Cincinnati Reds
14 minutes, sound
Copyright date and number: December 1, 1965, MP 15679

PLAY BALL, SON! 1946
Herb Lamb Productions, Inc.
Based on the book by Bert V. Dunne
Three reels, sound
Copyright date and number: April 30, 1946, MP 522

Baseball instructionals, position by position.

PLAY BALL, SON, 1966
Parthenon Pictures
Reel/3
22 minutes, sound

Guide for coaches of youth baseball teams.

PLAY BALL WITH BABE RUTH, 1920
(Babe Ruth Instructional Films)
One reel, silent, black and white
See: Babe Ruth Instructional Films

PLAY BALL WITH THE MINNESOTA TWINS, 1964
First National Bank of Minnesota
Martin Bovey Productions
30 minutes, sound

**PLAY BALL WITH THE OAKS,
1950**
The Tribune Publishing Co.
36 minutes, sound, color
Copyright date and number: August
28, 1950, MU 5159

The PCL Oakland Oaks are featured.

**ROBERTO CLEMENTE: A
TOUCH OF ROYALTY, 1973**
W & W Films, Inc.
30 minutes, sound, color
Written and directed by Don Fedynak

*Film tribute to the Hall of Fame outfielder.
Home video.*

**THE SCIENCE OF HITTING,
c. 1973**
30 minutes, sound, color
Narrated by Ted Williams

*Films of baseball stars are analyzed for stance,
swing, hip movement, and follow-through.*

**SPRING TRAINING OF THE
RED SOX, 1915**
Joseph J. Lannin
Written by Arthur Daniel Cooper
Copyright date and number: April 14,
1915, MU 310

TAKE IT BIG, 1926
Features Jim Thorpe, Irish Meusel,
Bob Meusel, Ernie Orsatti, Wheezer
Dell, Tillie Shafer, Mike Donlin, and
Chet Thomas

**TAKE ME OUT TO THE BALL
GAME, 1941**
Soundies Distributing Corp. of
America, Inc.
One reel, sound, black and white
Copyright date and number:
September 8, 1941, MP 11544

Musical production of the famous baseball song.

**TAKE ME OUT TO THE BALL
GAME, 1945**

Soundies Distributing Corp. of
America, Inc.
One reel, sound, black and white
Copyright date and number: March
19, 1945, MP 15731

Musical production of the song.

TED WILLIAMS, 1951
(Sportscope)
RKO Pathe, Inc.
8 minutes, sound
Copyright date and number: June 1,
1951, MP 1643

*Newsreel profile of the Boston Red Sox star
outfielder.*

**TED WILLIAMS SHOW: HOW
TO WATCH BASEBALL, 1950**
One reel, sound
Produced by Arthur Sampson and
Tim Cohane
Copyright date and number: February
8, 1950; March 1, 1950, MU 5094

THAT MAN RICKEY, 1952
(Sportscope)
RKO Pathe, Inc.
8 minutes, sound, black and white
Library of Congress number: Fi 52-
2025

*Newsreel profile of Hall of Fame executive
Branch Rickey.*

THIS IS BASEBALL, 1954
Emerson Yorke Studio
Series of films
One reel each, sound

Includes: And This is Pee Wee Reese.

THIS IS LITTLE LEAGUE, 1953
RKO Pathe, Inc.
16 minutes, sound
Copyright date and number:
November 4, 1953, MP 4576

*Highlights and history of the Little League
organization, founded in 1938 in Williamsport,
Pennsylvania.*

THROWING IN BASEBALL, 1947
Encyclopaedia Britannica Films, Inc.
One reel, sound
Copyright date and number: February
11, 1947, MP 1711

*Features instructions by Jimmy Dykes and
Hollis Thurston.*

TIGER WINS HIS STRIPES, 1966
20 minutes, sound

*Rookie earns his way onto a major league
roster.*

TITLE NOT KNOWN, 1898
Thomas A. Edison
One reel, silent, black and white

*U.S. Cavalrymen play baseball in a Spanish–
American War training camp.*

TOM LASORDA, 1973
Oxford Films
Tele-Sports
22 minutes, sound, color

*Profile of the minor league Albuquerque Dukes
manager.*

**THE TOOLS OF IGNORANCE,
1971**
Major League Baseball Productions
30 minutes, sound, color
Narrated by Pat Summerall

*Fundamentals and duties of a catcher as related
by Johnny Bench.*

TOURNAMENT, 1968
Asahi Shimbunsha/Asahi Television
News/Toho
97 minutes, sound, color
Directed by Kon Ichikawa

*Japanese-language documentary—titled,
Shishun—profiling the intensely followed high
school baseball tournament played each August
in Koshien Stadium near Osaka.*

TWO BALL GAMES, 1976
29 minutes, sound, color
Produced by David Gluck

Getting Close to the Game

In the long ago, hit-'em-where-they-ain't days of baseball, rooters, kranks, and other baseball-crazy Americans simply could not get close enough to a World Series game. Since baseball fans were still decades away from enjoying zoomed-in television replays or even radio play-by-play descriptions, they had to rely on their own unswerving devotion and sheer moxie to get a close-up view of a World Series game.

For the turn-of-the-century fan, a ticket into the ballpark also implied an entrance onto the field. It was common for fans at a World Series game to inch up to—and sometimes lean over—the foul lines for a better view. It was also customary for a fan to race onto the field to join in an argument with the umpires. And, in the case of the first World Series, it was even possible to get a close-up look of the game by peering over infielders' shoulders from the rim of the outfield grass. In those days, baseball fans were considered—not just in name only—an integral part of the game.

If World Series fans could not get into the ballpark by means proper or illegal, they climbed nearby trees and telegraph poles to get a view of the game. If a fan was unwilling to risk sliding down a pole that had been painted during the game by a club official (with paint containing no drying agent), then he milled around the admission gate or outside telegraph offices, clamoring not only for the score inning by inning, but for details of the game pitch by pitch. Oftentimes the swarming crowd outside the ballpark exceeded the number of fans inside.

From the moment aging pitcher Cy Young of the Boston Pilgrims faced Pittsburgh Pirates lead-off hitter Ginger Beaumont in the first-ever World Series game in 1903, the fall classic has been an extraordinary American rite. It galvanized the enthusiasms of a diverse people and brought them together in an autumnal gathering of the tribes. Standing shoulder to shoulder in virtually every major American city, watching the latest World Series results being posted on a bulletin board, were newly arrived immigrants and sons of the revolution alike. Those who knew nothing about baseball, who were perhaps unversed in the customs or even the language of the new world, were aware of the importance of the World Series.

So intense was the interest in the games that a minor industry was created to satisfy the demand for immediate play-by-play accounts of the World Series. Manually operated bulletin boards, which provided a simple inning-by-inning line score, were rapidly replaced by sophisticated electrical scoreboards offering pitch-by-pitch, batter-by-batter re-creations of telegraphed accounts of the games. Huge crowds stopped downtown traffic for hours every October as World Series fans watched the intricate flashing lights on a diamond scoreboard that codified the action of the games.

In 1908 the Essanay Company produced the first motion picture of a World Series game. That year a one-reel silent compilation of World Series highlights was shown in theaters across the United States. Although the results of the Chicago Cubs–Detroit Tigers World Series were already known (the Cubs won easily, four games to one), kranks and rooters nonetheless flocked to see the film. Even in a non–World Series city

55

The chaotic scene during the first game of the first World Series at the Huntington Avenue Grounds in Boston in 1903. The crowd had to be pushed back behind outfield ropes before the game could resume. (National Baseball Library.)

in the midwest, two theaters played Essanay's *World Championship Baseball* to a full house twice daily for a week.

Essanay's success notwithstanding, baseball officials were slow to comprehend the financial benefits to be reaped from the World Series films. In 1910, a mere $500 fee was charged for the rights to film the World Series highlights, the proceeds of which were divided among both clubs and baseball's National Commission. The following year the licensing fee was increased to a still modest $3500.

In 1913 Selig Polyscope Co. took over the filming of the World Series and expanded the highlights to four reels. That same year, Loew's Theaters devised a daring scheme to film each game of the New York Giants–Philadelphia Athletics World Series in its entirety for showing that

same evening in all nineteen of their theaters in New York and Brooklyn. After each 200-foot reel of baseball action was filmed, the reel was rushed from the Polo Grounds to a developing room to be processed in time for showing at seven o'clock that evening—or a mere three hours after the last out had been made. By the time the early reels were being shown in the theaters, the supply of later reels were arriving from the developing room. The logistics involved in the scheme must have rivaled the blockade of Mexico by the United States that year.

One can only imagine what the viewers experienced at Loew's that week in 1913. Without sound or even batter-by-batter captions to guide them, and with only the crude reportage of a single unedited camera to instruct them, even the most knowledgeable of kranks must have felt completely at sea. And yet, in 1913, novelty was all. One attended such affairs as much to pay homage to an emerging technology as to watch championship baseball being played.

Filmed highlights of the World Series were discontinued shortly after World War I, when newsreels became a popular source of news and sports information. In 1943, an enterprising former major leaguer, Lew Fonseca, initiated a program of filmed World Series highlights that was distributed yearly, free of charge, to community organizations all over the world. Though these films are widely popular among educational and home video audiences, they are essentially pro-motional products of Major League Baseball and do not offer an incisive documentary portrayal of the World Series.

Today, Americans can get as close to a World Series game as the television camera will take them. Not surprisingly, after nearly ninety years, we still find ourselves leaning over the foul lines and peering from behind infielder's shoulders—but it is done now through the miracle of precision close-ups and slow-motion replays. The World Series still inspires us to link arms in an October gathering of the tribes, except now we gather around our television sets—in offices, in taverns, and in the comfort of our own living rooms. ◆

A children's sandlot baseball game and an organized Little League game are contrasted to illustrate the benefits and disadvantages of each.

TY COBB, 1929
(Fox Movietone)
One reel, sound, black and white

Cobb affirms that he has no misgivings about his recent retirement from baseball.

WHEN DIAMONDS WERE A GIRL'S BEST FRIEND
Produced and directed by Janis L. Taylor

Co-produced by Meg Moritz
Film Department, Northwestern University, Evanston, Illinois

Documentary history of the 1940s All-American Girls Professional Baseball League.

WILLIE MAYS, 1954
(Sportscope)
RKO Pathe, Inc.
8 minutes, sound
Copyright date and number: October 27, 1954, MP 5631

Newsreel profile of the New York Giants outfielder and National League Most Valuable Player for 1954.

WORLD CHAMPIONSHIP BASEBALL, 1908
Essanay
One reel, silent, black and white

First ever theatrically released World Series film. Essanay also produced the highlights films for the 1909 through 1912 World Series.

THE WORLD SERIES GAMES, BOSTON VS. BROOKLYN, 1916
Selig Polyscope Co.
Four reels, silent, black and white
Copyright date and number: October 16, 1916, MP 742

Selig's coverage of the World Series began with the 1913 championship.

Baseball in Animated Cartoons —Feature

EXPLANATORY NOTES

1. Title of the cartoon episode, year of release.

2. Name of the cartoon series in parentheses, if applicable.

3. Name of releasing company.

4. Name of production company.

5. Length of the cartoon in reels or minutes, silent or sound, black and white or color.

6. Writer(s) of cartoon.

7. Director of cartoon.

8. Voices featured in cartoon.

9. Copyright date and registration number.

10. Annotation. Description of the cartoon. *Home video* (given when the cartoon is available in home video format).

The following catalog contains a comprehensive listing of theatrically released animated cartoons relating to baseball. Included are silent-era animated subjects, cartoon shorts from animated series, and special cartoon features relating to baseball.

Photographs for this section are provided courtesy of the Museum of Modern Art/Film Stills Archive, and Walt Disney Productions.

For animated cartoons produced for television, *see:* Baseball in Animated Cartoons—Television.

ABNER THE BASEBALL, 1961
Paramount Pictures Corp.
Two reels, sound, color
Written and narrated by Eddie Lawrence
Directed by Seymour Kneitel
Copyright date and number: April 1, 1961, LP 20352
See also: Baseball in Comedy and Light Verse—Recorded

ALICE IN THE BIG LEAGUE, 1927
(Alice in Wonderland)
Winkler Pictures, Inc.
R-C Pictures Corp.
Walt Disney
One reel, silent, black and white
Copyright date and number: August 22, 1927, LP 24553

THE BALL GAME, 1932
(Aesop's Fables)
Van Beuren Corp.
One reel, sound, black and white
Directed by John Foster and George Rufle
Copyright date and number: August 3, 1932, MP 3464

Two teams of insects vie in a comical baseball game. Home video. (In a Cartoon Studio.)

THE BALL PARK, 1929
(Aesop's Fables)
Pathe Exchange, Inc.
One reel, silent, black and white
Directed by Paul Terry
Copyright date and number: May 4, 1929, MP 163

Features a power-hitting ape and a trepidatious umpire.

BARNYARD BASEBALL, 1939
(Gandy Goose)
Twentieth Century-Fox
Terrytoons, Inc.
One reel, sound, black and white
Directed by Mannie Davis
Copyright date and number: July 14, 1939, MP 9929; October 14, 1966, R 395388

BASEBALL BASICS AND BLUNDERS, 1977
Paramount Communications
6 minutes, sound, color

Animated story demonstrating the rules of baseball.

BASEBALL BUGS, 1946
(Bugs Bunny)
Warner Bros.

One reel, sound, color
Written by Michael Maltese
Directed by Fritz Freleng
Animation by Gerry Chiniquy

Walt Disney produced a classic cartoon treatment of the Casey legend with his Casey at the Bat, *a segment from the full-length feature,* Make Mine Music. *(© 1946 Walt Disney Productions.)*

Fireball Snedeker peers in nervously as the Mighty Casey settles into the batter's box in Casey at the Bat. *(© 1946 Walt Disney Productions.)*

Copyright date and number:
December 26, 1946, MP 1497

Bugs Bunny is matched against a team of baseball-playing gorillas.

BASE BRAWL, 1948

(Screen Songs)
Paramount Pictures, Inc.
One reel, sound, color
Directed by Seymour Kneitel
Animation by Dave Tendlar and Tom Golden
Copyright date and number: January 23, 1948, LP 1472

"Bouncing ball" cartoon of the song, "Take Me Out to the Ball Game."

BATTY BASEBALL, 1944

MGM
One reel, sound, color
Directed by Tex Avery
Animation by Ray Abrams, Preston Blair, and Ed Love
Copyright date and number: April 13, 1944, MP 14919

BOBBY BUMPS' WORLD SERIES, 1917

(Bobby Bumps)
Paramount Pictures
J. R. Bray Productions
One reel, silent, black and white
Directed by Earl Hurd
Released October 8, 1917

BOULEVARDIER FROM THE BRONX, 1936

Warner Bros.
7 minutes, sound, color
Directed by Fritz Freleng
Animation by Cal Dalton and Paul Smith
Copyright date and number:
December 9, 1936, MP 7012; January 30, 1964, R 331007

A big-city team challenges a local club to a game of baseball.

BUDDY'S BEARCATS, 1934

Warner Bros.
One reel, sound, black and white
Directed by Jack King
Animation by Ben Clopton
Copyright date and number: July 7, 1934, MP 4844; June 20, 1962, R 296855

Actor Joe E. Brown—star of Alibi Ike *and* Elmer the Great—*is caricatured as a baseball play-by-play announcer.*

CASEY AT THE BAT, 1946

Walt Disney Productions
9 minutes, sound, color
Production supervisor: Joe Grant
Directed by Clyde Geronimi
Features the voice of Jerry Colonna
Released August 15, 1946

Segment from the feature, Make Mine Music. *Includes song, "Casey" (The Pride of Them All). (See:* Baseball in Music and Song—Recorded). *Home video. (Disney Cartoon Classics, Volume 12: Disney's Tall Tales.)*

CASEY AT THE BAT, 1966

(Living Poetry Series)
McGraw-Hill Book Co.
Lumin Films
8 minutes, sound, color
Copyright date and number:
December 29, 1966, MP 18236

CASEY AT THE BAT, 1968

Concord
6 minutes, color

CASEY AT THE BAT, 1976

AIMS Instructional Media, Inc.
7 minutes, color
Animation by John Wilson

CASEY BATS AGAIN, 1954

Walt Disney Productions
8 minutes, sound, color
Directed by Jack Kinney
Released June 18, 1954
Copyright date and number: October 28, 1953, LP 3779

Casey is the father of nine baseball-playing daughters, and their team needs Casey in the pinch.

DUD'S HOME RUN, 1920
(Us Fellers Cartoons)
J. R. Bray Company
One reel, silent, black and white
Written and directed by Us Fellers

FELIX SAVES THE DAY, 1922
(Felix the Cat)
M. J. Winkler
One reel, silent, black and white
Animation by Pat Sullivan and Otto Messmer

Felix is a good-luck mascot for the New York Yankees.

THE FOUL BALL PLAYER, 1940
(Stone Age)
Paramount Pictures
Max Fleischer
One reel, sound, black and white
Written by Jack Ward
Animation by Bill Nolan and Ralph Sommerville
Copyright date and number: May 24, 1940, LP 9664

GONE BATTY, 1954
(Looney Tune Cartoon)
Warner Bros.
Vitaphone Corp.
7 minutes, sound, color
Copyright date and number: September 4, 1954, MP 6472

Baseball as played by a team of short, fat men with beards, and a team of tall, skinny men with moustaches.

HOW TO PLAY BASEBALL, 1942
Walt Disney Productions
One reel, sound, color
Directed by Jack Kinney
Released September 4, 1942

Goofy demonstrates the finer points of inside baseball. Home video. (Disney Cartoon Classics, Volume 4: Sport Goofy.)

KIDDIE LEAGUE, 1959
(Woody Woodpecker)
Universal-International
Universal Film Exchange
One reel, sound, color
Created by Walter Lantz
Directed by Paul J. Smith
Copyright date and number: November 3, 1959, LP 19265

Baseball as played by diapered tots.

MEXICAN BASEBALL, 1947
(Gandy Goose)
Twentieth Century-Fox
Terrytoons, Inc.
One reel, sound, color
Directed by Mannie Davis
Released March 14, 1947

PLAY BALL, 1933
(Willie Whopper)
MGM
Celebrity Productions
One reel, sound, black and white
Animation by Ub Iwerks
Copyright date and number: November 1, 1933, MP 4370; July 12, 1961, R 278929

Babe Ruth is caricatured in this first cartoon in the "Willie Whopper" series.

PORKY'S BASEBALL BROADCAST, 1940
(Porky Pig)
Warner Bros.
One reel, sound, black and white
Directed by Fritz Freleng
Released July 6, 1940

Stuttering Porky Pig describes a madcap baseball game.

SLIDE, DONALD, SLIDE, 1949
(Donald Duck)
Walt Disney Productions
One reel, sound, color
Written by Nick George and Bill Berg
Directed by Jack Hannah
Released November 25, 1949

Goofy demonstrates the fine art of pitching in Disney's hilarious How to Play Baseball, *in which he manages to make a simple child's game seem too complicated to comprehend. (© 1942 Walt Disney Productions.)*

Copyright date and number: December 7, 1948, LP 2583

Baseball-loving Donald and a bee that admires classical music battle for control of the radio dial.

SOFTBALL GAME, 1936
(Oswald the Rabbit)
Universal Productions, Inc.
Walter Lantz
One reel, sound, black and white
Copyright date and number: January 23, 1936, MP 6147; December 30, 1963, R 328853

THREE STRIKES YOU'RE OUT, 1917
(Happy Hooligan)
Educational Film Corp. of America
International Film Service, Inc.
One reel, silent, black and white
Directed by William C. Nolan
Copyright date and number: April 26, 1917, LU 10659

Baseball in Television

The following section contains a comprehensive listing of dramatic, comic, and musical teleplays relating to baseball. Included in the catalog are live television dramas from the 1950s, original baseball musicals produced for television, made-for-television movies, television adaptations of baseball novels, books and short stories, baseball-related episodes from television series, and dramatizations of the events and personalities from baseball's past. Also included are baseball-related teleplays available in home video format.

Not included in this section are documentary and public affairs television programming. For a listing of these programs, *see:* Baseball in Documentary and Miscellaneous Television.

It is not altogether a coincidence that 1950s television—based almost entirely in New York—and New York City baseball (as represented by the Yankees, Giants, and Brooklyn Dodgers) enjoyed their respective golden ages concurrently. The excitement generated by live television drama was matched by the daily dramatics of the local major league teams, two of which seemed inevitably to be playing in the World Series, with one or the other of the famed New York center fielders leading the way. Perhaps for that reason, an astonishing number of programs from television's Golden Age has baseball as its theme.

It is regrettable, however, that much of 1950s television was never preserved on tape and has been permanently lost. The Museum of Broadcasting in New York houses the nation's largest collection of television broadcasts, a small number of which date from television's golden era. The Museum nonetheless contains a representative selection of baseball-related programs as listed in this catalog, as well as documentary and other historical programs such as complete World Series game broadcasts. In addition, scripts from virtually all dramatic television programs from 1976 to date can be found in the Library of the Annenberg School of Communications at the University of Pennsylvania in Philadelphia, including those relating to baseball. The Television Information Office offers an extensive research library specializing in all aspects of television programming history.

Titles to television programs as contained in this section are listed as copyrighted or as shown within the body of the program or as stated on the script. Programs without formal episode titles are found under "Broadcast of . . ." and are arranged chronologically.

Broadcast dates are listed, whenever possible, according to the listings as published in the Metropolitan New York edition of *TV Guide.*

Photographs in this section have been provided through the courtesy of Platypus Productions, Daniel Wilson Productions, Roger Gimbel Productions, Blatt/Singer Productions, Walt Disney Productions, and the publicity departments of Home Box Office, The Disney Channel, ABC, CBS, and NBC.

For home video and other television materials and collectibles, consult the Selected Guide to Sources and Dealers located at the back of the book.

EXPLANATORY NOTES

1. Title of the teleplay, year of broadcast.

2. Name of the television series in parentheses, if applicable.

3. Name of production company.

4. Broadcast network, program length in minutes, premiere broadcast date.

5. Writer(s) of program.

6. Director of program.

7. Producer of program.

8. Cast of program.

9. Copyright date and registration number.

10. Name of broadcast library holding a print of the teleplay.

11. Annotation. Description of the program. *Home video* (given when the television program is available in home video format).

ALL THOSE DREAMS, 1962
(The Donna Reed Show)
Todon of California, Inc.
ABC, 30 minutes
Cast: Donna Reed as Donna Stone, Carl Betz as Dr. Alex Stone, and Paul Petersen as Jeff Stone
Guests: Don, Ginger, and Kelly Drysdale
Copyright date and number: December 28, 1961, LP 26383

During a family trip to Chicago, Jeff attempts to interview Don Drysdale.

AUNT MARY, 1979
(The Hallmark Hall of Fame)
Henry Jaffe Enterprises
CBS, 120 minutes, December 5, 1979
Based on a story by Ellis A. Cohen
Directed by Peter Werner
Cast: Jean Stapleton as Mary Dobkin, Martin Balsam as Harry Strasberg, Harold Gould as Dr. Hoxley, Dolph

Sweet as Amos Jones, and Ernie Harwell as the announcer

True story about a physically challenged woman who coaches a children's sandlot baseball team.

THE BABE, 1985
ESPN, 90 minutes, October 18, 1985
Based on the play of the same name
Cast: Max Gail as Babe Ruth
See also: Baseball in Theater

THE BAD NEWS BEARS, 1979
CBS, 30 minutes, weekly series
Broadcast history: March 24, 1979 to October 6, 1979
Based on the motion picture
Cast: Jack Warden as Morris Buttermaker, Catherine Hicks as Dr. Emily Rappant, J. Brennan Smith as Mike Engelberg, Tricia Cast as Amanda Whurlitzer, Billy Jacoby as Rudi Stein, Sparky Marcus as Ogilvie, and Christoff St. John as Ahmad

Abdul Rahim
See also: Baseball in Film

BALL FOUR, 1976
CBS, 30 minutes, weekly series
Broadcast history: September 22, 1976 to October 27, 1976
Cast: Jim Bouton as Jim Barton, Jack Somack as Cap Capogrosso, David-James Carroll as Bill Westlake, Ben Davidson as Rhino Rhinelander, Bill McCutcheon as Coach Pinky Pinkney, Lenny Schultz as Birdman Siegel, Marco St. John as Rayford Plunkett, Jaime Tirelli as Orlando Lopez, and Sam Wright as C. B. Travis
See also: Baseball in Music and Song; Baseball in the Spoken Arts—Recorded

Locker-room comedy about a pitcher who is writing a series of articles on baseball life "off the field."

Jim Bouton's locker-room comedy, Ball Four, lasted just four episodes in the fall 1976 television season. Stranded in a stalled elevator, members of the Washington Americans decide to kill time by interviewing each other on Bouton's tape recorder. Pictured left to right: Ben Davidson (rear), David-James Carroll, Bouton, Charlotte Jones, Sam Wright, George Coe, Marco St. John, and Jaime Tirelli. (CBS, 1976.)

THE BALL GAME
(The Andy Griffith Show)
CBS, 30 minutes
Written by Rance Howard and Sid Morse
Cast: Andy Griffith as Andy Taylor, Ronnie Howard as Opie Taylor, and Don Knotts as Barney Fife

Andy umpires a town baseball game.

BANG THE DRUM SLOWLY, 1956
(The United States Steel Hour)
CBS, 60 minutes, September 26, 1956
Based on the novel by Mark Harris
Written by Arnold Schulman
Cast: Paul Newman as Henry Wiggen, Albert Salmi as Bruce Pearson, George Peppard as Piney Woods, Georgann Johnson as Holly,
Rudy Bond as Dutch, and John McGovern as Mr. Moors
See also: Baseball in Film; Baseball in Fiction; Baseball in Miscellaneous Recordings

Subsequently rebroadcast on ''The Golden Age of Television,'' PBS, September 27, 1981. Home video.

BASEBALL, 1979
(WKRP in Cincinnati)
MTM Enterprises, Inc.
CBS, 30 minutes, October 15, 1979
Written and directed by Hugh Wilson
Cast: Richard Sanders as Les Nessman, Gary Sandy as Andy Travis, Gordon Jump as Mr. Carlson, Loni Anderson as Jennifer Marlowe, and Howard Hesseman as Johnny Fever

Deprived of baseball as a child, Les is eager to excel in a company softball game.

BASEBALL BLUES, 1954
(The United States Steel Hour)
ABC, 60 minutes, September 28, 1954
Written by Steven Gethers
Cast: Frank Lovejoy as Mike Corriden, Billie Worth as Mae Corriden, Harry Bellaver as Pete, House Jameson as Mr. Denham, Edward Andrews as Eddie, Bert Thorn as Charlie, Lefty Gomez, and Frankie Frisch

A 40-year-old pitcher confronts his retirement from baseball and the necessity of a new career.

BASEBALL STORY, 1953
(Big Town)
CBS, 30 minutes, September 24, 1953
Written by Lawrence Kimble
Cast: Patrick McVey as Steve Wilson, and Jane Nigh
Copyright date and number: April 9, 1954, LU 3047

Newspaper reporter uncovers a tale of courage while investigating a suspected baseball fix.

BASEBALL VS. LOVE, 1961
(The Real McCoys)
Brennan-Westgate Productions
ABC, 30 minutes
Cast: Walter Brennan as Grandpa McCoy, Richard Crenna as Luke McCoy, and Kathy Nolan as Kate McCoy
Copyright date and number: March 31, 1961, LP 24306

Little Luke's baseball playing suffers when he falls in love.

BATTER UP, 1959
(The Real McCoys)
Brennan-Westgate Productions
ABC, 30 minutes
Cast: Walter Brennan as Grandpa McCoy, Richard Crenna as Luke

McCoy, and Kathy Nolan as Kate McCoy
Copyright date and number: April 2, 1959, LP 17701

Grandpa persistently interferes with Luke's coaching of a Little League team.

BATTER UP, 1968
(Gentle Ben)
Ivan Tors Films, Inc.
CBS, 30 minutes
Cast: Dennis Weaver as Tom Wedloe, Clint Howard as Mark Wedloe, and Rance Howard as Henry Boomhauer
Guest: Bob Gibson
Copyright date and number: January 28, 1968, LP 36644

Bob Gibson teaches a Little Leaguer the value of good sportsmanship. Home video.

BATTER UP, 1983
(Family Ties)
UBU Productions in association with Paramount Pictures
NBC, 30 minutes, November 30, 1983
Written by Lisa Bannick

Facing a possible forfeit due to a shortage of players, Jennifer must recruit the clumsiest girl in the neighborhood to play on her baseball team.

BAY CITY BLUES, 1983
MTM Enterprises, Inc.
NBC, 60 minutes, weekly series
Broadcast history: October 25, 1983 to November 15, 1983; July 1, 1984 to July 8, 1984
Created by Stephen Bochco and Jeffrey Lewis
Cast: Michael Nouri as Joe Rohner, Pat Corley as Ray Holtz, Peter Jurasik as Mitch Klein, Perry Lang as Frenchy Nuckles, Bernie Casey as Ozzie Peoples, Ken Olin as Rocky Padillo, Jeff McCracken as Vic Kresky, Dennis Franz as Angelo Carbone, Patrick Cassidy as Terry St. Marie, Tony Spiridakis as Lee Jacoby, Larry Flash

Jenkins as Lynwood "Linoleum" Scott, Mykel T. Williamson as Deejay Cunningham, Marco Rodriguez as Bird, and Kelly Harmon as Sunny Hayward

Dramatic series about life on a minor league baseball club in a small California town. Includes: "Bay City Blues" (premiere episode); "Beautiful Peoples"; "Zircons Are Forever"; "I Never Swung for My Father"; "Rocky IV-Eyes"; "Play It Again, Milt"; "Look Homeward Hayward"; "Going, Going, Gone."

BAY CITY BLUES, 1983
(Bay City Blues)
NBC, 60 minutes, October 25, 1983
See: Bay City Blues

Premiere episode of the series of the same name. Mickey Wagner has an opportunity to advance to the major leagues if he conquers his alcoholism.

BEAUTIFUL PEOPLES, 1983
(Bay City Blues)
NBC, 60 minutes, November 1, 1983
See: Bay City Blues

Aging black star Ozzie Peoples is honored with a day at Bluebird Stadium, but the goodwill does not extend beyond the playing field.

BEAVER THE ATHLETE, 1959
(Leave it to Beaver)
Gomalco Productions, Inc.
ABC, 30 minutes
Cast: Barbara Billingsley as June Cleaver, Hugh Beaumont as Ward Cleaver, Tony Dow as Wally Cleaver, and Jerry Mathers as Beaver Cleaver
Copyright date and number: June 11, 1959, LP 23585

Beaver prepares for the annual baseball game between the boys and the girls.

BEETHOVEN OR BASEBALL, 1964
(Karen)
Kayro-Vue Productions
NBC, 30 minutes, November 9, 1964

Cast: Debbie Watson as Karen Scott
Guest: Vince Scully as himself
Copyright date and number: November 9, 1964, LP 30012

BENTLEY GOES TO BAT, 1962
(Bachelor Father)
Bachelor Productions Co.
ABC, 30 minutes
Cast: John Forsythe as Bentley Gregg
Copyright date and number: April 17, 1962, LP 23452

Bentley teaches a tomboyish baseball player to adopt a more ladylike appearance.

THE BIG GAME
(The Flying Nun)
ABC, 30 minutes
Written by Clifford Goldsmith
Cast: Sally Field as Sister Bertrille
Guests: Don Drysdale and Willie Davis

Sister Bertrille finds a moral victory in her baseball team's 43–1 loss.

THE BIG LEAGUE, 1962
(The Living Word)
Salvation Army
Syndicated, 15 minutes

Baseball player stands by his religious principles.

BLEACHER BUMS, 1979
PBS, 90 minutes, October 14, 1979
Based on the play of the same name
See also: Baseball in Theater

THE BOYS AGAINST THE GIRLS
(Family Affair)
CBS, 30 minutes
Cast: Brian Keith as Bill Davis, Anissa Jones as Buffy, and Johnnie Whitaker as Jody

Girl-hating captain throws Buffy off of the boys' stickball team.

Elliott Gould stars in a whimsical adaptation —intended for younger viewers—of Casey at the Bat, *in which the mighty slugger must hit a home run to save Mudville's ramshackle stadium from being razed by a thievish businessman. (Platypus Productions, 1986. Photo: Lynn Houston.)*

CALLING WILLIE MAYS

(The Donna Reed Show)
ABC, 30 minutes
Cast: Donna Reed as Donna Stone, Carl Betz as Dr. Alex Stone, and Paul Petersen as Jeff Stone
Guest: Willie Mays

THE CAP, 1985

(Wonderworks)
Atlantis Films, Ltd. and the National Film Board of Canada
PBS, 30 minutes, March 25, 1985
Based on the story, "A Cap for Steve" by Morley Callaghan
Written and directed by Robert Duncan
Cast: Nicolas Podbrey as Steve Diamond, Michael Ironside as Dave Diamond, Jennifer Dale as Anna Diamond; and Andre Dawson and Duke Snider as themselves

Segment of 60-minute program, titled, "Two Alone." An unemployed father sells his son's prized autographed baseball cap.

CASEY, 1981

(The Hallmark Hall of Fame)
PBS, 60 minutes, May 6, 1981
Written by David and Sidney Carroll
Directed by Nick Havinga
Produced by David Susskind
Cast: Charles Durning as Casey Stengel

One-character performance dramatizing the life and philosophy of the Hall of Fame manager.

CASEY AT THE BAT, 1986

(Shelly Duvall's Tall Tales and Legends)
Platypus Productions, Inc./Gaylord Production Co.
Showtime, 60 minutes, March 21, 1986
Written by Andy Borowitz
Directed by David Steinberg
Cast: Elliott Gould as Casey, Carol Kane as Barbara, Hamilton Camp as Undercrawl, Rae Dawn Chong as Circe LeFemme, Bill Macy as Pop Gumm, Howard Cosell as Ernie, Bob Uecker as Joe, Jay Johnstone as Blake, and Tom Niedenfuer as Flynn

Comic melodrama in which Casey saves the Mudville Hogs baseball club from a villainous financier. Home video.

CATCH, 1981

(Lou Grant)
CBS, 60 minutes, January 5, 1981
Cast: Ed Asner as Lou Grant, Robert Walden as Joe Rossi, and Linda Kelsey as Billie Newman
Guest: Cliff Potts as Ted McCovey

Woman reporter falls in love with a baseball star.

CHANGES, 1984

(Silver Spoons)
NBC, 30 minutes, March 3, 1984

Girl pitcher has a crush on the boy catcher of the baseball team.

CHANGE UP, 1952

(Danger)
CBS, 30 minutes, September 30, 1952
Cast: Edward Binns

Gamblers attempt to fix a minor league game.

CHEERS, 1982

NBC, 30 minutes, weekly series
Broadcast premiere: September 30, 1982
Cast: Ted Danson as Sam Malone, and Shelly Long as Diane Chambers

Situation comedy about an ex-major league ballplayer who owns a Boston neighborhood tavern.

CHIEF TO CHIEF, 1977

(Carter County)
ABC, 30 minutes
Written by Sheldon Bull
Cast: Victor French as Chief Roy Mobey, Kene Holliday as Curtis Baker, and Richard Paul as Mayor Teddy Burnside

The fire and police departments are rivals in the annual softball game.

THE CLAMPETTS AND THE DODGERS, 1963

(The Beverly Hillbillies)
Filmways TV Productions,Inc.
CBS, 30 minutes
Cast: Buddy Ebsen as Jed Clampett, Irene Ryan as Granny, Donna Douglas as Elly May, and Max Baer, Jr. as Jethro Bodine
Guest: Leo Durocher
Copyright date and number: April 10, 1963, LP 25405

Leo is eager to sign Jethro to a big league contract until he learns that Bodine throws a "spitter" using possum fat.

CLEO AND THE BABE, 1982

(Voyagers!)
NBC, 60 minutes, November 14, 1982

Written and produced by Jill Sherman
Cast: Meeno Peluce as Jeffrey, and
Jon-Erik Hexum as Bogg
Guest: Bill Lucking as Babe Ruth

*Two boys travel back in time to visit the 1919
spring training camp of the Boston Red Sox,
where Babe Ruth contemplates quitting baseball
to take up a career in vaudeville.*

CLOSE DECISION, 1955
(Father Knows Best)
Screen Gems, Inc.
CBS, 30 minutes
Written by Roswell Rogers
Cast: Robert Young as Jim Anderson,
Jane Wyatt as Margaret Anderson,
Elinor Donahue as Betty Anderson,
and Billy Gray as Bud Anderson
Copyright date and number: March
27, 1955, LP 11960

*Bud admits he didn't tag a runner in a church
baseball game and is commended for his
honesty.*

COL. FLACK AND THE LITTLE
LEAGUERS, 1959
(Colonel Humphrey Flack)
CBS, 30 minutes
Cast: Alan Mowbray as Col.
Humphrey Flack
Copyright date and number: April 19,
1959, LP 14327

THE COMEBACK, 1956
(Crossroads)
Federal Telefilms, Inc.
ABC, 30 minutes, October 5, 1956
Credits: Bernard L. Schubert
Cast: Chuck Connors as Lou Brissie,
Don DeFore as Rev. C. E. Stoney
Jackson, and Grant Withers as Whitey
Martin
Copyright date and number: October
5, 1956, LP 7297

*Dramatization of Philadelphia A's pitcher Lou
Brissie's comeback from injuries suffered in
World War II.*

THE COMEBACK KID, 1980
ABC Circle Films
ABC, 120 minutes, April 11, 1980
Written by Joe Landon
Directed by Peter Levin
Cast: John Ritter as Bubba Newman,
Susan Dey as Megan Barrett, Doug
McKeon as Michael, James Gregory
as Scotty, and Michael Lembeck as
Tony

*Baseball player coaches a team of disadvantaged
youths.* Home video.

DAMN YANKEES, 1967
(NBC's TV Color Special)
NBC, 120 minutes, April 8, 1967
Cast: Lee Remick as Lola, Jerry
Lanning as Joe Hardy, Phil Silvers as
Mr. Applegate, Jim Backus as Van
Buren, Linda Lavin as Gloria, Fran
Allison as Meg, Ray Middleton as Joe
Boyd, and Joe Garagiola as the
announcer
See also: Baseball in Film; Baseball in
Theater; Baseball in Music and Song
—Recorded

DEATH ON THE DIAMOND,
1953
(Man Against Crime)
CBS, 30 minutes, July 17, 1953
Cast: Ralph Bellamy as Mike Barnett
Copyright date and number: July 17,
1953, LP 2851

*Barnett solves a murder involving a sensational
rookie.*

DENNIS AND THE DODGER,
1962
(Dennis the Menace)
Dariell Productions, Inc. in
association with Screen Gems
CBS, 30 minutes
Cast: Jay North as Dennis Mitchell,
Herbert Anderson as Henry Mitchell,
and Gloria Henry as Alice Mitchell
Guest: Sandy Koufax

Copyright date and number: May 7,
1962, LP 29091

DENNIS AND THE PEE WEE
LEAGUE, 1961
(Dennis the Menace)
Dariell Productions, Inc.
CBS, 30 minutes
Cast: Jay North as Dennis Mitchell,
Herbert Anderson as Henry Mitchell,
and Gloria Henry as Alice Mitchell
Copyright date and number:
November 13, 1961, LP 29068

A DIAMOND IS A BOY'S BEST
FRIEND, 1959
See: Moochie of the Little League

DON'T LOOK BACK: THE
STORY OF LEROY "SATCHEL"
PAIGE, 1981
ABC, 120 minutes, May 31, 1981
Written by Ronald Rubin
Directed by Richard A. Colla
Cast: Lou Gossett, Jr. as Satchel
Paige, Beverly Todd as LaHoma
Brown Paige, Cleavon Little as Rabbit
Thompson, Ernie Barnes as Josh
Gibson, Clifton Davis as Cool Papa
Bell, and Earle Willoughby as Dizzy
Dean

Film biography of the Hall of Fame pitcher.

DOUBLEPLAY FROM FOSTER
TO DUROCHER TO JOEY, 1963
(The Joey Bishop Show)
Bellmar Enterprises
NBC, 30 minutes
Cast: Joey Bishop as Joey Barnes
Guests: Phil Foster and Leo Durocher
Copyright date and number:
December 6, 1963, LP 30149

THE DROPOUT
(The Brady Bunch)
ABC, 30 minutes
Cast: Robert Reed as Mike Brady,
Florence Henderson as Carol Brady,

Louis Gossett, Jr., portrays the legendary Satchel Paige in Don't Look Back: The Story of Leroy "Satchel" Paige. *(ABC Theater, 1981.)*

Cast: Jimmy Stewart as Prof. James K. Howard, Dennis Larson as Teddy, and Jonathan Daly as P. J.

Prof. Howard prepares his unathletic son for the annual baseball game.

FEAR STRIKES OUT, 1955
(Climax!)
CBS, 60 minutes, August 18, 1955
Based on the book by James A. Piersall and Albert S. Hershberg
Written by Mel Goldberg
Cast: Tab Hunter as Jimmy Piersall, John Conte as Stubby, and Mona Freeman as Mary
See also: Baseball in Film

Dramatization of Red Sox outfielder Jimmy Piersall's comeback from mental illness.

FLASHING SPIKES, 1962
(Alcoa Premiere)
Avasta Productions
ABC, 60 minutes, October 4, 1962
Based on the novel by Frank O'Rourke
Written by Jameson Brewer
Directed by John Ford
Cast: James Stewart as Slim Conway, Patrick Wayne as Bill Riley, Tige Andrews as Gabby, Jack Warden as the commissioner, Don Drysdale as Gomer, Stefanie Hill as Mary Riley, Carleton Young as Rex Short, and Edgar Buchanan as Holman
Copyright date and number: October 4, 1962, LP 26556
See also: Baseball in Juvenile and Miscellaneous Fiction

Former pitching star, banned from baseball for having accepted a bribe, is accused of offering a bribe to a young ballplayer and friend.

THE GAME YOU LEARNED FROM YOUR FATHER, 1985
(Hardcastle and McCormick)
Stephen J. Cannell Productions
ABC, 60 minutes, March 18, 1985
Written by Patrick Hasburgh

and Barry Williams as Greg Brady
Guest: Don Drysdale

A compliment from Don Drysdale gives Greg a swelled head.

THE FATHER AND SON GAME, 1971
(The Jimmy Stewart Show)
NBC, 30 minutes, October 10, 1971

BALLADS TO OL' SATCHEL

In the sense that Satchel Paige has transcended the baseball diamond and has been assigned a permanent place in American folklore, the ageless Hall of Famer will indeed—as he often boasted he would—pitch forever. Except for Babe Ruth and Jackie Robinson, no other player has been as celebrated in story, song, and legend as the tall, lanky, sagacious black pitcher who, because something might be gaining on him, never cared much for looking back.

While the made-for-television movie *Don't Look Back: The Story of Leroy "Satchel" Paige* failed to measure up as either biography or baseball history, Lou Gossett, Jr., did convey the image of Satchel as part folkloric figure, part baseball hero. A more successful dramatization can be found in "The Ballad of Satchel Paige," a 1949 episode of the all-black radio series, *Destination Freedom*. In it, Oscar Brown, Jr., tells the story of Satchel Paige in the form of a ballad that he sings at intervals during the radio play.

In song Satchel Paige has been celebrated in Rev. Frederick Douglass Kirkpatrick's "Ballad of Satchel Paige," recorded in 1972, and in Raynola Smith's "Ballad of Satchel Paige (Don't Look Back)," recorded in 1982. The most perfect expression of Paige's oracular exuberance is found in Samuel Allen's eight-line poem "To Satch (or American Gothic)," written in 1963. In the poem Satchel Paige affirms that he may indeed pitch forever and that some day, after reaching up for a handful of stars, he'll "whip three hot strikes burnin' down the heavens / And look over at God and say / How about that!"

Directed by Kim Manners
Cast: Brian Keith as Judge Milton Hardcastle, and David Hugh-Kelly as Mark McCormick
Guests: Jeff MacKay as Duke McGuire, Rick Monday as the announcer, and Ron Cey as himself

Star pitcher is framed for murder by an unbalanced teammate who hopes to win his father's approval.

GOING, GOING, GONE, 1984
(Bay City Blues)
NBC, 60 minutes, July 8, 1984
See: Bay City Blues

On the eve of a deciding play-off game, Bluebird players openly revolt against the suspension of three fellow players for smoking

marijuana. *Presented as part two of the NBC Late Night Movie.*

GOOGAN, 1953
(The Doctor)
NBC, 30 minutes, February 22, 1953
Produced by Marion Parsonnet
Host: Warner Anderson
Cast: Ernest Truex, Virginia Gilmore, and Thomas Coley

A baseball manager seeks the advice and expertise of his son's imaginary friend.

THE GREAT BASEBALL SLIDE, 1955
(Our Miss Brooks)
CBS, 30 minutes
Cast: Eve Arden as Connie Brooks,

Gale Gordon as Osgood Conklin, and Dick Crenna as Walter Denton
Copyright date and number: April 19, 1955, LP 5089

HAROLD AT THE BAT, 1984
(Domestic Life)
CBS, 30 minutes, July 31, 1984
Cast: Martin Mull as Martin, Judith-Marie Bergan as Candy, and Megan Fellows as Didi

Harold's Little League team enters the play-offs.

HERMAN THE ROOKIE, 1965
(The Munsters)
Kayro-Vue Productions
CBS, 30 minutes
Cast: Fred Gwynne as Herman
Guests: Leo Durocher and Elroy Hirsch
Copyright date and number: April 5, 1965, LP 31365

Herman possesses incredible skills as a baseball player and athlete.

HERO FATHER, 1956
(Father Knows Best)
Screen Gems, Inc.
NBC, 30 minutes
Written by Dorothy Cooper
Cast: Robert Young as Jim Anderson, Jane Wyatt as Margaret Anderson, Elinor Donahue as Betty Anderson, Billy Gray as Bud Anderson, and Lauren Chapin as Kathy Anderson
Guest: Duke Snider
Copyright date and number: May 2, 1956, LP 10659

Jim arranges for Brooklyn Dodger outfielder Duke Snider and his touring all-star team to play in Springfield.

HEWITT'S JUST DIFFERENT, 1977
(ABC Afterschool Special)
Daniel Wilson Productions, Inc.
ABC, 60 minutes, October 12, 1977

Written by Jan Hartman
Cast: Perry Lang as Hewitt Calder, Moosie Drier as Willie Arthur, and Stack Pierce as Coach Andrus

Hewitt, a mentally retarded 16-year-old boy, is befriended by a younger neighborhood boy who needs Hewitt's advice and instruction in order to make the baseball team.

HIGH AND INSIDE, 1984
(Too Close for Comfort)
D. L. Taffner Productions
Syndicated, 30 minutes
Written by Larry Balmagia
Cast: Ted Knight and Nancy Dussault
Guest: Joe Cali as Mike Lassiter

A baseball player lies about his cocaine habit.

HIGH PITCH, 1955
(Shower of Stars)
CBS, 60 minutes, May 12, 1955
Musical director: David Rose
Cast: Marguerite Piazza as Dorothy Meadows, Tony Martin as Ted Warren, William Frawley as Gabby Mullins, Vivian Vance as Mrs. Mullins, and Mel Allen

A beautiful opera star buys a baseball club and falls in love with the team's slugger. An original musical produced for television.

THE HILLBILLY WHIZ, 1957
(The Phil Silvers Show)
CBS, 30 minutes
Cast: Phil Silvers as Sergeant Ernie Bilko, Maurice Gosfield as Duane Doberman, and Harvey Lembeck as Rocco
Guests: Dick Van Dyke, Yogi Berra, Whitey Ford, Phil Rizzuto, and Red Barber
Copyright date and number: September 26, 1957, LP 9632

Bilko discovers that one of his men could be a great baseball player.

A HOME RUN FOR LOVE, 1978
(ABC Afterschool Special)
ABC, 60 minutes, October 11, 1978
Based on the novel, *Thank You, Jackie Robinson* by Barbara Cohen
Produced by Martin Tahse
Cast: Ronnie Scribner, Charles Lampkin, and John LaFayette as Jackie Robinson
See also: Thank You, Jackie Robinson
(Baseball in Juvenile and Miscellaneous Fiction)

A fatherless white boy shares his love for baseball with an elderly black man.

THE HOSPITAL STAY
(What's Happening!)
ABC, 30 minutes
Written by Alan Eisenstock and Larry Mintz
Cast: Ernest Thomas as Roger Thomas, Danielle Spencer as Dee Thomas, Fred Berry as Rerun, and Heywood Nelson as Dwayne Nelson

Dee arranges a reunion of a dying ex–Negro League star and his daughter.

HOW CHARLIE FAUST WON A PENNANT FOR THE GIANTS, 1955
(TV Reader's Digest)
Alpha Television, Inc.
ABC, 30 minutes, April 11, 1955
Based on an article by Edwin Burkholder, published in the *Reader's Digest*, October 1950, pp. 79–82
Cast: Lee Marvin, Alan Reed, Lee Van Cleef, John Larch, and John Cliff
Copyright date and number: April 11, 1955, LP 17719

True story about the Giants' mascot of 1911 who warmed up every day expecting to pitch.

I NEVER SWUNG FOR MY FATHER, 1983
(Bay City Blues)
NBC, 60 minutes, November 15, 1983
See: Bay City Blues

Facing the play-offs with a shortage of pitchers, the Bluebirds obtain Joe Kresky, an aging ex-major leaguer who is hoping to make peace with his son—a fellow Bluebird player—whom he abandoned years earlier.

IT'S GOOD TO BE ALIVE, 1974
Metromedia Productions
CBS, 120 minutes, February 22, 1974
Based on the book by Roy Campanella
Written by Steven Gethers
Directed by Michael Landon
Cast: Paul Winfield as Roy Campanella, Ramon Bieri as Walter O'Malley, Lou Gossett, Jr. as Sam Brockington, Ruby Dee as Ruthe Campanella, Joe De Santis as Campanella's father, Ty Henderson as David Campanella, and Joe E. Tata as Pee Wee Reese

Dramatization of Hall of Famer Roy Campanella's life following a crippling automobile accident in 1959. Home video.

THE JACKIE JENSEN STORY, 1956
(Cavalcade of America)
ABC, 30 minutes, April 17, 1956
Cast: Jackie Jensen has himself, B. G. Norman as Jackie Jensen (age 13), Gary Gray as Jackie Jensen (age 17), Ross Elliott as Coach Ralph Kerchum, and Vivi Janiss as Mrs. Jensen

Jackie Jensen, shy and unobtrusive as a boy, advances to the major leagues with the help of a dedicated coach.

JASON AND BIG MO, 1973
(Room 222)
ABC, 30 minutes
Written by Richard Bluel
Cast: Lloyd Haynes as Pete Dixon, Denise Nicholas as Liz McIntyre, Michael Constantine as Seymour Kaufman, and Karen Valentine as Alice Johnson

A student is offered a professional baseball contract and becomes swell-headed.

JOEY AND THE LITTLE LEAGUE, 1956
(Fury)
NBC, 30 minutes, October 13, 1956
Cast: Bobby Diamond as Joey Newton, and Peter Graves as Jim Newton
Copyright date and number: October 13, 1956, LP 11507

A boy refuses to play on Joey's baseball team unless he can pitch.

JOEY AND THE LOS ANGELES DODGERS, 1964
(The Joey Bishop Show)
Bellmar Enterprises
CBS, 30 minutes
Cast: Joey Bishop as Joey Barnes
Guests: Don Drysdale and Vin Scully
Copyright date and number: February 14, 1964, LP 30128

THE KID FROM LEFT FIELD, 1979
Coleman/Silver-Kramer
NBC, 120 minutes, September 30, 1979
Directed by Adell Aldrich
Cast: Gary Coleman as J. R. Cooper, Robert Guillaume as Larry Cooper, Ed McMahon as Fred Walker, Gary Collins as Pete Sloane, and Tricia O'Neil as Marion Fowler

Remake of the 1953 film. (See: Baseball in Film.) Home video.

KINGFISH AT THE BALL GAME, 1953
(Amos 'n' Andy)
CBS, 30 minutes
Cast: Tim Moore as George "Kingfish" Stevens, and Spencer Williams as Andy Brown
Copyright date and number: April 16, 1953, LP 19757

THE LAST OUT, 1955
(Schlitz Playhouse of Stars)

CBS, 30 minutes, September 30, 1955
Cast: Thomas Mitchell as Sam Hawkins, Regis Toomey as Babe Bricker, Richard Erdman as Eddie McGuire, Edward Binns as Mike Gibson, Touch Connors as Lou Renaldi, and Robert Hyatt as Billy Crandall

Aging former ballplayer is a minor league groundskeeper whose constant interference is a source of irritation for the team's manager.

THE LEFT FIELD CAPER, 1963
(77 Sunset Strip)
Warner Bros. Pictures, Inc.
ABC, 60 minutes, April 26, 1963
Cast: Roger Smith as Jeff, Edward Byrnes as Kookie, and Robert Logan as J. R.
Guests: Ronnie Dapo as Danny Saunders, Diane Ladd as Helen Saunders, Ed Nelson as Dave Murcotte, and Bo Belinsky as himself
Copyright date and number: April 26, 1963, LP 27666

A Little Leaguer must decide if he wants his father—recently released from prison—to attend his baseball games.

LEO DUROCHER MEETS MISTER ED, 1963
(Mister Ed)
CBS, 30 minutes
Based on characters created by Walter Brooks
Cast: Alan Young as Wilbur Post
Guest: Leo Durocher
Copyright date and number: September 29, 1963, LP 28278

THE LIFE OF MICKEY MANTLE, 1956
(Kraft Television Theatre)
NBC, 60 minutes, October 3, 1956
Written by Nicholas E. Baehr
Cast: James Olson as Mickey Mantle

Dramatization of the Hall of Famer's early life.

THE LITTLE LEAGUE, 1955
(Make Room for Daddy)
Marterto Productions, Inc.
ABC, 30 minutes
Cast: Danny Thomas as Danny Williams, Jean Hagen as Margaret Williams, and Rusty Hamer as Rusty Williams
Copyright date and number: September 20, 1955, LP 7216

THE LITTLE LEAGUE, 1956
(The Loretta Young Show)
Lewislor Enterprises, Inc.
NBC, 30 minutes, September 16, 1956
Cast: Loretta Young as Helen Seaton, Mabel Albertson as Mert Seaton, Tommy Kirk as Mark Seaton, Ray Farrell as Petey Seaton, and Michael Garrett as Mr. Tyler
Copyright date and number: September 16, 1956, LP 9620

A dedicated mother teaches her son the fundamentals of baseball after the boy fails to make a Little League team.

LITTLE LEAGUE MOOCHIE, 1959
See: Moochie of the Little League

THE LITTLE LEAGUES, 1961
(Angel)
Burligame Productions, Inc.
CBS, 30 minutes
Cast: Annie Farge as Angel
Copyright date and number: April 28, 1961, LP 20023

LITTLE LEAGUE UMPIRE, 1957
(The Danny Thomas Show)
Marterto Enterprises, Inc.
ABC, 30 minutes
Cast: Danny Thomas as Danny Williams, Marjorie Lord as Mrs. Kathy Williams, and Rusty Hamer as Rusty Williams
Copyright date and number: March 28, 1957, LP 9509

James Olson, left, portrays Mickey Mantle in the 1956 dramatization, "The Life of Mickey Mantle," which centers on Mantle's close relationship with his father during the Hall of Famer's youth. (CBS, 1956.)

LITTLE PITCHERS HAVE BIG EARS, 1964
(Bewitched)
ABC, 30 minutes
Cast: Elizabeth Montgomery as Samantha Stephens, and Dick York as Darrin Stephens

Samantha helps a boy prove himself on the baseball diamond.

THE LITTLEST LEAGUER, 1957
(The Alcoa Hour)
NBC, 60 minutes, August 25, 1957
Written by Blanche Hanalis

Cast: Peter Lazer as Benjie Hauptmann, Nehemiah Persoff as Willie Hauptmann, Vivian Nathan as Marietta Hauptmann, Jacob Kalish as Grandfather, and Sal Maglie as himself

A 10-year-old gifted student is taken to a game at Ebbets Field—in an attempt to encourage an interest in nonintellectual pursuits—and he becomes a genuine baseball fanatic.

THE LONG DISTANCE CALL, 1962
(Leave it to Beaver)
Revue Studios

ABC, 30 minutes
Cast: Barbara Billingsley as June Cleaver, Hugh Beaumont as Ward Cleaver, Tony Dow as Wally Cleaver, and Jerry Mathers as Beaver Cleaver
Guest: Don Drysdale
Copyright date and number: June 16, 1962, LP 23481

Beaver and his pals place a long-distance telephone call to Don Drysdale.

LONG GONE, 1987
Home Box Office, 120 minutes, May 23, 1987

William L. Petersen stars as Stud Cantrell, player-manager for the Class-D Tampico (Florida) Stogies in Long Gone, *an adaptation of Paul Hemphill's novel of life in the 1950s minor leagues. (Home Box Office, 1987.)*

Based on the novel of the same name by Paul Hemphill
Written by Michael Norell
Directed by Martin Davidson
Cast: William L. Peterson as Stud Cantrell, Dermot Mulroney as Jamie Weeks, Larry Riley as Joe Louis Brown, and Virginia Madsen as Dixie Lee Boxx
See also: Baseball in Fiction

LOOK HOMEWARD HAYWARD, 1984
(Bay City Blues)
NBC, 60 minutes, July 8, 1984
See: Bay City Blues

During the play-offs, three Bluebird players are suspended for smoking marijuana in public. Presented as part one of the NBC Late Night Movie.

LOU GEHRIG'S GREATEST DAY, 1955

(You Are There)
CBS, 30 minutes, May 1, 1955
Written by Mel Goldberg
Directed by Bernard Girard
Narrated by Walter Cronkite
Cast: Sheila Bromley as Mrs. Lou Gehrig, Roy Engel as Grantland Rice, Paul Birch as Doc Painter, John Marley as Sam, and Dabbs Greer as Dave

Behind-the-scenes reenactment of "Lou Gehrig Day" at Yankee Stadium, July 4, 1939.

THE LOU GEHRIG STORY, 1956
(Climax!)
CBS, 60 minutes, April 19, 1956
Written by Mel Goldberg
Cast: Wendell Corey as Lou Gehrig, Jean Hagen as Eleanor Gehrig, and Harry Carey, Jr. as Bill Dickey

Dramatization of the final years of Gehrig's life. Home video.

A LOVE AFFAIR:.THE ELEANOR AND LOU GEHRIG STORY, 1978
Charles Fries Productions/Stonehenge Productions
NBC, 120 minutes, January 15, 1978
Based on the book, *My Luke and I* by Eleanor Gehrig and Joseph Durso
Written by Blanche Hanalis
Directed by Fielder Cook
Cast: Edward Herrmann as Lou Gehrig, Blythe Danner as Eleanor Gehrig, Patricia Neal as Mrs. Gehrig, Gerald S. O'Loughlin as Joe McCarthy, Ramon Bieri as Babe Ruth, Georgia Engel as Claire Ruth, James Luisi as Tony Lazzeri, and William Wellman, Jr. as Bill Dickey

Dramatization of Hall of Famer Lou Gehrig's life as told by his wife Eleanor. Home video.

LUCAS TANNER, 1974
NBC, 90 minutes, May 8, 1974
Directed by Richard Donner

Cast: David Hartman as Lucas Tanner, Rosemary Murphy as Margaret Blumenthal, Kathleen Quinlan as Joyce Howell, Nancy Malone as Nancy Howell, Ramon Bieri as Craig Willeman, and Joe Garagiola as himself'

Former baseball player and sportswriter becomes an English teacher at a high school in Missouri. Pilot for the television series.

LUCAS TANNER, 1974
NBC, 60 minutes, weekly series
Broadcast history: September 11, 1974 to August 20, 1975
Cast: David Hartman as Lucas Tanner, Rosemary Murphy as Margaret Blumenthal, Robbie Rist as Glendon Farrell, and Alan Abelew as Jaytee Drumm

LUCY AND THE LITTLE LEAGUE, 1963
(The Lucy Show)
Desilu Productions, Inc.
CBS, 30 minutes
Cast: Lucille Ball as Lucy Carmichael
Copyright date and number: March 14, 1963, LP 27721

LUCY AND VIV PLAY SOFTBALL, 1963
(The Lucy Show)
Desilu Productions, Inc.
CBS, 30 minutes
Cast: Lucille Ball as Lucy Carmichael and Vivian Vance as Vivian Bagley
Copyright date and number: May 9, 1963, LP 27884

THE MAN IN THE MASK, 1962
(The Donna Reed Show)
Todon of California, Inc.
ABC, 30 minutes
Cast: Donna Reed as Donna Stone, Carl Betz as Dr. Alex Stone, and Paul Petersen as Jeff Stone

Copyright date and number:
December 28, 1961, LP 24978

Don Drysdale teaches Jeff the intricacies of umpiring a girls' baseball game.

MAN ON SPIKES, 1955

(Goodyear TV Playhouse)
NBC, 60 minutes, July 17, 1955
Written by Eliot Asinof from his novel of the same name
Cast: Warren Stevens as Mike Kutner, Janet Ward as Ellen Kutner, Ned Glass as Al Tracy, William Zuckert as Herb Matthews, Frank Campanella as Jim, and Robert Morse as Pete
See also: Baseball in Fiction

A MAN'S GAME, 1952

(Philco TV Playhouse)
NBC, 60 minutes, June 1, 1952
Written by David Swift
Cast: Patricia Benoit and Vinton Hayworth

A big league manager travels to Alabama to scout catcher Chub Evans but signs Evans's fireball pitching sister instead. Subsequently musicalized for the "Kaiser Aluminum Hour" (1957).

A MAN'S GAME, 1957

(Kaiser Aluminum Hour)
NBC, 60 minutes, April 23, 1957
Written by David Swift
Music by Jack and Madeline Segal
Cast: Nanette Fabray as Josephine Evans, Lew Parker as Manager Lew Daniels, Stephen Shaw as Chub Evans, Gene Nelson as Tom Watts, Paul Ford as Rockman, and Fred Gwynne as Egghead

Musicalized version of the teleplay presented on the Philco TV Playhouse. Includes: "A Man's Game"; "Lament for the Whole Baseball World." (See: Baseball in Music and Song).

THE MAN WHO CAUGHT THE BALL AT COOGAN'S BLUFF, 1955

(Studio One)

CBS, 60 minutes, November 28, 1955
Written by Rod Serling
Cast: Alan Young as George Abernathy, Gisele MacKenzie as Mrs. Abernathy, Henry Jones as Sloane, Benny Baker as Harvey, Horace MacMahon as the Giants rooter, and Jerry Stiller as the Dodgers rooter

A shy, middle-aged baseball fan becomes a national celebrity after making a spectacular catch of a home-run ball.

MARGIE'S BASEBALL PLAYER, c. 1955

(My Little Margie)
NBC, 30 minutes
Cast: Gale Storm as Margie, and Charles Farrell as Vern

THE MIGHTY CASEY, 1955

(Omnibus)
CBS, 90 minutes, March 6, 1955
Opera based on the poem, *Casey at the Bat,* composed by William Schuman, libretto by Jerome Gury
Music conducted by Samuel Krachmalnuk
Cast: Danny Scholl as Casey, and Elise Rhodes as Merry
See also: Baseball in Theater

THE MIGHTY CASEY, 1960

(The Twilight Zone)
Cayuga Productions, Inc.
CBS, 30 minutes, June 17, 1960
Written by Rod Serling
Cast: Jack Warden as Mouth McGarry, Robert Sorrells as Casey, Abraham Sofaer as Dr. Stillman, Alan Dexter as Beasley, Don O'Kelly as Monk, Jonathan Hole as the doctor, and Rusty Lane as the commissioner
Published in story form in *From the Twilight Zone* by Rod Serling. Garden City, New York: Nelson Doubleday, 1962

Star pitcher, a robot in human form, loses the will to win after receiving a heart—and the ability to feel compassion. Home video.

MIKE'S LOSING STREAK

(Mayberry R.F.D.)
CBS, 30 minutes
Written by Dick Bensfield and Perry Grant
Cast: Ken Berry as Sam Jones, Buddy Foster as Mike Jones, and George Lindsey as Goober Pyle

Sam punishes his son by not allowing him to go to a baseball game.

MILLION DOLLAR INFIELD, 1982

CBS, 120 minutes, February 2, 1982
Written by Dick Wimmer, Philip Mishkin, and Rob Reiner
Directed by Hal Cooper
Cast: Rob Reiner as Monte Miller, Bonnie Bedelia as Marcia Miller, Robert Costanzo as Artie Levitas, Christopher Guest as Bucky Frische, Bruno Kirby as Lou Buonomato, and Mel Allen as the announcer

Four men engross themselves in their softball team in order to avoid responsibility for their adult lives.

MILLION DOLLAR ROOKIE, 1955

(Kraft Television Theatre)
NBC, 60 minutes, May 25, 1955
Written by Mel Goldberg
Cast: Buster Crabbe and Richard York

Former pitcher whose career was ruined because he beaned a player fears that his son—a rookie pitcher—will suffer the same fate.

MR. KENSINGTON'S FINEST HOUR, 1957

(General Electric Theatre)
Revue Productions, Inc.
CBS, 30 minutes, October 27, 1957
Based on the story by Lee McGiffin, published in the *Saturday Evening Post,* September 8, 1956, pp. 34–35
Cast: Charles Laughton as Edwin Kensington, Richard Eyer as Tommy Stevens, Phyllis Avery as Cary

Stevens, David Armstrong as McGill, and Charles Watts as Caldwell
Copyright date and number: September 5, 1957, LP 9870

A British consul befriends a Little Leaguer and inspires a Little League team.

MOOCHIE OF THE LITTLE LEAGUE, 1959
(Walt Disney Presents)
ABC, 120 minutes, in two parts
October 2, 1959, 60 minutes: "A Diamond Is a Boy's Best Friend"
October 9, 1959, 60 minutes: "Wrong Way Moochie"
Cast: Kevin Corcoran as Moochie, James Brown, Frances Rafferty, Reginald Owen, Stu Erwin, Alan Hale, Jr., Annette Gorman, and Donna Corcoran
Copyright date and number: September 11, 1959, LP 19453; September 18, 1959, LP 19454

Misadventures of an undersized, unathletic Little Leaguer. Released theatrically under the title, Little League Moochie.

MURDER AT THE WORLD SERIES, 1977
ABC Circle Films
ABC, 120 minutes, March 20, 1977
Written by Cy Cermack
Directed by Andrew V. McLaglen
Cast: Michael Parks as Larry Marshall, Bruce Boxleitner as Cisco, Hugh O'Brian as the Governor, Lynda Day George as Margot Mannering, Karen Valentine as Lois Marshall, Murray Hamilton as Harvey Murkison, and Gerald S. O'Loughlin as Moe Gold

Embittered ex-ballplayer seeks revenge against his former club.

MY SON, THE CATCHER, 1964
(The Donna Reed Show)
Screen Gems, Inc.
ABC, 30 minutes

Cast: Donna Reed as Donna Stone, Carl Betz as Dr. Alex Stone, and Paul Petersen as Jeff Stone
Guests: Don Drysdale, Willie Mays, and Leo Durocher
Copyright date and number: April 9, 1964, LP 29508

Jeff believes that baseball is more important than his education.

MY WAY, 1984
(E/R)
Embassy Television
CBS, 30 minutes, September 25, 1984
Written by Gary Gilbert
Directed by Peter Bonerz
Cast: Elliott Gould as Dr. Howard Sheinfeld
Guest: Harvey Vernon as Eddie "Cannon" Kostalski

Terminally ill former ballplayer asks a hero-worshiping Dr. Sheinfeld not to prolong his life.

THE NATIONAL PASTIME, 1961
(My Three Sons)
Gregg-Don, Inc.
ABC, 30 minutes, April 27, 1961
Cast: Fred MacMurray as Steve Douglas, Tim Considine as Mike Douglas, Don Grady as Robbie Douglas, Stanley Livingston as Chip Douglas, and William Frawley as Bub O'Casey
Copyright date and number: April 27, 1961, LP 20381

Chip's brothers attempt to talk him out of quitting his Little League team.

NO HITS, NO RUNS, NO OYSTERS
(The Ghost and Mrs. Muir)
ABC, 30 minutes
Written by John Fenton Murray and Elon Parkard
Cast: Hope Lange as Carolyn Muir, Edward Mulhare as Captain Daniel

Gregg, and Harlen Carrather as Jonathan Muir

Jonathan's confidence needs a boost after losing a baseball game.

THE ODD FATHER
(The Odd Couple)
ABC, 30 minutes
Written by Steve Zacharias and Michael Leeson
Cast: Tony Randall as Felix Unger, and Jack Klugman as Oscar Madison

Felix seeks Oscar's help when his daughter shows an interest in baseball.

OLD HEROES NEVER DIE, 1984
(The Fall Guy)
ABC, 60 minutes, May 2, 1984
Written by Michael Halperin
Cast: Lee Majors as Colt
Guests: Paul Winfield, Bill McKinney, Mills Watson, and Dick Bakalynn

Hero-worshiping Colt refuses to admit that a former baseball star is a compulsive liar and petty thief.

OLD MACDONALD HAD A CURVE, 1953
(Kraft Television Theatre)
NBC, 60 minutes, August 5, 1953
Written by Rod Serling
Directed by Harry Hermann
Cast: Olin Howlin as Maxwell (Firebrand Lefty) MacDonald, Jack Warden, and Cameron Prud'homme
Published in *Patterns* by Rod Serling. New York: Simon and Schuster, 1957, pp. 143–180

Sixty-seven-year-old ex-major leaguer rejoins his former team after developing a freakish curve ball.

ONE IN A MILLION: THE RON LEFLORE STORY, 1978
Roger Gimbel Productions/EMI Television

LeVar Burton portrays Detroit Tigers star Ron LeFlore's rise from ghetto youth and prison inmate to the Detroit Tigers outfield in One in a Million: The Ron LeFlore Story. *(Roger Gimbel Productions, 1978.)*

ABC, 120 minutes, September 26, 1978
Based on the book *Breakout* by Ron LeFlore and Jim Hawkins
Written by Stanford Whitmore
Directed by William A. Graham
Cast: LeVar Burton as Ron LeFlore, Madge Sinclair as Georgia LeFlore, Paul Benjamin as John LeFlore, Zakes Mokae as Pee Wee Spencer, John R. McKee as Ralph Houk; and Billy Martin, Al Kaline, Norm Cash, and Bill Freehan as themselves

Dramatization of Detroit Tigers star Ron LeFlore's advancement from prison to the major leagues. Home video.

O'TOOLE FROM MOSCOW, 1955
(Matinee Theatre)
NBC, 60 minutes, December 12, 1955
Written by Rod Serling
Cast: Leo Durocher as the manager of the Reds, and Chuck Connors

Misadventures of a baseball-loving Soviet citizen who defects to the United States in order to play for the Cincinnati Reds.

OUT AT HOME, 1962
(Room for One More)
Warner Bros. Pictures, Inc.
ABC, 30 minutes
Cast: Andrew Dugan as George Rose, Peggy McCay as Anna Rose, and Tim Rooney as Jeff Rose
Copyright date and number: June 23, 1962, LP 25572

Jeff must pass a history test or he can't play in a league championship game.

OUT AT THE OLD BALL PARK, 1960
(Have Gun—Will Travel)
CBS, 30 minutes, October 1, 1960
Cast: Richard Boone as Paladin
Guests: John Larch, J. Pat O'Malley, Jack Albertson, Ted Hamilton, Sandy Kenyon, and Perry Cook
Copyright date and number: October 1, 1960, LP 17614

Paladin agrees to umpire a game between a small-town nine and a team of touring all-stars.

OUT OF LEFT FIELD, 1961
(The Tom Ewell Show)
Four Star-Ewell-Caroll-Martin Productions
CBS, 30 minutes
Cast: Tom Ewell as Tom Potter
Guests: Larry Sherry and Stan Williams
Copyright date and number: February 21, 1961, LP 20151

A chance meeting leads to a real estate deal between Tom and two members of the Los Angeles Dodgers.

PEANUTS AND CRACKERJACKS, 1971
(Nichols)
NBC, 60 minutes, November 4, 1971
Cast: James Garner as Nichols, Stuart

Margolin as Mitchell, Margot Kidder as Ruth, and John Beck as Ketcham
Guests: Don Newcombe as the Army pitcher, and Art Passarella as the umpire

Light-hearted dramatization of a 1914 era game between a small-town nine and an Army baseball team.

PINCH HITTER, 1960
(The Ann Sothern Show)
Desilu Productions, Inc.
CBS, 30 minutes
Cast: Ann Sothern as Katy O'Connor
Copyright date and number: August 12, 1960, LP 23540

A youth is denied an opportunity to play on a sandlot baseball team.

PLAY BALL, 1964
(The Donna Reed Show)
Screen Gems, Inc.
ABC, 30 minutes
Cast: Donna Reed as Donna Stone, Carl Betz as Dr. Alex Stone, and Paul Petersen as Jeff Stone
Guests: Don Drysdale, Willie Mays, and Leo Durocher
Copyright date and number: September 24, 1964, LP 30751

PLAY IT AGAIN, MILT, 1984
(Bay City Blues)
NBC, 60 Minutes, July 1, 1984
See: Bay City Blues

Soon to be called up to the major leagues, outfielder Terry St. Marie is determined to keep his injured shoulder a secret. Presented as part two of the NBC Late Night Movie.

THE POOR LOSER, 1963
(Leave it to Beaver)
Revue Studios
ABC, 30 minutes
Cast: Barbara Billingsley as June Cleaver, Hugh Beaumont as Ward Cleaver, Tony Dow as Wally Cleaver, and Jerry Mathers as Beaver Cleaver

Copyright date and number: April 25, 1963, LP 25952

Beaver's feelings are hurt when his father obtains two tickets to a baseball game and takes Wally instead of him.

THE PRIMA DONNA, 1956
(The Screen Directors Playhouse)
NBC, 30 minutes, February 1, 1956
Written by Gene Raymond
Cast: Jeanette MacDonald as Martha, Alfred Caiazza as Johnny, Jerome Cowan as Lewis, Laraine Day as herself, and Leo Durocher as himself

A 13-year-old newsboy, who dreams of becoming a baseball star, resists the efforts of a concert artist to sponsor his development as an opera singer. An original musical produced for television.

THE RAG TAG CHAMPS, 1978
(ABC Afterschool Special)
ABC Circle Films
ABC, 60 minutes, March 22, 1978
Based on the novel by Alfred Slote
Written by E. Jack Kaplan
Cast: Larry Scott as Jake Wrather, Glynn Turman as Lenny Johnson, Madge Sinclair as Mrs. Bradbury, and Claudio Martinez as Jesus Sanchez

Boy leads his motley team to a championship.

ROCKY IV-EYES, 1984
(Bay City Blues)
NBC, 60 minutes, July 1, 1984
See: Bay City Blues

In the throes of a slump, a desperate Rocky Padillo dons corrective lenses and suffers the slurs of fans and rival players. Presented as part one of the NBC Late Night Movie.

ROOKIE OF THE YEAR, 1955
(Screen Directors Playhouse)
Hal Roach Studios
NBC, 30 minutes, December 7, 1955
Directed by John Ford
Cast: John Wayne as Mike Cronin, James Gleason as Ed Shafer, Patrick

During the early 1970s an emerging social issue was whether girls could, or should, play on all-boy Little League teams. In Rookie of the Year *eleven-year-old Sharon Lee (Jodie Foster) proudly and stubbornly overcomes the antagonism of her male teammates and the disapproval of parents in the community to win a place in the lineup and a victory for the team. (Daniel Wilson Productions, 1973.)*

Wayne as Lyn Goodhue, Ward Bond as Buck Garrison, and Vera Miles as Ruth
Copyright date and number: December 7, 1955, LP 7492

Small-town sports reporter sees an opportunity to advance his career by exposing the identity of a rookie player who was previously banned from baseball.

ROOKIE OF THE YEAR, 1973
(ABC Afterschool Special)

Daniel Wilson Productions, Inc.
ABC, 60 minutes, October 3, 1973
Based on the novel, *Not Bad for a Girl* by Isabella Taves
Cast: Jodie Foster as Sharon Lee
See also: Not Bad for a Girl (Baseball in Juvenile and Miscellaneous Fiction; Baseball in the Spoken Arts—Recorded)

Girl faces prejudice and antagonism in winning a place on her brother's baseball team.

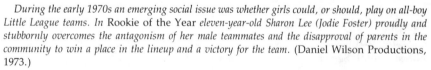

A ROSE IS A ROSE, 1961
(The Donna Reed Show)
Todon of California, Inc.
ABC, 30 minutes
Cast: Donna Reed as Donna Stone,
Carl Betz as Dr. Alex Stone, and Paul
Petersen as Jeff Stone
Copyright date and number:
September 14, 1961, LP 24437

Jeff is unable to attend a baseball game with his father because he has to rewrite an English composition.

RUSTY AND THE TOMBOY, 1960
(The Danny Thomas Show)
Marterto Enterprises, Inc.
CBS, 30 minutes
Cast: Danny Thomas as Danny
Williams, Marjorie Lord as Mrs.
Kathy Williams, and Rusty Hamer as
Rusty Williams
Copyright date and number: April 25,
1960, LP 18490

Danny arranges a date with Rusty and a girl baseball player.

THE SATURDAY GAME, 1971
(The Bill Cosby Show)
NBC, 30 minutes
Written by Art Wallace
Directed by Allan Sherman
Cast: Bill Cosby as Chet Kincaid
Guest: Milton Selzer

A young Chasidic Jew is torn between observing the Sabbath and playing an important Little League game.

SCREWBALL, 1950
(The Play's the Thing)
CBS, 60 minutes, April 28, 1950
Written by Mel Goldberg
Cast: Jack Gilford, Lee Grant, and
Edith King

A garage mechanic unflaggingly pursues his dream of playing major league baseball despite his advanced age and limited abilities. Restaged on June 18, 1951 and June 28, 1954.

SCREWBALL, 1951
(Studio One Summer Theatre)
CBS, 60 minutes, June 18, 1951
Cast: Dick Foran as Russ Adams,
Cloris Leachman, and Lefty Gomez

Restaged from April 28, 1950.

SCREWBALL, 1954
(Studio One)
CBS, 60 minutes, June 28, 1954
Cast: Jack Warden as Russ Adams,
Sally Gracie as Marge Adams, Leora
Thatcher as Mrs. Adams, Jeff Harris
as Chub, and Frankie Frisch as
himself

Restaged from June 18, 1951.

SECOND BASE STEELE, 1984
(Remington Steele)
MTM Enterprises, Inc.
NBC, 60 minutes, October 23, 1984
Written by Rick Mittleman
Cast: Pierce Brosnan as Remington
Steele, Stephanie Zimbalist as Laura,
and Doris Roberts as Mildred
Guests: Mickey Mantle and Whitey
Ford as themselves

Remington Steele investigates a murder at an adult fantasy baseball camp.

SHOELESS JOE, 1960
(Witness)
CBS, 60 minutes, October 27, 1960
Cast: Biff McGuire as Shoeless Joe
Jackson, and Royal Beal

A simulated Congressional panel investigates the role Shoeless Joe Jackson played in the 1919 "Black Sox" scandal.

THE SHORTSTOP, 1958
(How to Marry a Millionaire)
National Telefilm Associates, Inc. and
Twentieth Century-Fox
Syndicated, 30 minutes
Cast: Barbara Eden as Loco Jones
Copyright date and number: August
7, 1958, LP 18627

SISTER SLUGGER, 1960
(The DuPont Show with June
Allyson)
CBS, 30 minutes, March 14, 1960
Cast: June Allyson as Sister Mary
Ann, Sean McClory as Father Ray,
Donald Foster as Father Ryan, and
Richard Correll as Timmy Manners
Copyright date and number: March
14, 1960, LP 17644

Much beloved nun is a player–coach of a boy's softball team.

THE SKIPPY MANNOX STORY, 1963
(The Lloyd Bridges Show)
Four Star-Loring-Caron
CBS, 30 minutes, February 12,
1963
Cast: Lloyd Bridges as Mickey
Madden, Beau Bridges as Skippy
Mannox, Tony Fasce as Ape
Mahoney, Mickey Freeman as
Maginot Stillman, Ivan Dixon as
Shpritzen, Ed Sadowski, and Bo
Belinsky
Copyright date and number: February
12, 1963, LP 26870

Pitcher Skippy Mannox arrives on the scene to save the last place minor league Shenanigans.

SLIDE, DARLING, SLIDE, 1954
(Ford Theatre)
NBC, 30 minutes, December 23, 1954
Cast: Virginia Field, Allyn Joslyn,
Jane Darwell, and Anthony Caruso

An actress, bored with her part in a play, develops an interest in baseball.

SLUGGER SLASH, 1983
(Square Pegs)
CBS, 30 minutes, February 21, 1983
Produced by Anne Beatts
Guest: Steve Sax

High school "new wave" baseball star Johnny Slash is scouted by Steve Sax in behalf of the Los Angeles Dodgers.

THE SPITBALL KID, 1969
(Then Came Bronson)
NBC, 60 minutes, December 17, 1969
Based on a story by Alfred Brenner
Written by Lionel E. Siegel
Cast: Michael Parks as Jim Bronson
Guests: Kurt Russell as William P.
Lovering, David Sheiner as Eddie
Mickel, and Don Drysdale as the
Dodger scout

A promising industrial league pitcher learns that he telegraphs his pitches.

SPRING TRAINING, 1961
(Surfside 6)
Warner Bros. Pictures, Inc.
ABC, 60 minutes, April 3, 1961
Cast: Van Williams as Ken Madison,
Lee Patterson as Dave Thorne, and
Troy Donohue as Sandy Winfield
Guest: Will Hutchins as Arky Cooper
Copyright date and number: April 3,
1961, LP 25615

Arky Cooper, star pitcher of the Bears, is suspected of gambling.

STRIKE OUT, 1961
(Michael Shayne)
NBC, 60 minutes, March 10, 1961
Cast: Richard Denning as Michael
Shayne, and Jerry Paris as Tim
Rourke
Guests: James Best as Danny Blake;
and Vince Scully, Sandy Koufax, Ed
Roebuck, Larry Sherry, and Stan
Williams as themselves

The Los Angeles Dodgers rally to the defense of a fellow player injured in an automobile accident.

THE STRIKE-OUT KING
(The Partridge Family)
ABC, 30 minutes
Written by William S. Bickley
Cast: Shirley Jones as Shirley, David
Cassidy as Keith, and Danny
Bonaduce as Danny

PEN NAMES

One can tell quite a lot about the quality of a baseball film, television play, or novel by the character names given to the baseball players. Does the hero's name ring true or does it smack of sports-page mythology? In some works the writer chooses a character name that suggests a sense of modest, all-American virtuousness; for example, Joe Hardy (*Damn Yankees*), Roy Hobbs (*The Natural*), Billy Young (*Tiger Town*), Darryl Palmer (*The Slugger's Wife*), and Henry Wiggen (*Bang the Drum Slowly*). But in the main, authors and writers have strained to duplicate sports-page melodrama with such names as (to cite a few from television dramatizations): Mouth McGarry (*The Mighty Casey*, from ''The Twilight Zone''), Ape Mahoney (*The Skippy Mannox Story*), Rhino Rhinelander, Cap Capogrosso and Pinky Pinkney (all from *Ball Four*), and probably the worst name of all, Frenchy Nuckles, a pitcher featured in the cast of the woeful baseball series, *Bay City Blues*.

Other pulp-inspired character names can be found in films: Swat Anderson (*Hit and Run*), Monk Lanigan (*It Happens Every Spring*); plays: Manley Manners (*A Runaway Colt*), Rocket Reilly (*Triple Play*), Boomer, Ripper, Moose, Tank, and Duke (all from the cast of *Bullpen*); and novels: Rags Ragland (*The Seventh Babe*), Luke Playtowski (*Luke*), and Johnny Longboat from Roger Kahn's *The Seventh Game*.

Not every baseball hero, it is true, can enjoy a colorful name that has the ring of authenticity to it, but a few favorites come to mind: Crash Davis and Nuke LaLoosh (*Bull Durham*), Elmer (Hurry) Kane (*Elmer the Great*), Piney Woods and Dutch Schnell (*Bang the Drum Slowly*), and Sweetcorn Jackson (*Ain't Lookin': Chappie's Colored All-Stars*). Perhaps the best character name ever given to a baseball player belongs to a disheveled, alcoholic coach of an irreverent and rambunctious Little League team. A better name for ex–minor leaguer Morris Buttermaker (*The Bad News Bears*) probably does not exist.

Danny's Little League triumphs give him a swelled head.

TAKE ME OUT OF THE BALL GAME, 1967
(Family Affair)
CBS, 30 minutes
Cast: Brian Keith as Bill Davis,
Sebastian Cabot as French, Anissa
Jones as Buffy, and Johnnie Whitaker
as Jody
Copyright date and number;
November 13, 1967, LP 36422

TAKE ME OUT TO THE BALL GAME
(The Patty Duke Show)
ABC, 30 minutes
Written by Sidney Sheldon
Cast: Patty Duke as Patty/Cindy
Lane, William Schallert as Martin
Lane, and Paul O'Keefe as Ross

Ross's parents can't understand or appreciate his love for baseball.

Aging Detroit Tigers outfielder Billy Young (Roy Scheider) slides home safely in the climactic scene to Tiger Town, *in which a hero-worshiping youngster's unshakable faith in the fading star is vindicated. (© 1983 Walt Disney Productions.)*

TERRIBLE TEMPERED TOLLIVER, 1952

(Hollywood Opening Night)
NBC, 30 minutes, October 6, 1952
Cast: William Bendix and Peggy Ann Garner

Television version of Kill the Umpire *(1950).*
(See: Baseball in Film*).*

TIGER TOWN, 1983

Walt Disney Productions
The Disney Channel, 76 minutes,
October 9, 1983
Written and directed by Alan Shapiro
Cast: Roy Scheider as Billy Young,
Justin Henry as Alex, Ron McLarty as
Buddy, Bethany Carpenter as Nancy,
Ernie Harwell as himself, and Sparky
Anderson as himself

A fatherless boy refuses to lose faith in an aging Detroit Tiger star. Home video.

THE TWO-HUNDRED-MILE-AN-HOUR-FASTBALL, 1981

(The Greatest American Hero)
ABC, 60 minutes, November 4, 1981
Written and produced by Stephen J. Cannell
Cast: William Katt as Ralph Hinkley, and Robert Culp as Bill Maxwell
Guest: Don Drysdale as the announcer

Light-hearted melodrama in which superhero Ralph Hinkley foils a gambling syndicate by pitching the California Stars to a pennant.

THE UMPIRE, 1988

(Matlock)
Viacom, Inc./Fred Silverman Co.
NBC, 60 minutes, January 26, 1988
Written by Philip Mishkin
Directed by Harvey Shamberg
Cast: Andy Griffith as Ben Matlock

The losing team's manager is suspected of murdering the umpire of a men's fast-pitch softball game.

THE UNIFORM, 1978

(The Doris Day Show)
CBS, 30 minutes
Cast: Doris Day as Doris Martin, and Todd Starke as Toby Martin

Toby is jealous of his brother's Little League uniform.

THE UNNATURAL, 1985

(The Jeffersons)
CBS, 30 minutes, January 15, 1985
Guests: Reggie Jackson, Mike Witt, and Brian Downing

THE UNNATURAL, 1986

(Who's the Boss?)
Embassy Television
ABC, 30 minutes, April 8, 1986
Written by Ellen Guylas
Cast: Tony Danza as Tony, and Judith Light as Angela
Guests: Billy Martin, Steve Sax, and Bob Uecker

A chivalrous Tony grooves a pitch to a woman playing in her first softball game.

WARD'S BASEBALL, 1960

(Leave It to Beaver)
ABC, 30 minutes
Cast: Barbara Billingsley as June Cleaver, Hugh Beaumont as Ward Cleaver, Jerry Mathers as Beaver Cleaver, and Tony Dow as Wally Cleaver
Copyright date and number: April 9, 1960, LP 20731

Beaver plays catch with his father's prized autographed baseball.

WELCOME HOME LEFTY, 1952

(The Lux Video Theatre)
CBS, 30 minutes, June 23, 1952
Cast: Chester Morris

Major league star confronts the end of his career.

WHO'S ON FIRST?, 1963
(Our Man Higgins)
First Co. of Writers
ABC, 30 minutes, May 8, 1963
Cast: Stanley Holloway as Higgins,
Frank Maxwell as Duncan, and
Audrey Totter as Alice
Guest: Don Drysdale
Copyright date and number: May 1,
1963, LP 29594

*Higgins arranges for Don Drysdale to appear at
the opening of the local Little League season.*

WHO'S ON FIRST—AND SIXTH?, 1978
(Kaz)
CBS, 60 minutes, October 29, 1978
Cast: Ron Leibman as Attorney
Martin Kazinski, Patrick O'Neal as
Attorney Samuel Bennett, and Linda
Carlson as Katie McKenna
Guest: David Wilson as Dean Stover

*Big league pitcher faces mounting criticism for
his off-the-field behavior after a charge of
assault is filed against him.*

A WINNER NEVER QUITS, 1986
Columbia Pictures Corp.
ABC, 120 minutes, April 14, 1986
Written by Burt Prelutsky
Directed by Mel Damski
Cast: Keith Carradine as Pete Gray,
Huckleberry Fox as Nelson Gary, Jr.,
Mare Winningham as Annie, Dennis
Weaver as Wyshner, Jack Kehoe as
Bloom, Fionnula Flanagan as Mrs.
Wyshner, and Steve Rees as young
Pete Gray

*Film biography of one-armed outfielder Pete
Gray of the 1945 St. Louis Browns.*

*On the American League St. Louis Browns in
1945 was a remarkable athlete and inspiration to
Americans: one-armed outfielder Pete Gray,
whose life story is dramatized in* A Winner
Never Quits, *starring Keith Carradine. (Blatt/
Singer Productions, 1986.)*

WINNER TAKE ALL, 1962
(The Donna Reed Show)
Todon of California, Inc.
ABC, 30 minutes
Cast: Donna Reed as Donna Stone,
Carl Betz as Dr. Alex Stone, and Paul

Petersen as Jeff Stone
Copyright date and number:
December 28, 1961, LP 24970

*Alex counsels a neighbor who is disappointed in
his son's ability as a baseball player.*

WRONG WAY MOOCHIE, 1959
See: Moochie of the Little League

YOU CAN'T WIN 'EM ALL
(The Bob Newhart Show)
MTM Enterprises, Inc.
CBS, 30 minutes
Cast: Bob Newhart as Dr. Robert
Hartley

A has-been baseball player seeks psychoanalysis.

YOU COULD LOOK IT UP, 1952
(Gulf Playhouse)
NBC, 30 minutes, October 10, 1952
Based on the story by James Thurber
Cast: Ward Bond as Squawks Magrew
See also: Baseball in Radio

0 FOR 37, 1953
(Philco TV Playhouse)
NBC, 60 minutes, September 27, 1953
Cast: Arthur O'Connell, Eva Marie
Saint, and James Broderick

*A young ballplayer appreciates the value of
home and family after beginning a career in
professional baseball.*

ZIRCONS ARE FOREVER, 1983
(Bay City Blues)
NBC, 60 minutes, November 8, 1983
See: Bay City Blues

*After a brief stay in the majors, Mickey Wagner
returns to Bay City but is soon involved in a
fatal auto accident while driving under the
influence of alcohol.*

Appendix to Chapter 4

The appendix contains a listing of nonbaseball-related teleplays featuring a significant baseball-related character or scene. Also included in the catalog are nonbaseball-related teleplays in which a major league baseball player is cast in a starring or featured role. In most cases the relation to baseball—and not the program's plot or theme—is annotated.

For *Explanatory Notes* to this section, *see*: Baseball in Television.

THE APES OF RATH
(Get Smart)
NBC, 30 minutes
Cast: Don Adams as Maxwell Smart
Guest: Maury Wills

DALLAS COWBOYS CHEERLEADERS, 1979
ABC, 120 minutes, January 14, 1979
Cast: Jane Seymour as Laura Cole, and Laraine Stephens as Suzanne Mitchell

Features Yankees shortstop Bucky Dent in a minor role as Kyle Jessop.

DEMPSEY, 1983
CBS, 180 minutes, September 28, 1983
Cast: Treat Williams, Sam Waterston, and Michael McManus

In this dramatization of boxer Jack Dempsey's life, the character of Babe Ruth is depicted.

DRAGNET, 1969
NBC, 120 minutes, January 27, 1969
Cast: Jack Webb as Sergeant Joe Friday

Dodgers catcher John Roseboro is featured in a minor role as Sergeant Dave Bradford.

FATHER AND SON DAY
(Diff'rent Strokes)
NBC, 30 minutes
Cast: Gary Coleman as Arnold
Guest: Reggie Jackson

Arnold asks Reggie to be a surrogate father for a father–son athletic contest.

THE HARDCASE, 1960
(The Lawman)
ABC, 30 minutes, January 31, 1960

Los Angeles Dodgers' pitcher Don Drysdale appears in a western role.

THE HIT, 1975
(Police Woman)
NBC, 60 minutes, December 9, 1975
Cast: Angie Dickinson
Guest: Wes Parker

THE HUCKSTER, 1980
(Happy Days)
ABC, 30 minutes, February 5, 1980
Cast: Tom Bosley as Howard Cunningham, Ron Howard as Richie Cunningham, and Henry Winkler as Fonzie
Guest: Hank Aaron

Howard wants Hank Aaron to appear in a television commercial for his hardware store.

I LEFT MY HEART IN CINCINNATI
(The Partridge Family)
ABC, 30 minutes
Written by Dale McRaven
Cast: Shirley Jones as Shirley, David Cassidy as Keith, and Danny Bonaduce as Danny
Guest: Johnny Bench

I TAKE THESE MEN, 1983
CBS, 120 minutes, January 5, 1983
Cast: Susan Saint James and John Rubinstein

Steve Garvey of the Los Angeles Dodgers is included in a minor role.

JUST ANOTHER FOX IN THE CROWD, 1986
(Crazy Like a Fox)
CBS, 60 minutes, February 26, 1986
Cast: Jack Warden as Harry Fox
Guest: Hank Aaron

A vintage photograph of Hank Aaron provides a clue to an unsolved kidnapping.

LUCY AT MARINELAND, 1965
(The Lucy Show)
CBS, 30 minutes
Cast: Lucille Ball as Lucy Carmichael
Guest: Jimmy Piersall
Copyright date and number: June 10, 1965, LP 32200

MR. BELVEDERE, 1985
ABC, 30 minutes, weekly series
Broadcast premiere: March 15, 1985
Cast: Bob Uecker as George Owens

Uecker is a former major league catcher.

THE RETIRED GUN, 1959
(The Rifleman)
ABC, 30 minutes, January 20, 1959
Cast: Chuck Connors as Lucas McCain

Duke Snider of the Los Angeles Dodgers is featured in a western role.

SPARKY, 1979
(WKRP in Cincinnati)
CBS, 30 minutes, December 24, 1979
Written by Peter Torokvei and Steven Kampann
Guest: Sparky Anderson

Cincinnati Reds manager Sparky Anderson is featured as a host of a sports talk show.

TWITCH OR TREAT
(Bewitched)
ABC, 30 minutes
Cast: Elizabeth Montgomery as
Samantha Stephens
Guest: Willie Mays

THE UNDERGRADUATE
(The Brady Bunch)
ABC, 30 minutes
Cast: Robert Reed as Mike Brady,

Florence Henderson as Carol Brady,
and Barry Williams as Greg Brady
Guest: Wes Parker

Baseball in Documentary and Miscellaneous Television

The following section contains a listing of baseball-related television documentaries, public affairs programs, and miscellaneous telefilms of historical or cultural interest. Included in the catalog are player biographies and interviews, team histories, instructionals, educational programs produced for television, programs hosted by baseball players, and documentary profiles of famous moments and personalities from baseball's past. Also included are documentary and miscellaneous telefilms available in home video format.

Not included in this section are nonnetwork programs or series; or season, All-Star Game, and World Series highlights programs produced for local broadcast.

For *Explanatory Notes* to this section, *see*: Baseball in Television.

AMERICAN GAME, JAPANESE RULES, 1988
(Frontline)
PBS, 60 minutes, April 26, 1988
Written, produced, and directed by Ofra Bikel
Host: Judy Woodruff

Baseball is used to illustrate the differences between Japanese and U.S. business and cultural traditions.

BABE RUTH, 1962
(Biography)
Official Films, Inc.
Syndicated, 30 minutes
Host: Mike Wallace
Copyright date and number: February 11, 1962, MP 12776

BABE RUTH: A LOOK BEHIND THE LEGEND, 1963
ABC, 30 minutes, August 15, 1963
Written by Roger Kahn
Narrated by Horace McMahon

THE BASEBALL BUNCH, 1982
Major League Baseball Productions
ABC, 30 minutes, weekly series
Host: Johnny Bench
Features Tom Lasorda

Children's program featuring baseball instruction and comedy. Home video.

THE BASEBALL CORNER, 1958
ABC, 30 minutes, weekly series

Broadcast history: June 1, 1958 to August 27, 1958
Host: Buddy Blattner

Blattner narrates films, reports sports news, and conducts a panel of four guests.

BASEBALL: PROVING GROUND FOR CIVIL RIGHTS, 1959
(Heritage XIV)
NET, 30 minutes
Produced by WQED-TV, Pittsburgh

Branch Rickey outlines the contributions of baseball toward the eradication of racial and religious prejudice.

BASEBALL: PROVING GROUND FOR LIBERTY, 1959
(Heritage XIV)
NET, 30 minutes
Produced by WQED-TV, Pittsburgh

Branch Rickey discusses aspects of baseball that reflect democratic ethics.

BASEBALL ROOKIE'S BIG CHANCE, 1953
(March of Time)
NBC, 30 minutes, March 25, 1953
Copyright date and number: March 25, 1953, MP 3566
Museum of Modern Art, New York, number 005295

Profiles the spring training of rookie outfielder Jim Lemon of the Cleveland Indians.

BASEBALL: THE GAME, 1959
(Heritage XIV)
NET, 30 minutes
Produced by WQED-TV, Pittsburgh

Branch Rickey traces the history of baseball.

BASEBALL: THE MEN, 1959
(Heritage XIV)
NET, 30 minutes
Produced by WQED-TV, Pittsburgh

Branch Rickey outlines the characteristics of successful players and managers.

THE BASEBALL WORLD OF JOE GARAGIOLA, 1972
NBC, 15 minutes, weekly series
Broadcast history: June 12, 1972 to September 1, 1975

Magazine-style program preceding Monday night baseball broadcasts.

BASICALLY BASEBALL, 1977
Maryland Center for Public Broadcasting
PBS, 30 minutes, series of four programs

Baseball instructional programs featuring pitching, hitting, fielding, and specialties, as taught by Baltimore Orioles' stars Jim Palmer, Paul Blair, Boog Powell, and Brooks Robinson.

BIOGRAPHY OF A ROOKIE, 1961
Wolper-Sterling Productions, Inc.
Syndicated, 60 minutes, May 4, 1961

Narrated by Mike Wallace
Copyright date and number: April 7, 1961, MP 13123

Documentary profile of rookie outfielder Willie Davis of the Los Angeles Dodgers.

BIRTH OF A BALL CLUB, 1961
(The Summer Sports Spectacular)
CBS, 60 minutes, May 4, 1961
Host: Bud Palmer

Profile of the first spring training of the newly formed Los Angeles Angels.

BROADCAST OF APRIL 24, 1949
(Mr. I. Magination)
CBS, 30 minutes, April 24, 1949
Cast: Paul Tripp as Mr. I. Magination
Museum of Broadcasting, New York

Hall of Famer Rabbit Maranville is featured as a guest.

BROADCAST OF SEPTEMBER 21, 1952
(The Toast of the Town)
CBS, 60 minutes, September 21, 1952
Host: Ed Sullivan
Museum of Broadcasting, New York

Segment: The "All-American Look Baseball Team" is presented, including Mickey Mantle and Yogi Berra.

BROADCAST OF MARCH 27, 1955
(Omnibus)
CBS, 90 minutes, March 27, 1955

Segment: The life and training of New York Giants' minor league outfielder Al Stieglitz.

BROADCAST OF SEPTEMBER 20, 1955
(The Sixty-Four Thousand Dollar Question)
CBS, 30 minutes, September 20, 1955
Museum of Broadcasting, New York

Baseball is the subject of questioning.

BROADCAST OF OCTOBER 5, 1971

(Captain Kangaroo)
CBS, 60 minutes, October 5, 1971
Cast: Bob Keeshan as Captain Kangaroo, and Lumpy Brannum as Mr. Green Jeans

Episode devoted to children's baseball stories, including, "Green Jeans at the Bat," a re-creation of the famous ballad.

BROADCAST OF JUNE 19, 1979
(Dick Cavett Show)
PBS, 30 minutes, June 19, 1979
Guests: Leo Durocher, Mickey Mantle, Hank Aaron, and Tom Gorman

Ninety-minute panel discussion about baseball, broadcast in three nightly segments from June 19, 1979 to June 21, 1979.

A COMEDY SALUTE TO BASEBALL, 1985
OCC Productions
NBC, 60 minutes, July 15, 1985
Cast: Billy Crystal, Mickey Mantle, George Steinbrenner, Bob Uecker, Steve Garvey, Dwight Gooden, Reggie Jackson, and Tom Lasorda

Baseball players, managers, and owners lampoon themselves.

COUNTDOWN TO HISTORY: THE PETE ROSE STORY, 1985
Major League Baseball Productions
Syndicated, 30 minutes
Host: Johnny Bench
Narrated by Jim Gordon

Interview with Rose prior to his breaking Ty Cobb's career hit record.

DOUBLE PLAY, 1953
Syndicated, 15 minutes, regular series
Hosts: Leo Durocher and Laraine Day
See also: Baseball in Documentary and Miscellaneous Radio

Features interviews with baseball personalities.

AN EASY THROW TO FIRST, 1985

(The Sporting Life)
Foxwood Productions and the Educational Broadcasting Corp.
PBS, 30 minutes, June 11, 1985
Host: Jim Palmer

Affectionate look at the players—ages 75 to 92—of the "Three-Quarter Century Softball League" in St. Petersburg, Florida.

FLINCH DRILLS AND WHISK BROOMS, 1985
(The Sporting Life)
Foxwood Productions and the Educational Broadcasting Corp.
PBS, 30 minutes, May 7, 1985
Host: Jim Palmer

Documentary profile of a baseball umpire's school

THE GAME AND ITS GLORY: BASEBALL'S HALL OF FAME, 1982
Major League Baseball Productions
NBC, 60 minutes, August 7, 1982
Narrated by Donald Sutherland

History and highlights of baseball. Home video.

THE GLORY OF THEIR TIMES, 1977
PBS, 60 minutes, March 7, 1977
Based on the book by Lawrence S. Ritter
Narrated by Alexander Scourby
See also: Baseball in Miscellaneous Recordings; Baseball in the Spoken Arts—Recorded

Filmed interviews with star players from baseball's past. Home video.

HARDBALL, 1983
(Enterprises)
PBS, 30 minutes, February 24, 1983
Written and directed by David Espar
Narrated by Eric Sevareid

Documents the Oakland A's 1982 season on the field and in the front office.

TELEVISION FIRSTS

Without question, television has changed the face of major league baseball, as it has transformed much of modern culture. Day baseball is an anachronism, as are two-hour games, doubleheaders, and—because every move is under the unrelenting scrutiny of the camera—truly colorful or eccentric baseball players. And yet, with the aid of close-up views and slow-motion replays, today's fans have developed an intimate knowledge and appreciation of baseball that was not possible in the years before television. The following are some notable dates in baseball telecasting history:

May 17, 1939: *First telecast of a baseball game*—Columbia vs. Princeton at Baker Field in Philadelphia, on channel W2XBS, with announcer Bill Stern. A single camera, mounted on a platform on the third-base side of home plate, provided the only view of this collegiate baseball game. The contest was won in ten innings by Princeton, 2–1.

August 26, 1939: *First telecast of a major league game*—doubleheader, Cincinnati Reds at Brooklyn Dodgers, on channel W2XBS, with announcer Red Barber. A second camera was added to the telecast from Ebbets Field to provide an alternate—but still long-range—view of baseball action. The Dodgers won the first game of the doubleheader, 6–2, and the Reds took the second game, 5–1.

September 30, 1947: *First telecast of a World Series game*—Brooklyn Dodgers vs. New York Yankees at Yankee Stadium. Game One of the 1947 World Series was telecast by all three networks—NBC, CBS, and Dumont—with announcers Bill Slater, Bob Stanton, and Bob Edge. The Yankees won the game, 5–3, and went on to win the Series, four games to three.

August 11, 1951: *First color telecast of a major league game*—doubleheader, Boston Braves at Brooklyn Dodgers, on WOR-TV, New York, with announcers Red Barber and Connie Desmond. The Braves took the first game, 8–1, and the Dodgers won the nightcap, 8–4.

October 1, 1951: *First live coast-to-coast telecast of a baseball game*—New York Giants at Brooklyn Dodgers, on NBC, with announcers Ernie Harwell, Red Barber, Vin Scully, and Connie Desmond. The historic best-of-three National League Championship playoffs was broadcast coast to coast by a microwave relay system that had been developed just before the opening game. The Giants won game one, 3–1, and—by virtue of Bobby Thomson's memorable home run—later won the playoffs, two games to one.

October 13, 1971: *First prime-time World Series telecast*—Baltimore Orioles at Pittsburgh Pirates, on NBC. The fourth game of the 1971 World Series, scheduled as a night game as an experiment, was won, 4–3 by the Pirates. An estimated 61 million viewers convinced commissioner Bowie Kuhn to schedule all weekday games at night for the following year's World Series.

INSIDE BASEBALL: OFF THE PLAYING FIELD, 1956
(The Finder)
NET, 30 minutes
Produced by KETC-TV, St. Louis

Chronicles the lives of St. Louis Cardinal players outside of baseball.

IT'S ANYBODY'S BALL GAME, 1976

NBC, 60 minutes, April 3, 1976
Host and executive producer: Joe Garagiola
Guests: Roy Clark, Nipsey Russell, and Lonnie Stevens

Salute to the opening of the baseball season.

JACKIE ROBINSON, 1963
(Biography)
Official Films, Inc.

Syndicated, 30 minutes
Host: Mike Wallace
Copyright date and number:
September 28, 1963, MP 14465

JOE DIMAGGIO'S DUGOUT, 1952
NBC, 15 minutes, weekly series
Host: Joe DiMaggio

JONRON, 1984
(Presente!)
Milwaukee Public Television
PBS, 30 minutes, March 24, 1984
Written by Raul C. Galvan and
Aaron Bor
Produced and directed by Raul C.
Galvan

*History of Latino baseball players in the major
leagues.*

A LEAGUE OF THEIR OWN,
1987
PBS, 30 minutes, April 15, 1987
Written and directed by Mary Wallace
Produced by Kelly Candael and Kim
Wilson

*Members of the 1940s All-American Girls
Professional Baseball League reminisce about
their playing days.*

A MAN NAMED MAYS, 1964
(The Humble Report)
NBC, 60 minutes, July 21, 1964

*Documentary profile of Hall of Famer Willie
Mays. Includes interviews with Casey Stengel,
Alvin Dark, and Leo Durocher.*

M.V.P., 1971
Syndicated, 30 minutes, regular series
Host: Johnny Bench

*Sports talk show hosted by the Cincinnati Reds'
all-star catcher.*

THE OCTOBER CLASSIC, 1958
(The Twentieth Century)
CBS, 30 minutes, September 28, 1958
Narrated by Walter Cronkite
Copyright date and number:
September 25, 1958, LP 12651

*Red Smith and Phil Rizzuto describe memorable
World Series moments as they witnessed them.*

THE ODYSSEY OF A BONUS
BABY: THE COURTSHIP OF
RICK REICHARDT, 1964
NBC, 30 minutes, July 4, 1964

Produced and directed by John J.
Sughrue, Jr.
Museum of Broadcasting, New York

*Documents the process by which Rick Reichardt
reached his decision to sign with the Angels.*

ONLY THE BALL WAS WHITE,
1981
Chicago Public Television
PBS, 30 minutes, February 16, 1981
Based on the book by Robert Peterson
Directed and produced by Ken Solarz
Narrated by Paul Winfield

*Interviews and anecdotes about life in the
Negro Leagues.*

RED BARBER REMEMBERS, 1983
PBS, 30 minutes, October 1, 1983

*Former Dodger and Yankee announcer looks
back on his Hall of Fame broadcasting career.*

A TALE OF TWO SEASONS,
1984
TBS, 120 minutes, March 25, 1984
Produced by Glenn Diamond
Narrated by Red Barber

*Behind-the-scenes profile of the 1983 Atlanta
Braves season.*

THERE WAS ALWAYS SUN
SHINING SOMEPLACE: LIFE IN
THE NEGRO BASEBALL
LEAGUES, 1983
Southwest Texas Public Broadcasting
Council
PBS, 60 minutes, September 7, 1983
Produced and directed by Craig
Davidson
Narrated by James Earl Jones

*Includes interviews with great Negro League
players and early film footage of Negro League
games.*

THIS WEEK IN BASEBALL, 1977
Major League Baseball Productions
Syndicated, 30 minutes, weekly series
Narrated by Mel Allen

*Film highlights of the week in major league
baseball.*

VEECK: A MAN FOR ANY
SEASON, 1986
PBS, 30 minutes, April 12, 1986
Produced by WTTW-TV, Chicago
Narrated by Mary Frances Veeck

*Affectionate profile of club owner Bill Veeck's
life and philosophy.*

THE WAY IT WAS, 1974
Gerry Gross Productions in
association with KCET, Los Angeles
PBS, 30 minutes, weekly series
Broadcast premiere: October 3, 1974
Host: Curt Gowdy

*Topical panel discussions relating to baseball
and other sports.*

WHEN THE CHEERING STOPS,
1985
(The Sporting Life)
Foxwood Productions and the
Educational Broadcasting Corp.
PBS, 30 minutes, May 28, 1985
Host: Jim Palmer

*Interview with Hall of Famer Jim ''Catfish''
Hunter, who reflects on his life in and out of
baseball.*

YOUNG BASEBALL HEROES,
1986
(Faces of Japan)
TeleJapan USA in association with
Pacific Mountain Network
PBS, 30 minutes, October 23, 1986
Host: Dick Cavett

*Documentary profile of the importance and
significance of high school baseball in Japan.*

YOUR SPORTS SPECIAL, 1948
CBS, 15 minutes, weekly series
Broadcast history, October 8, 1948 to
November 4, 1949
Host: Dolly Stark

*Stark is a former major league umpire and
infielder.*

Baseball in Animated Cartoons —Television

EXPLANATORY NOTES

1. Title of the cartoon episode, year of broadcast.

2. Name of the cartoon segment or series in parentheses, if applicable.

3. Name of production company.

4. Broadcast network, segment or program length in minutes, premiere broadcast date, black and white or color.

5. Writer(s) of cartoon.

6. Director of cartoon.

7. Voices featured in cartoon.

8. Copyright date and registration number.

9. Annotation. Description of the cartoon. *Home video* (given when the cartoon is available in home video format).

The following catalog contains a comprehensive listing of baseball-related animated cartoons produced for television. Included are cartoon segments from animated series, and animated television specials relating to baseball.

All cartoon segments are listed at five minutes in length and are approximate. Cartoon segments from animated series generally vary from four to six minutes in length.

Photographs for this section are provided through the courtesy of Stan and Jan Berenstain, King Features Syndicate, and Nelvana Ltd.

For cartoons produced for theatrical release, *see:* Baseball in Animated Cartoons—Feature.

BASEBALL, 1965
(Roger Ramjet)
Ken Snyder Productions
Syndicated, 5 minutes, color
Features the voice of Gary Owens as
Roger Ramjet

BASE ON BAWLS, 1960
(Mr. Magoo)
UPA Pictures, Inc.
Syndicated, 5 minutes, black and white
Features the voice of Jim Backus as
Mr. Magoo
Copyright date and number:
November 11, 1960, LP 21999

BATS IN THE BALLPARK,
c. 1962
(King and Odie)
Total Television Productions, Inc. and
Leonardo Productions
CBS, 5 minutes, color
Features the voices of Jackson Beck as
King Leonardo, and Allan Swift as
Odie Colognie

Segment from series, "Tennessee Tuxedo and His Tales."

BATTERY UP, c. 1962
(Popeye)
King Features Productions
Syndicated, 5 minutes, color

Features the voice of Jack Mercer as
Popeye

THE BERENSTAIN BEARS PLAY
BALL, 1983
(Berenstain Bears)
NBC, 30 minutes, May 5, 1983
Written by Stan and Jan Berenstain
Produced by Joseph Cates
Features the voices of Ron McLarty as
Papa Bear, Pat Lysinger as Mama
Bear, Knowl Johnson as the son, and
Gabriela Glatzer as the daughter

Papa Bear believes his son is destined to become a baseball star, but it is his daughter who's the better baseball player. Home video.

© 1983 S.&J. BERENSTAIN

Sister Bear is a baseball standout, but it's Brother Bear who gets all the family attention in The Berenstain Bears Play Ball. *In this sensitive cartoon production, Sister Bear eventually gets her due when Papa Bear realizes that his daughter, and not Brother Bear, is the better ballplayer.* (S. & J. Berenstain, 1983.)

___

BIG LEAGUE FREDDIE, c. 1964
(The Flintstones)
Hanna-Barbera Productions
ABC, 30 minutes
Features the voices of Alan Reed as Fred Flintstone, and Mel Blanc as Barney Rubble

THE CASE OF THE BIG BALL GAME, 1961

___

(Courageous Cat and Minute Mouse)
Trans-Artists Productions, Inc.
Syndicated, 5 minutes, black and white
Credits: Bob Kane
Features the voice of Bob McFadden
Copyright date and number: February 23, 1961, LP 19389

CHARLIE BROWN'S ALL-STARS, 1966
(Peanuts)
CBS, 30 minutes, June 8, 1966
Written and created by Charles M. Schulz
Music by Vince Guaraldi
See also Baseball in Comic Art—Collected; Baseball in Miscellaneous Recordings

Comic adventures of a sandlot team that has lost 999 games in a row. Home video. (Snoopy's Home Video Library: Volume I.)

CLYDE CRASHCUP INVENTS BASEBALL, c. 1962
(Clyde Crashcup)
Format Films and Bagadasarian Film Corp.
CBS, 5 minutes
Features the voice of Shep Menken as Clyde Crashcup

Segment from the series, ''The Alvin Show.''

DINKY AT THE BAT, c. 1979
(Dinky Dog)
Hanna-Barbera Productions
CBS, 5 minutes, color
Features the voice of Frank Welker as Dinky

Segment from the series, ''The All-New Popeye Hour.''

THE HORSE THAT PLAYED CENTER FIELD, 1979
(ABC Weekend Special)
ABC, 60 minutes, in two parts
February 24, 1979, 30 minutes: Part I
March 3, 1979, 30 minutes: Part II
Features the voices of John Erwin as Lefty, and Joan Gerber as Karen
See also: Baseball in Juvenile and Miscellaneous Fiction

Gamblers abduct a baseball-playing horse before a crucial World Series game. Home video.

HOW TO BE A GOOD UMPIRE, c. 1964
(Mr. Know It All)
Hooper Productions in association with Jay Ward Productions
Syndicated, 5 minutes, color
Features the voice of Bill Scott as Bullwinkle Moose

Bullwinkle explains the skills required for good umpiring. Segment from the series, ''The Hoppity Hooper Show.''

KING OF SWAT, c. 1962
(Tooter Turtle)
Total Television Productions, Inc. and Leonardo Productions
CBS, 5 minutes, color
Features the voices of Allan Swift as Tooter Turtle, and Frank Milano as Lizard the Wizard

Lizard the Wizard transports Tooter Turtle back into time when Babe Ruth was baseball's King of Swat. Segment from the series, ''Tennessee Tuxedo and His Tales.''

No one wants to win a baseball game more than Charlie Brown, whose hapless sandlot team has lost 999 games in a row in Charlie Brown's All-Stars. *(CBS, 1966. © 1966 King Features Syndicate.)*

LADIES' DAY, c. 1963
(The Flintstones)
Hanna-Barbera Productions
ABC, 30 minutes
Features the voices of Alan Reed as
Fred Flintstone, and Mel Blanc as
Barney Rubble

*Barney dresses up as a woman in order to see a
baseball game for free.*

THE LATE T.C., 1962
(Top Cat)
Hanna-Barbera Productions
ABC, 30 minutes
Features the voices of Arnold Stang
as Top Cat, and Maurice Gosfield as
Benny
Copyright date and number: February
21, 1962, LP 30352

*Mickey Mantle hits a home run that lands on
Top Cat's head.*

THE LITTLE BIG LEAGUE,
c. 1967
(Winsome Witch)
Hanna-Barbera Productions
NBC, 5 minutes, color
Features the voice of Paul Frees as
Winsome Witch

*Segment from the series, ''The Secret Squirrel
Show.''*

MEXICAN BASEBALL, c. 1971
(Gandy Goose)
Terrytoons Productions
NBC, 5 minutes, color
Features the voice of Dayton Allen as
Gandy Goose

*Segment from the series, ''The Deputy Dawg
Show.''*

NINE STRIKES, YOU'RE OUT,
c. 1966
(The Atom Ant Show)
Hanna-Barbera Productions
NBC, 5 minutes, color

Team Earth is set to play the Outer Space All-Stars in the 1982 cartoon special, Take Me Up to
the Ball Game. *The earthlings quickly learn that the rules to this bizarre interplanetary baseball game
are stacked in favor of the home team All-Stars.* (© 1982 Nelvana Ltd.)

Features the voice of Howard Morris
as Atom Ant

OPERATION BARNEY, 1962
(The Flintstones)
Hanna-Barbera Productions
ABC, 30 minutes
Features the voices of Alan Reed as
Fred Flintstone, and Mel Blanc as
Barney Rubble
Copyright date and number: February
9, 1962, LP 32001

*Fred and Barney call in sick so they can attend
a baseball game.*

TAKE ME OUT TO THE BALL
GAME, 1962
(The Flintstones)
Hanna-Barbera Productions
ABC, 30 minutes, black and white
Features the voices of Alan Reed as
Fred Flintstone, and Mel Blanc as
Barney Rubble

Copyright date and number: April 20,
1962, LP 32011

TAKE ME OUT TO THE BRAWL
GAME, c. 1979
(The All-New Popeye Hour)
Hanna-Barbera Productions
CBS, 5 minutes, color
Features the voice of Jack Mercer as
Popeye

TAKE ME UP TO THE BALL
GAME, 1982
Nelvana Ltd.
CBS, 30 minutes, August 27, 1982
Songs by Rick Danko
Features the voice of Phil Silvers

*Team Earth plays the Outer Space All-Stars in
an interplanetary baseball game. Home video.
(Nelvanamation: Volume II.)*

Chapter

7

Baseball in Radio

The following section contains a comprehensive listing of baseball-related dramatic, comic, and musical radio plays. Included in the catalog are original radio dramas and comedies, radio adaptations of baseball-related films, novels, and short stories, and radio plays dramatizing the lives and histories of baseball players and teams. For a catalog of documentary and historical radio programs relating to baseball, *see:* Baseball in Documentary and Miscellaneous Radio.

Early radio, comprising the years 1925 to 1955, was a frenetic medium: Writers wrote scripts to several programs simultaneously; actors ran from studio to studio to appear in two or more programs within a single hour; and engineers transcribed programs for producers, sponsors, even for actors and announcers, but seldom for the networks themselves. As a result, lost in the bustle and excitement of live radio were the recordings of the programs themselves—and the opportunity for later generations to enjoy them.

Most audio recordings of early radio programming exist as a result of the efforts of a small but dedicated group of lay historians and collectors who have located and restored many of the huge 16-inch discs on which the programs were transcribed. These acetate discs are extremely fragile and deteriorate rapidly and must be dubbed onto magnetic tape or else the original radio recordings will be forever lost.

A surprisingly large number of early radio programs relating to baseball have survived and are available through the archives of the Library of Congress, the Museum of Broadcasting in New York, the G. Robert Vincent Voice Library at Michigan State University, and the National Baseball Hall of Fame and Museum in Cooperstown, New York. A significant collection of early radio programming can be found through the membership of such collectors' organizations as the Society to Preserve and Encourage Radio Drama, Variety, and Comedy (SPERDVAC), a not-for-profit society based in Hollywood, California. Its lending library contains many early radio programs of interest to baseball historians and enthusiasts.

Titles to radio programs contained in this section are listed as copyrighted or as stated on the script, as given within the body of the show, as shown on the labels of transcription discs, or as listed in radio reference books and logs. Programs without formal episode titles can be found under "Broadcast of . . ." and are arranged chronologically.

Broadcast dates are listed, whenever possible, according to the radio logs for the Metropolitan New York area.

EXPLANATORY NOTES

1. Title of the radio play, year of broadcast.

2. Name of the radio series in parentheses, if applicable.

3. Broadcast network, program length in minutes, premiere broadcast date.

4. Writer(s) of program.

5. Director of program.

6. Producer of program.

7. Cast of program.

8. Name of broadcast library holding a transcription of the program.

9. Annotation. Description of the program.

Red Barber and Connie Desmond. (Photofest.)

ADVENTURE OF THE WORLD
SERIES CRIME, 1943
(Ellery Queen)
NBC, 30 minutes, October 2, 1943
Cast: Sydney Smith as Ellery Queen
Pacific Pioneer Broadcasters,
Hollywood, California

THE ADVENTURES OF BABE
RUTH, c. 1947
Public Service Program, 15 minutes,
regular series
Written by Ben Freeman
Directed by Ronald Dawson
Produced by Woody Klose

*Sponsored by the U.S. Navy for high-school-
age boys, each program features the comic book
exploits of a richly mythologized Babe Ruth.*

"AIDA" AS A BASEBALL
GAME, 1947
(The Henry Morgan Show)
ABC, 30 minutes, April 2, 1947

*Segment: Includes a comedic interview with an
endorsement-minded ballplayer and the title
sketch in which an opera is described using
baseball terminology.*

ALIBI IKE, 1937
(The Lux Radio Theatre)
CBS, 60 minutes, April 19, 1937
Based on the motion picture
Host: Cecil B. DeMille
Cast: Joe E. Brown as Frank X.
Farrell, Helen Chandler as Dolly
Stevens, Roscoe Karns, and William
Frawley
Guests: Babe and Claire Ruth
Library of Congress number: Cassette
13630
See also: Baseball in Film; Baseball in
the Spoken Arts—Recorded

ALIBI IKE, 1945
(The Lady Esther Screen Guild
Theatre)
CBS, 30 minutes, June 18, 1945
Cast: Jack Carson

ALIBI IKE, 1947
(Studio One)
CBS, 60 minutes, May 20, 1947
Cast: Everett Sloane, Joe Di Santis,
and Anne Burr

ANGELS IN THE OUTFIELD,
1953
(The Lux Radio Theatre)
CBS, 60 minutes, April 6, 1953
Based on the motion picture
Host: Irving Cummings
Cast: George Murphy as Guffy
McGovern, Janet Leigh as Jennifer
Paige, and Donna Corcoran as
Bridget White
See also: Baseball in Film

AN ARM LIKE IRON, 1955
(Proudly We Hail)
Public Service Program, 30 minutes,
October 30, 1955

*Humorous story about an overly sensitive
pitcher who is prone to psychosomatic ailments.*

BABE RUTH: BIG MAN OF
BASEBALL, 1947
(The Radio Reader's Digest)
CBS, 30 minutes, April 24, 1947
Based on the article, "What Baseball
Owes to Babe Ruth" by Jack Sher,
published in the *Reader's Digest*, April
1947, pp. 1–5
Written by Robert Sloane
Cast: Howard Smith as Babe Ruth
Guests: Tom Shirley and Babe Ruth

Light-hearted dramatization of Babe Ruth's life.

THE BABE RUTH STORY, 1948
(The Camel Screen Guild Players)
NBC, 30 minutes, October 21, 1948
Based on the motion picture
Cast: William Bendix as Babe Ruth,
and Lurene Tuttle as Claire Ruth
See also: Baseball in Film

THE BALLAD OF SATCHEL
PAIGE, 1949
(Destination Freedom)
NBC, 30 minutes, May 15, 1949
Written by Richard Durham
Cast: Harris Gaines as Satchel Paige,
and Oscar Brown, Jr. as the balladeer

*Folkloric dramatization of star pitcher Satchel
Paige's life.*

BALL NINE, TAKE YOUR BASE,
1959
(Gunsmoke)
CBS, 30 minutes, August 2, 1959
Written by Vic Perrin
Cast: William Conrad as Matt Dillon,
Parley Baer as Chester, and Howard
McNear as Doc Adams

*After studying Chadwick's "Rulebook of Base
Ball," Doc agrees to umpire a game between a
local nine and a roughhouse team of touring all-
stars.*

BASEBALL, 1946
(The Land We Live In)
Syndicated, 30 minutes, April 15,
1946
Written by C. E. Barnhart
Produced by Ted Westcott

*Dramatization of the history of the St. Louis
Browns baseball club.*

BASEBALL, 1958
(NBC Monitor)
NBC, 25 minutes, in five parts
August 1958: 5 minutes each
Cast: Jim Jordan as Fibber McGee,
and Marian Jordan as Molly

Five "Fibber McGee and Molly" vignettes include: "Tall Tale"; "The Big Ball Game"; "A Little Pepper"; "How to Play the Game"; "Dangerous Game"; "Dispensable Shortstop."

THE BASEBALL ANNOUNCER, 1980
(Mutual Radio Theatre)
Mutual, 60 minutes, April 15, 1980
Cast: Robert Towers

BASEBALL COLOGNE, 1948
(Fibber McGee and Molly)
NBC, 30 minutes, May 18, 1948
Written by Don Quinn and Phil Leslie
Cast: Jim Jordan as Fibber, and Marian Jordan as Molly

McGee endeavors to invent a men's cologne that "captures the essence of baseball." Includes song, "Casey (The Pride of Them All)" by the King's Men.

BASEBALL EXPERT TEENY, 1957
(Fibber McGee and Molly)
NBC, 15 minutes, July 21, 1957
Cast: Jim Jordan as Fibber McGee, and Marian Jordan as Molly

BASEBALL HATTIE, 1951
(The Damon Runyon Theatre)
Syndicated, 30 minutes, episode 26
Based on the story by Damon Runyon
Written by Russell Hughes
Cast: John Brown as Broadway, and Lou Krugman as Armand

Woman baseball fan marries a roguish and intemperate star pitcher.

BASEBALL INSTRUCTOR, 1935
(Fibber McGee and Molly)
NBC, 30 minutes, July 22, 1935
Cast: Jim Jordan as Fibber, and Marian Jordan as Molly

BASEBALL OPENER, 1959
(NBC Monitor)
NBC, 25 minutes, in five parts
April 1959: 5 minutes each

Cast: Jim Jordan as Fibber McGee, and Marian Jordan as Molly

Five "Fibber McGee and Molly" vignettes include: "Two Box Seat Tickets"; "Nostalgic Memory"; "Chicago by Train"; "Phoning Old Peoria Friends"; "Wrong City Bus."

THE BASEBALL PLAYER MURDER, c. 1946
(Boston Blackie)
Syndicated, 30 minutes, episode 53
Cast: Richard Kollmar as Blackie, and Maurice Tarplin as Inspector Faraday
Guest: Clem McCarthy as the announcer

Star player Mike Allen is shot while sliding into second base, and a last-minute lineup switch provides Blackie with a clue.

BASEBALL SEASON BEGINS, 1948
(The Great Gildersleeve)
NBC, 30 minutes, April 7, 1948
Written by John Elliotte and Andy White
Cast: Harold Peary as Throckmorton P. Gildersleeve, and Una Merkel as Adelaide Fairchild

Gildersleeve agrees to search for a suitable location for a children's baseball field.

BASEBALL TEAM, 1952
(The Adventures of Ozzie and Harriet)
ABC, 30 minutes, April 18, 1952
Cast: Ozzie and Harriet Nelson

A flamboyant public relations man intends to change the game of baseball in order to bolster attendance for the local team.

THE BASEBALL UNIFORM, 1948
(The Life of Riley)
NBC, 30 minutes, May 1, 1948
Written by Ruben Ship and Alan Lipscott
Cast: William Bendix as Chester A. Riley, and Paula Winslowe as Mrs. Peg Riley

Riley brags about having been a great baseball player and produces an old uniform to prove it.

BIG BOY, 1947
(The Cavalcade of America)
NBC, 30 minutes, September 29, 1947
Written by Brice Disque, Jr.
Cast: Brian Donlevy as Babe Ruth

Dramatization of Babe Ruth's life.

BIG FOOT GRAFTON, c. 1949
(Richard Diamond, Private Detective)
NBC, 30 minutes
Written by Blake Edwards
Cast: Richard Powell as Richard Diamond, and Ed Begley as Lieutenant Walt Levinson

Second baseman for women's professional softball team is missing, and Diamond agrees to find her.

BIG LEAGUE BASEBALL FIBS, 1955
(Fibber McGee and Molly)
NBC, 15 minutes, June 22, 1955
Cast: Jim Jordan as Fibber McGee, and Marian Jordan as Molly

THE BLOOD RED DIAMOND, c. 1956
(It's a Crime, Mr. Collins)
Mutual, 30 minutes

A jealous catcher saturates a mitt with nitroglycerine to murder his spitball-pitching teammate.

BROADCAST OF SEPTEMBER 24, 1941
(The Eddie Cantor Show)
NBC, 30 minutes, September 24, 1941
Guest: Joe DiMaggio
Library of Congress number: Tape 12736-42 B

BROADCAST OF OCTOBER 5, 1941
(The Jack Benny Program)
NBC, 30 minutes, October 5, 1941
Cast: Jack Benny and Mary Livingstone

Jack and Mary attend a World Series game at Ebbets Field and discover that Jack's seat is already occupied by a diehard Dodgers' fan.

BROADCAST OF NOVEMBER 9, 1941
(The Jack Benny Program)
NBC, 30 minutes, November 9, 1941
Guest: Leo Durocher

Segment: Leo explains how the Dodgers lost the World Series.

BROADCAST OF APRIL 19, 1942
(The Texaco Star Theatre)
CBS, 60 minutes, April 19, 1942
Cast: Fred Allen
Guest: Leo Durocher

Segment: Fred and Leo discuss new "rules" whereby Leo and the Dodgers must treat umpires with strict courteousness.

BROADCAST OF JANUARY 2, 1944
(The Jack Benny Program)
NBC, 30 minutes, January 2, 1944
Cast: Jack Benny, Mary Livingstone, Dennis Day, and Phil Harris

Segment: Sketch titled, "The New Tenant," in which a baseball game is played by the United Nations All-Stars and the Axis Polecats.

BROADCAST OF APRIL 16, 1944
(The Fred Allen Show)
CBS, 30 minutes, April 16, 1944
Guest: Leo Durocher

Fred must pass a physical examination before he can play second base for the Dodgers.

BROADCAST OF JUNE 13, 1944
(The Abbott and Costello Show)
NBC, 30 minutes, June 13, 1944
Cast: Bud Abbott and Lou Costello

Segment: Includes the famous "Who's on First?" comedy routine. (See also: Baseball in Miscellaneous Plays and Sketches; Baseball in Comedy and Light Verse—Recorded.) See: The Naughty Nineties; The World of Abbott and Costello (Baseball in Film: Appendix).

BROADCAST OF APRIL 1, 1945
(The Radio Hall of Fame)
NBC, 60 minutes, April 1, 1945
Host: Deems Taylor
Features Paul Whiteman and His Orchestra
Guests: Garry Moore and Leo Durocher

Segment: A skit in which Durocher plays a refined and courteous manager.

BROADCAST OF OCTOBER 7, 1945
(The Jack Benny Program)
NBC, 30 minutes, October 7, 1945

Jack tries to find the World Series on the radio and gets every station but the one he wants. First of what became an annual sketch on the program.

BROADCAST OF NOVEMBER 25, 1945
(The Fred Allen Show)
NBC, 30 minutes, November 25, 1945
Cast: Fred Allen and Portland Hoffa
Guest: Leo Durocher

Fred wants Leo to quit his worrisome job as manager of the Dodgers and star in an operetta called, "The Brooklyn Pinafore." (See also: Broadcast of April 14, 1946).

BROADCAST OF APRIL 14, 1946
(The Fred Allen Show)
NBC, 30 minutes, April 14, 1946
Cast: Fred Allen and Portland Hoffa
Guest: Leo Durocher

Fred and Leo reprise the operetta, titled, "The Brooklyn Pinafore." (See also: Broadcast of November 25, 1945).

BROADCAST OF APRIL 14, 1946
(The Radio Hall of Fame)
ABC, 30 minutes, April 14, 1946
Guests: Roland Young and Joe DiMaggio

Segment: Humorous dialog in which Joe DiMaggio explains baseball to an Englishman.

BROADCAST OF OCTOBER 6, 1946
(The Jack Benny Program)
NBC, 30 minutes, October 6, 1946

Jack tries to get the World Series broadcast on his radio.

BROADCAST OF NOVEMBER 17, 1946
(The Jack Benny Program)
NBC, 30 minutes, November 17, 1946
Guests: Ronald Colman and Leo Durocher

BROADCAST OF APRIL 13, 1947
(The Jack Benny Program)
NBC, 30 minutes, April 13, 1947

Convinced by his press agent that he should acquire a baseball club—a la Bob Hope and Bing Crosby—Jack unwittingly purchases an all-women's team.

BROADCAST OF MAY 14, 1947
(Philco Radio Time)
ABC, 30 minutes, May 14, 1947
Cast: Bing Crosby
Guests: Groucho Marx, Warren Brown, and Hank Greenberg

Groucho tells Bing about "Marx's Bloomer Girls," where "a curve is on every bag." Includes song, "Goodbye, Mr. Ball." (See: Baseball in Music and Song.)

BROADCAST OF APRIL 25, 1948
(The Fred Allen Show)
NBC, 30 minutes, April 25, 1948

Guest: Leo Durocher
See also: The Fred Allen Show (Baseball in Miscellaneous Recordings)

After being given two tickets to a game at Ebbets Field, Fred is arrested for attempting to sell one to a Dodgers' fan.

BROADCAST OF JUNE 20, 1948
(The Jack Benny Program)
NBC, 30 minutes, June 20, 1948
Guests: Bob Feller, Bob Hope, and Marilyn Maxwell

BROADCAST OF OCTOBER 10, 1948
(The Jack Benny Program)
NBC, 30 minutes, October 10, 1948
Cast: Jack Benny, Mary Livingstone, Dennis Day, Eddie ''Rochester'' Anderson, and Don Wilson

Jack has the cast over to listen to the World Series on his radio, but a persistent echo rings in his ears.

BROADCAST OF APRIL 7, 1949
(The Kraft Music Hall)
NBC, 30 minutes, April 7, 1949
Host: Al Jolson
Guest: Groucho Marx

Segment: Groucho engages in play-on-words and repartee about the Bel Air Bloomer Girls.

BROADCAST OF APRIL 24, 1949
(The Adventures of Ozzie and Harriet)
CBS, 30 minutes, April 24, 1949
Cast: Ozzie and Harriet Nelson

Hoping to impress Harriet with his baseball prowess, Ozzie gets stuck in a catcher's mask.

BROADCAST OF MARCH 28, 1950
(The Henry Morgan Show)
NBC, 30 minutes, March 28, 1950
Cast: Henry Morgan and Art Carney

Segment: Comedic interview with a laconic baseball pitcher.

BROADCAST OF MAY 4, 1952
(The Jack Benny Program)
CBS, 30 minutes, May 4, 1952
Cast: Jack Benny and Mary Livingstone

Jack and Mary attend a baseball game.

BROADCAST OF OCTOBER 5, 1952
(The Jack Benny Program)
CBS, 30 minutes, October 5, 1952
Cast: Jack Benny and Mary Livingstone
Pacific Pioneer Broadcasters, Hollywood, California

BROADCAST OF OCTOBER 4, 1953
(The Jack Benny Program)
CBS, 30 minutes, October 4, 1953
Cast: Jack Benny, Mary Livingstone, Dennis Day, Eddie ''Rochester'' Anderson, and Don Wilson
Guest: Leo Durocher

Jack invites the cast over to watch the World Series on his television.

BROOKLYN BASEBALL CANTATA, 1941
(The Columbia Workshop)
CBS, 30 minutes, April 13, 1941
Written by Michael Stratton and George Kleinsinger
See also: Baseball in Theater; Baseball in Music and Song—Recorded

CASEY AT THE BAT, c. 1948
(Favorite Story)
Syndicated, 30 minutes
Written by Jerome Lawrence and Robert E. Lee
Host: Ronald Colman
Cast: Lionel Stander as Casey, Hal Berger as the manager, Anne Stone as Mrs. Casey, and Tommy Bernard as Timmy

A lovesick Casey strikes out when his wife leaves him because of his lack of ambition.

CASEY AT THE BAT, 1949
(Tell It Again)
CBS, 30 minutes, April 24, 1949
Directed, produced, and written by Ralph Rose
Cast: Marvin Miller as Casey, Ray Rowe, Gilbert Barnett, Ken Harvey, Martha Shaw, Peter Leeds, Alan Reed, Jr., and Shep Menken

In this adaptation, Casey is struck out by his adopted nephew—the son of a deceased former teammate.

CASEY AT THE BAT, 1951
(The Railroad Hour)
NBC, 30 minutes, July 9, 1951
Cast: Gordon MacRae as Casey, Dorothy Warenskjold as Mrs. Casey, Herb Vigran as the manager, Marvin Miller as the umpire, and Jeffrey Silver as the bat boy

CASEY AT THE BAT, 1953
(On Stage)
CBS, 30 minutes, April 1953
Written by E. Jack Neuman
Hosts: Cathy and Elliot Lewis
Cast: Hy Averback as Casey, Howard McNear, Byron Kane, Hal March, Peter Leeds, Sidney Miller, and Herb Butterfield

Casey falls into the clutches of a Svengali manager and strikes out deliberately in order to prove his independence to his bride-to-be.

CASEY, WHICH IS MYSELF, 1982
(National Radio Theatre)
National Public Radio, 60 minutes, March, 18, 1982
Written by William Brashler
Cast: Pat O'Brien as Casey Stengel

In this one-man show, Hall of Famer Casey Stengel reminisces about his days as baseball player and manager.

Baseball and the Bomb

What if nothing in life were certain, not even the verities of baseball? That's the question posed in *The Day That Baseball Died*, a 1946 allegory about the Hiroshima bomb and the uncertainities of life in the atomic age.

In this radio dramatization the baseball world is in chaos. All baseball leagues in the United States, Canada, Mexico, and Cuba have indefinitely suspended their schedules. A trial has been set to determine the future of baseball.

The cause of this upheaval is a pitch that was hurled by Red Besterski in the last inning of the deciding game of the World Series, a pitch likened to the A-bomb in its effect on the game.

The pitch is called Knuckleduster the Second, which Besterski had secretly developed over a span of six years. In the trial, witnesses describe their shocked reactions to the pitch, which, incredibly, had stopped three feet short of home plate.

With two out and the bases loaded, the batter had swung for an apparent third strike. Was he out? Or was the "antigravity" pitch illegally thrown? Witnesses described the violent argument that ensued: Players brawled on the field; horrified spectators rioted in the stands until, section by section, the stadium itself collapsed.

The inviolability of baseball had been breached. A secure and rational world was thrown into disarray.

Public opinion about the Knuckleduster pitch is highly charged and borders on hysteria. The trial gives voice to the uncertainties but does not resolve them.

This disturbing radio play ends abruptly and is left unconcluded. The dramatist is seemingly asking, as he hoped his radio audience did: Will we ever allow the bomb to fall again? ◆

THE DAY THAT BASEBALL
DIED, 1946
(The Columbia Workshop)
CBS, 30 minutes, September 28, 1946
Written by Irving Teitel
Cast: Art Carney as Red Besterski,
Santos Ortega as the Justice, and Bill
Slater as Belanger
Published in *Scholastic*, April 14, 1947,
pp. 21–23

The future of baseball is threatened when a pitcher for the Green Sox develops an antigravity pitch called, "Knuckleduster the Second."

DEATH ON THE DIAMOND,
1945
(Bulldog Drummond)
Mutual, 30 minutes, September 17,
1945

Star pitcher Twister Johnson has been murdered, and Drummond is certain that gamblers are involved.

ELMER THE GREAT, 1935
(The Lux Radio Theatre)
NBC, 60 minutes, June 30, 1935
Based on the motion picture
Host: Cecil B. DeMille
Cast: Joe E. Brown as Elmer Kane
See also: Baseball in Film; Baseball in
Theater. *See: Hurry Kane*

ELMER THE GREAT, 1936
(The Lux Radio Theatre)
CBS, 60 minutes, October 5, 1936
Based on the motion picture
Host: Cecil B. DeMille
Cast: Joe E. Brown as Elmer Kane,
and June Travis
Guests: Lou Gehrig and Carl Hubbell

Library of Congress number: Cassette
13644

Restaged from June 30, 1935.

ELMER THE GREAT, 1940
(Gulf Screen Guild Theatre)
CBS, 30 minutes, April 14, 1940
Cast: Bob Hope as Elmer Kane, Ann
Sheridan, and Eliva Ellman

ELMER THE GREAT, c. 1947
(Hollywood Startime)
CBS, 30 minutes
Cast: Harold Peary as Elmer Kane

ELMER THE GREAT, 1948
(Hallmark Playhouse)
CBS, 30 minutes, October 7, 1948
Based on the motion picture
Written by Jean Holloway

A FATEFUL BASEBALL GAME

Imagine how you would react if in a crucial moment of a World Series game you saw a thrown pitch suddenly stop six inches in front of home plate. In this scene from Irving Teitel's radio play, *The Day That Baseball Died*, a baseball announcer's recorded broadcast is replayed as courtroom evidence:

BELANGER (*Breathless, hysterical, shouting hoarsely into the mike*): . . .and now it's a riot that is completely out of control. There are individual fights going on all over the ball park, each the center of a milling, punching mass of baseball fans. All the players are slugging it out in the infield, which is a weaving nightmare of swinging fists and falling bodies. The roof of the east bleachers has collapsed, and through the shattered wreckage dazed and bruised baseball enthusiasts are still struggling . . . all the police who came pushing in just after the fateful pitch have disappeared into the middle of the mob—

SOUND (*Rending, ear-splitting crunch and crash.*)

BELANGER: And there goes the middle portion of the central stands in a cloud of dust and humanity—it's staggering! Here comes another flying wedge of police—uh, uh, the spearhead is down, there goes another one . . . now five of them have disappeared—this ball game will go down in history! This section of the stands is beginning to sway now [*panicky*] it's swaying dangerously now, a support is beginning to buckle and I'm going to get this microphone away from here before—look out!

SOUND (*Crunching, cracking, shattering noise that drowns all others, then cuts dead abruptly. Dead silence. Pause. On echo—off-mike cough and throat clearing.*)

JUSTICE: And this can be written into the records as an eyewitness account of the rioting at that, uh, fateful baseball game, Mr. Belanger?

BELANGER: Yes, your honor, the words you have heard are mine as recorded in our studios during the actual broadcast. I was greatly excited at the time and no doubt I missed a lot of points . . .

Cast: Bob Hope as Elmer Kane

ELMER THE GREAT, 1949
(Ford Theatre)
CBS, 60 minutes, April 15, 1949
Cast: Paul Douglas as Elmer Kane

ELMER THE GREAT, 1951
(The Theatre Guild on the Air)
NBC, 60 minutes, May 27, 1951
Cast: Paul Douglas as Elmer Kane

FIREBALL MCGEE, 1946
(Fibber McGee and Molly)
NBC, 30 minutes, May 21, 1946
Written by Don Quinn and Phil Leslie
Cast: Jim Jordan as Fibber, and Marian Jordan as Molly

Fibber is pitching for the Elks in an upcoming game against the Rotarians, but he can't understand why he doesn't have the control he once had. Includes song, "Casey (The Pride of Them All)" by the King's Men.

GAME CALLED OFF, 1929
(Majestic Theatre of the Air)
CBS, 30 minutes, October 6, 1929
Written by Ring W. Lardner

Written by Lardner expressly for the "Majestic Theatre of the Air," this is possibly the first baseball-related drama ever broadcast on radio. No script or recording of the broadcast is known to exist.

THE GIRL SHORTSTOP, 1953
(Guest Star)
Public Service Program, 15 minutes, September 1953
Narrated by Rod O'Connor
Cast: Eve Arden as Sally Lewis, Les Tremayne, Frank Nelson, and John Larch

Just when Sally Lewis has proven herself as good a shortstop as any male, she falls in love with the opposing pitcher, Fireball Finnegan.

THE GREAT MCGRAW, 1946
(The Cavalcade of America)
NBC, 30 minutes, April 15, 1946
Cast: Pat O'Brien as John McGraw
National Baseball Hall of Fame and Museum, Cooperstown, New York

Dramatization of the baseball life of Hall of Fame manager John McGraw.

HEX MARKS THE SPOT, 1947
(Grand Marquee)
NBC, 30 minutes, June 5, 1947
Written by Ralph Hunter and Mary McSkiving
Cast: Olan Soule as Steve Dalton, and Muriel Bremner as Emmy Huggins

Beautiful woman inherits a baseball team, including a zanily superstitious pitcher.

HURRY KANE, 1944
(Sports Stories of Grantland Rice)
NBC, 30 minutes, March 1944
Based on the story by Ring W.
Lardner, published in *Cosmospolitan*,
May 1927
Written by Gerald Holland
Host: Grantland Rice
Cast: Jim Backus as Elmer "Hurry"
Kane, John Gibson, Jackson Beck,
and Sam Wanamaker
See also: Elmer the Great (Baseball in
Film; Baseball in Radio; Baseball in
Theater)

**IT HAPPENS EVERY SPRING,
1949**
(The Lux Radio Theatre)
CBS, 60 minutes, October 3, 1949
Based on the motion picture
Cast: Ray Milland as Vernon Simpson
See also: Baseball in Film; Baseball in
Fiction

**IT HAPPENS EVERY SPRING,
1950**
(The Screen Directors' Playhouse)
NBC, 30 minutes, April 14, 1950
Based on the motion picture
Written by Richard Allen Simmons
Cast: Ray Milland as Vernon
Simpson, Ted deCorsia, Frank
Nelson, Parley Baer, Eddie Fields,
Frank Barton, Dan Riss, and Ann
Diamond

**LIZ AND IRIS PLAY BASEBALL,
1948**
(My Favorite Husband)
CBS, 30 minutes
Cast: Lucille Ball as Liz Cooper,
Richard Denning as George Cooper,
and Bea Benaderet as Iris

*Liz replaces her injured husband in the
company picnic baseball game.*

LOU GEHRIG, 1945
(Freedom of Opportunity)

Mutual, 30 minutes, June 29, 1945
National Baseball Hall of Fame and
Museum, Cooperstown, New York

Dramatization of Lou Gehrig's life.

MAJOR LEAGUE SCOUT, 1942
(The Adventures of Dick Cole)
Syndicated, 30 minutes, episode 16

*Children's melodrama in which a rival pitcher,
desperate to impress a big league scout, uses a
doctored baseball in a game against Dick Cole's
Farr Academy team.*

MARTIAN SAM, 1957
(X Minus One)
NBC, 30 minutes, April 3, 1957
Written by Ernest Kinoy
Cast: Mandel Kramer as Joe, Santos
Ortega as Rabbit, Bob Hastings as
Tommy, and Bill Zuckert as Curt

*Humorous story about a hapless baseball team
in the twenty-first century and its newest
player—an 18-inch-tall pitcher from Mars.*

MILLER HUGGINS, 1954
(The Hallmark Hall of Fame)
CBS, 30 minutes, May 2, 1954
Written by David Friedkin and Walt
Barnes
Host: Lionel Barrymore
Cast: Vic Perrin as Miller Huggins,
Charlotte Lawrence, Jack Kruschen,
John Dehner, Sam Edwards, and
Herb Vigran
Guest: Joe DiMaggio

*Conflict between a principled Miller Huggins
and an undisciplined Babe Ruth is dramatized.*

MOVIETIME USA, 1951
(The Lux Radio Theatre)
CBS, 60 minutes, September 24, 1951

Segment: A scene from The Pride of St.
Louis, *starring Dan Dailey as Dizzy Dean,
and Joanne Dru as Patricia. See also:* Baseball
in Film.

**MURDER AT THE BALL PARK,
1940**

(The Fred Allen Show)
NBC, 60 minutes, May 15, 1940

*Segment: Title sketch in which a farcical
Chinese detective solves a murder of an umpire
during a game*

MURDER IN THE BIG LEAGUE
(Five Minute Mysteries)
Syndicated, 5 minutes, episode 29

Star player is murdered by a jealous teammate.

**THE MYSTERY OF THE
PERFECT THROW FROM LEFT
FIELD AND THE CONGA
DANCER'S AUNT, 1942**
(WOR Summer Theatre)
Mutual, 30 minutes, August 13, 1942
Written by Bob Simon
Cast: Peter Donald as Daniel, Helen
Claire as Dolly, Ethel Remey as Mrs.
Jones, Jock MacGregor, Jerry Macy,
Junius Matthews, and Sidney Slon

*Comedic farce about an umpire who becomes a
detective.*

OLD INDISPENSABLE, 1944
(Sports Stories of Grantland Rice)
NBC, 30 minutes, March 4, 1944
Based on the story by Stanley Frank,
published in *Collier's*, October 16,
1943
Written by Gerald Holland
Host: Grantland Rice
Cast: Jack Hartley, Joe Julian, and
Reese Taylor

*Sore-armed major league pitcher, recently
inducted into the armed service, sacrifices his
career to pitch his army team to a
championship.*

ONE HIT, TWO ERRORS, 1948
(Hollywood Theatre of Stars)
Mutual, 30 minutes, October 12, 1948
Cast: Joe DiMaggio as Joe Collins,
and Dix Davis as Lefty Collins

*Light-hearted story in which two major league
scouts use subterfuge against each other in their
efforts to sign an unassuming small-town
slugger.*

A PITCH IN TIME, 1947

(Crime Club)
Mutual, 30 minutes, June 7, 1947
Cast: Walter Kinsella as Hank Harper, Ann Thomas as Mabel, Cameron Prud'homme as the chief of police, King Calder as Mike, Bill Smith as Sergeant Keefe, and Earl George as Red

A bumbling pitcher for a police officer's baseball club unwittingly captures a bank robber.

PLAY BALL, 1942

(The Columbia Workshop)
CBS, 30 minutes, April 19, 1942
Cast: John Connery, Jone Allison, Adelaide Klein, Ed Mayehoff, Chester Stratton, and Ed Lattimer

Life in a typical small town is revealed in the conversations of fans at an industrial league baseball game.

THE PRIDE OF THE YANKEES, 1943

(The Lux Radio Theatre)
CBS, 60 minutes, October 4, 1943
Based on the motion picture
Cast: Gary Cooper as Lou Gehrig, Virginia Bruce as Eleanor Gehrig, and Edgar Buchanan as Sam Blake
See also: Baseball in Film; Baseball in Comic Art—Collected: Appendix; Baseball in Miscellaneous Recordings

THE PRIDE OF THE YANKEES, 1946

(Hollywood Players)
CBS, 30 minutes, September 24, 1946
Based on the motion picture
Written by Forrest Barnes
Cast: Joseph Cotten as Lou Gehrig, and Rosemary De Camp as Eleanor Gehrig

THE PRIDE OF THE YANKEES, 1949

(The Screen Directors' Playhouse)
NBC, 30 minutes, September 30, 1949

Mel Allen. (Photofest.)

Based on the motion picture
Cast: Gary Cooper as Lou Gehrig, Lurene Tuttle as Eleanor Gehrig, Frank Lovejoy, Herb Vigran, Ted Von Eltz, and Jerry Hausner

THE RIME OF THE ANCIENT DODGER, 1948

(Destination Freedom)
NBC, 30 minutes, November 21, 1948
Written by Richard Durham
Cast: Studs Terkel as Sammy, Oscar Brown, Jr. as Jackie Robinson, and Everett Clark as Branch Rickey

Rhymed-verse story of Jackie Robinson as told by Sammy the Whammy, a streetwise Brooklyn Dodgers fanatic.

SACRIFICE PLAY, 1941

(First Nighter)
CBS, 30 minutes, July 8, 1941
Cast: Les Tremayne and Barbara Luddy

A woman's romantic interest turns a shy and modest pitcher into a conceited boor.

An Amazing Melodrama

Baseball has been treated reverently and whimsically in American popular culture, and even, on rare occasion, disdainfully. But it has probably never been treated more preposterously than in the 1950 radio mystery play *Wild Pitch.*

In this story Windy Noles is a minor league catcher with "a secret too deep to tell." In the clubhouse one day he learns that he has been called up to the major league New York Gulls. But the accompanying news that the Gulls had also purchased the contract of Big Ed Kowalski from another major league club clearly unsettles the catcher Noles. He is disconcerted by his sudden promotion and wonders if perhaps he isn't ready for the major leagues after all.

In his first game since joining the Gulls, Noles is paired with Kowalski as his batterymate. They work well for the first six innings until Kowalski begins to cross up his catcher by throwing different pitches than those signalled for by Noles. Conferring on the mound, Noles and Kowalski almost come to blows. The rookie catcher accuses Kowalski of subterfuge but seems helpless to take any action against the star pitcher.

Kowalski and Noles's squabbling and near fisticuffs continue for the next 23 games, during which time Noles, battling a slump deeper than even his own secret, becomes uncommunicative with his wife. To patch things up, she and he spend an evening dancing at a local club where they are soon met by a drunken Kowalski.

After a not-too-subtle attempt to walk away with Noles's wife, Kowalski spills the beans. According to Big Ed, Windy Noles was once a major league pitcher named Johnny Narron. One day while pitching batting practice, Noles—Narron—threw a wild pitch that killed Kowalski's brother, whom Narron—Noles—disliked as in-

tensely as Kowalski himself. "You killed him on purpose," Kowalski snarls at Johnny-Windy.

"I was just a wild southpaw who had a fastball like lightning!" disclaims Windy-Johnny. "Sure, I hated your brother. He was a loud-mouthed jerk like you. But I didn't kill him on purpose!"

The "secret too deep to tell" had been revealed. Shaken by the ordeal of having killed a man with a thrown pitch, Johnny Narron changed his identity and his uniform and transformed himself from a lithesomely built left-handed major league pitcher to a power-hitting, barrel-chested minor league catcher. For the next two years, despite being possibly the only left-handed throwing catcher in all of organized baseball, Noles manages to avoid arousing any suspicion concerning his remarkable resemblance to the missing and still-at-large Johnny Narron.

The next day Noles and Kowalski, with the pennant on the line, cast their differences aside. Nine tension-packed innings pass before Kowalski uncorks a wild pitch, hitting a batter squarely —but not lethally—on the head. Unnerved by the experience, Kowalski delivers a gopher ball on the next pitch and loses the crucial game for the New York Gulls.

In the runway after the game, Kowalski offers Noles his hand. "I know now it was an accident," says Big Ed, sheepishly, to his catcher. "I wasn't sure myself," replies Noles, "until I saw it today."

Perhaps still confused by his identity, his guiltlessness, and even which arm he throws with, Noles enters a clubhouse in which a happy, whooping, boisterous group of players are celebrating as if they'd won the pennant. Evidently Windy has just decided to change the team he plays for. ◆

SADE THINKS BASEBALL IS JUST A GAME, 1938
(Vic and Sade)
NBC, 15 minutes
Written by Paul Rhymer
Cast: Arthur Van Harvey as Vic, Bernadine Flynn as Sade, and William Idelson as Rush
Published in *Vic and Sade: The Best Radio Plays by Paul Rhymer*, edited by Mary Frances Rhymer. New York: Seabury Press, 1976

Two grown men argue childishly about baseball.

SAMMY SAUNDERS, BALLPLAYER, c. 1948
(Boston Blackie)
Syndicated, 30 minutes, episode 107
Cast: Richard Kollmar as Blackie, and Maurice Tarplin as Inspector Faraday
Guest: Bill Slater as the announcer

Gullible baseball player is manipulated by a female racketeer.

THE STRATTON STORY, 1950
(The Lux Radio Theatre)
CBS, 60 minutes, February 13, 1950
Based on the motion picture
Cast: James Stewart as Monty Stratton, and June Allyson as Ethel
See also: Baseball in Film

TAKE ME OUT TO THE BALL GAME, 1942
(Fibber McGee and Molly)
NBC, 30 minutes, April 21, 1942
Written by Don Quinn
Cast: Jim Jordan as Fibber, and Marian Jordan as Molly

McGee decides that the only way he and Molly can attend the sold-out opening game of the season is if he throws the ceremonial first pitch.

TAKE ME OUT TO THE BALL GAME, 1951
(The Red Skelton Show)

CBS, 30 minutes, June 3, 1951
Cast: Red Skelton, Rod O'Connor, and Lurene Tuttle

Boozy baseball player has a perfect explanation for his hitting heroics—the "hit the sign and win a free keg of beer" sign on the outfield fence.

THREE STRIKES, YOU'RE OUT, 1940
(The Columbia Workshop)
CBS, 30 minutes, April 18, 1940

THREE STRIKES, YOU'RE OUT!, 1949
(The Skippy Hollywood Theatre)
Syndicated, 30 minutes, episode 85
Directed by Les Mitchel
Cast: Barry Sullivan as Rube Walton, Al Garry as Monty Martin, Barbara Fuller as Sally, and Paul Conrad as Tony

Club owner's daughter falls in love with a superstitious pitcher.

TROUBLE IN THE RANKS, c. 1955
(Big Jon and Sparkie)
ABC, 15 minutes
Cast: Jon Arthur as Big Jon

First in a series of eight consecutive episodes in which Sparkie's friend, Ukey the cab driver, pitches the opening-day game for the Cincinnati Reds. Titles of subsequent episodes: "Sparkie's Telephone Troubles"; "A Proposed Solution to a Serious Problem"; "Twelve Down, Two to Go"; "Not Much Doing"; "The Pane in Mrs. Tuhill's Window"; "Tickets, Tickets, Who's Got the Tickets?"; "Opening Day, 1953."

WILD PITCH, 1950
(High Adventure)
NBC, 30 minutes, May 7, 1950
Cast: Jack Orrison as Windy Noles, Joyce Gordon, Maurice Tarplin, Jim Bowes, and Don Douglas

A pitcher changes his identity and converts to a catcher after hitting a batter with a thrown ball.

WORLD SERIES, 1958
(NBC Monitor)
NBC, 25 minutes, in five parts
October 1958: 5 minutes each
Cast: Jim Jordan as Fibber McGee, and Marian Jordan as Molly

Five "Fibber McGee and Molly" vignettes include: "Free Tickets"; "To Milwaukee by Train"; "Invitation to Dine"; "Outcome, Predictions"; "Wrong Tickets."

THE WORLD SERIES CAPER, 1973
(Dameron)
Syndicated, 30 minutes, episode 47
Written and produced by Jim French
Cast: Robert E. Lee Hardwicke as Dameron, and Sam Henry as B. B. Calendar

Private eye Dameron investigates a threat against star pitcher B. B. Calendar's life during the World Series.

YOU COULD LOOK IT UP, 1949
(Hallmark Playhouse)
CBS, 30 minutes, May 12, 1949
Based on the story by James Thurber, published in the *Saturday Evening Post*, April 5, 1941
Written by George Corey
Cast: William Frawley and Jerry Austin
See also: Baseball in Television

YOU COULD LOOK IT UP, c. 1951
(NBC Presents: Short Story)
NBC, 30 minutes
Based on the story by James Thurber

YOU COULD LOOK IT UP, 1957
(The CBS Radio Workshop)
CBS, 30 minutes, July 7, 1957
Based on the story by James Thurber
Written by Dee Engelbach
Cast: Ralph Bell, Sarah Fussell, Larry Haines, Joe Julian, and David Kerman

Baseball in Documentary and Miscellaneous Radio

This section contains a listing of selected historical, documentary, and miscellaneous radio programs relating to baseball. Included in the catalog are early appearances and interviews of baseball players, audio histories of baseball and baseball clubs, audio biographies of baseball players, and unclassified miscellaneous radio programs of historical significance.

Not included in the catalog are actual or recreated broadcasts of baseball games, or highlights of same.

For *Explanatory Notes* to this section, *see:* Baseball in Radio.

ALL-TIME, ALL-STAR BASEBALL TEAM, 1953
(American Cancer Society's Cancer Crusade)
Public Service Program, 15 minutes
Host: Joe Bolton
Guests: Joe E. Brown, Samuel S. Liebowitz, Harry Grayson, and Red Smith

Panel discussion of the greatest baseball players of all time.

BABE RUTH TRIBUTE, 1948
Mutual, 30 minutes, August 17, 1948

Eulogies by baseball officials and players, broadcast the day after Ruth's death.

THE BACK HOME HOUR, 1929
CBS, 60 minutes, weekly series
Features Billy Sunday

Sunday is the former major leaguer turned evangelist.

BASEBALL: HOW IT BECAME OUR GREAT NATIONAL GAME
WNYC-New York, 30 minutes
Host: Virginia Mathews
Rodgers and Hammerstein Archives, Performing Arts Research Center at Lincoln Center, New York

Interview with Dr. Robert S. Holzman.

BASEBALL ROUNDTABLE, 1956
(American Cancer Society's Cancer Crusade)
Public Service Program, 15 minutes
Announcer: Mort Lawrence

Guests: Jerry Coleman, Red Smith, Don Dunphy, and Phil Foster

Panel discussion in which strange plays in baseball are described.

BASEBALL, USA, 1954
(Milestones)
Syndicated, 30 minutes, June 12, 1954

Dramatization of the Baseball Centennial on June 12, 1939.

BOBBY BRAGAN SPORTS BRIEF, 1967
Spot Productions
Syndicated, one minute, regular series

Anecdotes and opinions by the former catcher and manager.

BROADCAST OF MARCH 19, 1930
(The Coca-Cola Top Notchers)
NBC, 30 minutes, March 19, 1930
Hosts: Graham McNamee and Grantland Rice
Features Leonard Joy's All-String Orchestra
Guest: Ty Cobb

In this premiere show, Grantland Rice interviews Ty Cobb, who reveals his greatest thrill, conditioning secrets, and the best hitter and pitcher he ever saw.

BROADCAST OF OCTOBER 10, 1935
(The Fleischmann Hour)
NBC, 60 minutes, October 10, 1935
Cast: Rudy Valle
Museum of Broadcasting, New York

Includes a guest appearance by Detroit Tigers' outfielder Goose Goslin.

BROADCAST OF SEPTEMBER 17, 1936
(The Kate Smith Show)
CBS, 60 minutes, September 17, 1936
Guest: Babe Ruth

First in a regular series of appearances for Ruth.

BROADCAST OF FEBRUARY 21, 1938
(For Men Only)
NBC, 30 minutes, February 21, 1938

Actress Tallulah Bankhead talks baseball with two members of the New York Yankees.

BROADCAST OF MARCH 3, 1938
(We, the People)
CBS, 30 minutes, March 3, 1938
Host: Gabriel Heatter
Guest: Daniel M. Casey

Former major leaguer Dan Casey claims to have been the inspiration for Casey at the Bat.

BROADCAST OF MARCH 24, 1938
(Good News of 1938)
NBC, 60 minutes, March 24, 1938
Host: Frank Morgan

Includes a guest appearance by Chicago Cubs' catcher and manager Gabby Hartnett.

BROADCAST OF AUGUST 20, 1939
(The People's Platform)
CBS, 30 minutes, August 20, 1939

Host: Lyman Bryson
Guests: Tallulah Bankhead, Ford Frick, Bill Corum, and Ed Ferguson

Baseball is the subject of discussion.

BROADCAST OF NOVEMBER 21, 1939
(Information Please)
NBC, 30 minutes, November 21, 1939
Guest: Moe Berg
Library of Congress number: LWO 17590 R354 A3-4

Quiz show in which the erudite Berg, a catcher for the Boston Red Sox, is a panelist.

BROADCAST OF AUGUST 8, 1941
(Information Please)
NBC, 30 minutes, August 8, 1941
Host: Clifton Fadiman
Panei: John Kiernan, Oscar Levant, and Franklin P. Adams
Guest: Larry McPhail

Baseball is the primary quiz subject.

BROADCAST OF FEBRUARY 4, 1942
(The Texaco Star Theatre)
CBS, 60 minutes, February 4, 1942
Cast: Fred Allen
National Baseball Hall of Fame and Museum, Cooperstown, New York

Segment: Tribute by Mrs. Lou Gehrig to baseball players in the armed services.

BROADCAST OF NOVEMBER 14, 1946
(Meet the Family)
ABC, 30 minutes, November 14, 1946
Host: Tom Breneman

Brooklyn Dodger outfielder Babe Herman and his family are interviewed.

BROADCAST OF JANUARY 26, 1947
(We, the People)

CBS, 30 minutes, January 26, 1947

Segment: Hank Greenberg, recently sold to the Pittsburgh Pirates, denies having wanted to leave the Detroit Tigers.

BROADCAST OF JULY 8, 1947
(Roundup of Sports)
ABC, 15 minutes, July 8, 1947
Announcer: Joe Hassel

Segment: Interview with sportswriter Arch Ward, founder of the All-Star Game.

BROADCAST OF AUGUST 17, 1948
(We, the People)
CBS, 30 minutes, August 17, 1948
Guests: Benny Bengough and Mrs. Lou Gehrig
National Baseball Hall of Fame and Museum, Cooperstown, New York

Tribute to Babe Ruth, broadcast the day after his death.

BROADCAST OF APRIL 17, 1949
(The Tex and Jinx Show)
NBC, 30 minutes, April 17, 1949
National Baseball Hall of Fame and Museum, Cooperstown, New York

Interview with Mrs. Lou Gehrig.

BROADCAST OF FEBRUARY 4, 1951
(The Big Show)
NBC, 90 minutes, February 4, 1951
Host: Tallulah Bankhead
Guests: Laraine Day and Leo Durocher

Segment: Laraine tells Tallulah what it is like being married to a baseball manager.

BROADCAST OF APRIL 15, 1951
(The Big Show)
NBC, 90 minutes, April 15, 1951
Host: Tallulah Bankhead
Guests: Phil Foster and Tommy Henrich

BROADCAST OF SEPTEMBER 30, 1954
(Bill Stern Sports)
ABC, 15 minutes, September 30, 1954
Guests: Tris Speaker and Frankie Frisch

Analysis of game two of the 1954 World Series by Speaker and Frisch. Includes postgame interviews with Johnny Antonelli, Jim Hearn, Paul Giel, Freddie Fitzsimmons, Jimmy Piersall, and Red Smith.

BROADCAST OF MARCH 20, 1960
(Campus Press Conference)
WNYC-New York, 30 minutes, March 20, 1960
Rodgers and Hammerstein Archives, Performing Arts Research Center at Lincoln Center, New York

Hall of Famer Jackie Robinson is interviewed.

CAN BASEBALL BE MADE AN EVEN BETTER GAME?, 1952
(American Cancer Society's Cancer Crusade)
Public Service Program, 15 minutes
Host: Bill Rogers
Guests: Jimmy Cannon, "Senator" Ed Ford, Dolly Stark, and Sid Gordon

The lively ball, official scorers, and curfew rules are discussed.

THE COLGATE SPORTS NEWSREEL, 1939
NBC, 15 minutes, weekly series
Broadcast history: October 8, 1939 to June 29, 1951
Host: Bill Stern

Features baseball and other sports stories and biographies, "some legend, some hearsay, but all so interesting we'd like to pass them along to you."

THE DIZZY DEAN SHOW, 1948
NBC, 15 minutes, weekly series
Broadcast history: July 3, 1948 to September 18, 1948

RADIO FIRSTS

Radio's long, colorful, and often folkloric link to baseball dates back to even before the wireless was manufactured for household use. In 1916, four years before radios were commercially produced, the man who was later to become the chairman of the board of the Radio Corporation of America (RCA), David Sarnoff, suggested that among the advantages of the new device might be to transmit baseball scores over the air. His foresight was demonstrated eleven years later when, on Opening Day 1924, the scores of baseball games were announced on radio station KDKA, Pittsburgh. The following are some notable dates in baseball radio history:

Opening Day, 1921: *First baseball news broadcast*—Results of major league games were announced three times each evening—beginning Opening Day, 1921—on station KDKA, Pittsburgh.

August 5, 1921: *First play-by-play broadcast of a major league game*—Phillies at Pittsburgh, on KDKA. Sitting inside the screen behind home plate, Harold Arlin called the game in which the Pirates, with a three-run rally in the bottom of the eighth, defeated the Phillies, 8–5.

August 5, 1921: *First home run described on radio*—In the first game ever broadcast, Phillies outfielder Cy Williams drove the Pirates starting pitcher, Hal Carlson, to the showers with a home run in the fourth inning. The game was eventually won by the Pirates, 8–5, with reliever Jimmy Zinn gaining the victory.

October 5, 1921: *First World Series radio broadcast*—New York Yankees vs. New York Giants. Game One of the 1921 World Series was announced live by famed sportswriter Grantland Rice on station KDKA, Pittsburgh. At the same time, Tommy Cowan broadcast an in-studio re-creation of the game on station WJZ, Newark, New Jersey, from details telephoned to him from a newspaper reporter situated in the press box at the Polo Grounds. Although the Yankees—in their first ever World Series—won the game, 3–0, the home-town rival Giants won the Series, five games to three in the best-of-nine championship.

April 23, 1924: *First regular play-by-play broadcasts of home games*—Chicago Cubs from Wrigley Field, on WMAQ, with announcer Hal Totten. Unlike other major league club owners, Cubs president William Wrigley encouraged radio broadcasts of home games, believing that play-by-play descriptions would promote fan interest in the team and increase attendance at the ballpark. For several seasons during the 1920s, as many as five Chicago radio stations carried Cubs home games.

Opening Day, 1932: *First former athlete to become a broadcaster*—Ex–major leaguer Jack Graney began broadcasting Cleveland Indians games on station WHK in 1932, ten years after he had retired as the Indians' left fielder. He continued calling play-by-play through the 1954 season. Graney was a far greater success in the announcer's booth than he was on the baseball diamond: He finished his 14-year career as the Indians' leadoff hitter with a lifetime batting average of .250.

Ol' Diz tells stories, gives tips to children, and forecasts the week's events in the world of baseball.

DON DRYSDALE'S BULLPEN, 1975
Public Service Program, 5 minutes, daily series

Drysdale relates humorous and inspirational stories from the world of baseball.

DOUBLE PLAY, 1953
Syndicated, 15 minutes, regular series
Hosts: Leo Durocher and Laraine Day
See also: Baseball in Documentary and Miscellaneous Television

Features interviews with baseball personalities.

THE GOLDEN AGE OF SPORTS, 1944
Mutual, 90 minutes, January 29, 1944
Guests: Red Barber, Connie Desmond, Harry Hershfield, Babe Ruth, and Frankie Frisch

Segment: Red Barber re-creates Ruth's "called home run."

Cleveland Indians outfielder Jack Graney was the first former athlete to become a play-by-play radio broadcaster. (National Baseball Library.)

THE GREAT AMERICAN PASTIME, c. 1972

(Kaleidoscope)
WJR-Detroit, 60 minutes
Narrated by Mike Whorf
G. Robert Vincent Voice Library,
Michigan State University

Audio history of baseball.

HERE'S BABE RUTH, 1943

NBC, 15 minutes, weekly series
Broadcast premiere: June 5, 1943
Host: Ben Grauer
Museum of Broadcasting, New York

Babe Ruth answers questions from children on how to play better baseball.

HIT THAT BALL, 1939

Mutual, 30 minutes, weekly series
Hosts: Tom Slater and Stan Lomax

Baseball players and sportswriters vie in a baseball trivia quiz contest.

THE JACKIE ROBINSON SHOW, 1950

ABC, regular series

Features opinions and insights by the Brooklyn Dodgers' star second baseman.

THE JOE DIMAGGIO SHOW, 1949

CBS, 30 minutes, weekly series
Directed by Dan Enright
Host: Jack Barry
Cast: Joe DiMaggio, Adelaide Klein, Leon Janney, Charles Irving, Jackson Beck, and Ted Brown

DiMaggio conducts a sports quiz, answers questions from the audience, and presents sketches from the lives of famous athletes.

LASORDA AT LARGE, 1985

Mutual, regular series
Host: Tom Lasorda

Radio commentary by the Los Angeles Dodgers' manager.

LEO DUROCHER: SPORTS QUESTION BOX, 1946

ABC, 15 minutes, weekly series

Durocher offers opinions and answers questions on the world of sports.

THE MAN IN THE IRON MASK, c. 1971

(Kaleidoscope)
WJR-Detroit, 60 minutes
Narrated by Mike Whorf
G. Robert Vincent Voice Library,
Michigan State University

Detroit Tigers' catcher Bill Freehan is queried about the life of a baseball player on and off the field.

MEMORIAL FOR COL. JACOB RUPPERT, 1939

Mutual, 30 minutes, January 15, 1939
Library of Congress number: Tape 12365

Eulogies by baseball officials and players,

including Babe Ruth, in tribute to the New York Yankees' owner.

A MOMENT IN SPORTS WITH DON NEWCOMBE, c. 1975

Public Service Program, 5 minutes, regular series

Former pitcher Don Newcombe interviews stars from the world of sports.

NBC BASEBALL ROUND-UP, 1937

NBC, 30 minutes, April 19, 1937
Host: Ford Bond
Guests: Jimmy Dykes, Rogers Hornsby, Frankie Frisch. Joe McCarthy, Jimmie Wilson, and Bill McKechnie
Museum of Broadcasting, New York

Panel discussion about baseball.

NOW BATTING FOR THE NEW YORK YANKEES, c. 1968

(Kaleidoscope)
WJR-Detroit, 60 minutes
Narrated by Mike Whorf
G. Robert Vincent Voice Library,
Michigan State University

Audio biography of Babe Ruth.

PLAY BALL: THE STORY OF PEE WEE REESE, 1948

CBS, 60 minutes, April 17, 1948
Guests: Red Barber, Branch Rickey, Leo Durocher, Babe Ruth, Honus Wagner, Clark Griffith, Rogers Hornsby, Harry Heilmann, and Pee Wee Reese

The reminiscences of family, friends, and baseball colleagues provide an audio biography of Brooklyn Dodgers' shortstop Pee Wee Reese.

QUIZZER BASEBALL, 1941

NBC, 30 minutes, weekly series
Host: Harry Von Zell
Team Captains: Glenda Farrell and Budd Hulick

Museum of Broadcasting, New York

Two three-member teams compete in a quiz show patterned on the game of baseball.

THIS GAME OF BASEBALL, 1953
CBS, 60 minutes, September 25, 1953
Narrated by Bing Crosby

Behind-the-scenes look at the duties and positions of various baseball personnel, on and off the field. Includes interviews with Mickey Mantle, Yogi Berra, Pee Wee Reese, Gil Hodges, Stan Musial, Phil Rizzuto, Warren Spahn, and others.

TRIBUTE TO LOU GEHRIG, 1941
NBC, 15 minutes, June 3, 1941
Announcer: Ty Tyson
Museum of Broadcasting, New York

Eulogies by baseball players and officials broadcast the day after Gehrig's death.

THE VOICES OF SUMMER, 1986
(Newsmark)
CBS, 30 minutes, May 23, 1986
Narrated by Ron Powers

Documentary appreciation of baseball radio broadcasting as an American folk art.

WELCOME BACK BASEBALL, 1950
CBS, 30 minutes, April 1950
Cast: Bing Crosby, Bob Hope, Dorothy Lamour, and Ralph Kiner

Gags and repartee saluting the opening of the baseball season. Includes song, "Take Me Out to the Ball Game" by Bing Crosby.

WORLD SERIES COMMENTARY, 1941
NBC, 15 minutes, limited series
Broadcast history: October 1, 1941 to October 6, 1941
Hosts: Paul Douglas and Frankie Frisch
Museum of Broadcasting, New York

Game-by-game analysis of the 1941 World Series.

WORLD'S FAIR SPORTS SCHOOL, 1939
NBC, 15 minutes, weekly series
Announcer: Bill Stern
Host: Christy Walsh
Museum of Broadcasting, New York

Children ask questions of baseball and other sports stars.

Chapter

9

Baseball in Theater

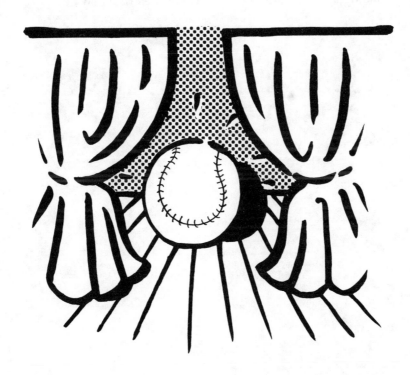

This section contains a comprehensive listing of baseball-related dramatic, comic, and musical plays produced for the legitimate stage. Included in the catalog are early baseball comedies, Broadway musicals, full-length operas and cantatas, plays dramatizing the lives of baseball players and events from baseball's past, and allegorical dramas in which baseball serves as a metaphor for the human condition.

For baseball-related skits, children's plays, and plays intended for the school or amateur stage, *see:* Baseball in Miscellaneous Plays and Sketches.

Scripts, musical scores, photographs, stage and costume designs, and, in a few instances, audio and video recordings of plays contained in this catalog can be located at the Billy Rose Theater Collection in the Performing Arts Research Center at Lincoln Center in New York. Additionally, the Schubert Archive in New York and the Museum of the City of New York house significant collections relating to theater in America.

A number of baseball-related plays are available in published form through Samuel French, Inc., the Dramatists Play Service, Inc., and various other publishers of theatrical plays.

EXPLANATORY NOTES

1. Title of the play, year of play's premiere.

2. Type of play, number of acts, author of play.

3. Premiere: Theater in which the play premiered, premiere date, number of performances in parentheses.

4. Production company.

5. Director of play.

6. Cast of play.

7. Publisher of play, year of publication if different than the year of premiere.

8. Annotation. Description of the play.

AIN'T LOOKIN' (CHAPPIE'S COLORED ALL STARS), 1980
Play by John Craig and George Luscombe
Based on the novel *Chappie and Me* by John Craig
Premiere: Toronto Workshop Productions Theatre, Toronto, Canada, May 29, 1980
Directed by George Luscombe
Cast: Ed Smith as Chappie Johnson, Rudy Webb as Sweetcorn Jackson, Anthony Sherwood as Cotton Nash, Leroy Gallier as Malachi Brown, Doug Johnston as Latimore Lee, and Paul Hubbard as Joe Giffen
See also: Chappie and Me (Baseball in Fiction)

ALL SHE CARES ABOUT IS THE YANKEES, 1984
Play in one act by John Ford Noonan
Premiere: American Kaleidoscope/West Side YMCA, New York, February 3, 1984
Cast: Jacqueline Knapp as Spanky

An agoraphobiac has an obsessive interest in baseball.

THE AMAZIN' CASEY STENGEL OR CAN'T ANYBODY HERE SPEAK THIS GAME?, 1981

Play in two acts by Michael Zettler and Shelly Altman
Premiere: American Place Theatre, New York, April 21, 1981 to May 3, 1981 (13 performances)
Directed by Stephen Zuckerman
Cast: Paul Dooley as Casey Stengel

"You ain't seen ball...like we play ball" sing members of The Dream Team, *the 1985 musical play produced at Goodspeed-at-Chester/Norma Terris Theatre in Connecticut. Pictured left to right: Teddey Brown, Edwin Battle, James Stovall, and Harry L. Burney III. (Goodspeed-at-Chester/Norma Terris Theatre, 1985. Photo: Diane Sobolewski.)*

One-character show dramatizing the life and philosophy of Casey Stengel.

AMERICAN HEROES, 1980
Musical play
Book by Michael Johnson, music and lyrics by Barry Mason, Michael Johnson, and Don Gould
Premiere: London, England

Outfielder Destiny Jones drops a fly ball during the final inning of the World Series and imagines he's been condemned to hell.

THE BABE, 1984
Play in three scenes by Bob and Ann Acosta
Premiere: Princess Theatre, New York, May 17, 1984
Corniche Productions, Ltd.
Directed by Noam Pitlik
Cast: Max Gail as Babe Ruth
See also: Baseball in Television

One-character show dramatizing the life of Babe Ruth.

BASEBALL PLAY, 1980
Play in one act by Steven Metcalfe
Premiere: Quaigh Lunchtime Theatre, New York, March 24, 1980
Directed by Jim Arnemann

BASEBALL WIVES, 1982
Comedy in two acts by Grubb Graebner
Premiere: American Renaissance Theatre, New York, May 6, 1982; The Harold Clurman Theatre, New York, September 29, 1982 to November 7, 1982 (45 performances)
Cast: Lynn Goodwin as Becky, Marcella Lowery as Janelle, and Carol Teitel as Doris

Wives of ballplayers cheer their husbands—and observe life—from the stands.

BINGO!, 1985
Musical play
Book by Ossie Davis and Hy Gilbert

Music by George Fischoff, lyrics by Hy Gilbert
Based on the novel, *The Bingo Long Traveling All-Stars and Motor Kings* by William Brashler
Premiere: AMAS Repertory Theatre, New York, October 24, 1985 to November 17, 1985
Directed by Ossie Davis
Cast: Norman Matlock as Bingo Long, David Winston Barge as Country Joe Calloway, James Randolph as Leon Price, John R. McCurry as "Pops" Foster, and Jackie Patterson as Louis Keystone
See also: The Bingo Long Traveling All-Stars and Motor Kings (Baseball in Film; Baseball in Fiction)

Includes: "Wheels Keep Turnin' "; "All in the Timin' "; Leon's Soliloquy" ("Get While the Gettin's Good"); "Gotta Give 'em a Show"; "We're a Team"; "The Bingo Long Traveling All-Stars and Motor Kings," (See: Baseball in Music and Song).

BLEACHER BUMS, 1977
A Nine-Inning Comedy conceived by Joe Mantegna
Written by Roberta Custer, Richard Fire, Dennis Franz, Joe Mantegna, Josephine Paoletti, Carolyn Purdy-Gordon, Michael Saad, Keith Szarabajka, and Ian Williams, under the direction of Stuart Gordon, with additional dialogue by Dennis Paoli
Premiere: Leo A. Lerner Theatre, Chicago, August 2, 1977
Published by Samuel French, Inc., New York.
See also: Baseball in Television

Life and baseball as seen by long-suffering Chicago Cubs' fans.

BOTTOM OF THE FOURTH, 1984
Play in one act by David M. Mead
Premiere: The New York Actors' Ensemble: Courtyard Playhouse,

New York, February 24, 1984
Cast: Joseph Callari, Jaye Moyer, Gordon W. Brown, Dayton Callie, Jaye Stewart, Rand Williams, and Blair Goold

Aging pitcher for the Boston Red Sox faces the biggest game of his career.

BOTTOM OF THE NINTH, 1982
Play in one act by Victor L. Cahn
Premiere: Perry Street Theatre, New York, January 20, 1982
Cast: Lou Miranda as Henry, and Emmett O'Sullivan-Moore as Frank

Two fans watch a spring training game in Florida.

BROOKLYN BASEBALL CANTATA, 1942
Comic operetta in one scene
Music by George Kleinsinger, lyrics by Michael Stratton
Premiere: Segment of "Of V We Sing": Concert Theatre, New York, February 11, 1942 to April 25, 1942 (76 performances)
See also: Baseball in Radio; Baseball in Music and Song—Recorded

The eternally optimistic Brooklyn Dodgers fans must wait yet another year.

BROTHER RAT, 1936
Comedy in three acts by John Monks, Jr. and Fred R. Finklehoffe
Premiere: Biltmore Theatre, New York, December 16, 1936 (577 performances)
Staged and produced by George Abbott
Cast: Wyn Cahoon as Joyce Winfree, Eddie Albert as Bing Edwards, Frank Albertson as Billy Randolph, José Ferrer as Dan Crawford, and Richard Clark as Harley Harrington
Published by Random House, Inc., New York, 1937
See also: Baseball in Film

Misadventures of a star baseball pitcher in a military school.

BULLPEN, 1984

Comedy in two acts by Steve Kluger
Premiere: Theatre/Theatre, Hollywood, California, July 4, 1984
Directed by Jeff Murray
Cast: James Purcell as Boomer, Gregg Henry as Ripper, Buddy Farmer as Moose, Wayne Kruse as Tank, Vinnie Guastaferro as Frito, and Lionel Mark Smith as Duke

The macho world of baseball is caricatured.

BUY ME SOME PEANUTS AND CRACKERJACK, 1979

Comedy in two acts by Dan Gurskis
Premiere: Merrick Theatre, Spingold Complex, Brandeis University, March 28, 1979 (five performances)
Directed by Brock Putnam
Cast: Steve Hofvendahl as Stan Helinski, David Fox as Whitely Shaughnessy, Steven Culp as Hillbilly Badilli, Hershell Norwood as Boom-Boom Baker, and Paul Mroczka as Mule Zuber

Misadventures of the Lackawanna Mud Hens baseball team.

CASEY AT THE BAT: A BASEBALL CANTATA, 1976

Cantata version of the opera, *The Mighty Casey*
Music by William Schuman, lyrics by Jeremy Gury
Premiere: April 6, 1976, by the National Symphony Orchestra and the Westminster Choir, under the direction of Antal Dorati
Published by Associated Music Publishers, Inc., New York
See also: The Mighty Casey

DAMN YANKEES, 1955

Musical comedy in two acts

Book by George Abbott and Douglass Wallop
Music and lyrics by Richard Adler and Jerry Ross
Based on the novel, *The Year the Yankees Lost the Pennant* by Douglass Wallop
Premiere: Forty-Sixth Street Theatre, New York, May 5, 1955 to October 12, 1957 (1,019 performances)
Directed by George Abbott
Cast: Stephen Douglass as Joe Hardy, Gwen Verdon as Lola, Ray Walston as Applegate, Shannon Bolin as Meg, Russ Brown as Van Buren, and Jimmie Komack as Rocky
Published by Random House, Inc., New York
See also: Baseball in Film; Baseball in Television; Baseball in Music and Song—Recorded

Includes: "The American League." (See: Baseball in Music and Song.) "Six Months Out of Every Year"; "The Game"; "Heart." (See: Baseball in Music and Song—Recorded.)

DIAMONDS, 1984

Musical revue in two acts
Book by Ralph G. Allen, Roy Blount, Jr., Richard Camp, Jerry L. Crawford, Sean Kelly, John Lahr, Harry Stein, John Weidman, and others
Music by Cy Coleman, Larry Grossman, John Kander, Doug Katsaros, Alan Menken, Jonathan Sheffer, Lynn Udall, and others
Lyrics by Gerard Alessandrini, Howard Ashman, Craig Carnelia, Betty Comden, Fred Ebb, Ellen Fitzhugh, Adolph Green, Karl Kenneth, Jim Wann, David Zippel, and others
Premiere: Circle in the Square Theatre (Downtown), New York, December 16, 1984
Directed by Harold Prince
Cast: Loni Ackerman, Susan Bigelow, Jackee Harry, Scott Holmes, Dick

Latessa, Larry Riley, Nestor Serrano, and Chip Zien

Includes: "Winter in New York"; "In the Cards"; "Vendors" (1–3); "Favorite Sons"; "What You'd Call a Dream"; "God Threw Out the First Ball"; "Hundreds of Hats"; "1919"; "Let's Play Ball"; "Song for a Hunter College Graduate"; "The Boys of Summer"; "Stay in Your Own Back Yard"; "Ka-razy"; "Diamonds Are Forever." (See: Baseball in Music and Song.)

THE DREAM TEAM, 1985

Musical play in two acts
Book by Richard Wesley
Music by Thomas Tierney, lyrics by John Forster
Premiere: Goodspeed-at-Chester: Norma Terris Theatre, Chester, Connecticut, April 23, 1985 to May 26, 1985
Directed and choreographed by Dan Siretta
Cast: Larry Riley as Luke Davenport, James McDaniel as Cal Davenport, Melodee Savage as Willa Taylor, S. Epatha Merkerson as Ruth McKinney, Harry L. Burney III as Slugfest Fontaine, Stanley Wayne Mathis as Choo Choo Brown, and Reginald VelJohnson as Abe Green

A black player in the late 1940s is signed by a major league club while his overage brother remains in the Negro Leagues. Includes: "Cloud of Joy"; "On the Road with the Roadrunners"; "Doncha Feel Proud?"; "Hey Star"; "A Whole New Ballgame"; "Dream Team"; "You Ain't Seen Ball"; "The Wonderful Game." (See: Baseball in Music and Song.)

ELMER THE GREAT, 1928

Comedy in three acts by Ring W. Lardner
Premiere: Lyceum Theatre, New York, September 24, 1928 (40 performances)
Produced by George M. Cohan
Staged by Sam Forrest
Cast: Walter Huston as Elmer Kane, Lida MacMillan as Mrs. Kane,

A member of a late-1940s all-black team is signed to a major league contract while his overage brother remains in the Negro Leagues in the musical play, The Dream Team. *(Goodspeed-at-Chester/Norma Terris Theatre, 1985. Photo: Diane Sobolewski.)*

Thomas V. Gillen as Nick, Mark Sullivan as Ben Beeson, and Tom Blake as Bull Wade
See also: Baseball in Film; Baseball in Radio. *See:* Hurry Kane *(Baseball in Radio)*

Gullible braggart becomes involved with gamblers.

FENCES, 1987
Play in two acts by August Wilson
Premiere: Forty-Sixth Street Theatre, New York, March 26, 1987
Directed by Lloyd Richards
Cast: James Earl Jones as Troy Maxson, Courtney B. Vance as Cory Maxson, Mary Alice as Rose Maxson, Ray Aranha as Jim Bono, Charles Brown as Lyons, and Frankie R. Falson as Gabriel

Pulitzer Prize-winning play dramatizing the struggle and conflicts between an embittered former Negro League star and his son, a promising football player, during the late 1950s.

THE FIRST, 1981
Musical play in two acts
Book by Joel Siegel, with Martin Charnin
Music by Bob Brush, lyrics by Martin Charnin
Premiere: The Martin Beck Theatre, New York, November 17, 1981 to December 12, 1981 (37 performances)
Directed by Martin Charnin
Cast: David Alan Grier as Jackie Robinson, Lonette McKee as Rachel Isum, David Huddleston as Branch Rickey, Trey Wilson as Leo Durocher, Bob Morrisey as Pee Wee Reese, Ray

Gill as Clyde Sukeforth, and Court Miller as Casey Higgins
Published by Samuel French, Inc., New York

Dramatization of Jackie Robinson's first year in the major leagues. Includes: "Jack Roosevelt Robinson"; "The National Pastime"; "The First"; "Bloat"; "It Ain't Gonna Work"; "The Brooklyn Dodger Strike"; "You Do-Do-Do It Good"; "Is This Year Next Year?"; "The Opera Ain't Over." (See: Baseball in Music and Song.)

THE FLATBUSH FAITHFUL, 1985
Play in three acts
Written and directed by Gene Nye
Premiere: Judith Anderson Theatre, New York, September 9, 1985
Produced by the Lion Theatre Company
Cast: Christopher McCann as Michael Brooks, Michael Guido as Vito Maggio, Jim Ricketts as Charlie Brewster, and Alvin Alexis as Willie Allen

The lives and destinies of four Brooklyn Dodger fans are revealed through a shared devotion to the team.

THE GIRL AND THE PENNANT, 1913
Comedy in four acts by Rida Johnson Young and Christy Mathewson
Premiere: Lyric Theatre, New York, October 23, 1913 (20 performances)
Cast: Florence Reed as Mona Fitzgerald, William Courtenay as Copley Reeves, William Roselle as Skeets Marvin, Calvin Thomas as Punch Reeves, Wallace Owen as Pitman, Tully Marshall as John Bohannan, and Malcolm Williams as Henry Welland
Published by Rosenfield, New York

Woman owner and her designing manager vie for financial control of the Eagles baseball club.

A MOMENTOUS MEETING

The story, though it has been told many times, not only bears repeating but warrants a lasting commemoration. The year is 1945. Jackie Robinson is seated in Dodger president Branch Rickey's office. A great athlete and a proud man is about to be asked to break baseball's color line. Here is the scene as played in the Broadway musical *The First:*

JACKIE: Mr. Rickey, all I want is to be treated fairly.
RICKEY: Judas Priest, son, you will *not* be treated fairly. *[He crosses to Jackie.]* You will be cursed. Your color will be cursed. Your family will be cursed. That vicious epithet, "nigger," will seem a veritable compliment. And if you are to break the color line and play in the major leagues, you must accept it all and accept it silently.
JACKIE: Mr. Rickey, are you looking for a black man who's afraid to fight back?
RICKEY: I'm looking for a ballplayer with guts enough *not* to fight back. For to fight, Robinson, is to lose. We are no army, we have few allies. The other owners? They will deny it, after the meeting they burnt their records in shame, but the vote was 15 to 1 against having Negroes in organized baseball. The players? 60 percent of all major league ballplayers were born in the South. Perfect fodder

for the bigots and hate-mongers who want to see you fail. And you cannot fail.
JACKIE: Mr. Rickey, do you realize what you're asking me to do?
RICKEY: Oh, yes. Do you? Robinson, we're in a ballgame. I'm on the opposing team, and I've been on you all day long. Sambo! Shine! Jigaboo! Junglebunny! And you've heard me—all day long. You're at shortstop, I'm on first. There's a slow grounder to second base—a double-play ball for sure. You cover the bag, get the throw, and I come in sliding—my spikes high. The umpire shouts, "Out!" and I jump up and all I see is your big, black face. "How do you like that, nigger boy!" I say. And I take a swing at your cheek. What do you do, Robinson? What do you do?

[Jackie's fists are clenched. After a moment, he relaxes.]

JACKIE: Mr. Rickey . . . I've got two cheeks.
RICKEY: *[Looking at Jackie admiringly.]* It won't be forever. One year. One silent season. I know it's not a perfect plan, but at the moment it's the only one we have.

HALL OF FAME, 1981
Play in one act by Joseph Hart
Cast: Brandwell Teuscher as Willie McGrath in one-character show
See: Triple Play (1981)

Aged umpire relates his opinions about life and baseball.

HALL OF FAME
Play in two acts by Allen Sternfield

Alcoholic man attempts to contrive the election of his dying father to baseball's Hall of Fame.

HIT AND RUN, 1981
Play in one act by Joseph Hart
Cast: Paul Astin as Carl, and

Ellwoodson Williams as Roy
See: Triple Play (1981)

Bittersweet reminiscences of two aging ex-ballplayers.

HOME IS WHERE YOU HANG YOURSELF, 1975
Comedy in one act by John von Hartz
Premiere: Segment of "Home/Work": Astor Place Theatre, New York, July 23, 1975 to August 31, 1975
Cast: Norman Thomas Marshall as Richard, Lynn Oliver as Sena, William Perley as Don, and Amy Wright as Betty

Young man attempts to hang himself whenever the New York Mets lose a game.

THE HOT CORNER, 1956
Comedy in three acts by Allen Boretz and Ruby Sully
Premiere: John Golden Theatre, New York, January 25, 1956 to February 12, 1956 (five performances)
Directed by Sam Levine
Cast: Sam Levine as Fred Stanley, Vicki Cummings as Mae Stanley, Daryl Grimes as Bobbie Stanley, Don Murray as Clarence "Lefty" McShane, and Cliff Tatum as George "Muldoon" Wilson
Published in manuscript by Samuel French, Inc., New York

Star pitcher refuses to cross a stadium picket

Christine Baranski stars as Connie Weaver in the lighthearted drama, Lady of the Diamond, *in which a woman baseball fanatic becomes a junkballing pitcher in the major leagues. (Studio Arena Theater, 1980.)*

Pulitzer Prize–winning composer William Schuman and librettist Jeremy Gury teamed up to write a full-scale opera, The Mighty Casey, *in 1953. Pictured is Paul Jackel as Mudville's mighty Casey in the 1986 production by the Glimmerglass Opera in Cooperstown, New York. (Glimmerglass Opera, 1986.)*

line on the final pennant-deciding game of the season.

INSIGNIFICANCE, 1982
Play in two acts by Terry Johnson
Premiere: Royal Court Theatre, London, England, July 8, 1982
Cast: Ian McDiarmid as The Professor, Judy Davis as The Actress, William Hootkins as The Senator, and Larry Lamb as The Ballplayer
Published by Methuen London Ltd., London
See also: Baseball in Film

Manhattan hotel room in the early 1950s is populated by four unnamed characters inspired by Albert Einstein, Marilyn Monroe, Joseph McCarthy, and Joe DiMaggio.

LADY OF THE DIAMOND, 1980
Play in three acts by Mark Berman
Premiere: Studio Arena Theatre, Buffalo, New York, September 26, 1980 (39 performances)
Directed by Jack O'Brien
Cast: Christine Baranski as Connie Weaver, Robert Spencer as the vendor, Robert Darnell as Hap "Coach" Farrell, Victor Arnold as Moose Katrina, and John Goodman as Bomber

Light-hearted depiction of a woman who pitches in a major league game.

LEADING OFF AND PLAYING SHORTSTOP
Play by Philip A. Bosakowski
Premiere: University Theatres, University of Iowa

Star shortstop, comtemptuous of his idol-worshiping fans, commits an obscenity during a World Series game.

LOU GEHRIG DID NOT DIE OF CANCER, 1970
Play in one act by Jason Miller
Premiere: Equity Theatre Informals: Library and Museum of the

A QUIET HERO

Such is the indelible effect of baseball upon our lives that a taciturn, otherwise undemonstrative father can, through a shared love for the game, eloquently communicate his humanity to his son. In Jason Miller's one-act play, *Lou Gehrig Did Not Die of Cancer*, a middle-aged man recalls the meaning of baseball in his father's life. Here's ex–Little League coach, Victor Spinilli, speaking to the mother of one of his former players:

[Phone rings.]

VICTOR: Hello . . . no, this is the ex-coach. *[Hangs up. Goes to bar.]* You're a strong woman . . . a little strange but strong . . . tell you what I'm going to do. I just got an idea. Since I am now the retired ex-coach of the Spinilli Spoilers, I have a little memento, souvenir my father gave me, a little gift for Jeffrey. *[Goes to desk, takes out baseball with signature on it.]* This is a baseball. It is a very special baseball. It is a special baseball because it was hit by Lou Gehrig on Sunday, June 14, 1939, into the left field D box seats at Yankee Stadium. Present, among the other thirty thousand people, were me and my father. You see, my father loved baseball and he loved Lou Gehrig. And on that Sunday, Lou Gehrig, not even knowing my father loved him, not even suspecting that my father loved him like a son, not even knowing my father was at the game, Lou Gehrig, hit this baseball right into my father's lap. It was the first and last time I ever believed in God. My father was in a trance. It was a miracle. After the game, my father and me waited outside until it was almost dark and the stadium was empty. My father said not one word. We waited alone in the darkness for Lou Gehrig. Finally, he came out and my father went over and spoke to him in Italian. Then, he did the most incredible thing, Lou Gehrig did the most amazing thing, he hugged my father

and then they were laughing together and I remember I started to cry, standing there watching Lou Gehrig hug my father. I don't know why to this day. They didn't notice me, though, and when he came over and shook my hand and handed me the autographed ball I just smiled up at him . . . and to this day I don't know what my father said to Lou Gehrig in the dark outside of Yankee Stadium. It's a strange feeling even now, you know.

MRS. MARTIN: Yes, I do.

VICTOR: And when Lou Gehrig died, a few years later, the day Lou Gehrig died, my father cried. And that was the first and last time I ever saw my father cry. Even when they lowered my mother in the ground, his face was dry. Even when the scouts came to see me play, even when the big league scouts came to see me play and I struck out three times and they wanted nothing to do with me, he said nothing. But, the day Lou Gehrig died, when he heard the news, he said one thing, "Lou Gehrig did not die of cancer, he died of a broken heart." Those are the exact and only words he said on that day . . . isn't it incredible, that my father could be hurt so much by the death of a stranger? Someone he never even . . . give this ball to Jeffrey . . . I've had it too long.

MRS. MARTIN: Are you sure you want Jeffrey to have this?

VICTOR: Things like this mean a lot to a boy and I don't need it anymore. I've outgrown it. You know what I like about you, Mrs. Martin? You listen, you really listen to someone. It makes someone want to talk.

Performing Arts at Lincoln Center, New York, March 2, 1970 (three performances)
Directed by Chet Carlin
Cast: Miriam Carlin, Charles Faranda, and Page Miller

Published in *Three One-Act Plays by Jason Miller*. New York: Dramatists Play Service, Inc., 1972

Young man confronts his failed dreams of becoming a baseball star.

MICKEY MANTLE RUINED MY LIFE, 1984

Comedy in one act by Roy London
Premiere: Segment of Olympic Arts Festival presentation of "Sporting Goods": The Ensemble Studio

Theatre, Los Angeles, California, June 30, 1984 to July 15, 1984
Cast: Charley Lang as Stefan Medlinski, and Lisa Robins as Gloria Vivanay

A male dancer declares his hatred of baseball after years of self-reproach.

THE MIGHTY CASEY, 1953

Opera in three scenes, based on the poem, *Casey at the Bat*
Composed by William Schuman, libretto by Jeremy Gury
Premiere: Julius Hartt Opera Guild, Hartford, Connecticut, May 4, 1953; Composer's Showcase, Museum of Modern Art, New York, May 11, 1961
Published by G. Schirmer, Inc., New York, 1954
Second revised edition published by G. Schirmer, Inc., New York, 1985
See also: Baseball in Television. See: Casey at the Bat: A Baseball Cantata

Includes: "Championship of the State"; "Strategy"; "Peanuts, Popcorn, Soda, Crackerjacks"; "The Mighty Casey"; "Autograph"; "You Look So Sweet Today"; "Last Half of the Ninth"; "Two Out"; "If Only Casey"; "A Prayer"; "Surprise"; "This Gladdened Multitude"; "You're Doin' Fine Kid (Catcher's Song)"; "Rhubarb"; "Hist'ry Hangs on a Slender Thread"; "Oh, Somewhere." (See: Baseball in Music and Song.)

NEVER SAY DIE, 1982

Play by Frank Higgins
Premiere: Classic Theatre, New York, July 27, 1982
Cast: Bill Smithrovich as Moose, Frederick Allen as Grandon, and Patrick O'Connell as Patrick

Study of three minor leaguers in varying stages of a career.

OLDTIMERS GAME, 1982

Play in two acts by Lee Blessing
Premiere: Actors Theatre of Louisville, Louisville, Kentucky,

March 18, 1982 (five performances)
Directed by Patrick Tovatt
Cast: Ray Fry as Old John Law, Dierk Toporzysek as Jesus Luna, Frederic Major, William McNulty, Mel Johnson, Michael Kevin, Anthony De Fonte, and Ken Latimer

Seriocomic look at life in a minor league clubhouse before a promotional game.

OUT!, 1986

Play in three acts by Lawrence Kelly
Premiere: Judith Anderson Theatre, New York, July 11, 1986 to July 27, 1986
Directed by Max Charruyer
Cast: Michael Countryman as Shoeless Joe Jackson, Rick Tolliver as Hap Felsch, Terry Hempleman as Lefty Williams, Richard Tabor as Buck Weaver, Paul Christie as Chick Gandil, Arnie Mazer as Swede Risberg, Steven Stahl as Eddie Cicotte, and John A. O'Hern as Fred McMullin

Locker-room dramatization of the 1919 "Black Sox" scandal.

PEANUTS AND CRACKER JACK, 1980

Comedy in two acts by Jerry Slaff
Premiere: Brooks Theatre: The Cleveland Playhouse, Cleveland, Ohio, April 11, 1980
(18 performances)
Directed by William Rhys
Cast: Dudley Swetland as Dave Wallis, and Kenneth Albers as Whitey Lamonica

Aging manager and a modern-era ballplayer engage in a verbal duel that ultimately leads to understanding and acceptance.

A PERFECT DIAMOND, 1984

Comedy in two acts by Don Rifkin
Premiere: TOMI Park Royal Theatre, New York, October 17, 1984
Cast: Michael Bofshever as Legs

Lannigan, Dan Desmond as Buck Beauregard, John Anthony Lack as Gentleman Jim Wilson, Jayne Bentzen as Tess Gallagher, and Steve Beauchamp as The Kid

A long-time manager contends with the changes in modern-day baseball, including rebellious ballplayers, female sportswriters, and the influences of big business.

RED HOT, 1981

Musical comedy in three acts
Book and lyrics by Lewis J. Stadlen and Mike Scott
Music by Elliot Finkel

Misadventures of a minor league baseball club owner.

ROOKIES, 1981

Play in one act by Joseph Hart
Cast: Ben Bettenbender as Christopher, and Sally Dunn as Alice
See: Triple Play (1981)

Rookie, slated to begin spring training, is stranded in a mountain cabin with his wife.

A RUNAWAY COLT, 1895

Play in four acts by Charles H. Hoyt
Premiere: Chicago, December 2, 1895; American Theatre, New York, 1895
Cast: Edwin Hollard as Manley Manners, Gage Clarke as Dolton Manners, and Adrian C. (Cap) Anson as the manager of the Chicagos
Published in *The Dramatic Works of Charles H. Hoyt*, Volumes 1–3. New York Public Library: 1901

Gamblers attempt to bribe pitcher Manley Manners using his brother as an accomplice.

SAY IT AIN'T SO, JOE!, 1983

Play in two acts by Richard Pioreck
Premiere: Arena Players Repertory Theatre, East Farmingdale, Connecticut, March 1983
Directed by Frederic De Feis
Cast: Artie Gerunda as Shoeless Joe

Larry Bazzell, left, stars as William (Dummy) Hoy in The Signal Season of Dummy Hoy *about the deaf ballplayer's struggle to win the acceptance of his teammates during his first minor league season in Oshkosh in 1886. Pictured at right is Rick Carter as Tyler, who resents Hoy's need for special signals by the pitcher and umpire, and Gregory Chase, center, as Selee. (Hudson Guild Theatre, 1987.)*

Jackson, and George Cerualo as Lefty Williams

Events surrounding the "Black Sox" scandal are dramatized.

THE SIGNAL SEASON OF DUMMY HOY, 1987

Play in two acts by Allen Meyer and Michael Nowak
Premiere: Hudson Guild Theatre, New York, December 13, 1987 to January 10, 1988
Directed by James Abar
Cast: Larry Bazzell as William (Dummy) Hoy, Nancy Travis as A. C., Katherine Diamond as Speaker Hoy, James Gleason as Dooley, and Ben Thomas as Judge

Light-hearted dramatization of deaf baseball player William (Dummy) Hoy's struggle to be accepted in his first minor league season in 1886.

SLUGGER, 1979

Play in two acts by Shelby Buford, Jr.
Premiere: PAF Playhouse, Huntington Station, New York, February 9, 1979 (35 performances)
Directed by Marshall W. Mason
Cast: Alan Feinstein as Mort Krelack, Sabra Jones as Marion Krelack, John

---

William (Dummy) Hoy as he appeared as a rookie for the Washington Nationals in 1888. The fleet-footed outfielder, who was deaf, played 14 years in the major leagues from 1888 to 1902, compiling a lifetime batting average of .288. It was on Hoy's account that umpires began using arm signals to indicate balls and strikes. He died in 1961, five months short of his 100th birthday, having lived longer than any other major leaguer. Hoy's solid statistics and inspirational baseball career are being given serious consideration by the old timers committee to baseball's Hall of Fame. (National Baseball Library.)

Ruth Holden (Lillian Ross), the manager's daughter, is in love with star pitcher Jimmy Buck (James Burtis), who is in love with the club owner's daughter. When manager Ed Holden is stranded in another city and can't make it to the Hyenas' big pennant game, daughter Ruth takes over as the skipper, names Jimmy Buck as the starting pitcher, and refuses to take him out during a shaky ninth inning. Ruth's faith in her hero is rewarded when Jimmy Buck declares his love in Solid Ivory, *a Broadway comedy produced in 1925. (Central Theatre, 1925.)*

Strasberg as Stinger, Jeff Daniels as Ernie, and Steve Spiegel as Butta

Portrayal of a failed minor leaguer in a small Texas town during the 1950s.

SOLID IVORY, 1925

Comedy in three acts by Theodore Westman, Jr.
Premiere: Stamford Theatre, Stamford, Connecticut, November 11, 1925; Central Theatre, New York, November 16, 1925 (32 performances)
Directed by Joseph H. Graham
Cast: Neil Pratt as Gil Hendricks,

William A. Norton as Ed Holden, Lillian Ross as Ruth Holden, Marie Adels as Shirley Griffin, James Burtis as Jimmy Buck, and Bert Robinson as Lefty Marvin

Romantic triangle involving the daughters of the manager and team owner and the star pitcher for the Hyenas baseball club.

SOMETHING ABOUT BASEBALL, 1988
Comedy in one act by Quincy Long
Premiere: Ensemble Studio Theatre, New York, Marathon '88, June 11, 1988 to July 18, 1988
Directed by Risa Braman
Cast: Steven Weber as the phenom, Richard Grusin as the manager, and Mercedes Ruehl as the German woman

An eccentric pitcher and an intellectual woman baseball fan engage in a discussion involving metaphysics and baseball.

The Barrymore of Baseball

In the Gay Nineties, when baseball games were played in the late afternoon and there were no such things as night games or all-night transcontinental airplane flights, a baseball player's evening was entirely his own. Some ballplayers spent their nights in roisterous saloons, trading purloined baseballs for drinks, and others visited dance halls and honky-tonks, trading on their baseball glory for the admiring company of feminine fans. Many ballplayers of the time turned to burlesque shows and vaudeville houses—and occasionally the legitimate theater—for their nighttime entertainment. In those gaslight days, before there were movies, many a ballplayer was attracted by the big marquees of Broadway.

None was more stagestruck than Cap Anson, the "Grand Old Man of Baseball," star manager (captain in those days) of the Chicago White Stockings from 1879 to 1898 and owner of a lifetime batting average of .333 and 3041 hits (he was the first player to surpass the 3000-hit mark). At 6 feet and 230 pounds, Anson was one of the larger players in major league baseball, but it was his perceived integrity and his dedication to physical conditioning that accounted for his stature in the game. Cap Anson was not only one of baseball's top drawing cards but he was considered the conscience of baseball at a critical stage in the game's formative years.

But his ambition to be an actor, like Rube Waddell's fascination with fire engines, was an unrestrainable weakness of Cap Anson. Even before he retired as an active player at the advanced age of 46 (advanced even for this day but almost supernaturally so at a time when ballplayers seldom played beyond their early thirties), Cap Anson was already seriously pursuing a career on the stage. Although he had suffered through several embarrassing walk-on appearances in which he became so flustered that he forgot his lines, Anson nonetheless answered his correspondence with a letterhead that contained the following bewildering conundrum:

A Better Actor Than Any Ball Player,
A Better Ball Player Than Any Actor.

The acting bug, you might say, simply gnawed at the big first baseman.

In 1895 popular playwright Charles H. Hoyt wrote a four-act comedic melodrama titled *A Runaway Colt* to be a starring vehicle for Anson. (The White Stockings were then sometimes known as the Colts because of the team's youthfulness—Anson excepted.) The play premiered in December 1895 in Chicago before the hometown fans and then moved to the American Theatre in New York that January. At long last, Cap Anson was a star on Broadway.

The melodrama—the first baseball play ever produced on Broadway—concerns a minister's son, ignominiously named Manley Manners, and his efforts to be a pitcher in the rough-and-tumble game of baseball, which, in those days, was held in considerable disrepute among the socially elite. Cap Anson visits the family to induce the elders to permit the lad to play for his ball club and to assure them of the wholesomeness of the noble game, especially as played under his tutelage. A friend of the family, a jealous lover of Manley Manners's fiancée, devises a villainous scheme that will bring shame to the pitcher and financial ruin to the fiancée's family. His plan is to restore the family's fortune on the condition that the woman agrees to accept his hand in marriage. He doesn't quite tie her to a railroad track, but it's the general idea.

A Runaway Colt contains a number of good-natured references to Anson's advanced age, his penchant for arguing with umpires, and, distressingly—considering Anson's well-publicized objections to allowing blacks to play in the 1880s major leagues—a racist reference, made in his presence, about a black clubhouse manager and "good luck mascot" of the team. Clearly the play was written to indulge the preferences of a hero-worshiping audience and was not intended to be an example of good theater or even, it seems, of good comedy.

The play lasted just over a month on Broadway, although Anson generally received good notices. The *New York Dramatic Mirror* said Anson was "quite as good as most of the people on the stage with him" although it added: "He speaks his lines with the directness of an artillery officer, no matter whether he is accepting an invitation to dinner or defending the good cause of professional baseball." The *New York Herald*, after praising Anson's charismatic presence, had to admit, ". . . he is prone to imitate an Illinois

Adrian C. "Cap" Anson of the 1880s Chicago White Stockings is the only major leaguer ever to have starred in a Broadway play. (National Baseball Library.)

Methodist preacher giving out the long metre doxology."

And no wonder, with lines such as these:

ANSON: Well, you mustn't worry, my boy. If you do, you can't get in condition to pitch good ball and I can't have my best young pitcher ruined.

MANLEY MANNERS: You think I'm going to be a good one?

ANSON: If you keep your head and don't worry you will. And you mustn't worry. [Your fiancée's jealous lover] can't do anything to you and if he tries it, I'll stand by you. (*Offers hand.*)

MANLEY: (*Takes hand.*) Thank you, Captain. In a case of trouble I'd rather have you for my friend than any man on earth! I *won't* worry and I'll pitch pennant ball for you as long as my arm lasts.

ANSON: I believe you, my boy. But let's change the subject. Do you know you're inclined at times to an illegal delivery? Don't get scared; I'm not scolding. I don't *scold* my boys, I try to *teach* them. Here, (*produces book*) let's read the rule together . . .

In the climax to the play, with the pennant, Manners's honor, and the fiancée's financial solvency at stake, our friend Cap hits a home run to win the day. In the play's script, the home run is an over-the-fence round-tripper. But a story (almost certainly apocryphal) was once told that Anson one day asked big league umpire Tim Hurst if he'd like to play the part of the umpire in a guest appearance later one night. Hurst agreed, and when Anson came sliding triumphantly home for an inside-the-park home run, Hurst supposedly forgot that he was on stage and shouted—as the catcher tagged the sliding Anson and the curtain fell—"You're out!"

The story is too good to be true and also too genuinely funny to have been included in such a sorry comedy as this one. Anson never again appeared in a Broadway play. He did, however, star in many small-town productions and travelling vaudeville shows after his playing days were over. In 1939, the great first baseman was elected to baseball's Hall of Fame. The records do not show that Anson ever won a Drama Critic's Award. ◆

STUFF, 1984
Comedy in one act by Jeff Morehead
Premiere: Segment of Olympic Arts Festival presentation of "Sporting Goods," The Ensemble Studio Theatre, Los Angeles, California, June 30, 1984 to July 15, 1984
Cast: Barry Michlin in a one-character show

A middle-aged man tells how he single-handedly won the World Series when he was eight years old.

TADPOLE, 1973
Comedy in three acts by Jules Tasca
Premiere: The Mark Taper Forum, Los Angeles, California, September 1973
Directed by Edward Parone
Cast: Lawrence Luckinbill as Jimmy Younkers, Ruth Nelson as Amy Younkers, George Furth as Skip Opar, Marian Mercer as Colleen Younkers, and Curt Conway as Andy Oldfield
Published by Dramatists Play Service, Inc., New York, 1974

Aging ballplayer refuses to relinquish his youth.

TRIPLE PLAY, 1937
Comedy in three acts by William Roos
Premiere: Plymouth Playhouse, Milford, Connecticut, August 23, 1937
Directed by Luther Greene
Cast: Joseph Cotten as Rocket Reilly, Edward Andrews as Johnny Ramsay, John Call as "Snake" Foote, Charles Powers as Mike, Dave Mallen as Mr. Blum, and Ruth Hammond as Jackie

Superstitious pitcher consults a fortune teller before a game and is told he will kill a man before midnight.

TRIPLE PLAY, 1981
Three one-act plays by Joseph Hart
Premiere: American Renaissance Theatre, New York, March 26, 1981
Directed by Lynn M. Thompson

Includes: Hit and Run; Rookies; Hall of Fame.

TWO OUTS, BOTTOM OF THE NINTH, 1982
Play in one act by Vince McKewin
Premiere: Los Angeles Repertory Theatre: McCadden Place Theatre, November 1982
Directed by Richard Holden
Cast: George Parrish, B. J. Ward, Paul Regina, Pamela Brull, Vince McKewin, and Richard Holden

Series of monologues by an umpire, catcher, shortstop, souvenir girl, pinch hitter, relief pitcher, and a ballplayer's wife.

THE UMPIRE, 1905
Musical comedy in two acts
Book and lyrics by Will M. Hough and Frank R. Adams
Music by Joseph E. Howard
Premiere: LaSalle Theatre, Chicago, December 2, 1905 (300 performances)
Cast: Cecil Lean as Johnny Nolan, and Florence Holbrook as Maribel Lewton
Published by Chas. K. Harris, New York

Umpire makes an outrageous decision in a crucial game and must flee for his life. Includes: "The Umpire is a Most Unhappy Man." (See: Baseball in Music and Song—Recorded.)

WHAT THE BABE SAID, 1982
Play in one act by Martin Halpern
Premiere: Denver Center Theatre Company, Denver, Colorado, April 9, 1982 to May 8, 1982
Cast: Rudy Bond as Sal Salerno, and Julian Gamble as Buck Benson
Published by Pioneer Drama Service, Inc., Denver, Colorado

An aging manager's personal faith is unshaken despite illness, job insecurities, and the ambivalence of his star center fielder.

YANKEE WIVES, 1982
Comedy in two acts by David Rimmer
Premiere: Old Globe Theatre, San Diego, California, March 4, 1982 (five peformances)
Directed by Jack O'Brien
Cast: Joan Pringle as Marceline Davis, Ronnie Claire Edwards as Sally Hite, Annette O' Toole as Wyla Lee, Barbara Anderson as Pam Monday, Deborah Taylor as Connie Antonelli, and Alice Playten as Ronnie Roberts

Affectionate look at baseball through the eyes of Yankee players' wives.

YANKS 3 DETROIT 0 TOP OF THE SEVENTH, 1975
Comedy in one act by Jonathan Reynolds
Premiere: American Place Theatre, New York, May 16, 1975 to September 21, 1975 (145

Sal Salerno (Rudy Bond), right, is an aging, ailing major league manager whose job is on shaky ground. His star centerfielder Buck Benson (Julian Gamble) not only seems incapable of playing with enough intensity but he also cannot understand his manager's passionate love for baseball in What the Babe Said, *a one-act play written by Martin Halpern. (Denver Center Theatre Company, 1982.)*

performances)
Directed by Alan Arkin
Cast: Tony Lo Bianco as Duke Bronkowski, Lou Criscuolo as Lawrence "Beanie" Maligma, and Mitchell Jason as Old Salt
Published in *Rubbers and Yanks 3 Detroit 0 Top of the Seventh*. New York: Dramatists Play Service, Inc., 1976.

In the late innings of a perfect no-hit game, a pitcher succumbs to the skepticism and uncertainties of a modern world.

THE YEAR BOSTON WON THE PENNANT, 1969

Play in two acts by John Ford Noonan
Premiere: Forum Theatre: The Repertory Theatre of Lincoln Center, New York, May 22, 1969 to June 21, 1969 (36 performances)
Directed by Tim Ward
Cast: Roy Scheider as Marcus Sykowski, William Myers as Man in a Raincoat, Marcia Jean Kurtz as Candy Cane Sykowski, and Jerome Dempsey as Leroy Starr
Published by Samuel French, Inc., New York

Allegory in which a one-armed pitcher attempts a comeback to the major leagues.

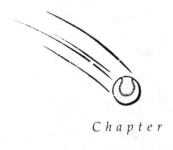

Chapter

10

Baseball in Miscellaneous Plays and Sketches

The following catalog contains a comprehensive listing of baseball-related sketches, children's plays, and plays intended for the school or amateur stage. Included in this section are early baseball farces and melodramas, vaudeville skits, pantomimes and black-outs, school pageants, and miscellaneous unclassified plays relating to baseball.

For *Explanatory Notes* to this section, *see:* Baseball in Theater.

ANGELA, OR THE UMPIRE'S REVENGE, 1888
Comic operetta
Scored by John Philip Sousa

A villainous umpire has designs on New York Giants' pitcher Eli Yale's girlfriend. Includes: "He Stands in the Box with the Ball in His Hands"; "The Umpire and the Dude"; "An Umpire I, Who Ne'er Say Die." (See: Baseball in Music and Song.)

AT THE BALL GAME, 1929
Doris M. Kenyon
Published in *Doris Kenyon's Monologues*
Philadelphia, pp. 65–72

AT THE SCHOOL BALL GAME
Katherine Ferguson
Published in *Six New Dramatic Stunts*
New York: National Recreation Association

THE BABE AND LIBBIE CUSTER, 1986
Play in one act by Bob Broeg
Premiere: Goldenrod Showboat, St. Louis, Missouri, July 15, 1986
Cast: Gilio Gherardini as Babe Ruth and Zoe Vonder Haar as Libbie Custer

Historical drama incorporating a fictionalized meeting between the Yankees' slugger and Mrs. George A. Custer.

BASEBALL, 1916
Vaudeville sketch by G. H. Kashner

BASEBALL?, 1957
Vernon Howard
Published in *Monologues for Boys and Girls*
New York: Sterling Publishing Co., p. 88

BASEBALL, 1965
Loren E. Taylor
Published in *Stunts and Skits*
Minneapolis, Minnesota: Burgess Publishing Co.

BASE-BALL AT SPRUCEVILLE, 1911
Farce by Richard Nesmith

THE BASE BALL BUG, 1908
Play in one act by T. P. Jackson

A BASE BALL CRANK, 1890
Farce by Ernest Howard

THE BASEBALL CRANK, 1902
Comedic monologue by Frank Dumont

BASE BALL CRANKS, 1893
Farce in three acts by Ernest Howard

THE BASEBALL FAN, 1951
Joyce Ingalls
Published in *Mixed Party Monologues and Some Encores*
Boston: Walter H. Baker Co., pp. 65–68

A woman's lack of understanding of baseball is caricatured.

THE BASEBALL GAME, 1941
Louis J. Huber
Published in *Vaudeville Skits*
Minneapolis, Minnesota: Northwestern Press

BASE BALL GAME, MADE PRACTICAL FOR THE STAGE, 1910
R. W. Tully

BASE BALL GIRL, 1910
Romantic American Operetta by S. A. Merinbaum and Harry Lahnde

BASEBALL-ITIS, 1910
Comedy in one act by V. H. Smalley

BASEBALL MINSTRELS, 1921
Helen Ferris
Published in *Producing Amateur Entertainments*
New York: Dutton, pp. 120–121

A BASE HIT, 1888
Play in three acts by Thomas W. King

Subsequently musicalized. See: A Base Hit (1889).

A BASE HIT, 1889
Musical comedy by Hubert Bown
Based on the play by Thomas W. King
Minneapolis, Minnesota: G. S. Richards and Co.

A BATTERY OF FUN, 1929
Vaudeville sketch
Premiere: New Palace Theatre, Chicago, January 27, 1929
Cast: Waite Hoyt and J. Fred Coots

BETTY AT THE BASEBALL GAME, 1921
Walter B. Hare
Published in *Readings and Monologues a la Mode*
Chicago: Denison, pp. 21–24

BETWEEN SHOWERS, 1913
Vaudeville sketch
Premiere: Grand Theatre, New York
Cast: Mike Donlin

MEN TALK

No one had a better ear for the bluster and badinage of baseball players' speech than Ring Lardner. He mastered the vernacular in such short stories as *Alibi Ike* and *Hurry Kane* and perfected it in his full-length collection, *You Know Me Al.* In a comedic sketch, written for the 1922 Ziegfeld Follies, Lardner presents two seldom-used relief pitchers—a veteran (played by Will Rogers) and a rookie—who trade insults and exchange observations about a subject that is uppermost in every baseball player's mind: women. Here is a sample from *The Bull Pen* as performed on the vaudeville stage:

BILL: Bob's wild. It's three and nothing on Sewell.

CY *(to Joe):* You better cut loose a little, kid. This may be our day.

JOE: Not both of us.

CY: Sure, providing he picks you first. *(Slight pause.)* But, listen, kid, if I was you I'd leave the dames alone. Wait till you've made good.

JOE: I ain't after no dames. But I can't help the looks they give me.

CY: No more than you can help the looks *God* give you. And he certainly didn't spread himself.

BILL: He's walked Sewell.

JOE: The *gals* seem to think I look O.K.

CY: How do you know?

JOE: The way they act. Do you remember that poor little kid in New Orleans?

CY: What kid?

JOE: The telephone gal in the hotel. She was down to the depot when we went away. But I ducked her. And that dame in Philadelphia.

CY: What do you owe *her?*

JOE: I don't owe you nothin', but she was out to the game every day, tryin' to flirt.

CY: Oh, *that* woman!

JOE: What woman?

CY: That's the woman that goes to the games in Philadelphia. You know those Philadelphia fans? Well, she's their sister.

BEULAH AT THE BALL GAME, 1926
Marie Irish
Published in *Fifty Humorous Monologues*
Dayton, Ohio: Paine Publishing Co., pp. 5–7

BLACK AND WHITE AND RED ALL OVER: RED SMITH ON BASEBALL, 1983
Theatrical presentation of baseball writings by Red Smith
Adaptation by Dennis Danziger and Ellen Sandler
Premiere: Itchey Foot Ristorante: The Mark Taper Forum, Los Angeles, California, May 8, 1983
Directed by John Frank Levey
Cast: Robert Ellenstein, Scott Lincoln, Billy Wiley, and Nathan Cook

BREAKING THE RECORD, OR THE NINETEENTH STRAIGHT, 1912
Vaudeville sketch
Premiere: Hammerstein's Theatre, New York
Cast: Rube Marquard and Blossom Seeley

Musical sketch starring New York Giants' pitching sensation Rube Marquard, who won 19 consecutive games in 1912—a record that still stands. Includes: ''The Marquard Glide.'' (See: Baseball in Music and Song.)

THE BULL PEN, 1922
Comedic sketch by Ring W. Lardner
Premiere: The Ziegfeld Follies of 1922: New Amsterdam Theatre, New York, June 5, 1922
Cast: Will Rogers as Cy Walters, Andy Toombes as Joe Webb, and Al Ochs as Bill Carney

Published in *Judge*, July 29, 1922; in *First and Last* by Ring W. Lardner
New York: Charles Scribner's Sons, 1934, pp. 333–339

Two unused relief pitchers bemoan their fate.

CAPTAIN OF THE BALL NINE, 1933
Marie Irish
Published in *Children's Comic Dialogues*
Minneapolis, Minnesota: Denison, pp. 53–55

THE CASE OF THE PHANTOM BASEBALL, 1978
Comedy in three acts by James E. Lawrence
Denver, Colorado: Pioneer Drama Service, Inc.

Farcical detective investigates a phenomenon in

which a baseball crashes through a window whenever a home run is hit several miles away.

CASEY, 1972
Musical play by William Shubert
Las Vegas, Nevada: Privately published

Musical based on the poem, Casey at the Bat.

CASEY AT THE BAT, 1978
Adaptation by Nancy Henderson
Published in *Celebrate America: A Baker's Dozen of Plays*
New York: Julian Messner

Ernest L. Thayer's ballad is recited while action is pantomimed.

CURVES, 1910
Vaudeville sketch by Bozeman Bulger
Premiere: Hammerstein's Theatre, New York
Cast: Christy Mathewson, Chief Myers, and May Tulley

A DOUBLE PLAY, 1909
Vaudeville sketch
Premiere: Majestic Theatre, New York, November 22, 1909
Cast: Mabel Hite and Mike Donlin

THE FAIREST PITCHER OF THEM ALL, 1971
Harold Cable
Published in *Plays for Modern Teen-Age Actors*
Boston: Plays, Inc.

In a parody of Snow White, Blanche is a pitcher for the Seven Dwarfs baseball team.

GLADYS AND BASEBALL
Mary G. Sharpe
Published in *Windows and Other Humorous Monologues*
Franklin, Ohio: Eldridge Publishing Co., pp. 36–39

A GREAT CATCH, 1910
Vaudeville sketch
Cast: Joe Tinker and Sadie Sherman

HERE'S THE PITCH, 1947
Musical comedy
Book by Craig P. Gilbert
Music by Courtney A. Crandall, lyrics by William M. Scudder
Premiere: Harvard University, Cambridge, Massachusetts, December 9, 1947; New York City Center, New York, December 19, 1947
Cast: Theodore Allegretti as Artie Hooper, Frederick Lamart as Horace Cornwall, William M. Reed as Fred Watson, and Thomas W. Zinsser as Susas Douglas

In this one-hundredth production of the Hasty Pudding Club, an 1890s small-town baseball team is the beneficiary of a traveling medicine salesman's ''Marvelous Magic Elixer.'' Includes: ''Baseball.'' (See: Baseball in Music and Song.)

HER FIRST BASEBALL GAME, 1925
Lilian Holmes Strack
Published in *Platform Readings*
Boston: Walter H. Baker Co., pp. 7–13

HOME RUN BILL, 1937
Louis J. Huber
Published in *Practical Pantomime*
Minneapolis, Minnesota; Northwestern Press, pp. 9–12

I HATE BASEBALL, 1951
Joyce Ingalls
Published in *Mixed Party Monologues and Some Encores*
Boston: Walter H. Baker Co., pp. 27–31

Wife complains about her husband's interest in baseball.

IN THE BLEACHERS, 1940
Marshall Stedman
Published in *Amusing Monologues*
San Francisco, California: Banner Play Bureau, pp. 32–33

IT'S A SILLY GAME, 1963
L. M. Brings
Published in *Rehearsal-less Skits and Plays*
Minneapolis, Minnesota: Denison

KILL THE UMP, 1948
Louis J. Huber
Published in *All in Fun*
Minneapolis, Minnesota: Northwestern Press, pp. 93–99

KIWANIS BASEBALL GAME, 1934
Arthur M. Depew
Published in *The Cokesbury Stunt Book*
Nashville, Tennessee: Cokesbury Press, pp. 217–220

LEARNING THE GAME, c. 1913
Vaudeville sketch by George Totten Smith
Music by Arthur Behim
Cast: Chief Bender and Kathryn Pearl

LITTLE LEAGUE HITTER, 1953
Joyce R. Ingalls
Published in *Teen Talk: Sixteen Character Sketches for Teen-aged Girls and Boys*
Boston: Walter H. Baker Co., pp. 68–72

Boy's confidence is boosted after an unexpected home run.

THE NATIONAL GAME, 1899
Play by George M. Cohan

THE NATIONAL GAME, 1911
Comedy-drama in Nine Innings by E. H. Clark and Lawrence J. McCarty

THE NIGHT BALL GAME, 1951
Joyce Ingalls
Published in *Mixed Party Monologues and Some Encores*
Boston: Walter H. Baker Co., pp. 73–76

New York Giants' outfielder Mike Donlin starred in a number of vaudeville sketches in the early 1900s, among them Stealing Home, *which costarred his wife and popular comedienne, Mabel Hite. Donlin also starred in a full-length baseball movie and later became a professional actor in dozens of Hollywood films. He was so taken with the stage that during his playing days he always carried a tattered theater program in his back uniform pocket as a good luck charm. (National Baseball Library.)*

Wife insists on talking while her husband listens to a baseball game on the radio.

ON THE BAT, 1960
Bernice W. Carlson
Published in *The Right Play for You*
Nashville, Tennessee: Abingdon

Three women misconstrue the rules of baseball to the point of wanting Babe Ruth arrested.

OPENING THE WORLD SERIES, 1945
Beatrice Plumb
Published in *The Modern Stunt Book* by Affa E. Preston, Beatrice Plumb, and Harry W. Githens
Minneapolis, Minnesota: Denison, p. 14

OUT AT HOME PLATE
H. R. Bennick
Published in *Separate Pamphlet Plays*
Minneapolis, Minnesota: Denison

A PENNANT FOR THE KREMLIN, 1966
Comedy in three acts by David Rogers
Based on the novel by Paul Molloy
Chicago: Dramatic Publishing Co.
See also: Baseball in Fiction

PLAY BALL!, 1940
Comedy in one act by Spranger Barry
New York: Samuel French, Inc.

Son of a wealthy stockbroker contemplates a career in professional baseball. Spranger Barry is a pseudonym for Stanley Kauffman.

PLAY BALL, 1940
Comedy in one act by Homer B. Hulbert
Minneapolis, Minnesota: The Northwestern Press

PLAY BALL, 1954
Musical play by Dinnie Mae Mackey
Richmond, Virginia: Mrs. J. M. Woolard

High school pageant in which girls express their desire to play baseball. Includes: "Play Ball" (1954). (See: Baseball in Music and Song.)

PLAY TO WIN, 1984
Musical play
Book, music, and lyrics by James de Jongh, Charles Cleveland, and Jimi Foster
Premiere: Theatreworks/USA: Promenade Theatre, New York, March 1984
Directed by Regge Life
Cast: Raymond Anthony Thomas as Jackie Robinson

Musical dramatization of Hall of Famer Jackie Robinson's life. For children.

A PRELIMINARY BASEBALL GAME, 1937
Willis N. Bugbee
Published in *Nutty Stunts*
Syracuse, New York: Willis N. Bugbee Co., p. 79

A QUIET MAN AT A BASEBALL GAME, 1921
Walter B. Hare
Published in *Bran' New Monologues and Readings and Verse*
Boston: Walter H. Baker Co., pp. 88–90

RIGHT OFF THE BAT, 1914
Vaudeville sketch
Cast: Mike Donlin and Marty McHale

Both ballplayers performed regularly on the vaudeville stage. McHale was billed as "The Baseball Caruso" and Donlin appeared in many motion pictures as well as in theater.

SEASONS IN THE SUN, 1982
Musical play in two acts
Book by Shubert Fendrich
Music and lyrics by Terry Jacks, Jacques Brel, Rod McKuen, Udo Jurgens, Paul and Alan Rolnick
Denver, Colorado: Pioneer Drama Service, Inc.

A dying rock musician and a newly retired baseball star contemplate their future. Includes: "Superstar." (See: Baseball in Music and Song.)

THE SPIRIT OF BASEBALL, 1937
Jewell J. Bader and M. M. Korn
Published in *From Little Acorns and Other Plays*
Chicago: Beckley-Cardy

SPITBALL, 1956
Bernice W. Carlson
Published in *Act it Out*
Nashville, Tennessee: Abingdon

THE STAIN OF GUILT, c. 1910
Vaudeville musical
Cast: John Rucker, Jas. A. Heenan, Geo. F. Miller, J. C. Turner, and Rube Waddell

The cover of The Stain of Guilt Songster *features vignette photographs of the cast, including three poses by Rube Waddell.*

STEALING HOME, 1908
Vaudeville sketch by Vincent Brynn
Premiere: Hammerstein's Theatre, New York, October 26, 1908
Cast: Mabel Hite and Mike Donlin

Musical skit starring the popular comedienne and the New York Giants' star.

STRIKE THREE!, 1938
Comedy in three acts by Robert Ray
Minneapolis, Minnesota: Northwestern Press

A businessman unwittingly sponsors an all-female baseball club.

STRIKING OUT!, 1983
Play in one act by Michael Bigelow Dixon and Valerie Smith
Premiere: South Coast Repertory, Newport Beach, California, April 9, 1983

THE SUFFRAGETTE PITCHER, 1913
Vaudeville sketch
Book and lyrics by Thomas J. Gray, music by W. Raymond Walker
Premiere: World Palace, Chicago, November 1913
Cast: Rube Marquard and Blossom Seeley

TAKE ME OUT TO THE BALL GAME, 1972
John Murray
Published in *Modern Monologues for Young People*

Boston: Plays, Inc.

A woman annoys her husband with her lack of understanding of baseball.

THAT'S MY OLD MAN!, 1950
Jack Neher and Dallas Pratt
Published in *Hi Neighbor!*
New York: National Association for Mental Health

Father and son resolve their conflicts through a shared enthusiasm for baseball.

THERE GOES THE OLD BALL GAME, 1974
Burlesque melodrama in two acts
Book, music, and lyrics by Dick Poston
Denver, Colorado: Pioneer Drama Service, Inc.

Villainous baseball manager and a female owner vie for financial control of a minor league team. Includes: "You Make a Hit With My Heart." (See: Baseball in Music and Song.*)*

THREE STRIKES, 1949
Louis J. Huber
Published in *Four Minutes of Fun*
Minneapolis, Minnesota: Northwestern Press, pp. 131–134

THREE STRIKES AND OUT, 1930
Farcical sketch by Lynn Mack
Franklin, Ohio: Farquhar Play Bureau

Lynn Mack is a pseudonym for Ross Farquhar.

THREE STRIKES—YOU'RE OUT!, 1932
Comedy in three acts by Wilbur Braun
New York: Samuel French, Inc.

TITLE NOT KNOWN, 1921
Vaudeville sketch by Ring W. Lardner
Songs by Herman Timberg
Cast: Cap Anson

The title of this sketch has not been identified nor has a script been located.

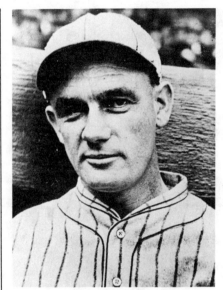

In the early 1900s vaudeville was the off-season home of many baseball stars and World Series heroes. One such player was Hall of Famer Rube Marquard, who won 19 consecutive games as a New York Giants pitcher in 1912. Along with his wife, actress Blossom Seeley, Marquard appeared in two popular vaudeville musicals, Breaking the Record *in 1912 and* The Suffragette Pitcher *in 1913. (National Baseball Library.)*

TWENTY MINUTES IN THE CLUB HOUSE, 1912
Vaudeville sketch
Cast: Tom Dillon, Bill Gleason, George Crable, and Frank Browning

TWO STRIKES, 1910
Comedy in two acts by Thacher Howland Guild
Boston: Walter H. Baker Co.

WANTED—A PITCHER, 1913
Comedy in one act by M. N. Beebe
Boston: Walter H. Baker Co.

WHO'S ON FIRST, 1975
Comedy in one act by James L. Seay
Elgin, Illinois: Performance
Publishing Co.

Adaptation of Abbott and Costello's famous baseball routine. (See also: Baseball in Comedy and Light Verse—Recorded.) See: "The Naughty Nineties"; "The World of Abbott and Costello" (Baseball in Film: Appendix); Broadcast of June 13, 1944 (Baseball in Radio).

WHO STOLE THIRD BASE?, 1957
Anne Coulter Martens

Published in *We're Speechless*
Boston: Walter H. Baker Co., pp. 5–18

Farcical pantomime of a women's softball game.

THE WORLD SERIES, 1944
Jerry Owen
Published in *Oh, Wilbur! Twenty-six Humorous Monologues*
Boston: Walter H. Baker Co., pp. 9–13

THE WORLD SERIES BROADCAST, 1932
No author given
Published in *My Operation and Other Uncommon Monologues*
New York: Fitzgerald Publishing Corp., pp. 17–23

YALLER! A BASEBALL STORY IN RIME
No author given
Published in *Win-a-Prize Readings*
Franklin, Ohio: Eldridge Publishing Co., pp. 91–93

Chapter

11

Baseball in Art and Sculpture

The following catalog contains a comprehensive listing of paintings and sculpture relating to Baseball. Included in this section are paintings, watercolors, drawings, and other works of baseball-related fine art and sculpture; public statuary relating to baseball; baseball-related folk art paintings; and works of art on the baseball theme by noted American artists.

Particular emphasis has been given to the listing of baseball-related paintings contained in the collections of museums and other fine art institutions; works of baseball art that have been exhibited in major fine art galleries; and baseball-related paintings and sculpture that have been reproduced in nonbaseball publications. Not included in this section are prints, lithographs, and other works issued in multiple editions. For these baseball-related works, *see:* Baseball in Miscellaneous Art and Illustrations.

Sporting scenes have been a popular subject for artists since the time of ancient Greece when Olympic athletes were celebrated in marble and decorative earthen trophies. Later, sports of the gentry—fox hunting, horse racing, yachting, fencing—were depicted in numerous European paintings and prints, especially by the English. But American artists were generally disinclined to explore sporting themes until the mid-1800s when they began painting idyllic pastoral vignettes—lush panoramic views of the American countryside. Included in a number of these early scenes was a game of baseball being played as a kind of joyous folk celebration. But even as late as the 1950s, baseball remained a relatively minor subject for artists. In 1953 Ethel Barrymore lamented in an article for *Look* magazine: "The inspiration to be found on a baseball field for great painting seems to me to be completely ignored. Think of the unconscious grace, the real poetry of motion of Hal Chase...the ease and apparent unawareness of impossible plays by Joe DiMaggio... and the speed of light achieved by Walter Johnson. Why was there no massive Degas to record them for us all?" Although baseball has recently become an enormously popular theme in American art, most paintings portray the melodramatics of game situations rather than the intrinsic beauty of the sport. Few contemporary baseball artists have approximated Degas's genius for rendering the grace, beauty, and athleticism of ballet. Indeed, too many recent baseball paintings are little more than sports-page iconography.

There exists no major collection of baseball art as cataloged in the following section. The National Art Museum of Sport in West Haven, Connecticut, houses a substantial collection of paintings and sculpture relating to virtually every kind of sports activity, including several that depict baseball. The National Baseball Hall of Fame in Cooperstown, New York, has recently expanded its collection of baseball-related art. The museum already features a substantial collection of original art illustrations, including two Norman Rockwell *Saturday Evening Post* covers on the baseball theme.

A growing number of art galleries have begun to specialize in sports and baseball-related art and sculpture. For further information regarding dealers and institutional resources of baseball art, consult the Selected Guide to Sources and Dealers located at the back of the book.

EXPLANATORY NOTES

1. Title of the painting or sculpture, year of completion.

2. Name of artist.

3. Medium, dimensions in inches (height preceding width).

4. Name of owner, museum collection, or gallery in which the work was exhibited.

5. Annotation. Description of the painting or sculpture. Bibliography of the best available reproduction.

ACTION AT SECOND, 1956
Fletcher Martin
Oil on canvas, 40 × 38 inches
Collection of Mr. and Mrs. Robert
Rittmaster, New York

Depicts an infielder leaping over a sliding runner. Reproduced in Fletcher Martin *by H. Lester Cooke, Jr. New York: Harry N. Abrams, Inc., 1977.*

ALL-AMERICAN ARENA, 1955
Saul Steinberg
Watercolor and ink

An aerial view of a baseball park is whimsically depicted. Reproduced in Life, *July 11, 1955.*

AMATEUR BASEBALL BOY
George Luks
Oil on canvas

Reproduced in Bulletin, Institute of Arts and Sciences, Brooklyn. *Volume 30: October 24, 1925, frontispiece.*

AMERIKA (BASEBALL), 1984
R. B. Kitaj
Oil on canvas, 60 × 60 inches
Marlborough Gallery, New York

Panoramic scene in which baseball players are engaged in an anarchy of various and unconnected activities.

ANGEL HERMOSA'S DOUBLE PLAY, 1974
Mark Rucker

Graphite on paper, 27½ × 22 inches
The University at Albany, State
University of New York

Prismatic depiction of baseball action. Reproduced in Diamonds Are Forever: Artists and Writers on Baseball *edited by Peter H. Gordon. San Francisco: Chronicle Books, 1987, p. 120.*

ARGUMENT AT THIRD, 1949
Paul Clemens
Oil on canvas, 12 × 15 inches
Collection of Mrs. Victor Hunter

Depicts three players arguing with an umpire. Reproduced in Look, *May 5, 1953, p. 106.*

Argument at Third *(1949), oil by Paul Clemens. (Collection of Mrs. Victor Hunter.)*

Babe Ruth *(1934), sculpture by Reuben Nak-ian. Like a laureled Greek god, this Babe Ruth does not swing from the heels but from the heavens. (National Baseball Library.)*

BABE RUTH, 1934
Reuben Nakian
Sculpture, plaster cast from a clay model, height 8 feet

Heroic representation of the Hall of Famer at the completion of his swing. Reproduced in The Life That Ruth Built *by Marshall Smelser. New York: Quadrangle/New York Times Book Co., 1975, p. 466.*

BABE RUTH
David L. Swasey
Oil on canvas, 30½ × 25 inches
The Old Print Shop, New York

On-the-field portrait of the Hall of Famer. Exhibited at the Grand Central Art Gallery, New York, 1951.

BABE RUTH
John Benson
Oil on canvas

Babe Ruth Birthplace Shrine and Museum, Baltimore, Maryland

On-the-field portrait of the Hall of Famer.

BABE RUTH
Harold Castor
Bronze sculpture, height 31 inches

Depicts the Hall of Fame slugger at the completion of his swing. Reproduced in Point 31: 1975, *Vol. 1, No. 2, p. 74.*

BABE RUTH
Dennis Luzak
Oil on canvas
National Baseball Hall of Fame and Museum, Cooperstown, New York

BABE RUTH, 1984
Armand LaMontagne
Acrylic on panel
Collection of Robert N. Anderson, Rhinebeck, New York
National Baseball Hall of Fame and Museum, Cooperstown, New York

Depicts Babe Ruth standing in a dugout, three bats in hand.

BABE RUTH, 1984
Armand LaMontagne
Painted basswood sculpture, life size
Collection of Robert N. Anderson, Rhinebeck, New York
National Baseball Hall of Fame and Museum, Cooperstown, New York

Super-realistic depiction of the Hall of Famer in a batting stance. Reproduced in the New York Times, *September 27, 1985, p. B 1.*

BABE RUTH, KING OF SWAT, 1939
Paul Clemens
Oil on canvas, 12 × 15 inches
Collection of Stanley E. Kramer

Whimsical depiction of Babe Ruth at the completion of a cork-screw swing. Reproduced in the Smithsonian, *July 1981, p. 145.*

BABE'S SIXTIETH, c. 1971
Ron Lessor
Oil on canvas, 21½ × 18 inches

BACK LOT BASEBALL, c. 1935
Henry Ives Cobb
Gouache, 13 × 16⅞ inches
Collection of Janice C. Oresman

BALL PARK—BOSTON, 1950
Raoul Dufy
Watercolor, 19½ × 25½ inches
Rose Art Museum, Brandeis University, Waltham, Massachusetts, gift of Mr. and Mrs. Edwin E. Hokin

Festive depiction of a game at Fenway Park. Also titled, Ball Game. *Reproduced in* Diamonds Are Forever: Artists and Writers on Baseball *edited by Peter H. Gordon. San Francisco: Chronicle Books, 1987, p. 19.*

Babe Ruth *(1984), sculpture by Armand LaMontagne. This realistic statue of the New York Yankee great is on permanent display at the Baseball Hall of Fame in Cooperstown, New York. (National Baseball Library.)*

The Babe Brought to Life

Befitting his place in American life and baseball history, two monumental works of sculpture have been created in tribute to Babe Ruth. One stands on permanent display in Cooperstown, New York, where it is the most photographed exhibit at the National Baseball Hall of Fame. The other statue, executed in 1934, is possibly the finest example of heroic sculpture ever created of a baseball subject. Unfortunately, the status and whereabouts of Reuben Nakian's masterpiece are completely unknown.

Except for their approximation in size—both sculptures are about eight feet in height—the two works could not be more vastly dissimilar. Armand LaMontagne's painted wood carving at the Hall of Fame is a super-realistic depiction of Babe Ruth in a batting stance in 1929 at age 34. Nakian's plaster statue (it was never cast in bronze) portrays the Babe as a mythic symbol, a modern incarnation of a laureled Greek god. His Babe Ruth does not swing from the heels but from the heavens. There's no Yankee lettering on the jersey, no buttons, no distinct definition to the baseball uniform. Instead, Nakian imbues his sculpture with the heroic motifs and images of classical mythology. And yet, undeniably, the sculpture is an American metaphor. Babe Ruth epitomizes a nation's upward gazing optimism, its youthful exuberance and unrestrained joy.

LaMontagne's sculpture, executed in 1984, was carved from a solid four-by-eight-foot block of laminated basswood. The 300-pound carving required an estimated 1,200 hours over a four-month period to complete. The result is a work of such breathtaking realism that it holds the viewer in a state of suspended reverie. It is the closest thing to actually having seen Babe Ruth at bat that most fans can ever know.

A year later LaMontagne was commissioned by Mrs. Tom Yawkey to carve a painted wood sculpture of the great Red Sox outfielder Ted Williams. That statue, depicting the Boston slugger at the completion of his swing, was donated to the Hall of Fame in 1985 and can also be viewed at the baseball shrine in Cooperstown.

Reuben Nakian's statue of Babe Ruth was sculpted from a ton of clay over a year's time and at the sculptor's expense. Nakian worked from fifteen large photographs of the Babe tacked to the walls of his studio and from a remembrance of the one Yankee game in which he saw Babe Ruth play—on September 30, 1927, the day Ruth hit his record-setting sixtieth home run of the season. The Babe never posed for the sculpture, although, considering the artist's extended working schedule, it is likely he was never asked.

It was Nakian's hope that the plaster model would be cast in bronze—an expensive process—and permanently installed in the rotunda at Yankee Stadium. However, his requests for contributions from New York Yankee executives and baseball officials, and even from baseball fans, went unheeded. After a widely publicized exhibition in a New York gallery, the statue—still unbronzed—was quietly retired from view.

A line from a 1934 newspaper story about the statue rings a painfully ironic note in light of the sculpture's uncertain whereabouts. The statue, wrote Will Wedge in the *New York Sun*, "is due to survive down the shadowy arches of time." Reuben Nakian never sculpted another baseball subject. He went on to become one of America's preeminent sculptors, enjoying major retrospective shows in the Museum of Modern Art in New York and at the Milwaukee Art Museum. He died in 1986 at age 89. His magnificent *Babe Ruth* has not reappeared since 1934 and remains missing today. ◆

THE BALL PLAYERS, c. 1877
William Morris Hunt
Oil on canvas, 16 × 24 inches
Detroit Institute of Arts, Detroit,
Michigan, gift of John L. Gardner
See also: Baseball (c. 1877)

Pastoral depiction of a sandlot baseball game. Reproduced in 200 Years of Sport in America *by Wells Twombly. New York: Rutledge Books/ McGraw-Hill Book Co., 1976, p. 46.*

BALL PLAYERS, 1962
William Winter
Oil on canvas, 22 × 34 inches
Collection of Mr. and Mrs. Gerry
Moses

BALTIMORE PITCHER, 1976
Michael Hart
Oil on canvas, 38 × 50 inches

BASEBALL, c. 1877
William Morris Hunt
Charcoal on paper, 13¾ × 19⅞ inches
Museum of Fine Arts, Boston, gift of the subscribers

Preliminary sketch for The Ball Players. *Reproduced in* The Late Landscapes of William Morris Hunt *by Marchal E. Landgren, with chronology and catalog by Sharman Wallace McGurn. University of Maryland Department of Art, 1975, plate 40.*

BASEBALL, c. 1960
Ernest Trova
Oil on canvas, 16 × 14 inches
The Gladstone Collection of Baseball Art

BASEBALL, 1965
Charles Garabedian
Flo-paque on paper, 36 × 77 inches

Panoramic view of baseball action is whimsically depicted. Reproduced in Diamonds Are Forever: Artists and Writers on Baseball *edited by Peter H. Gordon. San Francisco: Chronicle Books, 1987, pp. 24–25.*

BASEBALL, 1969
Roger Glazbrook
Oil on canvas
Collection of the artist

Depicts a runner sliding into second base. Reproduced in Sport in Art *by Robert Henkes. New York: Prentice Hall Press, 1986, p. 93.*

BASEBALL, 1986
Jack Earl
Ceramic sculpture
The America, building lobby, New York

Representation of a baseball on a grand scale. Reproduced in the New York Times, *October 27, 1986.*

BASEBALL
Philip Evergood
Watercolor, 21¾ × 30½ inches
Collection of Susan Dintenfass Subtle

BASEBALL
Richard Sparks
Oil
Collection of the artist

Depicts a batter at mid-swing. Reproduced in

The Ball Players *(c. 1877), oil by William Morris Hunt. While searching for subjects to paint in the fishing village of Kettle Cove (now Magnolia), Massachusetts during the mid-1870s, artist William Morris Hunt discovered this pastoral baseball scene. (Detroit Institute of Arts.)*

Sport in Art *by Robert Henkes. New York: Prentice Hall Press, 1986, color plate 5.*

BASEBALL
Robert Stanley
Oil on canvas
Collection of the artist

Depiction in silhouette of the famous John Roseboro–Juan Marichal brawl. Reproduced in Sport in Art *by Robert Henkes. New York: Prentice Hall Press, 1986, p. 90.*

BASEBALL BATTER, 1950
Clemente Spampinato
Bronze sculpture, height 18 inches
Collection of Barry Halper

Depicts Joe DiMaggio at the completion of his classic swing. Reproduced in the Smithsonian, *April 1987, p. 111.*

BASEBALL CATCHER AND BATTER, c. 1975
Michael Hart
Acrylic on canvas, 36 × 48 inches

Realist depiction of a catcher, umpire, and batter at the completion of his swing. Reproduced in the New York Times, *October 16, 1977.*

THE BASEBALL FAN
George Luks
Oil on canvas, 19½ × 15¼ inches

Portrait of a male wearing a baseball cap. Reproduced in International Studio, *March 1921, p. VI.*

BASEBALL GAME, 1892
Carle Joan Blenner
Oil on canvas, 9 × 14 inches
Collection of Herbert Allen, Jr., New York

Panoramic depiction of a pastoral baseball game. Reproduced in exhibition catalog, Americans. *New York: Schweitzer Gallery, 1966.*

A BASE BALL GAME, 1894
Hy Sandham
Oil on canvas
National Baseball Hall of Fame and

Museum, Cooperstown, New York

Panoramic depiction of baseball action at the Polo Grounds in New York.

THE BASEBALL GAME, c. 1908
George Bellows
Oil on canvas, 16 × 20½ inches
Muskegon Museum of Art, Muskegon, Michigan

Pastoral landscape in which a baseball game is depicted.

THE BASEBALL GAME, 1986
Andrew Radcliffe
Oil on canvas, 18 × 22 inches
Nancy Hoffman Gallery, New York

Pastoral depiction of a baseball game. Reproduced in Diamonds Are Forever: Artists and Writers on Baseball *edited by Peter H. Gordon. San Francisco: Chronicle Books, 1987, p. 9.*

BASEBALL GAME AT NIGHT, 1934
Morris Kantor
Oil on linen, 37 × 47 inches
National Museum of American Art, Smithsonian Institution, Washington, D.C., gift of Mrs. Morris Kantor

Atmospheric depiction of a small-town minor league game. Also titled, Baseball at Night. *Reproduced in* The Artist and the Sportsman *by Martha B. Scott. New York: Renaissance Editions, Inc., 1968, p. 44.*

BASEBALL MANAGER, 1963
Roy Lichtenstein
Magna on canvas, 68 × 58 inches
Collection of Mr. and Mrs. Joseph Helman, Frontenac, Missouri

Pop art close-up depiction of a baseball player. Reproduced in Roy Lichtenstein *by Diane Waldman. New York: Harry N. Abrams, Inc., 1971, plate 68.*

BASEBALL PARK
Ernest Lawson

Reproduced in First Biennial Exhibition of Contemporary American Paintings. *New*

York: Whitney Museum of American Art, 1932.

BASEBALL PITCHER, 1936
R. Tait McKenzie
Plaster medal sketch, diameter 4½ inches
University of Pennsylvania Archives, McKenzie Papers

Male nude representation of a baseball pitcher. Reproduced in R. Tait McKenzie: The Sculptor of Athletes *by Andrew J. Kozar. Knoxville, Tennessee: The University of Tennessee Press, 1975, p. 103.*

BASEBALL PITCHER, c. 1973
Fay Moore
Oil, 39½ × 31⅜ inches
University of Virginia, Charlottesville, Virginia

BASEBALL PITCHER (BLAZIN' ONE IN), 1950
Clemente Spampinato
Bronze sculpture, height 14½ inches
Campanile Galleries, Inc., Chicago

Depicts a pitcher at the beginning of a high leg-kick delivery. Reproduced in exhibition catalog. Sport and Western Sculpture *by Clemente Spampinato. Chicago: Campanile Galleries, Inc.*

BASEBALL PITCHER ON GREEN, 1976
Michael Hart
Oil on canvas, 36 × 52 inches

THE BASEBALL PLAYER, 1886
Jonathon Scott Hartley
Bronze sculpture, height 14 inches
The Gladstone Collection of Baseball Art

Depicts a baseball player reaching to catch a ball.

BASEBALL PLAYER, 1889
Douglas Tilden
Bronze statue, life size
Golden Gate Park, San Francisco,

Baseball Player (1889), sculpture by Douglas Tilden. In the early days of baseball, the pitcher threw the ball underhand, high or low, as directed by the batter. This heroic statue by Douglas Tilden, who was deaf, stands in Golden Gate Park in San Francisco.

California, gift of James D. Phelan
See also: Baseball Player (1889) (Baseball in Miscellaneous Art and Illustrations)

Heroic representation of an old-style underhand pitcher. Also titled, Ball Thrower *and* Baseball Thrower. *Reproduced in* Douglas Tilden: Portrait of a Deaf Sculptor *by Mildred Albronda. Silver Spring, Maryland: T. J. Publishers, Inc., 1980, p. 118.*

BASEBALL PLAYER, 1932
Vaclav Vytlacil
Tempera on canvas, 21 × 25¼ inches
The Gladstone Collection of Baseball Art

BASEBALL PLAYER, 1938
Guy Pène Du Bois
Ink and watercolor, 15¼ × 12 inches

Collection of Bert Randolph Sugar, New York

A pitcher is depicted contemplating his next pitch. Reproduced in Play Ball! A Century of Sports in Art. *New York: The Queens Museum, 1978, p. 9.*

BASEBALL PLAYER
William King
Aluminum sculpture, height 14 inches

BASEBALL PLAYER, c. 1975
Bernard Langlais
Wood relief, painted, 31¾ × 23 inches
Collection of Mr. and Mrs. Lew Wolff

A batter, catcher, and umpire are depicted.

BASEBALL PLAYER (AT BAT), 1982
Michael Hurson
Pencil, pastel, ink, and conte crayon on paper, 21 × 16½ inches
Collection of Elizabeth Murray, New York

Abstract depiction of a baseball batter. Reproduced in Diamonds Are Forever: Artists and Writers on Baseball *edited by Peter H. Gordon. San Francisco: Chronicle Books, 1987, p. 69.*

BASEBALL PLAYER (FIRST BASEMAN), c. 1915
Oronzo Cosentino
Bronze sculpture, height 21 inches
The Gladstone Collection of Baseball Art

Depicts a first baseman stretching to catch a ball. Reproduced in exhibition catalog, The Grand Game of Baseball, *essay by Shelly Mehlman Dinhofer. New York: Museum of the Borough of Brooklyn, 1987, plate 8.*

BASEBALL PLAYERS
Everett Shinn
Oil, 9¾ × 12 inches
ACA Galleries, New York

Pastoral depiction of a rural baseball game.

BASEBALL PLAYERS PRACTICING, 1875
Thomas Eakins
Watercolor and pencil on paper, 10¹³⁄₁₆ × 12⅞ inches
Rhode Island School of Design, Providence, Rhode Island, Jesse Metcalf and Walter H. Kimball funds

Realist depiction of a batter and catcher waiting for a pitch. Reproduced in Eakins Watercolors *by Donelson F. Hoopes. New York: Watson-Guptill Publications, 1971, plate 6.*

BASEBALL PLAYER WITH QUILTED PANTS, c. 1880
Archie Gunn
Watercolor, 27 × 15 inches
Collection of Bert Randolph Sugar, New York

BASEBALL SQUARE, c. 1971
Harry Nadler
Oil on canvas, 21½ × 18 inches

BASEBALL STING, c. 1910
Joseph Coll
Pen and ink on board, 13¼ × 16¾ inches
Collection of Mr. and Mrs. Bill Goff, New York

BASEBALL (WAITING FOR THE PITCH), c. 1931
Marjorie Phillips
Oil on canvas
The Phillips Collection, Washington, D.C.

Depicts a panoramic view of baseball action at Griffith Stadium in Washington, D.C. Also titled, The Baseball Game.

BATCOLUMN, 1975
Claes Oldenburg
Metal sculpture, height 39½ inches
National Museum of American Art,

Baseball's Masterpiece

It is fortunate that while Winslow Homer, William Glackens, and John Singer Sargent never rendered a work of baseball art, at least one American master did.

In 1875 Thomas Eakins, one of America's finest realist painters, visited Philadelphia's Jefferson Street Grounds to pursue his impassioned study of the city's skilled athletes. Having previously painted boxers, swimmers, and scullers, Eakins turned his attention to baseball players.

He found the "Athletic boys," as he called them, ". . . very fine in their build. They are the same stuff as bullfighters only bullfighters are older and a trifle stronger perhaps." As if to underscore the resemblance, Eakins rendered the batter in a matador-like pose as he waits confidently for the pitch.

The two players shown in *Baseball Players Practising*, though never certainly identified, are probably infielder Davy Force and catcher John Clapp. The Philadelphia Athletics were a formidable club in 1875, finishing second to the Boston "Champions" in the National Association standings.

In baseball's early days, when games were played during the afternoon, practice meant something different than it does today. Early morning practices were scheduled by managers in order to establish control over the players and to discourage them from staying out late the night before. As part of their daily routine, baseball players practiced briefly in the morning, changed out of their uniforms, and returned to the park to play the game later that day.

Today, of course, practice simply refers to the warming up ritual that occurs immediately before the game.

By rendering a practice scene rather than an actual game situation, Eakins was able to focus on the personality of the players rather than the dramatics of the sport. It is apparent by the generosity of light on the field, and by the obliviousness of the dark stands in the background, that Eakins was impressed by the special world in which baseball players moved. Both players, despite their rugged mustachios and tough-as-leather skin, are portrayed as veritable icons of dignified and aristocratic youth.

In this baseball masterpiece, Thomas Eakins reminds us that in 1875, as today, there was no existence on earth that seemed so favored and free as that of a big league baseball player. ◆

Baseball Players Practicing (1875), watercolor by Thomas Eakins. This most famous of baseball paintings depicts a Philadelphia Athletics batting practice scene. Artist Thomas Eakins's superb painting re-creates the special world that the ballplayers occupied. (Rhode Island School of Design.)

Batcolumn (1977), *metal statue by Claes Oldenburg. This 100-foot steel lattice statue stands at the Great Lakes Program Center in Chicago. (U.S. General Services Administration, Art-in-Architecture Program.)*

Smithsonian Institution, Washington, D.C., transfer from General Services Administration
See also: Bat Spinning at the Speed of Light

Study for the Batcolumn *monument erected in 1977. Reproduced in exhibition catalog,* The

Grand Game of Baseball, *essay by Shelly Mehlman Dinhofer. New York: Museum of the Borough of Brooklyn, 1987, plate 6.*

BATCOLUMN, 1977
Claes Oldenburg
Metal statue, height 100 feet

Social Security Administration, Great Lakes Program Center, Chicago, Illinois
See also: Batcolumn (1975)

Representation of a baseball bat on a grand scale. Reproduced in the New York Times, *September 22, 1985, p. E 22.*

BAT-E, 1985
Margaret Wharton
Wood and epoxy figure, 15 × 14 inches
Collection of Phyllis Kind, New York

Whimsical representation of a coiled baseball bat. Reproduced in Diamonds Are Forever: Artists and Writers on Baseball *edited by Peter H. Gordon. San Francisco: Chronicle Books, 1987, p. 37.*

BAT SPINNING AT THE SPEED OF LIGHT, 1967
Claes Oldenburg
Study for proposed monument, 17¾ × 12 inches
Collection of Sydney and Frances Lewis, Richmond, Virginia
See also: Baseball in Miscellaneous Art and Illustrations

One of several variant studies for Oldenburg's Batcolumn *statue. Reproduced in* Claes Oldenburg *by Barbara Rose. New York: Museum of Modern Art, 1970, p. 105.*

BATTER'S BOX
William Feldman
Oil
Spectrum Fine Art Ltd., New York

Depicts a batter waiting for a pitch.

BATTER UP!, 1922
George Luks
Composite drawing

Sketches of Babe Ruth, Ty Cobb, Irish Meusel, Jesse Barnes, Heinie Groh, Eddie Collins, and action drawing titled, Safe at Second! *Reproduced in* Vanity Fair, *August 1922, p. 70.*

A MONUMENT TO BASEBALL

In the city of monuments to American presidents, public servants, and war heroes, consideration was once given to the placement of a monument to baseball. Hearings were held in the United States House of Representatives during the early 1920s to decide on a suitable monument to the national game in Washington, D.C.

Reports were issued and recommendations were made. Sculptor James Earle Fraser was chosen to supervise submissions for the monument. But when details of the 1919 "Black Sox" scandal began to unfold in the newspapers around 1921, baseball fell into disrepute and plans for the monument were quietly discontinued.

Today, the nearest thing to a national baseball monument is Claes Oldenburg's colossal statue of a baseball bat in downtown Chicago. The 100-foot tall, 20-ton structure, titled *Batcolumn*, contains 1,608 pieces of welded steel in a diamond lattice pattern, symbolizing a baseball diamond.

But sculptor Oldenburg once had another, more grandiose plan to memorialize baseball. He envisioned having Chicago's Comiskey Park enclosed in a dome and established as a museum. Statues of the managers and players, each in a pose exactly as if a game were in progress, would be placed at every position in the field, in the coaching boxes, and within the dugouts. In this way, a typical baseball game would be permanently frozen in time.

Only one person would be seen moving about the field. He would be the park's groundskeeper, who would be given the title of Museum Curator.

BATTER UP
James Chapin
Oil on canvas, 59 × 40 inches
The Encyclopaedia Britannica Collection, New York

Depicts a batter, catcher, and umpire in a small-town baseball game. Reproduced in Contemporary American Painting *by Grace Pagano. New York: Duell, Sloan and Pearce, 1945, plate 20.*

BATTER UP, 1973
John Wesley
Oil on canvas, 66 × 66 inches
The Abrams Family Collection, New York

BEATEN BALL CLUB, 1949
Clyde Singer
Oil on canvas, 28 × 22 inches

Depicts a Mid-Atlantic minor league game in Youngstown, Ohio.

BECKETT AND BASEBALL, 1986
Harvey Breverman
Pastel on paper, 22 × 31 inches
Collection of the artist

Satirical depiction of playwright Samuel Beckett arguing with an umpire. Reproduced in Diamonds Are Forever: Artists and Writers on Baseball *edited by Peter H. Gordon. San Francisco: Chronicle Books, 1987, p. 125.*

BIG BROTHER'S BASEBALL HAT
Cary Nelson
Bronze, height 10 inches
National Art Museum of Sport, West Haven, Connecticut

BIG STRETCH, 1963
Joe Brown
Bronze sculpture, height 9 inches

Depicts a first baseman stretching to catch a throw. Reproduced in Joe Brown: Retrospective Catalogue 1932–1966. *Privately published, plate 94.*

BIRDIE TEBBETTS, 1978
Lance Richbourg
Oil on canvas, 83 × 99 inches
Collection of Schweber Electronics Corp.

Depicts a catcher tagging a sliding runner at home plate. Also titled, Untitled (Up-ended Catcher). *Reproduced in* Diamonds Are Forever: Artists and Writers on Baseball *edited by Peter H. Gordon. San Francisco: Chronicle Books, 1987, p. 106.*

BLOCKING THE PLATE, 1979
Lance Richbourg
Oil on canvas, 48½ × 97 inches

Dramatic depiction of a catcher tagging a sliding runner at home plate. Reproduced in New England, *May 6, 1981.*

BOB FELLER AND BALL, 1963
Kendall Shaw
Acrylic on canvas, 75 × 53 inches
Collection of the artist

BOB GIBSON
Lance Richbourg
Oil on canvas
O. K. Harris Works of Art, New York

Hall of Fame pitcher Bob Gibson is depicted at mid-delivery. Reproduced in the Washington Post, *April 7, 1983, p. E 1.*

Casey Stengel (1965), sculpture by Rhoda Sherbell. Ol' Casey's craggy wisdom and salty humor are lovingly portrayed by the artist in this polychromed plaster sculpture. (Queens Museum. Photo: Phyllis Bilick.)

BOREDOM ON THE BENCH, 1955

Saul Steinberg
Ink and colored pencil

Humorous cartoon depiction of baseball players sitting on a dugout bench. Reproduced in Life, *July 11, 1955.*

BOYS AT BAT, 1979

Eric Fischl
Oil on canvas, 84 × 69 inches
Collection of Edwin L. Stringer

Satirical depiction of a male nude swinging a phallic bat. Reproduced in Diamonds Are Forever: Artists and Writers on Baseball *edited by Peter H. Gordon. San Francisco: Chronicle Books, 1987, p. 143.*

BOYS PLAYING BALL, 1955

Chen Chi
Watercolor, 13 × 53 inches
Collection of the artist

Panoramic depiction of a New York city street baseball game. Reproduced in exhibition catalog, Sport in Art: From American Collections Assembled for an Olympic Year. *New York: Sports Illustrated and the American Federation of Arts, 1955, plate 13.*

BOY WITH BALL AND BAT, 1844

Artist Unknown
Oil on canvas, 23½ × 19 inches
The Gladstone Collection of Baseball Art

Portrait of a schoolboy holding a ball and bat.

BOY WITH BASEBALL, 1925

George Luks
Oil on canvas, 30 × 25 inches
Edward Joseph Gallagher III Memorial Collection

Portrait of a youngster and the symbol of his overriding passion. Reproduced in American Painting in the 20th Century *by Henry Geldzahler. New York: The Metropolitan Museum of Art, 1965, p. 23.*

BRONX CHEER: VIEW FROM LEFT FIELD WITH SELF PORTRAIT, 1984

Thom Corn
Acrylic and mixed-media
Real Art Ways, Hartford, Connecticut

Depicts a group of derisive fans. Reproduced in the Hartford Courant, *March 3, 1985, p. G 4.*

BROOKLYN BUMS CLUBHOUSE, 1955

Joseph Delaney

Charcoal on cardboard, 24 × 30 inches
Ewing Gallery of Art and Architecture, University of Tennessee

BROTHERHOOD OF EXCELLENCE, 1974

Art McKellips
Wood carving, bas-relief, 8 feet 2¼ inches × 7 feet 1½ inches
Atlanta Fulton County Stadium, Atlanta, Georgia

Depicts Babe Ruth with an arm around the shoulders of Henry Aaron.

CAMPANELLA, 1982

Lance Richbourg
Oil on canvas, 33 × 12 inches
O. K. Harris Works of Art, New York

Depicts Hall of Famer Roy Campanella at the completion of his swing. Reproduced in Sport in Art *by Robert Henkes. New York: Prentice Hall Press, 1986, p. 86.*

CAMPY AT THE PLATE, 1980

Elaine de Kooning
Acrylic on canvas, 30 × 39½ inches
Collection of the artist

Depicts a runner being congratulated by his teammates at home plate. Reproduced in Diamonds Are Forever: Artists and Writers on Baseball *edited by Peter H. Gordon. San Francisco: Chronicle Books, 1987, p. 103.*

CARL YASTRZEMSKI

William Dula
Oil on canvas
Collection of the artist

Photo-realist depiction of Red Sox outfielder Carl Yastrzemski at the completion of his swing. Reproduced in Sport in Art *by Robert Henkes. New York: Prentice Hall Press, 1986, p. 98.*

CASEY AT THE BAT, c. 1935

Paul Clemens
Charcoal drawing, 12 × 16 inches

Preliminary sketch for an essay series of four

paintings. Reproduced in Time, *October 31, 1938, p. 43.*

CASEY AT THE BAT, c. 1935
Paul Clemens
Essay series of four paintings
Federal Arts Project, Washington, D.C.

Depicts four scenes from the famous ballad.

CASEY AT THE BAT, 1985
Mark Lundeen
Bronze sculpture, life size
Collection of John McGivern II, Topeka, Kansas, and James Cole, Knoxville, Tennessee
See also: Baseball in Miscellaneous Art and Illustrations

Depicts Mudville's Mighty Casey leaning on a bat.

CASEY STENGEL, 1965
Rhoda Sherbell
Sculpture, polychromed plaster, height 46 inches
Queens Museum, New York, gift of Mervin Honig and Philip Schiavo

An oracular Casey Stengel is depicted in a New York Mets uniform. Reproduced in Champions of American Sport *by Mark Pachter. New York: Harry N. Abrams, Inc., 1981, p. 56.*

CASEY STRIKES OUT, 1962
William Copley
Copley Art Trust Collection

Stylized depiction of a batter, catcher, and umpire. Also titled, No Joy in Mudville. *Reproduced in* The New Painting *by Udo Kultermann. New York: Praeger, 1969, plate 112.*

CATCHER, 1940
William Zorach
Bronze sculpture, height 13½ inches
The Gladstone Collection of Baseball Art

Depicts a catcher crouched on one knee.

Reproduced in Gallery Notes. *Milwaukee Art Institute, Vol. 19, No. 6, March 1947.*

THE CATCHER, 1965
Joseph Hirsch
Oil on canvas, 18 × 10½ inches

CATCHER AT THE PLATE, c. 1953
Thomas Meehan
Oil

Expressionistic depiction of a crouching catcher. Reproduced in Sports Illustrated, *June 13, 1955, p. 63.*

CATCHER BEHIND THE SCREEN, 1953
Thomas Meehan
Oil, 38 × 19 inches
Collection of the artist

Abstract expressionist depiction of a catcher reaching for a pop foul. Reproduced in Sports Illustrated, *June 13, 1955, p. 64.*

CELEBRATION OF THE 1974 WORLD SERIES IN OAKLAND, 1986
Lance Richbourg
Mixed-media, 30 × 22 inches
The Butler Institute of American Art, Youngstown, Ohio

Panoramic depiction of jubilant fans dashing onto the field at the conclusion of the World Series. Reproduced in exhibition catalog, The Grand Game of Baseball, *essay by Shelly Mehlman Dinhofer. New York: Museum of the Borough of Brooklyn, 1987, overleaf.*

CHAMPION'S CHOICE, 1963
Leo Jensen
Mixed-media construction
Spectrum Fine Art Ltd., New York

Satirical representation of a baseball batter. Reproduced in Champions of American Sport *by Mark Pachter. New York: Harry N. Abrams, Inc., 1981, p. 21.*

CHRISTY MATHEWSON, 1920
Gertrude Boyle

Christy Mathewson *(1920), bust by Gertrude Boyle. A bronze casting of this heroic bust of the Hall of Fame pitcher can be viewed at the Baseball Hall of Fame in Cooperstown, New York. (National Baseball Library.)*

Bronze bust, life size
National Baseball Hall of Fame and Museum, Cooperstown, New York

Heroic bust portrait of the Hall of Famer. Reproduced in Champions of American Sport *by Mark Pachter. New York: Harry N. Abrams, Inc., 1981, p. 29.*

CHRISTY MATHEWSON
James F. Kernan
Oil on canvas
Keystone Junior College, LaPlume, Pennsylvania

On-the-field portrait of the Hall of Fame pitcher. Reproduced in Champions of American Sport *by Mark Pachter. New York: Harry N. Abrams, Inc., 1981, p. 26.*

CHRISTY MATHEWSON
C. R. Shaare
Oil on canvas, 28 × 21 inches
The Old Print Shop, New York

CHUCK KLEIN HITTING FOR THE 1929 PHILS, 1978
Lance Richbourg
Oil on canvas, 20 × 30 inches
Collection of Mrs. Sherwin Kamin

The Hall of Fame outfielder and slugger is depicted.

CLAUDIA AT DOUBLEDAY FIELD, 1984
Claudia DeMonte
Pulp, paper, acrylic, and mixed-media, 12 × 14 inches
Gracie Mansion Gallery

Depicts a formally dressed woman playing baseball. Reproduced in Diamonds Are Forever: Artists and Writers on Baseball *edited by Peter H. Gordon. San Francisco: Chronicle Books, 1987, p. 91.*

CLETIS BOYER CATCHING A BALL, 1963
Kendall Shaw
Acrylic on canvas, 96 × 41 inches
Collection of K. R. Moses, Metairie, Louisiana

Depicts a silhouetted player reaching to catch a ball. Reproduced in Art News Annual, *1965, p. 76.*

COMISKEY PARK, 1985
Buzz Spector
Pastel and paper relief, 8 × 10 inches
Collection of Bruce A. Ruzgis

Stylized aerial depiction of Chicago's Comiskey Park. Reproduced in Diamonds Are Forever: Artists and Writers on Baseball *edited by Peter H. Gordon. San Francisco: Chronicle Books, 1987, p. 18.*

CORRUGATED CATCHER, 1954
Saul Steinberg
Mixed-media, 30 × 20 inches
Collection of Anton Van Dalen, New York

Whimsical depiction of a baseball catcher as a modern American icon. Reproduced in Life, *July 11, 1955.*

COUNTY STADIUM—OCTOBER 7, 1957, 1958
Robert Gwathmey
Watercolor

Panoramic depiction of jubilant Milwaukee Braves players at the conclusion of Game 5 of the 1957 World Series. Reproduced in Sports Illustrated, *April 14, 1958, pp. 103–104.*

COUNTY STADIUM—OCTOBER 7, 1957, c. 1965
Robert Gwathmey
Oil on canvas, 32½ × 45½ inches
Terry Dintenfass Gallery, New York

Copied from an earlier watercolor. Also titled, World Series. *Reproduced in* Diamonds Are Forever: Artists and Writers on Baseball *edited by Peter H. Gordon. San Francisco: Chronicle Books, 1987, pp. 78–79.*

CROWD AT EBBETS FIELD, c. 1960
David Levine
Oil on canvas, 29 × 36 inches
Collection of the artist

DEATH OF AN UMPIRE
Elbert Davis
Oil on linen, 21½ × 41 inches
Collection of Italo Scanga and Stephanie Smedley Scanga

Depicts a lifeless figure in an empty ballpark. Reproduced in Diamonds Are Forever: Artists and Writers on Baseball *edited by Peter H. Gordon. San Francisco: Chronicle Books, 1987, p. 151.*

DESIGN FOR NEW MEXICO BASEBALL TEAM UNIFORMS, c. 1926
John Sloan
Watercolor, 10⅞ × 8⅜ inches
Kraushaar Galleries, New York

DIAGONAL SHADOW, 1980
Lance Richbourg
Oil on canvas, 68½ × 93 inches
O. K. Harris Works of Art, New York

Depicts home plate action amid a line of shadow and bright light.

DIARY SERIES: RED SOX, 1975
John Fawcett
Essay series of drawings
Ink and collage on paper, 14 × 11 inches each
O. K. Harris Works of Art, New York

THE DICK DONOVAN SURPRISE, 1963
Kendall Shaw
Acrylic on canvas, 68 × 96 inches
Collection of the artist

DIFFERENCE OF OPINION, 1982
Paul Clemens
Charcoal and pastel, 24 × 36 inches
Collection of Tom Lasorda

Depicts Dodger manager Tom Lasorda arguing with an umpire.

DIZZY DEAN
Fred Conway
Oil on canvas

Panoramic depiction of a just-completed game involving a controversial call. Reproduced in Look, *May 5, 1953, p. 105.*

DIZZY DEAN
Lance Richbourg
Oil on canvas
O. K. Harris Works of Art, New York

Hall of Fame pitcher Dizzy Dean is depicted at the completion of his delivery. Reproduced in the Washington Post, *April 7, 1983, p. E 15.*

DODGER LUMBER OF '54, 1985
Andy Jurinko
Oil on canvas, 62 × 80 inches
Collection of Robert Sui

Brooklyn Dodger greats Gil Hodges, Roy Campanella, Duke Snider, and Carl Furillo are shown in a group portrait. Reproduced in the New York Times, *April 23, 1987, p. B3.*

DOUBLE PLAY, 1953
Joe Brown
Sculpture, height 16 inches

Male nude representation of a baseball player pivoting for a double play. Reproduced in Joe Brown: Retrospective Catalogue 1932–1966. *Privately published, plate 182.*

DOUBLE PLAY, 1985
Tim Swartz
Watercolor on paper, 20 × 30 inches
Walker Gallery/The National Pastime, Cooperstown, New York

New York Yankees' shortstop Phil Rizzuto is depicted completing a double play.

DOWNTOWN CHICAGO, 1974
Mark Rucker
Oil on canvas, 49 × 35 inches
Collection of the artist

THE DREAM, 1979
Oscar De Mejo
Oil on masonite, 18 × 24 inches
Aberbach Fine Arts

A DREAM OF BEING, 1969
Sidney Tillim
Oil on canvas, 72 × 90 inches
Collection of the artist

Metaphorical depiction of a male watching a baseball game in the midst of feminine apathy and despair. Reproduced in Diamonds Are Forever: Artists and Writers on Baseball *edited by Peter H. Gordon. San Francisco: Chronicle Books, 1987, p. 149.*

EARL BATTEY CATCHING A BALL, 1963
Kendall Shaw
Acrylic on canvas, 63 × 27 inches
Collection of Mrs. Frances F. Shaw, Brooklyn, New York

Depicts a silhouetted player, glove extended, catching a ball.

THE EARLY YOUTH OF BABE RUTH, c. 1939
Philip Evergood
Oil on canvas, 20 × 24 inches
Hirshhorn Museum and Sculpture Garden, Smithsonian Institution, Washington, D.C., gift of Joseph H. Hirshhorn

Ironic depiction of a young Babe Ruth and two of his reformatory school friends gazing upon an idyllic vista. Reproduced in Diamonds Are Forever: Artists and Writers on Baseball *edited by Peter H. Gordon. San Francisco: Chronicle Books, 1987, p. 52.*

EBBETS FIELD, 1983
Andy Jurinko
Charcoal and pastel on paper, 30 × 44 inches
Collection of Kidder Peabody and Co.

EBBETS FIELD, BROOKLYN, 1940
Winthrop Duthie Turney
Essay series of two drawings
Charcoal on paperboard, 12 × 14½ inches
Elliot Galleries

ERNIE BANKS, 1979
Nicolas Africano
Oil, acrylic, wax, and canvas on masonite, 13 × 32½ inches
Collection of Mr. and Mrs. Douglas Cohen

Depicts a kneeling Ernie Banks posing for a photograph. Reproduced in Diamonds Are Forever: Artists and Writers on Baseball *edited by Peter H. Gordon. San Francisco: Chronicle Books, 1987, pp. 58–59.*

EVERY DAY IS D-DAY UNDER THE EL, 1968
Richard Merkin
Oil on canvas

Metaphorical representation of baseball's place in the American consciousness. Reproduced in

The New Painting *by Udo Kultermann. New York: Praeger, 1969, plate 113.*

EXECUTIONERS ON THE MOUND, 1955
Saul Steinberg
Watercolor and ink

Stylized depiction of a conference on the mound during a change of pitchers. Reproduced in Life, *July 11, 1955.*

EXPOS IN THE RAIN, 1985
Red Grooms
Gouache on paper, in five panels, 17 × 70 inches
Collection of Lysiane Luong and Red Grooms

Depicts a panoramic view of a spring training game as seen from the backstop bleachers. Reproduced in Diamonds Are Forever: Artists and Writers on Baseball *edited by Peter H. Gordon. San Francisco: Chronicle Books, 1987, pp. 60–61.*

THE FIRST ENCOUNTER, 1984
Richard Merkin
Oil on canvas, 54 × 68½ inches
Terry Dintenfass Gallery, New York

Symbolic representation of baseball as a subject matter in a casual conversation. Reproduced in Art News, *February 1984, p. 6.*

FOLLOW THRU, c. 1978
John Dobbs
Watercolor on paper, 4 × 4 inches
ACA Galleries, New York

Depicts a pitcher at the completion of his delivery. Reproduced in Diamonds Are Forever: Artists and Writers on Baseball *edited by Peter H. Gordon. San Francisco: Chronicle Books, 1987, p. 97.*

FOUR AT BAT, 1964
Kendall Shaw
Acrylic on canvas, 68 × 96 inches
Collection of the artist

Four-panel depiction in silhouette of Mickey Mantle, Roger Maris, Babe Ruth, and Lou Gehrig.

Futurist Picture of the Opening Game (1914), by James H. Daugherty. The caption to this synchronistic work, as written by the artist and published in the New York Sunday Herald, reads: "This is not a picture of a baseball game. It is a representation of the various sensations of the onlooker. The pitcher whirls about, a confusion of head, arms and legs. The ball flashes across the diamond in curves that make a snake look like a curtain rod. The batter swings the stick in flashing semi-circles, driving the ball like a comet over the first baseman's head into the field. The runners tear around the diamond in a hurricane of flying legs and arms. The ball comes skyrocketing back to the field to the third baseman's mitt as he fails to block a famous slide. One side of the grand stand is a crazy quilt of waving hats and yelling mouths; on the other side the fans present a checkerboard of gloom—the losing bets." (Whitney Museum of American Art.)

FULL SWING, 1970
Joe Brown
Bronze sculpture, height 10 inches.

FULL SWING, 1975
Joe Brown
Bronze statue, height 15½ feet
Veterans Stadium, Philadelphia, Pennsylvania

Depicts a batter at the completion of his swing.

FUTURIST PICTURE OF THE OPENING GAME, 1914

James H. Daugherty
Color reproduction for the *New York Sunday Herald*, 9¼ × 12 inches
Whitney Museum of American Art, New York

Synchronistic depiction of baseball action. Reproduced in the New York Sunday Herald, *April 12, 1914.*

GAME BALL, 1987
James Sullivan
Charcoal on paper, 30 × 22 inches
Nancy Hoffman Gallery, New York

Depicts a still life of a baseball atop a pedestal. Reproduced in Diamonds Are Forever: Artists and Writers on Baseball *edited by Peter H. Gordon. San Francisco: Chronicle Books, 1987, p. 30.*

GEORGE LUKS PLAYING BASEBALL, 1904
Robert Henri
Ink on paper, 7 × 4¾ inches
Whitney Museum of American Art, New York, gift of Edward W. Root

Humorous cartoon depiction of the artist playing sandlot baseball. Reproduced in exhibition catalog, Forms in Sport: 1842–1978, *foreword by Alexander deWitt Walsh. New York: Terry Dintenfass, Inc., 1978, p. 24.*

GIANTS VS. METS, 1964
Marjorie Phillips
Oil on canvas, 36 × 42 inches
The Phillips Collection, Washington, D.C.

Depicts a panoramic view of baseball action at the Polo Grounds in New York.

GIL HODGES
Cary Nelson
Bronze, height 15 inches
National Art Museum of Sport, West Haven, Connecticut

GOING DOWN SWINGING, 1983
John Dobbs
Oil on linen, 16 × 14 inches

Depicts a pitcher's view of a batter swinging at a pitch.

GOING TO LEFT, 1983
John Dobbs
Oil on linen, 36 × 40 inches
ACA Galleries, New York

Depicts a batter, catcher, and pitcher studying the flight of the ball.

GRANDSTAND PLAY, 1955
Saul Steinberg
Ink and colored pencil

Whimsical depiction of an outfielder leaping to catch a ball. Reproduced in Life, *July 11, 1955.*

THE GREATEST MOMENT IN BIG LEAGUE BASEBALL, 1941
Edward Laning
Oil on canvas
National Baseball Hall of Fame and Museum, Cooperstown, New York

Panoramic depiction of Joe DiMaggio at bat during his 56-consecutive-game hit streak. Reproduced in Life, *September 29, 1941, p. 64.*

HACK WILSON, MY FATHER AND MY UNCLE CLINT, 1986
Lance Richbourg
Watercolor on paper, 39 × 58½ inches
O. K. Harris Works of Art, New York

Chicago Cubs' Hall of Famer Hack Wilson and Boston Braves' outfielder Lance Richbourg, Sr. are depicted in a late 1920s dugout scene.

HANK AARON, 1984
Lance Richbourg
Oil on canvas, 69 × 58 inches
O. K. Harris Works of Art, New York

Depicts Hall of Famer Henry Aaron leaping to catch a fly ball.

HEADING FOR THE SHOWERS, 1977
Larry Zingale
Oil on canvas, 11 × 14 inches
America's Folk Heritage Gallery, New York

Depicts a folk art view of a pitcher leaving the field.

HENRY AARON, 1982
Ed Dwight
Bronze statue
Atlanta Fulton County Stadium, Atlanta, Georgia

Depicts the all-time home run leader at the completion of his swing.

Hank Aaron *(1984), oil by Lance Richbourg. (O.K. Harris Works of Art.)*

HOME, 1980
Lance Richbourg
Oil on canvas, 48 × 68 inches
O. K. Harris Works of Art, New York

Depicts a runner sliding safely into home plate. Reproduced in exhibition catalog, Time Out: Sport and Leisure in America Today. *Tampa, Florida: The Tampa Museum, 1983, p. 17.*

THE HOME RUN, 1938
Paul Clemens

Oil on panel, 14 × 18 inches
Juliana Force Collection, New York

Whimsical close-up depiction of a jubilant crowd scene.

THE HOME TEAM, c. 1905
Thomas Fogarty
Pen and ink, 15 × 15 inches
Marbella Gallery, Inc.

HONUS WAGNER, 1955
Frank Vittor

Honus Wagner *(1955), sculpture by Frank Vittor. This heroic statue in tribute to the Pirates Hall of Famer can be seen at Three Rivers Stadium in Pittsburgh. (National Baseball Library.)*

Bronze statue, height 9 feet
Three Rivers Stadium, Pittsburgh, Pennsylvania

Heroic depiction of the Hall of Famer at the completion of his swing. Reproduced in the Pittsburgh Post-Gazette, *July 22, 1972.*

HONUS WAGNER, 1979
Lance Richbourg
Oil on canvas, 62 × 83 inches
Collection of Sydney and Frances Lewis

Depicts the Pittsburgh Pirates' great in a heroic batting pose. Reproduced in exhibition catalog, Lance Richbourg. Paintings: The American Sport, February 24–April 4, 1981. *Los Angeles: Arco Center for Visual Art.*

HONUS WAGNER, 1984
Tim Swartz
Watercolor on paper, 20 × 30 inches
National Baseball Hall of Fame and Museum, Cooperstown, New York

Depicts the Hall of Famer striding toward first base upon hitting the ball.

HOOK-SLIDE, 1949
Joe Brown
Bronze sculpture, height 9 inches
The Gladstone Collection of Baseball Art

Depicts a baseball player sliding into a base. Reproduced in Joe Brown: Retrospective

Catalogue 1932–1966. *Privately published, plate 115.*

HURLER, 1935
Joe Brown
Sculpture, height 9 inches

Male nude representation of a pitcher delivering a baseball. Reproduced in Life, *May 19, 1941, p. 90.*

INJURED CATCHER, 1975
Leonard Dufresne
Acrylic on masonite, 9 × 6 inches
Collection of Sydney and Frances Lewis

Depicts a fallen catcher being administered to by a trainer. Reproduced in Diamonds Are Forever: Artists and Writers on Baseball *edited by Peter H. Gordon. San Francisco: Chronicle Books, 1987, p. 105.*

INSTANT REPLAY, 1974
Paul Spina
Pen and ink drawing, 12 × 14½ inches
Collection of the artist

IN THE DUGOUT, 1938
Paul Clemens
Oil on panel, 22 × 30 inches
WPA Federal Art Project, U.S. Treasury Department, Washington, D.C.

The Great Dutchman

In the baseball we dream about, relive, and play in our imaginations, some players seem always to excel and enthrall even in our personal mythology. Certainly the Babe and Jackie Robinson and Willie Mays and Ted Williams all do. In this masterful painting, executed in 1979, Lance Richbourg has given us yet another giant who grows ever taller in the mists.

Honus Wagner, bowlegged and ham-handed, is a likely subject for such mythic reinvention. As a shortstop for the Pittsburgh Pirates during the early 1900s, he was Gibraltar-steady and granite-hard: thick-muscled, sharp-featured, imposing. He was, at a time when America was a nation of tradesmen and laborers, the workingman's ball-player, not only because he played hard and uncomplainingly, but because Honus Wagner himself looked like a steelworker or stonemason. On the playing field as in baseball lore, Hans Wagner was a monument of solidity and strength.

Those who saw him play marvelled at his innate grace, all the more so because Honus's style of play tended to be headlong and unpredictable. It has frequently been told how Wagner scooped up handfuls of dirt and gravel with ground balls, as though he possessed little more than a raw intuitiveness for the game. But the truth is that Honus was such an exceptionally gifted ballplayer that he is probably the only man in the history of baseball who could have been elected to the Hall of Fame at any infield or outfield position he might have chosen to play. Not even Babe Ruth, who started his career as a pitcher, or Willie Mays, whose baseball sense was unsurpassed if not otherworldly, could attest to as much.

In the painting, the essence of both the grace and brute strength of Honus Wagner is conveyed. There is a dreamlike quality about the work, as if the artist has imagined the great Dutchman still playing somewhere in the arena of time, still finding the sweet spot, still ringing triples and doubles through the gaps of eternity. Indeed, Wagner is spotlighted in a metaphysical stillness, like one who has been benevolently cast in an enchanted spell: that of knowing forever the joy of being a baseball star.

While Lance Richbourg based *Honus Wagner* and other of his paintings on old black and white photographs from picture albums and magazine photos from the 1920s and 1930s, he knows firsthand the color and lore of baseball's past. His father, Lance Richbourg, Sr., played in the major leagues for eight seasons from 1921 to 1932,

Honus Wagner (1979), oil by Lance Richbourg. When the Great Dutchman retired in 1917 he had made more hits, scored more runs, and stolen more bases than anyone in the history of baseball. John McGraw considered the shortstop to be the greatest player ever to have played the game. (O.K. Harris Works of Art.)

mostly as an outfielder for the Boston Braves. From his youth Richbourg's life has been steeped in the textures and tonalities of his father's game, the red clay and the dry dust and the midafternoon shadows and the special sunlight that can be found nowhere else in the world but in a ballpark. Baseball is more than Richbourg's artistic genre, it is a cherished homeland—like the gaily-colored gardens of Renoir's France or Winslow Homer's mist-shrouded shores.

Richbourg's paintings are not so much a realistic depiction of baseball action as a revelation of a decisive moment in a game that has been suspended and transmuted in the artist's romantic inner vision. There are no false dramatics or cloying nostalgia in his paintings. The viewer is unconcerned whether the runner is out or safe or whether the catch was made or not; he wishes only to experience the fullness and roundness—the sound and feel—of his own reveries come to life.

When Honus Wagner's playing days were over, he remained for many years with the Pittsburgh Pirates as a coach. On occasion, before games, he joined in fielding or batting practice, and invariably a hush would prevail on the field. Every player—on the home and visiting teams alike—stopped whatever he was doing to watch in awe as the old Dutchman ranged deep into the hole at shortstop or cracked line drives against the wall. It happened wherever the Pirates played, for as long as Honus remained in the game—even when the players were more than a generation removed from Wagner's time.

Lance Richbourg has captured the sense of an ageless Honus Wagner taking batting practice untold seasons after his playing days had ended. One need not be aware of Wagner's Hall of Fame career, or even be a baseball enthusiast, to find *Honus Wagner* a compelling work of art. What is immortalized is not simply a baseball player but the joyous dreams of a whole baseball loving nation. As fans we are enchanted by Richbourg's work. As dreamers we are lost in a hush—and we are awed. ◆

Depicts a close-up view of a tense dugout scene. Reproduced in American Painting Today, *essay by Forbes Watson. Washington, D.C.: American Federation of Arts, 1939.*

INTO THIRD, 1983
John Dobbs
Oil on linen, 36 × 40 inches

Depicts a runner sliding head first into third base. Compositionally similar to Play at Third.

IVAN THROUGH A WINDOW, 1975
Mark Rucker
Oil on canvas, 50 × 36 inches
Collection of the artist

JOE DIMAGGIO, 1987
Tim Swartz
Watercolor on paper, 24 × 18 inches
Collection of Phillip D. Mote, Long Beach, California

The Yankee Hall of Famer is depicted at the completion of his swing.

JOE GARAGIOLA
Harold Castor
Bronze sculpture, height 27 inches
Renaissance Art Foundry and Gallery, Bridgeport, Connecticut

Depicts the St. Louis Cardinals' catcher, mask off, catching a pop-up. Reproduced in exhibition catalog, Castor. *New York: Sculptors Workshop, Inc.*

JULY FOURTH, 1951
Anna Mary Robertson (Grandma) Moses
Oil on canvas, 23⅞ × 30 inches
The White House, Washington, D.C.

Folk art depiction of an Independence Day picnic scene in which a baseball game is played. Reproduced in Grandma Moses *by Otto Kallir. New York: Harry N. Abrams, Inc., 1973, plage 95.*

KIRBY HIGBE (22–9), WHIT WYATT (22–10) AND THE PITCHING STAFF OF THE NATIONAL LEAGUE CHAMPION BROOKLYN DODGERS, 1941 MINUS TAMULIS, 1967
Richard Merkin
Mixed-media, 60 × 80 inches

In the Dugout *(1938), oil by Paul Clemens. (U.S. Treasury Department.)*

A FATHER REMEMBERED

When Lance Richbourg was born, his 40-year-old father was several years removed from his days as a Boston Braves rightfielder. While the artist never saw his father play in the major leagues, Richbourg nonetheless grew up knowing baseball not only as a game but as an impassioned way of life.

His father, Lance Richbourg, Sr., played eight seasons in the major leagues from 1921 to 1932, compiling a solid lifetime batting average of .308. In 1928, during his second year as a regular for the Braves, Lance Richbourg enjoyed the finest season of his career: 206 hits and a batting average of .337 in 148 games. On July 31 of the following year, Richbourg tied a modern major league record by hitting three triples in one game against the Cubs at Wrigley Field.

After his retirement from the major leagues, Richbourg spent many years playing and managing professional and semipro baseball all around the northwest Florida area. The younger Richbourg fondly remembers warming up pitchers and sweeping out the grandstands in those Florida panhandle games his father played.

Because he'd been around the game so much during his youth, the artist for years resisted baseball as a subject for his paintings. Then, after accepting a commercial art commission that involved baseball as a theme, the younger Richbourg turned to family picture albums to paint scenes from his father's major league days. Many of these paintings are warm tributes to his father and the passion and spirit with which he played the game.

Lance Richbourg, Sr., owned and operated a family cattle farm for many years near Laurel Hills, Florida, and he was the county superintendent of schools for 16 years before his death in 1974. The younger Richbourg presently teaches art at St. Michael's College in Winooski, Vermont. His paintings remain the finest examples of baseball-related art produced today.

Collection of Carol R. and Avram J. Goldberg

KOUFAX PITCHING I, 1963
Kendall Shaw
Acrylic on canvas, 53 × 75 inches

KOUFAX PITCHING II, 1964
Kendall Shaw
Acrylic on canvas, 51 × 51 inches
Collection of Mrs. E. P. Jones, New York

Silhouetted close-up depiction of a pitcher delivering a baseball. Reproduced in the New York Times Book Review, *May 8, 1966, p. 6 (part II).*

KRANEPOOL, 1975
Mark Rucker
Colored pencil, 24 × 18 inches
Collection of the artist

New York Mets first baseman Ed Kranepool is depicted.

Hack Wilson, My Father and My Uncle Clint *(1986), watercolor by Lance Richbourg. A pregame dugout scene during the late 1920s. Chicago Cubs slugger Hack Wilson and the artist's father, Lance Richbourg, Sr., of the Boston Braves, talk about hitting and other secrets of the game (O.K. Harris Works of Art.)*

L.A. DODGERS, 1978
Robert Kushner
Watercolor on paper, 67 × 30 inches
Collection of Thomas B. Solomon

Expressionistic depiction of baseball players. Reproduced in Diamonds Are Forever: Artists and Writers on Baseball *edited by Peter H. Gordon. San Francisco: Chronicle Books, 1987, p. 82.*

LANCE RICHBOURG SLIDES IN AT SULPHURDALE, 1975
Lance Richbourg
Oil on canvas, 78 × 108 inches

Depicts the artist's father, Lance Richbourg, Sr., sliding head-first into home plate. Reproduced in Palm, *Spring 1983, p. 23.*

THE LATE THROW, 1958
Edmond Kohn
Oil on masonite
Collection of Edmond O'Brien, Los Angeles, California

Close-up expressionistic view of a catcher tagging a sliding runner at home plate. Reproduced in Sports Illustrated, *August 25, 1958, pp. 52–53.*

LAYING DOWN THE BUNT, 1954
Thomas Meehan
Oil, 26 × 38 inches
Collection of the artist

LITTLE ALICE
Barbara Baldwin
Watercolor and crayon

Depicts a schoolgirl swinging a bat. Reproduced in the New York Times *(Connecticut section), February 8, 1987, p. CN 31.*

THE LONG BALL HITTER, 1957
Edmond Kohn
Oil on masonite
Collection of Edmond O'Brien, Los Angeles, California

Abstract expressionist portrait of a baseball player. Reproduced in Sports Illustrated, *April 15, 1957, p. 88.*

THE LONG STRETCH, 1949
Jacob Lawrence
Tempera on panel, 20 × 24 inches

African-American folk depiction of a close play at first base. Reproduced in exhibition catalog, Forms in Sport: 1842–1978, *foreword by Alexander deWitt Walsh. New York: Terry Dintenfass, Inc., 1978, p. 43.*

LOOKING FOR A CURVEBALL IN CUERNAVACA, 1983
Karl Wirsum
Acrylic on canvas, 44 × 49 inches
Krannert Art Museum, University of Illinois, Champaign

Abstract depiction of a baseball batter. Reproduced in Diamonds Are Forever: Artists and Writers on Baseball *edited by Peter H. Gordon. San Francisco: Chronicle Books, 1987, p. 57.*

LOU GEHRIG, 1942
William Westcott
Bronze bust, life size

Off-the-field bust portrait of the Hall of Famer.

MAHAFFEY SHUTS OUT CINCINNATI, 1984
Bruce Brown
Oil on canvas

The Long Stretch *(1949), tempera by Jacob Lawrence. The struggle for survival in the ghetto is the metaphorical thesis for many of Jacob Lawrence's works. In this extraordinary painting, a typical play in a baseball game represents not only the black man's desire to excel but his determination to survive. (Terry Dintenfass Gallery.)*

American Academy and Institute of Arts and Letters, New York

Expressionistic depiction of Phillies' pitcher Art Mahaffey striking out a batter. Reproduced in Sport in Art *by Robert Henkes. New York: Prentice Hall Press, 1986, p. 94.*

MAN ON FIRST, 1948
James Chapin
Oil on canvas, 28 × 24 inches
The Gladstone Collection of Baseball Art

Depicts a first baseman and a runner leading away from first base.

MAN ON SECOND, 1975
Leonard Dufresne
Acrylic on masonite, 9 × 6 inches
Collection of Sydney and Frances Lewis

Depicts a runner leading away from second base. Reproduced in Diamonds Are Forever: Artists and Writers on Baseball *edited by Peter H. Gordon. San Francisco: Chronicle Books, 1987, p. 123.*

MASK AND MITT, 1974
Mary Jo Schwalbach
Mixed-media assemblage, 24 × 48 inches

Satirical depiction of a catcher, umpire, and fans. Reproduced in the New York Times, *October 16, 1977.*

MCGRAW WATCHING TRAVIS JACKSON, 1982
Lance Richbourg
Oil on canvas, 53 × 68 inches
O. K. Harris Works of Art, New York

Depicts a 1920s New York Giants batting practice scene. Reproduced in Sport in Art *by Robert Henkes. New York: Prentice Hall Press, 1986, p. 86.*

MESSAGE FROM THE MANAGER, 1955
Saul Steinberg
Ink and colored pencil

Whimsical depiction of a manager flashing signs from the dugout. Reproduced in Life, *July 11, 1955.*

MICKEY MANTLE, 1972
Mary Jo Schwalbach
Mixed-media assemblage, 48 × 36 inches

Depicts the Hall of Famer in a fielding pose. Reproduced in Play Ball! A Century of Sports in Art. *New York: The Queens Museum, 1978, p. 20.*

MINE BASEBALL, 1937
Mervin Jules
Tempera
National Baseball Hall of Fame and Museum, Cooperstown, New York

Impressionistic depiction of Pennsylvania coal miners playing a late-afternoon baseball game. Reproduced in Time, *January 3, 1938, pp. 28–29.*

MINOR LEAGUE, 1946
Clyde Singer
Oil on canvas, 40 × 50 inches
The Butler Institute of American Art, Youngstown, Ohio

Depicts a Youngstown Gremlins Mid-Atlantic League game at Idora Park. Reproduced in Diamonds Are Forever: Artists and Writers on Baseball *edited by Peter H. Gordon. San Francisco: Chronicle Books, 1987, p. 65.*

THE MINORS: THE YORK WHITE ROSES VS. THE TRENTON PACKERS, 1940
Byron Thomas
Tempera, 16 × 41 inches

Richly detailed panoramic depiction of a small-town minor league game. Also titled, Night Ball Game. *Reproduced in* Life, *June 23, 1941, p. 51.*

MR. BASEBALL, c. 1957
Harry Rosin
Bronze sculpture
National Baseball Hall of Fame and

Lou Gehrig (1942), bust by William Westcott. (National Baseball Library.)

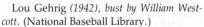

Museum, Cooperstown, New York

Depicts Hall of Fame manager Connie Mack with a scorecard in hand.

MY FATHER SLIDING IN, 1978
Lance Richbourg
Oil on canvas, 84 × 108 inches
Collection of American Republic Insurance Co.

Depicts Lance Richbourg, Sr., who played eight years in the major leagues, mostly as an outfielder for the Boston Braves, sliding into home plate. Reproduced in Arts Magazine, *November 1980, p. 20.*

MY FAVORITE ARTIST— STEINBERG, 1986
John Fawcett
Collage, 22 × 28¼ inches
The Gladstone Collection of Baseball Art

MY TURN AT BAT, 1987
Gerry Bergstein
Oil on canvas, 96 × 8 inches
Collection of the artist

A baseball bat is depicted as the allegorical Tree of Life. Reproduced in Diamonds Are Forever: Artists and Writers on Baseball *edited by Peter H. Gordon. San Francisco: Chronicle Books, 1987, p. 41.*

NATIONAL PASTIME, 1955
Ben Shahn
Drawing, ink on paper, 36 × 40¼ inches
Rosenfield Collection, Des Moines Art Center
See also: Baseball *(1968) (Baseball in Miscellaneous Art and Illustrations)*

Stylized depiction of a batter and catcher. Reproduced in Sport in Art *by Robert Henkes. New York: Prentice Hall Press, 1986, p. 91.*

THE NATIONAL PASTIME, 1987
Tim Swartz
Watercolor on paper, 20 × 30 inches
Collection of the artist

Depicts Hall of Fame manager Ed Barrow and a group of 1918 Red Sox players seated on a dugout bench.

NIGHT BALL GAME, 1946
Ferdinand E. Warren
Oil on canvas, 32 × 47 inches
Georgia Museum of Art, University of Georgia, Athens, Georgia

Panoramic depiction of a night game at Ebbets Field in Brooklyn. Also titled, Night Baseball. *Reproduced in* The Artist and the Sportsman *by Martha B. Scott. New York: Renaissance Editions, Inc., 1968, p. 79.*

NIGHT BASEBALL, 1951
Marjorie Phillips
Oil on canvas, 23¼ × 36 inches

The National Pastime (1987), watercolor by Tim Swartz. This evocative watercolor by Philadelphia-based artist Tim Swartz depicts manager Ed Barrow and a group of 1918 Boston Red Sox players in a spring training dugout scene. (Collection of the artist.)

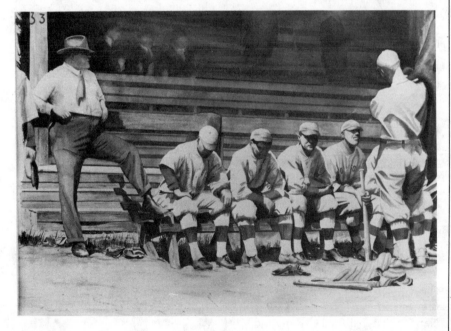

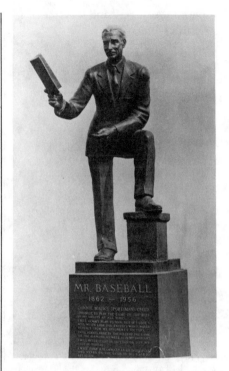

Mr. Baseball (c. 1957), sculpture by Harry Rosin. Hall of Famer Connie Mack, who managed the Philadelphia Athletics for 50 consecutive years, is shown with his proverbial scorecard in hand. (National Baseball Library.)

The Phillips Collection, Washington, D.C.

Depicts Joe DiMaggio waiting for a pitch during a game against the Senators at Griffith Stadium, Washington, D.C. Reproduced in Museums Discovered: The Phillips Collection *by Eleanor Green. Fort Lee, New Jersey: Penshurst Press, 1981, p. 148.*

NIGHT BASEBALL, 1962
Jay O'Meilia
Tempera on canvas, 24 × 30¼ inches
National Art Museum of Sport, West Haven, Connecticut

NIGHT BASEBALL
Jim Jonson
Acrylic on canvas, 45 × 50 inches

Collection of Abercrombie and Fitch, New York

Abstract expressionist depiction of a delivered pitch as seen from an umpire's view. Reproduced in The Art of Painting Sports *by Jim Jonson. New York: M. Grumbacher, Inc., 1975, p. 30.*

NIGHT GAME (PRACTICE TIME), 1979

Ralph Fasanella
Oil on canvas, 40 × 50 inches
Collection of the artist

Panoramic folk art depiction of pregame batting practice. Reproduced in Champions of American Sport *by Mark Pachter. New York: Harry N. Abrams, Inc., 1981, pp. 18–19.*

NIGHT GAME—YANKEE STADIUM, 1981

Ralph Fasanella
Oil on canvas, 60 × 74 inches

Depicts a panoramic folk art view of baseball action. Reproduced in Diamonds Are Forever: Artists and Writers on Baseball *edited by Peter H. Gordon. San Francisco: Chronicle Books, 1987, p. 15.*

1908: BRESNAHAN, 1984

Richard Merkin
Pastel on paper, 32½ × 46 inches
Terry Dintenfass Gallery, New York

Painterly interpretation of baseball nostalgia and mythology, as personified by Hall of Fame catcher Roger Bresnahan.

NOLAN RYAN, 1976

Mark Rucker
Oil on canvas, 70 × 50 inches
National Baseball Hall of Fame and Museum, Cooperstown, New York

Depicts the California Angels' star pitcher at mid-delivery.

OFF THE WALL, 1982

Lance Richbourg
Oil on canvas, 60 × 48 inches
O. K. Harris Works of Art, New York

Depicts an outfielder leaping to catch a ball.

Night Baseball *(1951), oil by Marjorie Phillips. Joe DiMaggio is at the plate in an early 1950s game against the Washington Senators at Griffith Stadium. (The Phillips Collection.)*

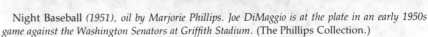

1908: Bresnahan *(1984), pastel by Richard Merkin. Hall of Fame catcher Roger Bresnahan is a symbol of baseball nostalgia and mythology in this pastel by Richard Merkin. (Terry Dintenfass Gallery.)*

Old Neighborhood (1979), oil by Ralph Fasanella. For contemporary folk artist Ralph Fasanella, the social harmony inherent in baseball and stickball has been a source of study and fascination for many years. "To me there's a purity in baseball," he once said. "You go up on a Sunday morning and people coming out of church, there's a kind of feeling of sunshine in the middle of a gloomy spot. They've got their nice clothes on. This is their day, their nice day . . . and the ball game is the center of it." In his 1979 painting, Old Neighborhood, Fasanella portrays a typical street scene on a late Sunday morning in New York City. (Collection of the artist.)

OLD LOW AND INSIDE
Ernie Barnes
Acrylic on canvas

Depicts a tall, lanky, black pitcher staring in for a sign.

OLD NEIGHBORHOOD, 1979
Ralph Fasanella
Oil on canvas, 28 × 36 inches
Collection of the artist

Folk art depiction of an inner-city neighborhood baseball game.

THE ORIOLES WIN THE SERIES,
c. 1967
George Hartman

Oil on canvas, 14 × 18 inches
D. Wigmore Fine Arts, New York

Depicts pitcher Dave McNally being congratulated by his Oriole teammates at the conclusion of the 1966 World Series. Reproduced in exhibition catalog, The Grand Game of Baseball, essay by Shelly Mehlman Dinhofer. New York: Museum of the Borough of Brooklyn, 1987, back page.

OUT AT HOME, 1940
Fletcher Martin
Oil on canvas, 20 × 40 inches
Collection of Mike Manuche, New York

Dramatic depiction of a catcher tagging a sliding runner at home plate. Reproduced in

Fletcher Martin *by H. Lester Cooke, Jr. New York: Harry N. Abrams, Inc., 1977, p. 40.*

OUT AT THIRD
Nelson Rosenberg
Watercolor and gouache, 15 × 22 inches
The Phillips Collection, Washington, D.C.

Expressionistic depiction of a third baseman making a play on a sliding runner. Reproduced in Diamonds Are Forever: Artists and Writers on Baseball edited by Peter H. Gordon. San Francisco: Chronicle Books, 1987, p. 104.

OUT OF PLAY
Lance Richbourg
Oil on canvas
O. K. Harris Works of Art, New York

Depicts a catcher leaping into a dugout to catch a pop foul.

PACIFIC STREET, 1981
Daniel O'Sullivan
Oil on canvas, 40¾ × 30¼ inches
Kraushaar Galleries

Depicts a group of youngsters playing baseball on a city street. Reproduced in exhibition catalog, The Grand Game of Baseball, essay by Shelly Mehlman Dinhofer. New York: Museum of the Borough of Brooklyn, 1987, plate 11.

PASTIME, 1984
Gerald Garston
Oil on canvas, 60 × 46 inches
Collection of Norman and Ruthellen Gahm

Folk-art-style depiction of a baseball player amid a patriotic motif. Reproduced in Diamonds Are Forever: Artists and Writers on Baseball edited by Peter H. Gordon. San Francisco: Chronicle Books, 1987, p. 136.

PASTORALE, 1983
Basil King
Oil on canvas, 35 × 49 inches
Collection of the artist

Depicts a pitcher at mid-delivery. Reproduced in Diamonds Are Forever: Artists and Writers on Baseball *edited by Peter H. Gordon. San Francisco: Chronicle Books, 1987, pp. 100–101.*

PHILADELPHIA STREET, 1936
Robert Gwathmey

A game of stickball is depicted.

PHIL NIEKRO, 1985
Ed Dwight
Bronze statue, height 12 feet
Atlanta Fulton County Stadium,
Atlanta, Georgia

Depicts the Atlanta Braves knuckleballer delivering a pitch. Reproduced in the New York Times, *October 4, 1986.*

THE PITCH, c. 1955
Ben Shahn
Brush drawing, 6¼ × 9¾ inches
Kennedy Galleries, Inc., New York

THE PITCH, 1980
Mark Levine
Bronze sculpture, height 7 inches
National Art Museum of Sport, West Haven, Connecticut

THE PITCHER
Adolph Weinman
Bronze sculpture

PITCHER
Mac Le Sueur

Reproduced in exhibition catalog, 92 Americans. *Minneapolis, Minnesota: Walker Art Center, c. 1943.*

PITCHER'S MOUND, HAGERSTOWN, MARYLAND, 1987
John Hull
Acrylic on canvas, 11 × 14 inches
Collection of Mr. and Mrs. Steven Roth

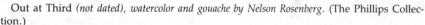

Out at Third (not dated), watercolor and gouache by Nelson Rosenberg. (The Phillips Collection.)

PLAY AT HOME, 1981
John Dobbs
Oil on linen, 32 × 36 inches

Depicts a runner sliding head first into home plate.

PLAY AT SECOND, 1983
John Dobbs
Oil on linen, 40 × 36 inches

Depicts an infielder leaping over a sliding runner.

PLAY AT SECOND BASE
Joe Brown
Bronze sculpture, height 10 inches

Depicts an infielder making a play on a sliding runner. Reproduced in the New York Times, *October 16, 1977.*

PLAY AT SECOND BASE, 1976
Joe Brown
Bronze statue, height 15½ feet
Veterans Stadium, Philadelphia, Pennsylvania

PLAY AT THE PLATE, 1982
John Dobbs
Oil on linen, 36 × 40 inches

Depicts a runner sliding into home plate.

PLAY AT THIRD, c. 1983
John Dobbs
Oil on canvas, 18 × 21 inches
ACA Galleries, New York

Depicts a runner sliding head first into third base. Compositionally similar to Into Third. *Reproduced in* Sport in Art *by Robert Henkes. New York: Prentice Hall Press, 1986, p. 88.*

POLO GROUNDS, 1947
Ralph Fasanella
Oil on canvas
Coe Kerr Gallery, New York

Panoramic folk art depiction of a baseball game amid a festive New York City scene. Reproduced in 200 Years of Sport in America *by Wells Twombly. New York: Rutledge Books/ McGraw-Hill Book Co., 1976, pp. 212–213.*

175

POLO GROUNDS, 1956
Ralph Fasanella
Oil on canvas, 40 × 30 inches
Collection of Mr. and Mrs. David
Ratner, New York

Depicts a folk art expressionistic view of baseball action at the Polo Grounds in New York. Reproduced in Fasanella's City *by Patrick Watson. New York: Knopf, 1973, p. 80.*

POP FLY, 1962
Mervin Honig
Oil on canvas, 32 × 42 inches
Collection of M. Donald Grant, New York

POP-FOUL (JIRO KANAI FROM LIFE), 1961
Joe Brown
Sculpture, height 12 inches

Male nude representation of a baseball player catching a fly ball. Reproduced in Joe Brown: Retrospective Catalogue 1932–1966. *Privately published, plate 38.*

PREMIUM PITCHER, 1949
Austin Briggs
Mixed-media on board, 12 × 16⅜
Collection of Mr. and Mrs. Bill Goff, New York

PROTECTORY GAMES, 1962
Ralph Fasanella
Oil on canvas, 44 × 30 inches
Collection of the artist

Folk art depiction of a school-yard baseball game. Also titled, Catholic Protectory I. *Reproduced in* Fasanella's City *by Patrick Watson. New York: Knopf, 1973, p. 70.*

PUT IT THERE
John George Brown
Oil on canvas, 24 × 16 inches
The Carnegie Museum of Art, Pittsburgh, Pennsylvania, gift of H. J. Heinz Co., 1949

Depicts a schoolboy catching a ball. Reproduced

in exhibition catalog, The Grand Game of Baseball, *essay by Shelly Mehlman Dinhofer. New York: Museum of the Borough of Brooklyn, 1987, plate 4.*

READY FOR THE PITCH, c. 1937
Marjorie Phillips
Oil on canvas, 35 × 22½ inches
National Baseball Hall of Fame and Museum, Cooperstown, New York

Depicts a close-up view of a batter, catcher, and umpire. Reproduced in Biennial Exhibition of Contemporary American Oil Paintings. *Washington, D.C.: Corcoran Gallery of Art, 1937.*

REFORM SCHOOL, 1961
Ralph Fasanella
Oil on canvas, 30 × 40 inches
Jay K. Hoffman Associates, New York

Folk art depiction of a school-yard baseball game. Reproduced in Twentieth Century American Folk Art and Artists *by Herbert W. Hemphill, Jr. New York: E. P. Dutton and Co., Inc., 1974, p. 181.*

REPORT FROM THE FIRE ZONE, SCROLL XV, 1986
Janet Braun-Reinitz
Acrylic on paper, 96 × 48 inches
Collection of the artist

Depicts silhouetted baseball players amid a tropical motif. Reproduced in Diamonds Are Forever: Artists and Writers on Baseball *edited by Peter H. Gordon. San Francisco: Chronicle Books, 1987, p. 152.*

RICHBOURG SLIDING IN (#2), 1982
Lance Richbourg
Oil on canvas, 54 × 68 inches
O. K. Harris Works of Art, New York

Depicts the artist's father sliding into home plate.

RICKEY HENDERSON (THE THIEF), 1983
Shar Tikkanen

French dyes on silk
National Baseball Hall of Fame and Museum, Cooperstown, New York

Depicts the Oakland A's base stealer breaking toward second base.

RIVERFRONT STADIUM: PHILLIES AND REDS, 1979
Nan Phelps
Oil on masonite, 34 × 48 inches
Galerie St. Etienne, New York

Panoramic folk art depiction of baseball action at Cincinnati's Riverfront Stadium. Reproduced in exhibition catalog, The Folk Art Tradition *by Jane Kallir. New York: Galerie St. Etienne, 1981, plate 25.*

ROBBIE PHELPS WITH BASEBALL BAT, 1969
Nan Phelps
Oil on canvas, 29⅞ × 14¾ inches
Galerie St. Etienne, New York

Folk art depiction of a youngster holding a baseball bat.

ROBERTO CLEMENTE
Juan Orcera
Bronze statue

The Hall of Fame outfielder is depicted in a batting stance. Reproduced in A Season in the Sun *by Roger Kahn. New York: Harper and Row, Publishers, Inc., 1977.*

RON KITTLE, 1985
Jim Nutt
Colored pencil on paper, 20 × 16 inches
Collection of Mr. and Mrs. John LeBourgeois

Whimsical abstract portrait of White Sox outfielder Ron Kittle. Reproduced in Diamonds Are Forever: Artists and Writers on Baseball *edited by Peter H. Gordon. San Francisco: Chronicle Books, 1987, p. 44.*

ROSE ARBOR, 1947
Henry Koerner
Oil on composition board, 27¾ × 35 inches

The Museum of Modern Art, New York, gift of John Jay Whitney

SAD SAM JONES, 1974
Richard Merkin
Tempera, 40 × 30 inches
Terry Dintenfass Gallery, New York

Stylized portrait of Sad Sam Jones, who pitched 22 seasons in the major leagues from 1914 to 1935.

SAFE, 1956
Ben Shahn
Ink drawing, 27¼ × 40¼ inches

SAFE AT FIRST, 1936
R. Tait McKenzie
Sculpture, plaster sketch, height 3 inches
J. William White Collection, University of Pennsylvania

Depicts a runner and a first baseman in a close play at first. Reproduced in R. Tait McKenzie: The Sculptor of Athletes *by Andrew J. Kozar. Knoxville, Tennessee: University of Tennessee Press, 1975, p. 102.*

ST. LOUIS NIGHT LIGHT, 1975
Mark Rucker
Oil on canvas, 49 × 35 inches
Collection of the artist

SANDLOT BASEBALL, 1947
Ralph Fasanella
Oil on canvas, 36 × 40 inches

Folk art depiction of an industrial league game. Reproduced in Fasanella's City *by Patrick Watson. New York: Knopf, 1973, p. 81. Compositionally similar to Sandlot Game #2.*

SANDLOT BASEBALL, 1968
Marilyn Mark
Oil on canvas, 16 × 31⅞ inches
National Art Museum of Sport, West Haven, Connecticut

SANDLOT GAME #2, 1967
Ralph Fasanella
Oil on canvas, 36 × 40 inches

Sandlot Game #2 *(1967), oil by Ralph Fasanella. (Collection of the artist.)*

Folk art depiction of an industrial league game. Compositionally similar to Sandlot Baseball.

SANDLOT IN THE BRONX
Ralph Fasanella
Oil on canvas

Depicts a folk art view of an inner-city neighborhood baseball game. Reproduced in Sports Illustrated, *April 9, 1956, p. 77.*

SANDLOT KID, 1964
Victor Salvatore
Bronze statue, life size
Doubleday Field, Cooperstown, New York

A schoolboy is depicted in a batting stance. Reproduced in the Smithsonian, *April 1984, p. 123.*

SANDLOTTER, 1947
Joe Brown
Sculpture, height 12 inches

An adolescent schoolboy is depicted in a batting stance. Reproduced in Joe Brown: Retrospective Catalogue 1932–1966. *Privately published, plate 36.*

SATURDAY AFTERNOON AT SPORTSMAN'S PARK, 1944
Edward Laning
Oil on canvas, 36 × 32 inches
The Gladstone Collection of Baseball Art

Depicts a panoramic view of baseball action at Sportsman's Park in St. Louis. Reproduced in Life, *September 3, 1945.*

SCARCELY IN PHILADELPHIA, 1975
Mark Rucker
Oil on canvas, 50 × 36 inches
Collection of the artist

Phillies pitcher Steve Carlton is depicted. Reproduced in exhibition catalog A History of

177

Baseball: A Bicentennial Exhibition. *New York: The Bronx Museum of the Arts, 1976, p. 6.*

SELF AS DOUBLEDAY, 1986
William King
Red vinyl sculpture, height 81 inches
Terry Dintenfass Gallery, New York

Whimsical depiction of a baseball player. Reproduced in Diamonds Are Forever: Artists and Writers on Baseball *edited by Peter H. Gordon. San Francisco: Chronicle Books, 1987, p. 87.*

SELF-PORTRAIT AS A RELIEF PITCHER FOR THE ROCHESTER RED WINGS, 1985
Richard Merkin
Pastel on paper, 12 × 9 inches
The Gladstone Collection of Baseball Art

Depicts a ruggedly stoical baseball player. Reproduced in Diamonds Are Forever: Artists and Writers on Baseball *edited by Peter H. Gordon. San Francisco: Chronicle Books, 1987, p. 93.*

SELF PORTRAIT AS A YANKEE KILLER
Larry Zingale
Oil on canvas, 22 × 28 inches
America's Folk Heritage Gallery, New York

Depicts a player in a Brooklyn Dodgers' uniform.

SELF-SATISFIED SOUTHPAW, 1955
Saul Steinberg
Ink and colored pencil

Whimsical depiction of a poised and confident pitcher standing atop a mound. Reproduced in Life, *July 11, 1955.*

THE SIGN, 1982
John Dobbs
Oil on linen, 20 × 16 inches

Depicts a center field view of a pitcher staring in for a catcher's sign.

SISLER AND SCHOENDIENST, 1967
R. B. Kitaj
Oil on canvas, 10 × 13⅞ inches

Reproduced in exhibition catalog, R. B. Kitaj: Hirshhorn Museum and Sculpture Garden, Smithsonian Institution. Washington, D.C.: Smithsonian Institution Press, 1981, plate 20.

SKETCH FOR BROOKLYN DODGERS MURALS, 1962
Stuyvesant Van Veen
Gouache on paper, 32 × 19¼ inches
Mary Ryan Gallery

Preliminary study for a series of seven murals in celebration of the Brooklyn Dodgers painted in the lobbies of the Ebbets Field apartment complex in Brooklyn.

SLIDE, 1964
Fay Moore
Oil on canvas, 36 × 39 inches
National Art Museum of Sport, West Haven, Connecticut

SLIDING IN, 1976
Lance Richbourg
Oil on canvas, 24 × 30 inches
Collection of Ivan and Marilynn Karp

SLIDING IN, YANKEE STADIUM, 1979
Lance Richbourg
Oil on canvas, 66 × 78 inches
Collection of Ken Rosenzweig

Panoramic scene of a runner sliding into home plate is depicted. Reproduced in Sport in Art *by Robert Henkes. New York: Prentice Hall Press, 1986, p. 88.*

SMOKEY JOE WILLIAMS, 1985
Deryl Daniel Mackie
Acrylic on canvas, 64 × 54 inches
Collection of the artist

Impressionistic depiction of the great Negro League pitcher. Reproduced in Diamonds Are Forever: Artists and Writers on Baseball

edited by Peter H. Gordon. San Francisco: Chronicle Books, 1987, p. 75.

THE SPECTACLE AT NIGHT, 1955
Saul Steinberg
Watercolor and ink

Panoramic aerial depiction of a baseball stadium. Reproduced in Life, July 11, 1955.

SPRING TRAINING, 1975
Robert M. Cunningham
Acrylic, 15½ × 21½ inches
Collection of the artist

SPRING TRAINING, 1981
Gerald Garston
Oil on canvas, 40 × 49 inches
Collection of Wiggin and Dana, New Haven, Connecticut

Folk-art-style group portrait of four baseball players. Reproduced in Diamonds Are Forever: Artists and Writers on Baseball *edited by Peter H. Gordon. San Francisco: Chronicle Books, 1987, p. 62*

SPRING TRAINING: FARM TEAM, 1977
James McMullan
Watercolor, 11¾ × 16¾ inches
Collection of the artist

SPRING TRAINING IN THE MOUNTAINS, 1985
Vincent Scilla
Oil on canvas, 20 × 24 inches
Collection of the artist

Folk art depiction of an outfielder making a play in front of a garishly painted advertising sign. Reproduced in Diamonds Are Forever: Artists and Writers on Baseball *edited by Peter H. Gordon. San Francisco: Chronicle Books, 1987, p. 23.*

SPRING TRAINING IN WEST PALM BEACH, 1985
Red Grooms
Watercolor, 14 × 17 inches

Abstract expressionistic view of a catcher tagging a sliding runner at home plate as seen from behind the backstop screen. Reproduced in Look, *May 5, 1953, p. 105.*

TOM SEAVER
Harold Castor
Bronze sculpture, height 27 inches
Renaissance Art Foundry and
Gallery, Bridgeport, Connecticut

Depicts the New York Mets' pitcher at the beginning of his delivery. Reproduced in exhibition catalog, Castor. *New York: Sculptors Workshop, Inc.*

T. P. AND JAKE, 1937
Thomas Hart Benton
Egg tempera on canvas mounted on
panel, 47½ × 30½ inches
Collection of Thomas P. Benton

Portrait of a farm boy—with a bat and baseball —and his dog. Reproduced in Thomas Hart Benton *by Matthew Baigell. New York: Harry N. Abrams, Inc., plate 112.*

TRYOUT, 1965
Sidney Goodman
Oil on canvas, 35 × 24½ inches
Collection of Mrs. Janet H. Shands

Depicts a batter waiting for a pitch in a starkly isolated stadium. Reproduced in exhibition catalog, Play Ball! A Century of Art in Sports. *New York: The Queens Museum, 1978, p. 16.*

TURNING THE DOUBLE PLAY, 1983
John Dobbs
Oil on linen, 16 × 14 inches

Depicts an infielder throwing a ball over a sliding runner.

2 BATS, BLACK AND WHITE—REPLICA, 1971
Claes Oldenburg
Soft sculpture, height 113¼ inches
Collection of the artist

Pop art representation of two curled baseball bats. Reproduced in Claes Oldenburg: Object

into Monument *by Barbara Haskell. Los Angeles: The Ward Ritchie Press, 1971, p. 71.*

TWO UMPIRES, 1938
Paul Clemens
Oil on panel, 10 × 16 inches
Collection of Mrs. Ethel Barrymore

Between-innings portrait of two umpires. Reproduced in Look, *May 5, 1953, p. 104.*

TY COBB, 1979
Lance Richbourg
Oil on canvas, 66 × 78 inches
Collection of Schweber Electronics Corp.

Realist depiction based on a famous photograph of Ty Cobb sliding into third base. Reproduced in Images and Issues, *Summer 1981, p. 65.*

TY COBB
Felix DeLeon
Bronze sculpture
Atlanta Fulton County Stadium,
Atlanta, Georgia

Depicts the Detroit Tigers' Hall of Famer hook-sliding into a base.

UNTITLED, 1872
(Baseball Player)
William Merritt Chase
Pencil drawing
The Gladstone Collection of Baseball Art

UNTITLED
(Baseball Is Like an Intricate Dance)
Jean Jones Watts
Pen and ink drawing

Stylized montage of baseball action as imagined by youngsters. Reproduced in Look, *May 5, 1953, p. 106.*

UNTITLED, 1953
(Baseball)
John Marin
Colored pencil on paper, 8½ × 10½ inches

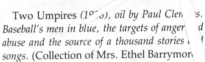

Two Umpires (1938), oil by Paul Clemens. Baseball's men in blue, the targets of anger and abuse and the source of a thousand stories and songs. (Collection of Mrs. Ethel Barrymore.)

The Gladstone Collection of Baseball Art

Stylized depiction of an infielder tagging a sliding runner. Reproduced in Diamonds Are Forever: Artists and Writers on Baseball *edited by Peter H. Gordon. San Francisco: Chronicle Books, 1987, p. 102.*

UNTITLED, c. 1955
(Batter)
Ben Shahn
India ink on paper, 4¾ × 9¼ inches

Whimsical depiction of a long-striding batter. Reproduced in exhibition catalog, Play Ball! A Century of Sports in Art. *New York: The Queens Museum, 1978, p. 10.*

UNTITLED, c. 1955
(Play at Home Plate)

CURIOSITIES IN BLUE

"Hangmen. That's what they are, you know. Hangmen!"

So said actress Ethel Barrymore upon first viewing Paul Clemens's 1938 painting, *Two Umpires*, a work Miss Barrymore later acquired for her own collection. To be sure, umpires have been the subject of abuse, derision, anger, outrage—and a thousand stories, legends, songs, and even a celebratory eulogy or two. A satirical verse, published in the *Washington Critic* in 1886, reflects a longstanding tradition in America. It reads in part:

> Mother, may I slug the umpire,
> May I slug him right away,
> So he cannot be here, mother,
> When the clubs begin to play?
>
> Let me clasp his throat, dear mother,
> In a dear, delightful grip,
> With one hand, and with the other
> Bat him several in the lip.
>
> Let me climb his frame, dear mother,
> While the happy people shout;
> I'll not kill him, dearest mother,
> I will only knock him out.

The men in blue were the subject of another, more popularly known work of art, Norman Rockwell's *Game Called Because of Rain*, which depicts three grave and unsmiling umpires surveying rain-laden clouds as though of coequal authority with Mother Nature. A number of poems and verses have satirized umpires, most notably Ogden Nash's hilarious "Decline and Fall of a Roman Umpire," in which an umpire is hounded out of the major leagues by a fan shouting Brooklynesque imprecations (". . . ya big bum ya, you're nothing but a big bum!"), and a blank-verse examination, "Kill the Umpire!" written in 1953 by Edwin Rolfe ("We hate him because whatever he says is true"). Two plays have made humorous sport of umpires, *The Umpire*, an immensely popular musical comedy presented

in 1905, and *Angela, or the Umpire's Revenge*, a comic melodrama written in 1888 and scored by John Philip Sousa.

A number of songs have lampooned umpires, including "The Umpire Is a Most Unhappy Man," from the aforementioned musical, *The Umpire*, and "Let's Get the Umpire's Goat," cowritten in 1909 by Jack Norworth, a year after his sensational hit "Take Me Out to the Ball Game." John Jacob Loeb wrote a humorous song recorded in 1950 by Phil Rizzuto, Roy Campanella, Ralph Branca, and Tommy Henrich, titled "The Umpire" ("The umpire, the umpire / The guy who calls ev'ry play / We ain't got no use for the umpire / Unless he calls 'em our way). Another song, "Kill the Umpire!" was part of a comic cantata written in 1942 by George Kleinsinger and Michael Stratton, titled *Brooklyn Baseball Cantata* ("Please, folks, don't hold it against me / I'm not an umpire because I want to be / It isn't that— / I've had a very unhappy childhood").

Two movies, both with the title of *Kill the Umpire*, have portrayed the men in blue. The latter of the two, released in 1950, starred William Bendix as an unemployed oaf whose passion for baseball leads to a life as an umpire. A novel, *The Conduct of the Game*, written in 1986 by John Hough, Jr., is the only full-length work of fiction to have used big league umpiring as a theme. It's a nostalgically written reminiscence of a man's coming of age from a small-town youth to a major league umpire.

In baseball, the umpire's word is law—unimpeachable (except by an overruling of the league president, not a common occurrence), irreversible (except by the crew chief, a somewhat more frequent occurrence), and inarguable (except by managers and players and the rest of the human race, but always to no avail). The only way to combat such absolute dictatorial power over a child's game is through invective, vilification, and ridicule. These are the great levelers that make mortals out of mere mediators.

Ben Shahn
India ink on paper, 4¾ × 9¼ inches

Depicts a catcher tagging a runner at home plate. Reproduced in exhibition catalog, Play Ball! A Century of Sports in Art. New York: The Queens Museum, 1978, p. 10.

UNTITLED, 1976
Phyllis Herfield
Colored pencil on paper, 19 × 24 inches
Collection of the artist

Series of vignettes depicting the musculature and movements of baseball players. Reproduced in Sport in Art by Robert Henkes. New York: Prentice Hall Press, 1986, p. 97.

UNTITLED
Artist Unknown
Oil on canvas, 16 × 23½ inches
The Gladstone Collection of Baseball Art

Folk art depiction of black youngsters playing baseball. Also titled, Black Baseball Players. Reproduced in Diamonds Are Forever: Artists and Writers on Baseball edited by Peter H. Gordon. San Francisco: Chronicle Books, 1987, p. 81.

UNTITLED (BASEBALL GAME), c. 1945
William Godfrey
Oil on canvas, 20 × 35 inches
National Baseball Hall of Fame and Museum, Cooperstown, New York

Panoramic depiction of a major league game in progress.

UPON NEVER HAVING SEEN KOUFAX PITCH, 1967
R. B. Kitaj
Oil on canvas, 14⅛ × 10 inches
Collection of Richard Gangel

VAN CORTLANDT PARK, 1909
Louis Michel Eilshemius
Oil on canvas, 22¼ × 28¼ inches

National Baseball Hall of Fame and Museum, Cooperstown, New York

Panoramic depiction of a pastoral baseball game.

VAN LINGLE MUNGO'S HAVANA, 1973
Richard Merkin
Tempera, 48 × 72 inches
Collection of Al Ordover, New York

VETERAN BUSH LEAGUE CATCHER, 1948
James Chapin
Oil on canvas, 50 × 40 inches
Collection of Dale C. Bullough

Heroic portrait of a baseball player as an American ideal. Also titled, Baseball Catcher. Reproduced in Diamonds Are Forever: Artists and Writers on Baseball edited by Peter H. Gordon. San Francisco: Chronicle Books, 1987, p. 73.

VILLANELLE
Ben Shahn
Brush and ink, 10½ × 8¼ inches
Collection of M. D. Feld

VISITING CARDINALS
Lance Richbourg
Oil on canvas
O. K. Harris Works of Art, New York

Depicts St. Louis Cardinals players seated in a dugout.

WAITING FOR A DECISION, c. 1953
Thomas Meehan
Oil

Expressionistic depiction of a catcher tagging a runner at home plate. Reproduced in Sports Illustrated, June 13, 1955, p. 63.

WALTER JOHNSON
U. S. Dunbar
Sculpture

Depicts the Hall of Fame pitcher at the beginning of his delivery.

WARREN SPAHN, 1966
Ellen Raskin
Acrylic on canvas, 30 × 30 inches
Collection of the artist

WHITENESS OF THE WHALE, 1984
Rupert Deese
Oil on canvas, 50 × 38 inches
Collection of Linda Komaroff

Depicts a baseball bat superimposed upon a stylized pattern. Reproduced in Diamonds Are Forever: Artists and Writers on Baseball edited by Peter H. Gordon. San Francisco: Chronicle Books, 1987, p. 38.

THE WIDE SWING, 1974
Harvey Dinnerstein
Oil on canvas, 24 × 32 inches
Collection of Phil Desind; The Butler Institute of American Art, Youngstown, Ohio

Depicts Joe DiMaggio at the completion of his swing. Reproduced in Diamonds Are Forever: Artists and Writers on Baseball edited by Peter H. Gordon. San Francisco: Chronicle Books, 1987, p. 77.

WILLIE GOING FOR THREE, 1983
Robert Stark
Oil on canvas, 16 × 20 inches
National Baseball Hall of Fame and Museum, Cooperstown, New York

Depicts Hall of Famer Willie Mays rounding second base.

WILLIE MAYS
Harold Castor
Bronze-polychrome sculpture, height 22 inches

The Hall of Famer is depicted at the completion of his swing. Reproduced in Point 31: 1975, Vol. 1, No. 2, p. 74.

Willie Mays (not dated), sculpture by Harold Castor. Willie Mays, in a Mets uniform, in the twilight of an illustrious career, is imbued with the exuberance and energy of a stickball playing youngster in this sculpture by Harold Castor. (Collection of the artist.)

Willie Mays (1985), watercolor by Tim Swartz. A close-up view of the consummate baseball player wholly and intensely devoted to his game. (Collection of Robert Sipko.)

WILLIE MAYS, 1978
Ron Cohen
Acrylic and oil on canvas, 68 × 64 inches
Collection of Barry C. Scheck and Lawrence A. Vogelman

Depicts Hall of Fame outfielder Willie Mays making an over-the-shoulder catch. Reproduced in Diamonds Are Forever: Artists and Writers on Baseball *edited by Peter H. Gordon. San Francisco: Chronicle Books, 1987, p. 96.*

WILLIE MAYS, 1985
Tim Swartz
Watercolor on paper, 20 × 30 inches
Collection of Robert Sipko, Mentor, Ohio

Depicts a close-up view of Hall of Famer Willie Mays in a batting stance.

WILLIE MAYS AT BAT, 1964
Kendall Shaw
Acrylic on canvas, 75 × 53 inches
Collection of Mr. and Mrs. Robert *...*yer, Winnetka, Illinois

Depicts a silhouetted Willie Mays striding into a pitch.

WILLIE MAYS—THE CATCH
Thom Ross
Essay sculpture in five panels

Serial depiction of Mays's over-the-shoulder catch in the 1954 World Series. Reproduced in Sports Illustrated, *October 6, 1986, p. 16.*

WILLIE MAYS—'TIS A BUNT, 1980
Ralph Fasanella
Oil on canvas, 50 × 60 inches
National Baseball Hall of Fame and Museum, Cooperstown, New York

A panoramic folk art view of baseball action is depicted. Also titled, Night Game—'Tis a Bunt.

WINNING SIDE
Lance Richbourg
Oil on canvas
O. K. Harris Works of Art, New York

Depicts Al Simmons of the Philadelphia Athletics scoring the winning run in the deciding fifth game of the 1929 World Series.

WORLD SERIES, c. 1933
Arnold Friedman
Oil on canvas, 20⅛ × 24⅛ inches
The Phillips Collection, Washington, D.C.

Depicts a panoramic view of baseball action as seen from the upper right field seats. Reproduced in Diamonds Are Forever: Artists and Writers on Baseball *edited by Peter H. Gordon. San Francisco: Chronicle Books, 1987, p. 129.*

WORLD SERIES #2, 1958
Robert Gwathmey
Watercolor and pencil on paper, 29 × 21 inches
Terry Dintenfass Gallery, New York

Depicts a group of expectant fans walking toward the stadium entrance. Reproduced in Diamonds Are Forever: Artists and Writers on Baseball *edited by Peter H. Gordon. San Francisco: Chronicle Books, 1987, p. 131.*

WORLD SERIES '75 (#1)
Stanley Meltzoff
Acrylic, 22 × 16 inches
Midtown Galleries, Inc., New York

Depicts a pitcher at mid-delivery amid a collage of pitching greats.

WRIGLEY FIELD, 1983
Andy Jurinko
Charcoal and pastel on paper, 30 × 44 inches

An aerial view of Chicago's Wrigley Field is depicted. Reproduced in Diamonds Are Forever: Artists and Writers on Baseball *edited by Peter H. Gordon. San Francisco: Chronicle Books, 1987, p. 12.*

YANKEE STADIUM, c. 1939

William Godfrey
Oil on canvas, 22 × 35½ inches
National Baseball Hall of Fame and
Museum, Cooperstown, New York

*Depicts a panoramic view of baseball action at
Yankee Stadium in New York.*

YANKEE STADIUM, 1980

Lance Richbourg
Oil on canvas, 66 × 84 inches
O. K. Harris Works of Art, New York

Depicts a panoramic view of baseball action.

YANKEES WIN SERIES, 4–3, 1952

Justin McCarthy

Watercolor on board, in five panels,
24½ × 30½ inches
The Gladstone Collection of Baseball
Art

*Essay series of watercolors depicting highlights
of the 1952 World Series between the Brooklyn
Dodgers and New York Yankees. Reproduced
in Diamonds Are Forever: Artists and
Writers on Baseball edited by Peter H.
Gordon. San Francisco: Chronicle Books, 1987,
p. 82.*

YOGI BERRA, 1974

Rhoda Sherbell
Bronze bust, life size
National Baseball Hall of Fame and

Museum, Cooperstown, New York

*Bust portrait of the New York Yankees Hall of
Famer.*

YOUNG BALL PLAYER

James Chapin
Oil on canvas
Associated American Artists, New
York

*Portrait of a confident college-age baseball
player. Reproduced in Time, March 11, 1940,
p. 57.*

YOUTH, 1865

David Gilmour Blythe
Oil on canvas, 8 × 12 inches
Collection of Dr. and Mrs. David Ray
Vilsack

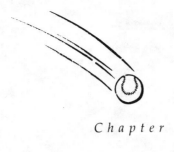

Chapter

12

Baseball in Miscellaneous Art and Illustrations

The following section contains a selected listing of prints, illustrations, and miscellaneous art relating to baseball. Included in the catalog are 19th-century lithographs depicting early baseball scenes, limited-edition fine art prints by noted artists, famous magazine covers and other illustrations, baseball-related sculpture issued in multiple editions, paintings by major league baseball players, and unclassified miscellaneous works of art relating to baseball.

Dimensions to lithographs and other surface prints refer to the outside size of the paper. Intaglio prints, such as etchings and engravings, are measured to the plate mark.

Lithographic prints refer to works that have been photomechanically reproduced in unlimited editions. In many instances a celebrated baseball illustration or limited edition art print has also been issued as a lithographic print in a popularly priced unlimited edition. It is important to note that only the original work or edition is listed in this catalog.

A number of art galleries and mail-order firms specialize in baseball and other sports art prints. For information regarding dealers and other sources of baseball-related art, consult the Selected Guide to Sources and Dealers at the back of this book.

For *Explanatory Notes* to this section, *see:* Baseball in Art and Sculpture.

ABSORPTION OF A BASEBALL PLAYER, 1889
Lithograph, 25½ × 12 inches
Library of Congress

AFTER CLASS AT CAMPO, 1968
Rex Brandt
Watercolor

Pastoral depiction of a collegian sandlot game. Reproduced in Rex Brandt's San Diego *by Rex Brandt. La Jolla, California: Copley Books, 1968.*

THE AMERICAN NATIONAL GAME OF BASE BALL, 1866
Currier and Ives
Lithograph, hand-colored, 19⅞ × 29⅞ inches
See also: Baseball—1865 (1929)

Panoramic depiction of a championship game played on August 3, 1865, between the Atlantics and the Mutuals, at the Elysian Fields in Hoboken, New Jersey. Reproduced in 100 Currier and Ives Favorites by Albert K. Baragwanath. New York: Crown Publishers, Inc., p. 101.

THE ARGUMENT, 1972
LeRoy Neiman

The American National Game of Base Ball *(1866), lithograph by Currier and Ives. This famous print depicts what Currier and Ives described as a "grand match for the championship," a game played on August 5, 1865 between the Atlantics and the Mutuals at the Elysian Fields in Hoboken, New Jersey. The game, won by the Atlantics, 13 to 12, was a championship game only in the sense that virtually every New York–area game played before 1871—when the first professional baseball club was formed—was a match or grudge game between two former "championship" clubs. To be sure, the Atlantics of Brooklyn were formidable enough to have handed the Cincinnati Red Stockings their first defeat in 1870 after the Reds had won 130 consecutive games during the 1868, '69, and '70 seasons. An original 1866 print of this often reproduced lithograph is an extremely rare and desired collector's item today.* (National Baseball Library.)

Babe Ruth (1984), oil by Joe Wilder. (Lynn Silverman.)

Photo-etching, 8¼ × 7⅜ inches
Edition of 150
See also: Baseball Players Suite #1–10

AWAITING THE DECISION, 1972
LeRoy Neiman
Photo-etching, 8¼ × 7⁷⁄₁₆ inches
Edition of 150
See also: Baseball Players Suite #1–10

THE BABE LOOKS ON, 1974
Norman F. Jackson
Oil on velvet
National Baseball Hall of Fame and Museum, Cooperstown, New York

Depicts an image of Babe Ruth gazing at a home run-hitting Hank Aaron.

BABE RUTH, c. 1948
S. J. Woolf
Charcoal on paper, 21¼ × 18⅝ inches
National Baseball Hall of Fame and Museum, Cooperstown, New York

Close-up portrait of the New York Yankees' slugger.

BABE RUTH, 1950
(He Showed Us How to Play the Game)
Harold Von Schmidt
Illustration
National Baseball Hall of Fame and Museum, Cooperstown, New York

Depicts the Hall of Famer signing autographs amid a crowd of youngsters. Reproduced in Saturday Evening Post, *July 22, 1950, p. 79.*

BABE RUTH
Robert Riger
Charcoal on paper
National Baseball Hall of Fame and Museum, Cooperstown, New York

Depicts the Hall of Fame slugger and a youngster sewing a numeral three on the back of his Little League jersey.

BABE RUTH, 1984
Jack Rudolf
Bronze figure, height 22 inches
Edition of 100
Renaissance Art Foundry and Gallery, Bridgeport, Connecticut

Depicts a caricature of the Hall of Famer. Rudolf is a Connecticut state representative.

BABE RUTH, 1984
Joe Wilder
Oil on canvas, 30 × 24 inches
Lynn Silverman, New York

Depicts the Hall of Famer at the completion of his swing. Reproduced in Athletes: The Paintings of Joe Wilder, M.D. *by Joe Wilder. New York: Harry N. Abrams, Inc., 1985, p. 16.*

BABE RUTH, AMERICAN ICON, 1987
Michael A. Schacht
Acrylic on paper
National Art Museum of Sport, West Haven, Connecticut, gift of the artist

BABE'S GREATEST MOMENT, 1976

Douglass Crockwell
Lithograph, 22 × 28 inches
National Baseball Hall of Fame and Museum, Cooperstown, New York

Depicts Babe Ruth pointing to center field. Reproduced in the Saturday Review, *September 18, 1976, back page.*

BACK TO NORMAL
Bill Crawford
Charcoal drawing
New York Yankees Baseball Club

BASEBALL, 1887
Aquarelle print, 24 × 17½ inches
Library of Congress

BASEBALL, 1902
Edward Penfield
Lithograph
Loring Art Gallery, Cedarhurst, New York

Depicts a pitcher's view of a batter and catcher.

BASEBALL, 1960
John Ross
Colored woodcut, 18 × 12 inches
The Metropolitan Museum of Art, New York, gift of the National Broadcasting Co.

BASEBALL, 1962
(Roger Maris)
Andy Warhol
Synthetic polymer paint silkscreened on canvas, 92 × 82 inches
William Rockhill Nelson Gallery of Art, Kansas City, Missouri

Pop art serial depiction of Roger Maris swinging a bat. Reproduced in Andy Warhol *by Rainer Crone. New York: Praeger Publishers, Inc., 1970, p. 156.*

BASEBALL, 1968
Ben Shahn
Wood engraving, 20½ × 26½ inches
New Jersey State Museum, Trenton, New Jersey, purchase 68-170

Wood engraving by Stefan Martin of Shahn's pen and ink drawing, National Pastime. *(See:* Baseball in Art and Sculpture.*) Reproduced in* Sport in Art *by Robert Henkes. New York: Prentice Hall Press, 1986, p. 92.*

BASEBALL
Ralph Fasanella
Silkscreen in colors, 31 × 43½ inches

Aerial folk art view of a baseball stadium. Reproduced in 200 Years of Sport in America *by Wells Twombly. New York: Rutledge Books/McGraw-Hill Book Co., 1976, back dust jacket.*

BASEBALL
Wayland Moore
Silkscreen in colors, 30½ × 24 inches
Edition of 300
Gallery Felice, New York

Depicts a batter swinging.

BASEBALL
Steven Stroud
Illustration
Famous Illustrators Gallery, Wilton, Connecticut

Depicts a batter waiting for a pitch. Reproduced in the New York Times *(Connecticut Weekly section), February 3, 1985, p. CN 21.*

BASEBALL, 1983
James Rizzi
Lithograph, three-dimensional hand-cut construction, 8 × 12 inches
Edition of 150
Published by John Szoke Graphics, Inc., New York

Folk art aerial depiction of a baseball game. Reproduced in Art News, *September 1983, back cover.*

BASEBALL ARGUMENT, 1939
Paul Clemens
Lithograph, 8 × 10 inches

Close-up depiction of two baseball players arguing with an umpire. Reproduced in A Treasury of American Prints *edited by Thomas Craven. New York: Simon and Schuster, 1939.*

BASEBALL—1865, 1929
Raoul Varin
Aqua-tint, 18 × 25 inches
Edition of 250
Published by A. Ackermann and Son, Inc., New York

Copied from the Currier and Ives lithograph, The American National Game of Base Ball *(1866).*

BASEBALL FIGURE—PITCHER, c. 1876
Isaac Broome
Parian porcelain, height 15 inches
New Jersey State Museum, Trenton, The Brewer Collection

Figurine depicting an early-day baseball player in uniform.

BASEBALL PARK
Ralph Fasanella
Silkscreen in colors, 31 × 43½ inches
Edition of 250
Gallery Felice, New York

Depicts a panoramic folk art view of baseball action.

BASEBALL PLAYER, c. 1875
Artist Unknown
Polychromed wood carving, height 70½ inches
Hood Museum of Art, Dartmouth College, Hanover, New Hampshire, gift of Abby Aldrich Rockefeller

Sporting goods store figure—attributed to artist Thomas V. Brooks—depicting a nineteenth-century baseball player.

BASEBALL PLAYER, 1889
Douglas Tilden
Bronze figure, height 34 inches
National Baseball Hall of Fame and Museum, Cooperstown, New York

Copied from the life-size statue in an edition of approximately six. See: Baseball Player (1889) (Baseball in Art and Sculpture).

Baseball Argument *(1939), lithograph by Paul Clemens. Artist Paul Clemens, who has described baseball as "the only game that has humor in it," presents a whimsical portrayal of a baseball argument in this 1939 lithograph. (Collection of the artist. Photo: Peter Glass.)*

Baseball Figure—Pitcher *(c. 1876), porcelain figure by Isaac Broome. (New Jersey State Museum.)*

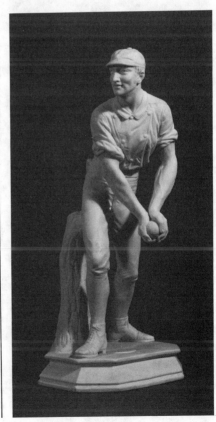

Baseball Player (c. 1875), wood carving attributed to Thomas V. Brooks. This wood carving of a baseball player served as a shop sign for a sporting goods store in the 1870s. (Hood Museum of Art, Dartmouth College.)

BASEBALL PLAYER, c. 1895
Samuel A. Robb
Polychromed wood carving, height 76 inches
Whitney Museum of American Art, New York, gift of Mr. and Mrs. Carl W. Haffeneffer

Tobacconist figure—carved between 1888 and 1903—depicting a mustachioed batter. Reproduced in 200 Years of American Sculpture *by the Whitney Museum of*

American Art. New York: David R. Godine, Publisher, 1976, p. 103.

BASEBALL PLAYER, c. 1905
Artist Unknown
Wood carving, height 8¾ inches
Collection of George O. Bird

Reproduced in American Folk Sculpture *by Robert Bishop. New York: E. P. Dutton and Co., Inc., 1974, p. 330.*

BASEBALL PLAYER
Artist Unknown

Baseball Player (c. 1895), wood carving by Samuel A. Robb. This wood carving of a mustachioed baseball batter stood in front of a tobacco store during the late 1800s. (Whitney Museum of American Art.)

Stone figure, height 11⅛ inches
Hirschl and Adler Galleries, New York

Depicts a schoolboy with bat, ball, and books. Reproduced in exhibition catalog, A History of Baseball: A Bicentennial Exhibition. *New York: The Bronx Museum of the Arts, 1976, p. 3.*

BASEBALL PLAYERS SUITE #1–10, 1972
LeRoy Neiman
Series of ten photo-etchings from original drawings
Edition of 150

Reproduced in The Prints of LeRoy Neiman *edited by Dr. Maury Leibovitz. New York: Knoedler Publishing, Inc., 1980.* See: The Argument: Awaiting the Decision; Batting Practice; The Hit; Next at Bat; The Pitch; Sliding Home; The Umps; Warm Up Swings (Mickey Mantle); Wind Up.

BASEBALL SCREEN PLAY, 1988
William Feldman
Lithograph, 21⅝ × 29⅝ inches
Edition of 500
Published by Bill Goff, Inc., New York

Depicts a panoramic view of baseball action as seen from behind the backstop screen.

BASEBALL TEAM, 1977
Phyllis Seltzer
Ozalid print, 26½ × 62 inches
Associated American Artists, New York

A BASE HIT, 1882
Currier and Ives
Lithograph, small folio size

BASS WOOD OF THE TINKERVILLE TOMCATS, 1987
Lavern Kelley
Painted wood figure, height 18 inches
Collection of the artist

A baseball batter is depicted. Reproduced in

Diamonds Are Forever: Artists and Writers on Baseball *edited by Peter H. Gordon. San Francisco: Chronicle Books, 1987, p. 141.*

BATSMAN, 1868
K. Muller and J. Deacon
Bronze figure, height 11 inches
Whitney Collections of Sporting Art,
Yale University

Depicts a batter waiting for a pitch.

BAT SPINNING AT THE SPEED OF LIGHT, 1975
Claes Oldenburg
Lithograph, 34 × 21 inches
Published by Landfall Press, Inc.,
Chicago
See also: Baseball in Art and Sculpture

One of several variant studies on the Batcolumn *theme. Reproduced in* Diamonds Are Forever: Artists and Writers on Baseball *edited by Peter H. Gordon. San Francisco: Chronicle Books, 1987, p. 40.*

BATTER UP
Lou Zansky
Lithographic print

Stylized depiction of a baseball batter.

THE BATTING CAGE, c. 1975
Clint Orlemann
Lithographic print of pencil sketch,
20 × 17 inches
Edition of 5000
Cincinnati Reds Baseball Club

Depicts Pete Rose and other Cincinnati Reds in a batting practice scene.

BATTING PRACTICE, 1972
LeRoy Neiman
Photo-etching, 8¼ × 7⅜ inches
Edition of 150
See also: Baseball Players Suite #1–10

BETWEEN INNINGS, 1971
Gerald Garston
Silkscreen, 20 × 20 inches

Philadelphia Museum of Art, gift of
Pucker-Safrai Gallery, Boston

Folk-art-style group portrait of three baseball players.

THE BIG TRAIN
Emanuel Haller
Etching
National Baseball Hall of Fame and
Museum, Cooperstown, New York

Depicts Hall of Fame pitcher Walter Johnson.

BILLY MARTIN CHANGES PITCHERS, 1983
Joe Wilder
Oil on canvas, 14 × 11 inches
Lynn Silverman, New York

Close-up view of New York Yankees' manager Billy Martin. Reproduced in Athletes: The Paintings of Joe Wilder, M.D., *by Joe Wilder. New York: Harry N. Abrams, Inc., 1985, p. 48.*

BROOKLYN BALTICS VS. LIBERTY NINE OF NEW BRUNSWICK, c. 1871
Artist Unknown
Watercolor on cloth, 23 × 30 inches
Collection of T. Dennie Williams and
Thomas D. Williams

Depicts a panoramic view of a pastoral baseball game. Reproduced in Diamonds Are Forever: Artists and Writers on Baseball *edited by Peter H. Gordon. San Francisco: Chronicle Books, 1987, p. 99.*

BROOKLYN DODGERS: TRAINING CAMP AT HAVANA, CUBA, 1947
(Dem Bums Abroad)
John Groth
Watercolor and ink, 29 × 39 inches
National Art Museum of Sport, West
Haven, Connecticut

Depicts the entire Brooklyn Dodgers squad engaged in various spring training drills. Reproduced in Collier's, *April 12, 1947, pp. 20–21.*

Casey at the Bat *(1985), bronze by Mark Lundeen. (National Baseball Library.)*

BUTCH HOBSON
Valerie Zint
Etching, hand colored, 25 × 18
inches
Midtown Galleries, Inc., New York

Boston Red Sox third baseman Butch Hobson is depicted in a fielding pose.

CASEY AT THE BAT, 1947
Edward Wilson
Lithograph
Published by Morrell Co., engraving
by Ketterlinus

Depicts the Mudville slugger swinging mightily at a pitch.

Clemente Catching One *(1968), oil by LeRoy Neiman. LeRoy Neiman, one of the nation's most prominent illustrators of sporting scenes, records the grace and ease of Hall of Fame outfielder Roberto Clemente of the Pittsburgh Pirates. (Collection of the artist.)*

CASEY AT THE BAT, 1985
Mark Lundeen
Bronze figure, height 18 inches
Edition of 30
Trails West Gallery, Laguna Beach, California

Copied after the statue of the same name. See: Baseball in Art and Sculpture.

CASEY STENGEL TEACHES SAMUEL JOHNSON HOW TO SPEAK, c. 1965
Al Herschfeld
Pen and ink and wash cartoon, 28 × 26 inches

The Margo Feiden Galleries; Mr. and Mrs. Philip S. Straniere

Depicts the New York Mets' manager instructing the eighteenth-century English lexicographer on the finer points of Stengelese.

THE CATCHER, 1981
Bob Scriver
Bronze figure, one-sixth life size
Edition of 100
Cincinnati Reds Baseball Club

Depicts Cincinnati Reds' catcher Johnny Bench.

CATCHER, 1984
John Dreyfuss
Bronze, height 14 inches
Edition of 12
Fendrick Gallery, Washington, D.C.

Stylized representation of a baseball catcher.

THE CATCHER
Bart Forbes
Watercolor
American Sport Art Museum and Archives, Daphne, Alabama

THE CHAMPIONS OF THE BALL RACKET: "AT THE CLOSE OF THE SEASON," 1885
Currier and Ives
Lithograph, small folio size

Racist cartoon depiction of blacks playing baseball.

THE CHAMPIONS OF THE BALL RACKET: "ON THE DIAMOND FIELD," 1886
Currier and Ives
Lithograph, small folio size

Racist cartoon depiction of blacks playing baseball.

CHRISTY MATHEWSON
Bart Forbes
Watercolor
American Sport Art Museum and Archives, Daphne, Alabama

CLEMENTE
Tom Clark
Acrylic

Depicts Hall of Famer Roberto Clemente trotting to his position in right field. Reproduced in The Temple of Baseball *edited by Richard Grossinger. Berkeley, California: North Atlantic Books, 1985.*

CLEMENTE CATCHING ONE, 1968
LeRoy Neiman
Oil on masonite, 14 × 7¾ inches

Stylized depiction of Hall of Famer Roberto Clemente catching a fly ball.

A COMPREHENSIVE VIEW OF BASEBALL, 1859
William T. Crane
Lithograph, 25⅜ × 20¾ inches
Library of Congress

THE CRITICAL MOMENT, 1904
A. B. Frost
Illustration

Comic depiction of a runner sliding into home plate in a rural baseball game. Reproduced in A Book of Drawings *by A. B. Frost. New York: Collier and Son, 1904.*

CROWD AT THE POLO GROUNDS, 1895
Jay Hambidge
Lithograph in colors, 18⅞ × 14 inches
Museum of the City of New York

DELAYED BALL GAME, 1946
Stevan Dohanos
Illustration

Depicts a group of baseball sandlotters waiting for a friend to finish his chores. First published in the Saturday Evening Post, *July 20, 1946. Reproduced in* American Realist *by Stevan Dohanos. Westport, Connecticut: North Light Publishers, 1980. p. 23.*

DENTON "CY" YOUNG
A. R. Thayer

Oil on canvas
National Baseball Hall of Fame and
Museum, Cooperstown, New York

*Heroic depiction of the Hall of Fame pitcher at
mid-delivery.*

DETERMINED MAN, c. 1983
Mike Lloyd
Acrylic on canvas
Orlando Gallery, Los Angeles,
California

*Depicts a pitcher in a Mets' uniform at the
completion of his delivery.*

THE DOCTOR, 1985
(Dwight Gooden)
Walt Spitzmiller
Lithograph

*Depicts Dwight (Dr. K) Gooden at mid-
delivery. Reproduced in the* New York Times,
November 9, 1985, p. 47.

DODGERS' JERSEY
Donald Moss
Illustration

*Still life depiction of a Dodgers' uniform jersey.
Reproduced in* 200 Years of Sport in America
*by Wells Twombly. New York: Rutledge Books/
McGraw-Hill Book Co., 1976, p. 217.*

DON SUTTON
Valerie Zint
Etching, hand colored, 25 × 18
inches
Midtown Galleries, Inc., New York

*Los Angeles Dodgers' pitcher Don Sutton is
depicted at mid-delivery.*

DOUBLE PLAY, 1952
Fletcher Martin
Lithograph, 12⅜ × 8⅜ inches
Edition of 250
Published by Associated American
Artists, New York

DREAM, 1979
Gene Locklear

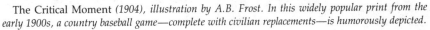

*The Critical Moment (1904), illustration by A.B. Frost. In this widely popular print from the
early 1900s, a country baseball game—complete with civilian replacements—is humorously depicted.*

Lithograph, 25½ × 17¼ inches
Edition of 300
Published by Allen E. Paul,
Richmond, Indiana

*Depicts a young boy and a dreamlike montage
of baseball stars above him. Locklear played in
the major leagues for the Reds, Padres, and
Yankees.*

THE DUGOUT, 1948
Norman Rockwell
Watercolor, 19 × 17⅞ inches
Brooklyn Museum, Brooklyn, New
York

*A crestfallen Chicago Cubs' dugout is
humorously depicted. Saturday Evening Post
cover of September 4, 1948.*

DWIGHT GOODEN, 1985
LeRoy Neiman
Illustration

*Close-up view of the New York Mets pitcher at
the completion of his delivery. Reproduced in*
Sports Illustrated, *October 21, 1985, p. 65.*

ED MATHEWS BATTING, 1968
LeRoy Neiman
Oil on masonite, 10 × 8 inches

*Stylized depiction of Hall of Famer Ed Mathews
at mid-swing.*

EMPLOYEES OF BLAKE'S BROTHERS PLAYING BALL AT HAMILTON PARK, 1869
J. R. Spencer
Drawing

EXPLOSIVE RUTH
Gene Locklear
Oil on canvas, 48 × 24 inches

*Stylized depiction of Babe Ruth striding into a
pitch.*

FAST BALL, 1964
Joe Sheppard
Lithographic print
Published by Rene Braverman

*Depicts an umpire's eye view of a delivered
pitch.*

Game Called Because of Rain *(1949), illustration by Norman Rockwell. Three stern and authoritative umpires are nonetheless subject to the whims of Mother Nature in this memorable Norman Rockwell cover for the* Saturday Evening Post. *(© 1949 Estate of Norman Rockwell.)*

FATE TAKES A HAND, 1969
Seymour Leichman
Lithograph, 30 × 22½ inches
Kennedy Galleries, Inc., New York

An angel is depicted aiding an outfielder's diving catch of a ball. Reproduced in 200 Years of Sport in America *by Wells Twombly. New York: Rutledge Books/McGraw-Hill Book Co., 1976, p. 238.*

FENWAY PARK TRIPTYCH, 1988
Andy Jurinko
Lithograph, 14 × 36 inches
Edition of 500
Published by Bill Goff, Inc., New York

Wide-angle panoramic view of baseball action at Fenway Park, Boston.

THE FIRST GAME, 1976
Robert Thom
Oil on canvas

National Baseball Hall of Fame and Museum, Cooperstown, New York

Depicts a batter, catcher, and umpire in a scene from the first National League game, April 22, 1876.

FIRST NIGHT GAME AT EBBETS FIELD, JUNE 15, 1938, 1986
Dick Perez
Oil on canvas, 29 × 35 inches
National Baseball Hall of Fame and Museum, Cooperstown, New York

Panoramic depiction of baseball action between the Cincinnati Reds and Brooklyn Dodgers in a game that featured Johnny Vander Meer's second consecutive no-hitter.

FIRST NIGHT GAME PLAYED IN MAJOR LEAGUES AT CINCINNATI, OHIO, MAY 24, 1935
Albert Dorne
Oil on canvas
National Baseball Hall of Fame and Museum, Cooperstown, New York

Panoramic depiction of baseball action as seen from the first-base bleachers.

FIRST NINE OF THE CINCINNATI BASEBALL CLUB, 1869
Lithograph, 18⅞ × 23 inches
Library of Congress

THE FIRST NINE OF THE RED STOCKINGS, 1869
Lithograph, 4½ × 6⅞ inches
Library of Congress

THE FIRST NINES, 1867
Lithograph, 4½ × 6⅝ inches
Library of Congress

THE FIRST PROFESSIONAL NIGHT GAME OF BASEBALL, 1930
Walter L. Greene
Oil on canvas

Collection of General Electric Co.
National Baseball Hall of Fame and Museum, Cooperstown, New York

Depicts a game in Des Moines, Iowa, May 2, 1930.

FOUL BALL, POLO GROUNDS, 1950
Stevan Dohanos
Illustration
National Baseball Hall of Fame and Museum, Cooperstown, New York

Depicts a ballplayer reaching into the stands for a foul ball. Saturday Evening Post *cover of April 22, 1950. Reproduced in* American Realist *by Stevan Dohanos. Westport, Connecticut: North Light Publishers, 1980, p. 42.*

FOUL! (FIELD PLAY), 1978
Bernarda Bryson Shahn
Etching, 16 × 14¾ inches
Midtown Galleries, Inc., New York

Comic depiction of a collision between two players.

A FOUL TIP, 1882
Currier and Ives
Lithograph, small folio size

Racist cartoon depiction of blacks playing baseball.

GAME CALLED BECAUSE OF RAIN, 1949
Norman Rockwell
Illustration
National Baseball Hall of Fame and Museum, Cooperstown, New York

Whimsical depiction of three umpires surveying rain-laden clouds. Also titled, The Three Umpires *and* Tough Call. Saturday Evening Post *cover of April 23, 1949.*

THE GASHOUSE GANG, 1976
Robert Thom
Oil on canvas
National Baseball Hall of Fame and Museum, Cooperstown, New York

*Depicts St. Louis Cardinals' star Pepper
Martin sliding into third base in a 1930s game.*

GEE THANKS, BROOKS!, 1971
Norman Rockwell
Lithographic print
Published by A-T-O, Inc.

*Depicts Hall of Famer Brooks Robinson
autographing a baseball for an appreciative
youngster.*

GIANTS WIN, 1914
Maurice Sievan
Ink, 7⅛ × 3⅜ inches
The Jewish Museum, New York, gift
of Mrs. Lee C. Sievan

GILMORE FIELD—1957, c. 1980
Stanley Cline
Watercolor, 16 × 20 inches

Depicts the home of the PCL Hollywood Stars.

THE GOLDEN ERA OF BASEBALL
Steve Towner
Oil on canvas
National Baseball Hall of Fame and
Museum, Cooperstown, New York

*Collage depiction of Babe Ruth and other
baseball greats in action.*

GRAMPS AT THE PLATE, 1916
Norman Rockwell
Illustration

*Comic depiction of an elderly man at bat in a
children's sandlot game. Saturday Evening
Post cover of August 5, 1916.*

GRAND OLD MAN
Ray G. Ellis
Watercolor
National Baseball Hall of Fame and
Museum, Cooperstown, New York

Hall of Fame manager Connie Mack is depicted.

THE GREAT AMERICAN PASTIME, 1981
James Rizzi
Serigraph, three-dimensional hand-
cut construction, 17½ × 23½ inches
Edition of 60
Published by John Szoke Graphics,
Inc., New York

*Folk art aerial depiction of a baseball game.
Reproduced in sales catalog,* The World of
James Rizzi. *New York: John Szoke Graphics,
Inc., 1982.*

GREEN SLIDING, 1980
Kim MacConnell
Silkscreen on diecut and folded
paper, 14½ × 22 inches
Holly Solomon Gallery

*Depicts a catcher tagging a runner sliding into
home plate. Reproduced in* Diamonds Are
Forever: Artists and Writers on Baseball
*edited by Peter H. Gordon. San Francisco:
Chronicle Books, 1987, p. 124.*

HALL OF FAME, c. 1980
Stan Albert
Oil on canvas
Sports Art USA, Studio City,
California

*Group portrait of Ruth, DiMaggio, Cobb,
Mays, and Koufax.*

HARVEY, 1982
George Lundeen
Bronze bust, height 15 inches
Edition of 30
Trails West Gallery, Laguna Beach,
California

*Bust portrait of Milwaukee Brewers' manager
Harvey Kuenn.*

HEAD QUARTERS, 76TH REGT.
N. Y. S. V. CAMP DOUBLEDAY,
LIEUT. COL. JOHN D. SHAUT,
COMMANDING, 1864
L. N. Rosenthal
Lithograph, hand colored

The Hidden Ball Trick *(1927), illustration
by Alan Foster. It seldom works—even on the
sandlots. But you get the idea that the hidden
ball trick will work this time in Alan Foster's
humorous cover for the* Saturday Evening
Post. *(The Saturday Evening Post. © 1927
The Curtis Publishing Co.)*

Published by Rosenthal Lith.,
Philadelphia

Depicts a baseball game in progress.

HEADS UP, D. H., 1980
Red Grooms
Etching and aquatint, 26¾ × 29¾
inches
Edition of 26
Marlborough Gallery, New York

HENRY AARON, 1978
William Forsyth
Oil on board, 22 × 30 inches

*Depicts the Hall of Fame slugger in the style of
a baseball card.*

HENRY LOUIS GEHRIG, 1987
Bronze figure, height 16 inches
World Wide Sports, St. Louis,
Missouri

Leroy Robert "Satchel" Paige *(c. 1983), lithograph by Harry Hammond. Rule No. 2 in Satchel Paige's six rules to staying young: "If your stomach disputes you, lie down and pacify it with cool thoughts." (Southern Art Associates, Ltd. Photo: Peter Glass.)*

The Hall of Famer is depicted at the completion of his swing.

HEROIC FIGURE, c. 1983
Mike Lloyd
Acrylic on canvas
Orlando Gallery, Los Angeles, California

198

Depicts a batter at the completion of his swing.

THE HIDDEN BALL TRICK, 1927
Alan Foster
Illustration

Humorous depiction of a sandlotter waiting to pull an old baseball ruse. Saturday Evening Post *cover of May 28, 1927.*

A HIT, 1938
Mervin Jules
Silkscreen, 15¼ × 20⅛ inches
Collection of the artist

THE HIT, 1972
LeRoy Neiman
Photo-etching, 8¼ × 7⅜ inches
Edition of 150
See also: Baseball Players Suite #1–10

HOME RUN, 1972
Stanley Kaplan
Etching, black and white, 11¾ × 8⅝ inches
Edition of 250
Published by Associated American Artists, New York

Stylized depiction of a baseball batter.

HOUSE OF DAVID, c. 1935
Artist Unknown
Lithograph, 21 × 13 inches
Collection of Marilyn and Ivan Karp

THE HOUSE OF DAVID, c. 1982
Andy Nelson
Lithograph, 15½ × 22½ inches
Edition of 500
Published by Mudville Baseball Art, McIntosh, Minnesota

Depicts a House of David player in uniform.

THE IMPOSSIBLE PLAY, 1949
Robert Riggs
Oil on panel, 10¾ × 31⅝ inches
Collection of Estelle C. and Arnold J. Kaplan

JACKIE ROBINSON
Tom O'Meara
Charcoal drawing
National Baseball Hall of Fame and Museum, Cooperstown, New York

JIM RICE, BOSTON RED SOX
Bart Forbes

Watercolor
American Sport Art Museum and
Archives, Daphne, Alabama

JOE DIMAGGIO
Malcolm Alexander
Bronze figure, height 12 inches
First Interstate Bank Athletic
Foundation, Los Angeles, California,
gift of the Helen Drue Gallery

The Hall of Famer is depicted at the completion of his swing.

JOE DIMAGGIO
Irene Schachter
Pastel
National Baseball Hall of Fame and
Museum, Cooperstown, New York

JOE MC CARTHY, 1940
Tony Sisti
Oil on canvas
National Baseball Hall of Fa.ne and
Museum, Cooperstown, New York

Off-the-field portrait of the Hall of Fame manager.

JOSE MORALES, 1977
Joe Wilder
Watercolor and pastel on paper, 13 ×
11 inches
Lynn Silverman, New York

Stylized depiction of the Montreal Expos' first baseman at the completion of his swing. Reproduced in Athletes: The Paintings of Joe Wilder, M.D. by Joe Wilder. New York: Harry N. Abrams, Inc., 1985, p. 53.

JUAN MARICHAL, 1966
LeRoy Neiman
Illustration
National Baseball Hall of Fame and
Museum, Cooperstown, New York

Depicts the Hall of Fame pitcher at mid-delivery.

LEO DUROCHER, 1973
David Levine

Ink on paper, 13½ × 11 inches
Forum Gallery, New York

LEO DUROCHER
LeRoy Neiman
Oil
Collection of Leo Durocher

LEO DUROCHER OF THE BROOKLYN DODGERS, 1947
John Groth
Watercolor and ink, 10 × 12 inches
National Art Museum of Sport, West
Haven, Connecticut

Depicts manager Leo Durocher conferring with his Dodger coaches. Reproduced in Collier's, April 12, 1947, p. 22.

LEROY ROBERT "SATCHEL" PAIGE, c. 1983
Harry Hammond
Lithograph, black and white, 18 × 24
inches
Edition of 500
Published by Southern Art Associates
Ltd., Dothan, Alabama

Depicts the Hall of Fame pitcher in a Cleveland Indians' uniform.

THE LITTLE BASEBALL PLAYER, 1860
J. G. Brown

THE LOCKER ROOM, 1957
Norman Rockwell
Illustration

Newly arrived rookie is greeted by a stoical Red Sox clubhouse. Also titled, The Rookie. Saturday Evening Post cover of March 2, 1957.

LOU BROCK'S 3000TH HIT, 1984
Mike Rabe
Acrylic on canvas
National Baseball Hall of Fame and
Museum, Cooperstown, New York

Panoramic depiction of the St. Louis Cardinals' Hall of Famer running toward first base.

LOU GEHRIG, c. 1948
S. J. Woolf
Charcoal on paper, 21¼ × 18⅝
inches
National Baseball Hall of Fame and
Museum, Cooperstown, New York

Close-up portrait of the Hall of Fame first baseman.

MANTLE AT HOME
LeRoy Neiman
Poster

Depicts Mickey Mantle sliding into home plate.

MASKED MAN, 1970
Ed Paschke
Lithograph, 12 × 6 inches
Phyllis Kind Gallery, New York

Parody of a famous photograph in which Babe Ruth is depicted as a tribal warrior. Reproduced in Diamonds Are Forever: Artists and Writers on Baseball edited by Peter H. Gordon, San Francisco: Chronicle Books, 1987, p. 139.

MAURY WILLS, JR., 1977
Joe Wilder
Oil on canvas, 10 × 8 inches
Lynn Silverman, New York

Depicts Texas Rangers' second baseman Bump Wills fielding a ball. Reproduced in Athletes: The Paintings of Joe Wilder, M.D. by Joe Wilder. New York: Harry N. Abrams, Inc., 1985, p. 48.

MIDDLE OF THE LINEUP, 1984
Joe Wilder
Oil on canvas, 14 × 10 inches
Lynn Silverman, New York

Depicts night game action as seen from the home plate bleachers. Reproduced in Athletes: The Paintings of Joe Wilder, M.D. by Joe Wilder. New York: Harry N. Abrams, Inc., 1985, p. 148.

THE MIGHTY BABE, 1976
Robert Thom
Oil on canvas

The Locker Room *(1957), illustration by Norman Rockwell. A newly arrived rookie visits the clubhouse of the Boston Red Sox in this 1957 Norman Rockwell cover for the* Saturday Evening Post. *Billy Goodman, right, can hardly suppress his amusement while veterans Haywood Sullivan, Jackie Jensen, and a weary Ted Williams look stoically on. (© 1957 Estate of Norman Rockwell.)*

National Baseball Hall of Fame and Museum, Cooperstown, New York

Depicts Babe Ruth pointing to center field.

THE MIGHTY CASEY, 1954
Paul Nonnast
Illustration

National Baseball Hall of Fame and Museum, Cooperstown, New York

The Mudville slugger is depicted doffing his cap in a scene from Casey at the Bat. *First reproduced in the* Saturday Evening Post, *July 3, 1954. Reproduced in* The Annotated Casey at the Bat *by Martin Gardner. New York: Clarkson N. Potter, Inc., 1967, p. 17.*

MIGHTY CASEY HAS STRUCK OUT, 1949
Albert Dorne
Illustration
Collection of Joe Cronin

Depicts the climactic scene from the famous baseball ballad. Reproduced in The Annotated Casey at the Bat *by Martin Gardner. New York: Clarkson N. Potter, Inc., 1967, p. 23.*

MITT, 1973
Claes Oldenburg
Lithograph, 13 × 15 inches
Published by Landfall Press, Inc., Chicago

Stylized depiction of a first baseman's glove. Reproduced in Diamonds Are Forever: Artists and Writers on Baseball *edited by Peter H. Gordon. San Francisco: Chronicle Books, 1987, p. 35.*

MY FAVORITE HITTERS, 1987
Gene Locklear
Acrylic on canvas, 36 × 24 inches
Collection of the artist

Depicts Pete Rose amid a montage of all-time great sluggers.

THE NATIONAL GAME: THREE "OUT" AND ONE "RUN." ABRAHAM WINNING THE BALL, 1860
Currier and Ives
Lithograph, 10 × 18 inches
The New York Public Library, Prints Collection

A baseball-playing Abraham Lincoln is depicted in this political cartoon.

THE NATIONAL PASTIME, 1984
(The Polo Grounds—Opening Day, April 29, 1886)
Dick Perez
Lithograph, 18½ × 26 inches
Edition of 200
Published by Perez-Steele Galleries, Fort Washington, Pennsylvania

My Favorite Hitters (1987), acrylic by Gene Locklear. Since his retirement from baseball, former Cincinnati Reds, New York Yankees, and San Diego Padres outfielder Gene Locklear has become an accomplished artist of baseball and other sports scenes. In this painting, Locklear reveals his own personal all-time favorites: Pete Rose, Reggie Jackson, Babe Ruth, Willie Mays, Rod Carew, Johnny Bench, Willie Stargell, Lou Gehrig, and others. Locklear, a Lumbee Indian, has also painted scenes from Native American history and his Carolina farm childhood, one of which was exhibited at the White House in Washington, D.C. (Collection of the artist.)

Panoramic depiction of baseball action as seen from the bleachers behind home plate.
Reproduced on the cover of The National Pastime: *Cooperstown, New York: Society for American Baseball Research, Spring 1984.*

NEW YORK FASHIONS FOR MARCH 1870, 1870
Lithograph
Published by E. Butterrick, New York
National Baseball Hall of Fame and Museum, Cooperstown, New York

Depicts players wearing baseball uniforms of the day.

NEXT AT BAT, 1972
LeRoy Neiman
Photo-etching, 8¼ × 7⅜ inches
Edition of 150
See also: Baseball Players Suite #1–10

NO RUNS, NO HITS, NO ERRORS (NOLAN RYAN), 1982
LeRoy Neiman
Serigraph, 28 × 38 inches
Houston Astros Baseball Club

100th Year of Baseball (1939), illustration by Norman Rockwell. To commemorate baseball's centennial year, the Saturday Evening Post *gave us this humorous Norman Rockwell cover depicting an 1890s-era pitcher. In baseball's early days only one umpire officiated a game; with a runner on base he took a position directly behind the pitcher. (© 1939 Estate of Norman Rockwell.)*

Depicts Nolan Ryan pitching his record-setting fifth no-hitter

OAKLAND COLISEUM NIGHT GAME

Tom Clark
Acrylic

Depicts a runner and first baseman in a close play at first. Reproduced in The Temple of Baseball *edited by Richard Grossinger. Berkeley, California: North Atlantic Books, 1985.*

ON DECK, 1973

Jay O'Meilia
Bronze figure, height 13½ inches
Edition of 15

Depicts a baseball player leaning on a bat. Reproduced in Antiques of Sport *by Jerry E. Patterson. New York: Crown Publishers, Inc., 1975, p. 121.*

100TH YEAR OF BASEBALL, 1939

Norman Rockwell
Illustration
National Baseball Hall of Fame and Museum, Cooperstown, New York

Comic depiction of an 1890s pitcher delivering a pitch. Saturday Evening Post *cover of July 8, 1939.*

OUT AT HOME, 1942

Fletcher Martin
Silkscreen in colors, 22¾ × 28 inches
Edition of 500
Published by Midtown Galleries, Inc., New York

Depicts an umpire, catcher, and runner in an action scene at home plate. Compositionally different from Martin's oil painting of the same title.

PANORAMA OF NEW YORK AND VICINITY, 1866

John Bachmann
Lithograph in colors, 35.13 × 22.4 inches

Published by John Bachmann, New York

Depicts a baseball game at Elysian Fields, Hoboken, New Jersey, 1865.

PETE ROSE, 1985

Andy Warhol
Screenprint, 40 × 31 inches
Cincinnati Museum of Art, Cincinnati, Ohio

Depicts Pete Rose in a batting stance in the style of a baseball card. Reproduced in Diamonds Are Forever: Artists and Writers on Baseball *edited by Peter H. Gordon. San Francisco: Chronicle Books, 1987, p. 71.*

PETE ROSE

John Petek
Bronze figure, height 17 inches
John Petek Art, Bozeman, Montana

Stylized depiction of Pete Rose in three images: crouched in a batting stance, at the completion of his swing, and being embraced by his son upon breaking the all-time career hit record.

PINSTRIPE WARRIOR, 1980

Bill Gallo
Lithograph, 18 × 22¼ inches
Edition of 300
National Baseball Hall of Fame and Museum, Cooperstown, New York

Depicts New York Yankees' catcher Thurman Munson throwing to second base.

THE PITCH, 1972

LeRoy Neiman
Photo-etching, 8¼ × 7⅜ inches
Edition of 150

See also: Baseball Players Suite #1–10

PITCHER, 1868

K. Muller and J. Deacon
Bronze figure, height 9²⁹⁄₃₂ inches
Whitney Collections of Sporting Art, Yale University

Depicts a pitcher about to deliver an underhand pitch.

THE PITCHER, 1982

Neil Kettlewell
Bronze figure, one-sixth life size
Edition of 100
Cincinnati Reds Baseball Club

Depicts Cincinnati Reds' pitcher Tom Seaver at mid-delivery.

PITCHER, 1984

John Dreyfuss
Bronze, height 33 inches
Edition of 12
Fendrick Gallery, Washington, D.C.

Stylized representation of a baseball pitcher. Reproduced in Diamonds Are Forever: Artists and Writers on Baseball *edited by Peter H. Gordon. San Francisco: Chronicle Books, 1987, p. 84.*

THE PITCHER THAT GOES OFTEN TO THE WELL, 1870

Lithograph, 6½ × 4⅞ inches
Library of Congress

PLAY AT SECOND, 1940

Alfred Bendiner
Lithograph, 12⁹⁄₁₆ × 17½ inches
Philadelphia Museum of Art, gift of Mrs. Alfred Bendiner

A sliding runner and an infielder are caricatured.

PLAY BALL, 1982

Michael Langenstein
Collage, 4 × 6 inches
Collection of Mr. and Mrs. Samuel A. Ramirez

Parody of Michelangelo's Creation of Man *in which the hand of God passes a baseball to Adam. Reproduced in* Diamonds Are Forever: Artists and Writers on Baseball *edited by Peter H. Gordon. San Francisco: Chronicle Books, 1987, p. 33.*

THE POLO GROUNDS, N.Y.: SEASON OF 1887, 1887

Lithograph in colors
Published by N.Y. Litho. Co.
Library of Congress

RAMPS AND PENNANTS
Robert Weaver
Acrylic, 15 × 20 inches
Midtown Galleries, Inc., New York

Still-life depiction of baseball pennants mounted below a stadium ramp.

RANK, 1964
Robert Rauschenberg
Lithograph, 16 × 16 inches
Collection of the artist

Collage depiction—incorporating baseball scenes—of 1960s turmoil. Reproduced in Diamonds Are Forever: Artists and Writers on Baseball edited by Peter H. Gordon. San Francisco: Chronicle Books, 1987, p. 68.

THE RECORD BREAKER, 1976
Robert Thom
Oil on canvas
National Baseball Hall of Fame and Museum, Cooperstown, New York

Depicts Hank Aaron hitting his 715th career home run.

REGGIE JACKSON, 1977
David Levine
Drawing, ink on paper, 10½ × 11 inches
Forum Gallery, New York

REGGIE JACKSON, 1978
Paul Calle
Lithograph, 25 × 34 inches
Edition of 600
National Art Museum of Sport, West Haven, Connecticut

Depicts New York Yankees' outfielder Reggie Jackson at bat during the 1977 World Series.

REGGIE JACKSON, 1981
Walt Spitzmiller
Lithograph, 36 × 27 inches
Edition of 72
National Art Museum of Sport, West Haven, Connecticut

REGGIE JACKSON, 1983
Joe Wilder
Oil on canvas, 16 × 12 inches
Lynn Silverman, New York

The California Angels' slugger is depicted at the completion of his swing. Reproduced in Athletes: The Paintings of Joe Wilder, M.D. by Joe Wilder. New York: Harry N. Abrams, Inc., 1985, p. 59.

REPRESENTATIVES OF PROFESSIONAL BASEBALL IN AMERICA, 1884
Lithograph in colors
Published by Root and Tinker
Library of Congress

RETIRED, c. 1965
Waite Hoyt
Oil on canvas
National Baseball Hall of Fame and Museum, Cooperstown, New York

Still life of ball, mitt, and spikes. Hoyt is a Hall of Fame pitcher.

ROBERTO CLEMENTE, c. 1973
Fernando Cano Co., Mexico
Metal sculpture, height 18½ inches
First Interstate Bank Athletic Foundation, Los Angeles, California

Stylized representation of the Hall of Famer swinging a bat.

ROBERTO CLEMENTE
Bob Dorsey
Oil on canvas
National Baseball Hall of Fame and Museum, Cooperstown, New York

Depicts a demonstrative Clemente after an unsuccessful turn at bat.

RONALD REAGAN STRIKES OUT ON FOREIGN POLICY, 1986
Edward Larson
Painted wood figure, height 26 inches
Zolla/Lieberman Gallery

Depicts a baseball-playing Ronald Reagan swinging a bat. Reproduced in Diamonds Are Forever: Artists and Writers on Baseball edited by Peter H. Gordon. San Francisco: Chronicle Books, 1987, p. 153.

SAFE, c. 1936
Jared French
Oil on canvas
National Baseball Hall of Fame and Museum, Cooperstown, New York

Depicts an infielder leaping over a sliding runner.

SAFE AT HOME, 1984
Joe Wilder
Oil on canvas, 18 × 14 inches
Lynn Silverman, New York

A runner sliding into home plate is depicted. Reproduced in Athletes: The Paintings of Joe Wilder, M.D. by Joe Wilder. New York: Harry N. Abrams, Inc., 1985, p. 44.

SAND-LOT, 1937
Joseph W. Golinkin
Watercolor, 25 × 22 inches

Pastoral depiction of a schoolboy baseball game. Also titled, Sandlot Baseball. Reproduced in American Sporting Scene by John Kieran. New York: The Macmillan Company, 1941, p. 85.

SANDY KOUFAX
Gerard Rende
Oil on canvas
National Baseball Hall of Fame and Museum, Cooperstown, New York

Depicts the Hall of Fame pitcher at mid-delivery.

THE SEAMLESS WEB, 1983
Mark Rucker
Gouache

Essay series depicting the evolution in baseball players' appearances and uniform styles. Reproduced on the cover of The National Pastime. Cooperstown, New York: Society for American Baseball Research, 1983.

The Saturday Evening **POST**

May 1, 1954 — 15¢

How Has
Secretary of Defense Wilson
Come Through His Year of Trial?
By BEVERLY SMITH

Stanley Musial (1954), illustration by John Falter. Stan Musial is not only one of the greatest players ever to have played the game of baseball—his lifetime batting average is .331 in a career that spanned 22 seasons—but he is also one of the most respected ballplayers ever to have worn a major league uniform. In John Falter's cover for the Saturday Evening Post *you can see one of the reasons why. (The Saturday Evening Post. © 1954 The Curtis Publishing Co.)*

THE SECOND GREAT MATCH
GAME FOR THE
CHAMPIONSHIP, 1867
J. L. Magee

Lithograph, hand colored
Published by J. L. Magee,
Philadelphia

*". . . between the Athletic Base Ball Club of Philadelphia, and the Atlantics of Brooklyn, on the grounds of the Athletics, Oct. 22nd, 1866."
Reproduced in* The National Pastime. *Cooperstown, New York: Society for American Baseball Research, Spring, 1984, p. 24.*

A SERIOUS TIME IN
BASEBALL'S HISTORY
Homer Davenport
Cartoon, pen and ink
New York Public Library, Prints
Collection

SEVENTH INNING—
EVERYBODY UP, 1913
Charles Dana Gibson
Pen and brush on paper, 22 × 24
inches
New York Public Library, Prints
Collection

Humorous cartoon depiction of baseball fans. Also titled, Everybody Up—Seventh Inning Stretch. *Reproduced in* Life, *July 10, 1913.*

SLIDING HOME, 1972
LeRoy Neiman
Photo-etching, 8¼ × 7¹⁄₁₆ inches
Edition of 150
See also: Baseball Players Suite #1–10

SLUGGER, 1978
William King
Aluminum figure, height 14 feet
Edition of 100

Panel cut-out depiction of a baseball player holding a bat. Reproduced in exhibition catalog, Forms in Sport: 1842–1978, *foreword by Alexander deWitt Walsh. New York: Terry Dintenfass, Inc., 1978, p. 62.*

SOFTBALL GAME AT HYDE
PARK, LONDON, 1944
Floyd Davis
Illustration

Depicts overseas Americans playing a game of softball before curious Britons. Reproduced in Life, *April 3, 1944.*

SOME SPORTS
Seymour Leichman
Lithograph, 18½ × 17½ inches
Kennedy Galleries, Inc., New York

STANLEY MUSIAL, 1954
John Falter
Illustration
National Baseball Hall of Fame and
Museum, Cooperstown, New York

*Depicts the Cardinals' Hall of Famer signing
autographs. Reproduced in the* Saturday
Evening Post, *May 1, 1954.*

STEVE GARVEY
LeRoy Neiman
Poster, 33¼ × 23 inches
Hammer Graphics Gallery, New York

*The Los Angeles Dodgers' first baseman is
depicted at the completion of his swing.*

STICKBALL
Ralph Fasanella
Silkscreen in colors, 29¾ × 30½
inches
Edition of 300
Gallery Felice, New York

Depicts a folk art view of a city street scene.

STOP ACTION LIGHTNING
(RON GUIDRY), 1980
Sheila Wolk
Lithograph, 24 × 32 inches
Edition of 300
Published by Bill Goff, Inc., New
York

*Sequential depiction—in three images—of New
York Yankee ace Ron Guidry's pitching motion.*

STUNT MAN III, 1962
Robert Rauschenberg
Lithograph
Detroit Institute of Arts, Detroit,
Michigan

TAKE ME OUT TO THE BALL
GAME, 1982

Karen Koblitz
Ceramic figure, 14 × 10 × 14 inches
Collection of Dr. Charles E. Wheeler

*Whimsical representation of Kansas City
Royals' outfielder Willie Wilson sliding safely
into home plate. Reproduced in exhibition
catalog,* Time Out: Sport and Leisure in
America Today. *Tampa, Florida: The Tampa
Museum, 1983, p. 31.*

TED WILLIAMS, 1968
Donald Moss
Acrylic on board

*Stylized depiction of the Hall of Famer
swinging a bat. Reproduced in* Champions of
American Sport *by Mark Pachter. New York:
Harry N. Abrams, Inc., 1981, p. 45.*

TOM SEAVER, 1977
Joe Wilder
Oil on canvas, 49 × 36 inches
Collection of Richard Waters

*Depicts the Cincinnati Reds' pitcher at mid-
delivery. Reproduced in* Athletes: The
Paintings of Joe Wilder, M.D. *by Joe Wilder.
New York: Harry N. Abrams, Inc., 1985, p. 3.*

TOM SEAVER, 1979
Andy Warhol
Acrylic and silkscreen on canvas
Collection of Richard L. Weisman

Pop art portrait of pitcher Tom Seaver.

TOM SEAVER, MET STAR, 1984
Joe Wilder
Oil on canvas, 30 × 22 inches
Lynn Silverman, New York

*The New York Mets' pitching star is depicted at
the completion of his delivery. Reproduced in*
Athletes: The Paintings of Joe Wilder,
M.D. *by Joe Wilder. New York: Harry N.
Abrams, Inc., 1985, p. 54.*

TONY GWYNN, 1987
Gene Locklear
Acrylic on canvas, 32 × 18 inches
Collection of the artist

*Montage depiction of San Diego Padres
outfielder Tony Gwynn.*

Untitled (America's Heartland) (1950),
*illustration by John Falter. Baseball has been
played on the frozen lakes of Alaska, in the teem-
ing streets of New York, and in the great indoors
of Houston. But in the heart of every baseball
fan, this is where baseball really belongs. (The
Saturday Evening Post. © 1950 The Curtis
Publishing Co.)*

TONY GWYNN AND TIM
FLANNERY, 1987
Gene Locklear
Acrylic on canvas, 42 × 24 inches
Collection of the artist

*Sandlotters are depicted amid a montage of San
Diego Padres stars.*

THE UMPS, 1972
LeRoy Neiman
Photo-etching, 8¼ × 7⅜ inches
Edition of 150
See also: Baseball Players Suite #1–10

UNION PRISONERS AT
SALISBURY, N.C., 1863
Otto Boetticher
Lithograph, hand colored, 27 × 52
inches
Published by Goupil and Co., New
York

Warm Up Swings (Mickey Mantle) *(1972), etching by LeRoy Neiman. (Collection of the artist.)*

The Winning Run (1885), lithograph by T. de Thulstrup. New York Giants catcher Buck Ewing's celebrated steal of home is depicted in this widely reproduced lithograph of a game played between the Giants and Chicago White Stockings on August 6, 1885. Ewing had announced his intention for all to hear before stealing second, third, and then home plate in a feat of baseball bravado that quickly became a part of American folklore of the late 1800s.

New York Public Library, Prints Collection

Panoramic depiction of Civil War prisoners playing a game of baseball. Reproduced in The National Pastime. *Cooperstown, New York: Society for American Baseball Research, Spring 1984, p. 24.*

UNTITLED, 1950
(America's Heartland)
John Falter
Illustration

Depicts a panoramic view of a country backyard baseball game. Saturday Evening Post *cover of September 2, 1950.*

WARM UP SWINGS (MICKEY MANTLE), 1972
LeRoy Neiman
Photo-etching, 8¼ × 7⅜ inches
Edition of 150

See also: Baseball Players Suite #1–10

Stylized depiction of New York Yankees' outfielder Mickey Mantle swinging several bats.

WILLIE MAYS, 1978
Leroy Neiman
Serigraph, 32 × 28 inches
Edition of 300

Hall of Famer Willie Mays is depicted at the completion of his swing. Reproduced in The Prints of LeRoy Neiman *edited by Dr. Maury Leibovitz. New York: Knoedler Publishing, Inc., 1980, p. 225.*

WILLIE STARGELL, 1981
Leroy Neiman
Serigraph, 37½ × 20½ inches
Edition of 300
Hammer Graphics Gallery, New York

Depicts the Pittsburgh Pirates' first baseman at the completion of his swing.

WILLIE STARGELL, 1987
Gene Locklear
Acrylic on canvas, 32 × 18 inches
Collection of the artist

Montage depiction of the Pittsburgh Pirates' Hall of Famer.

WIND UP, 1972.
LeRoy Neiman
Photo-etching, 8¼ × 7¼ inches
Edition of 150
See also: Baseball Players Suite #1–10

THE WINNING RUN, 1885
T. de Thulstrup
Lithograph

Depicts Buck Ewing's celebrated steal of home after having stolen second and third base.

THE WORLD CHAMPION YANKEES: VICTORY PARADE, 1977
Madeline Poster

Etching, 17 × 19¾ inches
Associated American Artists, New York

WRIGLEY FIELD (LOS ANGELES), c. 1980
Stanley Cline
Watercolor, 16 × 20 inches

Depicts the home of the Pacific Coast League Los Angeles Angels.

YANKEE STADIUM, 1937
Joseph W. Golinkin
Watercolor in two panels, 21½ × 56 inches

Collection of Manufacturers Hanover Trust Co.

Panoramic depiction of baseball action at Yankee Stadium. Reproduced in The American Sporting Scene *by John Kieran. New York: The Macmillan Company, 1941, pp. 76–77.*

YANKEE STADIUM REVISITED, 1987
William Feldman
Lithograph, 21⅝ × 29⅝ inches
Edition of 500
Published by Bill Goff, Inc., New York

Depicts a panoramic view of baseball action as seen from the center field bleachers.

YANKEE TEAM DOCTOR, c. 1956
Stevan Dohanos
Illustration

Depicts a New York Yankees' training room scene. Reproduced in American Realist *by Stevan Dohanos. Westport, Connecticut: North Light Publishers, 1980, p. 46.*

YOUR TURN, 1882
Lithograph, 6½ × 8⅜ inches
Library of Congress

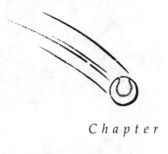

Chapter

13

Baseball in Comic Art—Collected

EXPLANATORY NOTES

1. Title of the book, year of publication.

2. Name of author.

3. Place of publication, name of publisher, book format (given when the book is available in paperback format only).

4. Annotation. Description of the contents.

The following catalog contains a comprehensive listing of publications of baseball-related comic art. Included in this section are collections of comic strips relating to baseball, collected comic illustrations depicting baseball scenes, and the first known pictorial baseball book—a collection of cartoon panels—published in 1867.

BASE BALL AS VIEWED BY A MUFFIN, 1867
S. Van Campen
New Bedford, Massachusetts: Taber Brothers, paperback
Lithographs by Ch. H. Crosby, Boston

This extremely rare collection of humorous panels is the first known pictorial book relating to American baseball.

BUTCHERED BASEBALL, 1952
Cartoons by R. Taylor, text by F. S. Pearson II
New York: A.S. Barnes and Co.

Baseball terminology is applied to nonbaseball scenes for humorous effect.

CHARACTER SKETCHES, PROMINENT FANS, BASEBALL STARS AND OTHER SPORTS, 1907
E. A. Bushnell
Hubbell Printing Co.

CHARLIE BROWN'S ALL-STARS, 1966
Charles M. Schulz
New York: World Publishing Co.

See also: Baseball in Animated Cartoons—Television; Baseball in Miscellaneous Recordings

---

Only three copies of this rare 1867 collection of cartoon panels—the first known pictorial book relating to American baseball—are known to exist. Shown is a typical panel from Base Ball as Viewed by a Muffin *as drawn by S. Van Campen. Seated at the table at left is the scorekeeper who also served as an umpire in some early baseball games.* (National Baseball Library.)

THE GARRY: A BOOK OF HUMOROUS CARTOONS: PICKINGS FROM THE DIAMOND, 1904
Garry Hermann
J. F. Collins, paperback

HOW MANY NEXT YEARS DO YOU GET IN BASEBALL: SHOE GOES TO WRIGLEY FIELD, 1988
Jeff MacNelly
New York: Bonus Books, paperback

Collection of Shoe comic strips relating to baseball and the Chicago Cubs.

IF I QUIT BASEBALL, WILL YOU STILL LOVE ME?, 1976
Jeff Millar and Bill Hinds
Sheed and Ward

Collection of Tank McNamara comic strips.

LEGENDARY BASEBALL STARS: PAPER DOLLS IN FULL COLOR, 1985
Tom Tierney
Mineola, New York: Dover Publications, paperback

Includes likenesses of 16 Hall of Famers and re-created baseball fashions from the 1890s to the 1970s.

LI'L LEAGUER, 1960
Al Liederman
New York: Pocket Books, paperback

LITTLE BIG LEAGUERS, 1967
Earl Hochman
Arrow Books, paperback

NIPPER, 1970
Morrie Turner
Westminster Press

ON THE SIDELINES, 1967
Earl Hochman
Arrow Books, paperback

RING LARDNER'S YOU KNOW ME AL, 1979
Ring W. Lardner
Cartoons by Will B. Johnstone and Dick Dorgan
New York: Harvest Books/Bruccoli Clark Publishers and Harcourt Brace Jovanovich, Inc.

See also: You Know Me Al: A Busher's Letters (Baseball in Fiction)

Collection of cartoon strips from 1922–1925 featuring pitcher Jack Keefe.

SANDLOT PEANUTS, 1977
Charles M. Schulz
New York: Holt, Rinehart and Winston

Collection of Peanuts comic strips relating to baseball.

SCROOGIE, 1976
Tug McGraw and Mike Witte
New York: New American Library/ Signet Books, paperback

Collection of comic strips inspired by the New York Mets' ace reliever.

SMITTY AT THE BALL GAME, 1929
Walter Berndt
Cupples and Leon Co.

Collection of Smitty comic strips relating to baseball.

Appendix to Chapter 13

EXPLANATORY NOTES

1. Title of the comic periodical, year of publication.

2. Name of the periodical series in parentheses, if applicable.

3. Name of publisher, date of publication.

4. Annotation. Description of the comic periodical.

The appendix contains a comprehensive listing of baseball-related comic periodicals. Included in this section are comic book series relating to baseball, comic book histories of baseball clubs and major league players, and comic periodicals featuring a fictitious baseball hero.

THE ALL-STAR STORY OF THE DODGERS, 1979
Stadium Communications: April 1979

THE AMAZING WILLIE MAYS, 1954
Famous Funnies

BABE, DARLING OF THE HILLS, 1949
Feature Publications: November–December 1949

Home-run-hitting woman leads her team to the World Series.

BABE RUTH SPORTS COMICS, 1949
Harvey Enterprises, Inc.
11 total in series: April 1949–February 1951

Includes a serial biography of Babe Ruth, baseball quizzes and instructionals, and true-life stories of sports heroes.

BASEBALL COMICS, 1949
Will Eisner Productions
One only in series: Spring 1949

Features the exploits of "Rube Rooky of the Major Leagues."

BASEBALL GREATS, 1946
(Sport Stars)
Parents Magazine Institute: issue no. 2

BASEBALL HALL OF FAME STORY
(True Comics)
True Comics/Parents Magazine Press: issue no. 3

BASEBALL HEROES, 1952
Fawcett Publications
One only in series

BASEBALL NUTS, 1982
(Popeye the Sailor)
Western Publishing Co., Inc.: issue no. 171

Popeye and Brutus are competitors in a marathon baseball game.

BASEBALL THRILLS, 1951
Approved Comics, Inc.
10 total in series: 1951–1952

BASEBALL WORLD SERIES STORY
(True Comics)
True Comics/Parents Magazine Press: issue no. 6

BOB FELLER STORY
(True Comics)
True Comics/Parents Magazine Press: issue no. 15

BROOKLYN DODGERS STORY
(True Comics)
True Comics/Parents Magazine Press: issue no. 17

CIRCLING THE BASES, 1947
A. G. Spalding and Bros.
Based on the motion picture
See also: Baseball in Documentary and Miscellaneous Films

DICK COLE, 1949
(Blue Bolt)
The Premium Group of Comics: July–August 1949

Dick Cole overcomes injuries and the jealousy of his teammates.

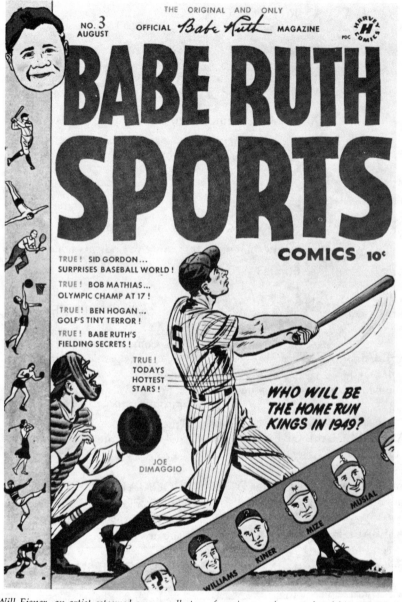

Will Eisner, an artist esteemed among collectors of comic magazines, produced his one and only baseball comic book in 1949. The magazine, Baseball Comics *(page 217, left), features the exploits of "Rube Rooky" and is a collector's item today.* Babe Ruth Sports Comics *(above) and* Swat Malone *(page 217, right) also had their turn at bat on the magazine stands.*

DON NEWCOMBE, BASEBALL HERO, 1950
Fawcett Publications

EDDIE STANKY, BASEBALL HERO, 1951
Fawcett Publications

GEORGE FOSTER: MAN OF DREAMS, MAN WITH A PURPOSE, 1982
George Foster Enterprises, Inc.

Inner title: *"George Foster: A Dream Comes True."*

HOME RUN, 1953
Magazine Enterprises
Three total in series

JACKIE ROBINSON, 1949
Fawcett Publications
Five total in series: 1949–1950

JACKIE ROBINSON, BASEBALL HERO, 1952
Fawcett Publications

JACKIE ROBINSON, ROOKIE OF THE YEAR, 1948
(Negro Heroes)
Parents Magazine Institute; issue no. 2

JOE DIMAGGIO STORY, 1948
(True Comics)
True Comics/Parents Magazine Press: May 1948

LARRY DOBY, BASEBALL HERO, 1950
Fawcett Publications

LIFE STORY OF LOU GEHRIG, 1940
(Sport Comics)
Street and Smith Publications: issue no. 1

LOU GEHRIG LIFE STORY, 1941
(World Famous Heroes Magazine)
Comic Corp. of America: issue no. 2

LOU GEHRIG STORY
(Real Heroes Comics)
Parents Magazine Institute: issue no. 6

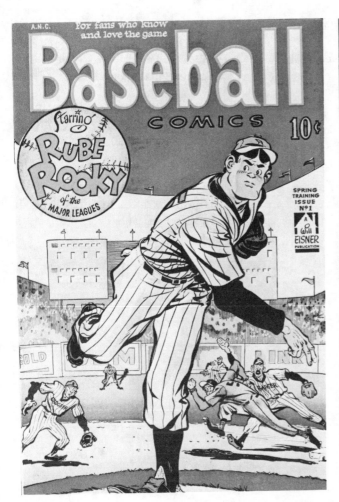

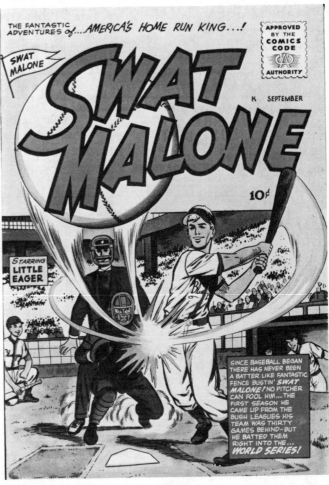

MEL ALLEN SPORTS COMICS,
1949
Visual Editions, Inc.
Six total in series

MY GREATEST THRILLS IN
BASEBALL BY MICKEY
MANTLE
Mission of California

NATIONAL LEAGUE, 1976
(Harvey Comics)
Harvey World: June 1976

PHIL RIZZUTO, BASEBALL
HERO, 1951
Fawcett Publications

THE PRIDE OF THE YANKEES,
1949
Magazine Enterprises
One only in series
See also: Baseball in Film; Baseball in
Radio; Baseball in Miscellaneous
Recordings

RALPH KINER, HOME RUN
KING, 1950
Fawcett Publications

RHUBARB
(Four Color Comics)
Dell Publishing Co., Inc.: issue
no. 423
See also: Baseball in Fiction, Baseball
in Film

ROY CAMPANELLA, BASEBALL
HERO, 1950
Fawcett Publications

THE STORY OF BASEBALL
(Real Life Comics)
Standard Publ.: issue no. 24

THE STORY OF BOB FELLER
(Real Life Comics)
Standard Publ.: issue no. 40

THE STORY OF GENE
BEARDEN, 1949
(Real Life Comics)
Visual Editions, Inc.: July 1949

THE STORY OF JIMMIE FOXX
(Real Life Comics)
Standard Publ.: issue no. 41

Includes ''The Story of 'Home Run' Baker.''

SWAT MALONE, 1955
Swat Malone Enterprises, Inc.
One only in series: September 1955

*Features the ''Fantastic Adventures of
America's Home Run King.''*

THE THRILLING TRUE STORY
OF THE BASEBALL GIANTS,
1952
Fawcett Publications

THE THRILLING TRUE STORY
OF THE BASEBALL YANKEES,
1952
Fawcett Publications

YOGI BERRA, BASEBALL
HERO, 1951
Fawcett Publications

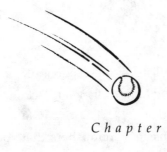

Chapter

14

Baseball in Fiction

The following catalog contains a comprehensive listing of full-length and collected adult fiction relating to baseball. Included in this section are serious and comic novels, detective stories, mysteries, and collections of baseball short stories by a single author. Not included are anthologies of baseball fiction by various authors, or fiction intended for younger readers. For a listing of these publications, *see:* Baseball in Juvenile and Miscellaneous Fiction.

For further information regarding book dealers and publishers that specialize in baseball-related fiction and other published materials, consult the Selected Guide to Sources and Dealers located at the back of the book.

EXPLANATORY NOTES

1. Title of the novel, year of publication.

2. Name of author.

3. Place of publication, name of publisher, book

format (given when the novel is available in paperback format only).

4. Annotation. Description of the novel.

ALL G.O.D.'S CHILDREN, 1975
John Craig
New York: William Morrow and Co., Inc.

Comic adventures of a perennial last-place club's pennant contending season.

ALL THE WAY HOME, 1984
Ellen Cooney
New York: G. P. Putnam's Sons

Woman softball player, injured in a motorcycle accident, returns home to coach a team.

ALMOST FAMOUS, 1982
David Small
New York: W. W. Norton and Co., Inc.

A star minor league player retreats from the mainstream of life after an auto accident ends his promising career.

BABE RUTH CAUGHT IN A SNOWSTORM, 1973
John Alexander Graham
Boston: Houghton Mifflin Co.

Manager organizes a minor league team comprised solely of players who love baseball.

BALLPARK, 1982
Michael Schiffer
New York: Simon and Schuster

Female sportswriter falls in love with a star baseball player.

BANG THE DRUM SLOWLY, 1956
Mark Harris
New York: Alfred A. Knopf, Inc.
See also: Baseball in Film; Baseball in Television; Baseball in Miscellaneous Recordings. *See: It Looked Like For Ever; The Southpaw; A Ticket for a Seamstitch*

Henry Wiggen befriends a second-string catcher who is dying of an incurable illness.

A BASEBALL CLASSIC, 1978
Merritt Clifton
Richford, Vermont: Samisdat, paperback

A wanderer quits his job as a mill worker to try out for a Class-A minor league club.

BASEBALL STORIES FOR GIRLS AND BOYS (PAST PUBERTY), 1982
Merritt Clifton
Richford, Vermont: Samisdat, paperback

Collection of four works of short fiction.

THE BATTING MACHINE, 1981
Mel Knopf
Great Neck, New York: Todd and Honeywell

Baseball-related science-fiction novel.

BEANBALL: A NOVEL OF BASEBALL AND MURDER, 1989
Tom Seaver and Herb Resnicow
New York: William Morrow and Co.

Baseball-related mystery fiction ghostwritten by Herb Resnicow.

BEHOLD, THY BROTHER, 1950
Murrell Edmunds
New York: Beechhurst Press

A black baseball player encounters opposition and prejudice as a rookie in the major leagues.

THE BIG LEAGUE, 1911
Charles E. Van Loan
Boston: Small, Maynard and Co.

Collection of nine stories relating to baseball.

THE BINGO LONG TRAVELING ALL-STARS AND MOTOR KINGS, 1973
William Brashler
New York: Harper and Row Publishers
See also: Baseball in Film; Baseball in Miscellaneous Recordings. *See: Bingo!* (Baseball in Theater)

Affectionate portrayal of a barnstorming team of black all-stars during the late 1930s.

THE BOYS OF WINTER, 1987
Wilfrid Sheed
New York: Alfred A. Knopf, Inc.

A SPECIAL SILENCE

There is no greater moment in a child's life as when he discovers for the first time an identity that is uniquely his own. For generations of children, baseball has been one such means of self-discovery. It can occur quite simply and instantaneously, as when a child swings a bat or throws a ball for the first time. Or it can happen during a rare moment, as when a child hits or throws a ball with uncommon authority. In David Small's outstanding novel, *Almost Famous*, a former minor leaguer recalls a moment during his childhood when his life became something special in its own right. Here's Ward Sullivan, on a visit to his mother's bedside, remembering a long-ago event along the shores of Maine:

"Listen," she said in that glittering voice that made the hairs on his neck stand up. "Beyond God a low window opens onto a mild gray summer evening. Mild and lovely such as I remember from my childhood in Dunnocks Head. Down the field I can see the *Arzamas*, the last ship, sitting on the ways. Do you remember that old ship?"

"Yes, I remember."

Yes, he remembered. Two old men in black suits. Both lean and white-haired. Maybe the old Captain standing on the edge of the field in the shadow of the house, he too in a black suit, only his coat laid in a neat bundle on the vivid green grass at his feet. No bigger than Keats, the kid said. Against the black butterfly of his vest his shirt glowed pure white.

Come on, Colby Jack! Show this rube your good stuff!

The black tails of Mr. Coombs' suit coat flapped as he slipped through the notches of his wind-up, moving jerkily as a figure striking an anvil on a Swiss clock. And the ball on the bright air, not fast, but heavy. And Ward, a boy of promise then, whaled hell out of it. The old men cackled delightedly when the ball jumped off the bat as if repelled by the wood, the boy now master of some secret law of physics known only to him and God. The ball rose in the light, winking like the evening star. It plummeted suddenly, with violent speed as if heavy as a shotput, a little white pea hurtling onto the deck of the half-built ship which wallowed in the tall weeds.

You little gnat! You hit that one a country mile!

And the special silence that followed. The old men looking at each other significantly, acknowledging this boy had the special gift too.

Copyright © 1982 by David Small, from *Almost Famous* (W. W. Norton, 1982). Reprinted by permission of the publisher.

Satirical examination of a Long Island writers' colony and its softball-playing rituals.

BREAKING BALLS, 1979
Marty Bell
New York: New American Library

Life on a major league ball club is caricatured.

CAN'T MISS, 1987
Michael Bowen
New York: Harper and Row, Publishers, Inc.

Misadventures of the first female to play in the major leagues.

THE CELEBRANT, 1983
Eric Rolfe Greenberg
New York: Everest House Publishers

America's loss of innocence is personified by Christy Mathewson and a hero-worshiping fan in this re-creation of early 1900s baseball.

CHANGING PITCHES, 1984
Steve Kluger
New York: St. Martin's Press

Comedic diary account of a year in the life of a big league team.

CHAPPIE AND ME, 1979
John Craig
New York: Dodd, Mead and Co.
See also: *Ain't Lookin'* (Baseball in Theater)

Novelized true story about a white youth who surreptitiously plays for a touring team of black all-stars.

CHEAT, 1984
Pat Jordan
New York: Villard Books

A jaded and unprincipled sports reporter writes unsparingly about a scandal involving a baseball player.

CHIN MUSIC, 1985
James McManus
New York: Crown Publishers, Inc.

Disturbing allegory about a Chicago White Sox pitcher's last hours before a nuclear conflagration.

THE CONDUCT OF THE GAME, 1986
John Hough, Jr.
San Diego, California: Harcourt Brace Jovanovich, Publishers

Nostalgic reminiscence of a young man's coming-of-age from small-town youth to big league umpire.

THE CURIOUS CASE OF SIDD FINCH, 1987

George Plimpton
New York: Macmillan Publishing Company

Humorous account of a mysterious Tibetan pitcher whose 168-mph fastball propels him upon a brief but brilliant career for the New York Mets.

DEAD IN CENTER FIELD, 1983

Paul Engleman
New York: Ballantine Books, paperback

Private investigator and former ballplayer Mark Renzler is hired to protect a baseball superstar. Mystery fiction.

DEATH ON THE DIAMOND, 1934

Cortland Fitzsimmons
New York: Frederick A. Stokes Co.
See also: Baseball in Film

THE DEVIL TO PLAY, 1974

Leonard Holton
New York: Dodd, Mead and Co.

Los Angeles police lieutenant investigates the shooting of a baseball player during a crucial game. Mystery fiction.

THE DIXIE ASSOCIATION, 1984

Donald Hays
New York: Simon and Schuster

Ex-convict joins a renegade minor league club composed of social and political outcasts.

THE DOUBLE SQUEEZE, 1915

Henry Beach Needham
Garden City, New York: Doubleday, Page and Co.

Collection of four stories relating to baseball, with an introduction by Connie Mack.

DUST IN THE AFTERNOON, 1940

Holmes Alexander
New York: Harper and Brothers Publishers

Major league star and his actress wife attempt to accommodate their marriage and their careers.

FIVE O'CLOCK LIGHTNING, 1982

William L. DeAndrea
New York: St. Martin's Press, paperback

McCarthy-era extremists are implicated in the threats against Mickey Mantle's life. Mystery fiction.

FOLLOW THE SHARKS, 1985

William G. Tapply
New York: Charles Scribner's Sons

Former Boston Red Sox pitcher is suspected of kidnapping his son from his estranged wife. Mystery fiction.

FROM BASEBALL TO BOCHES, 1918

H. C. Witwer
Boston: Small, Maynard and Co.
See also: A Smile a Minute; There's No Base Like Home

Letters from Cincinnati Reds pitcher Ed Harmon, now a World War I soldier, a la You Know Me Al.

THE FURTHER ADVENTURES OF SLUGGER MCBATT, 1988

W. P. Kinsella
Boston: Houghton Mifflin Co., paperback

Collection of ten short stories relating to baseball.

GAMEMAKER, 1980

David Keith Cohler
New York: Doubleday and Co., Inc.

A series of assassinations of professional athletes, including the star center fielder for the

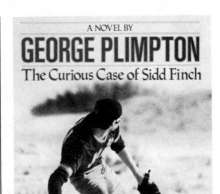

A NOVEL BY
GEORGE PLIMPTON
The Curious Case of Sidd Finch

On April 1, 1985 Sports Illustrated *published, as if it were a factual story, an article by George Plimpton about a Tibetan Buddhist monk named Sidd Finch who could throw a baseball accurately at the unheard of—and unhittable—speed of 168 mph. (His curve was clocked at 120!) The story, which ended with Finch considering an offer from the New York Mets, provoked a flood of calls and letters from disbelieving baseball fans who wanted to know—could this story possibly be true? Inquiring readers were advised to refer to the magazine's April Fools' publication date. More than one fan was thus brought back to earth, including a United States Senator. In 1987 Plimpton expanded "The Curious Case of Sidd Finch" into a whimsical and revealing novel of life in baseball and America. Finch is presented as a mystic and intellectual whose ideals are as unfathomable as his fastball, and whose presence in the major leagues threatens the delicate balance and the very future of the game. In all likelihood the next version of the Sidd Finch story will appear on the silver screen. (© 1987 Macmillan Publishing Company)*

―――――――――

New York Yankees, is the subject of an elite police force investigation. Mystery fiction.

GETTING BLUE, 1987

Peter Gethers
New York: Delacorte Press

Ballplayer Alex Justin's search for self-

discovery is traced over a span of four decades, from his days as a high school prospect to a big league star.

GOODBYE, BOBBY THOMSON! GOODBYE, JOHN WAYNE!, 1973

Alan S. Foster
New York: Simon and Schuster

An American male is disillusioned by the false notions of heroism adopted in his youth.

THE GRACE OF SHORTSTOPS, 1984

Rober Mayer
Garden City, New York: Doubleday and Co., Inc.

Evocative account of a Jewish immigrant youngster's journey of self-discovery through his enthusiasm for 1940s baseball and the Brooklyn Dodgers.

A GRAND SLAM, 1973

Ray Puechner
New York: Warner Paperback Library, paperback

A woman baseball player personifies the 1960s sexual revolution in this light-hearted novel.

THE GREAT AMERICAN NOVEL, 1973

Philip Roth
New York: Holt, Rinehart and Winston

Satirical re-creation of baseball lore as provided by a historian of the misfit Patriot League, a World War II era third major league.

THE GREATEST SLUMP OF ALL TIME, 1984

David Carkeet
New York: Harper and Row Publishers

A perennial pennant-contending team suffers from a rash of modern-day psychological maladies and eccentricities.

GUYS LIKE US, 1980

Tom Lorenz
New York: The Viking Press

Absurdist-comic novel about a group of men whose lives unravel while they obsessively involve themselves in their softball team.

HEART OF THE ORDER, 1986

Tony Ardizzone
New York, Henry Holt and Co.

Allegorical melodrama about a minor leaguer haunted by an unhappy past.

HEARTS AND THE DIAMOND, 1920

Gerald Beaumont
New York: Dodd, Mead and Co.

Collection of 11 stories relating to Pacific Coast League baseball during the early 1900s.

HIT AND RUN, 1982

Dave Klein
New York: Ace Charter, paperback

Latino baseball superstar is kidnapped. Mystery fiction.

HOME GAME, 1983

Paul Quarrington
Garden City, New York: Doubleday and Co., Inc.

A marooned sideshow circus troupe and a small-town fundamentalist sect settle their differences on the baseball diamond.

HOOPLA, 1983

Harry Stein
New York: Alfred A. Knopf, Inc.

Novelized re-creation of the events surrounding the 1919 "Black Sox" scandal.

THE IOWA BASEBALL CONFEDERACY, 1986

W. P. Kinsella
Boston: Houghton Mifflin Co.

Allegorical fantasy about a mythical baseball game between the 1908 Chicago Cubs and a small-town Iowa team.

IRONWEED, 1983

William Kennedy
New York: The Viking Press
See also: Baseball in Film: Appendix

Hero of the novel is Francis Phelan, a former big league baseball player, three-time murderer, and long-time bum.

IT HAD TO BE A WOMAN, 1979

Paul Newlin
New York: Stein and Day

Newly divorced baseball fan contemplates suicide in the manner of his childhood hero, Willard Hershberger.

IT HAPPENS EVERY SPRING, 1949

Valentine Davies
New York: Farrar, Straus and Young, Inc.
See also: Baseball in Film; Baseball in Radio

Humorous romance about a professor who invents a formula that makes a thrown ball impossible to hit.

IT LOOKED LIKE FOR EVER, 1979

Mark Harris
New York: McGraw-Hill Book Co.
See also: Bang the Drum Slowly; The Southpaw; A Ticket for a Seamstitch

A middle-aged Henry Wiggen confronts life outside of baseball.

KNAVE OF EAGLES, 1969

Robert Wade
New York: Random House, Inc.

Cuban-born major leaguer detained in Cuba during an unauthorized visit is retrieved by a private investigator. Mystery fiction.

THE LAST GREAT SEASON, 1979

Donald Honig
New York: Simon and Schuster

The owner of the 1942 New York Lions ruthlessly pursues a pennant.

THE LAST MAN IS OUT, 1969
Marvin Karlins
Englewood Cliffs, New Jersey:
Prentice-Hall, Inc.

*The results of twenty-first-century baseball
games are dictated by a computer. Science
fiction. Second edition retitled and issued under
a pseudonym: The New Atoms' Bombshell
by Robert Browne. New York: Ballantine
Books, 1980, paperback.*

LETTERS FROM LEFTY, 1966
Mickey Herskowitz
Houston, Texas: Houston Post Co.,
paperback
Second revised edition, Houston,
Texas: Inverness Press, Inc., 1980,
paperback

*Collection of fictional letters from a Houston
Colt 45's pitcher.*

LONG GONE, 1979
Paul Hemphill
New York: The Viking Press
See also: Baseball in Television

*Bittersweet story about a Class-D minor league
team during the mid-1950s.*

LOSE WITH A SMILE, 1933
Ring W. Lardner
New York: Charles Scribner's Sons

*Letters from rookie Danny Warner about his
life as a Dodgers' outfielder and roommate of
Casey Stengel. Originally published as a series
for the* Saturday Evening Post, *April 23,
1932 to September 3, 1932.*

THE LUCKY SEVENTH, 1913
Charles E. Van Loan
Boston: Small, Maynard and Co.

Collection of nine stories relating to baseball.

LUKE, 1976
Peter Winston
New York: Manor Books, Inc.,
paperback

*Melodramatic romance about a small-town
slugger gone wrong in the major leagues.*

MAN ON SPIKES, 1955
Eliot Asinof
New York: McGraw-Hill Book Co.
See also: Baseball in Television

*Episodic account of a ballplayer's life, from
youth to retirement.*

**THE MAN WHO BROUGHT
THE DODGERS BACK TO
BROOKLYN, 1981**
David Ritz
New York: Simon and Schuster

*Romantic fantasy in which two Brooklynites
accomplish the impossible.*

**THE MAN WHO WANTED TO
PLAY CENTER FIELD FOR THE
NEW YORK YANKEES, 1983**
Gary Morgenstein
New York: Atheneum Publishers,
Inc.

*Unhappy 33-year-old man reaffirms a
longstanding ambition to play in the major
leagues.*

MORTAL STAKES, 1975
Robert B. Parker
Boston: Houghton Mifflin Co.

*A private eye investigates a possible fix by a
star Boston Red Sox pitcher. Mystery fiction.*

MUCKALUCK, 1980
Richard Andersen
New York: Delacorte Press

THE NATURAL, 1952
Bernard Malamud
New York: Harcourt, Brace
See also: Baseball in Film; Baseball in
Miscellaneous Recordings; Baseball in
the Spoken Arts—Recorded

*The hero of this allegorical novel is Roy Hobbs,
the embodiment of American myth and baseball
lore.*

**THE NEW ATOMS'
BOMBSHELL, 1980**
See: The Last Man is Out

THE NEW KLONDIKE, 1926
Peggy Griffith
New York: Jacobsen-Hodgkinson
See also: Baseball in Film

*Based on the film of the same name, without
credit to the original story by Ring W. Lardner.*

ODDITORIUM, 1983
Hob Broun
New York: Harper and Row
Publishers

*Comic adventures of a barnstorming woman
baseball player.*

**THE ONLY GAME IN TOWN,
1954**
Charles Einstein
New York: Dell Publishing Co., Inc.,
paperback

*Former major leaguer returns as a manager
after years spent in the minor leagues.*

OUT AT HOME, 1985
Gary Pomeranz
Boston: Houghton Mifflin Co.

*Young man becomes entangled in a scheme to
influence the outcome of 1955 Chicago Cubs'
games.*

**A PENNANT FOR THE
KREMLIN, 1964**
Paul Molloy
New York: Doubleday and Co., Inc.
See also: Baseball in Miscellaneous
Plays and Sketches

*Light-hearted fantasy in which a major league
club is bequeathed to the government of the
Soviet Union.*

PRIDE OF THE BIMBOS, 1975
John Sayles
Boston: Little, Brown and Co.

*Comic misadventures of a barnstorming
carnival softball team.*

THE REAL DOPE, 1919
Ring W. Lardner

225

Indianapolis, Indiana: The Bobbs-Merrill Co.
See also: Treat 'em Rough: Letters from Jack the Kaiser Killer; You Know Me Al: A Busher's Letters

Further letters from busher Jack Keefe from a World War I camp. First published as a series for the Saturday Evening Post, July 6, 1918 to January 25, 1919.

RHUBARB, 1946
H. Allen Smith
New York: Doubleday and Co., Inc.
See also: Baseball in Film; Baseball in Comic Art—Collected: Appendix

Humorous fantasy about a cat that inherits a baseball team.

THE RIO LOJA RINGMASTER, 1977
Lamar Herrin
New York: The Viking Press

Former major leaguer attempts to start a new life as a player in the Mexican League.

ROAD GAME, 1986
Mark H. Burch
New York: Vanguard Press

Sportswriter covers Class-A minor league life in a small southern town.

THE RUNDOWN, 1977
James Magnuson
New York: The Dial Press

Club owner is suspected of kidnapping the team's star player, with whom he is involved in a contract dispute. Mystery fiction.

RUNNER MACK, 1972
Barry Beckham
New York: William Morrow and Co., Inc.

Allegory in which a black baseball player becomes a militant revolutionary.

ST. URBAIN'S HORSEMAN, 1971

Mordecai Richler
New York: Alfred A. Knopf, Inc.

SAM'S LEGACY, 1974
Jay Neugeboren
New York: Holt, Rinehart and Winston

Former Negro League star befriends a young down-on-his-luck gambler.

SCORE BY INNINGS, 1919
Charles E. Van Loan
New York: George H. Doran Co.

Collection of 10 stories relating to baseball.

THE SCREWBALL KING MURDER, 1978
Kin Platt
New York: Random House, Inc.

Private-eye Max Roper investigates the apparent murder of a flamboyant Los Angeles Dodgers' pitcher. Mystery fiction.

SCREWBALLS, 1980
Jay Cronley
New York: Doubleday and Co., Inc.

A baseball team is caricatured.

THE SENSATION, 1975
Norman Keifetz
New York: Atheneum Publishers, Inc.

Major league star is arrested for child molestation.

THE SENSUOUS SOUTHPAW, 1976
Paul R. Rothweiler
New York: G. P. Putnam's Sons

Baseball's first woman major leaguer is caricatured.

SEVEN GAMES IN OCTOBER, 1979
Charles Brady
Boston: Little, Brown and Co.

Detailed account of an FBI investigation into the extortion of a baseball star during the World Series. Mystery fiction.

THE SEVENTH BABE, 1979
Jerome Charyn
New York: Arbor House Publishing Co.

Whimsical satire about a gifted ballplayer's life in the major leagues and later as the first white player on an all-black team of touring all-stars.

THE 7TH GAME, 1977
Don Kowet
New York: Dell Publishing Co., Inc., paperback

Star pitcher's child is kidnapped in an attempt to fix the World Series. Mystery fiction.

THE SEVENTH GAME, 1982
Roger Kahn
New York: New American Library

Retrospective flashbacks and World Series dramatics relate the history of aging pitcher Johnny Longboat's life.

SHE'S ON FIRST, 1987
Barbara Gregorich
Chicago: Contemporary Books

Woman confronts prejudice and hostility from teammates and opposing clubs to become the first female to play in the major leagues.

SHOELESS JOE, 1982
W. P. Kinsella
Boston: Houghton Mifflin Co.

Allegorical fantasy about an Iowa farmer's obsession with Shoeless Joe Jackson.

SHORT SEASON AND OTHER STORIES, 1988
Jerry Klinkowitz
Baltimore, Maryland: Johns Hopkins University Press

Collection of 28 short stories involving a Class-A minor league baseball club.

A SMILE A MINUTE, 1919
H. C. Witwer
Boston: Small, Maynard and Co.
See also: From Baseball to Boches; There's No Base Like Home

Further letters from Cincinnati Reds pitcher Ed Harmon upon his return home from World War I, a la You Know Me Al.

THE SOUTHPAW, 1953
Mark Harris
Indianapolis, Indiana: The Bobbs-Merrill Co., Inc.
See also: Bang the Drum Slowly; It Looked Like For Ever; A Ticket for a Seamstitch

Humorous first person account of pitcher Henry Wiggen's rookie year.

SOUTHPAW, 1988
Frank King
New York: Lynx Books, paperback

A werewolf stalks a major league team. Horror fiction.

SPITBALLS AND HOLY WATER, 1977
James F. Donohue
New York: Avon Books, paperback

A black nun pitches a touring Negro League team to a victory over the 1927 New York Yankees.

THE SPOILER, 1987
Domenic Stansberry
Boston: Atlantic Monthly Press

Cynical small-town reporter investigates a minor league club owner's suspected criminal activities. Mystery fiction.

SQUEEZE PLAY, 1984
Paul Benjamin
New York: Avon Books, paperback

Former baseball player receives a threat against his life. Mystery fiction.

STAY LOOSE, 1959
Bud Nye
Garden City, New York: Doubleday and Co., Inc.

A computer is used to influence the outcome of baseball games.

STEALING HOME, 1979
Philip F. O'Connor
New York: Alfred A. Knopf, Inc.

The disunion and despair of a suburban family are revealed through its involvement with a Little League team.

STRICTLY AMATEUR, 1982
Tom McCormack
New York: Pinnacle Books, paperback

Black baseball superstar is kidnapped. Mystery fiction.

STRIKE THREE YOU'RE DEAD, 1984
R. D. Rosen
New York: Walker and Co.

Veteran outfielder attempts to solve the murder of a teammate. Mystery fiction.

SUDER, 1983
Percival L. Everett
New York: The Viking Press

Absurdist adventures of a slumping black ballplayer's escape from an oppressive personal life.

THE SUN FIELD, 1923
Heywood Broun
New York: G. P. Putnam's Sons

Humorous romance about a Ruthian slugger named Tiny Tyler.

THE SUNLIT FIELD, 1950
Lucy Kennedy
New York: Crown Publishers, Inc.

Romance fiction in which an immigrant 16-year-old girl learns the joy and promise of mid-1800s America through baseball.

TAKE ME OUT TO THE BALLGAME, 1980
Gary Morgenstein
New York: St. Martin's Press

Baseball-related mystery fiction.

THE TEN-THOUSAND-DOLLAR ARM AND OTHER TALES OF THE BIG LEAGUE, 1912
Charles E. Van Loan
Boston: Small, Maynard and Co.

Collection of nine baseball-related stories.

THERE'S NO BASE LIKE HOME, 1920
H. C. Witwer
New York: Doubleday, Page and Co.
See also: From Baseball to Boches; A Smile a Minute

Collection of letters by a newly married Cincinnati Reds pitcher to his friend, Joe, a la You Know Me Al.

THINGS INVISIBLE TO SEE, 1985
Nancy Willard
New York: Alfred A. Knopf, Inc.

Lyric allegory in which good and evil are rivals in a sandlot baseball game.

THE THRILL OF THE GRASS, 1984
W. P. Kinsella
New York: Penguin Books, paperback

Collection of 11 baseball-related works of short fiction.

A TICKET FOR A SEAMSTITCH, 1957
Mark Harris
New York: Alfred A. Knopf, Inc.
See also: Bang the Drum Slowly; It Looked Like For Ever; The Southpaw

A woman baseball fan develops an obsessive interest in star pitcher Henry Wiggen in this poignant novella.

BASEBALL BLACKOUT

When one considers that the New York Yankees did not add a black player, Elston Howard, to its club until 1955—eight years after Jackie Robinson had broken major league baseball's color line—and that the Boston Red Sox did not sign outfielder Pumpsie Green until 1959, then the bitterness of a former black ballplayer in Percival L. Everett's comic novel, *Suder*, is all the more painfully understandable. Here's ex–big leaguer Sid Willis speaking to a slump-ridden Craig Suder, third baseman for the Seattle Mariners:

Sid leans against the railing. "You know, I wasn't ever happy playing baseball."

"No?"

"No, and I resented the reason they let me into the majors."

"Why?" I ask.

"Well, when I started there wasn't but four or five blacks playing in the big leagues and they was all excellent—Jackie Robinson, Satchel Paige, and like that. And they brought me in because they was looking for a darky that wasn't so good."

"I don't follow you."

"I guess they figured they had to show that dark folks could be bad, too. I mean, every black playing was great and then came Sid Willis, Mr. Below Average. And I ain't even black."

"You ain't?"

"Hell, no. I'm a Narragansett Indian. I was born in Rhode Island."

"You sure look black."

"Well, I can't help that. Those damn white boys on the team would call me nigger and I'd tell them I was an Indian and they'd just laugh." He stops and looks up at the sky. "Then one season things just fell into place and I was hitting like three-fifty and they let me go."

"Why'd they do that?"

"Because all of a sudden I was another excellent dark-skinned ballplayer, that's why."

"That doesn't make any sense," I says.

"That's white folks." He looks at me with a single raised eyebrow. "This slump of yours—pretty bad?"

I nod. "I can't seem to get anything right. I can't seem to shake it."

"Problems in bed . . . with the wife?"

TODAY'S GAME, 1965
Martin Quigley
New York: The Viking Press

Fictionalized day in the life of a major league manager.

TOOT-TOOT-TOOTSIE, GOOD-BYE, 1981
Ron Powers
New York: Delacorte Press

Comic portrayal of a baseball announcer at the end of his career.

TREAT 'EM ROUGH: LETTERS FROM JACK THE KAISER KILLER, 1918
Ring W. Lardner

Indianapolis, Indiana; The Bobbs-Merrill Co.

See also: The Real Dope; You Know Me Al: A Busher's Letters

Letters from busher Jack Keefe, now a World War I soldier. First published as a series for the Saturday Evening Post, March 9, 1918 to June 8, 1918.

THE UNIVERSAL BASEBALL ASSOCIATION, INC., J. HENRY WAUGH, PROP., 1968
Robert Coover
New York: Random House, Inc.

A table-top baseball game is used metaphorically to portray man's desire to control his fate.

WIN OR ELSE!, 1954
D. J. Michael
New York: Lurton Blassingame, paperback

D. J. Michael is a pseudonym for Charles Einstein.

THE YEAR THE YANKEES LOST THE PENNANT, 1954
Douglass Wallop
New York: W. W. Norton and Co., Inc.

The Faustian legend retold: A middle-aged Washington Senators' fan sells his soul for baseball superstardom. See: Damn Yankees (Baseball in Film; Baseball in Television; Baseball in Theater; Baseball in Music and Song—Recorded).

A BET WITH DEATH

The theme of good versus evil is as old as literature itself, and writers down through the ages, from Old-Testament scribes to William Shakespeare, from Herman Melville to John Steinbeck, have explored its human significance. Certainly baseball, with its model heroes such as Christy Mathewson, Jackie Robinson, and Willie Stargell on the one hand, and its misanthropic Ty Cobb, Hal Chase, and Carl Mays on the other, will always merit its share of literary perspectives. In Nancy Willard's lyrical novel, *Things Invisible to See,* a decent-hearted soldier, stranded on an island during World War II, makes a bargain with impending Death. Here's the exchange that leads to the novel's compelling climax:

"My dad told me if you make a bet with Death, he has to accept."

"You want to make a bet with me?"

Ben nodded. "If you win, you can take me on the spot. If I win, I want to live to be a hundred."

"The die is cast," said Death, with a smile at his own joke. "I suppose you brought your own dice?"

"No."

"A chess set? A deck of cards? I am the grand master of all games, but I don't furnish the pieces."

"I only know one game," said Ben. "Baseball."

"Baseball," repeated Death. "I know the game. Never played it myself."

"Could you get a team together?" asked Ben.

Death was still.

"Your team against mine. The South Avenue Rovers versus the Dead Knights."

"I'm interested," said Death.

"Of course I'll need time to get the guys together. I don't even know where they are."

"I do," said Death.

"George Clackett? You know where George Clackett is?"

"He's on a destroyer in the Coral Sea."

"And Louis and Tony?"

"Cruising off Honolulu," said Death. "In a submarine," he added.

"And Charley?"

"In the sky. Off the coast of Africa."

"And Stilts?"

"Australia."

"And Henry?"

"Thorney Island, England."

"And Tom?"

"The Solomon Islands."

"There's no way to get us together," said Ben, "unless you end the war."

"I can arrange furloughs," said Death. "Shall we set the game for June twenty-seventh?"

"We'll need three weeks to warm up," said Ben.

Death shook his head.

"Time is rationed. There are terrible shortages. I can only give you two."

"Okay, two. How are you going to let everybody know?"

"Through the time-honored channel of dreams," replied Death. "And a little finagling with current events."

YOU KNOW ME AL: A
BUSHER'S LETTERS, 1916
Ring W. Lardner
New York: George H. Doran Co.
See also: Baseball in the Spoken Arts—

Recorded. *See: The Real Dope; Treat 'em Rough: Letters from Jack the Kaiser Killer. See: Ring Lardner's You Know Me Al* (Baseball in Comic Art—Collected).

Humorous letters from Jack Keefe about his life as a pitcher for the Chicago White Sox. First published as a series for the Saturday Evening Post, *March 7, 1914 to November 7, 1914.*

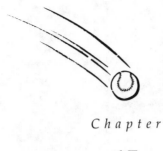

Chapter

15

Baseball in Juvenile and Miscellaneous Fiction

The following section contains a listing of baseball-related fiction for children and young people, and miscellaneous baseball fiction of literary or historical significance. Included in the catalog are collected short juvenile fiction, selected full-length juvenile fiction, anthologies of baseball fiction, series of baseball fiction for young people, fiction written as though by major league baseball players, and unclassified miscellaneous fiction relating to baseball.

For a supplementary listing of juvenile baseball fiction, refer to the *Guide to Baseball Literature* by Anton Grobani. (Detroit, Michigan: Gale Research Co.,

1975). Baseball stories for children and young people are also listed in a separate category in library card catalogs.

Many works of early baseball fiction for young people are sought-after collector's items today. For more information regarding dealers and other sources of rare and out-of-print baseball fiction, consult the Selected Guide to Sources and Dealers in the back of the book.

For *Explanatory Notes* to this section, *see:* Baseball in Fiction.

ALL EXCEPT SAMMY, 1966
Gladys Yessayan Cretan
Boston: Little, Brown and Co.

A child from a musically oriented family prefers baseball to playing an instrument.

ANDY, THE FIRST SWITCH PITCHER, 1982
Al Carmona
Encino, California: Privately published

Ambidextrous pitcher leads his team to the pennant.

THE ATAMI DRAGONS, 1984
David Klass
New York: Charles Scribner's Sons

THE BAD NEWS BEARS, 1976
Richard Woodley
New York: Dell Publishing Co., Inc., paperback
See also: Baseball in Film. *See:* The Bad News Bears Go to Japan; The Bad News Bears in Breaking Training.

Fictionalized treatment of the motion picture screenplay by Bill Lancaster.

THE BAD NEWS BEARS GO TO JAPAN, 1978
Richard Woodley

Based on the screenplay by Bill Lancaster
New York: Dell Publishing Co., Inc., paperback
See also: Baseball in Film. *See:* The Bad New Bears; The Bad News Bears in Breaking Training.

THE BAD NEWS BEARS IN BREAKING TRAINING, 1977
Richard Woodley
Based on the screenplay by Paul Brickman
New York: Dell Publishing Co., Inc., paperback
See also: Baseball in Film. *See:* The Bad News Bears; The Bad News Bears Go to Japan.

BANJO HITTER, 1951
Curtis K. Bishop
Austin, Texas: Steck Co.

First of many juvenile baseball books by this writer.

THE BARBARIAN, 1917
Brewer Corcoran
Boston: Page

BARON OF THE BULLPEN, 1954
Dick Friendlich

Philadelphia: Westminster Press

First of many juvenile baseball books by this writer.

BARTLEY, FRESHMAN PITCHER, 1911
William Heyliger
New York: D. Appleton and Co.

First of many juvenile baseball books by this writer.

BASEBALL FEVER, 1981
Johanna Hurwitz
New York: William Morrow and Co., Inc.

A youngster attempts to convince his scholarly father that baseball is a worthwhile activity.

BASEBALL JOE ON THE SCHOOL NINE, 1912
Lester Chadwick
New York: Cupples and Leon

First of many in the Baseball Joe series of juvenile fiction.

THE BASEBALL READER, 1951
Edited by Ralph S. Graber
New York: A. S. Barnes and Co.

Anthology of short and excerpted baseball fiction.

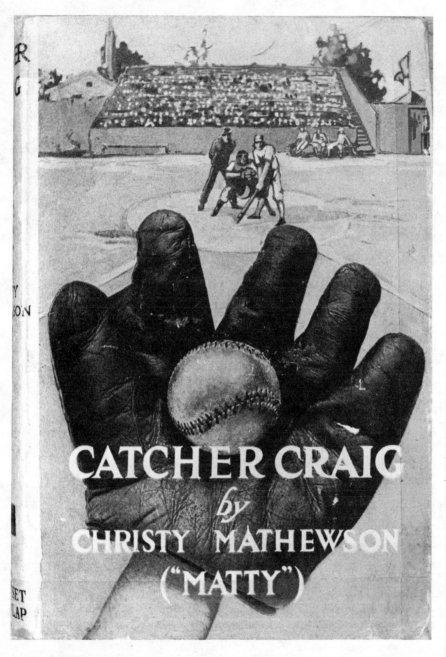

Hall of Fame Pitcher Christy Mathewson lent his name to a series of children's baseball adventures. Catcher Craig, *and the others in the "Matty" series, were ghost-written by John Wheeler. (National Baseball Library.)*

BASEBALL ROUNDUP, 1948
Edited by Leo Margulies
New York: Cupples and Leon

Anthology of ten juvenile stories relating to baseball.

BASEBALL STORIES, 1948
Edited by Frank Owen
New York: Lantern Press, Inc.

BASEBALL STORIES, 1959
Edited by Parke Cummings
New York: Hill and Wang, Inc.

Anthology of baseball-related short fiction.

BASEBALL'S DARKEST DAYS, 1966
Kenneth L. Grantham
New York: Exposition Press

BASEBALL 3000, 1981
Edited by Charles G. Waugh, Martin H. Greenberg, and F. McSherry, Jr.
New York: Lodestar Books

Anthology of science-fiction stories relating to baseball.

BASES FULL, 1928
Harold M. Sherman
New York: Grosset and Dunlap

First of six in the Home Run series of juvenile baseball books.

BATTERY MATES, 1978
William R. Cox
New York: Dodd, Mead and Co.

BEAN BALL BILL, AND OTHER STORIES, 1920
William Heyliger
New York: Grosset and Dunlap

Collection of baseball-related works of short juvenile fiction.

BEHIND THE PLATE, 1962
Yogi Berra and Til Ferdenzi
New York: Argonaut Books, Inc.

Juvenile fiction as told by the New York Yankees' catcher.

BENNY, 1977

Barbara Cohen

New York: Lothrop, Lee and Shepard

An American youth introduces baseball to a German refugee boy during the late 1930s.

THE BIG OUT, 1951

Arnold Hano

New York: A. S. Barnes and Co.

A banned baseball player organizes his own independent team.

THE BOYS' LIFE BOOK OF BASEBALL STORIES, 1964

Editors of *Boys' Life*

New York: Random House, Inc.

THE BRIDE AND THE PENNANT, 1910

Frank L. Chance

Chicago: Laird and Lee

Story of a young pitcher as told by the Cubs' Hall of Famer.

CAM JANSEN AND THE MYSTERY OF THE BABE RUTH BASEBALL, 1982

David A. Adler

New York: The Viking Press

CASEY'S REDEMPTION, 1958

Burgess Fitzpatrick

New York: Greenwich Book Publishing Co.

Fictionalized sequel to Casey at the Bat.

CATCHER CRAIG, 1915

Christy Mathewson

New York: Dodd, Mead and Co.

Full-length story as told by the Hall of Fame pitcher. Ghost-written by John Wheeler.

CENTER-FIELD JINX, 1961

Jackson V. Scholz

New York: William Morrow and Co., Inc.

CENTERFIELD RIVAL, 1974

Joe Archibald

Philadelphia: Macrae-Smith

CHANGING BASE, 1868

William Everett

Boston: Lee and Shepard

First known work of fiction to include baseball action.

CIRCUS CATCH, 1963

Bill Knott

Austin, Texas: Steck-Vaughn

First of many juvenile baaeball books by this writer.

CLARKVILLE'S BATTERY, 1937

Charles Lawton

New York: Cupples and Leon

Charles Lawton is a pseudonym for Noel Sainsbury.

CRACK OF THE BAT, 1952

Edited by Phyllis R. Fenner

New York: Alfred A. Knopf, Inc.

Anthology of 10 baseball-related works of short fiction.

THE CUB FAN'S CHRISTMAS WISH, 1983

Mike Foster and Bill Knight

Peoria, Illinois: privately published, paperback

DANGER IN CENTERFIELD, 1963

Willie Mays and Jeff Harris

New York: Argonaut Books, Inc.

Juvenile mystery fiction as told by the San Francisco Giants' outfielder.

THE DIAMOND CHAMPS, 1977

Matthew F. Christopher

Boston: Little, Brown and Co.

THE DIAMOND PINHEADS, 1966

J. A. Walpole

Theo, Guas' Sons, Inc., paperback

DOUBLE PLAY, 1870

William Everett

Boston: Lee and Shepard

Second known work of fiction to include baseball action.

DOUBLE PLAY, 1970

Stephen R. Lewinstein

Philadelphia: Westminster Press

DOUBLE PLAY, AND OTHER BASEBALL STORIES, 1932

Harold M. Sherman

New York: Grosset and Dunlap

Collection of short fiction relating to baseball.

DOUBLE-PLAY BALL, 1973

Bill Knott

Austin, Texas: Steck-Vaughn

DOUBLE PLAY ROOKIE, 1955

Joe Archibald

Philadelphia: Macrae-Smith

First of many juvenile baeball books by this writer.

THE FAIRPORT NINE, 1880

Noah Brooks

New York: Charles Scribner's Sons

Fourth known work of fiction to include baseball action.

FIELDER'S CHOICE, 1979

Edited by Jerome Holtzman

New York: Harcourt Brace Jovanovich

Anthology of 27 works of short and excerpted fiction relating to baseball.

THE FIFTH BASE, 1973

Joe Archibald

Philadelphia: Macrae-Smith

THE FIGHTING SHORTSTOP, 1959

Richard T. Flood
Boston: Houghton Mifflin Co.

THE FIGHTING SOUTHPAW, 1962

Whitey Ford and Jack Lang
New York: Argonaut Books, Inc.

Juvenile fiction as told by the New York Yankees' pitcher.

FIRST BASE FAULKNER, 1916

Christy Mathewson
New York: Dodd, Mead and Co.

Full-length story as told by the Hall of Fame pitcher. Ghost-written by John Wheeler.

FLASHING SPIKES, 1948

Frank O'Rourke
New York: A. S. Barnes and Co.
See also: Baseball in Television

First of eight juvenile baseball books by this writer.

FLEET-FOOTED FLORENCE, 1981

Marilyn Sachs
Garden City, New York: Doubleday and Co., Inc.

THE FOX STEALS HOME, 1978

Matthew F. Christopher
Boston: Little, Brown and Co.

FRANK ARMSTRONG'S SECOND TERM, 1911

Matthew M. Colton
New York: Hurst and Co.

FRANK MERRIWELL'S BASEBALL VICTORY, 1889

Burt L. Standish
New York: Street and Smith

First book-length Merriwell adventure and the first of many juvenile baeball books by this writer. Burt L. Standish is a pseudonym for Gilbert Patten.

GOOD FIELD, NO HIT, 1947

Duane Decker
New York: M. S. Mill Co.

First of many juvenile baseball books by this writer.

THE GOOF THAT WON THE PENNANT, 1976

Jonah Kalb
Boston: Houghton Mifflin Co.

GREAT BASEBALL STORIES, 1979

Edited by Jerry D. Lewis
New York: Tempo Books, paperback

Anthology of 24 baseball-related short stories.

A GREAT DAY FOR A BALLGAME, 1973

Fielding Dawson
Indianapolis, Indiana: The Bobbs-Merrill Co., Inc.

THE GREATEST VICTORY AND OTHER BASEBALL STORIES, 1950

Frank O'Rourke
New York: A. S. Barnes and Co.

Collection of 12 stories relating to baseball.

THE GREAT MATCH, 1877

No author given
Boston: Roberts

Third known work of fiction to include baseball action.

GREAT MCGONNIGLE SWITCHES PITCHES, 1980

Scott Corbett
Boston: Little, Brown and Co.

THE GREAT PETE PENNEY, 1979

Jean Bashor Tolle
New York: Atheneum Publishers, Inc.

Fantasy in which a girl pitches her team to victory with the aid of a magic ring.

HANG IN AT THE PLATE, 1974

Fred Bachman
New York: Henry Z. Walck, Inc.

HANG TOUGH, PAUL MATHER, 1973

Alfred Slote
Philadelphia: J. B. Lippincott Co.
See also: Baseball in the Spoken Arts—Recorded

THE HEAVENLY WORLD SERIES AND OTHER BASEBALL STORIES, 1952

Frank O'Rourke
New York: A. S. Barnes and Co.

Collection of nine stories relating to baseball.

HIGH FLY TO CENTER, 1972

Bill J. Carol
Austin, Texas: Steck-Vaughn Co.

Little League playing youngster learns the value and importance of family and friends.

THE HOME RUN KING: OR HOW PEP PINDAR WON HIS TITLE, 1920

Babe Ruth
New York: H. K. Fly Co.

THE HOME RUN TRICK, 1973

Scott Corbett
Boston: Little, Brown and Co.

HOORAY FOR SNAIL!, 1985

John Stadler
New York: Crowell Junior Books

Comical assortment of animals play an extraordinary baseball game. Illustrated by the author.

THE HORSE THAT PLAYED CENTER FIELD, 1969

Hal Higdon

New York: Holt, Rinehart and Winston
See also: Baseball in Animated Cartoons—Television

HOT SHOT AT THIRD, 1958
Joseph A. Moore
New York: Duell, Sloan and Pearce

HOW BASEBALL BEGAN IN BROOKLYN, 1958
LeGrand Henderson
New York: Abingdon Press

Comic folk tale about the origins of baseball in America. Illustrated by the author.

THE HUMMING BIRD, 1910
Owen Johnson
New York: Baker and Taylor

IN THE YEAR OF THE BOAR AND JACKIE ROBINSON, 1984
Bette Bao Lord
New York: Harper and Row, Publishers, Inc.

Immigrant Chinese girl learns about 1940s America through baseball.

THE IRON ARM OF MICHAEL GLENN, 1965
Robert C. Lee
Boston: Little, Brown and Co.

JACK HALL: OR THE SCHOOL DAYS OF AN AMERICAN BOY, 1888
Robert Grant
Boston: Gordan, Marsh

JACK LORIMER'S CHAMPIONS, 1907
Winn Standish
New York: A. L. Burt Co.

Rousing boy's adventure featuring Jack Lorimer of Millvale High. Winn Standish is a pseudonym for Walker L. Sawyer.

JACK WINTERS' BASEBALL TEAM, 1919
Mark Overton
New York: New York Book

JEFFREY'S GHOST AND THE LEFTOVER BASEBALL TEAM, 1984
David A. Adler
New York: Holt, Rinehart and Winston

JIMMY KIRKLAND OF THE SHASTA BOYS' TEAM, 1915
Hugh Fullerton
Philadelphia: John C. Winston Co.

First of three juvenile baseball books by this writer.

JINX GLOVE, 1974
Matthew F. Christopher
Boston: Little, Brown and Co.

THE JINX: STORIES OF THE DIAMOND, 1911
Allen Sangree
New York: G. W. Dillingham Co.

Collection of seven works of short baseball fiction.

JOCK AND JILL, 1982
Robert Lipsyte
New York: Harper and Row Publishers

High school pitcher confronts the pressures and complexities of modern athletic life.

JOHNNY NO HIT, 1977
Matthew F. Christopher
Boston: Little, Brown and Co.

THE KID FROM TOMKINSVILLE, 1940
John R. Tunis
New York: Harcourt, Brace and Co.

First of nine juvenile baseball books by this author.

Honesty is the best and the only policy in most early juvenile baseball stories, as seen in this snippet from Jack Lorimer's Champions, *published in 1907:*

"Runner safe!"
"No, sir, beg your pardon!" Ted Leighton cried as he ran up the diamond. "The runner's out! I'll leave it to himself!"
Clarkson wasn't pleased to have his decision questioned, and he scowled at the Doverdale captain.
"Back to your—" he began. But Captain Jack spoke up before he could finish the order.
"Captain Leighton is right, sir," he said. "I slid short, and he tagged me out."
"Decision reversed—runner out!—side out!" the umpire said, grumpily . . .

———

THE KING OF THE DIAMOND, 1960
Charles Spain Verrall
New York: Thomas Y. Crowell Co.

LAST SUNDAY, 1977
Robert Newton Peck
Garden City, New York: Doubleday and Co., Inc.

Humorous story about a girl mascot of a small-town baseball club.

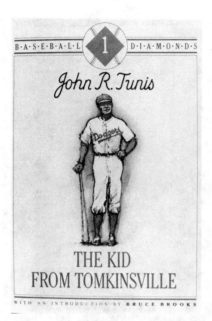

B·A·S·E·B·A·L·L ① D·I·A·M·O·N·D·S

John R. Tunis

THE KID
FROM TOMKINSVILLE

WITH AN INTRODUCTION BY **BRUCE BROOKS**

John R. Tunis, generally regarded as the dean of children's baseball fiction, wrote more than twenty books for young people, about half of which contain baseball action. His "Kid" books, featuring Brooklyn Dodgers star Roy Tucker, are among the most popular of all juvenile baseball books ever published. (Gulliver Books/Harcourt Brace Jovanovich. © 1987 Harcourt Brace Jovanovich, Inc.)

LEFT-HANDED SHORTSTOP, 1980

Patricia Reilly Giff
New York: Delacorte Press

Youngster places a cast on his arm to avoid having to reveal his poor baseball-playing abilities.

LEFTY LOCKE, PITCHER–MANAGER, 1916

Burt L. Standish
New York: Barse and Hopkins

LET'S GO TO A BASEBALL GAME, 1973

Robert Hood
New York: G. P. Putnam's Sons

LITTLE LEAGUE FAMILY, 1978

Leonard Wibberly
Garden City, New York: Doubleday and Co., Inc.

THE LUCKY BASEBALL BAT, 1954

Matthew F. Christopher
Boston: Little, Brown and Co.

First of many juvenile baseball books by this writer.

LUMPY: A BASEBALL FABLE, 1981

Tug McGraw
Philadelphia: Running Press, paperback

The story about how a baseball named Lumpy earns a place in the Hall of Fame. Includes a flexible phonodisc in which McGraw introduces the tale.

THE MAGIC MITT, 1959

Helen Kay
New York: Hastings House

MAKING THE NINE, 1904

Albertus True Dudley
Boston: Lee and Shepard

First of three juvenile baseball books by this author.

THE MAN ON THE BENCH, 1955

Wilfred McCormick
New York: David McKay Co.

First in the Rocky McClune series of juvenile baseball books.

MATT GARGAN'S BOY, 1975

Alfred Slote
Philadelphia: J. B. Lippincott Co.

MY FATHER, THE COACH, 1972

Alfred Slote
Philadelphia: J. B. Lippincott Co.
See also: Baseball in the Spoken Arts—Recorded

MYSTERY AT THE PITCHER'S MOUND, 1970

Albert I. Mayer
New York: Lantern Press, Inc.

MYSTERY COACH, 1973

Matthew F. Christopher
Boston: Little, Brown and Co.

NEW BLOOD AT FIRST, 1963

Bill Skowron and Jack Lang
New York: Argonaut Books, Inc.

Juvenile fiction as told by the New York Yankees' first baseman.

NICE GUY, GO HOME, 1968

Robert Weaver
New York: Harper and Row Publishers

NO ARM IN LEFT FIELD, 1974

Matthew F. Christopher
Boston: Little, Brown and Co.

NOONAN, 1978

Leonard Everett Fisher
Garden City, New York: Doubleday and Co., Inc.

Nineteenth-century youngster is struck on the head by a baseball and is transported a hundred years into the future.

NO PLACE FOR BASEBALL, 1973

Alex B. Allen
Chicago: Whitman

NOT BAD FOR A GIRL, 1972

Isabella Taves
New York: M. Evans
See also: Baseball in the Spoken Arts—Recorded. *See*: *Rookie of the Year* (1973) (Baseball in Television).

OLD TURTLE'S BASEBALL STORIES, 1982

Leonard Kessler
New York: Greenwillow Books

OLLIE'S TEAM AND THE MILLION DOLLAR MISTAKE, 1973
Clem Philbrook
New York: Hastings House

ON HOME GROUND, 1988
Alan Lelchuk
San Diego, California: Gulliver Books/
Harcourt Brace Jovanovich

Jewish immigrant youngster learns the value of friendship and the customs of 1940s America through his devotion to Jackie Robinson and the Brooklyn Dodgers. Illustrated by Merle Nacht.

ON THE DIAMOND, 1987
Edited by Martin H. Greenberg
New York: Bonanza Books

Anthology containing 27 baseball-related short stories and the complete novel, The Seventh Babe.

THE ORIGINAL COLORED HOUSE OF DAVID, 1981
Martin Quigley
Boston: Houghton Mifflin Co.

White youth surreptitiously joins a touring black all-star team and experiences the cruelties of racial prejudice in rural 1920s Minnesota.

OUR BASEBALL CLUB: AND HOW IT WON THE CHAMPIONSHIP, 1884
Noah Brooks
New York: E. P. Dutton and Co.

First-known work of fiction devoted exclusively to baseball.

OUR JIM, 1901
Edward S. Ellis
Boston: Dana Estes

PAUL THE PITCHER, 1984
Paul Sharp
Chicago: Childrens Press

FAMOUS FANS

In a 1973 essay titled, "My Baseball Years," novelist Philip Roth relates how the lore, legends, and personalities of baseball served as the "literature" of his boyhood, satisfying his literary appetite until he was introduced to Conrad's *Lord Jim* at age eighteen. In the sense that the continually evolving mythology of baseball appeals to the fictive mind, it can indeed be said that baseball is the most literary of American games. The following is an all-star lineup of famous writers and their favorite baseball teams:

Marianne Moore *(poet)*: Brooklyn Dodgers
George F. Will *(political columnist)*: Chicago Cubs
Stephen King *(horror story writer)*: Boston Red Sox
James T. Farrell *(novelist)*: Chicago White Sox
Thomas Wolfe *(novelist)*: New York Yankees
Will Durant *(historian)*: Los Angeles Dodgers
Philip Roth *(novelist)*: Brooklyn Dodgers
John Updike *(novelist/poet)*: Boston Red Sox
Mark Twain *(author/humorist)*: Hartford Blue Sox

PHYLLIS, 1957
Ed Key
New York: E. P. Dutton and Co.

PITCHER IN CENTER FIELD, 1974
A. E. Bunting
Chicago: Childrens Press

This book by Noah Brooks, published in 1884, is the first full-length work of fiction whose action and plot are devoted exclusively to baseball. (National Baseball Library.)

PITCHER IN LEFT FIELD, 1979
N. Waldman and J. Waldman
Englewood Cliffs, New Jersey: Prentice-Hall, Inc.

PITCHER POLLACK, 1914
Christy Mathewson
New York: Dodd, Mead and Co.

Full-length story as told by the Hall of Fame pitcher. Ghost-written by John Wheeler.

PITCHER'S CHOICE, 1972
Evelyn Lunemann
Westchester, Illinois: Benefic Press

THE PROFESSIONAL, 1974
Donald Honig
New York: Educational Services

Minor league pitcher learns what is required to advance to the major leagues.

RABBIT EARS, 1982
Alfred Slote
Philadelphia: J. B. Lippincott Co.

Ruth Marini, girl pitcher for the Los Angeles Dodgers, has been featured in three children's baseball books by Mel Cebulash. (© 1985 Lerner Publications Co.)

THE RED-HEADED OUTFIELD, AND OTHER BASEBALL STORIES, 1915
Zane Grey
New York: Grosset and Dunlap

Collection of 11 baseball-related stories.

RIGHT FIELD ROOKIE, 1967
Joe Archibald
Philadelphia: Macrae-Smith

ROOKIE FIRST BASEMAN, 1950
C. Paul Jackson
New York: Thomas Y. Crowell Co.

First of many juvenile baseball books by this writer.

ROOKIE SOUTHPAW, 1951
Burgess Leonard
Philadelphia: J. B. Lippincott Co.

First of six juvenile baseball books by this writer.

ROSIE'S DOUBLE DARE, 1980
Robie H. Harris
New York: Alfred A. Knopf, Inc.

Girl accepts a challenge to play on a boy's baseball team.

RUTH MARINI: DODGER ACE, 1983
Mel Cebulash
Minneapolis, Minnesota: Lerner Publications Co.

Female baseball pitcher wins a place on the Los Angeles Dodgers roster.

RUTH MARINI OF THE DODGERS, 1983
Mel Cebulash
Minneapolis, Minnesota: Lerner Publications Co.

The Los Angeles Dodgers sign a female pitcher to become the first woman to play in the major leagues. First in the Ruth Marini series of juvenile baseball books.

RUTH MARINI: WORLD SERIES STAR, 1985
Mel Cebulash
Minneapolis, Minnesota: Lerner Publications Co.

Baseball's first female player overcomes a midseason injury to pitch the Dodgers to a championship.

SEASON OF THE OWL, 1980
Miles Wolff, Jr.
New York: Stein and Day

SECOND BASE SLOAN, 1917
Christy Mathewson
New York: Dodd, Mead and Co.

Full-length story as told by the Hall of Fame pitcher. Ghost-written by John Wheeler.

THE SHORT-STOP, 1909
Zane Grey
Chicago: A. C. McClurg and Co.

SHOTGUN SHAW: A BASEBALL STORY, 1949
Harold Keith
New York: Thomas Y. Crowell Co.

SINGLE TO CENTER, 1974
Bill Knott
Austin, Texas: Steck-Vaughn

SLUGGER IN RIGHT, 1963
Roger Maris and Jack Ogle
New York: Argonaut Books, Inc.

Juvenile fiction as told by the New York Yankees' outfielder.

SLUGGING BACKSTOP, 1957
Wayne C. Lee
New York: Dodd, Mead and Co.

SOLDIERS AT BAT, 1942
Jackson V. Scholz
New York: William Morrow and Co.

First of many juvenile baseball books by this writer.

SOMETHING QUEER AT THE BALL PARK, 1975
Elizabeth Levy
New York: Delacorte Press

THE SOUTHPAW FROM SONORA MYSTERY, 1983
Elizabeth Van Steenwyk
Chicago: Childrens Press

Juvenile mystery fiction relating to baseball.

STEADY, 1942
Marion Renick
New York: Charles Scribner's Sons

First of six juvenile baseball books by this writer.

STRIKE THREE!, 1949
Claire Bee
New York: Grosset and Dunlap

First of nine juvenile baseball books by this writer.

THE SUBMARINE PITCH, 1976
Matthew F. Christopher
Boston: Little, Brown and Co.

SUPERBABY, 1969
Felix Mendelsohn
Los Angeles: Nash

University laboratory develops a bionic baseball player.

SUPERCHARGED INFIELD, 1985
Matthew F. Christopher
Boston: Little, Brown and Co.

TALL BASEBALL STORIES, 1948
Jiggs Amarant
New York: Association Press

Forty humorous tales as told by Wee Willie Little, ex-mascot of the Lightfoot Lillies.

THE TEAM THAT STOPPED MOVING, 1975
Matthew F. Christopher
Boston: Little, Brown and Co.

TEEN-AGE BASEBALL STORIES, 1948
Edited by Frank Owen
New York: Lantern Press, Inc.

TEEN-AGE STORIES OF THE DIAMOND, 1950
Edited by Abraham L. Furman
New York: Lantern Press, Inc.

THANK YOU, JACKIE ROBINSON, 1974
Barbara Cohen
New York: Lothrop, Lee and Shepard
See also: A Home Run for Love (Baseball in Television)

A fatherless white youngster shares his love for baseball and the Brooklyn Dodgers with an elderly black man.

The Magical Brooklyn Dodgers

Baseball as a connecting bridge between people of different ages, cultures, and religious faiths is a recurring theme in children's literature. Dozens of children's books have dealt with baseball's power to enrich a child's appreciation and understanding of the world around him. The most compelling of these tell the story of an immigrant child and his or her newfound American friends, who introduce the child to American customs, traditions, and history through a shared enthusiasm for baseball.

At least three such works focus on the special relationship between an immigrant child and the Brooklyn Dodgers of old. In Barbara Cohen's 1972 book, *Thank You, Jackie Robinson,* a fatherless ten-year-old Jewish boy resides in a world of baseball dreams and preoccupations in his mother's New Jersey inn, where Davy, a 60-year-old black man, works as a cook. Sammy possesses a photographic memory when it comes to baseball and can recite, batter by batter, entire Brooklyn Dodger games from two or three years before. When the boy discovers that Davy shares his enthusiasm for the Brooklyn Dodgers, the youngster forms a friendship with the older man and arranges for them to attend baseball games together at Ebbets Field in Brooklyn.

The boy's friendship with the stoical cook revolves, quite naturally, around his passionate love for baseball and the Dodgers. While sitting in the bleachers at the ballpark, Sammy dreams of catching a home run ball so that he and his older friend could take turns proudly displaying it in their respective homes. They agree that each should keep the ball for six months during the year. "And we'd go on and on like that for as long as we lived," says the boy.

"It would be Jackie Robinson's ball," Davy said. "It would be a ball that Jackie Robinson had hit."

"Well," [Sammy] replied judiciously, "we'd

The great Jackie Robinson and the 1947 Brooklyn Dodgers have inspired no fewer than three full-length works of children's baseball fiction. (National Baseball Library.)

take it no matter who hit it. I mean, I wouldn't care if it was Duke Snider or Roy Campanella that hit it.''

"Yeah, but as long as we're dreaming," Davy said, "we might as well dream good. We might as well make that ball perfect."

The dream is suddenly shattered when Davy suffers a stroke and is hospitalized. The boy, frantic with worry, attempts to find a way to rally the older man's spirits. Using his savings, Sammy purchases a regulation baseball at a

sporting goods store with the intention of getting Jackie Robinson's autograph for his friend. The boy visits Ebbets Field alone, and desperately implores every Dodger on the field to pass the ball along to his hero. Just as the boy is about to be escorted away by an usher, Robinson intercedes and not only signs the ball but induces the rest of his teammates to autograph the ball as well. "For Davy," Jackie writes. "Get well soon."

The boy gives the prized ball to the old man, but Davy does not recover from his illness. After his friend's death, neither the Dodgers nor baseball hold any appeal for the boy. For weeks Sammy cannot bring himself to listen to any Dodger games on the radio. The book concludes with the boy finally returning to the baseball broadcasts in a touching affirmation of life.

On Home Ground, written in 1987 by Alan Lelchuk, concerns a Jewish youngster whose family is newly immigrated from Russia during the late 1940s. The child quickly assimilates himself into the new country through a passionate enthusiasm for Jackie Robinson and the Brooklyn Dodgers. The father, a stern and unapproachable patrician, resists the customs of the new land and refuses to approve of his son's love for baseball. The book explores the conflict between father and son and the challenges placed before each to understand their common heritage despite differences in cultural points of view.

In Bette Bao Lord's exquisitely written book, *In the Year of the Boar and Jackie Robinson*, published in 1984, a little Chinese girl and her family immigrate to Brooklyn in 1947. The girl, who adopts the Americanized name of Shirley Temple Wong, attends school, gets lost, answers the wrong questions in class, and makes friends slowly. One day, Shirley finds herself—quite against her better judgement—in a children's stickball game. Without knowing what game she was playing, Shirley manages to hit the ball and score the winning run. The team captain—and Shirley's new-found best friend—chants in Shirley's honor:

> Hey, hey, you're just great
> Jackie Robinson crossed the plate.
> Hey, hey, you're a dream
> Jackie Robinson's on our team.

From that moment on, Jackie Robinson and baseball take on a special meaning to the Chinese girl. She learns the rules to baseball and follows the team's magical 1947 season on the radio. Shirley Temple Wong's eventful first year in America ends triumphantly with a personal visit by Jackie Robinson at her school's graduation.

This delightful book—and the two others like it—captures the innocent spirit of childhood, which seeks not only the company of heroes but the community of dreams. One reads these books wishing to have been a child in Brooklyn in the 1940s—when heroes had names like Jackie and Pee Wee and dreams died as hard as a late summer's sun. ◆

THIRD BASE THATCHER, 1923
Everett "Deacon" Scott
New York: Dodd, Mead and Co.

Everett Scott is a shortstop for the New York Yankees.

THE THREE AND TWO PITCH, 1948
Wilfred McCormick
New York: G. P. Putnam's Sons

First in the Bronc Burnett series of juvenile baseball books.

TIED IN THE NINTH, 1930
Merritt Parmalee Allen
New York: Century

TIGER ROOKIE, 1966
Edmund O. Scholefield
Cleveland, Ohio: The World Publishing Co.

First of three juvenile baseball books by this writer.

TREASURE AT FIRST BASE, 1950
Eleanor Clymer
New York: Dodd, Mead and Co.

TROUBLE AT SECOND, 1973
William C. Gault
New York: E. P. Dutton and Co.

TROUBLE AT SECOND BASE, 1966
William R. Cox
New York: Dodd, Mead and Co.

TUESDAY'S CHILD, 1984
Nancy Baron
New York: Atheneum Publishers, Inc.

Baseball-loving girl is forced against her will to give up baseball for ballet.

TURNING POINT, 1948
Ed Fitzgerald
New York: A. S. Barnes and Co.

First of four juvenile baseball books by this writer.

WAY TO GO, TEDDY, 1973
Donald Honig
New York: Franklin Watts
See also: Baseball in the Spoken Arts—Recorded

WEATHERBY'S INNING, 1903
Ralph Henry Barbour
New York: D. Appleton and Co.

First of many juvenile baseball books by this prolific author.

WILD PITCH, 1980
Matthew F. Christopher
Boston: Little, Brown and Co.

A girl is beaned by a boy who had previously professed a bias against female baseball players.

THE WINNING PITCH, 1948
Robert S. Bowen
New York: Lothrop, Lee and Shepard

First of many juvenile baseball books by this writer.

WONDER BOY, 1951
William Heuman
New York: William Morrow and Co.

First of 10 juvenile baseball books by this writer.

THE STORYBOOK DODGERS

It's not even close. More songs, stories, and legends have been written and told about the Brooklyn Dodgers than any other baseball club in the history of the game. No other team has been celebrated in American folklore as joyously or nostalgically as the beloved Bums of Flatbush.

In the canon of Brooklyn Dodgers mythology can be found a play (*The Flatbush Faithful*), an operatic cantata (*The Brooklyn Baseball Cantata*), two novels (*The Man Who Brought the Dodgers Back to Brooklyn* and *The Grace of Shortstops*), and several movies, notably, *It Happened in Flatbush, Roogie's Bump,* and *Whistling in Brooklyn*. Additionally, works that relate to the Brooklyn Dodgers as much as to Jackie Robinson—such as the play, *The First,* and the film, *The Jackie Robinson Story,* and many others —can be included as well.

In song the Brooklyn Dodgers have been saluted with "The Brooklyn Dodgers Jump" (as recorded by three of its players), "Dodgers Fan Dance, (I Used to Be A) Brooklyn Dodger," and "Let's Keep the Dodgers in Brooklyn," among others. The Brooklyn Dodgers, far and away, lead baseball's popular hit song parade.

Fittingly, though painfully, the Dodgers have been immemorialized with a series of murals in the lobbies of the Ebbets Field Apartments complex where Ebbets Field once stood. Today a visitor can see a still-life commemoration where home runs once flew.

THE WONDERFUL WORLD SERIES, 1956
Charles Spain Verrall
New York: Thomas Y. Crowell Co.

WON IN THE NINTH, 1910
Christy Mathewson
New York: R. J. Bodner Co.

Full-length story as told by the Hall of Fame pitcher. Ghost-written by John Wheeler.

WRONGWAY APPLEBAUM, 1984
Marjorie Lewis
New York: Coward-McCann

THE YOUNG PITCHER, 1911
Zane Grey
New York: Harper and Brothers

YOUNG READERS' BASEBALL STORIES, 1950
Edited by Charles Coombs
New York: Lantern Press, Inc.

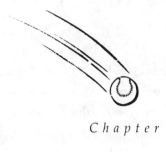

Baseball in Poetry and Light Verse

The following catalog contains a comprehensive listing of poetry and humorous verse relating to baseball. Included in this section are baseball-related poems by noted poets such as William Carlos Williams, Carl Sandburg, and Marianne Moore; parodies and light verse by such famous humorists as Edgar A. Guest and Ogden Nash; and baseball poetry as written by such ballplayers as Ed Charles and David Malarcher. Also included in the catalog is the most celebrated baseball poem ever written, *Casey at the Bat*, by Ernest Lawrence Thayer.

Particular emphasis has been given to the listing of baseball-related poems that have been published in nonbaseball collections, anthologies, and periodicals. Additional poems can be found in literary collections and anthologies that related primarily or exclusively to baseball. For a listing of these publications, *see:* Baseball in Poetry and Light Verse—Collected.

A number of booksellers and small presses specialize in literary publications relating to baseball. For further information regarding baseball poetry and other published materials, consult the Selected Guide to Sources and Dealers located at the back of the book.

One of the many representations of Casey at the Bat. (National Baseball Library.)

EXPLANATORY NOTES

1. Title of the poem, year of publication.

2. Name of poet.

3. Name of periodical or title of publication in which the poem appears.

4. Place of publication, name of publisher, book format (given when the publication is available in paperback format only).

5. Annotation. Description of the poem or a quotation from same.

THE ABOMINABLE BASEBALL BAT, 1982
X. J. Kennedy
Published in *Why Am I Grown So Cold? Poems of the Unknowable*, edited by Myra Cohn Livington
New York: Atheneum

AFTER THE GAME IS OVER, 1972
Daniel Curley
Published in *The Massachusetts Review*

ANALYSIS OF BASEBALL, 1971
May Swenson
Published in *More Poems to Solve*
New York: Charles Scribner's Sons

ANCIENT SPRINGS, 1924
Grantland Rice
Published in *Songs of the Open*
New York: The Century Co.

Celebration of the joys of baseball.

AND TO ALL A "PLAY BALL!" 1986
Judge Phyllis Orlikoff
Published in the *New York Times*, December 20, 1986, p. 1

Parody of "A Visit from St. Nicholas" in which a New York court judge sentences a parachutist

for criminal trespass during the 1986 World Series.

AN ATHLETE'S PRAYER, 1971
Ed Charles
Published in *Sports Poems* edited by R. R. Knudson and P. K. Ebert
New York: Dell Publishing Co., Inc., paperback

Charles played on the World Champion New York Mets in 1969.

AT THE BALL GAME, 1922
Roswell Martin Field
Published in *The Poems of Eugene Field*
New York: Charles Scribner's Sons

Mock-heroic poem describing Chicago Cubs players of the 1880s as Greek gods.

BABE RUTH, 1947
Damon Runyon
Published in *Poems for Men*
New York: Hawthorne Books, Inc.

Colloquial tribute to the Hall of Fame slugger.

THE BALLAD OF DEAD YANKEES, 1964
Donald Petersen
Published in *The Spectral Boy*
Middletown, Connecticut: Wesleyan University Press

Tribute to Ruth, Gehrig, Lazzeri, and Yankees of yore.

THE BALLAD OF OLD BILL WILLIAMS, c. 1935
Dr. Lucien Stark
Published in *The National Pastime*
Cooperstown, New York: Society for American Baseball Research, 1983

Narrative verse in tribute to umpires.

BALL GAME, 1968
Richard Eberhart
Published in *Shifts of Being*
New York: Oxford University Press

Caught off first, he leaped to run to second . . .

THE BALL GAME, 1982
Robert Creeley
Published in *The Collected Poems of Robert Creeley*
Berkeley: University of California Press
See also: Baseball in the Spoken Arts— Recorded

THE BALLGAME, 1983
Amiri Baraka
Published in *Divided Light: Father and*

Son Poems edited by John Shinder
The Sheep Meadow Press

THE BALLPARK AT MOIESE, 1980
Richard Hugo
Published in *White Center*
New York: W. W. Norton and Co.

Score tied in the 8th, the only fans, bison
high above the park . . .

BASE-BALL, 1767
John Newbery
Published in *A Little Pretty Pocket-Book*
London: privately published

The Ball once struck off,
Away flies the Boy
To the next destin'd Post
And then Home with Joy.
*The title to the poem is one of the earliest-
known references to the word "baseball."*

BASE BALL, 1911
S. D. Richardson
Published in *America's National Game*
by A. G. Spalding
New York: American Sports
Publishing Co., p. 457

Life is compared to a baseball game.

BASEBALL, 1969
Tom Clark
Published in *Stones*
New York: Harper and Row
Publishers

One day when I was studying with Stan
Musial . . .

BASEBALL, 1985
Frank Dempster Sherman
Published in *The Oxford Book of
Children's Verse in America* edited by
Donald Hall
New York: Oxford University Press

BASEBALL, 1985
Bill Zavatsky

Published in *For Steve Royal and Other
Poems*
Privately published: paperback

*A glorious Little League catch is remembered
20 years later.*

BASEBALL AND WRITING, 1961
Marianne Moore
Published in the *New Yorker*,
December 9, 1961; in *The Complete
Poems of Marianne Moore*. New York:
The Macmillan Company/The Viking
Press, 1967

*Kinetic tribute to the 1961 World Champion
New York Yankees.*
. . . In that galaxy of nine, say which
won the pennant? Each. It was he . . .

BASEBALL CANTO, 1973
Lawrence Ferlinghetti
Published in *Open Eye, Open Heart*
New York: New Directions
Publishing Corp.

Watching baseball
sitting in the sun
eating popcorn
reading Ezra Pound . . .

BASEBALL IN DE PARK, 1915
Arthur Guiterman
Published in *The Laughing Muse*
New York: Harper and Brothers
Publishers

*Humorous description of a baseball game played
by city youths.*

BASEBALL MEN, 1982
Merritt Clifton
Published in *Baseball Stories for Girls
and Boys (Past Puberty)*
Richford, Vermont: Samisdat,
paperback

BASEBALL NOTE, 1944
Franklin P. Adams
Published in *Nods and Becks*
New York: Whittlesey House

*The spring training holdout is humorously
lampooned.*

BASEBALL PITCHER, 1980
Mabel M. Kukendall
Published in *A Literature of Sports*
edited by Tom Dodge
Lexington, Massachusetts: D. C.
Heath and Co.

THE BASEBALL PLAYERS, 1984
Donald Hall
Published in *The Atlantic*, July 1984,
p. 94; in *Fathers Playing Catch with
Sons*. San Francisco: North Point
Press, 1985

THE BASEBALL SCORE, 1905
Eugene Field
Published in *Hoosier Lyrics*
Chicago: M. A. Donohue and Co.

*Light verse narrative in which local fans rejoice
at the news of another White Sox victory.*

BASE-BALL SONG, 1874
(Air: "The Old Oaken Bucket")
Henry Chadwick
Published in *Baseball: Diamond in the
Rough* by Irving A. Leitner
New York: Criterion Books, 1972

*Extracted from an entry in Chadwick's diary,
dated June 26, 1874.*

BASEBALL—THE NATIONAL
PASTIME, 1985
Ted T. Nichols
Published in *Practical Poems from the
Pen of the Practical Poet*
Westmont, Illinois: Privately
published, paperback

BASEBALL: 0 FOR 2, 1968
Edgar Simmons
Published in *Driving to Biloxi*
Baton Rouge: Louisiana State
University Press

The Mets are my companions in
New York . . .

Tinker-to-Evers-to-Cooperstown

No one disputes the power of poetry to move its readers to laughter or tears or quiet reflection. But can a poem—in this case an eight-line verse—elect a shortstop to the Hall of Fame?

In 1946 the old-timers committee at Cooperstown voted shortstop Joe Tinker, second baseman Johnny Evers, and first baseman Frank Chance—each from the legendary pennant winning Chicago Cubs teams of the early 1900s—into the Baseball Hall of Fame. That the famous double-play combination was elected together is as much a tribute to the power and influence of baseball folklore as to the baseball abilities, considerable though they were, of the three honorees.

To be sure, the three infielders immortalized in Franklin P. Adam's verse, "Baseball's Sad Lexicon," enjoyed remarkable Hall of Fame–caliber careers. First baseman Frank Chance, a raw-boned, burly ex-catcher, played 17 years in the majors during which he compiled a respectable, though not potent, .297 lifetime batting average. Chance twice led the league in stolen bases, with 67 in 1903 and 57 in 1906, making him among the most fleet-footed first basemen ever to have played the game. But it was his extraordinary abilities as a manager that earned him baseball immortality. In his seven full years as a player-manager for the Chicago Cubs, Frank Chance led his charges to three consecutive pennants in 1906–1908, and a fourth in 1910. In 1909 and 1911, his Cubs finished in second place.

Second baseman Johnny Evers, a nervous, combative, surly ballplayer, played 18 seasons in the major leagues, compiling a lifetime batting average of .270. The lantern-jawed Evers, whose nickname was "the Crab," was famously quick-minded on the field. It was Evers's alertness in the heat of battle that created the controversy surrounding the celebrated Merkle incident in 1908. Noting that Fred Merkle of the New York Giants had failed to tag second base on a game winning hit, Evers called for the ball and touched the bag. The resulting replay of the protested game enabled the Cubs to win the pennant over the Giants that year.

Joe Tinker, along with Honus Wagner of the Pittsburgh Pirates, was the game's top defensive

Chicago Cubs Hall of Fame infielders Joe Tinker and Johnny Evers. (National Baseball Library.)

Frank Chance, Hall of Fame first baseman and member of the legendary doubleplay combination. (National Baseball Library.)

shortstop during his fifteen seasons in the majors. He was a place hitter in an era when low scoring games prevailed—especially when teammate Three Finger Brown and New York Giants Christy Mathewson were opponents on the mound. By sawing the ends off power-hitter Frank Schulte's bat, Tinker was able to handle all manner of pitches in an assortment of clutch situations. While his lifetime batting average of .263 is not nearly as high as Frank Chance's .297, Tinker compiled significantly more long hits (doubles, triples, and home runs) in his career than did the first baseman: 409 for Tinker to Chance's 299.

The three infielders shared far more in common than simply exemplary careers and a hyphenated association in a famous poem. For one, Tinker, Evers, and Chance all possessed exceptional qualities of leadership. Indeed, Frank Chance was called "the Peerless Leader," which was attested by his being named player-manager after just two seasons as the Cubs' regular first baseman. Tinker and Evers also managed in the major leagues. Evers replaced Chance as the Cubs manager in 1913 and managed in 1921 and 1924 as well. Tinker was pilot for four years (1913–1916) for the Cubs, the Chicago Feds, and Cincinnati.

Each was durable, dependable, fleet-footed (Tinker stole home 17 times, Evers on 21 occasions), superstitious, hard-bitten, and fearless. None backed down from an inside pitch, a hard slide, or a fight. All three were notorious battlers, even among themselves. Shortstop Tinker and second baseman Evers played virtually their entire careers without speaking to each other after one such heated exchange.

Because they personified their times and the rough-and-tumble way the game was played, infielders Tinker, Evers, and Chance electrified the fans and captured the fancy of sportswriters everywhere. They were not, statistically speaking, the most proficient double-play combination of their era but they were—even before the poem's publication—by far the most celebrated.

And yet, it is unfortunate that they were elected concurrently to the Baseball Hall of Fame. Each infielder deserved to have his own quite meritorious career judged and celebrated individually without respect to sentiment or popular mythology. Their simultaneous induction into the baseball shrine obscures the merits of their individual achievements in light of the folkloric notoriety of Franklin P. Adams's verse.

For Joe Tinker, the metrical Tinker who preceded the poetical Evers-and-Chance, the simultaneous induction of the three infielders was particularly regrettable. Since, of the three, his statistics were the least spectacular, the integrity of his election to the baseball shrine—deserved as it was—was compromised.

Folklore and sentiment notwithstanding, Tinker and Evers proudly and gratefully welcomed the election. By the time they were inducted in 1946, Tinker and Evers—once sworn enemies, now quite frail and infirm—had renewed a warm friendship. They spoke of each other, admiringly, a little grudgingly on occasion, and they spoke *to* each other. There are some things even poems can't do. ◆

BASEBALL TYPES, 1975
Frank Jacobs
Published in *Mad: For Better or Verse*
New York: Warner Books, Inc.,
paperback

Series of eight humorous poems describing baseball players position by position.

BASEBALL'S CENTENNIAL, 1940
L. H. Addington
Published in *A Century of Baseball* by the staff of The Freeman's Journal Co.
Cooperstown, New York: The Freeman's Journal Co.

BASEBALL'S SAD LEXICON, 1910
Franklin P. Adams
Published in the *New York Evening Mail*, July 1910; in *In Other Words*.
New York: Doubleday, Page and Co.

The famous "Tinker-to-Evers-to-Chance" poem.

THE BASE STEALER, 1953
Robert Francis
Published in *The Orb Weaver*
Middletown, Connecticut: Wesleyan University Press
See also: Baseball in the Spoken Arts—Recorded

Poised between going on and back . . .

BATTING AVERAGE, 1982
P. J. Kemp
Published in *Baseball Stories for Girls*

and Boys (Past Puberty) by Merritt Clifton
Richford, Vermont: Samisdat, paperback

BEHIND UMPIRES' BACKS STARS RELAX, 1955
Ogden Nash
Published in *Life*, September 5, 1955, p. 85

Baseball players' off-the-field quirks are humorously treated.

THE BIG BRAIN, 1955
Ogden Nash
Published in *Life*, September 5, 1955, p. 90

Tribute to Stanford graduate and Pittsburgh Pirates' catcher Jack Shepard.

THE BINGE, 1962
Milton Bracker
Published in the *New York Times Magazine*, April 8, 1962, p. 33

Reasons for the increase in home runs are explored.

THE BODY BUILDER, 1955
Ogden Nash
Published in *Life*, September 5, 1955, p. 90

Tribute to Cleveland Indians' outfielder Larry Doby.

THE BUSH TO THE BIG LEAGUE, 1941
Grantland Rice

THE FAMOUS POEM

Newspaperman and poet Franklin P. Adams was a diehard New York Giants fan at a time when the legendary Chicago Cubs of Joe Tinker, Johnny Evers, and Frank Chance dominated the baseball world. Time and again he watched the celebrated Chicago Cubs infielders execute plays that would, as another newspaperman wrote, "set the crowd mad with applause." Remembering, a few years later, his constant disappointments of that era, Adams wrote an eight-line verse that has since become a part of American folklore. Here is the poem, "Baseball's Sad Lexicon," as published in the *New York Evening Mail* in July 1910:

These are the saddest of possible
  words,
  Tinker-to-Evers-to-Chance.
Trio of Bear Cubs fleeter than
  birds,
  Tinker-to Evers-to-Chance.
Ruthlessly pricking our gonfalon
  bubble,
Making a Giant hit into a double,
Words that are weighty with nothing but trouble.
  Tinker-to-Evers-to-Chance.

Published in *Only the Brave and Other Poems*
New York: A. S. Barnes and Co., Inc.

Intimations of mortality as symbolized by the inevitable loss of baseball stardom.

BYRON VS. DIMAGGIO, 1971
Peter Mienke
Published in *Sports Poems* edited by R. R. Knudson and P. K. Ebert
New York: Dell Publishing Co., Inc., paperback

BY WAY OF REVERY, 1924
Grantland Rice
Published in *Songs of the Open*
New York: The Century Co.

Nostalgic remembrance of a youthful Christy Mathewson and Honus Wagner.

CASEY AND THE METS, 1962
Milton Bracker
Published in the *New York Times Magazine*, April 8, 1962, p. 33

Parody of "Casey at the Bat" in tribute to Casey Stengel.

CASEY AT THE BAT, 1888
Ernest L. Thayer
Published in the *San Francisco Examiner*, June 3, 1888, p. 4

For collections of parodies of this most famous baseball verse, see: The Annotated Casey at the Bat *and* Mighty Casey: All-American *(Baseball in Poetry and Light Verse—Collected).*

CASEY'S REVENGE, 1985
Jack Kabat
Privately published, paperback

Parody sequel to Casey at the Bat.

CATCH, 1953
Robert Francis
Published in *The Orb Weaver*
Middletown, Connecticut: Wesleyan University Press

See also: Baseball in the Spoken Arts—Recorded

Two youngsters playing catch metaphorically illustrate the art and design of poetry.

THE CATCHER, 1913
Porter K. Johnston
Published in *Harper's Weekly*, September 6, 1913, p. 20

Low crouched and tense,
Criterion of the batter's prowess . . .

CHICK GANDIL'S GREAT HIT, 1914
Gilbert M. Eiseman
Washington, D.C.: Judd and Detweiler, Inc., paperback

This parody of "Casey at the Bat" celebrates Gandil's heroics in winning a game for the Washington Senators.

THE CHOW HOUND, 1955
Ogden Nash
Published in *Life*, September 5, 1955, p. 90

Cincinnati Reds' pitcher Joe Nuxhall's voracious appetite is humorously treated.

COBB WOULD HAVE CAUGHT IT, 1943
Robert Fitzgerald
Published in *A Wreath for the Sea: Poems 1935–1943*
New York: Arrow Books

In sunburnt parks where Sundays lie . . .

COEFFICIENTS OF EXPANSION (A GUIDE TO THE INFANT SEASON), 1969
Ogden Nash
Published in the *New Yorker*, April 26, 1969, p. 48; in *The Old Dog Barks Backwards*. Boston: Little, Brown and Co., 1972

Franchise shifts and expansion are humorously but bitterly denounced.

COUPLET, 1984
Donald Hall
Published in *The New Republic*, June 18, 1984, p. 34; in *Fathers Playing Catch with Sons*. San Francisco: North Point Press, 1985

Subtitled: "Old Timers' Day, Fenway Park, 1 May 1982."

CRIED THE LIP, 1969
Wallace Carroll
Published in *Sports Poems* edited by R. R. Knudson and P. K. Ebert
New York: Dell Publishing Co., Inc., 1971, paperback

Humorous verse in which Cubs manager Leo Durocher laments his team's loss of the pennant to the once lowly New York Mets.

THE CROWD AT THE BALL GAME, 1923
William Carlos Williams
Published in *Spring and All*
Paris: Contact Publishing Co.

The crowd at the ball game
is moved uniformly
by a spirit of uselessness
which delights them—

DA GREATA BASEBALL, 1912
T. A. Daly
Published in *Madrigali*
New York: Harcourt, Brace and Howe

Italian stereotype describes a baseball game.

DECEPTIVE BARGAINING, 1962
Milton Bracker
Published in the *New York Times Magazine*, April 8, 1962, p. 32

The spring training holdout is lampooned.

DECLINE AND FALL OF A ROMAN UMPIRE, 1957
Ogden Nash
Published in *Everyone But Thee and Me*
Boston: Little, Brown and Co.

Humorous narrative in which a courtly umpire is hounded by an uncouth fan.

THE DIAMOND DUDE, 1955
Ogden Nash
Published in *Life*, September 5, 1955, p. 91

New York Yankees' shortstop, Phil Rizzuto's expensive style of dress is lampooned.

DIVORCED MEN
Debra Bruce
Published in *Pure Daughter*
Fayetteville: University of Arkansas Press

Baseball symbolizes the gulf between a wife and her husband.

DON LARSEN'S PERFECT GAME, 1967
Paul Goodman
Published in *Hawkweed*
New York: Random House, Inc.

The human implications of Don Larsen's 1956 World Series perfect game are intimated. . . . This is a fellow who will have bad dreams . . .

An American Folk Hero

How a once-forgotten newspaper poem, written by an obscure humorist, came to be placed in the echelon of American folklore—along with such legendary tales as John Henry and Paul Bunyan —is itself a story of almost mythic proportions.

Like most folk stories, the legend of the Mighty Casey possesses just enough of a mystique to invite the tale-teller's constant enlargement and elaboration. Was Casey a budding young slugger destined for major league stardom or strictly a small-town hero? Was there a motive behind the famous strikeout? Where, precisely, was Mudville? And what happened to Casey after his shattering humiliation? Countless parodies and sequels have been offered in verse, literature, film, plays, and cartoons. But the only thing that can positively be said about the legendary Casey is that but for an incredible string of coincidences, the Mudville slugger might be utterly unknown today.

Casey at the Bat, written by Ernest Lawrence Thayer, was first published in the *San Francisco Examiner* on Sunday, June 3, 1888, under the pseudonymous byline of "Phin". The poem was assigned a modest place on a page of editorials, with the inauspicious title *Casey at the Bat: A Ballad of the Republic, Sung in the Year 1888*. Despite

"And when, responding to the cheers, he lightly doffed his hat, no stranger in the crowd could doubt 'twas Casey at the bat." Famed cartoonist Tad Dorgan drew this sketch of the mighty Casey for the July 5, 1908 edition of the San Francisco Examiner. *(San Francisco Examiner.)*

being reprinted in a few eastern newspapers—each time in a corrupted version with a misidentified author—the poem attracted little notice. Ernest L. Thayer's humorous ballad about a failed hero seemed destined to a permanent and irretrievable oblivion.

It would be many months before Casey was heard from again—but it would be years before author Thayer resurfaced. Sometime before the publication of the poem Thayer had quit the newspaper business and quietly returned home to manage a family-owned textile mill in Worcester, Massachusetts. Never again did the author of *Casey at the Bat* and other verses for the *Examiner* take the poet's pen in hand.

One summer evening in August 1889, after an exhibition game earlier that afternoon, members of the New York Giants and Chicago White Stockings attended a program of vaudeville at Wallack's Theater in New York. Before the performance, actor DeWolf Hopper, wishing to deliver a recitation in honor of his celebrity audience, hastily memorized a poem from a tattered newspaper clipping that had been given him for the occasion. An associate of Hopper's had suggested the poem after remembering that he had clipped it while on a visit to San Francisco the previous June.

In his comically histrionic style, Hopper recited the sad tale of the mighty slugger. Cap Anson, Buck Ewing, and the other players, expecting Casey to wallop a home run—as had everyone who was hearing the poem for the first time—reacted uproariously to the poem's denouement. In one fortuitous moment the world had discovered a new American folk hero and embraced its greatest declaimer.

So popular was Hopper's recitation of the poem that for the next forty-five years the actor repeated it, by his own estimation, over 10,000 times, mostly on the vaudeville stage. Hopper's

recordings of the ballad were also widely sold. Almost single-handedly, DeWolf Hopper won Casey a permanent place in American folklore.

After the poem's success was assured, dozens of persons proclaimed themselves as the true author of *Casey at the Bat*. George Whitefield D'Vys, a writer of privately-published baseball verse, was the most adamantly vocal in his claim to authorship. Spirited discussions took place in sporting journals and in letters-to-the-editor columns in an effort to determine the author of the poem. By the time Ernest Lawrence Thayer, at the urging of friends, publicly affirmed his authorship, there were so many claimants that it was years before Thayer was accepted as the ballad's true author.

Not only the poem's authorship but its inspiration was publicly contested. Dozens of ex-ballplayers—mostly small-town minor leaguers, some having a first, last, or nickname of Casey—claimed to have been the real life hero of the poem. Although Thayer denied that there was a living model for the ballad, most of these men, including former major leaguer Daniel Casey, insisted for the rest of their lives that it was they who had been the mighty slugger of the poem.

More incredibly, several cities and towns have put in a claim as the actual locale of the poem. The town board of Stockton, California, fifty-five miles east of San Francisco, recently issued a proclamation declaring itself as the original site of the poem. A plaque commemorating its part in baseball history has been placed at the entrance to the town's minor league stadium. Stockton has even gone so far as to rename its Class-A team the Mudville Nine!

In 1979 the Court of Historical Review and Appeals of the City and County of San Francisco, a nonbinding court which adjudicates matters relating to history, entered a judgment on the question concerning *Casey at the Bat*. In his whimsically worded decision, Judge Harry W. Low declared that the poem did not belong to any one author or place but ". . . to all the world. So [let] judgment be rendered accordingly."

Ernest Lawrence Thayer died in 1940 in Santa Barbara, California. Throughout his life he kept a disdainful distance from his famous creation, thinking its "persistent vogue [to be] simply unaccountable." He refused to accept any compensation for reprintings of the poem, informing publishers, "All I ask is never to be reminded of it again."

By remaining aloof from *Casey at the Bat*, Thayer actually encouraged its continuing mythification. Without royalties or a copyright to impede them, writers such as Grantland Rice had a field day concocting embellishments to the tale. No fewer than two published collections have been filled with poetical parodies and sequels concerning the famous Mudville slugger.

Despite the favorable conditions in which the poem has prospered, were it not for an actor's comedic genius, a ready friend's tattered clipping, an influential audience's explosive reception, and a nation's childlike fancy for tall tales and fondness for a child's game, it is likely that *Casey at the Bat* would be completely unheard of today. Even so, baseball would still have one other enduring legend to imprint upon the American consciousness—that of Abner Doubleday's mythical invention of the game. ◆

CASEY'S AT THE BAT...AGAIN

Poor Casey. He has been humiliated countless times at the hands of parodists and versifiers who glibly concoct new ways for the Mudville slugger to experience yet another devastating defeat. Occasionally a parodist will allow Casey to redeem his earlier strike out with a home run in the clutch, but it's never quite the same. Casey's triumph never attains the drama that his strike out did.

Two published collections of verse parodies (*The Annotated Casey at the Bat* and *Mighty Casey: All American*), contain dozens of sequels and recapitulations of the Mudville slugger's famous strikeout. A few parodies have been published in a single volume, such as *Casey's Revenge* and *I Was the Ump When Casey Came to Bat*. A children's book (*Casey's Redemption*) has sequelized the poem in story form, and an exceptional short story titled "McDuff on the Mound," written by Robert Coover, has told the story from the pitcher's point of view.

Walt Disney followed his wonderful cartoon version of the original poem with his own, less successful sequel (*Casey Bats Again*), in which the famous slugger's nine baseball playing daughters need him to hit in a pinch. At least four radio dramatizations, each offering a different explanation for the strikeout, have featured the mighty Casey, as has a recent television production, a freewheeling burlesque intended for younger viewers, that starred Elliott Gould. Four motion pictures have been based on the poem as well, the last and most successful of which starred Wallace Beery as a beer guzzling small-town slugger who, after refusing a bribe, strikes out anyway on an illegally thrown pitch.

Of the many dramatizations of the famous ballad, only one work has enlarged upon the theme without parodying it. In 1953 Pulitzer Prize winning composer William Schuman, along with librettist Jeremy Gury, wrote a full-scale opera about the famous slugger, titled *The Mighty Casey*. The musical score evokes the finest traditions of American folklore, romance, humor, and, not coincidentally, the ambience and rhythms of baseball. Though the opera is produced only rarely, most recently in Cooperstown, New York, it is the centerpiece of all Mudville folklore.

DORLAN'S HOME-WALK, 1915
Arthur Guiterman
Published in *The Laughing Muse*
New York: Harper and Brothers
Publishers

Humorous narrative in which a runner advances from first base to home while an argument is taking place.

DOUBLE-HEADER, 1977
John Stone
Published in *Traveling America with Today's Poets* edited by David Kherdian
New York: The Macmillan Company

A man relives his life and his dreams in an empty stadium at night.

THE DOUBLE-PLAY, 1965
Robert Wallace
Published in *Views from a Ferris Wheel*
New York: E. P. Dutton and Co.

Free-verse description of a shortstop-to-second-to-first double play.

DREAM OF A BASEBALL STAR, 1960
Gregory Corso
Published in *The Happy Birthday of Death*
New York: New Directions Publishing Corp.

Dantesque re-creation of Ted Williams's retirement from baseball.

DRIVING BY, 1979
Robert Wallace
Published in *Swimmer in the Rain*
Pittsburgh, Pennsylvania: Carnegie-Mellon University Press

An image of a night-time Little League game provides a motorist with a lasting impression.

THE DRUMMER BOY, 1955
Ogden Nash
Published in *Life*, September 5, 1955, p. 86

AMERICAN NOCTURNE

On occasion, while motoring along a highway, we might catch a glimpse of a youth-league base-ball game and wonder: What is the inning, who is playing, and what will be the outcome, not only of the game but of the lives of its players? In his poem, "Driving By," Robert Wallace intimates that the game is never completely behind us even after it disappears from view:

On August nights,
in little towns you sometimes see
from the throughways
bloom

the ball field lights—
domes
of smoky brilliance:
brighter than daylight colors,

figures through wire-mesh on the
    green,
figures in the plank stands,
a tiny moon
dropping out toward left.

They stay
much as we left them—
lichen of the blue American nights
from which we come.

Copyright © 1979 by Robert Wallace, from *Swimmer in the Rain* (Carnegie-Mellon University Press, 1979). Reprinted by permission of the publisher.

Humorous tribute to Detroit Tigers' outfielder and amateur drummer Charlie Maxwell.

THE ELECTRONIC AGE, 1962
Milton Bracker
Published in the *New York Times Magazine*, April 8, 1962, p. 32

A baseball fan's devotion to radio and television is humorously treated.

ELEGY FIVE, 1984
George Bowering
Published in *Kerrisdale Elegies*
Toronto, Canada: The Coach House Press, paperback

The fifth of ten elegies in this book-length poem relates exclusively to baseball.

ELEGY WRITTEN IN A WEST SIDE BALL YARD, 1916
Ring W. Lardner
Published in *Baseball Magazine*, July 1916

Parody of "Elegy in a Country Churchyard," originally published in the Chicago Tribune.

EMPATHY FOR DAVID WINFIELD, 1987
David Shapiro
Published in *Diamonds Are Forever: Artists and Writers on Baseball* edited by Peter H. Gordon
San Francisco: Chronicle Books

Now I feel good when Dave Winfield throws his bat . . .

FAIR OR FOUL, 1977
Lillian Morrison
Published in *The Sidewalk Racer*
New York: Lothrop, Lee and Shepard Co.

Life is wryly compared to baseball.
Our lives are loops
or line drives . . .

FAN, 1983
Walter Lew
Published in *Breaking Silence: An Anthology of Contemporary Asian American Poets* edited by Joseph Bruchac
The Greenfield Review Press

FANATICAL POEM ABOUT ICHI-BAN, AN ANTIQUE ROOT, 1909
Wallace Irwin
Published in *Letters of a Japanese Schoolboy*
New York: Doubleday, Page and Co., pp. 166–168

Humorous verse, written in pidgin English, about a man who is oblivious to everything except baseball.

FARMER STEBBINS AT THE BAT, 1890
Will Carleton
Published in *City Legends*
New York: Harper and Brothers

Narrative verse in which a boastful middle-aged man plays in a young men's baseball game.

FAST BALL, 1971
Fred Chappell
Published in *The World Between the Eyes*
Baton Rouge: Louisiana State University Press

FINALE, 1962
Milton Bracker
Published in the *New York Times Magazine*, April 8, 1962, p. 130

Salute to the return of the baseball season.

THE FORECAST: (AMERICAN LEAGUE), 1962
Milton Bracker
Published in the *New York Times Magazine*, April 8, 1962, p. 32

FOR HOYT WILHELM, 1985
Joel Oppenheimer
Published in the *New York Times*, January 13, 1985

Tribute to the knuckleball pitcher upon his election to the Hall of Fame.
the ball dances in
no steam no smoke . . .

FOR THE O-YANKS, 1979
Joel Oppenheimer
Published in *New Spaces: Poems 1975–1983*
Santa Barbara, California: Black Sparrow Press, 1985

Dedicated to the minor league Oneonta Yankees.
this green square
tilted on end
is perfect geometry . . .

FROM ALTITUDE, THE DIAMONDS, 1980
Richard Hugo
Published in *White Center*
New York: W. W. Norton and Co.

Life and baseball as seen from a reflective distance.

FROM THE BATTER'S BOX, 1980
David K. Harford
Published in *Anthology of Magazine Verse and Yearbook of American Poetry* edited by Alan F. Pater
Beverly Hills, California: Monitor Books

God is a screwball
Pitcher, I mean . . .

GAME CALLED, 1948
Grantland Rice
Published in *The Fireside Book of Baseball* edited by Charles Einstein
New York: Simon and Schuster, 1956

Rhymed eulogy to Babe Ruth.

GENTLE READER, 1970
Ron Loewinsohn
Published in *Meat Air: Poems 1957–1969*
New York: Harcourt Brace Jovanovich, Inc.

Free-verse description of a boy's spectacular catch and the exuberance of youth.

GEORGE HERMAN "BABE" RUTH, 1961
George Jessel
Published in *Elegy in Manhattan*
New York: Holt, Rinehart and Winston

Autobiographical narrative verse in which Ruth contemplates the meaning of his life.

GEORGE RUTH'S MIDDLE NAME, 1988
Gene Frumkin
Published in *Yankee*, August 1988, p. 115

In the dream I forgot
that George Ruth's middle name
was Herman.

GREAT GOD CASEY'S AT THE BAT, 1943
Robert P. Tristram Coffin
Published in *Primer for America*
New York: The Macmillan Company

Verse celebration of baseball and its heroes.

HERO, 1971
Ronald Gross
Published in *Sports Poems* edited by R. R. Knudson and R. K. Ebert
New York: Dell Publishing Co., Inc., paperback

hit a huge drive
to centerfield . . .

HE WAS FORMIDABLE, 1960
Robert Penn Warren
Published in *You, Emperors, and Others: Poems 1957–1960*
New York: Random House, Inc.

Eulogy to a small-town youth whose accidental death denied him baseball stardom.

HISTORIC UTTERANCE, 1962
Milton Bracker
Published in the *New York Times Magazine*, April 8, 1962, p. 33

Humorous commentary on Bobby Thomson's famous playoff home run.

HITS AND RUNS, 1918
Carl Sandburg
Published in *Cornhuskers*
New York: Holt, Rinehart and
Winston

I remember the Chillicothe ball players
grappling the Rock
Island ball players in a sixteen inning
game . . .

HITTING AGAINST MIKE CUTLER, 1972
Jonathan Holden
Published in *Design for a House: Poems*
Columbia: University of Missouri
Press

THE HOLLER GUY, 1955
Ogden Nash
Published in *Life*, September 5, 1955,
p. 85

Tribute to Chicago White Sox second baseman Nellie Fox.

HOMETOWN PIECE FOR MESSRS. ALSTON AND REESE, 1956
Marianne Moore
Published in the *New York Herald Tribune*, October 3, 1956; in *O to Be a Dragon*. New York: The Viking Press, 1959

Tribute to the Brooklyn Dodgers.

THE HOOFER, 1955
Ogden Nash
Published in *Life*, September 5, 1955,
p. 87

Pittsburgh Pirates outfielder Cal Abrams is humorously caricatured.

HOW TO PLAY NIGHT BASEBALL, 1972
Jonathan Holden
Published in *Design for a House: Poems*
Columbia: University of Missouri
Press

Poetical instructions for enjoying a summer evening's baseball game.
A pasture is best, freshly
mown . . .

IF CARL SANDBURG WERE A BASEBALL WRITER, 1975
Frank Jacobs
Published in *Mad: For Better or Verse*
New York: Warner Books, Inc.,
paperback

Parody of Sandburg's "Chicago."
Play Butcher of the League.
Goof Maker, Dropper of Flies . . .

I LOVE MARIS, 1962
Milton Bracker
Published in the *New York Times Magazine*, April 8, 1962, p. 32

Tribute to New York Yankees' outfielder Roger Maris.

IT IS AN OUTFIELDER, 1970
Ron Loewinsohn
Published in *Meat Air: Poems 1957–1969*
New York: Harcourt Brace
Jovanovich, Inc.

Free-verse description of a playground baseball game.

IT IS VERY DISTINCT AT THE BALLPARK, 1970
Ron Loewinsohn
Published in *Meat Air: Poems 1957–1969*
New York: Harcourt Brace
Jovanovich, Inc.

Poetical litany of decisive baseball impressions.

I WAS THE UMP WHEN CASEY CAME TO BAT, 1973
John J. Neville
New York: Winson Litho., Inc.,
paperback

Parody of Casey at the Bat *published in a single volume.*

JEEP, 1972
Charles Stetler
Published in *Kansas Quarterly*, vol. 4,
no. 3; in *A Geography of Poets: An Anthology of the New Poetry* edited by
Edward Field. New York: Bantam
Books, paperback

A fallen hero—Lee (Jeep) Handley of the Pittsburgh Pirates—is eulogized.

THE JOKESMITH, 1955
Ogden Nash
Published in *Life*, September 5, 1955,
p. 89

Tribute to St. Louis Cardinals pitcher Frank Smith.

JULY THE FIRST, 1983
Robert Currie
Published in *Poetspeak: In Their Words About Their Work* edited by Paul B.
Janeczko
Bradbury Press

JUNK BALL, 1971
Fred Chappell
Published in *The World Between the Eyes*
Baton Rouge: Louisiana State
University Press

KILL THE UMPIRE!, 1953
Edwin Rolfe
Published in the *Saturday Review*,
April 18, 1953, p. 46

KO, OR A SEASON ON EARTH, 1959
Kenneth Koch
New York, Grove Press, Inc.

Comic narrative poem about a Japanese baseball player who comes to America to pitch for the Dodgers.

THE LADY PITCHER, 1983
Cynthia Macdonald
Published in *Poetspeak: In Their Words*

About Their Work edited by Paul B. Janeczko
Bradbury Press

THE LAST TIME I SAW MARIS, 1962

Milton Bracker
Published in the *New York Times Magazine*, April 8, 1962, p. 130

Humorous tribute to New York Yankees' outfielder Roger Maris.

LEAVE US GO ROOT FOR THE DODGERS, RODGERS, 1942

Dan Parker
Published in *The Fireside Book of Baseball*
New York: Simon and Schuster, 1956
See also: Baseball in Music and Song

Humorous verse in which a socialite professes her enthusiasm for the Brooklyn Dodgers.

LINES COMPOSED IN EXALTATION OVER THE NORTH ATLANTIC, 1980

James A. Michener
Published in the *New York Times*, November 9, 1980, p. E 2.

Whimsical tribute to the 1980 World Series champion Philadelphia Phillies.

LINE-UP FOR YESTERDAY: AN ABC OF BASEBALL IMMORTALS, 1949

Ogden Nash
Published in *Sport Magazine*, January 1949, pp. 32–33; in *The Baseball Reader* edited by Charles Einstein. New York: Lippincott and Crowell, Publishers, 1980, pp. 256–259

Alphabetical tribute to the greats of baseball.

LISTENING TO BASEBALL IN THE CAR, 1986

Gail Mazur
Published in *Pose of Happiness*
Boston: David R. Godine, Publisher

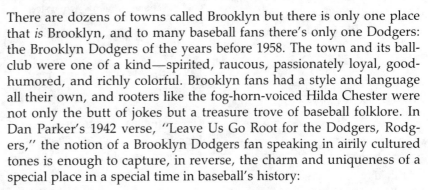

'DEM WONDERFUL BUMS

There are dozens of towns called Brooklyn but there is only one place that *is* Brooklyn, and to many baseball fans there's only one Dodgers: the Brooklyn Dodgers of the years before 1958. The town and its ball-club were one of a kind—spirited, raucous, passionately loyal, good-humored, and richly colorful. Brooklyn fans had a style and language all their own, and rooters like the fog-horn-voiced Hilda Chester were not only the butt of jokes but a treasure trove of baseball folklore. In Dan Parker's 1942 verse, "Leave Us Go Root for the Dodgers, Rodgers," the notion of a Brooklyn Dodgers fan speaking in airily cultured tones is enough to capture, in reverse, the charm and uniqueness of a special place in a special time in baseball's history:

Murgatroyd Darcy, the belle of Canarsie,
Went 'round with a fellow named Rodge.
At dancing the rhumba or jitterbug number,
You couldn't beat Rodge at this dodge.
Throughout the cold weather, the pair danced together,
But when the trees blossomed again,
Miss Murgatroyd Darcy, the belle of Canarsie
To Rodgers would sing this refrain:

Leave us go root for the Dodgers, Rodgers.
That's the team for me.
Leave us make noise for the boisterous boys
On the BMT.
Summer or winter or any season,
Flatbush fanatics don't need no reason.
Leave us go root for the Dodgers, Rodgers.
That's the team for me.

During a crucial moment in a game, a nonbeliever seeks providential assistance for her favorite team.

LITTLE-LEAGUE BASEBALL FAN, 1962

W. R. Moses
Published in *Identities*
Middletown, Connecticut: Wesleyan University Press

A spectator at a Little League game confronts his mortality after indulging in the joys of vicarious youth.

THE LOBBYIST, 1955

Ogden Nash
Published in *Life*, September 5, 1955, p. 86

Humorous caricature of Baltimore Orioles' outfielder Dave Philley.

THE LOVE SONG OF ABNER DOUBLEDAY, 1980

Brad Justus
Published in the *New York Times*, May 4, 1980

Parody of T. S. Eliot's, "The Love Song of J. Alfred Prufrock."

THE MAGICIAN, 1955

Ogden Nash
Published in *Life*, September 5, 1955, p. 88

Humorous tribute to Washington Senators' catcher and card-trickster Clint Courtney.

MANTLE, 1985
William Heyen
Published in *The Morrow Anthology of Younger American Poets*, edited by Dave Smith and David Bottoms
New York: Quill/William Morrow and Co.

Mantle ran so hard, they said,
he tore his legs to pieces.
What is this but spirit?

MATHEWSON TO RUTH, 1924
Grantland Rice
Published in *Songs of the Open*
New York: The Century Co.

Admonitory verse written as though from Christy Mathewson to Babe Ruth.

MEL ALLEN, MEL ALLEN, LEND ME YOUR CLICHE, 1955
Ogden Nash
Published in *You Can't Get There from Here*
Boston: Little, Brown and Co.

Playful parody of the cliche, "There's activity in the bullpen." Mel Allen is a Hall of Fame baseball announcer.

MISSOULA SOFTBALL TOURNAMENT, 1973
Richard Hugo
Published in *The Lady in Kicking Horse Reservoir*
New York: W. W. Norton and Co.

MIXED MEDIA, 1981
James Schevill
Published in *Anthology of Magazine Verse and Yearbook of American Poetry* edited by Alan F. Pater
Beverly Hills, California: Monitor Books

MY FATHER DREAMS OF BASEBALL, 1963
Laurence Lieberman
Published in *The Atlantic Monthly*, August 1963, p. 103; in *The*

Unblinding. New York: The Macmillan Company, 1968

On hot September nights, when sleep is scarce,
in place of sheep Dad counts home runs . . .

MYSTERY BASEBALL, 1972
Philip Dacey
Published in *The Prairie Schooner*: University of Nebraska Press, LIncoln; in *The Boy Under the Bed*. Baltimore, Maryland: Johns Hopkins University Press, 1981

The vagaries of fate, the uncertainties of life, are symbolized by an unseen tenth player on the baseball field.

NIGHT GAME, 1947
Rolfe Humphries
Published in *Forbid Thy Ravens*
New York: Charles Scribner's Sons

. . . Oh, this is good, I felt, to be part of this movement,
This mood, this music . . .

NIGHT GAME, 1977
Lillian Morrison
Published in *The Sidewalk Racer*
New York: Lothrop, Lee and Shepard Co.

NOTE TO THE YOUNG, 1962
Milton Bracker
Published in the *New York Times Magazine*, April 8, 1962, p. 130

The lucrativeness of a baseball career is humorously treated.

NUNS AT EVE, 1963
John Malcolm Brinnin
Published in *The Selected Poems of John Malcolm Brinnin*
Boston: Little, Brown and Co.
See also: Baseball in the Spoken Arts—Recorded

On St. Martin's evening green
Imaginary diamond . . .

OCTOBER CLASSIC, 1975
David Lehman
Published in *Poetry*, July 1975

"If only there were a way of knowing . . ."

ODE TO THE NEW YORK METS, 1969
John Lindsay
Published in the *New York Times*, October 10, 1969

Tribute to the world champions by the mayor of New York City.

ODE TO TY COBB, WHO STOLE FIRST BASE FROM SECOND, 1981
Ray Bradbury
Published in *The Haunted Computer and the Android Pope*
New York: Alfred A. Knopf, Inc.

Satirical commentary on Cobb's superhuman abilities.

OF KINGS AND THINGS, 1967
Lillian Morrison
Published in *The Ghosts of Jersey City*
New York: Thomas Y. Crowell Co.

A neighborhood stickball player is remembered.

THE OLD-FASHIONED BATTER, 1966
George E. Phair
Published in *The Glory of Their Times* by Lawrence S. Ritter
New York: The Macmillan Company, p. 243

The modern-day slugger is humorously compared to the batsman of old.

THE OLD-FASHIONED PITCHER, 1966
George E. Phair
Published in *The Glory of Their Times* by Lawrence S. Ritter
New York: The Macmillan Company, p. 225

THE UNSEEN TENTH MAN

It is one thing to envision in his glory a baseball player who has long been retired from the game, or, more probably, ourselves in a baseball glory that was never ours to enjoy. But it is another thing to imagine a player whom no one can see or identify —or quite comprehend. In his poem, "Mystery Baseball," Philip Dacey creates a haunting tableau in which an all-too-human game is played as a cosmic metaphor:

No one knows the man who throws out the sea-
　son's first ball.
　His face has never appeared in the newspapers,
　　except in crowd scenes, blurred.
　Asked his name, he mumbles something
　　about loneliness,
　　about the beginnings of hard times.

Each team fields an extra, tenth man.
　This is the invisible player,
　　assigned to no particular position.
　Runners edging off base feel a tap on their shoul-
　ders,
　　turn, see no one.
　Or a batter, the count against him, will hear whis-
　pered
　in his ear vague, dark
　rumors of his wife, and go down.

Vendors move through the stands
　selling unmarked sacks,

never disclosing their contents,
never having been told.
People buy, hoping.

Pitchers stay busy
　getting signs.
　They are everywhere.

One man rounds third base, pumping hard,
　and is never seen again.
　Teammates and relatives wait years at the plate,
　　uneasy, fearful.

An outfielder goes for a ball on the warning track.
　He leaps into the air and keeps rising,
　　beyond himself, past
　　the limp flag.

Days later he is discovered,
　descended, wandering dazed
　in centerfield.

Deep under second base lives an old man,
　bearded, said to be
　a hundred. All through the game,
　players pull at the bills of their caps,
　acknowledging him.

Humorous comparison between the modern pitcher and the hurler of old.

ONE TO NOTHING, 1961
Carolyn Kizer
Published in *The Ungrateful Garden*
Bloomington: Indiana University Press

Fans at a baseball game are satirized.
The bibulous eagle behind me at the ball game:
"Shucks a'mighty!" coming through the rye . . .

OPENING JUBILEE, 1913
Grantland Rice
Published in *Collier's*, April 12, 1913

THE ORIGIN OF BASEBALL, 1942
Kenneth Patchen
Published in *Collected Poems of Kenneth Patchen*
New York: New Directions Publishing Corp.
See also: Baseball in the Spoken Arts—Recorded

PENNANT FEVER, 1982
Helen B. Donato
Published in the *New York Times*, October 13, 1982, p. C2

Parody of "Sea Fever" by John Masefield.
I must go down to Ebbets Field again . . .

PITCHER, 1953
Robert Francis
Published in *The Orb Weaver*
Middletown, Connecticut: Wesleyan University Press

See also: Baseball in the Spoken Arts— Recorded

His art is eccentricity, his aim
How not to hit the mark he seems to aim
at . . .

PLAY BALL!, 1980
Robert Francis
Published in *Anthology of Magazine Verse and Yearbook of American Poetry*, edited by Alan F. Pater
Beverly Hills, California: Monitor Books

A POEM FOR ED "WHITEY" FORD, 1985
Jonathan Holden
Published in *The Morrow Anthology of Younger American Poets*, edited by Dave Smith and David Bottoms
New York: Quill/William Morrow and Co.

POLO GROUNDS, 1944
Rolfe Humphries
Published in *The Summer Landscape*
New York: Charles Scribner's Sons

Time is of the essence. This is a highly skilled
And beautiful mystery . . .

A POST CARD OUT OF PANAMA, 1980
William D. Barney
Published in *A Literature of Sports*
edited by Tom Dodge
Lexington, Massachusetts: D. C. Heath and Co.

Homage to the poet's unknown but nonetheless heroic baseball-playing father.

THE PUZZLER, 1955
Ogden Nash
Published in *Life*, September 5, 1955, p. 88

Humorous caricature of Cleveland Indians' first baseman Ferris Fain.

A QUERY, 1927
John Kieran
Published in the *New York Times*, October 2, 1927

Tribute to New York Yankees' slugger Babe Ruth.
. . . and I beg to ask: Was there ever a guy like Ruth?

REMEMBERING THE SPITBALL, 1986
J. E. Harris
Published in the *New York Times*, August 6, 1986, p. C2

Homage to a favorite uncle who taught a boy to throw a spitter.

REPORT OF THE BASEBALL GAME, 1905
Eugene Field
Published in *Hoosier Lyrics*
Chicago: M. A. Donohue and Co.

Light-verse narrative in which gamblers and fans bemoan a loss by the local team.

RONDEAU (FROM A HOUSING SITE IN FLATBUSH), 1962
Milton Bracker
Published in the *New York Times Magazine*, April 8, 1962, p. 32

Tribute to the Brooklyn Dodgers of old.

THE ROUNDHOUSE VOICES, 1979
Dave Smith
Published in *Goshawk, Antelope*
Champaign: University of Illinois Press

In full glare of sunlight I came here, man-tall but thin
as a pinstripe . . .

RURAL RECREATION, 1977
Lillian Morrison
Published in *The Sidewalk Racer*
New York: Lothrop, Lee and Shepard Co.

Humorous play on the word, "fungo."

THE SAGA OF OLD PETE, 1952
Parke Grindell
Published in *The Sun Shines Bright*
Bath, Maine: The Guerin Printing Co., paperback

Celebration of Grover Cleveland Alexander's 1926 World Series strikeout of Tony Lazzeri.

SAN FRANCISCO AT N.Y., 1962
Milton Bracker
Published in the *New York Times Magazine*, April 8, 1962, p. 32

Humorous tribute to San Francisco Giants' outfielder Willie Mays.

THE SEASON OPENS, 1927
Bert Leston Taylor
Published in *Motley Measures*
New York: Alfred A. Knopf, Inc.

SENATOR WALRUS ON SPRING POETRY, 1949
Al Graham
Published in *Collier's*, April 9, 1949

Humorous sonnet celebrating baseball.

SEPTEMBER VALENTINE, 1969
Frank Sullivan
Published in the *New York Times*, September 26, 1969, p. 71

Humorous tribute to the World Series-bound New York Mets.

7TH GAME: 1960 SERIES, 1967
Paul Blackburn
Published in *The Cities*
New York: Grove Press, Inc.

SIGN FOR MY FATHER, WHO STRESSED THE BUNT, 1985
David Bottoms
Published in *The Morrow Anthology of Younger American Poets*, edited by Dave Smith and David Bottoms

New York: Quill/William Morrow and Co.

SILVER NIGHTS, 1985
James S. LaVilla-Havelin
Published in *Diamonds Are Forever: Artists and Writers on Baseball* edited by Peter H. Gordon
San Francisco: Chronicle Books, 1987

There is no other place as green as this.

THE SINGLE MAN, 1955
Ogden Nash
Published in *Life*, September 5, 1955, p. 88

Milwaukee Braves' first baseman Joe Adcock's confirmed bachelorhood is humorously treated.

THE SONG OF SNOHOMISH, 1976
William S. Wallace
Published in the *New York Times Magazine*, August 8, 1976, p. 55

Composed entirely of baseball players' nicknames.

SOUTHPAW TRIPTYCH, 1962
Milton Bracker
Published in the *New York Times Magazine*, April 8, 1962, p. 130

Tribute to left-handers Warren Spahn, Luis Arroyo, and Whitey Ford.

SPITBALLER, 1971
Fred Chappell
Published in *The World Between the Eyes*
Baton Rouge: Louisiana State University Press

A poet because his hand goes first to his head & then to his heart.

SPRING TRAINING, 1984
Lynn Rigney Schott
Published in *The New Yorker*, March 26, 1984; in *The Temple of Baseball* edited by Richard Grossinger.

AT SEASON'S END

Occasionally a crowd at a night baseball game is asked to light candles in the darkened stadium in memory of a fallen baseball hero. In his apocalyptic poem, "The Stadium," William Heyen envisions a time when another kind of observance will be held—after baseball itself is no more:

The stadium is filled,
for this is the third night the moon
has not appeared as even a thin
     sickle.

We light the candles we were told to
     bring.
The diamond is lit red with torches.
Children run the bases.

A voice, as though from a tomb,
leads us to the last amen of a
     hymn.
Whole sections of the bleachers
     begin to moan.

The clergy files from the dugouts
to the makeshift communion rails
that line the infield grass.

We've known, all our lives,
that we would gather here in the
     stadium
on just such a night,

that even the bravest among us
would weep softly in the dark aisles,
catching their difficult breath.

Copyright © 1970 by William Heyen, from *Depth of Field* (Louisiana State University Press, 1970). Reprinted by permission of the author.

Berkeley, California: North Atlantic Books, 1985

THE STADIUM, 1970
William Heyen
Published in *Depth of Field*
Baton Rouge: Louisiana State University Press

Apocalyptic vision of a stadium scene in a world without baseball.

STICKBALL, 1971
Larry Thompson
Published in *It Is the Poem Singing into Your Eyes* edited by Arnold Adoff
New York: Harper and Row Publishers

STICKBALL, 1974
Chuck Sullivan
Published in *Esquire*, October 1974

STRIKE ZONE, 1971
Fred Chappell
Published in *The World Between the Eyes*
Baton Rouge: Louisiana State University Press

SUNSET BEFORE DAWN, 1975
David Malarcher
Published in *Voices from the Great Black Baseball Leagues* by John Holway
New York: Dodd, Mead and Co.

Tribute to black players whose careers ended before baseball's color barrier was broken. Malarcher was a Negro League star for many years.

TAO IN THE YANKEE STADIUM BLEACHERS, 1956
John Updike
Published in *The New Yorker*, August 18, 1956, p. 28; in *The Carpentered Hen and Other Tame Creatures*. New York:

Harper and Row, 1958

Distance brings proportion. From here
the populated tiers
as much as the players seem part of the
show . . .

TED WILLIAMS, AGE 63, TAKES BATTING PRACTICE, 1982
Merritt Clifton
Published in *Baseball Stories for Girls and Boys (Past Puberty)*
Richford, Vermont: Samisdat,
paperback

TED WILLIAMS ON THE ART OF HITTING, 1982
Merritt Clifton
Published in *Baseball Stories for Girls and Boys (Past Puberty)*
Richford, Vermont: Samisdat,
paperback

THIRD BASE COACH, 1971
Fred Chappell

Published in *The World Between the Eyes*
Baton Rouge: Louisiana State
University Press

A THIRD BASEMAN GIVES THANKS, 1964
Ed Charles
Published in *Baseball Digest*, May 1964, p. 43

Inspirational verse by the Kansas City A's third baseman.

TO A BASEBALL, 1971
No author given
Published in *Sports Poems* edited by
R. R. Knudson and P. K. Ebert
New York: Dell Publishing Co., Inc.,
paperback

TO SATCH (OR AMERICAN GOTHIC), 1963
Samuel Allen

Published in *Soon, One Morning*
edited by Herbert Hill
New York: Alfred A. Knopf, Inc.
See also: Baseball in the Spoken Arts—
Recorded

Tribute to Hall of Fame pitcher Satchel Paige.

TO THE DETROIT BASEBALL CLUB, 1887
Eugene Field
Published in *Hoosier Lyrics*
Chicago: M. A. Donohue and Co.,
1905

Verse tribute to the Detroit club after defeating the local White Stockings for the National League pennant.

TOMORROW!, 1962
Milton Bracker
Published in the *New York Times Magazine*, April 8, 1962, p. 32

Salute to baseball's opening day.

Bards of Baseball

Lurking in baseball's storied past are the ghosts of a thousand writers who have penned the life histories, how-to books, and inside-dope articles affixed to baseball players' names. The role of the ghost-writer in the history of baseball literature is so pervasive that the tradition still persists that the only book most ballplayers will ever read is his own ghost-written autobiography. He reads the book, it is said, because he wants to see how it ends.

In 1960, a journeyman long-reliever for the St. Louis Cardinals forever recast the image of the ballplayer as semiliterate with the publication of his best selling—and erudite—*The Long Season.* Studious looking and bespectacled (he was nicknamed the Professor), Jim Brosnan certainly fit the literary part. But no one in baseball, least of all his own teammates, could have anticipated Brosnan's wry, perceptive autobiographical account of a year in the life of a ballplayer. With that book, and his follow-up volume, *The Pennant Race*, in which he details his pennant clinching season with the Cincinnati Reds, Brosnan clearly deserves a place at the head of baseball's literary roundtable.

Although a few early-day ballplayers wrote, if somewhat floridly, by their own hand, the first baseball player to turn full-time professional writer was Sam Crane, a much-travelled, weak hitting utility infielder of the 1880s. When his ballplaying days were over, Crane took up a career as a sportswriter for the *New York Evening*

Journal and became a prolific freelancer for the baseball magazines as well. Moe Berg, the scholarly backup catcher of the 1920s and '30s, wrote several substantial articles and essays about baseball as befitting his intellectual nature and expertise.

Among contemporary ballplayers, Steve Boros, manager of the San Diego Padres in 1986, has prepared a novel, as yet unpublished, about his life in baseball. Billy Sample, an outfielder for the Texas Rangers and New York Yankees during the 1980s, is an excellent writer of essays dealing with baseball and social issues. Tom House, former pitcher for the Atlanta Braves and present coach of the Texas Rangers, recently put his PhD in psychology to good use by writing a book called *The Jock's Itch: The Fast-Track Private World of the Professional Ballplayer*, in which he examines the privileged society of major league baseball players.

A number of ballplayers have labored under the poetic muse. One of the earliest was Ed Kenna, who enjoyed a cup of coffee as a pitcher for the Philadelphia Athletics in 1902 (lifetime record: 1–1 with a 5.29 ERA) and who was nicknamed "the Pitching Poet." Kenna published a book of verse while toiling in the minor leagues, titled *Lyrics From the Hills*, a sample of which follows:

Ed Charles, third baseman for the world champion New York Mets of 1969, was known as the "Poet Laureate of the Infield." (National Baseball Library.)

> Fall time in the country, when the
>   Sunshine filters down
> The tangled maze of cloudland
>   And through the beeches brown;
> In the golden rays it scatters
>   On the dear, old dirty sod
> I can trace in wonderous letters
>   The mystic word of God.

David Malarcher, a star third baseman for the Chicago American Giants of the black leagues during the 1920s and '30s, wrote a number of verses in a formal, histrionic style. In his poem, "Sunset Before Dawn," Gentleman Dave, as he was known, pays tribute to black baseball stars who were born too soon to play in the integrated major leagues. The second verse reads:

> O, minds of fleetful thought!
>   O dead who lived too soon!
> What pity thou wert brought
>   To twilight ere the noon!

Cincinnati Reds pitcher Jim Brosnan authored two best-selling baseball books during the late 1950s and early '60s. (National Baseball Library.)

seasons as a major leaguer. After laboring ten years in the minor leagues in the Milwaukee Braves system, Charles was traded to the Kansas City Athletics where he batted .288 and hit 17 home runs in his rookie year in 1962. A deep feeling man, Charles was sensitive to the racism he encountered in his days as a peripatetic minor leaguer, and much of that sensitivity is reflected in the inspirational nature of his poetry. An excerpt of "A Third Baseman Gives Thanks" reads:

> Seeking a place with the stars of the game,
>   A niche in Baseball's Hall of Fame
> Where Babe, Ty and Jackie are proudly
>   enshrined,
>   White stars and black, arms entwined.
> Deep is my longing to rise to the heights.
>   Guide me then to higher flights
> Of fame and glory, victories won,
>   Homers winging into the sun . . .

Not exactly Shakespeare, it is true. And yet only the Bard of Avon could have admonished, "Ne'er leave striking in the field" (*Henry IV*). Not everyone can wield such an efficient bat, or, for that matter, such a poetic pen. ◆

Ed Charles, a third baseman for the world champion New York Mets in 1969, was called the "Poet Laureate of the Infield" during his eight

---

TWELVE PERFECT INNINGS, 1961
Weldon Myers
Commercial Press, paperback

Rhymed-verse narrative of Harvey Haddix's 12 perfectly pitched innings against the Milwaukee Braves, May 26, 1959.

TWO BASEBALL POEMS, 1975
Joel Oppenheimer
Published in *The Wrong Season*
New York: Award Books

Homage to two former minor leaguers and a vanishing way of life.

TWO HOPPER, 1984
Ron Ikan
Published in *Strings: A Gathering of Family Poems* edited by Paul B. Janeczko
Bradbury Press

TY COBB POEM, 1977
William Packard
Published in *First Selected Poems*
Pylon Press

THE TYCOON, 1955
Ogden Nash
Published in *Life*, September 5, 1955, p. 87

Hall of Famer Stan Musial's business acumen is humorously treated.

THE UMPIRE, 1909
Carolyn Wells
Published in *Harper's Weekly*, July 24, 1909, p. 25

UMPIRE, 1954
Walker Gibson
Published in *The Reckless Spenders*
Bloomington: Indiana University Press

Whimsical commentary on the semantics and logic peculiar to baseball.

THE UMPIRE, 1962
Milton Bracker
Published in the *New York Times Magazine*, April 8, 1962, p. 33

The anonymousness of being an umpire is humorously treated.

VILLANELLE, 1965
M. D. Feld
Published in *Sprints and Distances* edited by Lillian Morrison
New York: Thomas Y. Crowell Co.

. . . Unmask and be the sport of fate.

WAMBY: OR THE NOSTALGIC RECORD-BOOK, 1962
Milton Bracker
Published in the *New York Times Magazine*, April 8, 1962, p. 32

Limerick in tribute to Cleveland Indians' second baseman Bill Wambsganss, the only player to execute an unassisted triple play in World Series history.

WHAT EVERY HOME RUN HITTER KNOWS, 1962
Milton Bracker
Published in the *New York Times Magazine*, April 8, 1962, p. 32

WHEN FATHER PLAYED BASEBALL, 1917
Edgar A. Guest
Published in *Just Folks*
Chicago: The Reilley and Lee Co.

Humorous narrative in which a middle-aged man plays baseball for the first time since his youth.

WHERE, O WHERE?, 1962
Milton Bracker
Published in the *New York Times Magazine*, April 8, 1962, p. 130

Tribute to the baseball players of yore.

WILLIE MAYS, 1974
Paul Ramsey
Published in *Poetry: Points of Departure* edited by Henry Taylor
Cambridge, Massachusetts: Winthrop Publishers, Inc.

You know the records. They are there to read.

"WILL YOU SIGN MY BRAND-NEW BASEBALL, LOUIE?," 1976
David Allan Evans
Published in *Train Windows*
Athens: Ohio University Press

WILLY SMITH AT THE BALL GAME, 1934
George Sterling
Published in *The Book of American Poetry* edited by Edwin Markham
Great Neck, New York: Granger Book Co., Inc.

Mock heroic portrayal of baseball players as modern-day jousting knights.

YOGI, 1962
Milton Bracker
Published in the *New York Times Magazine*, April 8, 1962, p. 130

Tribute to Hall of Fame catcher Yogi Berra.

YOU CAN'T KILL AN ORIOLE, c. 1954
Ogden Nash
Published in holograph in *The Home Team: Our O's! Baseball and Baltimore* by James H. Bready
Privately published: paperback, 1984

The ghost of Wee Willie Keeler is roused by the return of major league baseball to Baltimore.

Baseball in Poetry and Light Verse— Collected

EXPLANATORY NOTES

1. Title of the book, year of publication.

2. Name of author.

3. Place of publication, name of publisher, book

format (given when the book is available in paperback format only).

4. Annotation. Description of the contents.

This section contains a listing of publications of collected baseball-related poetry and humorous verse. Included in the catalog are collections of poetry by a single author, anthologies of baseball poetry and verse, and literary publications relating exclusively to baseball.

ADAM'S AT BAT, 1987
Paul Weinman
Richford, Vermont: Samisdat, paperback

Collection of 19 baseball-related poems.

THE ANNOTATED CASEY AT THE BAT, 1967
Edited by Martin Gardner
New York: Clarkson N. Potter, Inc.
Second edition, Chicago: The University of Chicago Press, 1984
See also: Casey at the Bat (Baseball in Poetry and Light Verse)

Contains history, bibliography, original versions, and 25 parodies of this most famous baseball poem.

AUNT MINNIE'S SCRAPBOOK, 1949
Albert Kennedy (Rosey) Rowswell
Sharpsburg, Pennsylvania; paperback

Collection of anecdotes and verse by the Pittsburgh Pirates' announcer.

BALLADS OF BASEBALL, 1906
William A. Phelon

New York: Metropolitan Syndicate Press, paperback

Collection of humorous verse relating to baseball.

BASEBALL, 1971
Edited by Richard Grossinger
Issue No. 10 of *Io*
Cape Elizabeth, Maine: Io Publications, paperback

Anthology of baseball-related poetry, essays, and excerpted short fiction.

BASEBALL, 1982
Edited by Jim Villani and Rose Sayre
Issue No. 9 of *Pig Iron*
Youngstown, Ohio: Pig Iron Press, paperback

Anthology containing 39 baseball-related poems and 8 works of short fiction.

BASEBALL: A POEM IN THE MAGIC NUMBER 9, 1967
George Bowering
Toronto, Canada: The Coach House Press

Collection of nine baseball-related poems, printed in the shape of a pennant.

BASE-BALL BALLADS, 1910
Grantland Rice
Nashville, Tennessee: The Tennessean Company

Collection of baseball-related verse, including a parody sequel to Casey at the Bat *titled: "Casey's Revenge."*

BASEBALL DIAMONDS, 1980
Edited by Kevin Kerrane and Richard Grossinger
Garden City, New York: Anchor Press/Doubleday, paperback
See: Baseball I Gave You All the Best Years of My Life

BASEBALL FANTHOLOGY: HITS AND SKITS OF THE GAME, 1924
Edited by Edward Branch Lyman
New York: Privately published, paperback

Collection of baseball verse.

BASEBALL HISTORY IN LIMERICK VERSE AND IN SKETCH, 1981
D. C. Vogt

Milwaukee, Wisconsin: Greenfield House, paperback

Collection of puns and play on words in tribute to baseball players.

BASEBALL I GAVE YOU ALL THE BEST YEARS OF MY LIFE, 1976
Edited by Kevin Kerrane and Richard Grossinger
Berkeley, California: North Atlantic Books, paperback
See: Baseball Diamonds

Anthology of short fiction, essays, and over 60 baseball-related poems. Later re-edited and published under the title, Baseball Diamonds.

BASEBALL JOKES, STORIES AND POEMS, 1906
No author given
New York: M. J. Ivers and Co.

BASEBALLOGY, 1912
Edmund Vance Cooke
Chicago: Forbes and Co.

Collection of 25 light verses, including the poignant, "Game Called."

THE BEST OF SPITBALL, 1988
Edited by Mike Shannon
New York: Pocket Books, paperback

Anthology containing baseball-related poetry and short fiction.

BIG LEAGUE POETS, 1978
Mikhail Horowitz
San Francisco, California: City Lights Books, paperback

Collection of verse that describes famous poets as having been baseball players.

BULLPEN CATCHER, 1984
Paul Shuttleworth
Richford, Vermont: Samisdat, paperback
Second expanded edition, retitled, *Bullpen Catcher and Friends*

Richford, Vermont: Samisdat, 1985, paperback

Collection of poems about life in the minor leagues.

"CASEY AT THE BAT" AND OTHER MUDVILLE BALLADS, c. 1934
George Whitefield D'Vys
Cambridge, Massachusetts: J. Frank Facey, paperback

Contains 11 ballads about Casey, including a corrupted version of Thayer's poem, authorship of which D'Vys falsely claimed.

CASEY REMINISCENCES, 1911
Col. William H. Rowe, Jr.
Volunteer Press; paperback

Rhymed-verse history of baseball from 1871–1877.

CATCH, 1977
Edited by Virgil Smith
Kent, Ohio: Shelly's Press, paperback

Anthology of baseball-related poetry.

CHEERING SOME ONE ON, 1933
George Whitefield D'vys
Medford, Massachusetts: C. A. A. Parker, paperback
See also: Baseball in Music and Song

Collection of 36 baseball ballads.

CLASSIC SUMMER, 1982
D. Roger Martin
Richford, Vermont: Samisdat, paperback

Collection of 11 baseball-related poems.

CURT FLOOD AND OTHER BASEBALL POEMS, 1988
Tim Peeler
Conover, North Carolina: Third Lung Press, paperback

Collection of 17 poems relating to baseball.

DOUBLEHEADER, 1983
R. Gerry Fabian
Richford, Vermont: Samisdat, paperback

Collection of 18 baseball-related poems.

THE DREAMLIFE OF JOHNNY BASEBALL, 1987
Edited by Richard Grossinger
Berkeley, California: North Atlantic Books

Anthology containing essays, short fiction, and 12 poems relating to baseball.

FAN POEMS, 1976
Tom Clark
Plainfield, Vermont: North Atlantic Books, paperback

Collection of 33 baseball-related poems.

GREAT BASEBALL POEMS OF THE 1930'S FROM *BASEBALL MAGAZINE*, 1984
Edited by Ted T. Nichols
Privately published: paperback

Anthology containing more than 35 verses originally published in Baseball Magazine.

HE SWINGS A STRAIGHT STICK, 1985
Paul Weinman
Richford, Vermont: Samisdat, paperback

Collection of 14 baseball-related poems.

A LITTLE BOOK OF TIGERS, 1968
Leslie Shepard
Detroit, Michigan: Gale Research Co.

Collection of verse in tribute to the Detroit Tigers.

THE MANTLE/MAYS CONTROVERSY SOLVED, 1982
Mike Shannon
Kent, Ohio: Catcher Press, paperback

Collection of 27 baseball-related poems.

MARCH 6TH: THE HOME COMING OF CHARLES A. COMISKEY, JOHN J. MCGRAW, AND JAMES J. CALLAHAN, 1914

Ring W. Lardner and Edward C. Heeman

Chicago: The Blakeley Printing Co.

Collection of essays, verses, and songs saluting the arrival of the Chicago White Sox from their world tour of 1914.

MIGHTY CASEY: ALL-AMERICAN, 1984

Edited by Eugene C. Murdock

Westport, Connecticut: Greenwood Press

Contains a history and more than 75 parodies of Casey at the Bat.

MINNEAPOLIS REVIEW OF BASEBALL, 1981

Edited by Fred LaZebnik

Published regularly by subscription

Minneapolis, Minnesota; paperback

Quarterly devoted to baseball-related poetry and short fiction. First issue is dated Winter 1981.

MOSE'S BASEBALL POEMS, 1940

Al (Mose) Bland

Privately published; paperback

Collection of verses in tribute to the World Champion Cincinnati Reds.

ONE HUNDRED BASEBALL LIMERICKS, 1925

Charles M. Best

ON THE ROAD WITH THE BASE BALL BUGS, 1910

Jack Regan and Will E. Stahl

Chicago: J. Regan and Co., paperback

Collection of ballads and anecdotes.

PEP: THE RED-BOOK OF SPORTS FOR RED-BLOODED READERS, c. 1920

George S. Applegarth

Pittsburgh, Pennsylvania: Pittsburgh Gazette Times

Collection of light verse, including two Casey at the Bat *parodies: "The Man Who Struck Out Casey" and "Why Casey Fanned."*

PETE ROSE AGONISTIES, 1987

Mike Shannon

Conover, North Carolina: Third Lung Press, paperback

Collection of 19 poems relating to baseball.

PLAY BALL!, 1914

P. J. Conner

The Print Shop: paperback

POEMS AND OTHER BASEBALLS, 1976

George Bowering

Coatsworth, Ontario, Canada: Black Moss Press

RIGHT OFF THE BAT: BASEBALL BALLADS, 1911

William F. Kirk

New York: G. W. Dillingham Co.

Collection of 34 humorous verses as originally published in the New York Evening Journal.

ROSEY REFLECTIONS, 1945

Albert Kennedy (Rosey) Rowswell

Pittsburgh, Pennsylvania: Kerr Co.

Collection of ancedotes and verse by the Pittsburgh Pirates' announcer.

SPITBALL, 1981

Edited by Mike Shannon and W. J. Harrison

Published regularly by subscription

Covington, Kentucky: paperback

Quarterly devoted to baseball-related poetry and short fiction. First issue is dated Spring 1981.

THE TEMPLE OF BASEBALL, 1985

Edited by Richard Grossinger

Berkeley, California: North Atlantic Books

Anthology of articles, essays, and over 15 baseball-related poems.

US BASEBALLERS AND OUR BASEBALL TEAMS, 1923

Marshall Breeden

Los Angeles: Privately published

WHAT DO YOU HAVE TO LOSE?, 1987

William Heyen

Concord, New Hampshire: William B. Ewert, Publisher

Collection of six baseball-related poems by this important American poet. Printed in a limited edition of 100 copies.

YOU CAN'T TELL THE PLAYERS, 1979

Barton R. Friedman

Cleveland, Ohio: Cleveland State University Poetry Center, paperback

Collection of 33 poems about Brooklyn Dodgers' players from the 1940s and 1950s.

Baseball in Music and Song

The following catalog contains a comprehensive listing of published—but unrecorded—songs relating to baseball, baseball teams, and baseball players. Included in this section are 19th-century musical compositions relating to baseball, song tributes to major and minor league players and teams, comic songs with a baseball theme, songs included in musical plays and operas, songs in which baseball is used metaphorically, and songs celebrating baseball and its special place in the American consciousness.

In the 1800s baseball clubs traveled to the ballpark in horse-drawn transoms, and the singing of team songs was a popular way of passing the time along the way. The tradition carried over to the singing of tributes to the visiting team by their hosts at elaborate banquets held the evening before the game. Several of these songs were published in sheet music form as early as the 1840s, and not long afterward songs heralding local ballclubs sprouted up in towns and cities all over the baseball landscape.

In the 19th century, published sheet music enjoyed a prominence in the American marketplace that is all but forgotten today. In the years before the phonograph was invented, the parlor piano was virtually a standard piece of furniture in the American home. Nightly singalongs were a ritual in many families of those days, and sheet music, which sold for pennies each, was accumulated for all occasions and tastes. A popular subject among the inexhaustible themes and topics explored by songwriters was baseball. It was the songwriters of the 1800s who designated baseball "America's national game." Dozens of songs from that era made mention of baseball's singular place in American sporting life.

These early songsheets, many of which feature a colorful illustration of a baseball scene on its cover, are rare collectibles today. The Newberry Library in Chicago houses the J. Francis Driscoll Collection of sports and baseball songsheets, and the National Baseball Hall of Fame in Cooperstown, New York, contains a large collection of baseball sheet music, much of which is exhibited in a special display in the museum.

For further information regarding sources of sheet music and other musical collectibles, consult the Selected Guide to Sources and Dealers at the back of the book.

E X P L A N A T O R Y   N O T E S

1. Title of the song, year of publication.

2. Name of songwriter(s).

3. Dedication or inscription on songsheet cover (in quotation marks).

4. Publisher of the song, place of publication, licensing agency in parentheses.

5. Cover: Description of the songsheet cover.

6. Annotation. Description of the song or a quotation from same.

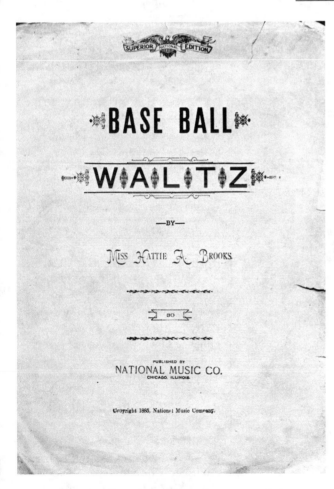

In the late 1800s the waltz was king—but so was baseball. It was only natural, then, that Miss Hattie A. Brooks of Chicago would compose this 1885 tune. (National Baseball Library.)

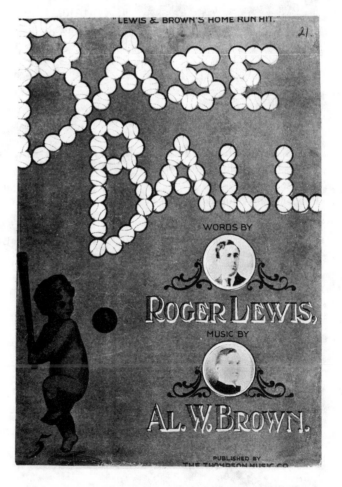

"One strike, two strikes, another strike you're out. Oh! what a shame!" The success of "Take Me Out to the Ball Game" during the early 1900s inspired a number of blatant imitations, including this 1908 song. (National Baseball Library.)

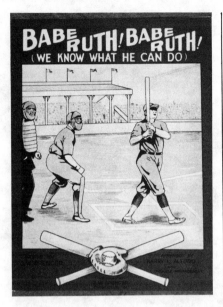

This paean to Babe Ruth was written in 1928: "He knocks 'em high, / he knocks 'em far, He gives that baseball an awful jar." (Michael Brown collection.)

ALL IN THE TIMIN', 1985
Words by Hy Gilbert, music by
George Fischoff
Published by George Fischoff
Publishing Co. (ASCAP)

Slugger explains the secret of his home run hitting success. Included in the musical play, Bingo! (See: Baseball in Theater.)

ALONG CAME RUTH, 1926
Irving Berlin, with special lyrics by
Christy Walsh, Addy Britt, and Harry
Link
Published by Henry Waterson, Inc.,
New York
Cover: Portrait of Babe Ruth

Originally this was the title song, written by Irving Berlin, of a 1914 Broadway play unrelated to baseball's Ruth. Later a new lyric was written in honor of the Babe.

THE AMERICAN LEAGUE, 1955
Richard Adler and Jerry Ross
Published by Frank Music Corp.,
New York

Included in the musical play, Damn Yankees. (See: Baseball in Theater.)

AMERICAN LEAGUE TWO-STEP, 1905
Grace Comiskey
Published by Newton Publishing Co.,
Chicago
Cover: Catcher's mask and mitt

AMERICA'S "PINCH HIT" MARCH, 1919
Bertha Stanfield Dempsey
"The Hit That Ended the World's
Greatest War"
Published by The McMillan Music
Co., Joplin, Missouri
Cover: Kaiser pitching, Uncle Sam
running to first base

THE A'S ARE THE CRAZE, 1938
Moe Jaffe
Published by Mills Music, Inc.
(ASCAP)

Fight song for the Philadelphia Athletics. Published in Batter Up. (See: Baseball in Music and Song—Collected.)

AT THE BALL GAME, 1949
Olof Thunstrom
Published by G. Schirmer, Inc., New
York

AT THE BASE BALL GAME, 1910
Chas. H. Graf
"March and Two Step"
Published by Chas. H. Graf,
Philadelphia, Pennsylvania
Cover: Cartoon depiction of baseball
action

AT THE OLD BALL GAME, 1941
Words and music by Max Bates,

Duncan Browning, and Harmon
Bickley
"World Series Edition—1940"
Published by Shelby Music Pub. Co.,
Detroit

AUTOGRAPH, 1954
Composed by William Schuman,
libretto by Jerome Gury
Published by G. Schirmer, Inc.

Included in the opera, The Mighty Casey. (See: Baseball in Theater.)

BABE, 1947
Words by Charles Tobias, music by
Peter de Rose
Published by Tobias and Lewis Music
Co., New York

Tribute to Babe Ruth.

BABE RUTH AT THE BAT, 1922
No author given
Words only published in *Delaney's
Song Book:* No. 89, p. 24
Published by Wm. W. Delaney, New
York

Verbatim parody of "Casey at the Bat." Originally published in the New York
American, *September 16, 1921.*

BABE RUTH! BABE RUTH! (WE KNOW WHAT HE CAN DO), 1928
Words by J. W. Spencer, arranged by
Harry L. Alford
Published by J. W. Spencer,
Olneyville, New York
Cover: Cartoon of Babe Ruth batting

BABE RUTH, HE IS A HOME RUN GUY, 1923
A. Atkins and Harry W. Trout
Published by H. J. Gott Music
Publisher, Chicago
Cover: Green panorama of baseball
field

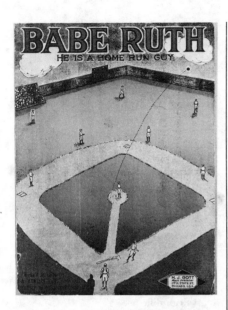

One of the earliest tributes to the Babe, published in 1923: "There's not a player in the land, who can hit a ball like Babe Ruth can." (National Baseball Library.)

BABE RUTH SONG, 1921
Words by G. D. Hart, music by
George Graff, Jr.
Published by World Music Publishing
Corp., New York

BACK TO THE BLEACHERS FOR MINE, 1910
Words by Harry Breen, music by
Albert Von Tilzer
Published by The York Music Co.,
New York

BACK UP THE DODGERS
Harry Simeone
Published by Words and Music, Inc.
(ASCAP)

"BALL DAYS" IN THE YEAR A.D. 1858, 1858
Henry Chadwick
Words only published in *The Game of Base Ball*
New York: George Munro and Co.,
1868

Come, my brave Yankee boys, there's
room enough for all,
So join in Uncle Samuel's sport—the
pastime of base ball.

BALL FOUR, 1976
Harry Chapin
Published by April Music, Inc.
(ASCAP)
See also: Baseball in Television

Theme from the television series of the same name.

THE BALL GAME
Published in *Music Education Series: The Home Edition, Volume 2* edited by
T. P. Giddings
Published by Ginn and Co., Boston

Children's baseball song.

THE BALL GAME ISN'T OVER 'TIL THE LAST MAN IS OUT, 1968
Sverre S. Elsmo
Published by Elsmo Bros. Publishers
Copyright date and number: October
26, 1968, EP 251744

A BALL PLAYER, 1967
Al Stillman and Paul Purcell
Published by Refrain Music Corp.
Copyright date and number: March 3,
1967, EP 229042

BALL THREE, 1962
Published by Boston Music

BAM IT'S GOING GOING GONE, 1939
"Deke" Moffitt and Harry Hartman
Cover: Panoramic photograph of
Crosley Field

Tribute to the Cincinnati Reds.

BASE BALL!, 1870
John Smith
"To the Root and Cady Base Ball
Club"

Published by Root and Cady, Chicago
Cover: Bats, ball, shoes, and cap in
center

More than fifteen musical valentines have been published in tribute to the immortal Babe Ruth. One of the earliest, "Oh! You Babe Ruth," was written in 1920 ("Babe Ruth's a treasure beyond earthly measure"), followed a year later by the "Babe Ruth Song" ("When Babe Ruth grabs his hickory, and ambles to the base, the pitcher hitches up his belt, and pulls a cheerless face"). An Irving Berlin song, "Along Came Ruth," was adapted in 1926 as a special tribute to the Babe ("We were looking for a home run hero, when along came Ruth"). And later, upon his death in 1948, a number of sentimental ballads were written in memory of the great slugger, among them "Safe at Home" ("He was called out, here below, but he's safe up there I know"). (National Baseball Library.)

BASE BALL, 1883
Words by Chas. F. Pidgin, music by
Chas. D. Blake
"Song and dance as sung by James H.
Dyer in Opera *Electric Spark,*
Atkinson's Jollities"
"To the Champion Boston Nine"
Published by Pidgin and Blake,
Boston

BASE BALL, 1908
Words by Roger Lewis, music by
Al. W. Brown
Published by The Thompson Music
Co., Chicago

BASEBALL, 1908
Harry P. Smith and Will A. Pratt
Published by Twentieth Century
Music Co., Chicago
Cover: View from grandstand behind
home plate; small photograph insert
at top left of Frank Chance

BASE-BALL, 1913
Words by Edmund Simonis, music by
Genevieve Scott
Published by The H. Kirkus Dugdale
Co., Washington, D.C.

BASEBALL, 1914
Composed by John Edward
Hamilton, arranged by G. Falkenstein
"A song setting forth our love for the
National Game"
Published by Falkenstein's Music
House, Fresno, California

*For the greatest of fun in the life of a lad is
e'er found in the ball, bat, and mitt.*

BASEBALL, 1919
Words by Alfred Bryan, music by
Jean Schwartz

Included in the Broadway musical, Hello
Alexander.

BASEBALL, 1939
(America's Favorite Game)

Tom Waring, Paul Gibbons, and
Craig Leitch
Published by Words and Music, Inc.,
New York

Humorous celebration of baseball.
Where Majors and Minors are not musical
keys,
And Giants are not any bigger than Bees.

BASEBALL, 1947
Words by William E. Scudder, music
by Courtney A. Crandall

Included in the play, Here's the Pitch. *See:*
Baseball in Miscellaneous Plays and Sketches.

BASEBALL, c. 1957
Jack Segal
Published by Mills Music, Inc.
(ASCAP)

BASEBALL
Thomas M. Adair and Gordon
Jenkins
Published by Gordon Jenkins, Inc.,
Kansas City, Missouri (ASCAP)

BASEBALL
Raymond A. Bloch
Published by Hollybrook Music Co.,
Inc. (ASCAP)

BASEBALL
Jerry Cohen and Larry Gold
Published by Writer Clearance (BMI)

BASEBALL
James Deuchar
Published by Gemrod Music (BMI)

BASEBALL
Jean Ferland and Daniel Mercure
Published by Ed Jaune, Ed Sibelieus
engraver. (BMI)

BASEBALL
Cari Jones and Goran Petrovic
Privately published (BMI)

BASEBALL

John Lewis
Published by MJQ Music (BMI)

BASEBALL
Ray Llewellyn
Published by World Broadcasting
Music (BMI)

BASEBALL
Stanley Henson
Published by Writer Clearance (BMI)

BASEBALL
Robert Hughes
Published by Zeal Music (BMI)

BASEBALL
Jean Robitaille
Published by Paroles Et Musique
(BMI)

BASEBALL
Harry Simeone
Published by Shawnee Press, Inc.,
Delaware Water Gap, Pennsylvania
(ASCAP)

BASE BALL
J. S. Zamecnik
Published by Sam Fox Publishing
Co., Inc. (ASCAP)

**BASE BALL, AMERICAN
ASSOCIATION VS. LEAGUE,
1886**
Words by the Dockstaders, music by
Geo. A. Cragg
No publisher given: Copyright 1886
by W. F. Shaw

*Comic nonsense song in which a man describes
a baseball game being played by 14 teams
simultaneously.*

BASEBALL AND WRESTLING
Danny Hutchins
Published by Writer Clearance (BMI)

BASEBALL, BASEBALL, 1959
James Sinclair
Published by Studio Music Corp.
Copyright date and number: June 1, 1959, EP 136551

BASE BALL BLUES, 1931
Written by Jack Alliance, arranged by Arthur Sizemore
Published through the courtesy of Alliance Finance Corp., Chicago

BASEBALL BLUES
David Bacha
Published by Writer Clearance (BMI)

BASEBALL BLUES
Walter Earl Brown and Ticker Freeman
Published by Sewanee Music, Inc. (ASCAP)

BASEBALL BLUES
Keith Mansfield
Published by Regline Music Co. (ASCAP)

BASEBALL BLUES
Skip Prokop
Published by Seven Mighty Elohim (BMI)

BASEBALL BOOGIE, 1977
William Wilson
Published by Bucksnort Music Co. (BMI)

BASEBALL BRAINS, 1909
Words by R. D. Heinbockel, music by W. D. Paulson
"A musical novelty by the bat and the ball as overheard on the diamond"
Published by Victor Kremer Co., Chicago

THE BASEBALL BUG, 1949
Words by Stephen P. J. Zappala, music by Lew Tobin

Copyright date and number: November 28, 1949, EU 186364

BASE BALL CAKE WALK, 1905
Al Senor Martin Adriansen
"Por Juan G. Evans"
Published by A. Wagner y Levien Sucs, Mexico
Registered for copyright by Lyon and Healy of Chicago
Cover: Cartoon of a boy hitting a baseball

BASEBALL CARDS, 1983
Words by Willie Fong Young and Fred Burch, music by Willie Fong Young

Included in the off-Broadway musical, American Passion.

BASE BALL DAY, 1913
Benjamin McNeill
Published by The H. Kirkus Dugdale Co., Washington, D.C.

THE BASE BALL FAN, 1892
Thomas H. West
"Great comic song with chorus"
Published by Will Rossiter, Chicago

THE BASE BALL FAN, 1911
George Culp
Published in *Joel Baggs' Songs*
Rochester, New York: The Rochester Herald Press, paperback

For I am a Fan, I'm a plumb crazy man,
At a Base Ball Game,
I sit with the boys,
And I help make the noise,
At a Base Ball Game.

THE BASEBALL FAN, 1913
Words by Clarence Allen, music by Genevieve Scott
Published by The H. Kirkus Dugdale Co., Washington, D.C.

THE BASE BALL FEVER, 1867
Words by H. Angelo, music by James W. Porter
"To Lew Simmons, Esq."
Published by Marsh and Bubna, Philadelphia
Cover: Illustration of a country baseball game

Humorous song in which baseball is described as a crazed fad.

THE BASEBALL GAME, 1913
Words by William J. Loughry, music by A. Melvin Crosby
Published by C. L. Partee Music Pub. Co., New York

The baseball game is starting, Old Hans Wagner's at the bat; Walter Johnson is the pitcher, In the outfield Cobb stands pat.

BASEBALL GAME
Irvin Graham
Privately published (ASCAP)

BASEBALL GAME
Jack Nitzsche
Published by Prestige Music (BMI)

BASEBALL GAME
Fred Steveken
Published by Steveken Publishing (BMI)

BASEBALL GAME OF LOVE, 1909
Words by Arthur Longbrake, music by Edith Barbier
Published by Jos. Morris Co., Philadelphia

When first I gaz'd into your eyes, Your image made a home run to my heart.

BASEBALL GAME OF LOVE
Dale Noe
Published by Acuff-Rose Publishing, Inc. (BMI)

A BASEBALL CRAZE

It is difficult to think of baseball as ever having been a fad like frisbee-throwing or hula-hooping, but that's essentially what it was during the early history of the game. In the mid-to-late 1800s, when Americans were looking for activities to fill their ever growing leisure hours, they turned with a passion to open-air athletics such as lawn tennis and bowling, badminton, yachting, bicycling—and baseball. The following song, "The Base Ball Fever," written in 1867, provides a humorous commentary on the madness surrounding the participation in what was already being called, "The American National Game:"

All 'round about we've queer complaints,
  Which needs some Doctor's patching;
But something there is on the brain,
  Which seems to me more catching.
'Tis raging too, both far and near,
  Or else I'm a deceiver,

I'll tell you what it is, now, please.
  It is the Base Ball fever.
Our Merchants have to close their stores,
  Their clerks away are staying.
Contractors too, can do no work,
  Their hands are all out playing;
There's scarce a day that folks don't run,
  As true as I'm a liver;
To see a match 'bout to be played,
  'Cause they've got the Base Ball fever.

. . . Our papers teem with base ball News,
  Four columns good and over;
Our stores now sell more bats and balls
  Than would three acres cover.
We've clubs no end, and players sharp,
  But I will bet my Beaver;
That I can catch, as well as they,
  For I have *kotcht* the fever.

Words by H. Angelo, music by James W. Porter. © Copyright 1867 by Marsh and Bubna.

BASEBALL GLOVE
Don Randi
Published by ABC Dunhill Music (BMI)

BASEBALL HOEDOWN
Ervin M. Drake
Published by Jericho Music Corp. (ASCAP)

BASEBALL IS IN THE AIR
Jack Lloyd and David D. Rose
Published by David Rose Publishing Co. (ASCAP)

Musical fragment intended for television.

BASEBALL IS YOUR GAME
Lester Lee
Privately published (ASCAP)

BASEBALL JAMBOREE
Benny Bell
Published by Madison Music (BMI)

BASEBALL JINGLE
Florence Kaye, Bill Grant, and Bernie Baum
Published by Unichappell Music (BMI)

BASE BALL JOE, 1868
Henry de Marsan
Words only published in *Henry de Marsan's New Comic and Sentimental Singer's Journal: No. 21, p. 131*
Published by Henry de Marsan, New York

Joe is a fun-loving Yale baseball player.
Mind you give a friendly call,
If to New Haven you should go,
Always glad to see you all,
Please to ask for Base Ball Joe.

BASEBALL LEAGUES, 1950
John W. Schaum
Published by Belwin, Inc., New York

Tribute to the major and minor leagues.

BASEBALL MAN
Herbert Baker
Published by Paul Weston (ASCAP)

THE BASEBALL MAN FOR ME, 1909
Oralie List
Published by Victor Kremer Co., Chicago

BASE BALL MARCH, 1886
C. F. Green
"Dedicated to all lovers of base ball"
"For piano or organ"
Published by Stopper and Fisk, Williamsport, Pennsylvania

BASEBALL MARCH
Hiroshi Shigeta
Published by Beechwood Music (BMI)

BASEBALL ONE STEP
L. E. De Francesco
Published by Sam Fox Publishing
Co., Inc. (ASCAP)

**BASEBALL ON THE BRAIN,
1910**
Words by J. T. Nealon, music by
E. E. Hummer
"A song for the fans"
Published by Nealon and Hummer,
Chicago
Cover: Skeletons playing baseball in
the moonlight

BASEBALL PLAYER
Hank Charles
Published by Writer Clearance (BMI)

THE BASE BALL POLKA, 1858
Composed by J. R. Blodgett of the
Niagara Base Ball Club
"Dedicated by The Niagara Base Ball
Club of Buffalo
To the Flour City Base Ball Club of
Rochester, N.Y."
Published by Blodgett and Bradford,
Buffalo, New York

*The earliest-known musical composition
relating to baseball.*

BASE BALL POLKA, 1867
Jas. M. Goodman
Published by C. F. Escher,
Philadelphia
Cover: Lithograph of game in
progress

BASE BALL POLKA, 1868
Miss Lizzie M. Hunter
"To the Erie City Base Ball Club"
Published by E. D. Ziegler, Erie,
Pennsylvania

**THE BASE BALL QUADRILLE,
1867**
Henry Von Gudera
"Respectfully dedicated to the Tri
Mountain Base Ball Club of Boston,
Champions of New England"
Published by Henry Tolman and Co.,
Boston
Cover: Lithograph by Bufford of a
player in uniform

BASEBALL QUICKSTEP, 1885
J. B. Ferguson
"To America's Base Ball Players"
Published by The John Church Co.,
Cincinnati

THE BASEBALL RAG, 1919
Words by Noel Coward, music by
Doris Doris
Published by Ascherberg, Hopwood
and Crew, London; and Leo Feist,
Inc., New York

BASEBALL RAP '82, 1982
Russell Mason
Published by Ruined Parquet Song
(BMI)

**BASEBALL'S A FASCINATING
PASTIME**
Herbert Baker and Ernest A.
Chambers
Published by Saul Ilson (ASCAP)

THE BASEBALL SCOUT, 1971
Scotty MacGregor
Published by Scotty MacGregor
Publications (ASCAP)

*Boy writes to a big league scout about his Little
League-playing sister.*

BASEBALL '77, 1977
(Summer of '77)
Richard Maier
Copyright date and number: July 21,
1977, EU 804902

BASE BALL SONG, 1874
Words and music by W. J. Bullock,
sole proprietor of Bullock's Royal
Marionettes
"To the Base Ball Clubs of the United
States"
Published by Oliver Ditson and Co.,
Boston

Let others hunt, or fish, or sail Afar o'er
ocean's foam
Give me the game that's played among the
sweet green fields of home.

THE BASEBALL SONG, 1888
M. Mullen
"Dedicated to all lovers of the
National Game"
Published by Willis, Woodward and
Co., New York
Cover: Batter, catcher, and umpire

Let others talk of Cricket
Or gunning in the thicket,
But Base-ball's the game for me.

BASEBALL: SONG, 1907
John Gordon Hitchfield
Published by J. G. Hitchfield, San
Francisco
Copyright date and number: June 17,
1907; September 16, 1907, No. 154771

THE BASEBALL SONG, 1971
Add Lovejoy
Published by Municorn Music Co.
(ASCAP)

*Celebration of the joys of attending a baseball
game. Published in* Johnny Bench Song
Book. *(See:* Baseball in Music and Song—
Collected.*)*

THE BASEBALL SONG, 1977
Randy Lee Glaser
Copyright date and number: January
21, 1977, EU 749053

BASEBALL SONG
Louis Atkey and Mark Telford
Published by Friendly Song (BMI)

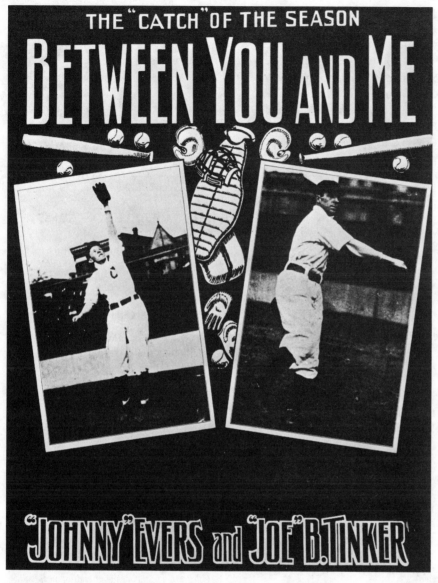

THE "CATCH" OF THE SEASON

BETWEEN YOU AND ME

"JOHNNY" EVERS and "JOE" B. TINKER

After their triumphant 1908 world championship, Chicago Cub stars Johnny Evers and Joe Tinker lent their names to this ghostwritten baseball tune. (National Baseball Library.)

THE BASEBALL SONG
Lee Erwin and Mel Howard
Published by Erwin Howard Music
Corp. (ASCAP)

BASEBALL SONG
Richard Neufeld

Published by Writer Clearance (BMI)

BASEBALL STRIKE BLUES
Jack Jacobs, Ken Melville, Dawn
Atkinson, and T. Abrahamson
Published by Humarock Music/
Rolling Fork Music (BMI)

**BASEBALL TENNIS BOXING
GOLF**
Lan Okun
Published by Okun Music Corp.
(ASCAP)

BASEBALL TIME
Jerome (Jerry) Bressler and Lyn
Duddy
Published by Ivanhoe Music, Inc.
(ASCAP)

**BASEBALL TIME IN
BROOKLYN, 1952**
Barney Young and Gloria Parker
Published by Godell Music, Inc., New
York

THE BASEBALL UMPIRE
Bobby Gregory
Published by American Music
Publishing Co. (ASCAP)

BASE BALL WALTZ, 1867
J. L. Truax
"To the Kent Base Ball Club, Grand
Rapids, Michigan"
Published by E. Moore, Grand
Rapids, Michigan

BASE BALL WALTZ, 1885
Miss Hattie A. Brooks
Published by National Music Co.,
Chicago

BASEBALL WORKOUT
William Johnson
Published by Investore Music (BMI)

BASES ARE LOADED
Published by Michael H. Goldsen,
Inc. (ASCAP)

BASES LOADED
Richard R. Hyman
Published by Eastlake Music, Inc.
(ASCAP)

BAT AND BALL, 1924
Published in *Intermediate Music* edited by T. P. Giddings
Published by Ginn and Co., Boston

Children's baseball song.

THE BAT AND THE BALL, 1867
Music by Max
Published by Oliver Ditson and Co., Boston

The earliest-known lyrical song relating to baseball.
We gather by nines for our national game.

BATTERIN' BABE, 1919
(Look at Him Now)
Words by Jack O'Brien, music by Billy Timmins
"The Home Run Song Hit of the Season"
"Dedicated to our own 'Babe' Ruth"
Published by Colonial Music Publishing Co., Boston
Cover: Photograph of Babe Ruth

He hears the call and then the ball is sailin' in the sky—
A mile away it kills a cow—(Vow)—
And if a bandit on the border gets a baseball in the eye
Put the blame on Babe.
Look at him now—(Wow). Look at him now.

BATTER UP
Jerome (Jerry) Bressler and Lyn Duddy
Published by Ivanhoe Music, Inc. (ASCAP)

BATTER UP
Ervin M. Drake
Published by Lindabet Music Corp. (ASCAP)

BATTER UP
Russell Freeman
Published by Encore Music (ASCAP)

BATTER UP
Chester Gierlach and Leonard Whitecup
Published by General Music Publishing Co., Inc. (ASCAP)

BATTER UP
Frank L. Ventre
Published by Sam Fox Publishing Co., Inc. (ASCAP)

BATTER UP
Published by West Coast Music (ASCAP)

BATTER UP, BATTER UP, PLAY BALL, 1955
Mason Mallory
Published by T. B. Harms Co. (ASCAP)

BATTING SLUMP, 1977
Collin Matthews
Published by Collin Matthews
Copyright date and number: March 10, 1977, EP 367466

BETWEEN YOU AND ME, 1908
A Home Run Hit by "Johnny" Evers and "Joe" B. Tinker
"The Catch of the Season"
Published by Will Rossiter, Chicago
Cover: Photographs of both Cub stars

Popular song as presented by the famous Cub infielders.

BIG CHARLEY! (THE YANKEE PITCHER MAN), 1942
Fred J. Bendel
Published by Fred J. Bendel, West Orange, New Jersey

Dedicated to "my friend, Charley Ruffing."

BIG LEAGUE BABY
Published by Leeds Music Corp., New York (ASCAP)

THE BINGO LONG TRAVELING ALL-STARS AND MOTOR KINGS, 1985
Words by Hy Gilbert, music by George Fischoff
Published by George Fischoff Publishing Co. (ASCAP)

Tribute to the fictional team of touring black all-stars. Included in the musical play, Bingo! (See: Baseball in Theater.)

BLOAT, 1981
Words by Martin Charnin, music by Bob Brush
Published by MPL Communications, Inc.

Included in play dramatizing Jackie Robinson's first year in the major leagues. See: The First. (Baseball in Theater)

BOSTON AMERICANS MARCH TWOSTEP, 1903
J. Ignatius Coveney
"Dedicated to the Boston American Baseball Team, champions of the world"
Published by Cecilian Music Co., Hyde Park, Massachusetts
Cover: Photograph of Jimmy Collins

THE BOYS OF SUMMER, 1984
Words by Ellen Fitzhugh, music by Larry Grossman

Included in the play, Diamonds. (See: Baseball in Theater.)

BRONX TOWN BILL IS A DYIN' (CAUSE THE DODGERS LOST IN THEIR LAST HOME GAME), 1948
Lew Mel, Jim Boyd, and Elmer Wickham
Published by Hill and Range Songs, Hollywood, California

Comic folk ballad about an overly zealous Brooklyn Dodgers' fan.

BROOKLYN DODGERS
Bennie Benjamin and George David
Weiss
Published by Leeds Music Corp.
(ASCAP)

**THE BROOKLYN DODGER
STRIKE, 1981**
Words by Martin Charnin, music by
Bob Brush
Published by MPL Communications,
Inc.

*Included in play dramatizing Jackie Robinson's
first year in the major leagues.* **See: The First**
(Baseball in Theater).

**BUCKY BOY, HIT OF UNCLE
SAM'S FOLLIES, 1925**
Al Stern
Published by Vasco Products, Inc.,
Washington, D.C.
Cover: Photograph of Bucky Harris

*Tribute to the player–manager of the
Washington Senators.*

BUTTER FINGERS, 1943
M. T. Canary
Published by M. T. Canary, Chicago

*A youngster's baseball clumsiness is
remembered.*

**BYE-BYE, BABY (GIANTS FIGHT
SONG), 1961**
Allyn Ferguson and Hugh Heller
Published by Heller-Ferguson, Inc.
Copyright date and number: October
2, 1961, EP 190732

**THE CARDINALS ARE
CHARGING, 1960**
Irving Bibo and Larry Kent
Published by Bibo Music, Inc.
Copyright date and number: June 29,
1960, EP 142304

CASEY AT THE BAT, 1920
Sidney Homer

Published in *Six Cheerful Songs to
Poems of American Humor*
Published by G. Schirmer, Inc., New
York
Cover: Cartoon of two boys admiring
a baseball player

CASEY AT THE BAT, 1935
Published in *The World's Best Famous
Poems and Stories*
Published by Frank Harding, New
York

CASEY AT THE BAT, 1965
Jo'n Milton Hagen
Published by Harmony House of San
Francisco
Copyright date and number: June 21,
1965, EP 206556

CATCH IT ON THE FLY, 1867
L. B. Starkweather
"Dedicated to the Chicago Excelsiors
and the Forest Citys of Rockford,
Illinois"
Published by Lyon and Healy,
Chicago

Come jolly comrade, here's the game
that's played in open air
Where clerks and all the indoor men can
profit by a share
'Twill make the weak man strong again
'Twill brighten every eye
And all who need such exercise should
catch it on the "Fly."

THE CHAMPION GALOP, 1868
Chas D. Blake
"Respectfully dedicated to the
Atlantic Base Ball Club of Brooklyn,
New York"
Published by Oliver Ditson and Co.,
Boston

**CHAMPIONSHIP OF THE
STATE, 1954**
Composed by William Schuman,
libretto by Jerome Gury
Published by G. Schirmer, Inc.

Included in the opera, The Mighty Casey.
(See: Baseball in Theater.)

THE "CHAMPS" OF 1912, 1912
Words by William D. Hurley, music
by Genevieve Scott
Published by H. Kirkus Dugdale Co.,
Washington, D.C.

CHEERING SOMEONE ON, 1936
Words by George Whitefield D'vys,
music by C. Austin Miles
Privately published
See also: Baseball in Poetry and Light
Verse—Collected

CHEER FOR THE CUBS, 1938
Moe Jaffe
Published by Mills Music, Inc.
(ASCAP)

Fight song for the Chicago Cubs. Published in
Batter Up. *(See: Baseball in Music and Song
—Collected.)*

CHEER THE RED SOX, 1967
Joseph A. McOsker
Published by Joseph A. McOsker
Copyright date and number: June 14,
1967, EP 236741

CIN-C-I-N-N-A-TI, 1938
Moe Jaffe
Published by Mills Music, Inc.
(ASCAP)

*Fight Song for the Cincinnati Reds. Published
in* Batter Up. *(See: Baseball in Music and
Song—Collected.)*

CLANCY WASN'T IN IT, 1890
B. H. Janssen
"To Buck Ewing, New York Player's
League"
"Comic Song"
Published by T. B. Harms and Co.,
New York

THE CLIMBERS RAG, 1910
Arthur Sizemore
Published by Stark Music Co.,

St. Louis, Missouri
Cover: Individual photographs of the
St. Louis Cardinals

CLOUD OF JOY, 1985
Words by John Forster, music by
Thomas Tierney

Included in the musical play, The Dream
Team. *(See:* Baseball in Theater.*)*

COME ON BABE, 1947
Isabel Horan and Grace Kohlepp
Published by Morty Berk

Tribute to Babe Ruth.

COME ON PLAY BALL WITH ME DEARIE, 1909
Words by Edward Madden, music by
Gus Edwards
"As sung in F. Ziegfeld Jr.'s Annual
Summer Review of 1909"
Published by Gus Edwards Music
Pub. Co., New York
Cover: Photograph of a women's
baseball game

A chorus girl invites a baseball player to
Come on play with me dearie
I'll "catch" whatever you "throw"
I know lots of places where we can "run
bases"
If you'll only wait for me after the show.

COME ON TO THE BASEBALL GAME, 1911
Words by Wm. A. Downs, music by
Lou Sievers
Published by Harold Rossiter Music
Co., Chicago

COME ON, YOU CUBS, PLAY BALL, 1937
Bernard H. Berquist
Published by Clarion Music Co.
(ASCAP)

COME OUT TO BRAVES FIELD
Words by Harry S. Faunce, music by
"Toots" Mondello

Published by F & M Music Publishing
Co., Boston
Cover: Photograph of night baseball
action.

Tribute to the Boston Braves.

CONNIE MACK IS THE GRAND OLD NAME, 1941
George M. Cohan
Published in the *Philadelphia Record*

Tribute to the Hall of Fame manager of the
Philadelphia Athletics.
Since the great William Penn,
Who's the best loved of men?
Connie Mack, Connie Mack,
Connie Mack.

CONNIE MACK, WE LOVE YOU, 1944
Frank Capano, Jr., Louis Herscher,
and Frank Capano
Published by Tin Pan Alley,
Philadelphia
Cover: Photograph of Connie Mack

THE DAY I PLAYED BASE BALL, 1878
Pat Rooney
Published by E. H. Harding,
New York

Title song of three-song collection. Inner title:
"Irish comic song written, composed and sung
by Pat Rooney."

D-D-D DODGERS, c. 1946
John O'Hara and Charles Turecamo

DE NEW JERUSALEM NINE, 1887
Words by Geo. Russell, music by
J. Little
Published by Louis H. Ross and Co.,
Boston
Cover: Title of song in decorative
script

DIAMONDS ARE FOREVER, 1984

Words by Fred Ebb, music by John
Kander

Included in the play, Diamonds. *(See:*
Baseball in Theater.*)*

THE DODGERS
David H. Broekman
Published by General Music
Publishing Co., Inc. (ASCAP)

THE DODGERS
Sammy Cahn and Jimmy Van Heusen
Published by Van Heusen Music
Corp. (ASCAP)

'DONCHA FEEL PROUD?, 1985
Words by John Forster, music by
Thomas Tierney

Negro League players bitterly ridicule a
teammate for signing with the New York
Yankees. Included in the musical play, The
Dream Team. *(See:* Baseball in Theater.*)*

DREAM TEAM, 1985
Words by John Forster, music by
Thomas Tierney

Included in the musical play, The Dream
Team. *(See:* Baseball in Theater.*)*

FAVORITE SONS, 1984
Words by Ellen Fitzhugh, music by
Larry Grossman

Parents comment on the abilities—and
disabilities—of their Little League-playing
children. Included in the play, Diamonds.
(See: Baseball in Theater.*)*

THE FED'S ARE HERE TO STAY, 1914
Augusta C. Gebhardt
"Dedicated to Chas. Weegham,
President"
Published by Augusta C. Gebhardt,
Chicago
Cover: Architect's rendering of the
Chicago Federal League baseball park

Tribute to the newly formed Federal League—a

Ring Lardner, who gave us such memorable stories as "Alibi Ike" and "Elmer the Great," wrote this utterly forgettable baseball song in 1911. The music was written by Chicago White Sox pitcher Doc White. (National Baseball Library.)

———————

third major league—which was disbanded the following year.

FINNEGAN THE UMPIRE, 1888
Monroe H. Rosenfeld
Supplement to No. 772: "The Boys of New York"

THE FIRST, 1981
Words by Martin Charnin, music by Bob Brush
Published by MPL Communications, Inc.

Title song of play dramatizing Jackie Robinson's first year in the major leagues. (See: Baseball in Theater.)

FIRST BASEMAN BLUES
Jack Fascinato
Privately published (ASCAP)

THE FIRST TIME, 1971
Add Lovejoy

Published by Municorn Music Co. (ASCAP)

Never forgotten is a child's first home run. Published in Johnny Bench Song Book. (See: Baseball in Music and Song—Collected.)

FORDHAM "RAM," 1905
J. Ignatius Coveney
"March and two step"
Published by Fordham University, Fordham, New York
Cover: Photograph of the Fordham baseball team

FOR WE WERE BOYS TOGETHER, 1890
Martin Saxx
"Respectfully dedicated to the Brotherhood Player's League"
Published by Louis H. Ross Co., Boston
Cover: Title of song in decorative script

THE GALLOPING A'S, 1929
Words by Wallace Legrande Henderson, music by Billy James
Published by Pennant Music Co., Philadelphia

For our 'Macks' are socking the old baseball . . .
Hurray, hurray for the Galloping A's . . .

GEE! IT'S A WONDERFUL GAME, 1911
Words by Ring W. Lardner, music by G. Harris (Doc) White
Published by Jerome H. Remick and Co., New York

Doc White pitched in the major leagues for 13 years, mostly for the White Sox. The pair composed another song, titled, "Little Puff of Smoke, Good Night." (See: Baseball in Music and Song: Appendix.)

GIANTS FIGHT SONG, 1961
See: "Bye-Bye, Baby (Giants Fight Song)"

THE GIANT'S MASCOT MARCH, 1895
Mark F. Richardson
"To the New York Base Ball Team"
Published by Duryee Brothers and Co., New York
Cover: Team photograph of the 1895 Giants

THE GIANTS OF 1908, 1908
Max Hoffman
Published by M. Witmark and Sons, New York
Cover: Photographs of Mike Donlin and John McGraw

GOD THREW OUT THE FIRST BALL, 1984
Words by Ellen Fitzhugh, music by Larry Grossman

Gospel song incorporating baseball terminology. Included in the play, Diamonds (See: Baseball in Theater).

———————

The New York Giants gave the pennant winning Chicago Cubs a run for their money in 1908, finishing the year in a tie as a result of the celebrated Merkle incident. The Cubs won the tiebreaker with the Giants and later the world championship over Ty Cobb and the Detroit Tigers. (National Baseball Library.)

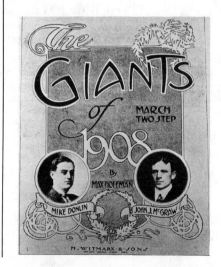

GOODBYE, MR. BALL, 1947
Bill Corum and Harold Smith

Humorous tribute to Pittsburgh Pirates' slugger Hank Greenberg. See also: Broadcast of May 14, 1947 (Baseball in Radio.)

GOTTA GIVE 'EM A SHOW, 1985
Words by Hy Gilbert, music by George Fischoff
Published by George Fischoff Publishing Co. (ASCAP)

A barnstorming team of black all-stars discovers that it must include show business antics in order to bolster attendance to its games. Included in the musical play, Bingo! (See: Baseball in Theater.)

GO YOU DODGERS
John T. Boudreau and Bob Mitchell
Published by Bulls Eye Music, Inc. (ASCAP)

GO, YOU WHITE SOX! GO, GO, GO!, 1959
Robert W. Billings
Published by Billings Publications
Copyright date and number: September 24, 1959, EP 134676

THE GRAND OLD GAME OF BASE BALL, 1912
Lawrence B. O'Connor
''The Great Base Ball March Song 'Hit' ''
Published by L. B. O'Connor Co., Boston
Cover: Illustration of a baseball batter at each corner

HAIL TO THE SENATORS!, 1943
Words by Stanley Rochinski, extra lyrics by Lindsay McPhail, music by Lindsay McPhail
''Official Song of the Washington American League Baseball Club''
Published by Lindsay McPhail, New York
Cover: Photograph of Clark Griffith

A BASEBALL SYMPHONY

Probably the most famous musical group in baseball history was Pepper Martin's Mudcat Band, a quintet of St. Louis Cardinal players who, along with Dizzy Dean, inspired the legendary Gashouse Gang of the 1930s. They appeared several times on the radio performing such tunes as ''Willie, My Toes Is Sore'' and ''Arkansas Traveler.'' The following is an all-time all-star lineup of notable (and not so notable) baseball musicians:

Maury Wills (*shortstop, Los Angeles Dodgers*): banjo
Carmen Fanzone (*second baseman, Chicago Cubs*): trumpet
Pepper Martin (*third baseman, St. Louis Cardinals*): guitar
Babe Ruth (*outfielder, New York Yankees*): saxophone
Charlie Maxwell (*outfielder, Detroit Tigers*): drums
Bob Kennedy (*outfielder, Cleveland Indians*): xylophone
Joe Pepitone (*first baseman, New York Yankees*): harmonica
Frankie Pytlak (*catcher, Cleveland Indians*): mandolin
Denny McLain (*pitcher, Detroit Tigers*): organ

HAMMERIN HANK
Richard R. Segall, Jr.
Published by Colgems EMI Music, Inc. (ASCAP)

Tribute to Hank Aaron.

HE HIT ONE!, 1966
Jane Jarvis and Harry C. Jackson
Published by Sportsmusic, Inc.

Tribute to the New York Mets. Published in Sing Along Baseball Song Book. (See: Baseball in Music and Song—Collected.)

HERE COME THE YANKS, 1938
Moe Jaffe
Published by Mills Music, Inc. (ASCAP)

Fight song for the New York Yankees. Published in Batter Up. (See: Baseball in Music and Song—Collected.)

(HE'S) DADDY'S LITTLE LEAGUER, 1976
Roland D. Wahl
Published by Yampa River Records
Copyright date and number: December 1, 1976, EP 361816

HE STANDS IN THE BOX WITH THE BALL IN HIS HANDS, 1888
Scored by John Philip Sousa

Included in the comic operetta, Angela, or The Umpire's Revenge. (See: Baseball in Miscellaneous Plays and Sketches.)

HEY PLAY BALL
Ray Charles
Published by Roncom Music Co. (ASCAP)

HEY STAR, 1985
Words by John Forster, music by Thomas Tierney

Included in the musical play, The Dream Team. (See: Baseball in Theater.)

HIGH-FLYING RED BIRDS, 1965
Words by Martin Quigley, music by Helen Graham
Privately published

Tribute to the St. Louis Cardinals.

HIST'RY HANGS ON A SLENDER THREAD, 1954
Composed by William Schuman, libretto by Jerome Gury
Published by G. Schirmer, Inc.

One of the earliest musical compositions relating to baseball was "Home Run Quick Step," published in 1861. (National Baseball Library.)

Pitcher ponders the consequences of his next pitch to the slugger Casey. Included in opera, The Mighty Casey. (See: Baseball in Theater.)

HIT THAT BALL
John T. Boudreau and Bob Mitchell
Published by Bulls Eye Music, Inc.
(ASCAP)

HIT THE BALL
Words by John Storm, music by
Harry Jay
Published by John Storm, Wheeling,
West Virginia
Cover: Cartoon illustration of a
baseball batter

HOMER, THE SEAGULL WHO LOVED BASEBALL, 1983
Red River Dave (McEnery)
Published by Scriptomuse Publishing
Co. (ASCAP)

Satirical ballad about outfielder Dave Winfield's

---

accidental killing of a seagull with a thrown ball.

HOME RUN GALOP, 1867
F. W. Root
"To the Atlantic Club of Chicago, the
boys who make 'em"
Published by Root and Cady, Chicago
Cover: Illustration of country baseball
scene

HOME RUN ON THE KEYS, 1937
Zez Confrey
See also: Baseball in Documentary and
Miscellaneous Films

Parody of "Kitten on the Keys" sung by Babe Ruth in a 1937 one-reel film.

HOME RUN POLKA, 1867
Mrs. Bodell
"Respectfully dedicated to the
National Base Ball Club of
Washington, D.C."
Published by Marsh and Bubna,
Philadelphia
Cover: Lithograph of "Massachusetts
game" in progress

HOME RUN QUICK STEP, 1861
John Zebley, Jr.
"Respectfully dedicated to the
Members of the Mercantile Base Ball
Club of Philad."
Published by Lee and Walker,
Philadelphia
Cover: Lithograph by Thomas Sinclair
of fans watching game

HOOP, HOOP, HOOPER UP FOR RED SOX, 1915
Words by Daniel J. Hanifen, music by
Bernard H. Smith
"Base Ball Song"
Published by Smith-Hanifen, Boston
Cover: Illustration of two red socks
hanging from a clothes line

Tribute to Hall of Fame outfielder Harry Hooper.

HUNDREDS OF HATS, 1984
Words by Howard Ashman, music by
Jonathan Sheffer

Nostalgic remembrance of a time when straw hats were thrown onto the field by jubilant fans. Included in the play, Diamonds. (See: Baseball in Theater).

HURRAH FOR OUR NATIONAL GAME, 1868
Written and composed by Walter
Neville of the Olympic B. B. Club of
New York
Published by C. H. Ditson and Co.,
New York
Cover: American eagle and shield

The patrons of Racket may feast on its
joys,
Whilst Cricket its lovers inflame,
Croquet's very well for young ladies and
boys
But give us the National Game.

HURRAY FOR OUR BASE BALL TEAM, 1909
Words by Fred C. Roegge, music by
Berte C. Randall
Published by Charles I. Davis Music
Pub., Cleveland
Cover: Photographs of American
League president Ban Johnson and
National League president H. C.
Pulliam

HUSKY HANS, 1904
Wm. J. Hartz
"A Stirring March and Two-Step
Resp. dedicated to Hans Wagner, 3
times Champion Batsman of the
National League"
Published by Carnegie Union,
Carnegie, Pennsylvania

Tribute to Hall of Famer Honus Wagner of the Pittsburgh Pirates.

I CAN'T GET TO FIRST BASE WITH YOU, 1935

Mrs. Lou Gehrig and Fred Fisher
"Dedicated to Lou Gehrig—Famous
First Baseman"
Published by Fred Fisher Music Co.,
New York
Cover: Photo of Lou Gehrig

Love song incorporating baseball terminology.
I've sacrificed and bunted my heart . . .

I CAUGHT A BALL AT THE BALL GAME
Published by Leeds Music Corp.,
New York (ASCAP)

IF ONLY CASEY, 1954
Composed by William Schuman,
libretto by Jerome Gury
Published by G. Schirmer, Inc.

Chorus and recitation of middle stanzas of
Casey at the Bat. Included in opera, The
Mighty Casey. (See: Baseball in Theater.)

I KNOW A FOUL BALL, 1933
Words by Ira Gershwin, music by
George Gershwin

Included in the musical revue, Let 'em Eat
Cake!, book by George S. Kaufman and Morrie
Ryskind.

I LIKE TO GO TO THE BALL GAMES, 1959
James Sinclair
Published by Studio Music Corp.
Copyright date and number: June 1,
1959, EP 136550

I'LL SEE YA' AT THE WORLD SERIES, 1950
Words by Jack Elliott, music by
Sonny Burke
Published by Robbins Music Corp.,
New York
Cover: Photograph of baseball action

And you can bet that even if I have to
crawl
I am gonna be there when they yell "Play
Ball!"

The sheet music to this 1935 ballad, written as though by Eleanor Gehrig to her famous husband Lou, appears to be as much an advertisement for cigarettes as a paean to love. (National Baseball Library.)

THE ILLINOIS LOYALTY SONG, 1907
Published by University of Illinois
Supply Store, Agents, Champaign,
Illinois
Cover: Photograph of baseball action

I LOVE TO PLAY BASEBALL, 1959
Ralph Killian
Published by Nordyke
Copyright date and number: May 18,
1959, EP 131101

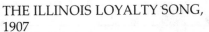

Even the great Irving Berlin struck out occasionally, as he did with this 1913 baseball novelty. (National Baseball Library.)

I'M A BASEBALL FAN
James K. Harbert
Published by Vantage Music (ASCAP)

I'M A JONAH, 1890
Words by Geo. D. Scott, music by
Chas. G. Heitinger
"A Base Ball Song"

292 Published by John F. Ellis and Co.,

Washington

Man claims to be a jinx.
At a party, a picnic, or a game of baseball
I hoodoo them all.

**I'M BASEBALL CRAZY (TIME'S
UP PLAY BALL)**
Nellie Peters and James S. White

Published by James S. White Co.,
Boston
Cover: Cartoon depiction of baseball
action

**I'M IN LOVE WITH THE
DODGERS, 1952**
Robert Sylvester, Billy Hickey, and
Murray Tannen
Published by Jo Golden Music
Publisher (BMI)

THE INDIAN SONG, 1938
Moe Jaffe
Published by Mills Music, Inc.
(ASCAP)

*Fight song for the Cleveland Indians. Published
in* Batter Up. *(See: Baseball in Music and
Song—Collected.)*

IN THE CARDS, 1984
Words by David Zippel, music by
Alan Menken

*Baseball card-collecting youngster dreams of
becoming a ballplayer. Included in the play,*
Diamonds. *(See: Baseball in Theater.)*

**IS THIS YEAR NEXT YEAR?,
1981**
Words by Martin Charnin, music by
Bob Brush
Published by MPL Communications,
Inc.

*Included in play dramatizing Jackie Robinson's
first year in the major leagues. See: The First
(Baseball in Theater).*

IT AIN'T GONNA WORK, 1981
Words by Martin Charnin, music by
Bob Brush
Published by MPL Communications,
Inc.

*Included in play dramatizing Jackie Robinson's
first year in the major leagues. See: The First
(Baseball in Theater).*

IT'S A GIRL'S GAME TOO!, 1971
Add Lovejoy

Published by Municorn Music Co. (ASCAP)

Girl affirms her right to enjoy baseball as much as boys. Published in Johnny Bench Song Book. *(See: Baseball in Music and Song—Collected.)*

IT'S A GRAND OLD GAME, 1931
Harry S. Faunce
Published by C. I. Hicks Music Jobbers, Boston
Cover: Photograph of Yankee Stadium

IT'S DETROIT, 1938
Moe Jaffe
Published by Mills Music, Inc. (ASCAP)

Fight song for the Detroit Tigers. Published in Batter Up. *(See: Baseball in Music and Song—Collected.)*

IT'S IN THE CARDS, 1938
Moe Jaffe
Published by Mills Music, Inc. (ASCAP)

Fight song for the St. Louis Cardinals. Published in Batter Up. *(See: Baseball in Music and Song—Collected.)*

I WAN-TA GO TO THE BALL-GAME, 1927
Tell Taylor
Published by Tell Taylor, New York

I WANT TO BE AT THE BALLGAME, 1967
Robert E. Miller
"A Great Marching Song"
Published by Midwestern Music Co., Chicago

I WANT TO GO OUT TO THE BALL GAME TO-DAY
M. H. West
Published by A. W. Perry's Sons, Sedalia, Missouri

I WANT TO GO TO THE BALL GAME, 1909
Words by C. P. McDonald, music by Al. W. Brown
Published by Victor Kremer Co., Chicago
Cover: Illustration of a young man and woman watching a baseball game

I WON'T GO HOME 'TIL THE LAST MAN'S OUT, 1912
Words by F. C. Brautigam, music by F. W. Rivarde and J. G. Kurtz
Published by Rivarde and Co., Rochester, New York

JACK RABBIT THE HOME RUN BUNNY
Ruth Roberts
Published by Michael Brent Publications, Inc. (ASCAP)

JACK ROOSEVELT ROBINSON, 1981
Words by Martin Charnin, music by Bob Brush
Published by MPL Communications, Inc.

Included in play dramatizing Jackie Robinson's first year in the major leagues. See: The First *(Baseball in Theater).*

JAKE! JAKE! (THE YIDDISHA BALL PLAYER), 1913
Words by Blanche Merrill, music by Irving Berlin
Published by Waterson, Berlin and Snyder Co., New York

JOHN J. MCGRAW (HE'S A CREDIT TO THE USA), 1923
Betty Conners
Privately published: New York

Tribute to the Hall of Fame manager of the New York Giants.

JOOSTA LIKE BABE-A-DA RUTH, 1928

James Kendis
Published by Mills Music, Inc., New York

Ethnic tribute to Babe Ruth.

KA-RAZY, 1984
Words by David Zippel, music by Doug Katsaros

Fans are crazy about baseball. Included in the play, Diamonds. *(See: Baseball in Theater.)*

KING OF CLUBS, 1912
(Ty Cobb)
Wm. Brede
Published by Will Rossiter, Chicago
Cover: Photograph of Ty Cobb

Tribute to the Hall of Fame outfielder for the Detroit Tigers.

LAMENT FOR THE WHOLE BASEBALL WORLD, 1957
Jack Segal and Madeline Segal
Published by Mills Music, Inc. (ASCAP)

Included in the musical, A Man's Game *(1957). (See: Baseball in Television.)*

LAST HALF OF THE NINTH, 1954
Composed by William Schuman, libretto by Jerome Gury
Published by G. Schirmer, Inc.

Recitation of first stanza of Casey at the Bat. *Included in opera,* The Mighty Casey. *(See: Baseball in Theater.)*

LEAVE US GO ROOT FOR THE DODGERS, RODGERS, 1942
Words by Dan Parker and Bud Green, music by Ted Berkman
Published by Green Bros. and Knight, New York
See also: Baseball in Poetry and Light Verse

In 1912, when this musical tribute was published, Ty Cobb batted .410 and stole 61 bases—and that represented an off-year for the Detroit Tigers star. The year before he had batted .420 and had swiped 83 bases. Needless to say, Ty Cobb was baseball's undisputed king of batsmen during the early 1900s. (National Baseball Library.)

LEON'S SOLILOQUY (GET WHILE THE GETTIN'S GOOD), 1985
Words by Hy Gilbert, music by George Fischoff
Published by George Fischoff Publishing Co. (ASCAP)

Aging pitcher wonders if he has enough left to pitch yet another year. Included in the musical play, Bingo! (See: Baseball in Theater.)

LES EXPOS SONT LÀ, 1969
(Expos Baseball Song)
English words by Pat McDougall

Published by Editions Musicales, Marco Enrq., Montreal

Tribute to the Montreal Expos.

LET'S GO METS, 1966
Jane Jarvis and Harry C. Jackson
Published by Sportsmusic, Inc.

Published in Sing Along Baseball Song Book. (See: *Baseball in Music and Song—Collected.*)

LET'S GO OUT TO THE BALLGAME, 1949
William Benson Richter
Published by William Benson Richter (ASCAP)
Cover: Photograph of Connie Mack

LET'S GO PADRES, 1969
Preston Foster
Published by Oz Music Publishers (ASCAP)

Official song of the San Diego Padres.

LET'S HAVE A BALL AT THE BALL GAME
Oscar Washington
Published by Solo Music Publishers, St. Louis, Missouri
Cover: Cartoon depiction of a youngster watching a baseball game

LET'S PLAY BALL, 1984
Gerard Alessandrini

Celebration of the joys of baseball. Included in the play, Diamonds. (See: Baseball in Theater.)

LET'S ROOT FOR THE METS
Vincent Lopez and Johnny Messner
Published by Vincent Lopez Music Co. (ASCAP)

LITTLE LEAGUER
Mundell Lowe
Published by Knollwood Music Corp. (ASCAP)

LITTLE LEAGUER BASEBALL MAN, 1960
Louise Lewis and Everett L. Whenham
Published by Skyway Records and Music Pub. Co.
Copyright date and number: February 17, 1960, EP 141514

LITTLE LEAGUERS
William C. Barnes
Published by Tylerson Music Co. (ASCAP)

THE LIVE OAK POLKA, 1860
J. H. Kalbfleisch
"And respectfully dedicated to the Live Oak Base Ball Club, Rochester, New York"
Published by Jos. P. Shaw, Rochester, New York
Cover: Lithograph of country baseball scene

Official song of the Rochester, New York baseball club.

MAGNATES MARCH, 1897
Henry Ditzel
"Respectfully dedicated to the Magnates of the National League and the American Association of Base Ball Clubs"
Published by Otto Sutro and Co., Baltimore, Maryland
Cover: Group photograph of 17 baseball club owners and officials

MAKE A NOISE LIKE A FAN, 1910
Words by A. Seymour Brown, music by Nat. D. Ayer
Published by Jerome H. Remick and Co., New York
Cover: Illustration of fans cheering baseball action

MANDA AT THE BASE BALL GAME

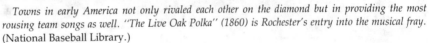

Towns in early America not only rivaled each other on the diamond but in providing the most rousing team songs as well. "The Live Oak Polka" (1860) is Rochester's entry into the musical fray. (National Baseball Library.)

Words by N. Campbell, music by Charles J. W. Jerreld
Published by H. Kirkus Dugdale Co., Washington, D.C.
Cover: Cartoon of a female baseball fan

A MAN'S GAME, 1957
Jack Segal
Published by Mills Music, Inc. (ASCAP)
See also: Baseball in Television

Title song of musical produced for television.

MARCH OF THE CARDINALS, 1937
George M. Cohan
"Official march of the St. Louis National Baseball Club"
Published by Jerry Vogel Music Co., Inc., New York

THE MARCH OF THE CHAMPS, 1941
Will H. Palmer
"The Official March of the Cincinnati Reds"
Published by The Modern Music Publ. Co., Cincinnati

THE MARCH OF THE MIDGET METS, 1966
Jane Jarvis and Harry C. Jackson
Published by Sportsmusic, Inc.

Published in Sing Along Baseball Song Book. (See: *Baseball in Music and Song—Collected.*)

THE MARQUARD GLIDE, 1912
Words by Rube Marquard and Thomas J. Gray, music by Blossom Seeley and W. Raymond Walker
"From a skit presented at

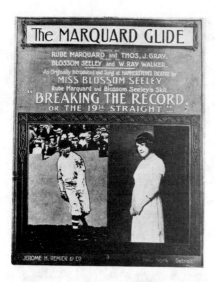

Pitcher Rube Marquard of the New York Giants was feted with this musical tribute after winning 19 consecutive games during the 1912 season and two more games in the World Series against the Boston Red Sox. The song was incorporated into a vaudeville sketch starring Marquard and his wife, Blossom Seeley. (National Baseball Library.)

Hammerstein's Theatre, *Breaking the Record, or the 19th Straight"*
Published by Jerome H. Remick and Co., New York
See also: Baseball in Miscellaneous Plays and Sketches

A dance melody in tribute to pitcher Rube Marquard, who won 26 games for the New York Giants in 1912.

MEET ME AT THE OLD BALL GAME, 1946
Wendall Hall
Published by Paul Pioneer Music Corp., Delaware Water Gap, Pennsylvania

MEET THE METS, 1966
Jane Jarvis and Harry C. Anderson
Published by Sportsmusic, Inc.

Published in Sing Along Baseball Song Book. (See: *Baseball in Music and Song—Collected.)*

296

A SONG AND A PRAYER

In 1860, not long before an eagerly awaited game with the celebrated Brooklyn Excelsiors, the Live Oak Base Ball Club of Rochester, New York, commissioned a local music teacher to compose a victory song. But what they really needed was a prayer.

For the Excelsiors, led by superstar pitcher James Creighton and rightfielder Asa Brainard, were the class of baseball. In June of that year, 1860, they embarked on the first tour ever made by a baseball club, with tales of Creighton's legendary fastball and underhand "wrist" pitch preceding them at every turn. Working their way upstate to Rochester, the Excelsiors handily defeated every club they met, including Albany, 24 to 6, the Victory Club of Troy, 13 to 7, and a strong Niagara Club, 50 to 19—the highest score ever recorded up to that time.

At last, the Live Oak Club—boasting their new team song "The Live Oak Polka"—welcomed their big city guests. Like the other upstate teams, the Rochester club proved to be an easy match for the Excelsiors, however, as they were walloped, 27 to 9.

Upon returning from their triumphant tour, the Excelsiors met the Atlantics of Brooklyn in a three-game "championship" match, played before the largest crowds ever assembled for a baseball game. On the strength of Creighton's expert pitching—and an abbreviated third game—the Excelsiors successfully completed baseball's first tour by defeating the Atlantics, two games to one.

THE MIGHTY CASEY, 1954
Composed by William Schuman, libretto by Jerome Gury
Published by G. Schirmer, Inc.

Members of the Mudville Nine introduce themselves. Title song of opera. (See: Baseball in Theater.)

THE MILLIONAIRES, 1908
D. C. Henninger
Published by Vandersloot Music Publishing Co., Williamsport, Pennsylvania
Cover: Photograph of the 1908 Williamsport baseball club

MISTER BASEBALL
John T. Boudreau and Johnny Lange

Published by Bulls Eye Music, Inc. (ASCAP)

THE MOST WELCOME SOUND, 1971
Add Lovejoy
Published by Municorn Music Co. (ASCAP)

The most welcome sound is the umpire's cry of "Play ball!" Published in Johnny Bench Song Book. (See: *Baseball in Music and Song—Collected.)*

MY OLD MAN IS BASEBALL MAD, 1910
Edward Clark
Published by Harry Von Tilzer Music Pub. Co., New York

Cover: Baseball bats arranged in the form of a player

THE NATIONAL GAME, 1909
Words by Chas. Horwitz, music by F. V. Bowers
Published by Jerome H. Remick and Co., New York

Production number of 11 pages, with parts for soloist and chorus. Included in the play, Commencement Days.

NATIONAL PASTIME
Lee J. Pockriss and Paul Vance
Published by Emily Music Corp./ Music of the Times Publishing Corp. (ASCAP)

THE NATIONAL PASTIME, 1981
Words by Martin Charnin, music by Bob Brush
Published by MPL Communications, Inc.

Included in play dramatizing Jackie Robinson's first year in the major leagues. See: The First (Baseball in Theater).

NEW YORK GIANTS' MARCH, 1895
W. A. Gardner
Published by W. A. Gardner, New York
Cover: Vignette portraits of New York Giants' players

NEW YORK METS CLAPPING SONG, 1966
Jane Jarvis and Harry C. Jackson
Published by Sportsmusic, Inc.

Published in Sing Along Baseball Song Book. (See: Baseball in Music and Song—Collected.)

1919, 1984
Jim Wann

Ballad about Shoeless Joe Jackson and the 1919 ''Black Sox'' scandal. Included in the play, Diamonds. (See: Baseball in Theater.)

NOW WHY DON'T YOU PLAY BALL THERE, 1910
(When Smithie Took the Widow to the Ball Game)
Words by E. Enkelman, music by Myron A. Bickford
Published by Belmont Music Co., Springfield, Massachusetts
Cover: Cartoon of a baseball batter

O'GRADY AT THE GAME, 1891
Geo. C. Edwards
''Sung with great success by Edward Leslie of Leclair and Leslie''
''Comic Song''
Published by Chas. W. Held, Brooklyn

OH, SOMEWHERE, 1954
Composed by William Schuman, libretto by Jerome Gury
Published by G. Schirmer, Inc.

Chorus and recitation of final stanza of Casey at the Bat. Included in opera, The Mighty Casey. (See: Baseball in Theater.)

OH! YOU ''BABE'' RUTH, 1920
Words by Wm. V. Hart, music by Ed. G. Nelson
Published by Hart Music Co., New York
Cover: Photograph of Babe Ruth

Musical tribute to the New York Yankees' slugger.

OH, YOU REDS!, 1919
Hayden Hendy
Published by Haden Hendy, Cincinnati, Ohio

Tribute to the National League champion Cincinnati Reds.

ONE TO NOTHING, 1885
Sydney Rosenfeld

Included in the American adaptation of the musical play, The Black Hussar, starring DeWolf Hopper and Digby Bell.

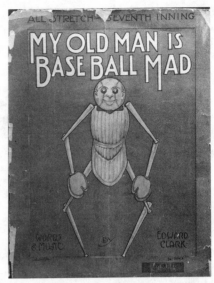

In 1910, when this whimsical song was published, baseball cards came with each pack of cigarettes, the great Mathewson reigned supreme on the mound, Cobb wreaked havoc on the bases, sixteen teams played in intimate ballyards during the day—and all of America was baseball mad. (National Baseball Library.)

ON THE ROAD WITH THE ROADRUNNERS, 1985
Words by John Forster, music by Thomas Tierney

Included in the musical play, The Dream Team. (See: Baseball in Theater.)

THE OPERA AIN'T OVER, 1981
Words by Martin Charnin, music by Bob Brush
Published by MPL Communications, Inc.

Included in play dramatizing Jackie Robinson's first year in the major leagues. See: The First. (Baseball in Theater.)

OUR BALL TEAM, 1897
John Griffin
''March and Two-Step''
Published by Holy Ghost College, Pittsburgh, Pennsylvania

A ROUGHHOUSE GAME

In the 1800s, baseball, especially small-town baseball, was often a lawlessly played, rough-and-tumble game. Not infrequently, the game was the dominion of ruffians and rowdies who played before crowds of gamblers and thugs. As one might suspect, some contests never reached a complete nine-inning conclusion, as the lyrics to an 1890 comic song, "Play Ball," attest:

. . . When our side got [to] fielding,
    McClosky made a muff,
And someone on the benches yelled,
    "McClosky you're a 'stuff' ";
At that, poor Mac got awful mad and
    grabbed a bat to fire,
It missed the man upon the stand and
    struck the poor umpire.
The captain of the "Neversweats"
    began to scrowl and frown,
Before the man had time to think,
    McClosky had him down.
Oh! I myself was scared to death, and
    from the field I fled,

And when the fight was at its height,
    the umpire to us said:
Play ball, play ball! You'd give a
    man a fit.
You muffers, you bluffers, you cannot play a bit.
To make [them] pay a quarter each,
    you have an awful gall.
All through the game they would
    exclaim: "Play ball, play ball!"

Words and music by William B. Glenroy.
© Copyright 1890 by Spaulding and Kornder.

Cover: Panorama of a college baseball game

Tribute to a Pittsburgh seminary team.

OUR BAMBINO, 1948
(Baseball's National Anthem)
Iva Phillips, Bud Averill, and Hayden Simpson
Published by Richardson Songs, Beverly Hills, California
Cover: Photograph of Babe Ruth swinging a bat

Tribute to Hall of Famer Babe Ruth.

OUR NOBLE GIANT NINE, 1889
Monroe H. Rosenfeld
Published by Hitchcock's Music Stores, New York

Tribute to the New York Giants.

PEANUTS, POPCORN, SODA, CRACKERJACKS, 1954
Composed by William Schuman, libretto by Jerome Gury
Published by G. Schirmer, Inc.

Vendors sing a litany of their wares. Included in opera, The Mighty Casey. *(See: Baseball in Theater.)*

THE PENNANT WINNER, 1900
A. Albin LeRoy
"March and Two-Step"
Published by John B. Meiler, Dayton, Ohio

PENNANT WINNER
John T. Boudreau and Bob Mitchell
Published by Bulls Eye Music, Inc. (ASCAP)

THE PIRATES ARE ON YOUR TRAIL, 1938
Moe Jaffe
Published by Mills Music, Inc. (ASCAP)

Fight song for the Pittsburgh Pirates. Published in Batter Up. *(See: Baseball in Music and Song—Collected.)*

PIZZA PARTY, 1971
Add Lovejoy
Published by Municorn Music Co. (ASCAP)

Youngsters enjoy baseball despite losing the game. Published in Johnny Bench Song Book. *(See: Baseball in Music and Song—Collected.)*

PLAY BALL, 1890
William B. Glenroy
Published by Spaulding and Kornder

Comic song about a rough-and-tumble small-town baseball game.

PLAY BALL!, 1922
Hal. Parker
"The Greatest Baseball Hit of the Century"
"There's a man named Holy Moses coming to our town"
Published by The New York Song and Music Mart, New York

Holy Moses, an evangelist, . . . is going to lick the devil in a three ring baseball game.

PLAY BALL, 1952
John A. McGee
Published by John A. McGee, Sarasota, Florida

PLAY BALL, 1954
Dinnie Mae Mackey
Published by Mrs. J. M. Woolard, Richmond, Virginia

Girls express their desire to play baseball.
What baseball needs is females
But they won't let us play . . .

Included in the play, Play Ball. (See: Baseball in Miscellaneous Plays and Sketches.)

PLAY BALL
Lee Erwin and Mel Howard
Published by Erwin Howard Music
Corp. (ASCAP)

PLAY BALL
Mel B. Kaufman
Published by Robbins Music Corp.,
New York (ASCAP)

PLAY BALL
Charles Martin and Art McKennan
Published by Beatrix Music, Inc.
(ASCAP)

PLAY BALL
Paul Reif
Published by Leo Feist, Inc. (ASCAP)

PLAY BALL
Henry Sylvern
Published by Templeton Publishing
Co., Inc. (ASCAP)

PLAY BALL MONTREAL, 1928
Words by Larry Andrews, music by
Fred Carbonneau
Published by Popular Music
Publishing Co., Ltd., Montreal,
Canada
Cover: Photograph of the 1928
Montreal baseball club

Tribute to the Montreal minor league team.

PLAYING FIRST BASE
Jeffrey A. Moss
Published by Festival Attractions, Inc.
(ASCAP)

PLAYING THE GAME, c. 1929
No author given
Published in *The Music Hour: Volume 3*
Published by Silver, Burdett and Co.,
New York

Children's baseball song.

This musical composition is a tribute to the fabled Cincinnati Red Stockings, the first professional club in baseball's history and winner of 56 consecutive games during the 1869 season. At center is pitcher Asa Brainard, who delivered his fastball with a menacing spin to it and who was often inclined to brush a batter back. Manager and centerfielder Harry Wright is pictured at top center. Shortstop George Wright, Harry's brother and the team's best fielder and hitter, is pictured at bottom, second from left. (National Baseball Library.)

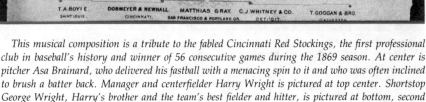

A PRAYER, 1954
Composed by William Schuman,
libretto by Jerome Gury
Published by G. Schirmer, Inc.

Casey's sweetheart offers a request in behalf of the Mudville Nine. Included in opera, The Mighty Casey. (See: Baseball in Theater.)

THE PRINCETON DUTCHMAN, 1906
(Der Dutchman aus Nassau)
John B. Thomas
Published by Edw. J. Van Marter,
Princeton

Dat Princeton man he trows such balls,
Dat Yalesmen cannot see.
Dat Yalesman ven he hits dat ball,
He hits it not at all.

PUT THE BALL OVER THE PAN, MCCANN, 1910
Words by A. G. Delamater, music by
Wm. Frederick Peters
"Song Hits from William Norris'
Successful Musical Farce *My Cinderella Girl*"
Published by Independent Music Co.,
Chicago

RAINY SATURDAY, 1971
Add Lovejoy
Published by Municorn Music Co.
(ASCAP)

Youngster bemoans a rained-out baseball game. Published in Johnny Bench Song Book. (See: Baseball in Music and Song—Collected.)

THE RED SOX SPEED BOYS, 1907
Words by Henry E. Casey, music by
Martin Barrett
Published by Martin Barrett,
Brookline, Massachusetts
Cover: Illustration of a baseball batter

The slow-footed Boston Red Sox are satirized.

THE RED STOCKINGS, 1869
(Polka, Schottisch, and March)

Mrs. Hettie Shirley Austin
"To the Ladies of Cincinnati"
Published by J. L. Peters, New York
Cover: Lithograph of Asa Brainard
pitching

Tribute to the Cincinnati Red Stockings, baseball's first professional team, who finished the 1869 season with a 56–0 record.

RHUBARB, 1954
Composed by William Schuman,
libretto by Jerome Gury
Published by G. Schirmer, Inc.

Fans and players protest umpire's called strike one against Casey. Included in opera, The Mighty Casey. (See: Baseball in Theater.)

THE ROOKIE, 1971
Add Lovejoy
Published by Municorn Music Co.
(ASCAP)

Humorous song about a youngster's lack of baseball ability. Published in Johnny Bench Song Book. (See: Baseball in Music and Song–Collected.)

ROOTERS, 1911
John F. Barth
"March-Two Step"
"Dedicated to all loyal rooters"
Published by The Eastman Co.,
Cleveland
Cover: Photograph of stands with
rooters cheering

ROOT FOR THE BOSTON RED SOX, 1938
Moe Jaffe
Published by Mills Music, Inc.
(ASCAP)

Fight song for the Boston Red Sox. Published in Batter Up. (See: Baseball in Music and Song–Collected.)

ROOT THE REDS HOME
Barney Rapp
Published by Buckeye Music, Inc.
(ASCAP)

ROSE POLKA, 1878
William A. Dietrich
"Dedicated to the California B. B.
Club"
Published by Sherman, Hyde and
Co., San Francisco, California
Cover: Team photograph of the
California club

THE ST. LOUIS BROWNS, 1938
Moe Jaffe
Published by Mills Music, Inc.
(ASCAP)

Fight song for the American League St. Louis Browns. Published in Batter Up. (See: Baseball in Music and Song–Collected.)

SCREWBALL BASEBALL
Scott Bradley
Published by Leo Feist, Inc. (ASCAP)

SHORTSTOP
Danny Hurd and Eddie Safranski
Privately published (ASCAP)

SILVER BALL MARCH, 1869
Chas. D. Blake
"Respectfully dedicated to the Lowell
Base Ball Club of Boston"
Published by Oliver Ditson and Co.,
Boston
Cover: Decorative pattern with ball
and bats

SLIDE, BILL, SLIDE, 1909
John B. Lowitz
"The 'Three Bagger' Baseball Song"
Published by The Trebuhs Publishing
Co., Inc., New York
Cover: Cartoon of runner sliding
head-first into home

SONG FOR A HUNTER COLLEGE GRADUATE, 1984
Words by Howard Ashman, music by
Jonathan Sheffer

Woman baseball fan shouts a continuous stream of obscenities at umpires and players. Included in the play, Diamonds. (See: Baseball in Theater.)

SONG OF THE "HAYMAKERS"
Nat Wood
"Respectfully dedicated to the Union Base Ball Club of Lansingsburgh"

Now let us show the lads we meet we play a noble game . . .

THE SONG OF THE "LOYAL GIANT ROOTERS," 1929
Dr. Charles B. Mandelbaum
"Dedicated to John J. McGraw and the New York Giants"
Privately published
Cover: Photograph of John McGraw

SOUTHPAW, 1971
Add Lovejoy
Published by Municorn Music Co. (ASCAP)

Humorous song about a left-handed youngster who uses a right-hander's mitt. Published in Johnny Bench Song Book. (See: Baseball in Music and Song—Collected.)

SPALDING'S BASE BALL TOURISTS AROUND THE WORLD GRAND MARCH, 1889
Fred T. Baker
Published by Wm. H. Boner and Co., Philadelphia

Tribute to the Chicago White Stockings' world tour of Australia, Egypt, and England, undertaken after the 1888 season.

THE SPECTATOR
Joseph Perrong
"March and Two Step"
Published by Edward A. Bowen, Malden, Massachusetts
Cover: Boy looking through a knot-hole in the fence

SPLENDID SPLINTER
David McKenna

Published by Maximum Music Corp. (ASCAP)

Tribute to Ted Williams.

STARS OF THE NATIONAL GAME, 1908
Words by James O'Dea, music by Anna Caldwell
Published by Jerome H. Remick and Co., New York
Cover: Cartoons representing each team in the major leagues

If I'm somewhat hanky-panky
O'er a game that's strictly Yankee . . .

STAY IN YOUR OWN BACK YARD, 1984
Words by Karl Kenneth, music by Lynn Udall
Additional music by Pam Drews

Evocation of baseball stars from the Negro Leagues. Included in the play, Diamonds. (See: Baseball in Theater.)

STEAL! SLIDE! ANYWAY!, 1889
Words by Virginia Duncan, music by James Mascotte
"Dedicated to The New York Base Ball Club"
Published by N. Weinstein, New York

Steal! Slide! Anyway! So we get around!
What are padded trousers for,
But plowing up the ground?

STRATEGY, 1954
Composed by William Schuman, libretto by Jerome Gury
Published by G. Schirmer, Inc.

Included in opera, The Mighty Casey. (See: Baseball in Theater.)

THE SUPERBUC SONG, 1972
Vince Lascheid
Published by Volkwein Bros., Inc.,

Pittsburgh, Pennsylvania

Tribute to the Pittsburgh Pirates.

SUPERSTAR, 1982
Words by Paul and Alan Rolnick, music by Udo Jurgens
Published by Pioneer Drama Service, Inc., Denver, Colorado

Baseball player's sweetheart declares her love. Included in the musical play, Seasons in the Sun. (See: Baseball in Miscellaneous Plays and Sketches.)

SURE! YOU'RE OFF YOUR BASE AGAIN, PAT MCCANN, 1893
Theo. H. Northrup
Published by National Music Co., Chicago

SURPRISE, 1954
Composed by William Schuman, libretto by Jerome Gury
Published by G. Schirmer, Inc.

Chorus and recitation of middle stanzas of Casey at the Bat. Included in opera, The Mighty Casey. (See: Baseball in Theater.)

THE SWINGIN' A'S, c. 1972
(A Victory March)
Harold Farberman

Tribute to the Oakland Athletics.

TALLY ONE FOR ME, 1877
John T. Rutledge
"Base Ball Song and Chorus"
Published by F. W. Helmick, Cincinnati
Cover: Illustration of a game in progress

A baseball player boasts about his way with the ladies.

TEAMWORK, 1971
Add Lovejoy
Published by Municorn Music Co. (ASCAP)

WORDS-ON-PLAY

It is positively astonishing to learn how quickly baseball jargon was incorporated into the American idiom. Terms such as *keystone base,* meaning second base, and *daisy cutter,* indicating a hard-hit ground ball, were commonly used almost from the day the New York Knickerbockers, baseball's first organized club, took the field in 1842. In the following lighthearted song, ''Tally One for Me,'' it is clear that the vernacular of baseball is already firmly established. The year of the song's publication was 1877:

> I'm the pride and pet of all the girls
>   That come out to the park,
> My ev'ry play out in the field,
>   You bet they're sure to mark.
> And when you see them smiling
>   And their hands go pit-a-pat,
> Just mark it down, for number one
>   Is going to the bat.

> I never knock the ball up high,
>   Or even make it bound,
> But always send it whizzing,
>   Cutting daisies in the ground.
> I always make a clean base hit,
>   And go around, you see.
> And that's the reason why I say,
>   Just tally one for me.

> I soon will stop my base-balling,
>   For my heart is led astray,
> 'Twas stolen by a nice young girl,
>   By her exquisite play.
> And after we are married,
>   Why, I hope you'll come to see,
> The ''tally'' I have made for life,
>   And mark it down for me.

Words and music by John T. Rutledge. © Copyright 1877 by F. W. Helmick.

Child realizes the importance of teamwork in baseball. Published in Johnny Bench Song Book. *(See:* Baseball in Music and Song– Collected.)*

THE TEMPLE CUP TWO-STEP MARCH, 1894
John W. Cavanagh
''Dedicated to Our Champions, the New York Base Ball Club''
Published by Howley, Haviland and Co., New York
Cover: Team photograph of the New York Giants

Tribute to the winner of the Temple Cup—the predecessor to the modern-day World Series.

THERE'S GOLD IN THEM THERE PHILS, 1938
Moe Jaffe
Published by Mills Music, Inc. (ASCAP)

Fight song for the Philadelphia Phillies.

Published in Batter Up. *(See:* Baseball in Music and Song–Collected.)*

THEY ALL KNOW COBB, 1913
William Murphy
''Base Ball Song and Chorus''
Published by Wm. Murphy, Endicott, New York
Cover: Illustration of Ty Cobb swinging a bat

A man attends his first baseball game and is ridiculed for being unaware of Ty Cobb's notoriety.

THIRD BASE ROCK
H. Cannon and Saul Ilson
Published by Absegami Music Co. (ASCAP)

THIS GLADDENED MULTITUDE, 1954
Composed by William Schuman, libretto by Jerome Gury
Published by G. Schirmer, Inc.

Chorus and recitation of middle stanzas of Casey at the Bat. *Included in opera,* The Mighty Casey. *(See:* Baseball in Theater.)*

THIS IS BASEBALL, 1962
Words by Solita Palmer, music by James Ployhar
Published by Marlen Music Co., Beverly Hills, California
Cover: Emblems of the major league teams

''THREE CHEERS!'' BASE-BALL IS A GRAND OLD GAME, 1912
Words by Clarence Gaskill, music by Billy Parker
Published by Emmett J. Welch, Philadelphia

TIGERS ON PARADE, 1934
J. Fred Lawton and Will E. Dulmage
''Introduced by Harry A. McDonald''
''Dedicated to Mickey Cochrane and the Tigers''

Published by Hartway Publishing Co., Detroit

Tribute to the American League champion Detroit Tigers.

TRI-STATE MARCH TWO-STEP, 1906
Harry J. Lincoln
Published by Vandersloot Music Co., Williamsport, Pennsylvania
Cover: Illustration of a baseball batter

THE TRIUMPHANT MARCH, 1909
Chas. W. Glass and Geo. R. Hunt
"Respectfully dedicated to the Pittsburg Baseball Club and their new home Forbes Field"
Published by Lechner and Schoenberger Co., Pittsburgh, Pennsylvania
Cover: Panoramic view of Forbes Field

TURN ME LOOSE AT THE BALLGAME
Charles Weir
Published by Will Lewis, Chicago

A TWO BAGGER, 1910
Charles Stutzman
"Two Step and March"
Published by Stutzman Music Co., Williamsport, Pennsylvania
Cover: Comic drawing of baseball action

TWO OUT, 1954
Composed by William Schuman, libretto by Jerome Gury
Published by G. Schirmer, Inc.

Chorus and recitation of middle stanzas of Casey at the Bat. Included in opera, The Mighty Casey. (See: Baseball in Theater.)

TYRO BASE BALL MARCH, 1870
Alice Rice

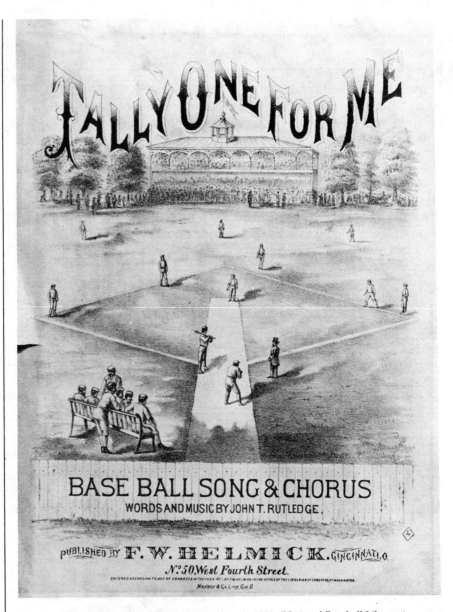

This lighthearted baseball song was written in 1877. (National Baseball Library.)

"Dedicated to the Tyro Base Ball Club of Detroit"

THE UMPIRE AND THE DUDE, 1888
Scored by John Philip Sousa

Included in the comic operetta, Angela, or The Umpire's Revenge. *(See: Baseball in Miscellaneous Plays and Sketches.)*

AN UMPIRE I, WHO NE'ER SAY DIE, 1888
Scored by John Philip Sousa

THE FIRST "WORLD SERIES"

The present-day World Series was not baseball's first officially sanctioned championship series. In 1894—nine years before the modern World Series was inaugurated in 1903—a Pittsburgh sportswriter, William C. Temple, arranged for a 42-inch tall loving cup to be awarded to the winner of a best-of-seven series between the first and second place teams of the National League. That year Ned Hanlon's Baltimore Orioles, whose lineup featured six future Hall of Famers (Dan Brouthers, Hughie Jennings, John McGraw, Wee Willie Keeler, Joe Kelley, and Wilbert Robinson) finished first over John Montgomery Ward's New York Giants, led by two 36-game winning pitchers, Jouett Meekin and Hall of Famer Amos Rusie. In the series, however, the Giants defeated the legendary Orioles, four games to none. Not long afterwards, a song "The Temple Cup Two-step March" was written in tribute to the triumphant victors of the $500 trophy.

The Temple Cup series continued for the next three years, but disagreements over the division of gate receipts by the two competing clubs spelled the demise of the championship series. Except for this quirk in baseball history, the name of today's fall classic might more closely resemble hockey's Stanley Cup than the present, as yet not quite international, World Series.

Included in the comic operetta, *Angela, or the Umpire's Revenge*. (See: *Baseball in Miscellaneous Plays and Sketches*.)

UNA SCHOTTISCHE, 1874
M. J. Messer
"To the Una Base Ball Club, Charlestown, Junior Champions, 1870–72–73"
Published by G. D. Russell and Co., Boston
Cover: Illustration of a pitcher

UNION BASE BALL CLUB MARCH, 1867
T. M. Brown
"To the Members of the Union Base Ball Club, Champions of Missouri"
Published by Rich. J. Compton, St. Louis, Missouri
Cover: Vignettes of team members

UP THE HILL WITH GIL!, 1968
Alfred E. Motta
Published by Baba Motta
Copyright date and number: May 21, 1968, EP 245536

VENDORS (#1–3), 1984
Words by Betty Comden and Adolph Green, music by Cy Coleman

Song fragments about ballpark peanut vendors. Included in the play, Diamonds. *(See:* Baseball in Theater.*)*

VICTORY FOR THE BEES, 1938
Moe Jaffe
Published by Mills Music, Inc. (ASCAP)

Fight song for the National League Boston Bees. Published in Batter Up. *(See:* Baseball in Music and Song–Collected.*)*

VICTORY SONG, 1971
Add Lovejoy
Published by Municorn Music Co. (ASCAP)

Victory march for baseball-playing youngsters. Published in Johnny Bench Song Book *(See:* Baseball in Music and Song–Collected.*)*

WANNA GO OUT TO THE BASEBALL GAME, 1950
Winnie E. Hodge
Published by Shamrock Music Publishers, Inc., Houston, Texas
Cover: Names of major and minor league teams

WATCH THE SENATORS, 1938
Moe Jaffe
Published by Mills Music, Inc. (ASCAP)

Fight song for the American League Washington Senators. Published in Batter Up. *(See:* Baseball in Music and Song–Collected.*)*

WE PLAY BASEBALL!, 1979
Larry Nestor
Published by Lardon Music, River Grove, Illinois

WE'RE A TEAM, 1985
Words by Hy Gilbert, music by George Fischoff
Published by George Fischoff Publishing Co. (ASCAP)

A barnstorming baseball team vows to remain together regardless of the consequences. Included in the musical play, Bingo! *(See:* Baseball in Theater.*)*

WE'RE GOING TO SEE A BASE BALL GAME!, 1910
Phil Capwell and Ed C. Mahony
Published by A. C. Harriman Co., Boston
Cover: Photograph of a baseball stadium crowd

WE'RE THE BOYS FROM BROOKLYN, 1938
Moe Jaffe
Published by Mills Music, Inc.
(ASCAP)

Fight song for the National League Brooklyn Dodgers. Published in Batter Up. *(See: Baseball in Music and Song–Collected.)*

WHAT YOU'D CALL A DREAM, 1984
Craig Carnelia

Businessman imagines himself a baseball star. Included in the play, Diamonds. *(See: Baseball in Theater.)*

WHEELS KEEP TURNIN', 1985
Words by Hy Gilbert, music by George Fischoff
Published by George Fischoff Publishing Co. (ASCAP)

A barnstorming team laments the hardships of life on the road. Included in the musical play, Bingo! *(See: Baseball in Theater.)*

WHEN BASEBALL GOES WEST
Irvin Graham
Published by Mark Warnow Music
(ASCAP)

THE WHITE SOX ARE COMING HOME, 1938
Moe Jaffe
Published by Mills Music, Inc.
(ASCAP)

Fight song for the Chicago White Sox. Published in Batter Up. *(See: Baseball in Music and Song–Collected.)*

THE WHITE SOX (MARCH TRIUMPHAL), 1907
T. F. Durand
Published by Tomaz F. Deuther, Music Publishers, Chicago
Cover: Team photograph of the 1907 White Sox

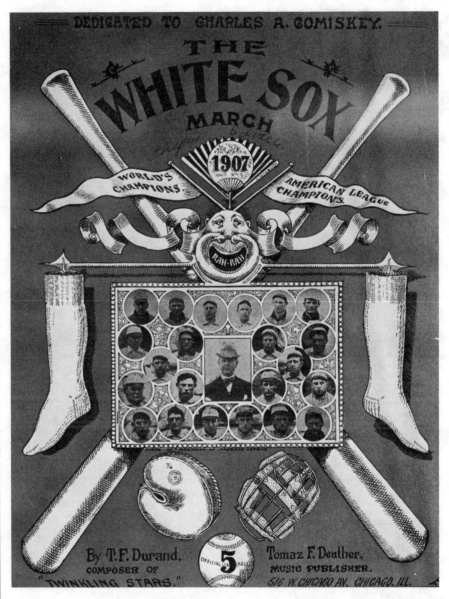

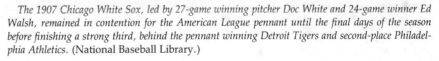

The 1907 Chicago White Sox, led by 27-game winning pitcher Doc White and 24-game winner Ed Walsh, remained in contention for the American League pennant until the final days of the season before finishing a strong third, behind the pennant winning Detroit Tigers and second-place Philadelphia Athletics. (National Baseball Library.)

A WHOLE NEW BALLGAME, 1985
Words by John Forster, music by Thomas Tierney

Included in the musical play, The Dream Team. *(See: Baseball in Theater.)*

WHO NEEDS BASEBALL?
Published by Frank Music Corp., New York (ASCAP)

Baseball terminology has been woven into many popular love songs, including this 1911 romantic ballad. (National Baseball Library.)

———

WHO WOULD DOUBT THAT I'M A MAN?, 1895
Words by M. S., music by A. F. Groebel
"Dedicated to the New Woman"
"Base Ball Song"

Specially adapted from the comic opera, *The Mormons*
"Greatest hit of the season"
Published by Weidig and Co., Cincinnati
Cover: Picture of a woman in a baseball uniform

WIN MERCER TWO-STEP, 1896
Geo. J. Becker
Published by George J. Becker, Washington, D.C.
Cover: Off-the-field photograph of Win Mercer

Tribute to Washington pitching ace Win Mercer.

WINTER IN NEW YORK, 1984
Words by Fred Ebb, music by John Kander

Fans complain of cold weather and the lack of baseball. Included in the play, Diamonds. *(See: Baseball in Theater.)*

WITH THE BASES LOADED I STRUCK OUT
Published by Peer International Corp., New York (BMI)

THE WONDERFUL GAME, 1985
Words by John Forster, music by Thomas Tierney

Included in the musical play, The Dream Team. *(See: Baseball in Theater.)*

WORLD'S CHAMPION'S MARCH, 1911
Joseph Palladino
Published by Joseph Palladino, Camden, New Jersey
Cover: Portrait of Connie Mack

Tribute to the Philadelphia A's.

WORLD SERIES
Robert J. Farnon
Published by Chappell and Co., Inc. (ASCAP)

WORLD SERIES BLUES
Stanley Davis
Published by Balladier Music Co. (ASCAP)

YANKEES! MY BOYS!, 1949
Nan Reid Parsons

306

Tribute to Casey Stengel and the New York Yankees.

YOU AIN'T SEEN BALL, 1985
Words by John Forster, music by Thomas Tierney

Included in the musical play, The Dream Team. (See: Baseball in Theater.)

YOU BETTER PLAY BALL WITH ME, 1936
Charlie Tobias, Carmen Lombardo, and John Jacob Loeb
Published by Donaldson Douglas and Gumble, New York
Cover: Cartoon of a woman baseball player

YOU CAN'T GO WRONG, 1938
Moe Jaffe
Published by Mills Music, Inc. (ASCAP)

Fight song for the National League New York Giants. Published in Batter Up. *(See: Baseball in Music and Song—Collected.)*

YOU DO-DO-DO IT GOOD, 1981
Words by Martin Charnin, music by Bob Brush
Published by MPL Communications, Inc.

Included in play dramatizing Jackie Robinson's first year in the major leagues. See: The First *(Baseball in Theater).*

YOU LOOK SO SWEET TODAY, 1954
Composed by William Schuman, libretto by Jerome Gury
Published by G. Schirmer, Inc.

Ballad about Casey's sweetheart. Included in the opera, The Mighty Casey. *(See: Baseball in Theater.)*

YOU MAKE A HIT WITH MY HEART, 1974
Dick Poston
Published by Pioneer Drama Service, Inc., Denver, Colorado

Slugger tries unsuccessfully to declare his love without using baseball terminology. Included in the burlesque melodrama, There Goes the Old Ball Game. *(See: Baseball in Miscellaneous Plays and Sketches.)*

YOU OUGHT TO SEE THE DODGERS, 1961
Archie Gillam
Published by Nordyke
Copyright date and number: May 20, 1961, EP 153426

YOU'RE DOIN' FINE KID (CATCHER'S SONG), 1954
Composed by William Schuman, libretto by Jerome Gury
Published by G. Schirmer, Inc.

Catcher tells pitcher how to pitch to the slugger Casey. Included in opera, The Mighty Casey. *(See: Baseball in Theater.)*

YOU'RE GONNA WIN THAT BALL GAME, UNCLE SAM!, 1943
Words by George Moriarty, music by Carl Bonner
Published by Forster Music Publ., Chicago (ASCAP)
Cover: Cartoon of Uncle Sam swinging a bat

World War II patriotic song incorporating baseball terminology.

YOU'RE HITTING A THOUSAND IN THE GAME OF LOVE, 1915
Words by Bill Cahalin and J. Keirn Brennan, music by Ernest R. Ball
Published by M. Witmark and Sons, New York

YOU'VE MADE A HOMERUN WITH ME, 1911
Words by Thomas J. Gray, music by Edna Williams
Published by Jos. W. Stern, New York

Appendix to Chapter 18

The appendix contains a listing of non–baseball-related songs written by major league baseball players.

For *Explanatory Notes* to this section, *see:* Baseball in Music and Song.

DEAR OLD HOME OF CHILDHOOD, 1911
Words by Ed Walsh, music by Tell Taylor
Published by Tell Taylor, Grand Opera House, Chicago
Cover: Photograph of Ed Walsh

Hall of Fame pitcher Ed Walsh won 40 games for the 1908 White Sox.

I'LL CHANGE YOUR SHADOWS TO SUNSHINE, 1912
Words by Thos. H. Griffith, music by Elmer B. Griffith
Published by Thos. H. Griffith, New Bedford, Massachusetts

Cover: Small insert photograph of Tommy Griffith in uniform

Outfielder Tommy Griffith played 13 years in the major leagues, mostly for the Brooklyn Dodgers.

LITTLE ALLIGATOR BAIT, 1918
Words by George Moriarty, music by Robert Bruce Allan
Published by Will Rossiter, Chicago

George Moriarty managed, umpired, and played 13 years in the major leagues.

LITTLE PUFF OF SMOKE, GOOD NIGHT, 1910
Words by Ring W. Lardner, music by G. Harris (Doc) White

Published by Victor Kremer Co., Chicago
Cover: Small insert photograph of Doc White

Doc White, for many years a star pitcher for the Chicago White Sox, won 27 games in 1907.

REMEMBER ME TO MY OLD GAL, 1911
Words by George Moriarty, music by Al. W. Brown and J. Brandon Walsh
Published by Harold Rossiter Music Co., Chicago

"Successfully introduced by those three great ball players Chief Bender, Coombs, and Morgan, the heroes of the World's Series." Moriarty also wrote, I Can't Miss That Ball Game. (See: Baseball in Music and Song—Recorded.)

Chapter

19

Baseball in Music and Song— Collected

E X P L A N A T O R Y   N O T E S

1. Title of the book, year of publication.

2. Name of author.

3. Place of publication, name of publisher, book

format (given when the book is available in paperback format only).

4. Annotation. Description of the contents.

The following catalog contains a listing of publications of collected baseball-related songs. Included in this section are published collections of team fight songs, collected baseball songs for young people, and anthologies of songs relating to baseball.

BASEBALL IN MUSIC AND SONG, 1954
Edited by Harry Dichter
Philadelphia: Musical Americana, paperback

Facsimile reproductions of 14 nineteenth-century songsheets. Includes: "The Base Ball Fever"; "Base Ball Polka"; "The Base Ball Quadrille"; "Home Run Galop"; "Home Run Polka"; "Home Run Quick Step"; "Hurrah for Our National Game"; "Live Oak Polka"; "The Red Stockings"; "Slide, Kelly, Slide"; "Tally One for Me"; "The Temple Cup"; "Una Schottische"; "Union Base Ball Club March." (See: Baseball in Music and Song.)

BATTER UP, 1938
Moe Jaffe
New York: Mills Music, Inc., paperback

Collection of 16 songs, one for each major league team. Includes: "A's Are The Craze"; "Cheer for the Cubs"; "Cin-c-i-n-n-a-ti"; "Here Come the Yanks"; "The Indian Song"; "It's Detroit"; "It's in the Cards"; "The Pirates Are on Your Trail"; "Root for the Boston Red Sox"; "The St. Louis Browns"; "There's Gold in Them There Phils"; "Victory

for the Bees"; "Watch the Senators"; "We're the Boys from Brooklyn"; "The White Sox Are Coming Home"; "You Can't Go Wrong." *(See: Baseball in Music and Song.)*

DOZENS O' DIAMOND DITTIES, 1959
Patsy (Hotso) Casey
San Francisco, California: Privately published, paperback

Collection of 30 baseball-related songs.

FENWAY TO CANDLESTICK IN SONG, 1983
Patsy (Hotso) Casey
South Pasadena, California: Privately published

Collection of 150 baseball and religiously inspired songs.

JOHNNY BENCH SONG BOOK, 1971
Add Lovejoy
Cincinnati, Ohio: Municorn Music Co., paperback

Includes: "The Baseball Song"; "The Most

Welcome Sound"; "The First Time"; "Teamwork"; "Rainy Saturday"; "Southpaw"; "The Rookie"; "It's a Girl's Game Too!"; "Pizza Party"; "Victory Song." *(See: Baseball in Music and Song.)*

(NEW YORK METS OFFICIAL 1966) SING ALONG BASEBALL SONG BOOK, 1966
Jane Jarvis and Harry C. Jackson
New York: Sportsmusic, Inc., paperback

Collection of 17 popular song parodies, including the following baseball-related songs: "Meet the Mets"; "Let's Go Mets"; "New York Mets Clapping Song"; "The March of the Midget Mets"; "He Hit One!" (See: Baseball in Music and Song.)

TAKE ME OUT TO THE BALL GAME AND OTHER FAVORITE SONG HITS, 1906–1908, 1984
Edited by Lester S. Levy
Mineola, New York: Dover Publications, paperback

Contains reproductions of original sheet music to the title song and 22 nonbaseball favorites.

Baseball in Music and Song— Recorded

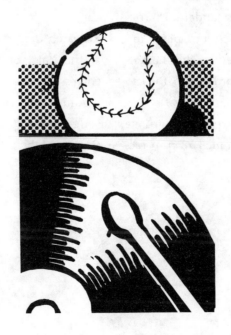

The following catalog contains a comprehensive listing of recorded songs relating to baseball, baseball players, and teams. Included in this section are commercially released recordings of early baseball songs, comic songs with a baseball theme, song tributes to major league baseball players and teams, original cast and soundtrack recordings from musical plays and movies relating to baseball, songs in which baseball is used metaphorically, and songs that celebrate baseball's special place in American culture.

Sound recordings released between 1877 and 1930 differ markedly from those known today. The first sound recordings were cylindrical in shape—4½ inches long and 2¼ inches in diameter—and were operated manually in a spring-wound phonograph at 120 to 160 revolutions per minute. By 1894 one- and two-sided flat recording discs were commercially available in sizes of eight, ten, and twelve inches in diameter. These recordings were also operated manually at speeds ranging from 60 to more than 100 revolutions per minute.

By 1930 all record discs were produced for electric phonographs and were issued at standard 78 rpm speeds. In 1948, twelve- and ten-inch long-play "microgroove" records were introduced to the marketplace. The seven-inch 45 rpm record—with the 1½ inch center hole—was issued commercially a year later. The success of the 33 and 45 rpm microgroove records rendered the venerable ten-inch 78 rpm record all but extinct by the late 1950s.

For records issued before 1930, a detailed description of the disc type and size will be found in the catalog entry. For records produced since 1930, standardized record speeds are given instead of disc size. All records listed as 78 rpm (78), 33 rpm (33), and 45 rpm (45), are ten inches, twelve inches, and seven inches in diameter, respectively, unless otherwise noted. All seven-inch records having a small center hole are listed as extended play (ep) recordings regardless of the number of tracks on the record. All other records are standard commercial recordings unless otherwise noted.

In recent years, sound recordings relating to baseball have been the subject of increased interest among some baseball historians, archivists and collectors, who are intrigued by their historical value and cultural significance. The National Baseball Hall of Fame and Museum in Cooperstown, New York, features a substantial collection of baseball recordings of all types. Additionally, baseball-related recordings can be found in the Recorded Sound Division of the Library of Congress, the Rodgers and Hammerstein Archives of Recorded Sound at the Performing Arts Research Center at Lincoln Center in New York, and at the Yale, Stanford, and Syracuse University archives of recorded sound. For further information regarding sources and dealers of recorded baseball songs, consult the Selected Guide to Sources and Dealers at the back of the book.

EXPLANATORY NOTES

1. Title of the song, year of record's release.

2. Name of recording artist(s) or group. If the name is italicized, the artist is also the sole writer of the song.

3. Title of the long-play or extended-play record, if applicable.

4. Name of record label company, rpm in parentheses, record label release number.

5. Name of songwriter(s).

6. Publisher of the song, year of publication in parentheses, licensing agency in parentheses.

7. Cover: Description of the songsheet cover.

8. Reverse: Title of song on the record's reverse, name of recording artist(s) or group in parentheses if different than the artists indicated above.

9. Annotation. Description of the song.

AFTER THIRTY-NINE YEARS, 1984
John Frigo
Phonograph (45) SP-002
Published by Albertina Music (BMI)
Reverse: "Cubbie Blue" (Danny Long)

Celebration of the Chicago Cubs' National League Eastern Division championship, their first championship of any kind in 39 years.

AIN'T NO STOPPING US NOW, 1980
(Phillies Version)
Gene McFadden and John Whitehead
TSOP (45)
Special lyrics by Ron Hunter

Tribute to the Philadelphia Phillies.

THE AMAZING METS, 1969
Featuring the voices of the New York Mets
Buddah (33) Mets 1969

Includes: "We're Gonna Win the Series"; "Mets Are Here to Stay"; "Heart"; "The Song for the '69 Mets"; "La La La La"; "Mets—Hallelujah"; "God Bless America"; "The Mets Ball Game"; "We've Got the Whole World Watching Us"; "Green Grass of Shea."

AMAZIN' WILLIE MAYS, 1954
The King Odom Quartette
Perspective (78) 5001
Reverse: "Basin Street Blues"

Tribute to the New York Giants' outfielder.

ASTROTURF, 1979
Howie Newman
On *Baseball's Greatest Hits*
Major League Records 7-inch ep (33) 3302
Published by Chin Music (BMI)

Artificial turf is humorously lampooned.

BABE RUTH, THE WINNER OF THEM ALL, c. 1975
Cathy Lynn

Heart and Soul (45) BR 1
Published by Alpha-PHI Music, Inc. (ASCAP)
Reverse: "The Greening of America"

Pop tribute to the Hall of Fame slugger.

BALLAD OF A BALL GAME, 1986
Christine Lavin
On *Beau Woes (and Other Problems of Modern Life)*

Humorous folk ballad in which a woman plays baseball for the first time.

THE BALLAD OF DON LARSEN, 1956
Red River Dave (McEnery)
TNT (45) 9010
Reverse: "Adios, Mi Amor, Mi Corazon"

Folk ballad celebrating New York Yankee pitcher Don Larsen's 1956 World Series perfect game.

Way high above the bleachers in the "gallery of the blue"
There was Ruth and "Mighty Matty" and the "Big Train" watching too;
And I know that they were pulling for that kid upon the mound—
The day that young Don Larsen pitched the 27 down.

THE BALLAD OF FERNANDO VALENZUELA, 1981

Los All Stars
Screwball 7-inch ep (45) EB 001
Published by Right Song Music/Elvis Presley Music (BMI)

Tribute to the Los Angeles Dodgers' pitching sensation.

THE BALLAD OF MAURY WILLS, 1964

Maury Wills
Dot (45) 16529
Written by Fred Thompson
Published by Sun-Vine Music Corp. (BMI)
Reverse: "The Wayfarin' Stranger"

A religious ballplayer doesn't mind stealing bases for a living. Wills is a shortstop for the Los Angeles Dodgers.

THE BALLAD OF ROBERTO CLEMENTE, 1973

Paul New

BBB (45) 233
Published by Judith (ASCAP)
Also available: "Baladas de Roberto Clemente" BBB (45) (Spanish version)

Memorial tribute to the Pittsburgh Pirates' Hall of Famer.

BALLAD OF SATCHEL PAIGE, 1972

Rev. Frederick Douglass Kirkpatrick
On *Ballads of Black America*
Folkways (33) 7751

Folk song in tribute to the Hall of Fame pitcher.
So remember everybody, my name is Satchel Paige
I gonna pitch on forever, regardless of my age.

BALLAD OF SATCHEL PAIGE (DON'T LOOK BACK), 1982

Raynola Smith
Cain and Able (45) 3118
Written by Settie Truitt

Tribute to the Hall of Fame pitcher.

THE BALL GAME, 1953

Wynona Carr
Specialty (45) 855
Published (1953) by Venice Music, Inc. (BMI)
Reverse: "I Know By Faith"
Also available: (1953) Fidelity (78) 855;
On *Greatest Gospel Gems* (various artists) Specialty (33) 2144

Up-tempo gospel song in which life is compared to a baseball game.

BALL GAME BLUES

Minnie Matles
Vocalion (78) 04431

THE BALL GAME IS OVER

Phil Celea
Tin Pan Alley (45)

THE BAMBINO, THE CLIPPER AND THE MICK, 1982

Terry Cashman

In some Chicago taverns during the magical—but ultimately heartbreaking—season of 1969, this was the only song ever played on the jukebox. But 1969 belonged to the Miracle Mets, while the Cubs experienced yet another late-season swoon. (Universal Records, 1969.)

Lifesong (45) 45097

"Talkin' Baseball" tribute to the New York Yankees.

BASEBALL
Fannie Flagg
RCA (78) ANLI 2640

BASEBALL, 1954
Lee Sullivan
Bison (78) 105
Written by Ethel Opp
Published by Ethel Opp Music (BMI)
Reverse: "Those Cleveland Indians"

BASEBALL
Modern Jazz Quartet
On *Modern Jazz Quartet Live at the Lighthouse*
Atlantic (33) 1486

BASEBALL, 1980
Michael Franks
Warner Bros. (45) 49556
Published by Warner-Tamerlane Pub. Corp/Mississippi Mud Music Co. (BMI)
Also available: On *One Bad Habit*
Warner Bros. (33) BSK 3427

Double entendres incorporating baseball terminology.

BASEBALL, 1982
General Caine
Tabu (45) ZS5-02947
Written by Mitch McDowell
Published by Interior Music/Irving Music, Inc. (BMI)
Reverse: "Girls"
Also available: Tabu 12-inch single (33) 4Z9-03178; Tabu 12-inch single (33) AS1492; On *Girls* Tabu (33) FZ-37997

Pop vocal celebration of baseball.

BASEBALL
Kagny and Rockwell
On *Mind Control*

Motown (33) 6104
Written by Ashby and Rockwell

BASEBALL
Sue Raney and the Bob Florence Group
On *Ridin' High*
Discovery (33) 913
Written by Michael Franks

BASEBALL (AMERICA'S NATIONAL PASTIME), 1981
The Mudville Nine
Lifesong (45) LS 45087
Written by Stan Satlin
Published by Blendingwell Music, Inc. (ASCAP)

Reverse: "Willie, Mickey and 'The Duke' " (Terry Cashman)

Celebration of the joys of baseball.

BASEBALL AND THE BRAVES, 1982
Terry Cashman
Lifesong (45) 45110
Also available: (1984) Metrostar (45) 84451

"Talkin' Baseball" tribute to the Braves.

BASEBALL AND THE BUCS, 1982
Terry Cashman
Lifesong (45) 45109

"Talkin' Baseball" tribute to the Pirates.

"Put me in, coach, I'm ready to play..." John Fogerty's 1985 hit song, "Centerfield," makes wonderful use of baseball history and folklore in conveying the songwriter's joyous intention to rejoin the mainstream of life after years of reclusive retreat. (Warner Bros., 1985.)

BASEBALL AND THE CUBS, 1982
Terry Cashman
Lifesong (45) 45104

"Talkin' Baseball" tribute to the Cubs.

BASEBALL AND THE METS, 1982
Terry Cashman
Lifesong (45) 45108

"Talkin' Baseball" tribute to the New York Mets.

BASEBALL AND THE O'S, 1982
Terry Cashman
Lifesong (45) 45105
Also available: On *The Earl of Baltimore* Lifesong picture disc (33) 8138 PD

"Talkin' Baseball" tribute to the Baltimore Orioles.

BASEBALL AND THE PHILS, 1982
Terry Cashman
Lifesong (45) 45096

"Talkin' Baseball" tribute to the Phillies.

BASEBALL AND THE SOX, 1982
Terry Cashman
Lifesong (45) 45106

"Talkin' Baseball" tribute to the Red Sox.

BASEBALL AND THE STROS, 1982
Terry Cashman
Lifesong (45) 45112

"Talkin' Baseball" tribute to the Houston Astros.

BASEBALL AND THE TRIBE, 1982
Terry Cashman
Lifesong (45) 45099

"Talkin' Baseball" tribute to the Cleveland Indians.

BASEBALL BABY, c. 1958
Johnny Darling
Deluxe (45) 6167
Written by Gibson and Minion
Reverse: "I Don't Want to Wind Up in Love"

The game of love is told using baseball terminology.

BASEBALL BALLET, 1982
Terry Cashman
Lifesong (45) 45117
Written by Terry Cashman and Michael Mugrage
Published by Blendingwell Music, Inc. (ASCAP)
Reverse: "Cooperstown (The Town Where Baseball Lives)"
Also available: (1982) Lifesong (45) 45119; On *Talkin' Baseball—American League* Lifesong (33) 8136; On *Talkin' Baseball—National League* Lifesong (33) 8137

Pop vocal in which the intrinsic beauty of baseball is celebrated.

BASEBALL, BASEBALL, 1954
Jane Morgan
Kapp (45) 104
Written by David Kapp, Allan Roberts, and Albon Timothy
Published by John Fields Music Co., Ltd./Leeds Music Corp. (ASCAP)
Reverse: "Fair Weather Friends"

Humorous song in which a woman complains that her lover talks only about baseball.

BASEBALL, BASEBALL, 1969
Nate Oliver, Gene Oliver, and Willie Smith
On *Cub Power*
Quill (33) 1001
Written by John Frigo
Published by Marjon Publ. Co. (ASCAP)

The joys of attending a baseball game are celebrated.

BASEBALL BLUES, 1921
Palmetto Jazz Quartet
Okeh (78) 8023

BASEBALL BLUES, c. 1948
Clarence Samuels
Aristocrat (78) 1003

BASEBALL BLUES, 1972
Claire Hamill
Island (45) 1202
Published by Ackee Music, Inc. (ASCAP)
Also available: On *One House Left Standing* Island (33) SW 9316

Camp love song incorporating baseball terminology.

BASEBALL BOOGIE, c. 1945
The Delta Rhythm Boys
Festival 10-inch ep (78) EPM 201 (Australian import)

Boogie-woogie celebration of the joys of attending a baseball game.

BASEBALL BOOGIE, 1946
Brownie McGhee
Alert (78) 413
Reverse: "Dissatisfied Woman"

Tribute to Hall of Famer Jackie Robinson.

BASEBALL BOOGIE, c. 1947
Buster Dobson Quintet
Bandwagon (78) 505
Vocals by Jackie Walters
Written by Brownie McGhee

BASEBALL BOOGIE, 1950
Mable Scott
King (78) 4368
Written by Bill Williams
Published (1950) by Trio Music Co., Inc./Fort Knox Music Co. (BMI)
Reverse: "I Found My Baby"
Also available: On *Fine, Fine Baby* Jukebox Lil (33) 606 (Swedish import)

Double entendres incorporating baseball terminology.

BASEBALL CARD LOVER, 1977
Ritchie Ray
Rhino (45) 004
Published by Kinko Music (BMI)
Also available: On *Rhino Royale*
Rhino (33) RNLP 002

Camp rock-and-roll song about a man who literally loves his baseball cards.

BASEBALL CROWD
No artist given
Major (78) 4103-B

BASEBALL FURIES' CHASE, 1979
Barry DeVorzon
A&M (45) 2129
Published by Ensign Music (BMI)
Reverse: "Theme from 'The Warriors' "
Also available: On *The Warriors* A&M (33)

THE BASEBALL GAME, 1965
Original cast
On *You're a Good Man Charlie Brown*
MGM (33) S1E-9
Based on the comic strip, "Peanuts" by Charles M. Schulz
Music and lyrics by Clark Gesner
Published by Jeremy Music, Inc. (ASCAP)

Charlie Brown mourns a lost opportunity to finally win a baseball game.

THE BASEBALL GAME, 1966
Studio cast
On *You're a Good Man Charlie Brown*
Leo (33) 900
Also available: MGM (33) LES-9000

THE BASEBALL GAME, 1966
Soundtrack from television production
On *You're a Good Man Charlie Brown*
Atlantic (33) SD-7252

THE BASEBALL GIRL, 1909
Ray Cox

Edison Amberol 4-minute cylinder 196
Also available: (1913) Edison Amberol 4-minute cylinder 1747

Girl arrives in the seventh inning of a game and berates the umpire. Included in the Broadway play, The Never Homes *(1911).*

THE BASEBALL GLIDE, 1940
Frank Luther, Zora Layman, and the Century Quartet
On *Decca Presents "Take Me Out to the Ball Game"*
Decca album No. 120 (78) 3210-3212
Written by Andrew B. Sterling, music by Harry Von Tilzer
Published (1911) by Harry Von Tilzer Music Publ. Co., New York

Song describes dance steps using baseball terminology. Title on the record label is given as, "That Baseball Glide."

BASEBALL HE LOVES, 1961
Cathy Carr
Roulette (45) 4367
Written by Ben Raleigh and John Gluck, Jr.
Published by Kahl Music Pub./Big Seven Music (BMI)
Reverse: "Yearning"

Girl complains about her boyfriend's preoccupation with baseball and other school athletics.

BASEBALL IN K.C., 1982
Terry Cashman
Lifesong (45) 45111

"Talkin' Baseball" tribute to the Kansas City Royals.

BASEBALL IN ST. LOO, 1982
Terry Cashman
Lifesong (45) 45107

"Talkin' Baseball" tribute to the St. Louis Cardinals.

BASEBALL IS MORE THAN A GAME

The George Romanis Sound Composition (45) 1100
Written by George Romanis and Floyd Huddleston
Published by Romanis Music (ASCAP)

Pop tribute to baseball.

BASEBALL MAGIC, 1976
Soundtrack
On *The Bingo Long Traveling All-Stars and Motor Kings*
MCA (33) 2094
Written by William Goldstein

Pop instrumental.

BASEBALL MEDLEY
Gladys Goodding
V Disc (78) 431-B
Reverse: "Who's on First?" (Abbott and Costello)

Selection of baseball tunes by the organist for the Brooklyn Dodgers.

BASEBALL MERENGUE
Ricardo Rico
Monogram (78) M-932

BASE BALL PAPA, 1951
Billy Mitchell
On *Library of Negro Music: Novelty Series, Volume Five*
Blue (78) 126
Written by Dootsie Williams
Published by Dootsie Williams Music (BMI)
Reverse: "Red Spring Boogie"

Humorous double entendres incorporating baseball terminology.

BASEBALL POLKA, 1950
George Cates and His Orchestra with the Buccaneers
Coral (45) 60249
Written by Larry Fotine, Dick Hardt, and Moe Jaffe

Published (1950) by General Music Publishing Co., Inc., New York

BASEBALL POLKA
Johnny Vadnal and His Orchestra
Victor (78) 25-1167
Written by Larry Fotine, Dick Hardt, and Moe Jaffe

BASEBALL POLKA, c. 1958
Harmony Bells Orchestra
Dana (45) 3210
Written by Walter Dana
Published by Dana Pub. (BMI)
Also available: Dana (78) 3210

THE BASEBALL SONG, c. 1962
The Craftsmen
Scout (45) 435
Written by Al Trace and Ben Trace
Published by Le-Mor Music Co. (ASCAP)
Reverse: ''Let's Go Angels''

The joys of attending a baseball game are celebrated.

BASEBALL SPECIAL
Knuckles O'Toole
Grand Award (45) 1004

Includes: ''Take Me Out to the Ball Game.''

BASEBALL'S BEST, 1963
Bob Mitchell
Cappe Enterprises (33)

Includes: ''Charge, Dodgers, Charge''; ''Take Me Out to the Ball Game.''

BASEBALL'S GREATEST HITS, 1979
Howie Newman
Major League Records 7-inch ep (33) 3302
Published by Chin Music (BMI)

Includes: ''Astroturf''; ''Utility Infielder Blues''; ''Wait Until Next Year''; ''Traded''; ''Blasted in the Bleachers.''

BASEBALL'S RED MACHINE, 1982
Terry Cashman
Lifesong (45) 45101
Also available: On *One Stop Along the Way* Lifesong (33) 8140;
(1985) Metrostar (45) 4585-2

''Talkin' Baseball'' tribute to the Reds. Also titled, ''Cincinnati's Red Machine.''

BASEBALL (THE MAJOR LEAGUE BASEBALL SONG), 1971
Richard Wolfe
Lycoming (45)
Published (1971) by Bayberry Music, Inc. and Hastings Music Corp., New York
Cover: Official insignia of Major League Baseball

The joys of baseball are celebrated.

BASEBALL THEME
Vince Guaraldi Trio
On *A Boy Named Charlie Brown*
Fantasy (33) 8430
Written by Vince Guaraldi
Published by Shifty Music (BMI)

THE BASES WERE LOADED, 1950
Sugar Chile Robinson
Capitol (78) 1060
Written by Irving Gordon
Published by Morley Music Co. (ASCAP)
Reverse: ''Sticks and Stones''

Boogie-woogie description of a baseball game.

THE BATTLING BOSTON BRAVES
Artist not given
Valor (78) 1500
Reverse: ''Take Me Out to the Ball Game''

BE A BELIEVER IN DODGER FEVER, 1979
The Paid Attendance
Homerun (45) 504
Written by Sonny Marrow
Published by Solid Smoke Songs, San Francisco

BE A BELIEVER IN GIANT FEVER, 1978
The Paid Attendance
Homerun (45) 500
Written by Sonny Marrow
Published by Solid Smoke Songs, San Francisco

BE A BELIEVER IN PHILLY FEVER, 1979
The Paid Attendance
Homerun (45) 503
Written by Sonny Marrow
Published by Solid Smoke Songs, San Francisco

BE A BELIEVER IN RED SOX FEVER, 1979
The Paid Attendance
Homerun (45) 502
Written by Sonny Marrow
Published by Solid Smoke Songs, San Francisco

BE A BELIEVER IN YANKEE FEVER, 1979
The Paid Attendance
Homerun (45) 501
Written by Sonny Marrow
Published by Solid Smoke Songs, San Francisco

BEAT 'EM BUCS, 1960
Benny Benack
Robbee (45) 108
Written by S. Bloom and J. Negri
Published by Mary Jo Pub. Co. (ASCAP)
Reverse: ''The Charge of the Buccaneers''

Tribute to the Pittsburgh Pirates.

BEAT 'EM BUCS, CHA, CHA, CHA
The Lovaliers
Surprise (45) 101

BEE THAT WON THE BASEBALL GAME
Tom Durden
D (45) 1076
Reverse: ''Heart of a Fool''

THE BIG BLUE WRECKING CREW, 1984
No artist given
On *We Are the Tenth Man and Other Songs of the Dodgers*
Rhino (33) EP 607
Written and lead vocals by Rick Segall and John Bahler
Published by Fat Finger Music (BMI) and Power Alley Music (ASCAP)

Tribute to the Los Angeles Dodgers.

BIG FRANK, c. 1963
Jimmie Maddin and His Little Leaguers
Golden West (45) 1001
Written by Jimmie Maddin, Paul Vandervoort II, and Del Kacher
Published by EDM Music Pub. (ASCAP)
Reverse: ''Danke Schoen''

Novelty tribute to Frank Howard, ''the Paul Bunyan of the bat.''

BILLYBALL, 1980
No artist given
Oakland A's unnumbered cassette
Features the voice of Billy Martin

Official song of the Oakland A's.

BILLY'S TURNAROUND GANG, c. 1974
Jerry Hayes
Toro (45) 107

Reverse: ''I Want to Play Ball for Billy''

Tribute to Billy Martin and the Texas Rangers.

THE BINGO LONG SONG, 1976
(Steal On Home)
Thelma Houston
Motown (45) 1385
Written by Berry Gordy and Ron Miller
Published by Jobete Music Co., Inc./ Leeds Music Corp. (ASCAP); Stone Diamond Music Corp./Duchess Music Corp (BMI)
Also available: On *The Bingo Long Traveling All-Stars and Motor Kings* (Soundtrack) MCA (33) 2094

THE BIRD MAGIC MAN, 1964
The Roy Ross Singers
On *Pennant Fever*
RGA (33) M-300
Written by Robert Goodman

Tribute to Hank Bauer, manager of the Baltimore Orioles.

BLASTED IN THE BLEACHERS, 1980
Howie Newman
Major League Records (45) 4502
Published by Chin Music (BMI)
Reverse: ''One Day on the Gas Line''
Also available: On *Baseball's Greatest Hits* Major League Records 7-inch ep (33) 3302

Humorous song about a beer-guzzling baseball fan.

BLEACHER BOOGIE, 1984
Little Tino and the Hawaiians
Teenage (45) 711
Written by Martin Gross and John Evans
Published (1984) by Teeno Music (BMI)
Reverse: ''Crazy 'Bout Those Tigers''

Spirited celebration of baseball and rock-and-roll.

BLESS YOU BOYS, 1984
(This is the Year)
Curtis Gadson and Loren Woods
Go-4-It (45) AR 6900
Written by Randall Jacobs, Curtis Gadson, and Tom DeLisle

Tribute to the world champion Detroit Tigers.

BLUE JAY JEANNE
Kelly Girls
Blue Jay (78) 110

Official song of the Philadelphia National League Club.

THE BLUE JAYS
Paul's People
Little Guy (45) 007
Written by Michael Lococo
Published by Cataract Music (BMIC)
Reverse: Same (instrumental)

Official song of the American League Toronto Blue Jays.

BOBBY THE BOMBER, 1918
Byron G. Harlan
Columbia 10-inch double-faced record A 2587
Reverse: ''What Yankee Doodle Says He'll Do, He'll Do'' (Peerless Quartet)

World War I song in which a baseball pitcher hurls bombs as accurately as he had previously tossed strikes across the plate.

BREWER FEVER, 1980
Perfect Pitch
Milwaukee Brewers (45) unnumbered

Pop tribute to the Milwaukee Brewers.

BREWERS ALL THE WAY, 1982
Terry Cashman
Lifesong (45) 45113

''Talkin' Baseball'' tribute to the Brewers.

BROOKLYN BASEBALL CANTATA, 1949
Robert Merrill
RCA Victor album No. DC 42 (78)

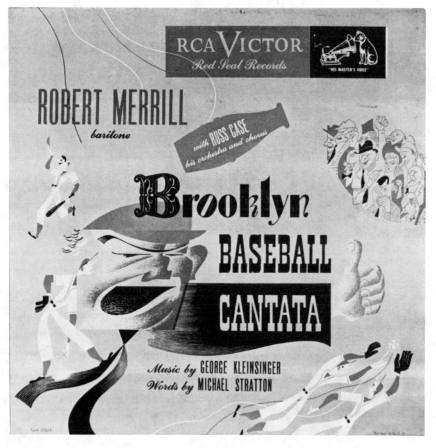

Brooklyn's colorful and passionate baseball fans are the subject of this comic operetta, first produced on Broadway in 1942 and recorded by Robert Merrill in 1949. (RCA Victor, 1949.)

1412/13 (two-record set)
Written by Michael Stratton, music by George Kleinsinger
Published by Mills Music, Inc., New York
See also Baseball in Radio; Baseball in Theater

THE BROOKLYN DODGERS JUMP, 1949

Ralph Branca, Carl Furillo, and Erv Palica
Leslie (78) 918
Written by Joseph A. Ricciardello
Published by Bars (ASCAP)

Branca, Furillo, and Palica are Brooklyn Dodger teammates.

BROTHER NOAH GAVE OUT CHECKS FOR RAIN, 1907

Arthur Collins
Edison 2-minute wax cylinder 9642
Written by Arthur Longbrake
Published (1907) by Jos. Morris, Philadelphia
Cover: Cartoon of a deacon batting in a church baseball game
Also available: (1907) Victor 10-inch single-faced record 5204; (1908) Victor 10-inch double-faced record 16241

A deacon tells how baseball might have been played in the Bible.

BUC FEVER, 1966

Johnny Valor, with Prince Valiant and the Knights
St. Clair (45) 999
Written by Valor and Kruspiri
Published by Jules-Tone Music (BMI)
Reverse: ''Green-Weenie Dog''

Tribute to the Pittsburgh Pirates.

BUDDY, SUNNY AND THE SCOOP, 1982

Terry Cashman
Lifesong (45) 45100

''Talkin' Baseball'' tribute to the Texas Rangers.

BUNKER HILL, 1964

The Roy Ross Singers
On *Pennant Fever*
RGA (33) M-300
Written by Robert Goodman

Tribute to pitcher Wally Bunker of the Baltimore Orioles.

CALIFORNIA ANGELS 'A-OK!,' 1966

Jack Halloran Singers
Vista (45) 452
Written by Shirley and Dick Winslow
Published (1966) by Walt Disney Music Co.
Cover: Illustration of Anaheim Stadium

Official song of the California Angels.

CALL TO THE BULLPEN, 1964

The Roy Ross Singers
On *Pennant Fever*
RGA (33) M-300
Written by Robert Goodman

Tribute to the relief pitchers of the Baltimore Orioles.

CANNED HEAT, 1984

No artist given
On *We Are the Tenth Man and Other Songs of the Dodgers*

Rhino (33) EP 607
Written and lead vocals by Rick Segall
and John Bahler
Published by Fat Finger Music (BMI)
and Power Alley Music (ASCAP)

Tribute to the Los Angeles Dodger pitchers.

CASEY AT THE BAT
Four Moods
Life (78) 58822
Reverse: Part II

CASEY AT THE BAT, 1982
Muddy and the Diamonds
C-ductions (45) RSDP 782
Written by R. Stover
Published by C-lect Publishing (BMI)
Reverse: "The Mudville Story"

Pop vocal about the mighty Casey.

CASEY (THE PRIDE OF THEM ALL), 1946
Jerry Colonna
Capitol (78) 249
Written by Ray Gilbert, Ken Darby,
and Eliot Daniel
Published (1945) by Southern Music
Publ. Co., Inc., New York
Reverse: "Josephine Please No Lean
on the Bell"

*Humorous song included in the Walt Disney
production,* Make Mine Music. *See: Casey
at the Bat* (Baseball in Animated Cartoons—
Feature.)

CATFISH
Joe Cocker
On *Stingray*
A&M (33)
Written by Bob Dylan and Jacques
Levy
Published (1975) by Jackelope Pub.
Co., Inc./Ram's Horn Music (ASCAP)

*Folk ballad in tribute to pitcher Jim "Catfish"
Hunter of the New York Yankees.*

THE CATFISH KID, 1976
(Ballad of Jim Hunter)

FAMOUS FANS

If we had a pitcher whose fastball hummed, we'd want a team that could hum—on key—right along with it. The following is an all-star lineup of famous musicians and their favorite baseball teams:

Huey Lewis *(rock singer):* San Francisco Giants

Itzhak Perlman *(concert violinist):* New York Yankees

George Thorogood *(rock singer):* New York Mets

Jose Feliciano *(folk singer):* California Angels

Helen Traubel *(opera soprano):* St. Louis Browns

Glenn Frey *(rock singer):* Los Angeles Dodgers

Samuel Sanders *(concert pianist):* New York Yankees

Steve Goodman *(folk singer):* Chicago Cubs

John Fogerty *(rock singer):* Oakland A's

Big Tom White
Moon (45) 6021-18
Written by Bobby Hollowell
Published by Clay Music Corp. (BMI)
Reverse: "Shake, Rattle and Roll"

*Tribute to the Hall of Fame pitcher Jim
"Catfish" Hunter.*

CENTERFIELD, 1985
John Fogerty
Warner Bros. (45) 7-29053
Published by Wenaha Music Co.
(ASCAP)
Reverse: "Rock and Roll Girls"
Also available: On *Centerfield* Warner
Bros. (33) 1-25203

Baseball is used metaphorically to portray a

---

*man's desire to re-enter the mainstream of life
after years of retreat.*

CHARGE, 1960
See "Dodgers Charge"

CHARGE, DODGERS, CHARGE, 1963
Bob Mitchell
On *Baseball's Best*
Cappe Enterprises (33)
Published by Bulls-Eye Music, Inc.
(ASCAP)

Organ instrumental.

THE CHARGE OF THE BUCCANEERS, 1960
Benny Benack
Robbee (45) 108
Written by J. Negri and L. Martin
Published by Mary Jo Pub. Co.
(ASCAP)
Reverse: "Beat 'em Bucs"

Tribute to the Pittsburgh Pirates.

CHARLIE HUSTLE, 1974
Jim Wheeler
Nu-Sound (45) 1030
Written by E. Miller
Published by Teardrop Music
(ASCAP)
Reverse: "Going Back to Carson City"

*Tribute to Cincinnati Reds' outfielder
Pete Rose.*

CHARLIE HUSTLE, 1979
Pamela Neal
Free Flight (45) 11557
Written by Mark Glabman and
Pamela Neal
Published by Adventure Music
(ASCAP)
Reverse: "Magic Again"
Also available: Free Flight picture disc
(33) JM-11555

Disco tribute to Pete Rose.

CHAVEZ RAVINE, c. 1963
Danny Michaels
Chambers (45) BB 200
Written by Michaels and Jay
Published by Druther Music (BMI)
Reverse: ''Give the Ball to Calhoun''

Tribute to the Los Angeles Dodgers.

CHICAGO CUBS SONG: HEY, HEY! HOLY MACKEREL!, 1969
Bleacher Bum Eight
On *Cub Power*
Quill (33) 1001
Written by John Frigo and I. C. Haag
Published (1969) by Marjon Music
Pub. Co. (ASCAP)

Dixieland instrumental.

CHICAGO CUBS SONG: HEY, HEY! HOLY MACKEREL!, 1969
The Len Dresslar Singers
Universal (45) 76936M

Pop vocal tribute to the Chicago Cubs.

CHICAGO CUBS SONG: HEY, HEY! HOLY MACKEREL!, 1969
Nate Oliver, Gene Oliver, and
Willie Smith
On *Cub Power*
Quill (33) 1001

CHOCOLATE STRAWBERRY, 1987
Darryl Strawberry with U.T.F.O.
Whistle and Richie Rich
Macola 12-inch single (33) 1041
Written by Richie Rich and the
Kangol Kid

Rap music tribute to the New York Mets star outfielder Darryl Strawberry.

CINCINNATI'S RED MACHINE, 1982
See: ''Baseball's Red Machine''

CLEMENTE LAND, 1973
Jim Wheeler

Nu-Sound (45) 1024
Written by E. Miller
Published by Teardrop Music
(ASCAP)
Reverse: ''I Like Your Style''

Memorial tribute to Pittsburgh Pirates' outfielder Roberto Clemente.

THE COMMITTEE, 1984
Steve Vaus
On *Sounds of Success: Music of a Winning Season*
San Diego Padres (33) unnumbered

Tribute to the San Diego Padres.

COOPERSTOWN (THE TOWN WHERE BASEBALL LIVES), 1982
Terry Cashman
Lifesong (45) 45117
Published by PKM Music (ASCAP)
Reverse: ''Baseball Ballet''
Also available: On *Talkin' Baseball—American League* Lifesong (33) 8136;
On *Talkin' Baseball—National League* Lifesong (33) 8137

Pop vocal celebrating baseball's Hall of Fame.

CRAZY 'BOUT THOSE TIGERS, 1984
Little Tino and the Hawaiians
Teenage (45) 711
Written by Martin Gross
Published (1984) by Teeno Music
(BMI)
Reverse: ''Bleacher Boogie''

Rock-and-roll tribute to the Detroit Tigers.

CUBBIE BLUE, 1984
Danny Long
Phonograph (45) SP-002
Published by Albertina Music (BMI)
Reverse: ''After Thirty-Nine Years''
(John Frigo)

Tribute to the Chicago Cubs.

CUB POWER, 1969
The Chicago Cubs and the Bleacher

Bum Eight
Featuring Nate Oliver, Gene Oliver,
and Willie Smith
Quill (33) 1001

*Includes: ''Hey, Hey! Holy Mackerel!'';
''Pennant Feeling''; ''Baseball, Baseball'' (Nate Oliver, Gene Oliver, and Willie Smith); ''Take Me Out to the Ball Game''; ''Hey, Hey! Holy Mackerel!'' (Bleacher Bum Eight).*

CUBS ON PARADE, 1908
Edison Military Band
Edison 2-minute wax cylinder 9889
Written by H. R. Hempel
Published (1907) by Tomas F.
Deuther, Chicago
Cover: Cartoon of dancing bears

Tribute to the World Champion Chicago Cubs.

CUBS ON PARADE, 1908
Zonophone Concert Band
Zonophone 10-inch single-faced
record 1099

DADDY PLAYED FIRST BASE, 1970
Homer and Jethro
RCA (45) 9866
Written by Haynes, Burns, and
Perkins
Published by Cedarwood Pub. Co.,
Inc., House of Cash, Inc. (BMI)
Reverse: ''You Smell Like Turtles''

Humorous parody of ''Daddy Sang Bass.''

DAMN YANKEES, 1955
Original cast
RCA (33) 1021
Also available: (1955) RCA 7-inch ep
(33) EOC-1021 (three-record set);
(1955) RCA (33) LSO-1021
(rechanneled stereo); RCA (33) AYL
1-3948 (rechanneled stereo) reissue
See also: Baseball in Film; Baseball in
Television; Baseball in Theater

*Includes ''Six Months Out of Every Year'';
''The Game''; ''Heart.''*

DAMN YANKEES, 1955
Studio cast
Capitol (33) SN-7515
Reverse: "The Pajama Game"

DAMN YANKEES, c. 1955
Various artists
Mercury 7-inch ep (45) 3324

DAMN YANKEES, 1958
Soundtrack
RCA (33) 1047

DANCING IN THE SUMMER SUN, 1986
Straightface
Baseball in Sunshine (45) unnumbered
Written by Randy Rice
Published (1986) by Seen My Sawn Music (BMI)
Reverse: "Twist of Fate"

Celebration of the joys and traditions of daytime baseball at Wrigley Field in Chicago.

DANCING WITH RONNIE CEY, 1981
The Zanies
Dore (45) 974
Reverse: "I Hate Baseball"

Pop instrumental tribute to the Los Angeles Dodgers' third baseman.

DANCIN' WITH THE PHILLIES, 1977
Dave Cash, Larry Bowa, Mike Schmidt, Greg Luzinski, and Garry Maddox
Grand Prix (45) 207
Reverse: "Phillies Fever"

Tribute to the Philadelphia Phillies by several of its players.

DANDY SANDY, 1964
Jimmy Durante
On *The Sounds of the Dodgers*
Jaybar (33) 1

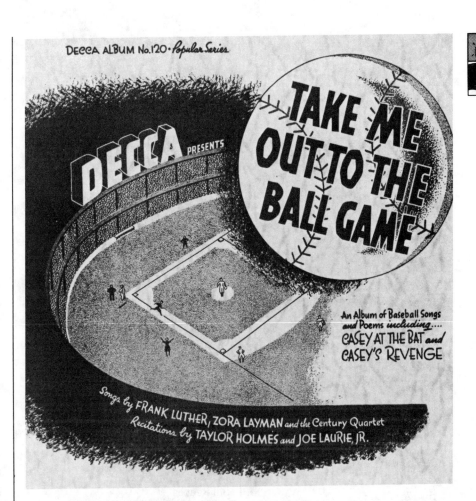

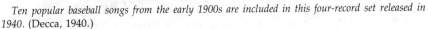

Ten popular baseball songs from the early 1900s are included in this four-record set released in 1940. (Decca, 1940.)

Written by Jackie Barnett and Sammy Fain
Published by Jaybar-Fain

Humorous tribute to Los Angeles Dodgers' pitcher Sandy Koufax.

DECCA PRESENTS "TAKE ME OUT TO THE BALL GAME," 1940
Frank Luther, Zora Layman and the Century Quartet
Recitations by Taylor Holmes and Joe Laurie, Jr.
Decca album No. 120 (78) 3210-3212 (four-record set)

Includes: "Take Me Out to the Ball Game"; "Gee But It's Great at a Baseball Game"; "Home Run Bill"; "Take Your Girl to the Ball Game"; Let's Get the Umpire's Goat"; "I Can't Miss That Ball Game"; "Oh Didn't It Rain"; "That Baseball Glide"; "He's a Fan, Fan, Fan"; "I Want to Go to the Ball Game"; "Casey at the Bat"; "Casey's Revenge."

DID YOU SEE JACKIE ROBINSON HIT THAT BALL?, 1949
Buddy Johnson and His Orchestra
Decca (45) 9-24675
Written by Buddy Johnson
Published (1949) by Sophisticate

Music, Inc. (BMI)
Also available: Decca (78) 24675; On
Say Ella Jukebox Lil (33) 604 (Swedish
import)

*Pop vocal tribute to the Brooklyn Dodgers' Hall
of Famer.*

DID YOU SEE JACKIE ROBINSON HIT THAT BALL?, 1949
Count Basie and His Orchestra
RCA Victor (45) 47-2990
Reverse: "Shoutin' Blues"
Also available: RCA Victor (78)
20-3514
On *The Complete Count Basie: Volume 19*
Ajazz (33) 409

DOBY AT THE BAT, c. 1948
Fatman Humphries
Abbey (78) 3016

*Tribute to Cleveland Indians' outfielder Larry
Doby, the first black to play in the American
League.*

DOBY'S BOOGIE, c. 1948
Freddy Mitchell Orchestra
Derby (78) 713

Tribute to Larry Doby.

DODGER BLUE, 1977
Sue Raney
Blue Label Records 7-inch ep (33)
unnumbered
Written by Dave Frishberg
Published by Swiftwater Music
(ASCAP)
Reverse: "Van Lingle Mungo"

Pop vocal tribute to the Los Angeles Dodgers.

DODGER BLUE, 1981
Los Bahos
Mystic 7-inch picture record (45) MP 45
Published by Doug Moody Music (BMI)
Reverse: "Fernando"

*Spanish-language tribute to the Los Angeles
Dodgers.*

DODGER BLUE, 1983
Dave Frishberg
On *The Dave Frishberg Songbook,
Volume No. 2*
Omnisound (33) N 1051

DODGER CALYPSO, 1962
The Dodgermen
Milt Jim (45) 1001
Credits: Deutsch
Reverse: "Dodgers Song"

DODGERS CHARGE, 1960
Bob Grabeau
Magnolia (45) 1
Written by Gerald Bowne, Horace
Heidt, and Ivan Ditmar
Published (1960) by Amco, Inc.
(ASCAP)
Reverse: "Angel Town"

*Tribute to the 1959 world champion Dodgers.
Label states the song title as, "Charge."*

DODGERS CHARGE (1960 VERSION), 1960
Bill Reeves
Magnolia (45) 1001
Written by Gerald Bowne, Horace
Heidt, and Ivan Ditmar
Published by Amco, Inc. (ASCAP)
Reverse: *Casey at the Bat*
(Vin Scully)

DODGERS FAN DANCE, 1941
Harry James Orchestra
Columbia (78) 36222
Written by Harry James and Jack W.
Matthias
Published by Paramount Music Corp.
(ASCAP).
Reverse: "Lament to Love"

D-O-D-G-E-R-S SONG, 1962
(Oh, Really? No, O'Malley)
Danny Kaye
Reprise (45) 20105

Written by Sylvia Fine and Herbert
Baker
Published by Dena Music, Inc.
(ASCAP)
Reverse: "Myti Kaysi at the Bat"

*Humorous song describing a crucial game
between the Dodgers and Giants.*

DODGERS SONG, 1962
The Dodgermen
Milt Jim (45) 1001
Credits: Deutsch
Reverse: Dodger Calypso

DODGER STADIUM, 1964
Maury Wills, Willie Davis, and
Stubby Kaye
On *The Sound of the Dodgers*
Jaybar (33) 1
Written by Jackie Barnett
Published by Jaybar Music

*Wills and Davis are Los Angeles Dodgers
teammates.*

DOIN' THE GOOSE, 1984
Glenn Erath
On *Sounds of Success: Music of a
Winning Season*
San Diego Padres (33) unnumbered

*Tribute to Padres' relief pitcher Rich (Goose)
Gossage.*

DON NEWCOMBE REALLY THROWS THAT BALL
Teddy Brannon Orchestra
Regal (78) 3236

Tribute to the Brooklyn Dodgers' pitcher.

DONTCHA JUST KNOW IT, 1984
Stormy Weather
Canterbury (45) CP-2100
Published by Ace Publishing (BMI)
Reverse: "The Land of Wrigley"

Tribute to the Chicago Cubs.

DON'T TAKE YOUR HORSE TO THE BALL GAME, 1958
Patti Moore and Benny Lessy

On *Hilarity in Hollywood* (various artists)
Hilarity (33) 1-001
Written by Mac Maurada, music by Norman Hawes
Published by Pell Mell Music/Hel-Mac Music (ASCAP)

Comic nonsense song.

DR. K, 1986
Dwight Gooden and the MCL Rap Machine
Vine St. 12-inch single (33) 004 EP
Written by M. Owens and L. Barry
Published by Port St. Joe Music (BMI)

Rap tribute to the New York Mets' star pitcher Dwight Gooden.

DREAMS CAN COME TRUE: ODE TO RAY, 1984
Mutimer and Friends
On *Sounds of Success: Music of a Winning Season*
San Diego Padres (33) unnumbered

Tribute to the San Diego Padres and its late owner Ray Kroc.

A DYING CUB FAN'S LAST REQUEST, 1981
Steve Goodman
Red Pajamas (45) 1001
Published by Big Ears Music, Inc./Red Pajamas Music, Inc. (ASCAP)
Reverse: "Take Me Out to the Ball Game"
Also available: (1983) On *Affordable Art* Red Pajamas (33) 002

Humorous song about a dying man's wish to be buried in Wrigley Field.

THE EARL OF BALTIMORE, 1982
Terry Cashman
Lifesong (45) 45119
Published by PKM Music (ASCAP)
Reverse: "Baseball Ballet"

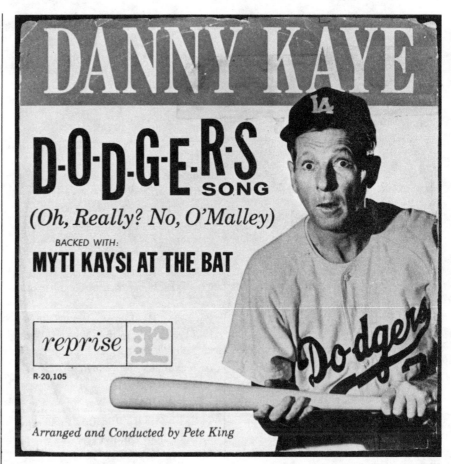

The inimitable Danny Kaye describes a crucial Dodger-Giant game in this humorous song recorded in 1962. (Reprise, 1962.)

Also available: Lifesong picture disc (33) 8138

Tribute to Earl Weaver upon his retirement as manager of the Orioles.

EL CIELO ES AZUL, 1982
The Sketch
Loose Leaf (45) 103
Written by Elliott Morabia and Joey Nasar
Published by Split Music (BMI)
Reverse: "Sky Blue"

Spanish-language tribute to the Los Angeles Dodgers.

EXPOS ALL THE WAY, 1982
Terry Cashman
Lifesong (45) 45115

"Talkin' Baseball" tribute to the Montreal Expos.

EXTRA INNINGS, 1968
Denny McLain
Capitol (45) 2282
Written by Robert Schneider and Ernie Skuta
Published by Beechwood Music Corp. (BMI)
Reverse: "Lonely is the Name"

Also available: On *Denny McLain at the Organ* Capitol (33) ST-2881

Organ instrumental by the Detroit Tigers' pitching star.

THE FANS' MARCH, 1909
John J. Kimmel
Zonophone 10-inch double-faced record 5184
Reverse: ''Tipperary March''
Also available: (1909) Edison 2-minute wax cylinder 10172; (1909) Indestructible 2-minute wax cylinder 1065

Accordion instrumental saluting baseball fans.

FERNANDO, 1981
Stanley Ralph Ross
Horn (45) 10
Written by Stanley Ralph Ross and Jimmie Haskell
Published by Hollywood Boulevard Music (ASCAP)
Reverse: ''Speedy Fernando''

Tribute to Fernando Valenzuela of the Los Angeles Dodgers.

FERNANDO, 1981
Los Bahos
Mystic 7-inch picture record (45) MP 45
Published by Doug Moody Music (BMI)
Reverse: ''Dodger Blue''

Spanish-language tribute to Fernando Valenzuela.

FERNANDO, EL TORO, 1981
Lalo Guerrero
Ambiente 7-inch ep (45) 001 (blue wax)
Written by Mark Guerrero
Published by Ynez Avenue Music (BMI)
Reverse: ''Ole! Fernando''

Tribute to Fernando Valenzuela.

FERNANDO SUPERSTAR, 1983
Claudio Merloni
Royal Blue Sky (45) unnumbered
Published by Royal Blue Sky Music (BMI)
Reverse: Same (Spanish version)

Tribute to Fernando Valenzuela.

THE FIGHTIN' PHILS, 1950
Delaware County String Band of Pennsylvania
Reel (78) 1000
Written by Bix Reichner and Elliot Lawrence
Published (1950) by Elliot Music Co., Inc. (ASCAP)
Cover: Phillies caricature leaning on a bat
Reverse: ''The Red We Want Is the Red We've Got in the Old Red, White and Blue''
Also available: Rainbow (78) 11188

Tribute to the Philadelphia Phillies.

THE FIGHTIN' PHILS, 1950
Mike Pedicin Quintet
Malvern (45) 1000
Reverse: ''Always, Always, Always''

THE FIRST BASEBALL GAME, 1947
Johnny Mercer
Capitol (78) 15096
Written by Don Raye and Gene DePaul
Published by Leeds Music Corp. (ASCAP)
Reverse: ''Sweetie Pie''

Humorous song about how the first baseball game might have been played in the Bible.

THE FIRST BASEBALL GAME, 1961
Nat King Cole
Capitol (45) 4555
Reverse: ''Goodnight, Little Leaguer''

FOLLOW THE DODGERS, 1951
Gladys Goodding
Sports (78) 7115
Vocals by the Bank of Manhattan Chorus
Published by Schwartz Music Co., Inc. (ASCAP)

Official song of the Brooklyn Dodgers.

FOR ALL THE YEARS, 1984
(A Tribute to Phil Niekro)
Terry Cashman
Metrostar (45) 84451
Published by Metrostar Music (ASCAP)
Reverse: ''Baseball and the Braves''

Pop vocal tribute to the Atlanta Braves' knuckleballer.

FOREVER DODGER BLUE, 1982
Terry Cashman
Lifesong (45) 45098

''Talkin' Baseball'' tribute to the Dodgers.

THE GAME, 1955
See: Damn Yankees

A ballplayer, no matter how tempted or distracted he may be, must always keep his mind on the game at hand.

GEE BUT IT'S GREAT AT THE BASEBALL GAME, 1940
See: ''It's Great at a Baseball Game''

GENE AUTRY'S DREAM, 1983
Robb Corless
California Angels unnumbered cassette
Written by Marc Adams and Robb Corless

Country-and-western tribute to the California Angels.

GIANTS BY THE BAY, 1982
Terry Cashman
Lifesong (45) 45102

''Talkin' Baseball'' tribute to the Giants.

Songs to Baseball Heroes

One of the greatest pleasures of being a baseball fan is watching a newfound baseball star explode upon the scene. Except for a major league team's late-season pennant drive, nothing galvanizes a baseball city more than a charismatic hometown hero having a sensational rookie year.

One way to determine how enthusiastically a city embraces its newest baseball star is to count the number of songs that have been written and recorded about the player during his rookie year. Using such a gauge, pitcher Fernando Valenzuela of the Los Angeles Dodgers is the most celebrated rookie ever to play in the major leagues.

When the 20-year-old left-hander won his first eight games without a defeat in 1981, all of Los Angeles, and especially the Hispanic community of East Los Angeles, went wild over the Mexican-born pitcher. His every appearance was played before capacity crowds that were ebullient, excited, and lustily vocal. Outside Dodger Stadium hundreds of street vendors hawked T-shirts, bumper stickers, and phonograph recordings in tribute to the young star. Although the recorded songs were not original or musically distinctive, they nonetheless expressed the unrestrained joy of having discovered a genuine baseball hero.

Important as Fernando's ethnic heritage was to a city with a Mexican population larger than any in the world except Mexico City, it was not the only reason for the enthusiastic reception given him by Los Angeles. For one, Fernando, like Babe Ruth, was portly but athletically graceful, boyishly charming but deadly serious on the field. Just as the Babe, as an outfielder, never missed a cutoff man or threw to the wrong base, Fernando always seemed to have total mastery of the game. He possessed the poise not so much of a veteran but of a skilled artisan. In his 1981 rookie season, Fernando Valenzuela didn't simply pitch games, he crafted them.

And just as Babe Ruth rescued baseball from the perilous throes of the 1919 "Black Sox" scandal, Fernando was a bright and rising star during the strike-shortened 1981 season. The lingering effects of the long and bitter baseball players' strike were almost completely mitigated by Fernando's fortuitous arrival on the baseball scene.

While Fernando was feted by over a dozen songs in his honor, the first widely popular recorded tribute to a baseball star was "Joltin' Joe DiMaggio" in 1941, the year of his incredible 56-game hitting streak. The first rookie ever celebrated in recorded song was Jackie Robinson in 1947, with Buddy Johnson's "Did You See Jackie

---

Fernando Valenzuela was feted with over a dozen songs in his honor during his explosive 1981 rookie year, including this Carmen Moreno recording. (Kelly Records, 1981.)

Robinson Hit That Ball?'' and Brownie McGhee's ''Baseball Boogie,'' a jubilant tribute to the first black major leaguer. Larry Doby, the first black to play in the American League, was honored with ''Doby's Boogie'' and ''Doby at the Bat'' a year later.

But the player who generated the most excitement and celebration in the black community was Willie Mays in 1954, when, as a 23-year-old centerfielder, he hit a league-leading .345 and crashed 41 home runs to guide the New York Giants to a World Series championship. While Jackie Robinson was held in awe and revered by the black community, Willie Mays was embraced as a favorite son by the old men sitting on the stoops and as an older brother by the urchins playing stickball in the streets. Jackie Robinson was anointed by the gods to bear the burdens of destiny. But Willie Mays was sprung as if from a catapult, to catch—over his shoulder with cap flying—the bright golden orb of a people's joys and dreams.

It is difficult to appreciate Willie Mays's baseball career without knowing the effect his meteoric 1954 season had on all America. As with Valenzuela nearly 30 years later, dozens of products and giveaways, from comic books to ''Say Hey'' baseball caps, flooded the baseball landscape. And at least a dozen recorded song tributes including Mays's own ''Say Hey (The Willie Mays Song)'' were released that year. Young Willie Mays, just returned from military service and about to embark on an amazing baseball career, had become a full-blown American institution. He has remained one ever since.

Hank Aaron's assault on Babe Ruth's career home run record did not go unrecorded by the songwriters' pen. Former major leaguer Bill Slayback recorded and cowrote the most famous of the half dozen or so Aaron tributes, ''Move Over Babe (Here Comes Henry)'' in 1974. Pittsburgh Pirates pitcher Nellie Briles enjoyed popular success during the off-season of 1973 with his recording of ''Hey Hank I Know You're Gonna Do It,'' in which he implores the Atlanta Braves slugger not to hit home run number 715 off of him—an impossibility, as it turned out, because Briles was traded to the American League Kansas City Royals before the historic 1974 season.

Not every baseball rookie celebrated in popular song has a long and prosperous career. In 1980, the year before Fernando's arrival, Joe Charboneau enjoyed a fine rookie season as an outfielder for the Cleveland Indians, hitting 23 home runs to win the American League Rookie of the Year award. But the song, ''Go Joe Charboneau'' was not a harbinger of success for the slugger. By 1983 Charboneau was out of baseball, a forgotten hero who no longer heard the cheers—or the melodies. ◆

THE GIANTS' MARCH, 1947
Ray Bloch and His Military Band
Signature (78) 15122
Vocals by the Grenadiers
Written by Buddy Kaye, James Lozito, and Fred Wise
Reverse: ''The Umpire Is a Most Unhappy Man''

Tribute to the New York Giants.

GIMME THAT GAME OF BASEBALL
Harry Lipton
Pandemonium (78)

GO, CUBS, GO, 1984
Steve Goodman
WGN (45) 784
Published by Big Ears Music/Red

Pajamas Music (ASCAP)

Official theme song of the Chicago Cubs.

GO FERNANDO, 1981
Everardo y Su Flota
Profono (33) 3051

Contains nine Spanish-language tributes to pitcher Fernando Valenzuela of the Los Angeles Dodgers.

GO FERNANDO, 1981
Carmen Moreno
Kelly (45) 101
Written by Dan Dalton, Carmen
Moreno, and John Reynolds
Published by Bresnahan Music (BMI)

*Tribute to Los Angeles Dodgers' pitcher
Fernando Valenzuela.*

GO! GO! GO! CHICAGO CUBS!,
1969
Marie R. Fuller
Fuller Records (45) 711
Published by Marie R. Fuller, Park
Forest, Illinois

GO, GO, GO, SOX, 1960
Bob Elson
Magnolia (45) 1002
Written by Gerald Bowne, Horace
Heidt, and Ivan Ditmar
Published (1960) by Amco, Inc.

Tribute to the Chicago White Sox.

GO-GO PHILLIES, c. 1964
The Umpires
Jaclyn one-sided record (45) 101
Written by Barry Abbott and Johnny
Bond
Published by Tempter (BMI)

*Rock-and-roll tribute to the Philadelphia
Phillies.*

GO JOE CHARBONEAU, 1980
Section 36
Carrot (45) 11803
Written by Don Kriss and Stan Bloch
Published by Carrotunes (BMI)
Reverse: Part II

*Tribute to the rookie sensation for the Cleveland
Indians.*

GOODNIGHT, LITTLE
LEAGUER, 1961
Nat King Cole
Capitol (45) 4555

Written by Dorcas Cochran and Russ
Black
Published by Bradshaw Music, Inc.,
Hollywood, California (BMI)
Reverse: ''The First Baseball Game''

*Sentimental ballad about the dreams of a
baseball-loving child.*

GRAND OLD MAN OF
BASEBALL, 1950
Four Buddies
Eagle (78)
Written by Teddy Troy
Published (1950)) by Troy Music Co.,
Philadelphia
Cover: Photograph of Connie Mack

*Tribute to the Hall of Fame manager of the
Philadelphia Athletics.*

GREAT BIG CASEY
Four Buddies
Eagle (78) 103

GREAT BIG CASEY
Charlie Moore and Bill Napier
King (45)

GREEN GRASS OF SHEA, 1969
Featuring the voices of the New York
Mets
On *The Amazing Mets*
Buddah (33) Mets 1969
Written by Stan Vincent
Published by Kama Sutra/Duckson
Music (BMI)

Tribute to the New York Mets.

HAIL GIANTS, c. 1962
Nick Alexander and the Bat Boys
Embee (45) 1002
Written by Bob Britton and Maury
Wolohan
Published by Paul Barrett Music, Inc.
(BMI)
Reverse: ''Win, Giants, Win''

Tribute to the San Francisco Giants.

HAMMERING HANK, 1973
Blast Furnace Band and the
Grapevine Singers
Clintone (45) 012
Written by Sam Dees and C. Yelder
Published by Moonsong (BMI)

*Pop vocal tribute to Atlanta Braves' slugger
Hank Aaron.*

HANK DONE IT AGAIN, c. 1974
Willie Dixon
Yambo (45)
Reverse: ''That Last Home Run''

Tribute to Hank Aaron.

HEART, 1955
See: Damn Yankees

*To win at baseball—and life—''you gotta have
heart.''*

HEART, 1955
Eddie Fisher
RCA (45) 6097
Reverse: ''Near to You''

HEART, 1955
Four Aces
Decca (45) 29476
Reverse: ''Sluefoot''

HEART, 1969
Featuring the voices of the New York
Mets
On *The Amazing Mets*
Buddah (33) Mets 1969

HERE COME THE YANKEES,
1967
Sid Bass Orchestra and Chorus
Columbia (45) 44083
Written by Lou Stallman and Bob
Bundin
Published (1967) by Blackwood
Music, Inc. (BMI)

Pop vocal tribute to the New York Yankees.

HERE WE GO PADRES, 1983
The Other Brothers
Ardmore Media Production Co.
unnumbered cassette
Written by Paul T. Coffman

Tribute to the San Diego Padres.

HE'S A FAN, FAN, FAN, 1940
Frank Luther, Zora Layman and the
Century Quartet
On *Decca Presents "Take Me Out to the
Ball Game"*
Decca album No. 120 (78) 3210-3212
Written by Florence Holbrook and
Cecil Lean
Published (1909) by M. Witmark and
Sons, New York

*Humorous song about a baseball fanatic.
Included in the musical comedy, Bright Eyes
(1920).*

HEY HANK I KNOW YOU'RE GONNA DO IT, 1974
Nellie Briles
Capitol (45) 3851
Written by Mark Barkan and Donald
Oriolo
Published by Cypher Music, Inc. /
Pambar Music Ltd./ Vin Joy Music
Co./Vin Lou Music, Inc. (ASCAP)

*Pittsburgh Pirates' pitcher asks Hank Aaron to
hit his historic 715th home run off of a pitcher
other than himself.*

HEY, HEY! HOLY MACKEREL!, 1969
*See: "Chicago Cubs Song: Hey, Hey!
Holy Mackerel!"*

HEY PADS, 1984
Glenn Erath
On *Sounds of Success: Music of a
Winning Season*
San Diego Padres (33) unnumbered

Tribute to the San Diego Padres.

HIT DE LONG BALL
Four Happy Fellas
Tabb (45) 1012
Written by Ben Barton and Edward
Martin
Published (1957) by Barton Music
Corp. (ASCAP)
Reverse: "It's Illegal, It's Immoral"

*Calypso song in which a batter is implored to
hit a home run.*

HOME OF THE BRAVES, 1970
Tim McCabe
Published (1970) by Lowery Music
Co., Inc.

HOME OF THE PADRES
Tim McCabe
Blue Orpheus (45)

HOME RUN, c. 1960
Chance Halladay
Bull Dog (45) 103
Written by Bobby Please
Published by Wares Music and Star
Kaye Music (BMI)
Reverse: "Deep Sleep"

*The game of love is told using baseball
terminology.*

HOME RUN BILL, 1940
Frank Luther, Zora Layman and the
Century Quartet
On *Decca Presents "Take Me Out to the
Ball Game"*
Decca album No. 120 (78) 3210-3212
Written by Alfred Bryan, music by
Jerome Shay
Published (1911) by Chas. K. Harris,
New York
Cover: Illustration of batter, catcher,
and umpire

*Humorous ballad about a slugger who fans in a
pinch.*

HOME RUN KING, 1977
Gene Clark

RSO (45) 876
Published by Irving Music, Inc. (BMI)
Also available: On *Two Sides to Every
Story* RSO (33) 1-3011

HOME RUN MAN, 1966
Jimmy Martin
Decca (45) 32031
Written by Martin and White
Published by Champion Music Corp.
(BMI)
Reverse: "You're Gonna Change"

*The game of love is told using baseball
terminology.*

HOMERUN WILLIE, 1977
Larry Hosford
Warner Bros. (45) 8445
Published by His and Hers/On Fire
Music (BMI)

*Poignant ballad about an aging but still heroic
Willie Mays.*

HOUSTON LOVES THE ASTROS
Steve and the Astro Fans
Bellaire (45) 5079
Written by Barbara Livitz and Linda
Miller
Published by Melody Lane
Publications (BMI)

Tribute to the Houston Astros.

HURRAH FOR OUR BASEBALL TEAM!, 1910
Fred Lambert
Zonophone 10-inch double-faced
record 5644
Reverse: "Mary, You're a Big Girl
Now"

I CAN'T MISS THAT BALL GAME, 1940
Frank Luther, Zora Layman and the
Century Quartet
On *Decca Presents "Take Me Out to the
Ball Game"*
Decca album No. 120 (78) 3210–3212
Written by George Moriarty, music
by Joseph Cooper

Published (1910) by Harry Cooper
Music Pub. Co, New York
Cover: Children peeking through a
knot-hole in the fence

*The joys of attending a baseball game are
celebrated. Songster Moriarty played 13 years
in the major leagues, primarily as an infielder
for the Detroit Tigers.*

I HATE BASEBALL, 1981
A. Player and the Zanies
Dore (45) 974
Written by Glen Erath, Joe Bauer, and
Cindy Bauer
Published by Meadowlark Music, Inc.
(ASCAP)
Reverse: "Dancing with Ronnie Cey"

*Satirical song in which a baseball player
professes his distaste for the game.*

I LIKE BASEBALL, 1980
New Marines
Pro America (45) unnumbered
Written by Brad Thiel
Reverse: "From These Parts"

*"New wave" reverse parody in which baseball
and all things American are embraced.*

I LOVE MICKEY, 1956
Teresa Brewer and Mickey Mantle
Coral (45) 61700
Written by Teresa Brewer, Ruth
Roberts, and William Katz
Published (1956) by Willow Music
Corp., New York
Cover: Photograph of Teresa Brewer
and Mickey Mantle
Reverse: "Keep Your Cotton Pickin'
Paddies Offa My Heart"
Also available: Coral (78) 61700

*Female baseball fan expresses her admiration for
New York Yankees' slugger Mickey Mantle.*

I LOVE THE NEW YORK YANKEES, 1983
Kimm Fedena
Yankee Girl (45) 701
Written by Paula Gay Lindstrom

Published by Yankee Girl Music
(ASCAP)

I'M A BALLPLAYER
Lenny Randle and the Ballplayers
Ballplayers (45)
Reverse: "Kingdome"

Randle is a member of the Seattle Mariners.

I'M A CUBBIE FAN, 1984
No artist given
Breezeway (45) 2521
Written by P. Kamoske, S. Barri, and
P. Sloan
Published (1984) by Saw Rite Music
(BMI)/MCA Music, Inc. (ASCAP)

Tribute to the Chicago Cubs.

IS THERE A LITTLE LEAGUE IN HEAVEN?
Charlie Walker
Mission (45) CW 3
Written by George Wells and Billy
Stone
Published by Tidewater Music/Little
David Music (BMI)
Reverse: "We Thank God for the
Roses"

*Sentimental ballad in which a father expresses
his religious faith in the face of his baseball-
loving son's impending death.*

IT'S A BEAUTIFUL DAY FOR A BALL GAME, 1960
The Harry Simeone Songsters
20th-Fox (45) 197
Written by Ruth Roberts, William
Katz, Gene Piller, and Harry Simeone
Published (1960) by Famous Music
Corp. (ASCAP)
Cover: Photograph of baseball action
Reverse: "Won't You Marry Me?"

*Celebration of the joys of attending a baseball
game.*

IT'S A BEAUTIFUL DAY FOR A BALL GAME c. 1980
Helen Dell

*George Moriarty, the only major leaguer to
have earned membership in the American Society of Composers, Authors, and Publishers
(ASCAP), was truly a jack of all baseball trades.
He played as an infielder for the Detroit Tigers,
managed two years for Detroit, and was a big
league umpire for many years. "I Can't Miss
That Ball Game," written by Moriarty in 1910
and recorded by Frank Luther and Zora Layman
in 1940, is yet another of Moriarty's contributions to baseball. (National Baseball Library.)*

Malar (45) MAS 2024
Reverse: "Take Me Out to the Ball
Game"

Organ instrumental.

IT'S GREAT AT A BASEBALL GAME, 1906
Billy Murray
Zonophone 10-inch single-faced
record 493
Written by Fred Fisher and George
Whiting
Published (1906) by Conn and Fisher
Music Pub. Co., Chicago

*The joys of attending a baseball game are
celebrated.*

BASEBALL'S GOLDEN BOY

In 1956 everybody loved Mickey Mantle. He was baseball's golden boy: a shy, muscular, small-town slugger who had taken New York and all of baseball by storm. He was the most feared home run hitter in the major leagues and the rightful heir to the once irreplaceable Joe DiMaggio in the Yankee Stadium center field. That year, 1956, was the season Mickey Mantle won the American League triple crown: most home runs (52), most RBIs (130), and highest batting average (.353), as the Yankees waltzed to their seventh American League pennant in eight years. That was also the year his life story was portrayed on television and a song was written and recorded in his honor. Here are the lyrics to "I Love Mickey," as sung by recording star Teresa Brewer and baseball star Mickey Mantle, with Mantle supplying—in not quite perfect pitch—the parenthetical queries:

I love Mickey! (Mickey who?) The fella with the celebrated swing.

I love Mickey! (Mickey who?) The one who drives me batty every spring.

If I don't make a hit with him, my heart will break in two.

I wish that I could catch him and pitch a little woo-oo!

I love Mickey! (Mickey who?) Mickey you.
I love Mickey! That's who-oo.
I love Mickey! Mickey Mantle I love you.

I love Mickey! (Mickey who?) His muscles are a mighty sight to see.

I love Mickey! (Mickey who?) The one I want to steal right home with me.

I'd sacrifice most anything to win his manly charms.

I'd like to be a fly ball and pop into his arms-oo!

I love Mickey! (Mickey who?) Mickey you.
I love Mickey! That's who-oo.
I love Mickey! (Not Yogi Berra?) Mm Mm I love you.

Words and music by Teresa Brewer, Ruth Roberts, and William Katz. © Copyright 1956 by Willow Music Corp. All rights reserved.

Also available: On *Return of the Wanderer* Lifesong (33) 35356

Bittersweet homage to the passing of youth.

I WANNA BE A YANKEE, 1982
Carmen Cassanova
EGI (45) 1115
Published by Irmil Music (BMI)
Reverse: "Boys Life—Girls Dream"

A baseball fan professes a desire to be a member of the New York Yankees.

I WANT TO GO TO THE BALL GAME, 1940
Frank Luther, Zora Layman and the Century Quartet
On *Decca Presents "Take Me Out to the Ball Game"*
Decca album No. 120 (78) 3210–3212
Written by Albert Von Tilzer, Ned Nye, and Charles Richel
Published (1909) by Broadway Music Corp., New York

Woman expresses her desire to attend a baseball game.

I WANT TO PLAY BALL FOR BILLY c. 1974
Jerry Hayes
Toro (45) 107
Reverse: "Billy's Turnaround Gang"

Tribute to Texas Rangers' manager Billy Martin.

IT'S GREAT AT A BASEBALL GAME, 1940
Frank Luther, Zora Layman and the Century Quartet
On *Decca Presents "Take Me Out to the Ball Game"*
Decca album No. 120 (78) 3210–3212

Song title on the record label is given as, "Gee But It's Great at the Baseball Game."

(I USED TO BE A) BROOKLYN DODGER, 1978
Dion (DiMucci)
Lifesong (45) 1785
Written by Dion DiMucci, Dan Beck, M. Tiernan, and R. Steele
Published by Blendingwell Music, Inc./County Line Music/Megabucks Music Co. (ASCAP)
Reverse: "Sweetheart Theme"

JOHNNY PODRES HAS A HALO 'ROUND HIS HEAD, c. 1955
Allen Swift
Jubilee (45)
Written by Horace Linsley and Allen Swift
Reverse: "Temper Is a Terrible Thing"

Tribute to Johnny Podres, who pitched the Brooklyn Dodgers to their first World Series championship.

JOLTIN' JOE DIMAGGIO, 1941
Les Brown and His Orchestra

Okeh (78) 6377
Vocals by Betty Bonney
Written by Alan Courtney and Ben Homer
Published (1941) by Alan Courtney Music Co.
Reverse: ''The Nickel Serenade''
Also available: (1949) Columbia (78) 38554

Tribute to the New York Yankees' outfielder during his 56-game hitting streak.

JOLTIN' JOE DIMAGGIO, 1941
Bob Chester and His Orchestra
Bluebird (78) 11316
Vocals by Bob Haymes
Reverse: ''This Love of Mine''

THE KANSAS CITY ROYALS ARE ON THE GO, 1977
Gene McKown
Column One (45) 1007
Written by Gene McKown and Marshall K. Admire
Published by Kuan Yin Publishing Co., Inc.

KINGDOME
Lenny Randle and the Ballplayers
Ballplayers (45)
Reverse: ''I'm a Ballplayer''

Tribute to the Seattle Mariners by one of its players.

KNOCK IT OUT OF THE PARK
Sam and Dave
Atlantic (45) 2733
Written by W. Martin and Dave Crawford
Published by Cotillion (BMI)
Reverse: ''You Easily Excite Me''

The game of love is told using baseball terminology.

LA LA LA LA, 1969
Featuring the voices of the New York Mets

Mickey Mantle led the hit parade on and off the baseball diamond in 1956. (Willow Music Corp., 1956.)

On *The Amazing Mets*
Buddah (33) Mets 1969

THE LAND OF WRIGLEY, 1984
Stormy Weather

Canterbury (45) CP-2100
Published by Alladin Publishing (BMI)
Reverse: ''Dontcha Just Know It''

Rock-and-roll tribute to the Chicago Cubs.

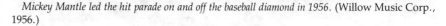

THE ONE MAN SHOW

You know you've had a good season when you win the Most Valuable Player award over a player who batted .406, hit a league leading 37 home runs, and drove in 120 runs. In 1941 Joe DiMaggio, by virtue of a .357 average, 125 RBIs, 30 home runs, and a memorable hitting streak, beat out the incomparable Ted Williams for the American League MVP. That was the year DiMaggio hit in an incredible 56 consecutive games, compiling 91 hits in 223 at bats during the streak for a 56-game batting average of .408. DiMaggio's hitting heroics captured the fancy of the entire nation and inspired a song that made the pop hit parade. Here are the lyrics to "Joltin' Joe DiMaggio," as written by Alan Courtney and Ben Homer:

> He started baseball's famous streak,
> That's got us all aglow,
> He's just a man and not a freak,
> Joltin' Joe DiMaggio.
> Joe Joe DiMaggio,
> We want you on our side.
>
> He'll live in baseball's hall of fame,
> He got there blow by blow,
> Our kids will tell their kids his name:
> Joltin' Joe DiMaggio.

> (We dream of Joey with the light brown bat).
> Joe Joe DiMaggio,
> We want you on our side.
>
> Tied the mark at forty four,
> July the first, you know.
> Since then he's hit a good twelve more,
> Joltin' Joe DiMaggio.
> Joe Joe DiMaggio,
> We want you on our side.
>
> Now they speak in whispers low,
> Of how they stopped our Joe.
> One night in Cleveland, oh-oh-oh!
> Goodbye streak DiMaggio.
> Joe Joe DiMaggio,
> We want you on our side.
>
> Coast to coast that's all you hear,
> Of Joe the one-man show.
> He's glorified the horsehide sphere,
> Joltin' Joe DiMaggio.
> Joe Joe DiMaggio,
> We want you on our side.

Joe DiMaggio's 56-game hitting streak in 1941 captivated a nation. (National Baseball Library.)

LET'S ALL GO TO THE BALL GAME, 1962
Kris Arden
Keepsake (45) 1006
Written by Bill Welsh and Gordon Vanderburg
Published (1962) by Keepsake Serenades (ASCAP)
Reverse: "Off to Seattle"

The joys of attending a baseball game are celebrated.

LET'S GET THE UMPIRE'S GOAT, 1940
Frank Luther, Zora Layman and the Century Quartet

On *Decca Presents ''Take Me Out to the Ball Game''*
Decca album No. 120 (78) 3210–3212
Written by Nora Bayes and Jack Norworth
Published (1909) by Jerome H. Remick and Co., New York
Cover: Cartoon of fans berating an umpire

Baseball fans berate the umpire. Included in the Ziegfeld Follies of 1909.

LET'S GO ANGELS, c. 1962
The Craftsmen
Scout (45) 435
Written by Al Trace and Ben Trace
Published by Le-Mor Music Co. (ASCAP)
Reverse: ''The Baseball Song''

Tribute to the American League Los Angeles Angels.

LET'S GO GO GO WHITE SOX, c. 1959
Captain Stubby and the Buccaneers
Drum Boy (45) 121
Written by Al Trace, Ben Trace, and Lil Wally
Published by Le-Mor Music Co. (ASCAP)
Reverse: ''The Old Ball Game''

Tribute to the American League champion ''Go-Go'' Chicago White Sox.

LET'S GO METS!, 1986
Featuring the voices of the New York Mets
Vestron 12-inch single (33)
See also: Baseball in Documentary and Miscellaneous Films

LET'S GO TO THE BALL GAME
Wayne Cody
Keystone (78) 10001

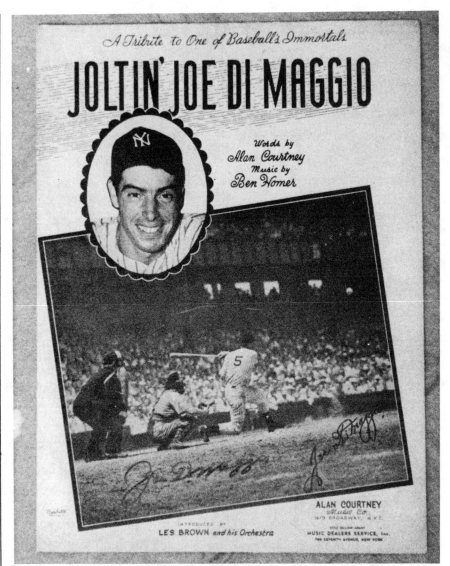

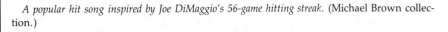

A popular hit song inspired by Joe DiMaggio's 56-game hitting streak. (Michael Brown collection.)

LET'S KEEP THE DODGERS IN BROOKLYN, 1957
Phil Foster
Coral (45) 61840
Written by Roy Ross, Sam Denoff, and Bill Persky
Published by Famous Music Corp.
Reverse: ''Listen All You Bachelors''

A Brooklyn Dodgers' fan asks that his favorite team not move to Los Angeles.

LET'S PLAY BALL, 1984
Buzz Barnaba
San Diego Padres (45) JP 001
Published by Dick Badger (BMI)
Reverse: ''The Operator''

Tribute to the San Diego Padres.

LITTLE BOY'S HERO, 1983
Larry Stewart
AFR (45) UR-4233
Published by Pyne Tar Publishing, Inc. (BMI)
Reverse: "Pine Tar Wars" (C. W. McCall)

Sentimental ballad about a baseball hero who hits a home run for a blind boy.

LITTLE LEAGUE, 1951
Leroy Holmes
MGM (45)
Written by Emerson Yorke, music by

Solita Palmer
Published (1947) by Carl Fischer, Inc. (ASCAP)
Reverse: "Take Me Out to the Ball Game"
Also available: MGM (78) 11016

Official march of Little League baseball.

LITTLE LEAGUE
Bunker Hillbillies
Seville (45) 106
Written by Mary Spaulding
Published by Rush Music (BMI)
Reverse: "Take Me Out to the Ball Game"

Celebration of the joys of playing in a youth baseball league.

LITTLE LEAGUER, 1955
Art Kassel and His Orchestra
Double-Play (45) D4-45-101 A
Written by Art Kassel
Published by Kassel Airs Music Co. (ASCAP)
Cover: Illustration of the official Little League emblem
Reverse: "Little League Field Ceremonies"
Also available: Double-Play (78) D4-101 A

A DODGER DIRGE

It still hurts to think of it. Two short years after having won their first ever World Series and 67 years after joining the National League—and all of the 10,253 lively, electrifying, disheartening, and daffy games in between—the Dodgers were leaving Brooklyn. It may seem in retrospect that the citizens of the borough did not sufficiently marshall their forces to prevent the move. Perhaps Brooklynites simply believed that it was not possible for the Dodgers to move to Los Angeles—or thought it too horrific a possibility to contemplate. Whatever the case may have been, the song "Let's Keep the Dodgers in Brooklyn" seems more a fan's way of not crying than the rallying cry of an aroused citizenry. Here's the lyrics to the 1957 song as recorded by Brooklyn comedian Phil Foster:

Say, did you hear the news about what's happening in Brooklyn?
We really got the blues about what's happening in Brooklyn.
It ain't official yet, we hope official it won't get,
But beware, my friend, and let me warn ya,
They're thinkin' of takin' the Bums to California.

Let's keep the Dodgers in Brooklyn,
A house is not a home without some love,
Don't let them leave our premises, L.A. would be their nemesis,
'Cause Brooklyn fits the Dodgers like a glove.

Brooklyn would be like a pair of socks that's holey
Without Jackson and Cimoli,
Like a bed without a pillow
Without Erskine and Furillo,
Like a ship without a harbor
Without Podres and the Barber,
Like the sun when it don't shine
Without Zimmer and Labine,
Like the birds without a bee
Without Alston and Pee Wee

. . . So send the Phils to Trenton, the Giants to St. Paul,
But keep the Dodgers in Brooklyn,
The greatest borough of all!

A LONG RUN HOME, 1981
Rick Cerone
Reel Dreams (45) 1002
Written by Carl Henry and Bill Hudak
Published by Carl Henry Music (BMI)

A baseball player regrets a lost opportunity for love. Cerone is a catcher for the New York Yankees.

LOVE GOES ON LIKE A BALLGAME
Tom Anderson
MGM (78) 1163-53

LOVE IS BIGGER THAN BASEBALL, 1973
Dexter Redding
Capricorn (45) 0033
Written by Jackie Avery and Carolyn Brown
Published by Redwal Music (BMI)
Reverse: "God Bless"

The importance of love is explained using baseball terminology.

LOVE IS BIGGER THAN BASEBALL, 1975
J. Allen
United Artists (45) x708

(LOVE IS LIKE A) BASEBALL GAME, 1968
The Intruders
Gamble (45) 217
Written by Kenny Gamble and Leon Huff
Published by Razor Sharp Music (BMI)
Reverse: "Friends No More"
Also available: On *Cowboys to Girls* Gamble (33) 5004; On *Super Hits* Philadelphia International (33) 32131

The game of romance is explained using baseball terminology.

THE MAN CALLED BENCH, 1983
Cliff Adams

High Spiral (45) 287
Written by Cliff Adams and T. Wakim
Published by High Spiral Music (BMI)
Reverse: "When Rock 'n Roll Was King"

Tribute to Cincinnati Reds catcher Johnny Bench.

MEET THE METS, 1964
Glenn Osser and His Orchestra
Michael Brent Records (45) NYM 1
Written by Ruth Roberts and William Katz
Published (1961) by Michael Brent Publications, Inc. (ASCAP)

Pop vocal tribute to the New York Mets.

MEN IN BLUE, 1984
Jody Davis, Leon Durham, Keith Moreland, Gary Woods, and Rick Sutcliffe
PR Records (45) 6
Written by J. Ritz and A. Petrowski
Published by Yarmouth Publishing (BMI)
Reverse: "Good Ol' Time Tonight"

Tribute to the Chicago Cubs by five of its players.

METS ARE HERE TO STAY, 1969
Featuring the voices of the New York Mets
On *The Amazing Mets*
Buddah (33) Mets 1969

METS BALL GAME, 1969
Featuring the voices of the New York Mets
On *The Amazing Mets*
Buddah (33) Mets 1969
Special lyrics by Stan Vincent and Mike Duckman

Parody of "Take Me Out to the Ball Game."

METS—HALLELUJAH, 1969
Featuring the voices of the New York Mets

This is one club that never really needed an introduction. Since 1962, when they lost 120 out of 160 games, they've been known the world over as those Amazin' Mets. (Michael Brent Records, 1964.)

On *The Amazing Mets*
Buddah (33) Mets 1969

THE MIGHTY BABE IS SAFE AT HOME, 1948
See: "Safe at Home"

MINOSO AL BATE, 1955
Tico (45)
Published by Barry Guy Enterprises, Inc. (ASCAP)

Latin rhythm tribute to Chicago White Sox outfielder Minnie Minoso.

THE MOTOR CITY TEAM, 1982
Terry Cashman
Lifesong (45) 45103

"Talkin' Baseball" tribute to the Detroit Tigers.

MOVE OVER BABE (HERE COMES HENRY), 1973
Bill Slayback
Karen (45) 714
Written by Ernie Harwell and Bill Slayback
Published by Iramac Music (ASCAP)

343

MOVE OVER BABE
(HERE COMES HENRY)

RECORDED BY
BILL SLAYBACK

KAREN RECORDS
714

Hank Aaron's assault on Babe Ruth's career home run record was celebrated with a half dozen recorded songs, including this one by Detroit Tigers pitcher Bill Slayback. (Karen Records, 1973.)

Tribute to Hank Aaron as he approached Babe Ruth's career home-run record. Slayback is a pitcher for the Detroit Tigers.

MOVE OVER BABE (HERE COMES HENRY), 1973
Richard (Popcorn) Wylie
Carla (45) 715

MOVIN' WITH THE GIANTS, 1965
Box and Bleacher Society
Mammoth (45) 823
Written by Alf Brinton
Published by Superchief Music (BMI)
Reverse: "Willie's Waheeda"
(Guajira)

Jazz vocal tribute to the San Francisco Giants.

MY SON THE PONY LEAGUER, c. 1960
Sammy Watkins Orchestra and the Big League Singers
Boys Baseball (45) unnumbered
Written by Sammy Watkins
Published by Big League Records (ASCAP)
Reverse: "We're the Best Ball Team (in the Neighborhood)"

NACAHOMA MURPHY, 1986
Wade Hester
Dog Gone 12-inch single (33) 1010
Published by Hesterdays Music (BMI)

Tribute to Atlanta Braves outfielder Dale Murphy.

THE NATIONAL GAME MARCH, 1925
John Philip Sousa's Band
Victor 10-inch double-faced record 19741
Written by John Philip Sousa
Published by Sam Fox Pub. Co., New York
Cover: Illustration of a batter and catcher
Reverse: "Black Horse Troop"

Dedicated to Judge Kennesaw Mountain Landis, commissioner of baseball.

THE NATIONAL GAME MARCH, 1926
New York Military Band
Edison Diamond Disc 51631
Reverse: "Black Horse Troop"

THE NATIONAL GAME MARCH
Eastman Wind Ensemble
On *Sousa on Review*
Mercury (33) SRI-75064

THE NATIONAL GAME MARCH, 1976
Detroit Concert Band
On *Sousa American Bicentennial Collection*
H & L (33) 62962

NATIONAL PASTIME, 1972
Gary Buck
RCA (45) 0013
Written by Michael Donovan
Published by Dunbar Music (BMI)

The game of love is explained using baseball terminology.

NEAR A DUGOUT, 1964
The Roy Ross Singers
On *Pennant Fever*
RGA (33) M-300
Written by Robert Goodman

Tribute to the Baltimore Orioles from a woman's point of view.

NEW BASEBALL BOOGIE, 1948
Brownie McGhee
Savoy (78) 5561
Reverse: "Good Thing Gone"

Tribute to Hall of Famer Jackie Robinson.

NIGHT GAME, 1975
Paul Simon
On *Still Crazy After All These Years*
Columbia (33) PC 33540
Published by Paul Simon (BMI)

Baseball is used metaphorically to portray the loneliness and finality of failure.

1984 CUBBIES, 1984
No artist given
Duke (45) 101

Tribute to the Chicago Cubs.

O'BRIEN TO RYAN TO GOLDBERG, 1949
Soundtrack
On *Take Me Out to the Ball Game*
Curtain Calls (33) 100/18
Vocals by Gene Kelly, Frank Sinatra, and Jules Munshin
Written by Betty Comden, Adolph Green, and Roger Edens

Filmic double-play combination engages in humorous self-boasting.

OH! DIDN'T IT RAIN, 1924
Frank Crumit
Victor 10-inch double-faced record 19469
Written by Eddie Leonard
Reverse: "No One Knows What It's All About"

Humorous song lamenting a rained-out game at Yankee Stadium.

OH! DIDN'T IT RAIN, 1925
Ernest Hare
Okeh 10-inch double-faced record
40305
Reverse: "Dear Old Lady"

OH! DIDN'T IT RAIN, 1940
Frank Luther, Zora Layman and the
Century Quartet
On *Decca Presents "Take Me Out to the
Ball Game"*
Decca album No. 120 (78) 3210–3212

OIL CAN, 1985
John Lincoln Wright and the
Designated Hitters
Lincoln Records (45) 003
Written by John Lincoln Wright
Published by Lincoln Lines (BMI)
Reverse: "Yaz's Last At Bat";" Ol'
.275"

*Tribute to Dennis "Oil Can" Boyd of the
Boston Red Sox.*

OK BLUE JAYS, 1983
The Bat Boys
Kosinec/Lenz (45) BJ 01
Published by Don't Blink Music, Inc.
(CAPAC)

Tribute to the Toronto Blue Jays.

THE OLD BALL GAME, c. 1959
Captain Stubby and the Buccaneers
Drum Boy (45) 121
Written by Al Trace, Ben Trace, and
Lil Wally
Published by Le-Mor Music Co.
(ASCAP)
Reverse: "Let's Go Go Go White Sox"

*The joys of attending a baseball game are
celebrated.*

THE OLD BALL GAME, c. 1984
King Hannibal
Real Good (45) 100-2

A MUSICAL LINEUP

By going around the horn, so to speak, and touching each base, we can come up with a pretty fair musical lineup of baseball stars. Here's an all-time all-star team of baseball player songs:

Left-handed pitcher: *"Dandy Sandy"* (1964), Sandy Koufax
Right-handed pitcher: *"Ballad of Satchel Paige"* (1982), Leroy "Satchel" Paige
Catcher: *"One Stop Along the Way"* (1983), Johnny Bench
First baseman: *"I Can't Get to First Base With You"* (1935), Lou Gehrig
Second baseman: *"Did You See Jackie Robinson Hit That Ball?"* (1947), Jackie Robinson
Third baseman: *"Charlie Hustle"* (1979), Pete Rose
Shortstop: *"Husky Hans"* (1904), Honus Wagner
Left fielder: *"Move Over Babe (Here Comes Henry)"* (1973), Hank Aaron
Center fielder: *"Homerun Willie"* (1977), Willie Mays
Right fielder: *"Batterin' Babe"* (1919), Babe Ruth
Manager: *"Grand Old Man of Baseball"* (1950), Connie Mack

Written by King Hannibal and Della Gartrell
Published by Captain Music (BMI)
Reverse: "Don't Go Looking"

*Baseball terminology symbolizes a repudiation
of a cocaine freebasing habit.*

OLE! FERNANDO, 1981
Lalo Guerrero

Ambiente 7-inch ep (45) 001 (blue wax)
Published by Ladera Music
Publishing (BMI)
Reverse: "Fernando, El Toro"

*Tribute to Los Angeles Dodgers' pitcher
Fernando Valenzuela.*

ONE GAME AT A TIME, 1976
Ron Cey
Long Ball (45) 100
Written by Clyde Curtis Ligons
Published by Long Ball Records
(ASCAP)
Reverse: "Third Base Bag"

*Pop vocal incorporating baseball terminology.
Cey is a third baseman for the Los Angeles
Dodgers.*

ONE STOP ALONG THE WAY, 1983
(The Ballad of Johnny Bench)
Terry Cashman
Lifesong (33) 8140
Published by Metrostar Music
(ASCAP)

*Title track of the album is a tribute to Johnny
Bench upon his retirement from baseball.
Includes: "Cincinnati's Red Machine";
"Broadcast Highlights of Johnny Bench's
Career."*

ORIOLES MAGIC (FEEL IT HAPPEN), 1980
Perfect Pitch
Baltimore Orioles (45) 3001

ORIOLE VICTORY SONG
Ray Charles Singers
Cotillion (78) EB 2532

OUR NATIONAL PASTIME, 1974
Rupert Holmes
Epic (45) 5-11117
Published by Leeds Music Corp./
Widescreen Publ., Inc. (ASCAP)
Reverse: "Phantom of the Opera"
Also available: On *Widescreen* Epic
(33) KE 32864

Humorous commentary—incorporating baseball terminology—on the ritualization of romance.

OUR OLD HOME TEAM, 1963
Nat King Cole
On *Those Lazy-Hazy-Crazy Days of Summer*
Capitol (33) T-1932

Celebration of the joys of attending a baseball game.

PADRES ALL THE WAY, 1983
Terry Cashman
Lifesong (45) 45123
Also available: On *Sounds of Success: Music of a Winning Season* San Diego Padres (33) unnumbered

PADRES POP, 1984
No artist given
Creative Music 7-inch ep (45) CF 11
Written by C. Furgatch
Reverse: "We're Winning Again"

Title of the extended-play recording is, "Oh Doctor! You Gotta Hang a Star on That Baby!"

PADRES WIN AGAIN, 1984
Eric Show
On *Sounds of Success: Music of a Winning Season*
San Diego Padres (33) unnumbered

Tribute to the San Diego Padres by one of its pitchers.

PAUL RICHARDSON PLAYS ORGAN FOR THE PHILLIES, 1972
Paul Richardson
Philadelphia Phillies (33) AZ 99961

Includes: "Take Me Out to the Ball Game."

PENNANT DREAM
The Orange Express
Uranus Corp. (45) unnumbered
Reverse: "Se Comuirto en Relidad"

Tribute to the San Diego Padres.

PENNANT FEELING, 1969
Nate Oliver, Gene Oliver, and Willie Smith
On *Cub Power*
Quill (33) 1001
Special lyrics by Gene Oliver

Tribute to the Cubs by three of its players.

PENNANT FEVER, 1964
The Roy Ross Singers
RGA (33) M-300
Written by Robert Goodman

Tribute to the Baltimore Orioles. Includes: "Pennant Fever"; "Bunker Hill"; "Ramblin' Scramblin' "; "Win or Lose"; "The Bird Magic Man"; "That Yankee Game"; "Would You Rather"; "Call to the Bullpen"; "Near a Dugout"; "Please Leave Us Alone"; "Refuse to Lose."

PENNANT FEVER, 1964
The Roy Ross Singers
On *Pennant Fever*
RGA (33) M-300
Written by Robert Goodman

Title track of the album is a musical tribute to the Baltimore Orioles.

PENNANT FEVER, 1969
Featuring the voices of the Chicago Cubs
Chess (45) 2075
Written by Davenport and Cooly
Special lyrics by Kal Mann
Published by Jay and Cee Music Corp. (BMI)
Reverse: "Slide"

Tribute to the Chicago Cubs.

PETE'S HIT RECORD, 1985
Gale Watson
Genius (45) 4192
Written by M. Shannon and J. Hazelbaker
Published by Wheelsongs Music Pub. (BMI)

Tribute to Pete Rose upon becoming the all-time career hit leader.

THE PHILADELPHIA FILLIES, 1971
Del Reeves
United Artists (45) 50802
Written by Jim Mundy
Published by Acuff-Rose Publications, Inc. (BMI)
Reverse: "Belles of Broadway"

The virtues of Philadelphia's women are told using baseball terminology.

PHILLIES FEVER, 1977
Dave Cash, Larry Bowa, Mike Schmidt, Greg Luzinski, and Garry Maddox
Grand Prix (45) 207
Written by Walt Kahn, Lorenzo Wright, and Rich Wing
Reverse: "Dancin' with the Phillies"

Tribute to the Phillies by five of its players.

THE PINE TARRED BAT, 1983
(The Ballad of George Brett)
Red River Dave (McEnery)
Longhorn (45) 2004
Published by Scriptomuse and Golden Gelt Music (ASCAP)
Reverse: "The Clinging Lovers of Kenya"

PINE TAR WARS, 1983
C. W. McCall
AFR (45) UR-4233
Written by Larry Stewart and Larry Isley
Published by Pyne Tar Publishing, Inc. (BMI)
Reverse: "Little Boy's Hero" (Larry Stewart)

Novelty tribute to George Brett and his controversial pine-tarred bat.

PLAY BALL, 1951
Frank Devol
Capitol (78) 1460
Written by Hector D. Marchese
Published by Roger Music, Inc.

Reverse: "Theme for John and Marsha"

The joys of attending a baseball game are celebrated.

PLAY BALL, 1951
Frankie Yankovic and His Yanks
Columbia (45) 39327
Reverse: "Shenandoah Waltz"

PLAY BALL, c. 1955
Jimmie Maddin
Skyway (45) 103
Written by Paul Vandervoort II, and
Benny Carter
Published by Skyway Record and
Music Pub. Co. (BMI)
Reverse: "Spring Fever Blues"

Jazz vocal celebration of baseball.

PLAY BALL YOU ALL
El Rojo and the Left Fielders
Redd-E (45) 5006
Written by Walter Bishop and Mel
Allen
Published (1952) by Jefferson Music
Co., Inc. (ASCAP)
Cover: Photograph of Mel Allen

PLAYING CATCH WITH THE
BABE, c. 1979
Jess DeMaine
Thurman (45) 82579

*Memorial tribute to New York Yankees' catcher
Thurman Munson.*

PLEASE JIMMY PIERSALL,
c. 1960
Jimmy Piersall and the Three
Heartbreakers
G.C. (45) 609
Written by Richard Mullan and
Hamish Menzies
Published by Jamige Music Co.
Reverse: "The Rookie of the Year"

*Piersall assures his fans that he will remain a
feisty ballplayer.*

PLEASE LEAVE US ALONE,
1964
The Roy Ross Singers
On *Pennant Fever*
RGA (33) M-300
Written by Robert Goodman

*Humorous plea from an Orioles' fan to players
from the opposing teams: "Please leave the
Orioles alone."*

POLISH BASEBALL POWER,
c. 1970
Sig Sakowicz
Mishawaka (45) 1702
Published by Hiawatha Pub. Co.
(ASCAP)

*Tribute to major league players of Polish
descent.*

POP FLY
Kay Thomas
Black and White (78) 784
Features the Maxwell Davis Orchestra

RAIN DELAY, 1982
Terry Cashman
On *Talkin' Baseball—American League*
Lifesong (33) 8136
Written by Terry Cashman and
Michael Mugrage
Published by Blendingwell Music,
Inc. (ASCAP)
Also available: On *Talkin' Baseball—
National League* Lifesong (33) 8137

*Life is compared to a rain-delayed baseball
game.*

RAMBLIN' SCRAMBLIN', 1964
The Roy Ross Singers
On *Pennant Fever*
RGA (33) M-300
Written by Robert Goodman

Tribute to the Baltimore Orioles.

THE RED SOX ARE WINNING,
1968
Earth Opera
On *Earth Opera*

Elektra (33) EKS- 74016
Written and vocals by Peter Rowan
Published by Nina Music (BMI)

*Young man tries to hold on.to baseball and
innocence during the Vietnam war.*

REFUSE TO LOSE, 1964
The Roy Ross Singers
On *Pennant Fever*
RGA (33) M-300
Written by Robert Goodman

Tribute to the Baltimore Orioles.

REGGIE FOR CHRISTMAS, 1982
Hozay Smith and the Hammerhead
Reel Dreams (45) 1005
Written by Jack Camarda, Carl
Henry, and Bill Hudak
Published by Carl Henry Music (BMI)
Reverse: "Silent Night"

*Humorous tribute to New York Yankees'
outfielder Reggie Jackson.*

ROBBIE-DOBY BOOGIE, c. 1948
Brownie McGhee
Savoy (78) 5550

*"Dedicated to Jackie Robinson and Larry
Doby."*

ROBERTO'S GONE, 1973
Jim Owen
Ace of Hearts (45) 0476
Published by Vector Music, Inc. (BMI)

*Memorial tribute to Pittsburgh Pirates
outfielder Roberto Clemente.*

THE ROOKIE OF THE YEAR,
c. 1960
Jimmy Piersall and the Three
Heartbreakers
G. C. (45) 609
Written by Richard Mullan and
Blanche Albritton
Published by Jamige Music Co.
Reverse: "Please Jimmy Piersall"

*In the game of romance, a ballplayer is a rookie
of the year. Piersall is an outfielder for the
Cleveland Indians.*

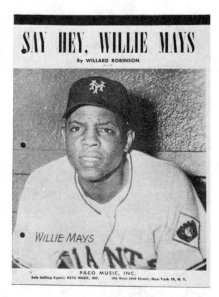

More than a half dozen songs were recorded in tribute to a new baseball hero during Willie Mays's electrifying 1954 season. (Michael Brown collection.)

SAFE AT HOME, 1948
(A Tribute to Babe Ruth)
Tex Fletcher
Flint (78) 1788
Written by Jack Rollins and Perry Alexander
Published (1948) by Dubonnet Music Publishing Co.
Cover: "A Tribute to our Beloved 'Babe' Ruth"

Memorial tribute to New York Yankees' Hall of Famer Babe Ruth.

SAFE AT HOME, 1948
The Jesters
Twentieth Century (78) 3
Reverse: "Take Me Out to the Ball Game"

THE SAN FRANCISCO GIANTS SONG, 1960
Paul Walti
Warner Bros. (45) 5138

Written by Bill Richardson
Published by M. Witmark and Sons (ASCAP)
Reverse: "The San Francisco Forty-Niners Song" (Aaron Edwards)

SAY HEY!, 1954
(A Tribute to Willie Mays)
The Nite Riders
Apollo (45) 460
Written and lead vocals by James "Doc" Starkes
Published by Bess Music (BMI)
Reverse: "Women and Cadillacs"

Tribute to New York Giants' outfielder Willie Mays.

SAY HEY (THE WILLIE MAYS SONG), 1954
Willie Mays and the Treniers
Epic (78) 9066
Written by Kleiner, Douglass, and Warner
Published by Jack Spina/Jane Douglass White (ASCAP)
Reverse: "Out of the Bushes" (The Treniers)
Also available: On *Okeh Rhythm and Blues* Epic (33) EG-37649

SAY HEY WILLIE
Ricky Segall
Bell (45) 45429
Published by Colgems EMI Music, Inc. (ASCAP)

Tribute to Willie Mays.

SAY HEY, WILLIE MAYS, 1954
The Wanderers
Decca (45) 29230
Written by Willard Robison
Published by Willard Robison (ASCAP)
Reverse: "Don't Drop It"

Joyous harmony celebrating the arrival of a new baseball star.

SAY HEY, WILLIE MAYS, 1954
Johnny Long
Coral (45) 61238

SEASONS IN THE SUN, 1985
(A Tribute to Mickey Mantle)
Terry Cashman
Metrostar (45) 4585-3
Published by Metrostar Music (ASCAP)
Reverse: "The Bambino, the Clipper and the Mick"

Pop music tribute to Hall of Famer Mickey Mantle.

SECOND BASE BLUES
John Hall and the Piemen
Otty (45) 101
Reverse: "Sunday Morning Softball"

SIGN A BALL FOR ME, 1981
Bill Momone
Globe Export 7-inch picture disc (33) unnumbered
Written by Steve Gardner
Reverse: Same (Spanish version)

Tribute to pitcher Fernando Valenzuela of the Los Angeles Dodgers.

SIX MONTHS OUT OF EVERY YEAR, 1955
See: Damn Yankees

Wife complains about her husband's preoccupation with baseball.

SKY BLUE, 1982
The Sketch
Loose Leaf (45) 103
Written by Elliott Morabia and Joey Nasar
Published by Split Music (BMI)
Reverse: "El Cielo Es Azul"

Tribute to the Los Angeles Dodgers.

SLIDE, KELLY, SLIDE, 1893
George J. Gaskin
North American Brown Wax cylinder 146

Written by John W. Kelly
Published (1889) by Frank Harding,
New York
Cover: Title of song in bold letters
Also available: Edison 2-minute wax
cylinder 1547

This tribute to Mike (King) Kelly is the earliest-known baseball-related song issued on a phonorecord.

SOCKIT TO 'EM TIGERS, c. 1968
York Mills Trio
Detroit Sound (45) 233
Written by Leonard Moss
Published by Detroit Sound Music
Co. (BMI)

SOLILOQUY OF A DODGER FAN, 1964

Stubby Kaye
On *The Sound of the Dodgers*
Jaybar (33) 1
Written by Jackie Barnett
Published by Jaybar Music

Humorous commentary on the fickleness of baseball fans who live and die for their team.

SOMEBODY'S KEEPING SCORE, 1964
Maury Wills
On *The Sound of the Dodgers*
Jaybar (33) 1
Written by Jackie Barnett and Sammy Fain
Published by Jaybar-Fain

Gospel song incorporating baseball terminology.

THE SONG FOR THE '69 METS, 1969
Featuring the voices of the New York Mets
On *The Amazing Mets*
Buddah (33) Mets 1969

SONG OF ROBERTO, 1973
Mario Martinelli
Chatham (45) 10
Written by Thomas E. Morgan and
Hamilton Whitlinger
Published (1973) by New Chatham Music

Tribute to Hall of Famer Roberto Clemente.

A Toast to King Kelly

Baseball's first hit song, and the most popular of all baseball songs until "Take Me Out to the Ball Game" was written in 1908, was an 1889 comic sendup of one of baseball's first true superstars. At once charming and audacious, flamboyant, frolicsome . . . and intoxicated, Mike (King) Kelly was the darling of the Gay Nineties baseball world. No other player of his time matched his competitive savvy or equalled his magnetic presence. As baseball's "King of the Diamond," Mike Kelly may have been the closest thing to a perfect amalgam of Ty Cobb and Babe Ruth that the world has ever known.

It is a measure of King Kelly's extraordinary baseball fame that the song, "Slide, Kelly, Slide" was such a popular hit. Like Ty Cobb, Kelly was known for his fearless, sometimes ferocious style of play, his peculiar grip of the bat (hands separated, like Cobb's), his daring base running despite having only slightly better than average speed, and his hitting heroics, as evidenced by a .388 batting average and an incredible 155 runs scored in 118 games in 1886. And like Cobb, Mike Kelly constantly sought new and innovative ways to gain the winning edge, such as being the first outfielder to back up the infield and the first catcher to back up first base. He was the first to develop the fadeaway or hook slide, which also was known as the "Chicago" slide, after the White Stockings for which Kelly played. Kelly was also credited by Cap Anson as having been the creator of the hit-and-run play.

Like Babe Ruth, King Kelly enjoyed a special relationship with the fans. While playing right field, he exhibited to the bleacherites the same lusty gregariousness so favored by his teammates. He possessed, again like Ruth, an engaging sense of self-perspective: he relished the role of seeming bigger than life while preferring the company of the common man. And though

349

One of the game's first superstars was catcher-outfielder Mike (King) Kelly, the darling of Chicago and Boston baseball fans during the 1880s and '90s. (National Baseball Library.)

Kelly, like the Babe, succumbed to frequent episodes of self-indulgence and intemperance, the fans always forgave him; indeed, were eager to forgive him. It was fortunate for the ballplayer that the fans forbore his trespasses because King Kelly was capable of so many of them.

So popular was the catcher-outfielder that for years the poem *Casey at the Bat* was customarily printed as *Kelly at the Bat*. King Kelly often gave a boisterous recitation of the ballad while holding sway over his admirers in a saloon. Next to his love of baseball and fondness for whiskey was

Kelly's fascination with the theater. Dressed in a dapper black coat and top hat, pearl-studded ascot, and sporting a luxurious handlebar mustache, King Kelly affected an actor's jaunty style. He never managed, however, to acquire an actor's skill. His appearances on the vaudeville stage were doleful exercises in unbridled histrionics.

Stories about King Kelly's baseball antics, quirky stratagems, and unabashed cheating have won a special niche in baseball folklore. In the 1800s only one umpire officiated a game and Kelly was not above cutting across the diamond while running from first to third when the umpire's back was turned. He also invented the ploy of dropping his catcher's mask on home plate or in the base path to slow down or trip up an oncoming runner. Once, while playing right field in the twelfth inning of a game that would soon be called on account of darkness, Kelly squinted into the twilight and leaped high in the air to catch a third out fly ball that ended the game in a tie. Whooping for joy, King Kelly darted off the field and disappeared into the clubhouse where jubilant teammates congratulated him for his great catch. Asked if he knew where the ball was —since it could not be located in his glove— Kelly responded: "How the hell would I know? The ball was hit a mile over me head!"

On another occasion, while sitting in the dugout nursing a hangover, a pop foul was hit Kelly's way. Noting that the ball was beyond the reach of his backup catcher, Kelly roared, "Kelly now catching for Chicago!" and hauled in the pop fly. In the ensuing argument, Kelly gleefully pointed out that a substitution could be made at any time by simply notifying the umpire beforehand. Needless to say, Kelly's stunt inspired a rules change.

More brazenly, Kelly once faked an injury while sliding into third base as the front half of a double steal. While his teammates gathered around him, Kelly whispered instructions to the runner at second base. On the next pitch he bolted for home. Stopping short of home plate, King Kelly was easily tagged out by the catcher. But by spreading his legs apart, he allowed his teammate to slide into home safely behind him with the winning run. The ruse was quintessential Kelly.

By today's standards, most of Kelly's antics seem amateurish and a little perverse. And yet, unlike Cobb, Kelly's deceits never aroused the animosity of his opponents. Kelly was admired and esteemed by baseball fans, his teammates, and even the opposing clubs.

It was only natural, then, that the song "Slide, Kelly, Slide" became such an enormous success. Its popularity, however, cannot be explained by its lyrics, which are painfully banal, but simply by its comic premise. The song tells the story of an inept and buffoonish player, also named Kelly, who reaches first base only by virtue of a dropped third strike, who is implored by jeering fans not to attempt a steal of second base, and who gets bonked on the nose by a foul tip. The very notion of a bumbling Mike Kelly who is browbeaten by the fans at the ballpark struck the baseball fans of the day as ludicrously funny. The song created a national sensation, and the term *slide, Kelly, slide!* became an American byword to be shouted whenever danger or an emergency is imminent. Even a hundred years later, this Kellyesque term remains an enduring part of the American idiom.

King Kelly played 16 seasons in the major league, mostly for Chicago and, later, Boston. In the end, his alcoholism undermined his abilities and Kelly descended into the life of a baseball vagabond. One day, suffering from pneumonia, King Kelly was carried into a hospital on a stretcher. He is said to have whispered, "Boys, I think I've just made me last slide." He died days later, penniless, at the age of 36. In 1945 Michael Joseph (King) Kelly was elected to baseball's Hall of Fame. ◆

THE SOUND OF THE DODGERS, 1964
Jimmy Durante, Stubby Kaye, Willie Davis, Maury Wills, and Vin Scully
Jaybar (33) 1

Includes: "Dodger Stadium" (Wills, Davis, Kaye); "Somebody's Keeping Score" (Wills); "What Is a Dodger?" (Scully); "Soliloquy of a Dodger Fan" (Kaye); "Dandy Sandy" (Durante); "That's the Way the Ball Bounces" (Davis); "The Story of the L.A. Dodgers" (Scully).

SOUNDS OF SUCCESS: MUSIC OF A WINNING SEASON, 1984
Various artists
San Diego Padres (33) unnumbered

Tribute to the 1984 San Diego Padres. Includes: "Thunderin' Lumber"; "Doin' the Goose"; "The Garv"; "Talkin' Number One"; "Padres Win Again"; "Hey Pads"; "Steve Garvey National Anthem"; "Tiger Safari"; "The Committee"; "We Are Still the Champions"; "Dreams Can Come True . . . Ode to Ray."

SOUTHPAW SPECIAL
Al Trace and the Silly Symphonies
National (78) 7007

SPEEDY FERNANDO, 1981
Stanley Ralph Ross
Horn (45) 10
Written by Stanley Ralph Ross and Jimmie Haskell
Published by Hollywood Boulevard Music (ASCAP)
Reverse: "Fernando"

Tribute to pitcher Fernando Valenzuela of the Los Angeles Dodgers.

STAN THE MAN, 1961
Steve Bledsoe and the Blue Jays
Scope (45) J 90 W
Written by Loomis, Loomis, and Stevens
Published by Studio Music (BMI)
Reverse: "Peabody's Tomb"

Tribute to St. Louis Cardinals' Hall of Famer Stan Musial.

STAN THE MAN, 1963
Marty Bronson
Norman (45) 543
Written by Frank Harris
Published by Missouri Music (BMI)
Reverse: "I'm Just a Country Boy"

Tribute to Stan Musial.

AN AFFECTIONATE LAMPOON

It's not an anthem to a legendary base stealer or even a serenade to a beloved baseball hero, but simply an affectionate lampoon of the most idolized ballplayer of his time. To make sport of catcher-outfielder Mike (King) Kelly was the highest form of praise, as the handsome Irishman was himself a fun loving good sport. Here are the lyrics to "Slide, Kelly, Slide," about a player who—as King Kelly's complete opposite—just can't seem to do anything right:

I play'd a game of baseball, I belong to Casey's Nine!
The crowd was feeling jolly, the weather it was fine . . .
The game was quickly started, they sent me to the bat:
I made two strikes, says Casey, "What are you striking at?"
I made the third, the catcher muff'd, and to the ground it fell:
Then I run like a devil to first base, when the gang began to yell:

Slide, Kelly, slide! Your running's a disgrace!
Slide, Kelly, slide! Stay there, hold your base!
If someone doesn't steal you, and your batting doesn't fail you,
They'll take you to Australia! Slide, Kelly, slide!

'Twas in the second inning, they call'd me in, I think,
To take the catcher's place, while he went to get a drink;
But something was the matter, sure I couldn't see the ball;
And the second one that came in, broke my muzzle, nose and all . . .

They sent me out to centerfield, I didn't want to go;
The way my nose was swelling up, I must have been a show!
They said on me depended vict'ry or defeat,
If a blind man was to look at us, he'd know we were beat.
"Sixty-four to nothing!" was the score when we got done,
And ev'rybody there but me said they had lots of fun.
The news got home ahead of me, they heard I was knock'd out;
The neighbors carried me in the house, and then began to shout:

(Repeat chorus).

Words and music by J. W. Kelly. © Copyright 1889 by Frank Harding, Publisher.

STEVE GARVEY NATIONAL ANTHEM, 1984
Steve Vaus
On *Sounds of Success: Music of a Winning Season*
San Diego Padres (33) unnumbered

Tribute to the San Diego Padres' first baseman.

THE SUMMER THERE WAS NO BASEBALL, 1981
Randy Haspel
Home Run (45)

Lament over the loss of baseball due to the major league players' strike.

SUNDAY MORNING SOFTBALL
John Hall and the Piemen
Otty (45) 101
Reverse: "Second Base Blues"

SWAT MILLIGAN (CLOBBER THAT BALL), 1960
Ernie Sheldon
Columbia (45) 41637
Written by Ernie Sheldon and Bob Barron
Published by Bryden Music, Inc., New York (BMI)
Reverse: "The True Song of Billy the Kid"

Nonsense song about a mighty slugger.

TAKE ME OUT TO THE BALL GAME, 1908
Haydn Quartet
Victor 10-inch single-faced record 5510
Written by Jack Norworth, music by Albert Von Tilzer
Published (1908) by York Music Co., New York
Cover: Large baseball and silhouettes of fans

The chorus to this song has become baseball's anthem.

The Anthem of Baseball

In the permanent collection of the National Baseball Hall of Fame are a few small scraps of yellowed paper that are as deserving of their honored place as a bat used by Babe Ruth or a uniform worn by Jackie Robinson.

Upon the sheets are scribbled the lyrics to a song which has been sung at nearly every baseball game for over three generations. And though the accomplishments of Ruth and Robinson have kept their luster through the years, few fans know the name of the man who wrote baseball's greatest song.

In 1908 Jack Norworth, a vaudeville performer and songwriter, was standing in a crowded New York subway car when he noticed a placard that read, "Baseball Today—Polo Grounds." Norworth was seized with an idea, and for the next thirty minutes he wrote feverishly on handy sheets of paper. Although he had never been to the Polo Grounds and had never attended a major league game, Norworth left the train having penned the most famous baseball song ever written.

"Take Me Out to the Ball Game," with music by Albert Von Tilzer, was an immediate hit on the vaudeville circuit and in sheet music stores. It also inspired a "golden age" of baseball songs, mostly sorry imitations that could only affect the innocence of the original.

Even George M. Cohan, a genuine baseball fanatic, attempted to capitalize on the trend. He cowrote a song titled "Take Your Girl to the Ball Game," the unsuccess of which Norworth cheerfully pointed out at every opportunity. Years later, at a dinner in Norworth's honor, the songwriter said of Cohan's effort: "Who ever heard of a baseball song with 'in the stands it's so grand if you're holding her hand at the old ball game'? Nobody holds hands at a baseball game!"

Norworth finally attended a big league game in Brooklyn in 1942. Today he is chiefly remembered for having cowritten the popular classic "Shine on Harvest Moon," his only other hit song. ◆

Little did anyone know in 1908 that this "Sensational Base Ball Song" would become an immediate smash hit and the anthem of the game. (National Baseball Library.)

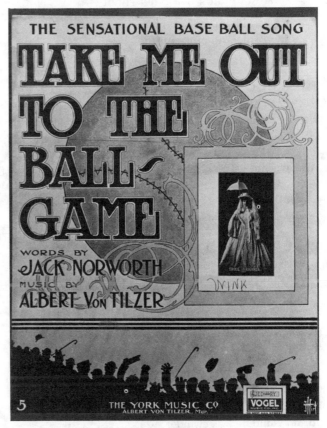

BASEBALL'S GREATEST HIT

Although every baseball fan is familiar with the lilting chorus to "Take Me Out to the Ball Game," few can recite the actual verses to the song. Early printings of the song's sheet music give the baseball fanatic's name as Kitty Casey and contain several clumsily worded lines that were later amended and refined. Here is the final version of the song that immortalizes that redoubtable woman—now named Nelly Kelly—who didn't care if she never got back:

> Nelly Kelly loved baseball games,
> Knew the players, knew all their names,
> You could see her there ev'ry day,
> Shout "Hurray," when they'd play.
> Her boy friend by the name of Joe
> Said, "To Coney Isle, dear, let's go,"
> Then Nelly started to fret and pout,
> And to him I heard her shout.
>
> Take me out to the ball game,
> Take me out with the crowd,

Buy me some peanuts and crackerjack,
I don't care if I never get back.
Let me root root root for the home team,
If they don't win it's a shame,
For it's one two three strikes, you're out
At the old ball game.

Nelly Kelly was sure some fan,
She would root just like any man,
Told the umpire he was wrong,
All along, good and strong.
When the score was just two to two,
Nelly Kelly knew what to do,
Just to cheer up the boys she knew,
She made the gang sing this song.

(Repeat chorus).

Words and music by Jack Norworth and Albert Von Tilzer. © Copyright 1908 by York Music Co. © Copyright 1936 by Jack Norworth. Reprinted by permission of Jerry Vogel Music Company, Inc.

TAKE ME OUT TO THE BALL GAME, 1908
Harvey Hindermyer
Columbia 10-inch single-faced record 3917
Also available: (1909) Columbia 10-inch double-faced record A 586; (1909) United 10-inch double-faced record A 586 (large center hole)

TAKE ME OUT TO THE BALL GAME, 1908
Fred Lambert
Zonophone 10-inch single-faced record 1185
Also available: (1909) Zonophone 10-inch double-faced record 5371

TAKE ME OUT TO THE BALL GAME, 1908
Edward Meeker
Edison 2-minute wax cylinder 9926

TAKE ME OUT TO THE BALL GAME, 1929
Dan Hornsby Novelty Quartet
Columbia 10-inch double-faced record 15444-D
Reverse: "Hinky Dinky Dee"

Title song segues into the last stanzas of "Casey at the Bat."

TAKE ME OUT TO THE BALL GAME, 1938
The Old Timer's Orchestra
Bluebird (78) B-7457

TAKE ME OUT TO THE BALL GAME, 1938
Dick Robertson
Decca (78) 1735
Reverse: "My Gal Sal"

TAKE ME OUT TO THE BALL GAME, 1939

Frankie Masters and His Orchestra
Vocalion (78) 4915
Reverse: "Scatter-Brain"

TAKE ME OUT TO THE BALL GAME, 1940
Frank Luther, Zora Layman and the Century Quartet
On *Decca Presents "Take Me Out to the Ball Game"*
Decca album No. 120 (78) 3210-3212

TAKE ME OUT TO THE BALL GAME, 1941
Ella Logan
Columbia (78) 36257
Reverse: "The Mountains O'Mourne"

Joyous swing vocal.

TAKE ME OUT TO THE BALL GAME, 1948

The Jesters
Twentieth Century Records (78) 3
Reverse: ''(The Mighty Babe Is) Safe at Home''

TAKE ME OUT TO THE BALL GAME, 1949
Andrews Sisters and Dan Dailey
Decca (45) 24605
Reverse: ''In the Good Old Summertime''
Also available: Decca (78) 24605; MCA (45) 65016

TAKE ME OUT TO THE BALL GAME, 1949
Gene Kelly and Betty Garrett
MGM (78) 30193
Also available: On *Million Dollar Vaudeville Show* Lion (33) 70089

TAKE ME OUT TO THE BALL GAME, 1949
Soundtrack
Curtain Calls (33) 100/18
See also: Baseball in Film

*Includes: ''Take Me Out to the Ball Game'';
''O'Brien to Ryan to Goldberg.''*

TAKE ME OUT TO THE BALL GAME, 1949
Soundtrack
On *Take Me Out to the Ball Game*
Curtain Calls (33) 100/18
Vocals by Gene Kelly and Frank Sinatra

TAKE ME OUT TO THE BALL GAME, 1950
Tommy Henrich, Ralph Branca, Phil Rizzuto, and Roy Campanella
Golden Record 7-inch record (78) SR 107 (yellow wax)
Reverse: ''The Umpire''
Also available: Golden Record (33) BR 25; Wheaties (78) GM6

TAKE ME OUT TO THE BALL GAME, 1951

Pete Dailey
Capitol (78) 1588
Reverse: ''Harmony Rag''

TAKE ME OUT TO THE BALL GAME, 1951
Leroy Holmes
MGM (45)
Reverse: ''Little League''
Also available: MGM (78) 11016

TAKE ME OUT TO THE BALL GAME, 1951
Tony Martin
RCA Victor (78) 20-4216
Reverse: ''Casey at the Bat''

TAKE ME OUT TO THE BALL GAME, 1951
Helen Traubel
Arthur Fiedler conducting the RCA Victor Orchestra
RCA Victor (78) 49-3790
Also available: RCA (33) 7005

TAKE ME OUT TO THE BALL GAME, 1955
Stuart McKay and His Woods
RCA (45) 6168
Reverse: ''A Foggy Day''

Jazz novelty.

TAKE ME OUT TO THE BALL GAME, c. 1955
Four Roses Society
On *Sing with the Four Roses Society*
RCA (33) K80P

TAKE ME OUT TO THE BALL GAME, 1960
Bing Crosby
On *Join Bing and Sing Along: 33 Great Songs*
Warner Bros. (33) 1363

TAKE ME OUT TO THE BALL GAME, 1962
Jane Morgan

On *Jane Morgan at the Cocoanut Grove*
Kapp (33) 3268

TAKE ME OUT TO THE BALL GAME, 1963
Boston Pops Orchestra
Conducted by Arthur Fiedler
On *Song Fest*
RCA (33) LM/LSC 2677
Also available: On *And Now a Word from Our Sponsor* RCA (33) LM/LSC 2599

TAKE ME OUT TO THE BALL GAME, 1963
Bobby Gregg and His Friends
Epic (45) 5-9601
Reverse: ''Scarlet O'Hara''

TAKE ME OUT TO THE BALL GAME, 1963
Bob Mitchell
On *Baseball's Best*
Cappe Enterprises (33)

Organ instrumental.

TAKE ME OUT TO THE BALL GAME, 1969
Bleacher Bum Eight
On *Cub Power*
Quill (33) 1001

Dixieland instrumental.

TAKE ME OUT TO THE BALL GAME, 1972
Paul Richardson
On *Paul Richardson Plays Organ for the Phillies*
Philadelphia Phillies (33) AZ 99961

Richardson is the organist for the Philadelphia Phillies.

TAKE ME OUT TO THE BALL GAME, 1975
Buzz Capra and the Atlanta Braves
Atlantis (45)

TAKE ME OUT TO THE BALL GAME, 1978
Harry Caray
Churchill (45) 7714
Reverse: "Na Na, Hey Hey, Kiss Him Goodbye"

Caray is the play-by-play broadcaster for the Chicago White Sox.

TAKE ME OUT TO THE BALL GAME, 1978
Gene Kelly
On *Gene Kelly: Song and Dance Man*
Stet (33) DL 15010

First issue of the song, originally recorded in the late 1940s.

TAKE ME OUT TO THE BALL GAME, 1979
Roy Ayers
On *Fever*
Polydor (33) 1-6204
Vocals by Carla Vaughn

TAKE ME OUT TO THE BALL GAME, 1979
Larry Croce and the Disneyland Children's Sing-Along Chorus
On *Disney's Children's Favorites: Volume One*
Disney (33)

TAKE ME OUT TO THE BALL GAME, c. 1980
Helen Dell
Malar (45) MAS 2024
Reverse: "It's a Beautiful Day for a Ball Game"

Instrumental by the organist for the Los Angeles Dodgers.

TAKE ME OUT TO THE BALL GAME, 1980
The Grasshoppers
On *The Chipmunk Song*
Merry (33) MR- 6022

Children's version is sung "Chipmunk" style.

TAKE ME OUT TO THE BALL GAME, 1982
Bruce Springstone
Clean Cuts (45) 902
Reverse: "Bedrock Rap"
Also available: Clean Cuts 12-inch single (45) 1202

Parody of Bruce Springsteen.

TAKE ME OUT TO THE BALL GAME
Steve Goodman
Red Pajamas (45) 1001
Reverse: "A Dying Cub Fan's Last Request"
Also available: (1983) On *Affordable Art* Red Pajamas (33) 002

TAKE ME OUT TO THE BALL GAME, 1983
Doc and Merle Watson
On *Doc and Merle Watson's Guitar Album*
Flying Fish (33) 301

Bluegrass instrumental.

TAKE ME OUT TO THE BALL GAME, 1984
Joe West
On *Blue Cowboy*
Colonial (33)

West is a National League umpire.

TAKE ME OUT TO THE BALL GAME
No artist given
Valor (78) 1500
Reverse: "The Battling Boston Braves"

TAKE ME OUT TO THE BALL GAME
H. B. Barnum
RCA Victor (45) 8155
Reverse: "Coming 'Round the Mountain"

TAKE ME OUT TO THE BALL GAME
Bunker Hillbillies
Seville (45) 106
Reverse: "Little League"

TAKE ME OUT TO THE BALL GAME
Mike Campbell and Tom Garvin
On *Blackberry Winter*
ITI Records (33) 009

TAKE ME OUT TO THE BALL GAME
Freddy Cannon
On *Freddy at Palisades Park*
Swan (33) 507

TAKE ME OUT TO THE BALL GAME
Don Elliott
Savoy (45) 1103
Also available: Savoy (78) 1103

TAKE ME OUT TO THE BALL GAME
Ferko String Band
Palda (78) 113
Reverse: "Baby Face"

TAKE ME OUT TO THE BALL GAME
The Fireside Gang
On *Everybody Sing!*
Golden Tone (33) C 4044
Also available: On *Let's All Sing* Mayfair (33)

TAKE ME OUT TO THE BALL GAME
Terry Gibbs
On *Swing's the Thing*
Savoy (33) MG-12062

TAKE ME OUT TO THE BALL GAME
Ken Griffin
Rondo (45) 45197
Reverse: "The Skaters Waltz"

Also available: Rondo (78) 197
On *The Wizard of the Organ* Rondo 10-inch ep (33)

TAKE ME OUT TO THE BALL GAME
Bill Heyer
Epic (45) 9050
Reverse: "Lazy Afternoon"
Also available: Epic (78)

TAKE ME OUT TO THE BALL GAME
Hoosier Hot Shots
Columbia (78) 20432
Also available: Melotone (78) 6-10-51; Conqueror (78) 8745

TAKE ME OUT TO THE BALL GAME
Bernie Leighton
On *Dizzy Fingers*
Cameo (33) 1005

TAKE ME OUT TO THE BALL GAME
The Mark-ettes
Big 20 (45) 869
Reverse: "The Hut Sut Song"

TAKE ME OUT TO THE BALL GAME
Freddy Martin and His Orchestra
On *54 Great Waltzes*

TAKE ME OUT TO THE BALL GAME
Loumell Morgan Trio
V Disc (78) 478

TAKE ME OUT TO THE BALL GAME
Billy Mure
On *Strictly Cha Cha*
Everest (33) SD-1120

TAKE ME OUT TO THE BALL GAME
Knuckles O'Toole

On *Baseball Special*
Grand Award (45) 1004

TAKE ME OUT TO THE BALL GAME
Andre Previn and Russ Freeman
On *Double Play*
Contemporary (33) OJC-157

TAKE ME OUT TO THE BALL GAME
Dave Remington
On *Dixie on the Rocks*
Vee Jay (33) 3009

TAKE ME OUT TO THE BALL GAME
Frank Rosolino
On *Trombone Album* (various artists)
Savoy (33) 2253 (two-record set)

TAKE ME OUT TO THE BALL GAME
Six Fat Dutchmen
On *Oldtime Waltzes*
Dot (33) 25599

TAKE ME OUT TO THE BALL GAME
F. Stanley
Oxford (78) 1185

TAKE ME OUT TO THE BALL GAME
Cal Tjader and Don Elliott
On *Vibrations*
Savoy (33) MG-12054

TAKE ME OUT TO THE BALL GAME
Shay Torrent
Anonymously labeled (45) 22547

Organ instrumental.

TAKE ME OUT TO THE BALL GAME
Woodhul's Old Tyme Masters
Victor (78) 28-0439

TAKE ME OUT TO THE BALL GAME
George Wright
King (78) 15039 AA
Also available: On *Encores Volume Two* HiFi (33)

TAKE ME OUT TO THE BALL GAME
Ben Yost Singers
Varsity (78) 525

TAKE ME TO THAT BALL GAME, MAMIE
Colonial Orchestra
Victor (78) 762
Vocals by Ray Winter
Written by B. Witkowski and R. Halle

TAKE YOUR GIRL TO THE BALL GAME, 1940
Frank Luther, Zora Layman and the Century Quartet
On *Decca Presents "Take Me Out to the Ball Game"*
Decca album No. 120 (78) 3210-3212
Written by George M. Cohan, Wm. Jerome, and Jean Schwartz
Published (1908) by Cohan and Harris Publishing Co., New York
Cover: Illustration of a man and woman watching a baseball game.

Get your seat in the shade,
Buy some cool lemonade . . .
Tell her each player's name
And all her life she'll be thankful to you.
Included in the Broadway play, The American Idea *(1908).*

TALKIN' BASEBALL, 1981
See: "Willie, Mickey and 'The Duke' "

TALKIN' BASEBALL— AMERICAN LEAGUE, 1982
Terry Cashman, with Ernie Harwell, Roy Firestone, and Larry King
Lifesong (33) 8136

"Mr. Cub" Ernie Banks extols the virtues of teamwork in sports and in life in this 1981 pop song. (Wanna Records, 1981.)

Includes: "Willie, Mickey and 'The Duke' "; "Baseball Ballet"; "Generic Baseball Announcer" (Firestone); "Rain Delay"; "Cooperstown"; "Rhubarb"; "Definition of Baseball" (Harwell); "Baseball in Brooklyn" (King); and edited versions of "Talkin' Baseball" songs for the American League teams.

TALKIN' BASEBALL—NATIONAL LEAGUE, 1982
Terry Cashman, with Ernie Harwell, Roy Firestone, and Larry King
Lifesong (33) 8137

Includes: Same material as "Talkin' Baseball— American League" except for edited versions of songs for the National League teams.

TALKIN' NUMBER ONE, 1984
Steve Vaus
On *Sounds of Success: Music of a Winning Season* (various artists)
San Diego Padres (33) unnumbered
Also available: On *A Dedicated Season*
Music Makers (33) unnumbered

Tribute to the San Diego Padres.

TEAMWORK, 1981

Ernie Banks
Wanna (45) 45814

Written by Stan Hollenbeck
Published by Wanna Good Time Publishing (BMI)

The virtues of baseball teamwork are extolled.

THE TENTH MAN, 1984
No artist given
On *We Are the Tenth Man and Other Songs of the Dodgers*
Rhino (33) EP 607
Written (1983) and lead vocals by Rick Segall and John Bahler
Published by Fat Finger Music (BMI) and Power Alley Music (ASCAP)

Salute to the fans of the Los Angeles Dodgers.

THANKS MISTER BANKS, 1979
Roger Bain
Barking Gecko (45) NR 10655
Published by Geck Songs (BMI)
Reverse: "Weather Girl"

Tribute to Chicago Cubs' Hall of Famer Ernie Banks.

THAT BASEBALL GLIDE, 1940
See: "The Baseball Glide"

THAT BASEBALL RAG, 1913
Arthur Collins
Victor 10-inch double-faced record 17377
Written by Dave Wolff, music by Clarence Jones
Published (1913) by Harold Rossiter Music Co., Chicago
Cover: Child looking through a knothole in the fence
Reverse: "Rolling" (Peerless Quartet)

THAT FASCINATING BASEBALL SLIDE, 1912
Elsie Janis
Victor 10-inch single-faced record 60090 (purple label)

A woman declares her love for star pitcher Spitball Mike.

THAT FASCINATING BASEBALL SLIDE
Fred Lambert
Zonophone 10-inch record 1185
Also available: Zonophone 10-inch record 5371

THAT LAST HOME RUN, c. 1973
Willie Dixon's Chicago Blues All Stars
Spoonfull (45) unnumbered
Vocals by McKinley Mitchell
Published by Rathsino Music (BMI)
Reverse: "All Star Bougee"
Also available: Yambo (45)

Blues vocal tribute to Atlanta Braves' slugger Hank Aaron.

THAT YANKEE GAME, 1964
The Roy Ross Singers
On *Pennant Fever*
RGA (33) M-300
Written by Robert Goodman

Musical account of a come-from-behind victory by the Baltimore Orioles over the New York Yankees on June 23, 1964.

THERE GOES THE BALLGAME, 1977
Soundtrack
On *New York, New York*
EMI/United Artists (33) LK BL-750
Vocals by Liza Minnelli
Written by John Kander and Fred Ebb

THERE GOES THE BALLGAME
David Schnitter
On *Thundering*
Muse (33) 5197

THERE MUST BE SOMETHING INSIDE, 1985
(A Tribute to Pete Rose)
Terry Cashman
Metrostar (45) 4585-2
Published by Metrostar Music (ASCAP)
Reverse: "Baseball's Red Machine"

Pete Rose's inner fortitude and determination are celebrated.

THERE USED TO BE A BALLPARK, 1973
Frank Sinatra
On *Ol' Blue Eyes Is Back*
Reprise (33) FS 2155
Written by Joe Raposo
Published by Sergeant Music Co.,
Jonico Music, Inc. (ASCAP)

Haunting ballad of years gone by and innocence lost.

THIRD BASE BAG, 1976
Ron Cey
Long Ball (45) 100
Written by Clyde Curtis Ligons
Published by Long Ball Records
(ASCAP)
Reverse: "One Game at a Time"

The joys of being a big-league third baseman are celebrated. Cey is a member of the Los Angeles Dodgers.

THOSE CLEVELAND INDIANS, 1954
Lee Sullivan
Bison (78) 105
Written by Ethel Opp
Published by Ethel Opp Music (BMI)
Reverse: "Baseball"

THREE STRIKES AND YOU'RE OUT
Lew Burdette
Dot (45) 15672
Reverse: "Mary Lou"

Burdette is a pitcher for the Milwaukee Braves.

THREE STRIKES AND YOU'RE OUT
Cowboy Copas
King (78) 605
Reverse: "Things Are Gonna Be Different"

THREE STRIKES AND YOU'RE OUT
F. Mitchell
Derby (45)
Also available: Rock 'n Roll (78)

THUNDERIN' LUMBER, 1984
Steve Vaus
On *Sounds of Success: Music of a Winning Season*
San Diego Padres (33) unnumbered

Tribute to the San Diego Padres.

TIGER SAFARI, 1984
Glenn Erath and Steve Horn
On *Sounds of Success: Music of a Winning Season*
San Diego Padres (33) unnumbered

Tribute to the San Diego Padres, the Tigers' opponents in the 1984 World Series.

TING-A-LING DOUBLE PLAY, 1975
Larry Bowa and Dave Cash
Molly (45)
Written by Tommy Monte and Danny Luciano

Bowa and Cash are the double-play combination for the Philadelphia Phillies.

TITLE TOWN U.S.A., c. 1980
Acappella Gold
Iron City (45) 301 (yellow wax)
Written by Ron Crawley
Published by Golden Heron (ASCAP)

Tribute to the baseball Pirates and football Steelers.

TOMMY'S SONG, 1981
Sean Patrick Brady
Fox (45) 101-9 (blue wax)
Written by Sean Patrick Brady and
Willard R. Fox
Published by Will Fox Records and
Pub. Co.(ASCAP)
Reverse: "You'll Never Know"

Tribute to Tom Lasorda, manager of the Los

Angeles Dodgers.

TONY, THE KILLER AND CAREW, 1982
Terry Cashman
Lifesong (45) 45114

"Talkin' Baseball" tribute to the Minnesota Twins.

TRADED, 1979
Howie Newman
On *Baseball's Greatest Hits*
Major League Records 7-inch ep (33)
3302
Published by Chin Music (BMI)

Humorous song about a ballplayer's disbelief at having been traded.

THE UMPIRE, 1950
Tommy Henrich, Ralph Branca, Phil
Rizzuto, and Roy Campanella
Golden Record 7-inch record (78) SR
107 (yellow wax)
Written by John Jacob Loeb
Published by John Jacob Loeb Music
Publishing Co. (ASCAP)
Reverse: "Take Me Out to the Ball
Game"
Also available: Golden Record (33) BR
25

Humorous song in which baseball players express their contempt for umpires.

THE UMPIRE IS A MOST UNHAPPY MAN, 1906
Edward M. Favor
Edison 2-minute wax cylinder 9352
Written by Will M. Hough, Frank R.
Adams, and Joseph E. Howard
Published (1905) by Chas. K. Harris,
New York

Umpire is humorously berated by fans. Included in the musical comedy, The Umpire. (See: Baseball in Theater.)

THE UMPIRE IS A MOST UNHAPPY MAN, 1906
Bob Roberts

359

For three years before moving into Chavez Ravine in 1962, the Los Angeles Dodgers played in the Memorial Coliseum—home of the 1932 Olympics—with its special baseball attraction: the leftfield "monster," a 42-foot high wire-mesh fence that stood only 251 feet away from home plate. Although the city did not yet have a major league stadium, Los Angeles fans welcomed the Dodgers anyway with tunes like this fight song from about 1959. (American International.)

Victor 10-inch single-faced record
4746

THE UMPIRE IS A MOST UNHAPPY MAN, 1947
Ray Bloch and His Orchestra
Signature (78) 15122
Vocals by the Chickering Four
Reverse: "The Giant's March"

THE UMPIRE IS A MOST UNHAPPY MAN, 1947
Joseph E. Howard
On *I Wonder Who's Kissing Her Now*
Deluxe Albums (78) 18

UTILITY INFIELDER BLUES, 1979
Howie Newman
On *Baseball's Greatest Hits*
Major League Records 7-inch ep (33) 3302
Published by Chin Music (BMI)

Humorous salute to baseball's forgotten men.

VAN LINGO MUNGO, 1977
Sue Raney
Blue Label Records 7-inch ep (33)
unnumbered
Written by Dave Frishberg
Published (1970) by Red Day Music/
Daramus, Inc. (ASCAP)
Reverse: "Dodger Blue"

Nostalgic homage to baseball players' names, revealing America as a melting pot.

VAN LINGO MUNGO, 1981
Dave Frishberg
On *The Dave Frishberg Songbook, Volume No. 1*
Omnisound (33) N 1040

VIDA BLUE, 1971
Albert Jones
Tri-City (45) 327
Written by Tom Newton and Choker Campbell
Published (1971) by Luzar Publishing (BMI)
Reverse: Same (Tom Newton)

Tribute to the Cy Young Award winner and American League Most Valuable Player for 1971.

VIDA BLUE, c. 1971
Jimmy Bee
United Artists (45) 50843
Reverse: Part II

Tribute to pitcher Vida Blue of the Oakland A's.

VIVA FERNANDO, 1981
Gene Page Orchestra
Domain (45) 1019
Written by B. Panella and J. Cameron
Published by Cord Music/Rio Napoli Music (ASCAP)
Reverse: Same (Spanish version)

Tribute to Los Angeles Dodgers' pitcher Fernando Valenzuela.

WAIT UNTIL NEXT YEAR, 1979
Howie Newman

On *Baseball's Greatest Hits*
Major League Records 7-inch ep (33)
3302
Published by Chin Music (BMI)

Bittersweet elegy to another disappointing baseball year.

WARREN SPAHN, 1979
The Blackholes
Blackhole (45) 0604
Written by Mark Shurilla
Published by Blackhole Music, Inc. (BMI)
Reverse: "Captain Payday"
Also available: Armada (45) 104

Tribute to the Hall of Fame pitcher for the Braves.

WE ARE STILL THE CHAMPIONS, 1984
Glenn Erath and Karen McDermott
On *Sounds of Success: Music of a Winning Season*
San Diego Padres (33) unnumbered

Tribute to the San Diego Padres.

WE ARE THE TENTH MAN AND OTHER SONGS OF THE DODGERS, 1984
No artist given
Rhino (33) EP 607

Includes: "The Tenth Man"; "Where the Blue Is"; "The Big Blue Wrecking Crew"; "Canned Heat".

WE LOVE THE DODGERS, c. 1960
Jimmie Maddin
American International (45) 525
Written by Maddin, Vandervoort II, and Gordon
Published by Dijon Music (BMI)
Reverse: "Bird Dog"

WE PLAY BASEBALL, c. 1980
Larry, Tommy, and Annie
Toddlin' Town (45) 840
Written by Larry Nestor

Published (1979) by Lardon Music/
Yorkwood Music (BMI)
Reverse: "Step to the Rear of the
Spaceship"

**WE'RE GONNA WIN THE
SERIES, 1969**
Featuring the voices of the New York
Mets
On *The Amazing Mets*
Buddah (33) Mets 1969

WE'RE NUMBER ONE!, 1979
Bobbi Blake
M.S.R. (45) 2773
Written by John McBride
Published by Eve-Joy Music (ASCAP)
Reverse: "Grin and Bear It"

**WE'RE THE BEST BALL TEAM
(IN THE NEIGHBORHOOD),**
c. 1960
Sammy Watkins Orchestra and the
Pony League Singers
Boys Baseball (45) unnumbered
Written by Sammy Watkins
Published by Big League Records
(ASCAP)
Reverse: "My Son the Pony Leaguer"

WE'RE WINNING AGAIN, 1984
No artist given
Creative Music 7-inch ep (45) CF 11
Written by C. Furgatch
Reverse: "Padres Pop"

*Tribute to the San Diego Padres. Title of the
extended-play recording is, "Oh Doctor! You
Gotta Hang a Star on That Baby!"*

**WE'VE GOT THE WHOLE
WORLD WATCHING US, 1969**
Featuring the voices of the New York
Mets
On *The Amazing Mets*
Buddah (33) Mets 1969

WHAT ARE WE WAITING FOR?
Danny Topaz

Zapot (45)
Written by Dan Shapiro and Danny
Topaz
Published by Beatrix Music, Inc.
(ASCAP)

Tribute to the San Diego Padres.

**WHEN THE BRAVES CAME TO
MILWAUKEE**
Fran Allison
Keepsake 12-inch record (78)

**WHEN YOU WERE MICKEY
MANTLE AND I WAS STAN
THE MAN**
Ken Carlysle
Inglewood (45) 133222

WHERE THE BLUE IS, 1984
No artist given
On *We Are the Tenth Man and Other
Songs of the Dodgers*
Rhino (33) EP 607
Written and lead vocals by Rick Segall
and John Bahler
Published by Fat Finger Music (BMI)
and Power Alley Music (ASCAP)

Tribute to the Los Angeles Dodgers.

THE WHIPPETS RAG, 1982
Garrison Keillor
On *The Family Radio*
Prairie Home Companion (33) 606
(two-record set)

*Humorous song about the Lake Wobegon
Whippets, the most inept baseball team ever.*

THE WHITE SOX SONG
Shay Torrent
Anonymously labeled (45) 22547

Organ instrumental.

WHITE SOX STOMP, 1943
Jimmy Yancey
Jazztone (78) 1023
Reverse: "Shave 'em Dry"
Also available: Jazztone (78) 1224; Pax
(33) 6012

**WHO'S GONNA WIN THE
PENNANT THIS YEAR?**
The Toppers
Decatur (78) 10017
Written by Paul Germano, Gary Van
Dyke, and Herman Bandes
Published (1953) by Chick Kardale
Music Co., New York

**WILLIE, MICKEY AND "THE
DUKE," 1981**
(Talkin' Baseball)
Terry Cashman
Lifesong (45) 45086
Published by Blendingwell Music,
Inc. (ASCAP)
Reverse: "It's Easy to Sing a Love
Song"
Also available: Lifesong (45) 45108;
Lifesong picture disc (33) 8135
On *Talkin' Baseball—American League*
Lifesong (33) 8136
On *Talkin' Baseball—National League*
Lifesong (33) 8137

*Pop vocal tribute to Willie Mays, Mickey
Mantle, Duke Snider, and other players from
the 1950s.*

WILLIE (STARGELL), c. 1975
Al Perry
Love (45) 2015
Published by Perigold Publ. (BMI)
Reverse: "Close to Loving You"

Tribute to the Pittsburgh Pirates' slugger.

**WILL YOU BE READY (AT THE
PLATE WHEN JESUS THROWS
THE BALL), 1980**
Elmo and Patsy
Oink (45) KP 3801
Written by R. Brooks
Published by Kris Pub. (SESAC)
Reverse: "The Lover"
Also available: On *Will You Be Ready?*
Oink (33) KPL 8021

*Satirical gospel song incorporating baseball
terminology.*

WIN, GIANTS, WIN, c. 1962
Nick Alexander and the Bat Boys
Embee (45) 1002
Written by Bob Britton and Maury
Wolohan
Published by Paul Barrett Music, Inc.
(BMI)
Reverse: "Hail Giants"

WIN OR LOSE, 1964
The Roy Ross Singers
On *Pennant Fever*
RGA (33) M-300
Written by Robert Goodman

Tribute to the Baltimore Orioles.

WOULD YOU RATHER, 1964
The Roy Ross Singers
On *Pennant Fever*
RGA (33) M-300
Written by Robert Goodman

Tribute to the Baltimore Orioles in which the question is posed: "Would you rather have a winning team or exploding scoreboards and flashy uniforms?"

YANKEE CLIPPER, 1949

Charlie Ventura and His Orchestra
RCA Victor (78) 20-3552
Written by Williams, Crayhon, and
Ventura
Reverse: "Boptura"

Tribute to New York Yankees' outfielder Joe DiMaggio.

THE YANKS ARE THE CHAMPS, 1977
The Fowls
Rotten Rat (45) 1018
Written by Gary J. Mellis and Michael
Latham
Published by Ogfile Music (BMI)
Reverse: "The Yanks Are Back"

YASTRZEMSKI SONG, 1967
Jess Cain
On *The Impossible Dream*
Fleetwood (33) 3024

Tribute to outfielder Carl Yastrzemski of the Boston Red Sox.

YAZ'S LAST AT BAT, 1985
John Lincoln Wright and the

Designated Hitters
Lincoln Records (45) 003
Written by John Lincoln Wright
Published by Lincoln Lines (BMI)
Reverse: "Oil Can"

Tribute to outfielder Carl Yastrzemski of the Boston Red Sox.

YOU ARE THE STARS, 1985
Steve Vaus and the voices of the San
Diego Padres
San Diego Padres (45) unnumbered
Written by Steve Vaus
Published (1984) by Music Makers
Reverse: "Studio Outtakes"

Tribute to the fans of the San Diego Padres.

YOU'RE GONNA THRILL ME MORE THAN A BASEBALL-BALL, c. 1982
Billy Wiggle and the Wigglers
On *Rock-It-Billy*
Mac (33) 005 (Belgium import)
Written by Arthur Arts

Up-tempo vocal incorporating baseball terminology.

Appendix to Chapter 20

The appendix contains a listing of nonbaseball-related songs that include a significant reference to baseball or baseball players. In most cases the relation to baseball—and not the song's topic or theme—is annotated.

For *Explanatory Notes* to this section, *see:* Baseball in Music and Song—Recorded.

DID HE RUN?, 1909
Columbia (Peerless) Quartet
Columbia 10-inch double-faced record
A 664
Written by Junie McCree, music by
Albert Von Tilzer
Published by York Music Co.
Reverse: "The Yama Yama Man"
(Ada Jones)

In one verse, Merkle's "boner" of the previous year is satirized.

ELEVEN MONTHS AND TEN MORE DAYS, 1929
Vernon Dalhart
Columbia (78) 15572-D
Written by Arthur Fields and Fred Hall
Also available: Harmony (78) 1095; Clarion (78) 5027

In one verse, playing baseball in a prison is humorously treated.

IN THE OLD TOWN HALL, 1921
Billy Murray
Victor 10-inch record 18810

Includes a reference to Babe Ruth.

MRS. ROBINSON, 1968
Simon and Garfunkel
Columbia (45) 44511
Written by Paul Simon
Reverse: "Old Friends/Bookends"

Includes the famous line, Where have you gone, Joe DiMaggio? A nation turns its lonely eyes to you, *suggesting that America had lost its heroes.*

PARADISE BY THE DASHBOARD LIGHT, 1978
Meat Loaf
Epic-Cleveland International (45)
50588
Features the voice of Phil Rizzuto
Written by J. Steinman
Reverse: " 'Bat' Overture"
Also available: Epic 12-inch single (33)
AS 477; Memory Lane (45) 15 2371

Couple makes love in an automobile while a baseball game is on the radio.

PORCH SONG, 1982
Garrison Keillor
On *The Family Radio*
Prairie Home Companion (33) 606
(two-record set)
Features the radio voice of Herb Carneal

Humorous song in which a lazy man listens to a baseball game while sitting on the front porch.

SUMMER DAYS, 1911
Edith Chapman and Henry Burr
Columbia 10-inch double-faced record
A 1033
Reverse: "Any Girl Looks Good"

Summer days, those good old summer days
Time for baseball weather—see them get together!
Gee, I'm always itching to see Matty pitching
In those summer days.

SUMMER DAYS, 1911
Billy Murray and Chorus
Edison Amberol cylinder

THAT'S MY HAP-HAP-HAPPINESS, 1927
The Happiness Boys (Billy Jones and Ernest Hare)
Victor 10-inch double-faced record
20500
Reverse: "Cock-a-Doodle"
Also available: Edison 10-inch
Diamond Disc 51973

Happiness is going to a baseball game because when the bags are full it's great, and "Babe" Ruth walks to the plate.

THEY'RE ALL GOOD AMERICAN NAMES, 1911
Fred Duprez
U.S. Everlasting 2-minute cylinder
372

One verse is completely composed of last names of Irish baseball players.

THEY'RE ALL GOOD AMERICAN NAMES, 1911
Eddie Morton
Victor 10-inch double-faced record
16938
Reverse: "If He Comes In, I'm Goin' Out"

THEY'RE ALL GOOD AMERICAN NAMES, 1911
Bob Roberts
Edison Amberol 4-minute cylinder
722
Also available: Indestructible
2-minute cylinder 1483

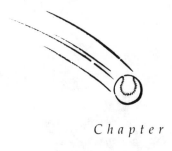

Chapter

21

Baseball in Miscellaneous Recordings

The following section contains a listing of historical, documentary, and miscellaneous spoken-word recordings relating to baseball. Included in the catalog are phonorecorded interviews with baseball players, audio histories of baseball and baseball teams, instructional recordings, and unclassified miscellaneous recordings relating to baseball.

Not included are team yearly highlights, radio transcriptions and other commercially unreleased recordings, or sports anthology recordings that do not relate exclusively to baseball.

For *Explanatory Notes* to this section, *see:* Baseball in Music and Song—Recorded.

ALLSTAR TIPS, c. 1964
Steady (33) 131
Narrated by Marty Glickman

Baseball instructionals by Willie Mays, Mickey Mantle, Roger Maris, Al Kaline, Whitey Ford, Sandy Koufax, Bill Mazeroski, Pete Ward, Jim Gentile, Ken Boyer, Frank Robinson, and Don Drysdale. Previously released in a series of 16 cardboard picture records, titled, Columbia Sports Champions.

AL SCHACHT, 1982
On *Jim Thorpe*
Mark 56 (33) 842 (two-record set)

Schacht reminisces about his minor league days with Thorpe.

"BABE" AND "LOU," THE HOME RUN TWINS, 1926
Babe Ruth and Lou Gehrig
Perfect 10-inch double-faced record 12382
Also available: On *Babe Ruth on Radio* Radiola (33) MR 1019; Famous Voices (78) FV1; Rare Records 7-inch ep (33) Y-901

Comic repartee between the two most celebrated sluggers of their time.

BABE RUTH ON RADIO
Radiola (33) MR 1019

Includes: " 'Babe' Ruth's Home Run Story"; " 'Babe' and 'Lou' " (The Home Run Twins); and excerpts of radio speeches and interviews by Babe Ruth.

"BABE" RUTH'S HOME RUN STORY, 1920
By "Babe" Himself (Babe Ruth)
Perfect 10-inch double-faced record 022443
Reverse: "Abadele Fox Trot" (Duane Sawyer and His Novelty Orchestra)
Also available: On *Babe Ruth on Radio* Radiola (33) MR 1019

There is conjecture that the Babe did not actually record the comic monologue but was impersonated by a professional actor.

BABE RUTH: THE LEGEND COMES TO LIFE, 1974
Fleetwood (33) 3079
Narrated by Curt Gowdy

Audio biography of the Hall of Famer.

THE BALL HIT THE BAT, 1975
Fleetwood (33) 3089

"The story of baseball through the eyes and hearts of the fans of baseball." Features the voices of many baseball stars.

BANG THE DRUM SLOWLY, 1973
Soundtrack
Paramount (33) PAS 1014
Music by Stephen Lawrence
See also: Baseball in Film; Baseball in Television; Baseball in Fiction

BASEBALL—AN ACTION HISTORY, 1958
Columbia Masterworks (33) KL 5270
Narrated by Buddy Blattner

Audio history and highlights of baseball. Includes paperback book.

BASEBALL IN BROOKLYN, 1982
Larry King
On *Talkin' Baseball—American League*
Lifesong (33) 8136
Also available: On *Talkin' Baseball—National League* Lifesong (33) 8137

Personal narrative on what it was like being a Dodgers' fan in the 1950s.

BASEBALL IN THE GREAT YANKEE TRADITION
Columbia 7-inch ep (33) 548

Includes interviews with Mickey Mantle, Ralph Houk, Mel Stottlemyre, Elston Howard, Joe Pepitone, Tom Tresh, Frank Crosetti, and Jerry Coleman.

BASEBALL MORA
Ichiro Wakahara Terugiku
On *Today's Popular Songs*
King 7-inch ep (45) KEB-13 (Japanese import)

Japanese-language party song incorporating double entendres.

THE BEST OF WAITE HOYT IN THE RAIN, 1963
Waite Hoyt
Personality (33) 537
Also available: King (33) 879

Actual radio broadcasts in which the Hall of Famer and Cincinnati announcer tells stories during rain delays.

THE BINGO LONG TRAVELING ALL-STARS AND MOTOR KINGS, 1976
Soundtrack
MCA (33) 2094
Music composed by William Goldstein
See also: Baseball in Film; Baseball in Fiction

Includes: "The Bingo Long Song (Steal On Home)"; "Baseball Magic."

BLACK DIAMONDS, 1978
Visual Educational Corp. set of three cassettes No. 5303
Narrated by Stephen Banker

Interviews with stars of the Negro Leagues, including Hall of Famers Satchel Paige, Cool Papa Bell, Judy Johnson, Roy Campanella, and Ernie Banks.

BROADCAST HIGHLIGHTS OF JOHNNY BENCH'S CAREER, 1983
On *One Stop Along the Way*
Lifesong (33) 8140

Includes World Series highlights, Bench's 2000th major league hit, and record-breaking home runs.

CHARLIE BROWN'S ALL-STARS, 1978
Charlie Brown Records (33) 2602
Based on the *Peanuts* animated television cartoon
Written by Charles M. Schulz
Music by Vince Guaraldi
Also available: Charlie Brown Records (33) 3702
See also: Baseball in Animated Cartoons—Television; Baseball in Comic Art—Collected

A CONVERSATION WITH ROBERTO CLEMENTE, 1973
Soundtrack
G & C Record Co. (33) 30417

Soundtrack of the television program, "A Conversation With Clemente," October 8, 1972, WIIC-TV, Pittsburgh.

CURT GOWDY TALKS WITH CARL YASTRZEMSKI, 1967
Fleetwood (33) FCLP 3026

Recorded interview with the Triple Crown winner and American League Most Valuable Player for 1967.

A DAY TO REMEMBER, 1969
Columbia 7-inch ep (33) CSM 1020

Highlights of Mickey Mantle Day at Yankee Stadium, June 8, 1969.

DEFINITION OF BASEBALL, 1982
Ernie Harwell
On *Talkin' Baseball—American League* Lifesong (33) 8136
Also available: On *Talkin' Baseball—National League* Lifesong (33) 8137

Narrative on what baseball means to America, written and recited by the Hall of Fame broadcaster.

DODGER RECORD LIBRARY, 1966
Series of 12 records
Union Oil 7-inch ep (33) unnumbered
Narrated by Vin Scully

Interviews with 21 players and Dodger manager Walt Alston, general manager Buzzie Bavasi, and club president Walter F. O'Malley.

DON DRYSDALE'S WORLD'S SCORELESS INNING RECORD, 1968
Danny Goodman (33) unnumbered
Narrated by Vin Scully

Highlights of Drysdale's 58⅔ consecutive scoreless innings pitched.

THE EVILS OF DRINK
Billy Sunday
Rare Records 7-inch ep (33) R-1001

Reissue of a recorded sermon by the major leaguer turned evangelist.

THE FRED ALLEN SHOW
Radiola (33) MR 1146
See also: "Broadcast of April 25, 1948" (Baseball in Radio)

Includes the complete broadcast of the April 25, 1948 show with guest Leo Durocher.

THE GIANTS WIN THE PENNANT, 1952
Liggett and Myers Tobacco Co. (78) unnumbered

Radio account of the last half of the ninth inning of the 1951 playoff game between the Dodgers and the Giants in which Bobby Thomson hit his famous home run.

THE GLORY OF THEIR TIMES, 1966
Lawrence S. Ritter
Spoken Arts (33) unnumbered
Also available: Sonic Recording Products (33) K-441
See also: Baseball in Documentary and Miscellaneous Television; Baseball in the Spoken Arts—Recorded

Contains actual interviews on which the classic book was based. Includes: Chief Myers, Rube Marquard, Sam Crawford, Davy Jones, Goose Goslin, Edd Roush, Fred Snodgrass, and Lefty O'Doul.

THE GREATEST GAME NEVER PLAYED, 1982
Technisonic (33) 82-1037/38
Features the voices of Jack Buck and Lindsey Nelson

Broadcast highlights of a computerized all-time all-star baseball game.

GREAT MOMENTS IN CUBS BASEBALL, 1971
Major Official Productions (33) 839A-2314
Features the radio voices of Vince

Lloyd, Lou Boudreau, Jack Brickhouse, and Gene Elston

Audio history and highlights of the Chicago Cubs.

HANK AARON: THE LIFE OF A LEGEND, 1974
Fleetwood (33) 3081
Narrated by Curt Gowdy

Highlights, interviews, and audio appreciation of baseball's home run king.

HEAR HOW TO PLAY BETTER BASEBALL, c. 1970
Ralph Houk
Carlton (33) CHH 16

Baseball fundamentals by the New York Yankees' manager.

THE HERITAGE OF THE CLEVELAND INDIANS, 1959
Sports Records (33) 101/02

Highlights and history of the Cleveland Indians.

HOW TO PLAY BASEBALL
Joe E. Brown
RCA Victor 12-inch records (78) Y 351 (two-record set)

Baseball instructionals are incorporated in a light-hearted narrative.

THE IMPOSSIBLE DREAM, 1967
Fleetwood (33) 3024
Written by John Connelly
Narrated by Ken Coleman

Poem and radio highlights saluting the 1967 Boston Red Sox. Includes "Yastrzemski Song" by Jess Cain. (See: Baseball in Music and Song —Recorded.)

THE IMPOSSIBLE PIRATES: SIXTY YEARS OF BASEBALL, 1960
Thorn-Beach (33) 1001
Narrated by Bob Prince

Highlights and history of the Pittsburgh Pirates. Features Rosey Rowswell, Chet Smith, Joe E. Brown, Branch Rickey, Danny Murtaugh, and others.

INSIDE MAJOR LEAGUE BASEBALL, 1971
Sports Illustrated (33) 81671

Features interviews with Willie Mays, Ted Williams, Frank Howard, Jim Fregosi, Billy Martin, Dave McNally, and Bill Freehan.

JIM THORPE, 1982
Mark 56 (33) 842 (two-record set)

Audio biography of the famed athlete and baseball player. Includes an interview with Al Schacht.

JOHNNY BENCH, 1971
Continental (33) CS 3102 (two-record set)
Narrated by Paul Sommerkamp

Interviews and audio biography of the Cincinnati Reds' all-star catcher.

LAST INNING SANDY KOUFAX, 1965
Mister Marty 7-inch ep (33) unnumbered
Features the radio voice of Vin Scully
Also available: Danny Goodman 7-inch ep (33) 1

Radio broadcast of the last half-inning of Koufax's perfect game against Chicago, September 9, 1965.

THE LEGENDARY BABE RUTH, 1969
Learning Plans cassette no. 010 466-100 46

Audio appreciation of Hall of Famer Babe Ruth.

LITTLE JOHNNY STRIKEOUT, 1949
Featuring Joe DiMaggio
Capitol (45) 30126/27 (two-record set)
Narrated by Bill Terry
Story and songs by John Jacob Loeb

Also available: Capitol (78) DBS-3051 (two-record set)

Dramatization of a little boy's difficulty in mastering the game of baseball.

LITTLE LEAGUE FIELD CEREMONIES, 1955
Art Kassel and His Orchestra
Double-Play (45) D4-45-101 AX
Reverse: "Little Leaguer"
Also available: Double-Play (78) D4-101 AX

Contains: "Star Spangled Banner"; "Little League Pledge"; "Little Leaguer" (one chorus).

LOOK, LISTEN, AND LEARN BASEBALL, 1956
Picturecs (33) BB 350
Narrated by Vin Scully

Instructionals by Brooklyn Dodger stars Carl Erskine, Duke Snider, Gil Hodges, Jackie Robinson, Roy Campanella, Clem Labine, and Walter O'Malley. Includes paperback book.

MEL ALLEN'S BASEBALL GAME, 1959
RCA Victor (33) LBY 1025
Narrated by Mel Allen
Also available: "Buck Canel's Baseball Game" RCA Camden (33) CAL 1045 (Spanish version)

Children learn to keep score and announce a baseball game.

THE MUDVILLE STORY, 1981
Mike Wynn
C-ductions (45) RSDP 782
Written by Bob Carruesco
Published by C-lect Publishing (BMI)
Reverse: "Casey at the Bat"

Narrative in which Stockton, California is purported to have been the Mudville of the famous poem.

MY FAVORITE HITS
Mickey Mantle
RCA Victor (33) LPM-1704

Joe DiMaggio helps a youngster master the art of playing baseball in this rare 1949 recording issued especially for children. (Capitol Records, 1949.)

Collection of nonbaseball-related songs as selected by the Yankee outfielder.

MY GREATEST THRILL IN BASEBALL, c. 1956
Donut Corp. of America 7-inch record (78) 1
Narrated by Joe O'Brien

Features Gil Hodges, Whitey Ford, and Johnny Antonelli.

THE NATURAL, 1984
Soundtrack
Warner Bros. (33) 25116-1
Music composed by Randy Newman

See also: Baseball in Film; Baseball in Fiction; Baseball in the Spoken Arts—Recorded

NO-HITTER BY BILL SINGER, 1970
Los Angeles Dodgers 7-inch ep (33) unnumbered
Features the radio voice of Vin Scully

Broadcast highlights of the July 20, 1970 game against Philadelphia.

OL' .275, 1985
John Lincoln Wright and the Designated Hitters

Lincoln Records (45) 003
Written by John Lincoln Wright
Published by Lincoln Lines (BMI)
Reverse: "Oil Can"

Rhymed-verse tribute to a baseball-loving father.

THE ONLY GAME, c. 1965
Cleve Hermann
Sports (45) 101
Written by Cleve Hermann, Gary Paxton, and Ben Benay
Published by Garpax Music, Inc., Limelite Music
Reverse: "Story of a Giant"

Narrative tribute to baseball and what it means to America.

PHILLIES—THE FIRST 100 YEARS, 1977
Instant Replay Productions, Inc. (33)
Narrated by Harry Kalas

Highlights and history of the Philadelphia Phillies.

"PIANO LEGS!," 1971
Norman Vincent Peale
On *The Undefeated*
Guideposts (33) 122

Inspirational narrative of the life of Lou Gehrig.

PLAY BALL, c. 1949
Challenger (78) BB 6

PLAYTIME BASEBALL SERIES, 1952
Series of four records
Columbia 6-inch records (78) PV 800-803 (red wax)

Baseball instructionals include: Ralph Kiner (hitting); Phil Rizzuto (bunting); Yogi Berra (catching); Bob Feller (pitching).

PLAYTIME BASEBALL SERIES, 1953
Series of four records

Columbia 6-inch records (78) PV 804-807 (red wax)

Baseball instructionals include: George Kell (third base); Richie Ashburn (base running); Bobby Thomson (batting); Ned Garver (pitching).

THE PRIDE OF THE YANKEES, c. 1980
Radiola (33) MR 1106
See also: Baseball in Film; Baseball in Radio; Baseball in Comic Art—Collected: Appendix

Contains the complete one-hour broadcast of "The Lux Radio Theatre," October 4, 1943.

PROFESSIONAL BASEBALL—THE FIRST 100 YEARS, 1969
Fleetwood (33) 3036
Narrated by James Stewart and Curt Gowdy
Also available: Fleetwood 7-inch ep (33)

Highlights and interviews in commemoration of the one-hundredth year of professional baseball.

THE REAL BABE RUTH
Robert Creamer and Roger Kahn
The Center for Cassette Studies
cassette no. 38497

Discussion of the myths surrounding Babe Ruth.

RED JONES STEEERIKES BACK, 1969
Red Jones
Motown (33) MS 691

Former umpire tells 17 humorous baseball anecdotes.

ROBERTO CLEMENTE MEMORIAL ALBUM, 1973
Triple B (33) T-1001

Contains tributes and eulogies by President Richard M. Nixon, club executive Joe L. Brown, manager Danny Murtaugh, and others. Includes a song by Rafi Monclova.

SLUGGER AT THE BAT, 1949
Jackie Robinson and Pee Wee Reese
Columbia 10-inch ep (33) JL-8009
Reverse: "Stampede" (Gene Autry)
Also available: Columbia (78) MJV-57 (two-record set)

THE SLUGGER'S WIFE, 1985
Soundtrack
MCA (33) 5578
See also: Baseball in Film

STAN-THE-MAN'S HIT RECORD, 1963
RCA Victor (33) PR-141

Instructionals by Hall of Famer Stan Musial. Includes a paperback booklet.

STORY OF A GIANT, c. 1965
Cleve Hermann
Sports (45) 101
Written by Cleve Hermann and Kenneth Johnson
Published by Garpax Music, Inc., Limelite Music
Reverse: "The Only Game"

Rhymed-verse tribute to Willie Mays.

THE STORY OF THE L.A. DODGERS, 1964
Vin Scully
On *The Sound of the Dodgers*
Jaybar (33) 1
Written by Mel Durslag

Humorous narrative describing the ups and downs of the Dodgers.

TIPS ON HOW TO BECOME A BETTER HITTER
Ted Williams
Sears and Roebuck (45) ZTSC-68481

Batting fundamentals by Hall of Famer Ted Williams.

WHAT IS A DODGER?, 1964
Vin Scully
On *The Sound of the Dodgers*
Jaybar (33) 1
Written by Sidney Skolsky

Recitation describing baseball and the Dodgers. "What is a Dodger? A Dodger is a way of life."

WORLD SERIES, 1980
Fleetwood (33) 3108
Narrated by Curt Gowdy

Highlights and history of great World Series games.

THE YANKS ARE BACK, 1977
The Fowls
Rotten Rat (45) 1018
Reverse: "The Yanks Are the Champs"

Spoken-word tribute to the New York Yankees.

YAZ 3000, 1979
Fleetwood (33) 3113

Audio biography of Boston Red Sox outfielder Carl Yastrzemski, including radio accounts of his 400th home run and his 3000th base hit.

YES WE CAN, 1980
Golden West Broadcasters Radio Productions (33) unnumbered
Features the radio voices of Dick Enberg, Don Drysdale, Al Wisk, Buddy Blattner, and Don Wells

Highlights and history of the California Angels.

Appendix to Chapter 21

The appendix contains a listing of nonbaseball-related songs recorded by major league baseball players.

For *Explanatory Notes* to this section, *see:* Baseball in Music and Song—Recorded.

ALBIE PEARSON, c. 1967
Albie Pearson
Vibrant (33) 1501-VPS

The former California Angels' outfielder sings 10 contemporary gospel songs.

ALL I WANT IS SOMEONE TO LOVE
Lee Maye
Cash (45) 1065
Reverse: ''Pounding''

ANYTIME, ANYDAY, ANYWHERE, 1961
Albie Pearson
Capitol (45) 4619
Reverse: ''I'm Still in Love with You''

AT THE PARTY
Lee Maye
Tower (45) 243
Reverse: ''When My Heart Hurts No More''

CARELESS HANDS
Lee Maye and Barbara Lynn
Jamie (45) 1295
Reverse: ''Just Lay It on the Line'' (Barbara Lynn)

'CAUSE YOU'RE MINE ALONE, 1957
Arthur Lee Maye
Flip (45) 330
Reverse: ''Hey, Pretty Girl''

Lee Maye, who enjoyed success as a recording artist before becoming a major leaguer, played 13 years in the big leagues, primarily as an outfielder for the Milwaukee Braves.

CRAWDAD HOLE, c. 1963
Maury Wills, with John Roseboro and Tommy Davis
Glad-Hamp (45) 2009
Reverse: ''Bye Bye Blues''

Wills, Roseboro, and Davis are Los Angeles Dodgers' teammates.

CROSS YOUR HEART (WITH LOVE), 1961
Elroy Face
Robbee (45) 111
Reverse: ''Bells, Bells''

Elroy Face is the ace reliever for the Pittsburgh Pirates.

DENNY MCLAIN AT THE ORGAN, 1968
Denny McLain
Capitol (33) ST-2881

Halcyon days for pitcher Denny McLain. After a triumphant 1968 season in which he compiled a 31-6 record for the world champion Detroit Tigers, McLain sought the bright lights of Las Vegas and Hollywood where he performed at the organ and recorded an album of nonbaseball tunes. A few years later, McLain was out of baseball and in 1985 was imprisoned for loan-sharking, extortion, bookmaking, and possession of cocaine. McLain has since established, with the help of his wife and family, a new life away from the spotlight. (Capitol Records, 1968.)

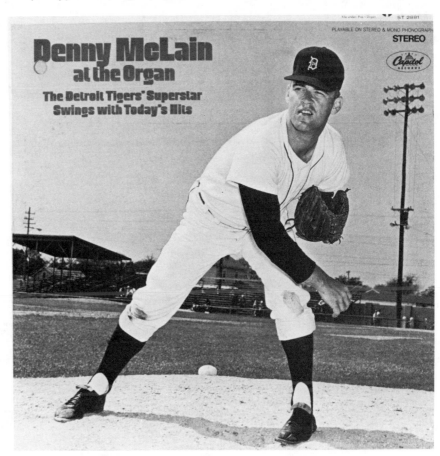

In 1963 Los Angeles Dodgers pitcher Don Drysdale made a bid to become a teen idol with this romantic ballad. (Reprise Records, 1963.)

———————

Includes "Extra Innings" and 11 nonbaseball tunes. McLain won 31 games as a pitcher for the Detroit Tigers in 1968.

DENNY MCLAIN IN LAS VEGAS, 1969
Denny McLain
Capitol (33) ST-204

McLain, at the organ, plays a selection of nonbaseball songs.

GLORIA, 1956
Arthur Lee Maye and the Crowns
Specialty (45) 573
Reverse: "Oh-Rooba-Lee"
Also available: Yvette (45) 300;
On *Original Rock Oldies—Golden Hits: Vol. 1* Specialty (33) 2129

GOOD OL' TIME TONIGHT, 1984
Jody Davis, Leon Durham, Keith Moreland, Gary Woods, and Rick Sutcliffe
PR Records (45) 6
Written by J. Ritz and A. Petrowski
Published by Yarmouth Publishing (BMI)

Reverse: "Men in Blue"

Davis, Durham, Moreland, Woods, and Sutcliffe are Chicago Cubs' teammates.

HALF WAY
Lee Maye
Lenox (45) 5566
Reverse: "I Can't Please You"

HE'LL HAVE TO GO, 1969
Lee Maye
Buddah (45) 141
Reverse: "Jes' Lookin' "

LITTLE RED SCOOTER
Tony Conigliaro
RCA Victor (45) 8577
Reverse: "I Can't Get Over You"

Conigliaro is an outfielder for the Boston Red Sox.

LOCKED IN, 1970
Al Fitzmorris
Reverse: "Winds of My Life"

Fitzmorris is a Kansas City Royals' pitcher.

LOVE ME ALWAYS, 1955
Arthur Lee Maye and the Crowns
RPM (45) 429
Reverse: "Loop De Loop De Loop"

LOVING FOOL
Lee Maye
Jamie (45) 1276
Reverse: "How's the World Treating You?"

MULLDIGGER, 1984
Thad Bosley
B & E (45) 901
Published by Thad Bosley Publ. (BMI)
Reverse: "Mulldigger" (instrumental version)

Bosley is an outfielder for the Chicago White Sox.

ONE LOVE, 1963
Don Drysdale
Reprise (45) 20162
Reverse: "Give Her Love"

Drysdale is a Hall of Fame pitcher for the Los Angeles Dodgers.

ONLY A DREAM
Lee Maye
Jamie (45) 1284
Reverse: "The Breaks of Life"

ONLY YOU
Arthur Lee Maye
With the Johnny Otis Orchestra
Dig (45) 146
Reverse: "Gee"

The above is a re-pressing of a previously unavailable recording.

PLEASE DON'T LEAVE ME, 1955
Arthur Lee Maye and the Crowns
RPM (45) 438
Reverse: "Do the Bop"

PLEASE SAY YOU LOVE ME, 1955
Arthur Lee Maye and the Crowns
RPM (45) 420
Reverse: "Cool Lovin' "

POETRY, 1975
Tony Conigliaro
Magna Glide (45) 5N-326
Reverse: "Midnight in Boston"

SET MY HEART FREE, 1954
Arthur Lee Maye and the Crowns
Modern (45) 944
Reverse: "I Wanna Love"

SH-BOOM
Arthur Lee Maye
With the Johnny Otis Orchestra
Dig (45) 149
Reverse: "Sincerely"

The above is a re-pressing of a previously unavailable recording.

SHE WAS WAITING ON THE CORNER
Nelson Briles
Pip (45) 6505
Reverse: "Me and My Rock n' Roll Heroes"

Briles is a pitcher for the Pittsburgh Pirates.

STOP THE WORLD
Lee Maye
Pic (45) 126
Reverse: "At the Party"

THAT'S THE WAY THE BALL BOUNCES, 1964
Willie Davis
On *The Sound of the Dodgers*
Jaybar (33) 1
Written by Jackie Barnett and Sammy Fain
Published by Jaybar-Fain

Romantic pop tune unrelated to baseball. Davis is a Los Angeles Dodgers' outfielder.

THIS IS THE NIGHT FOR LOVE
Arthur Lee Maye and the Crowns
Dig (45) 124
Reverse: "Honey, Honey"
Also available: Yvette (45) 300

TO BASEBALL WITH LOVE, 1983
Ed Nottle
Nott's Landing (33)

Collection of nonbaseball-related songs as sung by the Oakland A's coach.

TODAY TODAY
Lee Maye
Pic (45) 115
Reverse: "Touch Me on My Shoulder"

TRULY, 1955
Arthur Lee Maye and the Crowns
RPM (45) 424

Reverse: "Oochie Pachie"
Also available: RPM (78) 424

WABASH CANNON BALL
Dizzy Dean
Colonial (45) 2118/9
Reverse: "You Don't Have to Be from the Country"

The Hall of Fame pitcher and broadcaster's signature song, often sung during rain delays.

THE WAYFARIN' STRANGER, 1964
Maury Wills
Dot (45) 16529
Reverse: "The Ballad of Maury Wills"

WE ARE THE CHAMPIONS, 1981
Big Blue Wrecking Crew (Steve Yeager, Rick Monday, Jay Johnstone, and Jerry Reuss)
Elektra (45) 47253
Reverse: "Theme from 'New York, New York' "

Yeager, Monday, Johnstone, and Reuss are Los Angeles Dodgers' teammates.

WHAT IS A WOMAN, WHAT IS A MAN
Nellie Briles
Ram (45) 1002

WHEN YOU TAKE MORE THAN YOU GIVE
Tony Conigliaro
RCA Victor (45) 8793
Reverse: "I Was There"

WHISPERING WIND
Arthur Lee Maye
Dig (45) 133
Reverse: "A Fool's Prayer"

WHY DON'T THEY UNDERSTAND
Tony Conigliaro
Penn-tone (45) PT 25

In the days before free-agency, when ballplayers sold insurance or automobiles or ran bowling alleys during the off-season, Milwaukee Braves outfielder Lee Maye was recording rock-and-roll songs. Indeed, he was a successful recording artist even before he made the major leagues, with such hit tunes as "Please Say You Love Me," recorded in 1955, and "Gloria," released in 1956. In 1959 Maye broke into the Braves outfield lineup with a .300 batting average in 51 games. The finest year in his 13 seasons in the major leagues was in 1964, when he batted .304 in 153 games and led the league with 44 doubles. Today, singer Lee Maye performs in the Los Angeles area, and many of his early 78 rpm recordings are collector's items among connoisseurs of early rhythm-and-blues. (National Baseball Library.)

Reverse: "Playing the Field"
Also available: RCA (45) 8523

WILL YOU BE MINE
Lee Maye
Imperial (45) 5790
Reverse: "Honey Honey"
Also available: Cash (45) 1063

Baseball in the Spoken Arts— Recorded

This section contains a listing of recorded poetry, fiction, and talking books relating to baseball. Included in the catalog are commercially released phonorecords and cassette tape recordings of baseball books, novels, and short stories; anthologized recordings of baseball-related poetry; and talking books for the blind.

For *Explanatory Notes* to this section, *see:* Baseball in Music and Song—Recorded.

ALIBI IKE, 1977
Story by Ring W. Lardner, read by Henry Morgan
On *Alibi Ike, Haircut, The Love Nest*
Newman Communications Corp. cassette no. 10031
See also: Baseball in Film; Baseball in Radio

BABE: THE LEGEND COMES TO LIFE, 1974
Book by Robert W. Creamer, read by Leon Janney
American Printing House for the Blind (six-record set)

BALL FOUR, 1970
Book by Jim Bouton and Leonard Shecter, read by John Cannon
American Foundation for the Blind TB 3442 (nine-record set)
See also: Baseball in Television

THE BALL GAME, 1967
Poem by Robert Creeley, read by himself
On *Today's Poets—Volume Three*
Scholastic (33) LA-2-FS 11003
See also: Baseball in Poetry and Light Verse

BASEBALL: AN INFORMAL HISTORY, 1969
Book by Douglass Wallop, read by Ed Kallay
American Printing House for the Blind TB 2946 (six-record set)

BASEBALL IS A FUNNY GAME, 1960
Book by Joe Garagiola, read by Leon Janney
American Foundation for the Blind TB 3510 (five-record set)

BASEBALL'S ZANIEST STARS, 1971
Book by Howard Liss, read by Ed Kallay
American Printing House for the Blind

THE BASE STEALER, 1967
Poem by Robert Francis, read by Paul Hecht
On *Reflections on a Gift of Watermelon Pickle and Other Modern Verse*
Scholastic (33) FS 11007
See also: Baseball in Poetry and Light Verse

THE BASE STEALER, 1975
Poem by Robert Francis, read by himself
On *Robert Francis Reads His Poems*
Folkways (33) 9729
See also: Baseball in Poetry and Light Verse

THE BOYS OF SUMMER, 1973
Book by Roger Kahn, read by Paul Clark
American Printing House for the Blind (ten-record set)
See also: Baseball in Documentary and Miscellaneous Films

CATCH
Poem by Robert Francis, read by David Wayne

On *A Gathering of Great Poetry for Children, Third Grade and Up*
Caedmon (33) TC 1237
See also: Baseball in Poetry and Light Verse

A FALSE SPRING, 1975
Book by Pat Jordan, read by Paul Clark
American Printing House for the Blind (four-record set)

THE GLORY OF THEIR TIMES, 1966
Book by Lawrence S. Ritter, read by John Cannon
Six-record set
See also: Baseball in Documentary and Miscellaneous Television; Baseball in Miscellaneous Recordings

HANG TOUGH, PAUL MATHER, 1973
Novel by Alfred Slote, read by Barry Bernson
American Printing House for the Blind (two-record set)
See also: Baseball in Juvenile and Miscellaneous Fiction

I NEVER HAD IT MADE, 1972
Book by Jackie Robinson, read by Fred Morsell
American Printing House for the Blind (four-record set)

KISS IT GOODBYE, 1973
Book by Shelby Whitfield, read by John Clark
American Printing House for the Blind (three-record set)

THE MICK, 1985
Book by Mickey Mantle and Herb Gluck, read by Bob Askey
Newman Communications Corp. set of two cassettes no. 68035
Newstrack, Inc.

MICKEY MANTLE OF THE YANKEES, 1958
Book by Gene Schoor, read by Milton Metz
American Printing House for the Blind (two-record set)

MY FATHER, THE COACH, 1972
Novel by Alfred Slote, read by Ed Kallay
American Printing House for the Blind (two-record set)
See also: Baseball in Juvenile and Miscellaneous Fiction

THE NATURAL, 1986
Novel by Bernard Malamud, read by Ken Howard
Listen For Pleasure cassette no. 7157-7 (two-cassette set)
See also: Baseball in Film; Baseball in Fiction; Baseball in Miscellaneous Recordings

Abridged reading of the classic novel.

NOT BAD FOR A GIRL, 1972
Novel by Isabella Taves, read by Terry Hayes Sales
American Printing House for the Blind
See also: Baseball in Juvenile and Miscellaneous Fiction

NUNS AT EVE
Poem by John Malcolm Brinnin, read by himself
On *Spoken Arts Treasury of 100 Modern American Poets Reading Their Poems, Volume Thirteen*

Spoken Arts (33) 1052
See also: Baseball in Poetry and Light Verse

THE OLD BALL GAME: BASEBALL IN FOLKLORE AND FICTION, 1971
Book by Tristram Potter Coffin, read by Ed Kallay
American Printing House for the Blind (five-record set)

THE ORIGINS OF BASEBALL, 1960
Poem by Kenneth Patchen, read by himself
On *Selected Poems of Kenneth Patchen*
Folkways (33) FL 9717
See also: Baseball in Poetry and Light Verse

PITCHER, 1975
Poem by Robert Francis, read by himself
On *Robert Francis Reads His Poems*
Folkways (33) 9729
See also: Baseball in Poetry and Light Verse

SEEING IT THROUGH, 1970
Book by Tony Conigliaro, read by Van Vanoe
American Printing House for the Blind (six-record set)

THE SUMMER GAME, 1972
Book by Roger Angell, read by Leon Janney
American Printing House for the Blind (five-record set)

TO SATCH (OR AMERICAN GOTHIC), 1966
Poem by Samuel Allen, read by James Earl Jones

On *A Hand Is on the Gate*
Folkways (33) 9740
See also: Baseball in Poetry and Light Verse

Original cast recording of black poetry and songs as presented at the Longacre Theatre, New York.

VIDA—HIS OWN STORY, 1972
Book by Vida Blue and Bill Libby, read by Paul Clark
American Printing House for the Blind (three-record set)

WAY TO GO, TEDDY, 1973
Novel by Donald Honig, read by Ed Kallay
American Printing House for the Blind (two-record set)
See also: Baseball in Juvenile and Miscellaneous Fiction

WHY THE BIG BALL GAME BETWEEN HOT GROUNDERS AND THE GRAND STANDERS WAS A HOT GAME
Story by Carl Sandburg, read by himself
On *Carl Sandburg Reading His Rootabaga Stories, Volume Three*
Caedmon (33) TC 1306

Folkloric children's tale about the magic "home run shirt" and the "spitball shirt" made by a "snoox" and a "gringo."

YOU KNOW ME AL: A BUSHER'S LETTERS, 1985
Novel by Ring W. Lardner, read by Barry Kraft
Book of the Road cassette no. 007 (two-cassette set)
See also: Baseball in Fiction. *See:* "Ring Lardner's You Know Me Al" (Baseball in Comic Art—Collected)

Abridged reading of the humorous letters from Chicago White Sox pitcher Jack Keefe.

Chapter

23

Baseball in Comedy and Light Verse— Recorded

The following catalog contains a comprehensive listing of recorded spoken-word comedy and humorous verse relating to baseball. Included in this section are early baseball comedy routines, monologs, skits, parodies—and two of the most celebrated examples of baseball humor: *Casey at the Bat* and *Who's on First?*

Many of the earliest recordings listed in this section feature a comedy routine in which an ethnic stereotype attends a baseball game for the first time. Early-1900s America was a hotbed of ethnic humor, and the newly invented Gramophone allowed the popular vaudeville comedians of the day to record virtually every conceivable variation on the ethnic theme. Of the many hundreds of comedy recordings released during the first decades of the 1900s, the vast majority of them were ethnic routines. Baseball was just one of the many subjects given the ethnic treatment by the vaudeville comics of that era.

For *Explanatory Notes* to this section, *see:* Baseball in Music and Song—Recorded.

ABE KABIBBLE AT THE BALL GAME, 1920
Harry Hershfield
Columbia 10-inch double-faced record A 2907
Reverse: "Abe Kabibble Dictates a Letter"

Jewish stereotype attends a baseball game for the first time.

ABNER THE BASEBALL (A FANTASY), 1957
Eddie Lawrence
Coral (45) 61821
Music arranged by Bernie Wayne
Also available: On *The Kingdom of Eddie Lawrence* Coral (33) 57203
See also: Baseball in Animated Cartoons—Feature

Heart-warming story about how a baseball named Abner earns a place in the Hall of Fame.

AT THE BASEBALL GAME
The Three Stooges
On *Madcap Musical Nonsense*
Golden Records (33) GLP 43
Also available: (1983) Rhino picture disc (33) 808; Grizzly (33) 76103

Slapstick visit to a baseball game.

AXEL AT THE BALL GAME, 1926
Axel Christensen

Broadway 10-inch double-faced record 8079-A
Reverse: "Axel Receives a Letter"

Swedish stereotype plays baseball for the first time.

BABE RUTH VISITS LAKE WOBEGON, 1985
Garrison Keillor
On *Gospel Birds and Other Stories of Lake Wobegon*
Prairie Home Companion set of two cassettes no. 1212/13

Comedic monolog about a visit to the fictional town of Lake Wobegon by Babe Ruth and his touring all-stars.

THE BALL GAME
Ethel Olson
Brunswick (78) 40051
Reverse: "Story of a Bookcase"

Baseball routine by the Norwegian woman comic.

BALLS, 1959
Jean Shepard
On *Jean Shepard and Other Foibles*
Elektra (33)

Humorous narrative on what it was like being a White Sox fan during the 1940s.

BASEBALL, 1968
Bill Cosby

On *To Russell, My Brother, Whom I Slept With*
Warner Bros. (33) 1734

BASEBALL, c. 1978
Bill Dana
On *Jose . . . Supersport*
Puente (33) 1

Updated and slightly altered version of "The Baseball Star."

THE BASEBALL COORDINATOR, c. 1968
Tim Conway and Ernie Anderson
On *Are We On?*
Liberty (33) 3512

Comic interview with a bumbling traveling secretary.

THE BASEBALL EXPERT
Joey Adams and Al Kelly
Coral 10-inch ep (78) 69045
Written by Cindy Heller and Joey Adams
Published by Musictime USA (BMI)
Reverse: "How Now Brown Cow"
Also available: Coral (78) 61169

BASEBALL-FOOTBALL, 1975
George Carlin
On *An Evening with Wally Londo Featuring Bill Slazo*
Little David (33) 1008

Comedic comparison between the gentle nature of baseball and the brutality of football.

BASEBALL GAME, 1916
Joe Weber and Lew Fields
Columbia 10-inch double-faced record
A 2092
Reverse: "The Marriage Market Scene"

Vaudeville sketch containing repartee and play on words.

THE BASEBALL GAME
The Newlyweds
Par-ty (45) 1006

Party record incorporating baseball-related double entendres.

BASEBALL IN BALTIMORE
Groucho Marx
On *An Evening with Groucho*
A&M (33) SP 6010 (two-record set)

THE BASEBALL STAR
Bill Dana
On *Jose Jimenez Talks to Teenagers of All Ages*
Kapp (33) 1304

Comic interview with a baseball "bonus baby."

THE BIG GAME, c. 1958
Bill Fern
Sport (45) 505

Novelty "break-in" description of a nonsensical baseball game.

BLITZ AND BLATZ AT THE BALL GAME, 1910
Bob Roberts and Fred Duprez
Indestructible (Columbia) 2-minute cylinder 1137

THE BOY IN THE BLEACHERS, 1916
Ralph Bingham
Victor 12-inch double-faced record 35490
Reverse: "My 'Possum Hunt"

Rhymed-verse recitation about a little boy's comical behavior at a baseball game.

A BROOKLYN BASEBALL FAN, 1954
Phil Foster
Coral (45) 61200
Reverse: "The Kids on the Corner"
Also available: Coral (78) 61200; Coral (45) EC 81088; On *Fun Time* (various artists) Coral (33) 57072; On *Phil Foster at Grossinger's* Epic (33) 3632

Comic monolog about a diehard Dodgers fan.

CASEY AT THE BAT, c. 1899
Russell Hunting
Edison cylinder 3802

First-known recording of this famous baseball ballad.

CASEY AT THE BAT, 1906
DeWolf Hopper
Victor 12-inch single-faced record 31559
Also available: (1909) Victor 12-inch single-faced record 31559 (reissue); (1913) Victor 12-inch double-faced record 35290; (1926) Victor 12-inch double-faced record 35783; On *The Old Curiosity Shop* (various artists) RCA Victor (33) 1112

Hopper recited this famous ballad over 10,000 times—by his own account—mostly in vaudeville and variety revues. It is possible that Casey at the Bat *might be utterly forgotten today were it not for Hopper's popularization of the poem. Hopper also starred in a motion picture of the same title. (See: Baseball in Film.)*

CASEY AT THE BAT, 1940
Taylor Holmes
On *Decca Presents "Take Me Out to the Ball Game"*
Decca album No. 120
Decca 12-inch record (78) 15048

Reverse: "Casey's Revenge" (Joe Laurie, Jr.)

CASEY AT THE BAT, c. 1950
Mel Allen
Golden Record (33) BR 25
Reverse: "The Umpire"/"Take Me Out to the Ball Game" (Tommy Henrich, Ralph Branca, Phil Rizzuto, and Roy Campanella)

CASEY AT THE BAT, 1951
Tony Martin
RCA Victor (78) 20-4216
Reverse: "Take Me Out to the Ball Game"

CASEY AT THE BAT, 1954
Lionel Barrymore
MGM 10-inch ep (78) S 35
Also available: On *Million Dollar Vaudeville Show* Lion (33) 70089

CASEY AT THE BAT, 1960
Vin Scully
Magnolia (45) 1001
Reverse: "Dodgers Charge"
(Bill Reeves)

CASEY AT THE BAT, 1961
Vincent Price
On *America the Beautiful: The Heart of American Poetry*
Columbia (33) 91 A 02013

CASEY AT THE BAT, 1965
Jackie Gleason
Capitol (45) 5420
Reverse: "I Had but 50¢"

The famous ballad as recited by "Reginald Van Gleason, III."

CASEY AT THE BAT, 1969
Ray Arkie
Canta 7-inch ep (33) 2512
Reverse: "Casey's Revenge"

CASEY AT THE BAT, 1969
Heggeness and West
Clowd (45) 7403
Reverse: "Doctor Gorrie's Press
Conference"

Double-talk version of the famous ballad.

CASEY AT THE BAT, 1978
Foster Brooks
Horizon Records
Reverse: "Riley on the Mound"

CASEY AT THE BAT, 1980
Johnny Bench
On *Casey at the Bat: Johnny Bench*
Moss Music Group (33) 1127
Features the Cincinnati Pops, Erich
Kunzel, conductor
Composed by Frank Proto
Reverse: "Peter and the Wolf, Opus
67," narrated by Tom Seaver

The famous ballad as recited by the Cincinnati Reds' all-star catcher.

CASEY AT THE BAT, 1980
Tug McGraw
On *Tug McGraw Narrates Casey at the Bat*
Ruth (33)
Features Peter Nero and the Philly
Pops

The Philadelphia Phillies' star reliever recites the comic poem.

CASEY AT THE BAT, c. 1982
No artist given
Aim (33) 02052 C

Recitation of the poem is followed by a reading of "The Story of Casey at the Bat" in which Casey becomes a slugger after discovering the benefits of drinking milk.

CASEY AT THE BAT
Eddie Albert, Vincent Price, Hal
Holbrook, Ed Begley, and Frederick
O'Neal
On *Classics of American Poetry for the Elementary Curriculum*
Caedmon (33) TC 2041 (two-record

The famous baseball ballad, Casey at the Bat, *has been recorded numerous times through the years. Comic actor DeWolf Hopper assured its place in American folklore with his popular recordings of the early 1900s. In 1954 Lionel Barrymore produced this rare recording of the poem, complete with musical background and sound effects. (MGM Records, 1954.)*

set)

CASEY AT THE BAT
Ed Begley
On *Favorite American Poems*
Caedmon (33) TC 1207

CASEY AT THE BAT
Gene "Poppa" Kelly
Klubhouse (78) D9 QB 10049/50
Reverse: "Casey's Revenge"

CASEY AT THE BAT
Paul Sparer and John Randolph

On *Story Poems*
Lexington (33) 7610/7615
Also available: On *American Story
Poems* Educational Audio Visual (33)
7299-2

CASEY AT THE BAT, YESTERDAY AND TODAY, 1971
No artist given
Cameron McKay 7-inch ep (33)
unnumbered

Includes: "An authentic recording of the famous poem as it was performed around the turn of the century"; "The famous Mudville inning as it might be recorded by today's TV sportscasters.''

CASEY'S REVENGE, 1940
Joe Laurie, Jr.
On *Decca Presents ''Take Me Out to the Ball Game''*
Decca album No. 120
Decca 12-inch record (78) 15048
Reverse: *Casey at the Bat*
(Taylor Holmes)

Parody of Casey at the Bat.

CASEY'S REVENGE, 1969
Ray Arkie
Canta 7-inch ep (33) 2512
Reverse: *Casey at the Bat*

CASEY'S REVENGE
Gene ''Poppa'' Kelly
Klubhouse (78)) D9 QB 1049/50
Reverse: *Casey at the Bat*

CASEY UMPIRING A BALL GAME, 1895
Russell Hunting
Brown Wax cylinder, 120 rpm

A man named Casey umpires a game he has never seen or played before.

CHARLIE AT THE BAT, 1961
Larry Verne
Era (45) 3051
Reverse: *Pow, Right in the Kisser*

Arrogant slugger strikes out, a la Casey at the Bat.

DEATH AND BASEBALL, 1979
Mal Sharpe
On *The Meaning of Life*
Rhino (33) 006

Man-on-the-street interview in which the question is asked, ''Would you take a dead body to a baseball game?''

DOG BALL, 1982
Stevens and Grdnic

On *Retail Comedy at Wholesale Prices*
Laff (33) 222

Play-by-play of a game in which live dogs are pitched and batted.

AN ENGLISHMAN AT A BALL GAME, 1923
Harry A. James
Gennett 10-inch double-faced record 5092
Reverse: ''An Englishman's Idea of American Wit''

FLANAGAN AND ''THE REILLEYS'' AT A BASEBALL GAME, 1908
Steve Porter
Edison Amberol 4-minute cylinder 4

THE GARV, 1984
Hudson and Bauer
On *Sounds of Success: Music of a Winning Season*
San Diego Padres (33) unnumbered

Satirical interview with an overly solicitous Steve Garvey.

GENERIC BASEBALL ANNOUNCER, 1982
Roy Firestone
On *Talkin' Baseball—American League*
Lifesong (33) 8136
Also available: On *Talkin' Baseball—National League* Lifesong (33) 8137

Parody of a typical minor league play-by-play announcer and his endless sales pitches.

GERMAN BASEBALL, 1957
Eddie Lawrence
Coral (45) 61799
Reverse: ''Golden Boskos''

Nonsense interview with a manager of a German baseball team.

GETZEL AT A BASEBALL GAME
Michael Rosenberg

Banner (78) 2046
Reverse: ''Shepsel in Florida''

Yiddish-language comedy routine.

HANK'S 715TH, 1974
Gary Hoffar
Jemkl (45) 3294
Reverse: ''Memories of Yesterday''
(Ellison Pinder)

Novelty ''break-in'' tribute to Hank Aaron.

HOME RUN BILL'S DEFENSE, 1917
Ralph Bingham
Victor 12-inch double-faced record 35626
Reverse: ''Hold Up at Buck Run''

INTERNATIONAL BASEBALL GAME, c. 1943
(British Bull Dogs vs. Swastikas)
Woodhouse and Hawkins
Bluebird (78) 4684
Reverse: Part II

Baseball as played by the leaders of the Axis powers and the Allies.

JIMMY AND MAGGIE AT A BASEBALL GAME, 1906
Ada Jones and Len Spencer
Victor 10-inch single-faced record 4865

A man takes a woman to her first baseball game.

LOCO BASEBALL, 1957
Eddie Lawrence
Coral (45) 61713
Reverse: ''The New Philosopher''
Also available: On *The Old Philosopher* Coral (33) 57103

Play-by-play description of a nonsensical baseball game.

THE MAN WHO FANNED CASEY, 1909
Digby Bell
Victor 12-inch single-faced record 31733
Also available: (1909) Victor 12-inch double-faced record 35139; (1910) Edison Amberol 4-minute cylinder 430; (1913) Victor 12-inch double-faced record 35290

Parody of Casey at the Bat.

METS PHILOSOPHER, c. 1963
Eddie Lawrence

Coral (45) 62367
Reverse: "We Love Yuh Mets"

Humorous lampoon of the New York Mets, in the style of Lawrence's famous, "The Old Philosopher."

MR. AND MRS. FLANNIGAN AT A BASEBALL GAME, 1907
Steve Porter
Columbia cylinder BC 85082

MYTI KAYSI AT THE BAT, 1962
Danny Kaye
Reprise (45) 20105

Written by Sylvia Fine and Herbert Baker
Published by Dena Music, Inc. (ASCAP)
Reverse: "D-o-d-g-e-r-s Song"

Parody of Casey at the Bat.

NISHIMOTO AT THE BAT, 1953
Harry Kari and His Six Saki Sippers
Capitol (45) F 2516
Written by Harry Stewart
Reverse: "The Love Bug Will Bite You"
Also available: Capitol (78) 2516

EVERYBODY'S FAVORITE TEAM

In case you've ever wondered, the position-by-position lineup of Abbott and Costello's comedy classic "Who's on First?" reads like this: Tomorrow (pitcher), Today (catcher), Who (first base), What (second base), I Don't Know (third base), I Don't Give a Darn (shortstop), Why (left field), and Because (center field). In all the years they performed the sketch, Abbott and Costello never made a reference to a rightfielder. That's probably because the position belongs—unquestionably—to an exclamation point named Babe Ruth. The following is a sample from the classic routine, as performed by Abbott and Costello on one of their best-selling recordings:

ABBOTT: You know, strange as it may seem, they give ballplayers peculiar names nowadays. On the St. Louis team Who's on first, What's on second, I Don't Know is on third.
COSTELLO: That's what I want to find out. I want you to tell me the names of the fellows on the St. Louis team.
ABBOTT: I'm telling you. Who's on first, What's on second, I Don't Know is on third.
COSTELLO: You know the fellows' names?
ABBOTT: Yes.
COSTELLO: Well, then, who's playin' first?
ABBOTT: Yes.
COSTELLO: I mean the fellow's name on first base.
ABBOTT: Who.
COSTELLO: The fellow's name on first base for St. Louis.
ABBOTT: Who.
COSTELLO: The guy on first base.
ABBOTT: Who is on first base.
COSTELLO: Well, what are you askin' me for?
ABBOTT: I'm not asking you, I'm telling you. Who is on first.
COSTELLO: I'm askin' you, who is on first?
ABBOTT: That's the man's name.
COSTELLO: That's whose name?
ABBOTT: Yes.
COSTELLO: Well, go ahead, tell me.
ABBOTT: Who.
COSTELLO: The guy on first.
ABBOTT: Who.
COSTELLO: The first baseman.
ABBOTT: Who is on first.
COSTELLO (*trying a different approach*): Have you got a first baseman on first?
ABBOTT: Certainly.
COSTELLO: Well, all I'm tryin' to find out is what's the guy's name on first base.
ABBOTT: Oh, no, no. What is on *second* base!

A Baseball Classic

In the pantheon of famous first basemen who have contributed to the legends and lore of baseball are such greats as George Sisler, Frank Chance, Bill Terry, Stan Musial, Willie Stargell, Don Mattingly, and the man they called the Iron Horse, the pride of baseball, Lou Gehrig. But the list would not be complete if we failed to include a first sacker who has made his own mark in baseball history, the improbable first baseman—usually of the Browns, sometimes of the Wolves—by the inquiring name of Who.

It is likely that as long as baseball is played, Bud Abbott and Lou Costello's comedy classic, "Who's on First?," will enjoy a special place in baseball lore. Even now, decades after the two comics last performed the sketch, it is still being discovered by new generations of baseball fans and connoisseurs of American humor.

"You know, they give ballplayers peculiar names nowadays." Bud Abbott, left, and Lou Costello performing their classic comedy routine. (National Baseball Library.)

No one knows precisely who wrote or originated "Who's on First?" or how Abbott and Costello, as two garden-variety burlesque comics, came to include the routine into their act. Pitter-patter sketches, incorporating play on words, had long been a staple of stand-up comedy. At one time, early in their partnership, Abbott and Costello performed a skit that played on the words "watts" and "volts" in a manner quite similar to "Who's on First?" To wit: Abbott: "Do you know what volts are?" Costello: "What are volts?" Abbott: "That's right. Watts are volts." Costello: "Well, go ahead, tell me. What are volts?"—and so on. It is apparent that "Who's on First?" evolved from a tradition of such play-on-word routines and that Abbott and Costello, much to their lasting credit, took an otherwise shopworn routine and tranformed it into a comedic work of art.

The two comics spent several years together as roustabout vaudevillians before they were signed to appear regularly on the popular radio program "The Kate Smith Show" in 1939. They set out immediately to perform the baseball skit—now polished and flawlessly timed—during their segment of the show. But the producer, thinking the sketch unfunny, barred the comics from performing it on the program. Weeks passed when Abbott and Costello, desperate to work the routine into the show, confessed somewhat untruthfully that they had run out of material and would not be able to appear on that week's program. The producer, of course, would not hear of it and suggested they try the detested baseball routine. They did, and it created a sensation with the radio audience. Abbott and Costello were asked to perform the sketch time and again in the years that followed.

Abbott and Costello estimated that they performed the skit approximately 10,000 times in radio and television appearances and in live performances. (Curiously, DeWolf Hopper gave the same figure for the number of occasions he recited *Casey at the Bat*). The routine was included in their 1945 film *The Naughty Nineties* and was part of a film compilation celebrating the two comics, *The World of Abbott and Costello*, released in 1965. The routine has also been preserved in countless records and audio cassettes.

In 1956 a gold-plated record, honoring the famous baseball routine, was placed on display at the Baseball Hall of Fame in Cooperstown, New York. Today, visitors can watch a film segment of the two comics performing their comedy classic continuously throughout the day. ◆

Parody of Casey at the Bat *in which the sad tale of DiMaggio Nishimoto is told.*

NOBODY WILL EVER PLAY BASEBALL, 1960
Bob Newhart
On *The Button-Down Mind of Bob Newhart*
Warner Bros. (33) 1379

Imagines how Abner Doubleday might have fared if he had offered his invention to a contemporary party-game manufacturer.

RILEY ON THE MOUND, 1978
Foster Brooks
Horizon Records
Reverse: *Casey at the Bat*

Ballad about the pitcher who struck out the famous Casey, as written and recited by Brooks.

"STRIKE" LONG BALL, 1981
Bill Neale
Forr (45) 444
Reverse: Same

Novelty "break-in" commentary on the strike by major league baseball players.

THAT HOLLER GUY!, 1958
Joe Garagiola
United Artists (33) UAL 3032

THROUGH A HOLE IN THE FENCE, 1911
Murray K. Hill

Victor 10-inch double-faced record 16844
Reverse: "Come, Josephine, In My Flying Machine" (Ada Jones)
Also available: (1911) Victor 10-inch double-faced record 16954

Rhymed-verse recitation comparing life to a game of baseball.

THE TOUGH BOY ON THE RIGHT FIELD FENCE, 1909
Digby Bell
Victor 12-inch record 31731
Also available: (1909) Edison Amberol 4-minute cylinder 156

TWO TOP GRUSKIN
Ed (Archie) Gardner
Top Ten (78) 6

UNCLE JOSH AT A BALL GAME, 1897
Cal Stewart
Columbia 2-minute wax cylinder 14005
Also available: (1900) Edison Grand Concert cylinder B 129; (1902) Columbia 10-inch single-faced record 71; (1908) Indestructible (Columbia) 2-minute cylinder 923; (1908) Columbia 10-inch double-faced record A 286; (1909) Edison 2-minute wax cylinder 10168; Harvard 7-inch record (78) 71; Silvertone (78)

UNCLE JOSH PLAYING A GAME OF BASEBALL, 1897
Cal Stewart
Edison 2-minute cylinder 3881
Also available: (as 'Uncle Josh Playing Baseball''): (1903) Zonophone 9-inch single-faced record 5848; (1903) Victor 10-inch single-faced record 2348 (also available as an 8-inch record); (1908) Victor 10-inch double-faced record 16228

Folksy description of a middle-aged man's attempt to play in a youth baseball game.

UNCLE JOSH'S FOOTBALL AND BASEBALL GAME, 1899
Cal Stewart
Columbia Grand cylinder 14041

THE VOYAGE, 1982
The Zanies
Dore (45)

A series of puns, incorporating baseball players' names, tells a tale of a ship at sea.

WE LOVE YUH METS, c. 1963
Eddie Lawrence
Coral (45) 62367
Reverse: "Mets Philosopher"

Humorous lampoon of the New York Mets, in the style of Lawrence's famous, "The Old Philosopher."

WHAT'S THE SCORE, PODNER, c. 1954

Cactus Pryor
4 Star (45) 1676
Published by 4 Star Sales (BMI)
Reverse: "Tweedle Dee"

Biting parody of Dizzy Dean broadcasting a baseball game.

WHO'S ON FIRST?
Abbott and Costello
Castle (78) 1253
Also available: Enterprise (78) 501;

(1960) Campbell (45) 1001; Nostalgia Lane (33) 800-GR 1001; Anonymously labeled 10-inch ep (33) unnumbered (label states: "Presented to National Baseball Hall of Fame, Cooperstown, N.Y., 1956.")
See also: Baseball in Miscellaneous Plays and Sketches. *See: The Naughty Nineties; The World of Abbott and*

Costello (Baseball in Film: Appendix); "Broadcast of June 13, 1944" (Baseball in Radio)

WHO'S ON FIRST, 1978
Hudson and Judson
Cream (45) 7824
Reverse: "The Pits"
Also available: Cream (33) 1008

Later and slightly altered version of Abbott and Costello's famous routine.

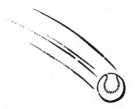

Selected Bibliography

Publications listed in Everything Baseball *or mentioned in the annotations are not included in the Selected Bibliography.*

MONOGRAPHS

American Society of Composers, Authors, and Publishers. *Index of Performed Compositions.* New York: ASCAP, 1978. Supplement, 1981.

Barnouw, Erik. *A History of Broadcasting in the United States:* Volumes 1–3. New York: Oxford University Press, 1966, 1968, 1970.

Bergan, Ronald. *Sports in the Movies.* New York: Proteus Books, 1982.

Bordman, Gerald. *American Musical Theatre.* New York: Oxford University Press, 1978.

———. *The Oxford Companion to American Theatre.* New York: Oxford University Press, 1984.

Brooks, Tim, and Marsh, Earle. *The Complete Directory to Prime Time Network TV Shows.* New York: Ballantine Books, 1979.

Bruccoli, Matthew J., and Layman, Richard, editors. *Ring W. Lardner: A Descriptive Bibliography.* Pittsburgh, Pennsylvania: University of Pittsburgh Press, 1976.

Buxton, Frank, and Owen, Bill. *The Big Broadcast.* New York: The Viking Press, 1972.

Cappio, Alfred P. *Slide, Kelly, Slide: The Story of Michael J. Kelly.* Paterson, New Jersey: The Passaic County Historical Society, 1962.

Coffin, Tristram Potter. *The Old Ball Game: Baseball in Folklore and Fiction.* New York: Herder and Herder, 1971.

Dunning, John. *Tune in Yesterday: The Ultimate Encyclopedia of Old-Time Radio, 1925–1976.* Englewood Cliffs, New Jersey: Prentice-Hall, Inc., 1976.

Einstein, Charles, editor. *The Fireside Book of Baseball.* New York: Simon and Schuster, 1956.

———. *The Second Fireside Book of Baseball.* New York: Simon and Schuster, 1958.

———. *The Third Fireside Book of Baseball.* New York: Simon and Schuster, 1968.

Eisner, Joel, and Krinsky, David. *Television Comedy Series: An Episode Guide to 153 TV Sitcoms in Syndication.* Jefferson, North Carolina: McFarland and Co., Inc., 1984.

Gianakos, Larry James. *Television Drama Series Programming:* Volumes 1–4. Metuchen, New Jersey: The Scarecrow Press, Inc., 1978, 1980, 1981, 1983.

Green, Abel, and Laurie, Joe, Jr. *Show Biz From Vaude to Video.* New York: Henry Holt and Co., 1951.

Grobani, Anton. *Guide to Baseball Literature.* Detroit, Michigan: Gale Research Co., 1975.

Guernsey, Otis L., Jr., editor, and others. *The Burns Mantle Theatre Yearbook:* Volumes 1919 to 1983. New York: Dodd, Mead and Co.

Higgs, Robert J. *Laurel and Thorn: The Athlete in American Literature.* Lexington, Kentucky: The University Press of Kentucky, 1981.

Keller, Dean H. *Index to Plays in Periodicals.* Metuchen, New Jersey: The Scarecrow Press, Inc., 1971.

Kinkle, Roger D. *The Complete Encyclopedia of Popular Music and Jazz, 1900–1950:* Volumes 1–4. New Rochelle, New York: Arlington House Publishers, 1974.

Kreider, Barbara. *Index to Children's Plays in Collections.* Metuchen, New Jersey: The Scarecrow Press, Inc., 1972.

Lahue, Kalton C. *Continued Next Week: A History of the Moving Picture Serial.* Norman, Oklahoma: University of Oklahoma Press, 1964.

———. *World of Laughter: The Motion Picture Comedy Short, 1910–1930.* Norman, Oklahoma: University of Oklahoma Press,1966.

———. *Motion Picture Pioneer: The Selig Polyscope Company.* New York: A. S. Barnes and Co., 1973.

Lauritzen, Einar, and Lundquist, Gunnar. *American Film Index:* Volumes 1–2. Stockholm, Sweden: Film-Index, 1976, 1984.

Lenburg, Jeff. *The Encyclopedia of Animated Cartoon Series.* Westport, Connecticut: Arlington House Publishers, 1981.

Lowe, Benjamin. *The Beauty of Sport.* Englewood Cliffs, New Jersey: Prentice-Hall, Inc., 1977.

Maltin, Leonard. *The Great Movie Shorts.* New York: Bonanza Books, 1972.

———. *Of Mice and Magic: A History of American Animated Cartoons.* New York: New American Library, 1980.

———. *TV Movies: 1985–86.* New York: New American Library/Signet, 1984.

Marill, Alvin H. *Movies Made for Television: The Telefeature and the Mini-Series, 1964–1984.* New York: New York Zoetrope, Inc., 1984.

Minus, Johnny, and Hale, Willia Storm. *Film Superlist: 20,000 Motion Pictures in the Public Domain.* Hollywood, California: Seven Arts Press, Inc., 1973.

Monro, Isabel Stevenson, and Monro, Kate M. *Index to Reproductions of American Paintings.* New York: The H. W. Wilson Co., 1984.

Motion Picture, Broadcasting, and Recorded Sound Division, Library of Congress. *The George Kleine Collection of Early Motion Pictures in the Library of Congress: A Catalog.* Washington, D.C.: Library of Congress, 1980.

Munden, Kenneth W., and Krafsur, Richard P., editors. *The American Film Institute Catalog of Motion Pictures:* Volumes 1–2. New York: R. R. Bowker Co., 1971, 1976.

National Video Clearinghouse. *The Video Source Book.* Syosset, New York: The National Video Clearinghouse.

Oriard, Michael V. *Dreaming of Heroes.* Chicago: Nelson-Hall, Inc., 1982.

Osborne, Jerry. *Rock, Rock & Roll 45's:* Fourth Edition (Osborne and Hamilton's Original Record Collector's Price Guide). Phoenix, Arizona: O'Sullivan Woodside and Co., 1983.

Osborne, Jerry, and Hamilton, Bruce. *Blues, Rhythm and Blues, Soul:* First Edition (Osborne and Hamilton's Original Record Collector's Price Guide). Phoenix, Arizona: O'Sullivan Woodside and Co., 1980.

Overstreet, Robert M. *The Comic Book Price Guide:* Fifteenth Edition. Cleveland, Tennessee: Overstreet Publications, Inc., 1985.

Parish, James Robert. *Actors' Television Credits: 1950–1972.* Metuchen, New Jersey: The Scarecrow Press, Inc., 1973.

Parish, James Robert, and Trost, Mark. *Actors' Television Credits, Supplement I.* Metuchen, New Jersey: The Scarecrow Press, Inc., 1978.

Price, Tom. *Performances Logs of Marian and Jim Jordan: 1917–1980.* Salinas, California: Privately published, 1980.

———. *Radio Program Timelines.* Salinas, California: Privately published, 1980.

Racquet and Tennis Club. *Dictionary Catalogue of the Library of Sports in the Racquet and Tennis Club.* Boston: G. K. Hall, 1971.

Reichler, Joseph L., editor. *The Baseball Encyclopedia:* Fifth Edition. New York: Macmillan Publishing Co., Inc., 1982.

Research Institute of the College Art Association. *The Index of Twentieth Century Artists: 1933–1937.* New York: Arno Press.

Ritter, Lawrence S. *The Glory of Their Times.* New York: Macmillan Publishing Co., Inc., 1966. Second enlarged edition published New York: William Morrow and Co., Inc., 1984.

Rosenberg, Bernard, and White, David Manning. *Mass Culture: The Popular Arts in America.* Glencoe, Illinois: The Free Press/The Falcon's Wing Press, 1957.

Rust, Brian. *The Complete Entertainment Discography.* New Rochelle, New York: Arlington House, 1973.

Seymour, Harold, *Baseball: The Early Years.* New York: Oxford University Press, 1960.

———. *Baseball: The Golden Age.* New York: Oxford University Press, 1971.

Shissler, Barbara Johnson. *Sports and Games in Art.* Minneapolis, Minnesota: Lerner Publications Co., 1966.

Smart, James R. *Radio Broadcasts in the Library of*

Congress: 1924–1941. Washington, D.C.: Library of Congress, 1982.

Smith, Myron J. *Baseball: A Comprehensive Bibliography.* Jefferson, North Carolina: McFarland and Co., Inc., 1986.

Smith, William James, editor, and others. *Granger's Index to Poetry:* Editions 1–7. New York: Columbia University Press.

Society for American Baseball Research. *Baseball Research Journal:* Volumes 1–11. Cooperstown, New York: Society for American Baseball Research, 1975–1985.

Spalding, A.G. *America's National Game.* New York: American Sports Publishing Co., 1911.

Spears, Jack. *Hollywood: The Golden Era.* Cranbury, New Jersey: A. S. Barnes and Co., Inc., 1971.

Stecheson, Anthony. *The Stecheson Classified Song Directory.* Hollywood, California: The Music Industry Press, 1961.

Swindell, Larry. *The Last Hero: The Biography of Gary Cooper.* Garden City, New York: Doubleday and Co., Inc., 1980.

Terrace, Vincent. *Radio's Golden Years.* San Diego and New York: A. S. Barnes and Co., Inc., 1981.

Thomas, Bob. *Bud and Lou: The Abbott and Costello Story.* Philadelphia: J. B. Lippincott Co., 1977.

United States Copyright Office. *Motion Pictures:* Volumes 1–4. Washington, D.C.: Library of Congress, 1951, 1953, 1960, 1971.

Voigt, David Quentin. *American Baseball: Volumes 1–2.* Norman, Oklahoma: University of Oklahoma Press, 1966, 1970.

———. *America Through Baseball.* Chicago: Nelson-Hall, 1976.

Walls, Howard L. *Motion Pictures, 1894–1912.* Washington, D.C.: Library of Congress, 1953.

Writers' Program. *The Film Index:* Volume I. New York: MOMA Film Library and The H. W. Wilson Co., 1941.

Yaakov, Juliette, editor, and others. *Play Index:* Editions 1–6. New York: The H. W. Wilson Co.

Zucker, Harvey Marc, and Babich, Lawrence J. *Sports Films: A Complete Reference.* Jefferson, North Carolina: McFarland and Co., Inc., 1987.

PERIODICALS

Anon. "Broadway Is Hot for Baseball Shows; Keyed to Public Sports Growth." *Variety,* June 3, 1981. Summary of baseball-related plays in production.

Barnes, Ken. "Baseball's Greatest Hits (And Misses)." *Records and Radio,* October 26, 1984, p. 22. Informal review of recently recorded baseball songs.

Cantwell, Robert. "The Music of Baseball." *Sports Illustrated,* October 3, 1960. Significant history of baseball in music and song.

———. "Sport Was Box Office Poison." *Sports Illustrated,* September 15, 1969, pp. 108–112. Substantial history of sports-related films.

———. "America Is Formed for Happiness." *Sports Illustrated,* December 22, 1975, pp. 54–71. Significant history of early American sports and games.

Cashman, Terry. "Twenty Years and Twenty Minutes." *Inside Sports,* June 30, 1981, pp. 15–16. Informal account of how the song, "Willie, Mickey and 'The Duke' " came to be written.

Catton, Bruce. "The Great American Game." *American Heritage,* April 1959, pp. 17–20. Essay in appreciation of baseball.

Dichter, Harry. "Baseball in Words and Music." *Musicgram:* National Sheet Music Society, Inc., February 1965, pp. 88–91. Informal survey of early baseball-related songs.

Drohan, John. "50,000 Songs on Sports in Driscoll Collection." *The Sporting News,* January 22, 1947, pp. 14–15. Informal survey of baseball-related songs in the J. Francis Driscoll collection.

Elmore, Richard. "Sports in American Sculpture." *International Studio,* November 1925, pp. 98–101. Incisive history of sports in modern sculpture.

Gold, Eddie. "Baseball Movies." *Baseball Research Journal* (Society for American Baseball Research, Cooperstown, New York), 1983, pp. 126–129. Informal survey of baseball-related motion pictures.

Hall, Donald. "From Short to Second to Verse." *Inside Sports,* May 1982, pp. 14–15. Critical survey of baseball-related poetry.

Holbrook, Stewart H. "Frank Merriwell at Yale Again—and Again and Again." *American Heritage,*

June 1961, pp. 24–27. Informal history of the Gilbert Patten series of juvenile sports stories.

Morehouse, Ward. "Actor-Athletes Struck It Rich as Thespians." *The Sporting News,* March 23, 1960. Informal history of baseball players in vaudeville.

Mott, Margaret M. "A Bibliography of Song Sheets: Sports and Recreations in American Popular Songs —Part II." *Notes:* Music Library Association, Volume 7, No. 4, September 1950, pp. 522–533. Comprehensive listing of baseball-related songsheets.

Okrent, Daniel. "The All-Star Team." *New York Times Book Review,* May 3, 1981, p. 13. Informal survey of baseball-related fiction.

Ripley, John W. "Baseball's Greatest Song." *American Heritage,* June/July 1983, pp. 76–79. Significant history of baseball-related nickelodeon song slides.

Rosenthal, Harold. "Take Me Out to the Ball Game Written on Subway in '08." *The Sporting News,* March 16, 1958. Informal account of how this most famous baseball song came to be written.

Smith, Ken. "Baseball's Got Rhythm." *Baseball Magazine,* September 1942, pp. 465–466. Informal history of barbershop-singing baseball players.

Spears, Jack. "Baseball on the Screen." *Films in Review,* April 1968, pp. 198–217. Exhaustive history of baseball-related films. Later revised and included as a chapter to, *Hollywood: The Golden Era.* Cranbury, New Jersey: A. S. Barnes and Co., Inc., 1971.

Talese, Gay. "Platter Up." *New York Times Magazine,* October 7, 1956, pp. 77–78. Informal review of recently recorded baseball songs.

Taylor, Mark. "Baseball as Myth." *Commonweal,* May 12, 1972, pp. 237–239. Significant interpretation of Robert Coover's novel, *The Universal Baseball Association, Inc., J. Henry Waugh, Prop.*

Walsh, Jim. " 'Take Me Out to the Ball Game' Still Champion." *Variety,* April 8, 1953. Informal history of early baseball-related songs.

———. "Baseball Recordings." *Hobbies,* December 1971, pp. 37–38. Exhaustive history of early baseball-related phonorecordings. Includes a definitive discography.

———. "More About Baseball Recordings and the National Baseball Museum." *Hobbies,* July 1972, pp. 37–38. Informal addendum to the December 1971 article.

Selected Guide to Sources and Dealers

The following is a selected listing of institutional and commercial sources for materials cataloged in *Everything Baseball*. While every effort has been made to provide a representative selection in all categories, the reader is encouraged to use the listing as a guide only and to inquire at other suitable libraries and dealers.

MUSEUMS, LIBRARIES, SOCIETIES

American Film Institute. 1815 H Street, N.W., Washington, DC 20006. Film archives and nonlending library, symposia, exhibitions. General membership by subscription to *American Film* magazine.

The Library of Congress. Washington, DC 20540. Extensive collections in all fields: film, broadcasting, recorded sound, sheet music, prints, photographs, fiction and poetry. Library open to the public; some collections restricted to scholars only.

The Museum of Broadcasting. 1 East 53rd Street, New York, NY 10022. Television and radio broadcast archives: audio/visual noncirculating library, symposia, exhibitions. Museum and membership open to the public.

National Art Museum of Sport. University of New Haven, Marvin K. Peterson Library. 300 Orange Avenue, West Haven, CT 06516. Gallery and permanent collection of baseball and sports-related art and sculpture, research library, newsletter. Museum and membership open to the public.

National Baseball Hall of Fame and Museum/ National Baseball Library. Cooperstown, NY 13326. Exhibition and permanent collection of baseball-related artifacts of historical interest;

representative collections in all categories: film, broadcasting, recorded sound, sheet music, art and sculpture, prints, photographs, fiction, poetry, books and periodicals; research library and archives. Museum and library open to the public.

National Library of Sports. 180 West San Carlos Street, San Jose, CA 95113. Extensive sports and baseball collection of books, periodicals, and stadium programs; research library. Library and membership open to the public.

Newberry Library. Special Collections Department. 60 West Walton Street, Chicago, IL 60610. Contains the J. Francis Driscoll music collection of baseball and sports songsheets. Noncirculating library, open to scholars.

North American Society for Sport History (NASSH). 101 White Building, Pennsylvania State University, University Park, PA 16802. Academic research exchange, scholarly journals, symposia. Membership open to the public.

Notre Dame Sports and Games Research Collection. Memorial Library. University of Notre Dame, South Bend, IN 46556. Extensive archives of sports-related artifacts of historical interest; books and periodicals collection. Noncirculating library, open to scholars.

Society for American Baseball Research (SABR). P.O. Box 10033, Kansas City, MO 64111. Research lending library, information exchange; monographs, journals, bulletins, symposia. Membership open to the public.

Society for the Preservation and Encouragement of Radio Drama, Variety and Comedy (SPERDVAC). P.O. Box 1587, Hollywood, CA 90078. Radio recordings archives and lending library, information exchange; journals, bulletins, symposia. Membership open to the public.

United States Sports Academy. One Academy Drive, Daphne, AL 36526. Graduate school of the sport sciences; gallery and archives of baseball and sports art. Museum open to the public.

ART DEALERS AND MARKET SOURCES

Gallery 53/Smithy Art Works. 53 Pioneer Street, Cooperstown, NY 13326. Fine art gallery; baseball art and sculpture.
Gene Locklear Gallery. Union Chapel Road, Pembroke, NC 28372. Baseball art by former major leaguer Gene Locklear.
Mudville Baseball Art. 215 Broadway, McIntosh, MN 56556. Limited edition art prints, baseball illustrations.
Perez-Steele Galleries. P.O. Box 1776, Fort Washington, PA 19034. Limited edition collectors' art prints.
Walker Gallery/The National Pastime. 81 Main Street, Cooperstown, NY 13326. Limited edition collectors' art prints, fine art.

BOOKSELLERS: BASEBALL FICTION, POETRY, HISTORY

ATC/Sports Books. 321 East Superior Street, Duluth, MN 55802. New and used baseball and sports books. Catalog.
Austin Book Shop. P.O. Box 36, Kew Gardens, NY 11415. Rare, out-of-print baseball books. Catalog.
Bill's Books. 3323 Lindbergh Avenue, Steven's Point, WI 54481. New and used baseball books. Catalog.
Sports Books, Etc. 7073 Brookfield Plaza, Springfield, VA 22150. Baseball and sports books and home video. Catalog.

PUBLISHERS: BASEBALL FICTION, POETRY, LITERARY JOURNALS

Minneapolis Review of Baseball. 1501 4th Street,

Minneapolis, MN 55454. Journal of baseball poetry and short fiction. By subscription.
North Atlantic Books. 2320 Blake Street, Berkeley, CA 94704. Publishers of baseball literary anthologies. Catalog.
SABR Review of Books. P.O. Box 10033, Kansas City, MO 64111. Journal of baseball literary criticism. By subscription.
Samidat. P.O. Box 129, Richford, VT 05476. Publishers of baseball poetry. Catalog.
Spitball: The Literary Baseball Magazine. 6224 College Vue Place, Cincinnati, OH 45224. Journal of baseball poetry and short fiction. By subscription.

FILM, TELEVISION, ANIMATED CARTOONS, HOME VIDEO

Collectors Book Store. 1708 North Vine Street, Hollywood, CA 90028. Film photographs, posters, collectibles.
Eddie Brandt's Saturday Matinee. P.O. Box 3232 (6310 Colfax Avenue), North Hollywood, CA 91609. Film photographs, posters, collectibles; mail-order home video rentals. Catalog.
Movie Collector's World. P.O. Box 309, Fraser, MI 48026. Periodical: film and home video collectibles. By subscription.
Movie Star News. 134 West 18th Street, New York, NY 10011. Film photographs, posters, collectibles.
Movies Unlimited. 6736 Castor Avenue, Philadelphia, PA 19149. Mail-order home video sales. Catalog.
National Video Clearinghouse. 100 Lafayette Drive, Syosset, NY 11791. Publishers: The Video Source Book.

THEATER

Larry Edmund's Bookshop. 6658 Hollywood Boulevard, Hollywood, CA 90028. Theater and film books and scripts, photographs, posters.
Theatre Arts Bookshop. 405 West 42nd Street, New York, NY. Theater books and scripts, posters, playbills.

SOUND RECORDINGS, MUSIC

Disc-overies. P.O. Box 255, Port Townsend, WA 98368. Periodical: phonorecords and music collectibles. By subscription.
Michael Brown. 12 Yorktown Road, East Brunswick, NJ 08816. New and used baseball-related phonorecords and sheet music.

COLLECTIBLES

National Baseball Hall of Fame and Museum. P.O. Box 590, Cooperstown, NY 13326. Gift items, selected books, lithographs. Catalog.
Sports Collectors Digest (SCD). 700 East State Street, Iola, WI 54990. Periodical: Baseball and sports collectibles. By subscription.

Index

Aaron, Hank, 53, 89, 160, 165, 190, 197, 203, 289, 334, 335, 336, 343–44, 345, 358, 371, 390

Abbott, Barry, 335

Abbott, Bud, 44, 45, 108, 147, 391, 392–93, 394

Abbott, George, 15, 129

Abelew, Alan, 77

Abrahamson, T., 284

Abrams, Cal, 258

Acosta, Ann, 128

Acosta, Bob, 128

Adair, Thomas M., 280

Adams, Claire, 45

Adams, Cliff, 343

Adams, Don, 89

Adams, Ernie, 33

Adams, Frank R., 138, 359

Adams, Franklin P., 248, 249–50, 251, 252

Adams, Joey, 387

Adams, Marc, 332

Adcock, Joe, 263

Addington, L. H., 251

Adler, David A., 235, 237

Adler, Richard, 129, 278

Admire, Marshall K., 339

Adriansen, Martin, 281

Africano, Nicolas, 163

Albers, Kenneth, 134

Albert, Eddie, 12, 27, 43, 128

Albert, Stan, 197

Albertson, Mabel, 75

Albritton, Blanche, 347

Albuquerque Dukes, 54

Aldis, Will, 37

Aldrich, Robert, 11

Alessandrini, Gerard, 294

Alexander, Grover Cleveland, 40, 262

Alexander, Holmes, 223

Alexander, Jace, 16

Alexander, Malcolm, 199

Alexander, Perry, 348

Alford, Harry L., 278

All-American Girls Professional Baseball League, 57, 96

Allan, Robert Bruce, 311

Allegretti, Theodore, 145

Allen, Alex B., 238

Allen, Clarence, 281

Allen, Dayton, 101

Allen, Fred, 108–9, 370

Allen, Frederick, 134

Allen, Mel, 74, 78, 96, 217, 260, 347, 371

Allen, Merritt Parmalee, 243

Allen, Samuel, 73, 264, 384

Allen, Woody, 44

Alliance, Jack, 281

Allison, Fran, 71

Allison, Jone, 113

Allison, May, 17

Allyson, June, 38, 82, 113

Alston, Walt, 258, 370

Altman, Shelly, 127

Amarant, Jiggs, 241

American Association, 295

American League, 21, 30, 50, 278, 290, 300, 303, 304, 305, 325, 330, 334, 338, 340, 341, 357, 360, 370

American Legion Junior Baseball, 52

Andersen, Richard, 225

Anderson, Eddie, 109

Anderson, G. M. (Bronco Billy), 9, 38

Anderson, Harry C., 296

Anderson, Herbert, 71

Anderson, Loni, 68

Anderson, Sparky, 84, 89

Andrews, Edward, 68, 138

Andrews, Larry, 299

Andrews, Tige, 72

Angell, Roger, 384

Angelo, H., 281, 282

Anson, Cap, 134, 136–38, 147, 254, 349

Antonelli, Johnny, 120, 372

Applegarth, George S., 273

Appling, Luke, 38

Archer, Lou, 4

Archibald, Joe, 235, 240

Arden, Eve, 73, 111

Ardizzone, Tony, 224

Arkin, Alan, 43, 139

Arlin, Harold, 121

Armstrong, David, 79

Armstrong, Robert, 25

Arroyo, Luis, 263

Arthur, Jean, 39

Arthur, Jon, 114

Arts, Arthur, 362

Ashburn, Richie, 373

Ashby (songwriter), 321

Ashby, Hal, 35

Ashman, Howard, 290, 300–301

Asinof, Eliot, 225

Asner, Ed, 70

Astin, Paul, 131

Atkey, Louis, 283

Atkins, A., 278

Atkinson, Dawn, 284

Atlanta Braves, 36, 53, 96, 175, 265, 321, 332, 334, 335, 344, 356, 358

Austin, Hettie Shirley, 300

Austin, Jerry, 115

Averback, Hy, 109

Averill, Bud, 298

Avery, Jackie, 343